LEGAL INFORMATICS

This groundbreaking work offers a first-of-its-kind overview of legal informatics, the academic discipline underlying the technological transformation and economics of the legal industry. Edited by Daniel Martin Katz, Ron Dolin, and Michael J. Bommarito, and featuring contributions from more than two dozen academic and industry experts, chapters cover the history and principles of legal informatics and background technical concepts – including natural language processing and distributed ledger technology. The volume also presents real-world case studies that offer important insights into document review, due diligence, compliance, case prediction, billing, negotiation and settlement, contracting, patent management, legal research, and online dispute resolution. Written for both technical and non-technical readers, *Legal Informatics* is the ideal resource for anyone interested in identifying, understanding, and executing opportunities in this exciting field.

Daniel Martin Katz is Professor of Law, Illinois Tech – Chicago Kent College of Law where he directs The Law Lab. He also serves as an external affiliated faculty at CodeX, the Stanford Center for Legal Informatics and the Academic Director of the Bucerius Center for Legal Technology and Data Science. A scientist and technologist, Professor Katz applies an innovative, polytechnic approach to teaching law to help create lawyers for today's biggest societal challenges. Both his teaching and scholarship integrate science, technology, engineering, and mathematics.

Ron Dolin is a Senior Research Fellow and Lecturer on Law at Harvard Law School, focusing on the impact of technology on the practice and nature of law. He received a B.A. in math and physics, a Ph.D. in computer science, and a J.D. He has worked at JPL, CERN, and Google, and is a licensed attorney in California. Dolin's research includes developing legal quality metrics, examining the impact of standardized benchmarks on the legal system, and analyzing the legal market from the perspective of The Innovator's Dilemma.

Michael J. Bommarito is an entrepreneur, educator, and investor in the legal and technology industries. His experience spans R&D, technology, business, and operations – ranging from top Am Law firms and $B+ AUM investment firms to idea-stage startups. He is affiliated with the University of Michigan, Stanford University, Michigan State College of Law, and the Illinois Tech – Chicago Kent College of Law. His research has been published in *Science, Physica A, Artificial Intelligence and Law,* and *Quantitative Finance*.

Legal Informatics

Edited by

DANIEL MARTIN KATZ

Illinois Tech – Chicago Kent Law
Bucerius Law School
Stanford CodeX

RON DOLIN

Harvard Law School

MICHAEL J. BOMMARITO

Stanford CodeX

CAMBRIDGE UNIVERSITY PRESS

CAMBRIDGE
UNIVERSITY PRESS

University Printing House, Cambridge CB2 8BS, United Kingdom

One Liberty Plaza, 20th Floor, New York, NY 10006, USA

477 Williamstown Road, Port Melbourne, VIC 3207, Australia

314–321, 3rd Floor, Plot 3, Splendor Forum, Jasola District Centre,
New Delhi – 110025, India

79 Anson Road, #06–04/06, Singapore 079906

Cambridge University Press is part of the University of Cambridge.

It furthers the University's mission by disseminating knowledge in the pursuit of education, learning, and research at the highest international levels of excellence.

www.cambridge.org
Information on this title: www.cambridge.org/9781107142725
DOI: 10.1017/9781316529683

© Cambridge University Press 2021

This publication is in copyright. Subject to statutory exception and to the provisions of relevant collective licensing agreements, no reproduction of any part may take place without the written permission of Cambridge University Press.

First published 2021

A catalogue record for this publication is available from the British Library.

ISBN 978-1-107-14272-5 Hardback

Cambridge University Press has no responsibility for the persistence or accuracy of URLs for external or third-party internet websites referred to in this publication and does not guarantee that any content on such websites is, or will remain, accurate or appropriate.

Contents

List of Figures	page viii
List of Tables	xi
List of Contributors	xii

	PART I INTRODUCTION TO LEGAL INFORMATICS	1
1.1	Motivation and Rationale for this Book Michael J. Bommarito II, Daniel Martin Katz, and Ron Dolin	3
1.2	Technology Issues in Legal Philosophy Ron Dolin	5
1.3	The Origins and History of Legal Informatics Michael J. Bommarito II	24
	PART II LEGAL INFORMATICS: BUILDING BLOCKS AND CORE CONCEPTS	31
	A. INFORMATION REPRESENTATION, PREPROCESSING, AND DOCUMENT ASSEMBLY	33
2.1	Representation of Legal Information Katie Atkinson	35
2.2	Information Intermediation Ron Dolin	41
2.3	Preprocessing Data Michael J. Bommarito II	55
2.4	XML in Law: The Role of Standards in Legal Informatics Ron Dolin	61
2.5	Document Automation Marc Lauritsen	69

B. ARTIFICIAL INTELLIGENCE, MACHINE LEARNING, NATURAL LANGUAGE PROCESSING, AND BLOCKCHAIN — 85

2.6 AI + Law: An Overview — 87
Daniel Martin Katz

2.7 Machine Learning and Law — 94
Daniel Martin Katz and John J. Nay

2.8 Natural Language Processing for Legal Texts — 99
John J. Nay

2.9 Introduction to Blockchain and Cryptography — 114
Nelson M. Rosario

C. PROCESS IMPROVEMENT, GAMIFICATION, AND DESIGN THINKING — 121

2.10 Legal Informatics-Based Technology in Broader Workflows — 123
Kenneth A. Grady

2.11 Gamification of Work and Feedback Systems — 136
Stephanie Kimbro

2.12 Introduction to Design Thinking for Law — 155
Margaret Hagan

D. EVALUATION — 177

2.13 Measuring Legal Quality — 179
Ron Dolin

PART III USE CASES IN LEGAL INFORMATICS — 201

A. CONTRACTS AND PATENTS — 203

3.1 Contract Analytics — 205
Noah Waisberg

3.2 Contracts as Interfaces: Visual Representation Patterns in Contract Design — 213
Helena Haapio and Stefania Passera

3.3 Distributed Ledgers, Cryptography, and Smart Contracts — 239
Nina Gunther Kilbride

3.4 Patent Analytics: Information from Innovation — 257
Andrew W. Torrance and Jevin D. West

B. LITIGATION AND E-DISCOVERY — 289

3.5 The Core Concepts of E-discovery — 291
Jonathan Kerry-Tyerman and A. J. Shankar

3.6	Predictive Coding in E-discovery and the NexLP Story Engine Irina Matveeva	315
3.7	Examining Public Court Data to Understand and Predict Bankruptcy Case Results Warren E. Agin	335
	C. LEGAL RESEARCH, GOVERNMENT DATA, AND ACCESS TO LEGAL INFORMATION	355
3.8	Fastcase, and the Visual Understanding of Judicial Precedents Ed Walters and Jeff Asjes	357
3.9	Mining Information from Statutory Texts in a Public Health Domain Kevin D. Ashley	371
3.10	*Gov2Vec*: A Case Study in Text Model Application to Government Data John J. Nay	393
3.11	Representation and Automation of Legal Information Katie Atkinson	397
	D. DISPUTE RESOLUTION AND ACCESS TO JUSTICE	407
3.12	Online Dispute Resolution Dave Orr and Colin Rule	409
3.13	Access to Justice and Technology: Reaching a Greater Future for Legal Aid Ronald W. Staudt and Alexander F. A. Rabanal	416
3.14	Designing Legal Experiences: Online Communication and Resolution in Courts Maximilian A. Bulinski and J. J. Prescott	430
	PART IV LEGAL INFORMATICS IN THE INDUSTRIAL CONTEXT	449
	A. CHALLENGES FACING INNOVATION IN LAW	451
4.1	Adaptive Innovation: The Innovator's Dilemma in Big Law Ron Dolin and Thomas Buley	453
4.2	Legal Data Access Christine Bannan	467
	B. LARGE FIRM AND CORPORATE LEGAL INFORMATICS CASE STUDIES	481
4.3	A History of Knowledge Management at Littler Mendelson Scott Rechtschaffen	483
4.4	Legal Operations at Google Mary O'Carroll and Stephanie Kimbro	501

Figures

1.3.1	This nilometer on Elephantine Island in Aswan, Egypt is one of the first applications of informatics in the law	page 25
1.3.2	*Corpus Juris Civilis*, republished in 1627 with commentary by Johann Fehe	27
2.1.1	CATO abstract factor hierarchy	39
2.2.1	Term vector spaces: (a) simple query; (b) complex query	49
2.3.1	A simplified, illustrative workflow for preprocessing data	56
2.5.1	Functions of document automation	70
2.5.2	Realms of knowledge management	70
2.6.1	Subfields within artificial intelligence	89
2.8.1	Example of a network of similar bills under consideration by Congress	101
2.8.2	Number of presidential proclamations or determinations, trivial proclamations, memoranda, and executive orders, from 1928 through 2015	106
2.8.3	Positive correlations between topics represented as lines	107
2.8.4	Part-of-speech tagging for a sentence in a state bill	108
2.8.5	Named entity recognition for the last part of the bill sentence	109
2.8.6	Syntactic dependencies	110
2.8.7	Co-reference resolution	110
2.8.8	Word2Vec algorithm	112
2.10.1	Anna's process	125
2.10.2	Chart of email steps	126
2.10.3	Anna's email process	126
2.10.4	Example workflow	129
2.10.5	Process stick for Anna's activities	132
2.12.1	Six levels of legal design work that can improve users' experience with the legal system, from least ambitious to most	173
2.13.1	88.4% of what? Failed to settle on 11.6% of losing cases?	180
2.13.2	Additive scoring (a) vs. (unweighted) multiplicative scoring (b)	193
2.13.3	Weighted multiplicative scoring	195
2.13.4	Geographical relevance of 0, 0.05, and 1	196
3.2.1	The emerging view of the purpose and functions of contracts	217
3.2.2	Linear timelines	226
3.2.3	Circular timeline	227
3.2.4	Processes with different paths	228
3.2.5	Variables over time	228
3.2.6	Synchronous progress of multiple processes or events	229
3.2.7	Flowchart	230
3.2.8	Table with bulleted lists	231

List of Figures

3.2.9	Table with color-coding and icons to show key differences	232
3.2.10	Swimlane	233
3.2.11	Icons in a tenancy agreement	235
3.2.12	Delivery diagram	236
3.2.13	Two different timelines, two different understandings	237
3.2.14	Decision tree evaluating average expected value of alternative decisions	238
3.3.1	A cryptographic hash	240
3.3.2	Linked timestamping storage in hash trees (Merkle trees)	242
3.3.3	Linked timestamping of case law	242
3.4.1	US Patent No. 6,164,870	259
3.4.2	A CIPO patent landscape of shale oil and gas technologies	274
3.4.3	Federal judicial districts by mean importance of patents litigated there	276
3.4.4	An example citation network	285
3.4.5	Automatic categorization	286
3.5.1	The EDRM	292
3.6.1	Visualization of the machine learning process	321
3.6.2	Mathematical objects in SVM with decision boundaries	323
3.6.3	A news article containing last names, nicknames, abbreviations, and metonymy	324
3.6.4	LSI-created word associations	326
3.6.5	Subdivisions within a cluster	328
3.6.6	Nested cluster diagram	329
3.6.7	Dendrogram	329
3.6.8	Entities extracted from an article about airline fare increases	330
3.6.9	NexLP Enron email communication network and content summary for emails discussing Enron	332
3.6.10	Example of emails under investigation	333
3.6.11	Failure of simple keyword search for "William Brown"	333
3.6.12	Story Engine summarizes data and discovers relevant details	333
3.7.1	This chart shows the number of cases in the data set for each disposition code	341
3.7.2	Case volume and success rate by judicial district, grouped vertically by federal circuit	343
3.7.3	Example of a decision tree	344
3.7.4	A small section of the final decision tree	345
3.7.5	Importance scores for model features	346
3.7.6	Confusion matrix for the three test sets, combined	347
3.7.7	Probability output to percentage conversion graph	349
3.8.1	A problem search	360
3.8.2	Fastcase search filters	361
3.8.3	Boolean search	361
3.8.4	Image from Fastcase's Interactive Timeline	367
3.8.5	Y-axis changed to show court level	368
3.8.6	"Same-sex marriage" Interactive Timeline, with arrowing indicating *Lawrence v. Texas*	369
3.8.7	Close-up of Figure 3.8.6, "Same-sex marriage" case relevance	370
3.9.1	LENA statutory network comparing Texas and Pennsylvania statutes on epidemic emergencies with infectious diseases	377
3.9.2	Heat map of agent strength in statutory networks	378
3.9.3	Schematic view of phases of coding text by the SPH team	379
3.9.4	Sample public health emergency statutory provision	380
3.9.5	Results of initial machine learning	383

3.9.6	Results of successively applying more states' classification models	387
3.9.7	Sample comparison of statutory provision texts	390
3.9.8	Interactive ML tool screen	390
3.9.9	Results of evaluation of the interactive ML approach	391
3.10.1	Sentence probabilities across bills for first data (a) and last data (b)	396
3.11.1	CATO abstract factor hierarchy	398
3.11.2	IBP logical model	400
3.11.3	Example abstract argumentation framework	401
3.11.4	Visualization of automobile exception domain addressing the question "Can an automobile be searched without a warrant?"	406
3.13.1	Conditional logic to determine judicial district in IL	421
3.13.2	Conditional logic to determine the end-user's full name	422
3.13.3	Example of map feature (i.e., decision tree)	422
3.13.4	Report feature – readability score	423
3.13.5	A2J Guided Interview progress bar in Spanish	423
3.13.6	Example of a question screen in A2J Author	423
3.13.7	A2J Author usage on LHI, 2008–2016	427
3.14.1	Matterhorn litigant access	434
3.14.2	Eligibility for review	435
3.14.3	Judge's reviews of a litigant's request	436

Tables

2.5.1	Document automation range of functions	*page* 71
2.5.2	Document assembly products, past and present	77
2.5.3	Worksheet for document automation goals	82
2.10.1	Process study sheet	125
3.2.1	Examples of pattern structures	222
3.2.2	Categorization of contract visualization patterns	223
3.5.1	Hash values for the Gettysburg Address	303
3.6.1	LSI-computed areas of interest in Enron emails	327
3.6.2	Main named entity types	329
3.7.1	Prediction accuracy of model for different groupings of probability numbers	348
3.9.1	Comparing similarly purposed provisions from Pennsylvania (left) and Florida (right)	385
3.9.2	Results of models trained on Florida (FL), Pennsylvania (PA), and combined (FL + PA) data sets applied to PA (left) and FL (right) test sets	386
3.10.1	Synthetic summary for three topics, "Enacted" or "Failed," in the House or the Senate	395
3.11.1	Base-level factors in CATO	399
3.11.2	CATO as ADF	402
3.11.3	IBP logical model as an ADF	402

Contributors

Warren E. Agin Adjunct Professor, Boston College Law School; Managing Director for Digital Strategy and Solutions, Elevate Services

Kevin D. Ashley Professor of Law, University of Pittsburgh

Jeff Asjes Product Manager, Fastcase

Katie Atkinson Professor of Computer Science, University of Liverpool

Christine Bannan Policy Counsel, Open Technology Institute, New America

Michael J. Bommarito II Fellow, CodeX – Stanford Center for Legal Informatics

Thomas Buley Vice-President of Product, Guideline

Maximilian A. Bulinski Research Fellow, University of Michigan Law School

Ron Dolin Lecturer on Law, Harvard Law School; Senior Research Fellow, Center on the Legal Profession, Harvard Law School

Kenneth A. Grady Adjunct Professor, Michigan State University College of Law

Helena Haapio Associate Professor of Business Law, University of Vaasa; International Contract Counsel, Lexpert Ltd.

Margaret Hagan Director Legal Design Lab, Stanford Law School Lecturer, Stanford Institute of Design (d.school)

Daniel Martin Katz Professor of Law, Illinois Tech – Chicago Kent College of Law Academic Director, Bucerius Center for Legal Technology & Data Science; Affiliated Faculty, CodeX – Stanford Center for Legal Informatics

Jonathan Kerry-Tyerman Vice-President of Business Development, Everlaw

Nina Gunther Kilbride Principal, Corpening Labs

Stephanie Kimbro Former Research Fellow, Stanford Law School; Independent Consultant, Virtual Law Practice

Marc Lauritsen President, Capstone Practice Systems

Irina Matveeva Adjunct Professor, Illinois Tech; Head of Machine Learning, NexLP

John J. Nay CEO & Co-Founder, Skopos Labs

Mary O'Carroll Director of Legal Operations, Google; President, CLOC

Dave Orr Senior Product Manager, Google

Stefania Passera Legal Tech Lab, Helsinki University

J. J. Prescott Professor of Law, University of Michigan Law School

Alexander F. A. Rabanal Associate Director, The Law Lab @ Illinois Tech – Chicago Kent College of Law

Scott Rechtshaffen Chief Knowledge Officer, Littler Mendelson

Nelson M. Rosario Adjunct Professor, Illinois Tech – Chicago-Kent College of Law Principal, Smolinski Rosario Law P.C.

Colin Rule Vice-President for Online Dispute Resolution, Tyler Technologies

A. J. Shankar Founder and CEO, Everlaw

Ronald W. Staudt Professor of Law Emeritus, Illinois Tech – Chicago Kent College of Law

Andrew W. Torrance Paul E. Wilson Distinguished Professor of Law, University of Kansas School of Law

Noah Waisberg CEO and Co-founder, Kira Systems

Ed Walters CEO and Co-founder, Fastcase

Jevin D. West Associate Professor, Information School, University of Washington

PART I

Introduction to Legal Informatics

1.1

Motivation and Rationale for this Book

Michael J. Bommarito II, Daniel Martin Katz, and Ron Dolin

From document review in litigation, to compliance, case prediction, billing, negotiation and settlement, contracting, patent management, due diligence, legal research, and beyond, technology is transforming the production of legal work and in turn the economics of the legal industry. Legal informatics is the academic discipline that underlies many of these transformational technologies, and despite all of these technical advances, no modern comprehensive treatment of the field has been offered to date. With contributions from more than two dozen academic and industry experts, this book offers readers a first-of-its-kind introductory overview of the exciting field of legal informatics.

While technology is not new to law, previous rounds of technology adoption by lawyers have largely been driven by technologies that are more generally applicable to all knowledge workers (e.g., the use of word processing, email, smartphones, cloud computing, etc.). Excitingly, many of the current innovations in legal technology are actually retrofitted to the specific work that lawyers undertake.

The design of this new generation of legal technology is increasingly built on and linked to the field of legal informatics. Across a wide range of substantive examples, readers will be exposed to both the theoretical and applied challenges that underlie the field. Although the book is aimed at those with limited technical knowledge, we hope it will encourage readers to seek additional technical skills. We also hope that the book will assist an emerging class of engineers – legal technologists – in applying their technical skills to the field of law with an understanding of underlying legal requirements.

In addition to being an aid to law and/or technology practitioners, this book is also meant to serve as a textbook for teaching legal informatics. A new book of this breadth and depth cannot feasibly be written by one or two individuals. The dozens of expert contributors necessary imply a complexity among and between chapters. There is an inevitable redundancy of material (e.g., defining precision and recall). To some degree, we left in some of the repetition in order to allow for the atomicity of individual chapters. This gives more freedom to instructors to select chapters that fit their focus and expertise, be it breadth or depth. Any book such as this that discusses modern technology is almost inevitably somewhat out of date before it is published. That being said, our goal was to explain underlying concepts such that the timeliness of the examples is not crucial.

It is our hope to see the development of US graduate programs and associated degrees at all levels in legal informatics, similar to medical informatics programs, up to and including PhD programs. We also hope to see, increasingly, appropriate career paths for legal technologists whose value is recognized as central to modern strategic planning and business models, system design and integration, and creative problem solving, on par with any senior-level professional. As we emphasize throughout the text, the importance of an understanding of both law and technology for a modern legal system cannot be overstated.

1.2

Technology Issues in Legal Philosophy

Ron Dolin

I INTRODUCTION: TECHNOLOGICAL IMPLEMENTATION OF LAW

"How do these techniques of policy inform the practice of policy makers?"

Lawrence Lessig, *Code 2.0*

The *philosophy of law* is the study of the nature of law: What is law? What are the criteria of a functioning legal system? What is the relationship between law and morality? A course on legal technology and legal informatics focuses on the *technological* implementation of a legal system. As we move away from static, printed documents toward virtual, distributed, integrated systems, software ("code") plays an increasingly important role in the legal system. Obviously code has applications far beyond implementing law. Yet, as Lawrence Lessig points out in *Code 2.0*, non-law code also regulates behavior, often in a more fundamental way than laws do.[1] As discussed in this chapter, code is architectural in nature and effectively limits behavior similarly to laws of physics. Only in science fiction do we entertain the notion of faster-than-light travel, perpetual motion, or evading gravitational forces. Similarly, we tend to accept the limitations of code that prevent us from, say, lending out our e-books, though such lending would certainly be legal. Even if we are aware of these limits and do not like them, most of us have no capacity to change them. As far as our behavior is concerned, code may as well be the law.[2]

This increase in the role of software calls into question the manner in which fundamental legal functions such as the interpretation, enforcement, and creation of rules are moving beyond the institutions traditionally established to implement them. This raises issues such as which groups, following which norms, are regulating our behavior. The ability to block legal behavior in order to prevent potentially illegal behavior also raises the issue of whether software *ought* to allow us to act *illegally* because we have either the custom or the right, at times, to do so – whether to jaywalk, to speed, or to act in civil disobedience. Where technology changes the nature of preventive possibilities, we have to take another look at the balance between prevention and punishment to regulate behavior.

---

[1] Lawrence Lessig, *Code 2.0* (New York, NY: Basic Books, 2006), available at: http://codev2.cc.
[2] *Ibid*. Lessig's *Code 2.0* is referenced repeatedly throughout this chapter, in part because it highlights the necessity of dealing with some of the philosophical issues related to legal technology. In addition, many of Lessig's points will be more readily available to readers of a legal informatics survey course if they are more succinctly presented. The reader is encouraged to seek the original source.

A complementary perspective on law that derives from legal informatics is looking at the logic, structure, data, and measurement of law. Formulas are not new to law – anyone who has studied torts has encountered the negligence calculation by Judge Learned Hand, commonly written as B = PL, which dates back to 1947.[3] The economics of law, empirical legal studies, and even investigations of AI and the law, go back several decades. An informatics approach to law, as in other fields such as medicine, looks at law through the lens of data flow. Which types of data structures and algorithms might be associated not only with legal documents and legal information, but also with courts, legislation, law firms, or policing, in general? How might we quantify, analyze, and predict legal quality and outcomes, and how might we measure the accuracy of these quantifications? Finally, what might be the proper boundaries for the applications of automation in the legal system, and what are the trade-offs between efficiency, quality, access, and fairness that impact our decisions?

At first blush, some of these questions might be seen as no more basic than any policy issue arising in any substantive law course. But as millions of disputes are handled automatically, as increasingly complex problems are handled algorithmically, and as AI assists *pro se* litigants, document review, and settlement negotiations via estimates of outcomes, the law is increasingly being handed over to machines based on quantitative analyses. Whether we consider standard philosophical themes such as the rule of recognition and the role of institutions, or new questions related to the proper role of machines in regulating human-to-human interactions, technology increasingly impacts law at the philosophical level. Ronald Dworkin stated that law "is defined by attitude, not territory or power or process."[4] In legal informatics, it is not clear where, or in what manner, that attitude resides.

This chapter is not intended to be a comprehensive study of all the topics it touches. Instead, it is an effort to introduce the reader to the relationship between legal technology and philosophy. It also serves to introduce many common themes across legal technology within a framework of the legal system, rather than through a technology orientation.

II LEGAL INSTITUTIONS, EFFECTIVENESS, AND TECHNOLOGICAL DISRUPTION

"Many, if not all, legal philosophers have agreed that one of the defining features of law is that it is an institutionalized legal system."

Joseph Raz, *The Institutional Nature of Law*

Institutions are a defining component of a mature legal system.[5] They are "'stable, valued, recurring patterns of behavior'. As structures or mechanisms of social order, they govern the behaviour of a set of individuals within a given community. Institutions are identified with a social purpose, transcending individuals and intentions by mediating the rules that govern living behavior."[6]

Modern society allocates the role of interpretation, enforcement, and creation of law to associated institutions – typically the judiciary, police, and legislature, respectively. For various reasons addressed throughout this chapter, the issue of the *effectiveness* of the

---

[3] United States v. Carroll Towing Co., 159 F.2d 169 (2d Cir. 1947) ("if the probability be called P; the injury, L; and the burden, B; liability depends upon whether B is less than L multiplied by P: *i.e.*, whether B > PL").
[4] Ronald Dworkin, *Law's Empire* (Cambridge, MA: Harvard University Press, 1986), pp. 413, 470.
[5] Joseph Raz, "The Institutional Nature of Law," *The Modern Law Review* 38 (5) (1975): 489–503.
[6] "Institution," *Wikipedia*, available at https://en.wikipedia.org/wiki/Institution (accessed June 9, 2020).

implementation of a legal system surfaces repeatedly. This point was raised as a fundamental assumption by Joseph Raz in defining legal systems:

> "We are familiar with the distinction between legal systems which are in force in a certain society and those which are not. There is a legal system in force now in Great Britain and there is one in force in Norway. But the legal system once in force in the Roman Republic is no longer in force, nor is the legal system proposed by a group of scholars for country X in fact in force in that country. Whether or not a system is in force in a society depends on its impact on the behaviour of people in the society. The precise nature of the criterion determining if a system is in force is a disputed issue with which I will not be concerned. But whatever it is, it concerns the attitudes and responses of all or certain sections in the society to the legal system: Do they know it, do they respect it, obey it? etc. This seems to me to be a very significant fact ... A legal system exists if and only if it is in force. The significance of the point is that it brings out that normative systems are existing legal systems because of their impact on the behaviour of individuals, because of their role in the organisation of social life. Consequently when we look at legal systems as systems of laws, when we consider their content and disregard the question of whether they are in fact in force, whether they exist, we should look for those features which enable them to fulfil a distinctive role in society. These will be the features which distinguish legal systems from other normative systems."[7]

Therefore, as we review the intended role of basic legal institutions, we also need to examine their effectiveness. Technology has a complex impact on legal implementation. On the one hand, it may serve to sustain institutions when it enables them to function more efficiently (though doing so may come at a societal cost). On the other hand, technology may serve as a disruptive force as it increasingly regulates behavior outside the legal system, potentially more quickly than the legal system is able to accommodate.[8] The rate of change of technology tends to increase, while the rate of change of the legal system tends to get bogged down by its increasing complexity.

The central theme of technological disruption as applied here is that systems tend to cater to higher ends of a market, leaving behind the lower end; the ability to handle the complexity at the high end comes with a burden of cost and inefficiency that the lower end cannot afford and does not require. This leaves an opening for the displacement of the status quo with a more efficient model that only needs to address the lesser needs at the lower end. Over time, the new model grows in sophistication and moves upmarket, all the while maintaining the higher levels of efficiency.

A Defining an Effective Legal System

In identifying or defining legal systems, not all institutions are equally determinative. In particular, a necessary requirement of "municipal legal systems" is that they contain "primary norm-applying organs":

---

[7] Raz, "The Institutional Nature of Law," *supra* note 5 at 489–490.
[8] For a full discussion of the notion of the sustaining and disruptive impacts of technology, *see* Clayton M. Christensen, *Innovator's Dilemma: When New Technologies Cause Great Firms to Fail* (Cambridge, MA: Harvard Business Review Press, 1997). This book is discussed at length in Chapter 4.1 – Adaptive Innovation: The Innovator's Dilemma in Big Law, *infra*. The disruption described here is more of the "adaptive" nature, as legal systems are more likely to transform than to go away. By definition, whatever serves the purpose of defining and applying societal norms, while maintaining supremacy over other systems, *is* the legal system.

"the type of institutions we are looking for are those which combine norm-making and norm-applying in a special way. Let us call these institutions primary (norm-applying) organs, to indicate their importance ... They are institutions with power to determine the normative situation of specified individuals, which are required to exercise these powers by applying existing norms, but whose decisions are binding even when wrong."[9]

In other words, the institution of the judiciary is perhaps the key component of a legal system.

Raz addresses the issue of the uniqueness of a legal system as compared to any other normative system and arrives at several requirements. It is a *necessary* feature of all legal systems (1) that they contain norms *establishing primary institutions*; (2) that a law belongs to them only if the primary institutions are under a *duty* to apply it; and (3) that primary institutions have *limits to discretion* set by the norms.[10] In addition to these necessary conditions, he identifies three *sufficient* conditions that define a legal system. Legal systems are: (1) *comprehensive*, in that they may regulate any type of behavior; (2) *supreme*, in that they have precedence over all other normative systems available to its citizenry; and (3) *open*, in that they enforce external rules, such as conflicts of laws, contracts, and corporate bylaws.[11]

If we analyze these requirements *without* the presumption of effectiveness, however, several of them are problematic in their implementation in many modern legal systems. As is common in disruption, systems, values, and procedures develop around certain presumptions that, while perhaps true originally, become less so over time. For example, assumptions about caseloads, per capita resources, legal complexity, and technological capability have not remained static. Many implementation methodologies are no longer justifiable in the face of the inefficiencies they create and their inability to scale. However, a move toward efficiency usually impacts quality – sometimes for the better, but sometimes not.

B Interpretation and Application

How effective is the judiciary, the institution responsible for legal interpretation and application? American courts, for example, are increasingly overloaded and backlogged, leading to severe access to justice (A2J) issues across a range of problems for literally millions of people annually. Civil litigants involved in common disputes such as family law, consumer debt, and property law are often forced to represent themselves, usually poorly, due to a lack of personal and societal resources.[12] In criminal law, public defenders are vastly overloaded.[13] In addition, commercial, online transactions are often cross-jurisdictional or international, involving small monetary amounts, and result in millions of disputes annually – almost exclusively handled outside any court system.

One result of this excessive caseload has been a push for, and increase in, online dispute resolution (ODR) systems that automate as much of the dispute resolution process as

---

[9] Raz, "The Institutional Nature of Law," *supra* note 5 at 493–494.
[10] *Id.* at 499.
[11] *Id.* at 500–502.
[12] See Staudt and Rabanal – Access to Justice and Technology: Reaching a Greater Future for Legal Aid, *infra*.
[13] See, e.g., Alexa van Brunt, "Poor People Rely on Public Defenders Who Are Too Overworked to Defend Them," *Guardian*, June 17, 2015, available at: www.theguardian.com/commentisfree/2015/jun/17/poor-rely-public-defenders-too-overworked; Laurence A. Benner, "Eliminating Public Defender Workloads," *Criminal Justice* 26 (2) (2011), available at: www.americanbar.org/content/dam/aba/publications/criminal_justice_magazine/cjsu11_benner.authcheckdam.pdf.

possible, both domestically and internationally.[14] Even under the assumption that ODR systems are high quality (which many certainly are), they are not a panacea for all the problems facing the traditional legal system institutional model:

1. ODR is usually outside courts – as in ADR – and lacks many of the attributes associated with a judicial system.
2. ODR within courts needs to address automation issues (see below).
3. There is an ecosystem of barriers to the adoption of efficient solutions, such as a desire to protect the profession (another institution)[15] and the bureaucracy of the judiciary.[16]
4. There are problems for which there are no known norms.

Many people's actual experience with the judiciary is quite lacking in access or quality. A norm-applying institution cannot be said to fulfill the requirements of a legal system model if norms are so frequently not applied in case after case, and the system is so inefficient that it becomes increasingly ineffective. However, a technological approach such as ODR, while addressing the efficiency issue, also needs to maintain quality of outcomes. Judicial institutions do not mechanically apply norms to facts:

> "legal systems consist of laws which the courts are bound to apply and are not at liberty to disregard whenever they find their application undesirable, all things considered. It does not follow that the courts are to be regarded as computing machines, always applying pre-existing rules regardless of their own views of which rules or which decisions are the right ones. But it does follow that they are to apply a certain body of laws regardless of their views on its merits and are allowed to act on their own views only to the extent that this is allowed by those laws."[17]

Judges have a duty to apply the law, and though they have some discretion, that discretion is limited by law. This raises the question of the ability of automated systems to fulfill this function (to whatever degree possible). From a technology perspective, the problem is not that judges *are not* mechanical, but rather the assumption that computers necessarily *are* mechanical. This is perhaps an overly simplistic notion of software.[18] Some existing systems use game theory and transparent applications of algorithms to assist with settlement and mediation negotiations. Current technology solutions used for A2J and consumer law, utilizing varying degrees of expert systems and other AI, focus on triage. A sophisticated algorithm for ODR should be able to assess whether it should defer to a human adjudicator. The point is that computer-based dispute resolution systems exist, are growing in sophistication, and are orders of magnitude more efficient than the status quo.

Efficiency risks a decline in quality, a risk that courts are loath to accept. For example, the US Supreme Court has addressed the issue of whether criminal sentencing guidelines,

---

[14] See Orr and Rule – Online Dispute Resolution, *infra*. As one of many examples of courts adopting an ODR framework, the UK is moving lower-value claims online; see The Civil Justice Council, "Online Dispute Resolution: For Low Value Civil Claims," 2015, available at: www.judiciary.gov.uk/wp-content/uploads/2015/02/Online-Dispute-Resolution-Final-Web-Version1.pdf.
[15] See Dolin – Measuring Legal Quality, section on "Access to Justice: UPL vs. Technology," *infra*.
[16] See, e.g., Ron Dolin, "Feedback on Technology Governance, Strategy, and Funding Proposal: Executive Summary for California Judicial Branch," Slide Presentation, June 16, 2014, available at: www.slideshare.net/RonDolin/court-report.
[17] Raz, "The Institutional Nature of Law," *supra* note 5, at 497.
[18] A humorous, yet insightful, analysis of the issues of machine free will and robotic judges is given in "Free Will Hunting," *Futurama*, Season 7, Episode 9, Comedy Central, 2012.

a formulaic, efficient approach to consistency, can or should be mandatory.[19] They found that the factual elements of a crime used to extend a sentence beyond the guidelines must be found to be true by a jury, beyond a reasonable doubt, and that such a requirement can be met only if the guidelines are advisory rather than mandatory. In weighing the balance of efficiency with quality (in this case, fairness), the Court found that quality takes precedence, at least where the stakes are sufficiently high. Of course, when the cost of acting fairly means frequently not acting at all in many cases due to an overburdened institution, courts are squeezed – limiting their effectiveness one way or the other.

At the end of the day, as we increase efficiency and move toward automation, we need to measure both procedural and outcome fairness to retain the effective application of norms within the institution of the judiciary.

C Enforcement

While institutions that apply norms to disputes may be the key defining characteristic of municipal legal systems, institutions for enforcing norms are also necessary.[20] Regulation through law's exercise of power is institutionalized through mechanisms such as a police force. Similar to applying the law, *efficient* enforcement comes with risks. As an example, consider predictive policing:

> "Predictive policing tries to harness the power of information, geospatial technologies and evidence-based intervention models to reduce crime and improve public safety. This two-pronged approach – applying advanced analytics to various data sets, in conjunction with intervention models – can move law enforcement from reacting to crimes into the realm of predicting what and where something is likely to happen and deploying resources accordingly."[21]

Unconditionally accurate prediction is possible only for systems that are "well-isolated, stationary, and recurrent (like our solar system). Such systems are quite rare in nature, and human society is most emphatically not one of them."[22] Prediction is never an exact science, and predictive algorithms draw conclusions based on the input of prior patterns.[23] One potential downside of predictive policing is a predisposition to suspicion, in part because the technology can be used to predict not just where and when crimes may occur, but *who* may commit them, imperfectly.[24] Also, where similar technology may influence estimates of

---

[19] A string of cases from 2000 to 2007 concluded that, although sentencing guidelines may be presumed to be reasonable, they may not be considered mandatory. The findings of facts related to the details of how a crime was committed and the character of the perpetrator are inputs to the guidelines, and require the "beyond reasonable doubt" standard – that is, a jury. See *Apprendi v. New Jersey*, 530 U.S. 466 (2000) (the jury-trial right "has never been efficient; but it has always been free."); *Ring v. Arizona*, 536 U.S. 584 (2002); *Blakely v. Washington*, 542 U.S. 296 (2004); *United States v. Booker*, 543 U.S. 220 (2005) (mandatory guidelines inconsistent with jury trial, as required); *Rita v. United States*, 551 U.S. 338 (2007) (guidelines presumed reasonable).

[20] Raz, "The Institutional Nature of Law," *supra* note 5, at 493: "There is no doubt that norm-enforcing institutions play an important role in all modern legal systems." The article proposes that a society in which enforcement is handled privately rather than institutionally, once a dispute has been discharged by the norm-applying institution, would still be considered to have a legal system. Although that might be true in theory, no examples are given, as one might imagine.

[21] National Institute of Justice, "Predictive Policing," available at: www.nij.gov/topics/law-enforcement/strategies/predictive-policing/Pages/welcome.aspx.

[22] Stanford Encyclopedia of Philosophy, "Karl Popper," November 13, 1997, available at: https://plato.stanford.edu/entries/popper/#ScieKnowHistPred.

[23] See Katz – AI + Law: An Overview, *infra*.

[24] www.washingtonpost.com/local/public-safety/police-are-using-software-to-predict-crime-is-it-a-holy-grail-or-biased-against-minorities/2016/11/17/525a6649-0472-440a-aae1-b283aa8e5de8_story.html.

recidivism, errors could keep someone in jail longer than otherwise necessary.[25] The potential use of AI across the criminal justice system is a balance between perpetuation of past patterns and effective intervention.[26]

In addition to sustaining innovation within standard institutions, enforcement through disruptive innovation also occurs outside them. This raises issues of trust and the legitimacy of new enforcement mechanisms. "People accept the police's right to dictate appropriate behaviour not only when they feel a duty to obey officers, but also when they believe that the institution acts according to a shared moral purpose with citizens."[27] When regulation comes through law and the enforcement is generally accepted as beneficial, compliance follows. As discussed below, technology increasingly regulates behavior. Where such regulation originates outside the legal system, the notion of "shared moral purpose" is not necessarily included.

D Creation

Finally, in addition to interpretation and enforcement, technology increasingly impacts the creation of enforced rules, law or not. While the activity of legislation is often categorized more as political science than law, that distinction assumes a particular social order that may be lacking in the evolution of software as a regulatory entity.[28]

As Lessig points out, the notion of technology (code) regulating behavior is not surprising to an engineer. If code regulates, then, given that law is "supreme," the legal system has the authority to regulate code. Lessig believes that the existing institutional structure, however, is not effectively doing so, as neither the legislature nor the judiciary are equipped to handle such oversight. What is the relationship of the coders to the regulated?

> "Of course, for the computer scientist code is law. And if code is law, then obviously the question we should ask is: Who are the lawmakers? Who writes this law that regulates us? What role do we have in defining this regulation? What right do we have to know of the regulation? And how might we intervene to check it?"[29]

Is this just a problem with the current political climate, or is there something more fundamental about the way that technology impacts law? Perhaps the current technological implementation reveals a shortcoming in the pre-technological institutional structures that may be incapable of effectively responding to the growing complexity within a reasonable time and a sufficiently comprehensive manner. If so, would we expect this difficulty to appear in other legal systems?

---

[25] For potential benefits, see, e.g., Nancy Ritter, "Predicting Recidivism Risk: New Tool in Philadelphia Shows Great Promise," *NIJ Journal* 271 (2013), available at: www.nij.gov/journals/271/pages/predicting-recidivism.aspx; "New Models to Predict Recidivism Could Provide Better Way to Deter Repeat Crime," *The Conversation*, September 9, 2015, available at: http://theconversation.com/new-models-to-predict-recidivism-could-provide-better-way-to-deter-repeat-crime-44165. For limitations on these practices, see, e.g., Julia Dressel and Hany Farid, "The Accuracy, Fairness, and Limits of Predicting Recidivism," *Science Advances* 4 (1) (2018), available at: http://advances.sciencemag.org/content/4/1/eaao5580.full.

[26] See, e.g., Chelsea Barabas, Karthik Dinakar, Joichi Ito, Madars Virza, and Jonathan Zittrain, "Interventions Over Predictions: Reframing the Ethical Debate for Actuarial Risk Assessment," *Proceedings of Machine Learning Research* 81 (2018).

[27] Jonathan Jackson, Ben Bradford, Mike Hough, Andy Myhill, Paul Quinton, and Tom R. Tyler, "Why do People Comply with the Law? Legitimacy and the Influence of Legal Institutions," *The British Journal of Criminology* 52 (6) (2012), 1051–1071.

[28] Efficiency of institutionalized rule creation (e.g., legislation) is beyond the scope of this chapter. See, e.g., Jamie Susskind, *Future Politics: Living Together in a World Transformed by Tech* (New York, NY: Oxford University Press, 2018), p. 516.

[29] Lessig, *Code 2.0*, supra note 1, at 323.

E The Implications of Efficiency

Efficiency may be a primary requirement of a modern legal system in order to allow the implementation to be *effective*. This raises two issues, along the lines of sustaining and disruptive innovation. The first issue is the application of efficiency to existing institutions (i.e., sustaining innovation) – the inevitable technological implementation presents a potential conflict with quality. Efficiency without quality is useless. A legal system's full set of requirements would not be satisfied by settling all disputes with a coin toss, no matter how efficient that may be. Wherever efficiency is integrated into the implementation of legal functions, especially with automation, a mechanism for measuring and enforcing quality also becomes a requirement of a valid legal system.[30]

The second issue is the application of efficient regulation outside the standard institutions (i.e., disruptive innovation). Efficiency is agnostic with regard to institutions, except where such structures happen to streamline fundamental legal functions; institutions may not be as necessary. For example, a self-driving car could self-enforce its legal mandates without requiring the police or the judiciary; software implements the driving regulations, and the software is out of the control of the occupants, who therefore have no capacity to break the rules. The question is how technological efficiency may impact the structure of the legal system. Are the same institutions necessary and sufficient, and, if so, how might they need to be re-implemented? In addition, in what way does technology (e.g., software) serve as a new form of regulatory structure, and is it *effectively* subordinate to the existing legal system?

In terms of re-implementing a legal system, progress often begins with digitizing current practice, followed by redesigning processes. Lessig points out that changes in efficiency inherently force changes in the legal system and in the law: "The power to regulate is a function of architecture as much as of ideology; architectures enable regulation as well as constrain it. To understand the power a government might have, we must understand the architectures within which it governs."[31]

The impact of implementation architecture is not limited to the regulation of cyberspace as an increasing amount of normal life occurs online. A change in implementation also impacts what we have already been doing. The inefficiencies that have existed created a constraint on practice (e.g., the cost of wide-scale surveillance made doing so prohibitive). Removing the inefficiencies enables a new scale of prior practice such that the new implementation can no longer be said to be the same beast. Technological efficiency results in orders-of-magnitude differences. These changes not only necessitate a revisit and rebalance of prior principles, but also create fundamental new ways that regulation can be implemented, potentially requiring the development of new principles.

III REGULABILITY[32]

"We are entering an age when the power of regulation will be relocated to a structure whose properties and possibilities are fundamentally different."

Lawrence Lessig, *Code* 2.0

---

[30] *See* Dolin – Measuring Legal Quality, *infra*.
[31] Lessig, *Code* 2.0, *supra* note 1, at 282.
[32] This section is principally a brief summary of Lessig's *Code* 2.0 chapter 7 and the related appendix. Minor changes have been made for the purpose of integration into this chapter; the reader is encouraged to seek the original source.

The regulation of behavior is facilitated by four *modalities*: law, norms, markets, and architecture. Architecture can be created or natural. Created architecture includes hard (physical) and soft (virtual, software) limitations on behavior, such as a door lock, a speed bump, or a maximum speed hard-coded into a self-driving car. Natural architecture is the limits set by nature, such as the speed-of-light limit on physical motion and information transmission. Thus, one aspect of regulation is *agency*, where it is a consequence of intentionality.

Another aspect of regulation is *temporality* – the time at which the regulatory mechanism impacts the potential actor's behavior. Some involve an *ex post* consequence such as legal punishment or societal ostracization. Others involve an *ex ante* impact such as markets requiring payment prior to allowing an activity, or a physical limitation that prevents an action from occurring at all. However, although some regulations may have an *objective ex post* consequence, the potential actor who anticipates such a consequence may act accordingly in advance so as to avoid the potential result, as when general deterrence prevents the "Bad Man" from breaking the law so as to avoid punishment. Thus, the temporality of the *subjective* impact of the regulation may be different than the objective consequence. Laws and norms are most effective when made subjective, internalized. Only subjectively perceived, known consequences (i.e., objectively transparent and predictable) can be accurately internalized. Architecture, however, does not need to be known to regulate behavior, since it prevents actions regardless of an actor's perception or knowledge.

The various regulatory modalities are not independent, and law can be used to influence the others. Although federal commandeering of states is unconstitutional under the Tenth Amendment, many other forms of indirect control by law are available.[33] For example, in *Rust v. Sullivan*, the US Supreme Court held that the government could mandate in "government-funded" clinics that staff could not mention abortion in family planning discussions with patients.[34] Thus the law can hide its role, in this case under the misperception of medical advice; the patient may never realize that abortion is even a potential option. Where regulation lacks transparency, the regulated may not realize that it is created rather than natural, or that they could possibly challenge it, or who is responsible for creating it. What if the law directs code, such as encryption back doors, tracking online users and usage, hidden computer searches, etc.?

> "Indirectly, by regulating code writing, the government can achieve regulatory ends, often without suffering the political consequences that the same ends, pursued directly, would yield.
>
> We should worry about this. We should worry about a regime that makes invisible regulation easier; we should worry about a regime that makes it easier to regulate. We should worry about the first because invisibility makes it hard to resist bad regulation; we should worry about the second because we don't yet ... have a sense of the values put at risk by the increasing scope of efficient regulation."[35]

Thus, as code regulates behavior both within and outside of the legal system, the issue of transparency gains prominence in new ways.

---

[33] See, e.g., *New York v. United States*, 505 U.S. 144 (1992).
[34] *Rust v. Sullivan*, 500 U.S. 173 (1991) (Medical staff could be directed to address questions regarding abortion as follows: "The project does not consider abortion an appropriate method of family planning").
[35] Lessig, *Code 2.0*, *supra* note 1, at 136–137.

IV TRANSPARENCY

"I don't know this law," said K. "So much the worse for you, then," said the policeman. "It probably exists only in your heads," said K ... But the policeman just said dismissively, "You'll find out when it affects you." Franz joined in, and said, "Look at this, Willem, he admits he doesn't know the law and at the same time insists he's innocent."

Franz Kafka, *The Trial*

There are several transparency issues that arise from the technological implementation of regulations. One issue focuses on the legal system – what do we mean by access to law within a society that increasingly expects to find information online? Another issue has to do with the nature of the regulatory modalities that enable or disable not only our actions, but our very awareness of potential choices, which may be blocked before most of us have even considered them as possibilities, irrespective of their potential legality. Finally, technology increasingly brings to light instances in which norms and laws are in conflict, inviting us to acknowledge our ongoing and seemingly acceptable illegal behaviors. The question is whether we ever have a *right* to act illegally such that an architectural approach to preventing such activity is overly restrictive.

A Access to Law and the Rule of Recognition

Described by H. L. A. Hart, the *rule of recognition* in a legal system is the rule that determines which rules are binding.[36] *Primary rules* are those that regulate day-to-day activities, while *secondary rules* establish how to recognize, change, and adjudicate the primary rules.[37] Characteristics of the secondary rules, and thus by implication, the primary rules, include resolution of normative uncertainty, dexterity, efficiency, supremacy, and more.[38] But what about transparency?

Legal information, be it case law and other court documents, statutes and regulations, or even legally mandated compliance standards, may or may not be found online, may or may not be copyrighted, and may or may not be behind a paywall.[39] Regardless of whether there is a single rule of recognition or a "shared plan" of secondary rules that direct governmental officials as to the scope and discretion of their decision making, transparency of both primary and secondary rights and responsibilities is a presumed characteristic in a valid legal system. For example, in one examination of the modern applicability of the rule of recognition, the author allocates the requirement of transparency to a footnote, seemingly due to the obviousness of its necessity:

> "Because a plan that is completely secret cannot be shared, we should also add that a shared plan be at least "publicly accessible," namely, that the participants could discover the parts of the plan that pertain to them and to others with whom they are likely to interact if they wished to do so. In the interests of brevity, I have omitted this condition in the discussions that follow."[40]

---

[36] Herbert Lionel Adolphus Hart and Leslie Green, *The Concept of Law*, eds. Joseph Raz and Penelope A. Bulloch (Oxford: Oxford University Press, 2012).

[37] Scott J. Shapiro, "What Is The Rule of Recognition (And Does It Exist)?" Public Law & Legal Theory Research Paper 181, Yale Law School, (2009), 3–4, available at: https://papers.ssrn.com/sol3/papers.cfm?abstract_id=1304645.

[38] *Id.* at 8–11.

[39] *See* Bannan – Legal Data Access, *infra*.

[40] Shapiro, "What Is The Rule of Recognition (And Does It Exist)?," *supra* note 37, at 19, note 55.

If the rule of recognition assumes that legal systems make rules transparently accessible, then we need to address what "accessibility" means. Within a technologically modern implementation of law, there is an expectation of the manner in which information is located and the format with which it is made accessible (e.g., via an API). At some point, if we cannot find something online, download it, or perhaps incorporate it into our preferred (legal-advice) app, then it does not *effectively* exist. By contrast, patent law on prior art, for example, seems to define publication ("available to the public") by rather archaic standards compared to modern expectations of search engines.[41] One might wonder if there may come a time when the definition of "published" may be whether or not Google has something indexed. A lack of access to legal information presents an impediment to access to justice, and is thus intimately associated with the notion of the rule of recognition.[42] It is difficult to argue that the laws that bind us are transparently and effectively available to us when access is blocked by fees, copyright, or format.

B Regulation by Software

Transparency plays a different role among the different modalities of regulation. Norms and customs need to be taught and internalized to function. And while the mechanisms of establishing valuations within a market may not be transparent, a fair exchange requires both parties to know what they would be exchanging in order to decide whether to participate in the interaction. For the legal system, as we said, the rule of recognition assumes transparency or availability of primary and secondary rules. But, as Lessig makes clear, architecture, and software in particular, need not be transparent to be effective, including effectively preventing legal behavior.

Lessig refers to transparent code as *open* and opaque code as *closed*.[43] What types of *legal* software require transparency? For example, the application of game theory to dispute resolution requires that disputants understand the algorithm and trust that it is accurately implemented. In e-discovery, an understanding of the algorithms impacts how document search can proceed, that responsive documents are produced, and that only mutually agreeable privileged documents are held back.[44] Beyond legal software, non-legal code increasingly sets up architectural limits on our behavior, potentially without our knowledge or ability to modify:

> "For most of us, it is just as [in]feasible to change the way [closed] Microsoft Word functions as it is to change the way [open] GNU/Linux operates.
>
> But the difference here is that there is – and legally can be – a community of developers who modify open code, but there is not – or legally cannot be – a community of developers who modify closed code, at least without the owner's permission. That culture of developers is the critical mechanism that creates the independence within open code. Without that culture, there'd be little real difference between the regulability of open and closed code.

---

[41] *See* Title 35, United States Code, Section 102, and related case law. For example, in *Suffolk Technologies, LLC v. AOL Inc.*, 752 F. 3d 1358 (2014), a non-indexed and non-searchable newsgroup post was deemed prior art.

[42] *See* Bannan – Legal Data Access, *infra*.

[43] Lessig, *Code* 2.0, *supra* note 1, at 139. More generally, for code to be considered open, Lessig requires that we have an ability not only to *know* the code, but also to *modify* it, at least among self-selecting non-profit developers. For the purposes of this chapter, we will sometimes refer only to the transparency component of open or closed code.

[44] *See, e.g.,* "meet and confer"-type rules, such as Federal Rule of Civil Procedure 26(f). *See also* Kerry-Tyerman and Shankar – The Core Concepts of E-Discovery, *infra*.

This in turn implies a different sort of limit on this limit on the regulability of code. Communities of developers are likely to enable some types of deviations from rules imposed by governments. For example, they're quite likely to resist the kind of regulation by the French to enable the cracking of financial safety. They're less likely to disable virus protection or spam filters."[45]

Our ability to change the code through a group of developers who perhaps follow some type of normative creed is quite different from the framework of norm application, enforcement, and creation through legal institutions. A valid legal system certainly does not require that all its subjects normatively agree with all the rules imposed on them, or even that they have recourse to change the rules. But certainly a valid legal system requires that those subjected to rules at least have an effective manner in which to become aware of the rules before being required to follow them. Moreover, a democratic system attempts to provide a mechanism to change them.

With closed code, we are blocked from the ability to change or know the rules, other than those rules that prevent us from doing something we sought to do. But even with open code, the norms of this non-governmental subclass called "developers" directly impact architectural-based regulations. What is the interaction among members in this class to set norms, and the interaction between this class and standard legal system institutions that interpret and enforce law? What is the relationship between this class and jurisdictions? How are norms within this group regulated? For example, how does one "join" the IETF[46] or any technical standards body (e.g., ACM, IEEE, OASIS)? What are the various (and often conflicting) goals of the members, and how are decisions made? What is the relationship between the creation and the adoption of a given standard (e.g. TCP/IP, P3P, HTML, Dublin Core, LegalXML)?[47]

Example Problem: Modeling Book Lending

What does the US Constitution say about exclusive rights to sell books? In what way might exclusivity promote progress? Under what legal authority are libraries, public or private, allowed to lend books? Although lending books might reduce sales somewhat, presumably these two principles are not in (strong) conflict.

Suppose that lending a physical book requires at least a day to be given, read, and returned. Now suppose that books have gone electronic, and e-book lending is handled via almost instantaneous global passing around of simple tokens (e.g., assume for simplicity that everyone already has an encrypted copy of the e-book, but can only access/decrypt it with a valid key). Thus, when a person stops reading an e-book, she simply turns off her reader, thereby automatically releasing the token to an online lending pool of legally acquired e-books (e.g., virtual library, peer-to-peer network).

Suppose it took one physical book for, say, 10 people to be able to read it (though not simultaneously). Assume that, on average, 1000 people can share a single e-book. For example, suppose 10,000 people around the world try to read the same e-book, but only 10 would be reading at exactly the same time. Thus, while it would take 1000 physical books, only 10 e-books (tokens) would be needed among all 10,000 people. In either case, no copy

---

[45] Lessig, *Code 2.0, supra* note 1, at 151.
[46] Internet Engineering Task Force. *See generally,* IETF, "Mission and principles," available at: www.ietf.org/about/mission.
[47] *See* Dolin – XML in Law: The Role of Standards in Legal Informatics, *infra,* for a discussion of the role of XML and other standards in the legal system.

of the book would be read by more than one person at any given moment. As a result, the author would receive two orders of magnitude fewer sales with e-books than with physical books, even ignoring that there's less incentive to personally own an e-book when it's freely available from a library and the experience is largely equivalent.

Would this still be legal under the first sale doctrine as written? Under the constitution, even though granting exclusivity is a right, not a duty, would e-lending undermine the notion of promoting the arts (e.g., is exclusivity still effectively valid)? If not, what changed? Certainly not the statute, the constitution, the exclusivity, nor the lending. Is this reconcilable while retaining the same level of anonymity available to someone who either checks out physical books from a library or reads them inside the library?

One could write a formulaic version of the various statutes and constitutional authority under the physical book model. By parameterizing the analysis as a function of lending time, at a certain point the statute would no longer be consistent with the intended goal of IP exclusivity as an incentive to create new ideas. What were the assumptions in the statute that were rendered invalid by the introduction of new technology? How realistic is this model – how could it be improved? What other regulations' validity is based on expired or soon-to-be expired assumptions due to either existing or upcoming technology?

C Latent Ambiguities

Section II referenced the issue that technology and efficiency can bring to light issues for which there are no known norms. Lessig discusses several examples of latent ambiguities, including search, copyright, privacy, and free speech.[48] All of these point to societal norms brought into stronger and more apparent conflict due to the impact of technological changes on presumptions that are no longer valid (e.g., privacy vs. security). These conflicts include, for example, the way that technology can enable search without the need to be physically invasive, or the tracking and aggregation of individuals' behaviors on a mass scale without their knowledge or permission. The example of copyright infringement highlights the issue of the ability of regulation to block behavior that may be either legal or was effectively permissible, to some degree, in the pre-digital age.

Infringement of IP rights (copyrights, trademarks, patents, trade secrets) seems, at first blush, counter to both the law and to social norms. However, there are exceptions. Legal exceptions include fair use, first sale, etc. Social exceptions based on behavior seem to include some degree of small-scale copying. As a deterrent, civil liability is often used instead of, or in addition to, criminal liability, neither of which is necessarily worth pursuing for minor violations.

Copyright regulation provides an example of the changing nature of regulation. Pre-technological regulations to limit infringement incorporated market modalities, taking into account the costs of copying and the degradation of analog downstream copies. But the move to digital made the market impact negligible. One response was a U.S. Department of Commerce "White Paper" that sought to maintain the same balance of regulatory modalities, in a manner similar to dealing with prior analog copying.[49]

---

[48] Lessig, Code 2.0, supra note 1, chapters 9–12.
[49] Bruce A. Lehman, *Intellectual Property and the National Information Infrastructure: The Report of the Working Group on Intellectual Property Rights* (Washington, DC: Information Infrastructure Task Force, 1995).

"Balance is attractive, and moderation seems right. But something is missing from this approach. The White Paper proceeds as if the problem of protecting intellectual property in cyberspace was just like the problem of protecting intellectual property in real space. It proceeds as if the four constraints [law, norms, market, and architecture/code] would operate in the same proportions as in real space, as if nothing fundamental had changed.

But something fundamental has changed: the role that code plays in the protection of intellectual property. Code can, and increasingly will, displace law as the primary defense of intellectual property in cyberspace. Private fences, not public law."[50]

A private fence presumes that the property being protected is wholly private. This approach, however, can and often does preclude forms of legally allowable, and societally beneficial, sharing of intellectual property (e.g., fair use), let alone the minor violations that hitherto have been tolerable and also beneficial.

Trying to resolve latent ambiguities raises the question of whether the existing legal institutions are effective vehicles for addressing these challenges. Lessig raises the issue of whether lawyers are properly trained or sociologically appropriate agents for this:

"I've argued that cyberspace will open up three important choices in the context of intellectual property: whether to allow intellectual property in effect to become completely propertized (for that is what a perfect code regime for protecting intellectual property would do); and whether to allow this regime to erase the anonymity latent in less efficient architectures of control; and whether to allow the expansion of intellectual property to drive out amateur culture. These choices were not made by our framers. They are for us to make now.

I have a view, in this context as in the following three, about how we should exercise that choice. But I am a lawyer. Lawyers are taught to point elsewhere – to the framers, to the United Nations charter, to an act of Congress – when arguing about how things ought to be. Having said that there is no such authority here, I feel as if I ought to be silent."[51]

What is the role of a lawyer, a legal technologist, a designer, or an engineer in a modern legal system? What types of training might they require? How much understanding of both law and technology are required to know which options exist, and which policies are both advantageous and practical? What forces influence their decisions, and to whom might they be accountable? Perhaps the government could establish indirect market forces to incentivize code to address the issues that Lessig raises about copyright. It might seem obvious that an institution or committee responsible for setting technical policy would benefit from including technical expertise among its members.[52] It might be less obvious, however, that such expertise may be increasingly necessary for non-technical policy. For example, the determination of whether the regulation of speech is overbroad requires an understanding of what might be feasible at any given time in a quickly changing technological landscape, one in which much speech has moved to online platforms.[53]

---

[50] Lessig, *Code 2.0*, *supra* note 1, at 175.

[51] *Id.* at 197.

[52] See, e.g., Ron Dolin, "Search Query Privacy: The Problem of Anonymization," *Hastings Science and Technology Law Journal* 2 (137) (2010). At that time, there were no technical experts listed among the members of the Article 29 Working Party, responsible for setting data privacy rules in the EU.

[53] Lessig, *Code 2.0*, *supra*, note 1. Lessig discusses issues around the use of an "H2C" HTML tag ("Harmful-To-Children") that establishes a potentially appropriate balance between content providers, regulators, parents, and free speech. The issue here is how the potential use of technological standards (or any technological solution, really) gets communicated to decision makers who may or may not understand the underlying technology. In addition, the creation of a standard does not necessarily yield sufficient market adoption, as with P3P or LegalXML. *See additionally* Dolin – XML in Law: The Role of Standards in Legal Informatics, *infra*, which discusses several aspects of the use of standards in the legal system.

Should we be allowed to block legal behavior such as lending or personal copying in order to prevent the possibility of illegal behavior such as infringement, with no indication that such behavior is likely on an individual basis? Even if we could perfect prevention to focus only on illegal acts and never prevent legal ones, would that be acceptable? In other words, do we ever have the *right* to break the law?

D The Right to Break the Law?

"Death penalty for parking tickets!"

Steve Martin

Do we have the right to break the law? How does architectural prevention impact the notion of proportional punishment as a deterrent? One way of viewing punishment is that it is an attempt to make the cost of doing something illegal greater than the benefit, such that a rational actor will refrain from the illegal activity. Another perspective is that we have a tolerance for various types of illegal activity that permits a certain level of freedom to be naughty. Between varying levels of punishment, selective enforcement, and prosecutorial discretion, we allow a degree of illegal behavior unless it becomes sufficiently problematic that it needs to be reined in.

Consider the following types of law breaking: (1) the "Bad Man," (2) speeding, (3) jaywalking and dog walking, and (4) civil disobedience. In terms of the modalities of regulation, each case proffers a different profile in appropriate levels of punishment, the interplay between criminal and civil remedies, and the potential role of prevention. In terms of transparency, the issue is whether and to what degree we may want to intentionally architect the ability to act illegally, and which norms are at play in the process.

1 The "Bad Man"

In Oliver Wendell Holmes' *The Path of the Law*, he describes the "Bad Man" who carries no moral dictates.[54] His desired actions do not conform with either the law or social norms. Instead, his behavior is regulated by legal deterrence (and, apparently, a presumption of rationality), by architectural prevention, or perhaps by the market:

> "You can see very plainly that a bad man has as much reason as a good one for wishing to avoid an encounter with the public force, and therefore you can see the practical importance of the distinction between morality and law. A man who cares nothing for an ethical rule which is believed and practised by his neighbors is likely nevertheless to care a good deal to avoid being made to pay money, and will want to keep out of jail if he can ... If you want to know the law and nothing else, you must look at it as a bad man, who cares only for the material consequences which such knowledge enables him to predict."[55]

Certainly the Bad Man presents a case for the potential benefit of prevention as perhaps more efficient than consequence-based deterrence. But many people break the law regularly and think little of it.

---

[54] Oliver Wendell Holmes, Jr., "The Path of the Law," *Harvard Law Review* 10 (457) (1897).
[55] *Ibid.*

2 Speeding

An example of conflicting customs vs. laws involves speeding. Most drivers go faster than the posted speed limit with some regularity. Speed laws serve to protect drivers and the public at large. There are certain accepted norms of speeding such that the police are known not to issue citations within some range beyond the posted speed limit, though technically they could. However, as we move toward increased technological innovations related to driving, the interplay between law and software becomes more interesting.

Example Problem: Speeding and Transparency

When I drive along Highway 280, I notice most people driving over the speed limit. I also often notice people pulled over getting tickets. With current smartphone APIs, could you design an app that would allow you to keep your speeding violation costs, including any additional insurance premiums, to, say, $250/year, within a 90% probability? What data would it need (if it is not currently available, why not)? Would building such an app be ethical, legal? Should such a system put a limit on how far above the speed limit it would incorporate into its calculations, based on public safety?

With the onset of self-driving cars, suppose that we wanted to simplify the entire moving violation mechanism and allow people to prepay for some level of violation by regularly billing them (fees to the state or county) and then, via automobile software, only allow them to drive within that fee-level violation range. Suppose one could drive at the speed limit for free. Perhaps one could drive more recklessly, say, by prepaying a larger amount each billing cycle, or by compensating for one day's excesses with a week's worth of driving the speed limit. Would this change the probabilities of accidents and tickets, or their costs?

Wouldn't this just make more efficient, transparent, and rational what already goes on, but without the added expense of the traffic police/court system? After all, the wealthy can afford to pay penalties easier than the poor already, so have less to lose from the occasional penalty. Would this incentivize governments to change speed limits to anything different than the current model incentivizes? Would it change highway safety mechanisms and budgets? How would this model be impacted if penalties were assessed based on income? Where in this system is legal application, enforcement, and creation?

This simple example demonstrates some of the societal norms made transparent through an open application of regulation by code.

3 Jaywalking and Dog Walking

Regarding the rule of recognition, "legal systems can, and typically do, contain some rules that are not themselves practiced by members of the group. Jaywalking, for example, is prohibited in New York City even though most everyone does it."[56] The rationale for laws against jaywalking is likely more to protect the jaywalker than to prevent denting cars; while norms may allow it, architecture may serve to prevent jaywalking where it may be particularly dangerous. In contrast, the prohibition of walking a dog off-leash is not necessarily for the purpose of protecting the dog. Norms frequently permit it, and it is difficult to prevent architecturally. But in both cases, the penalties are somewhat minimal, and minimally enforced, to the degree that the rules against them are commonly disregarded. There are

---

[56] Shapiro, "What Is The Rule of Recognition (And Does It Exist)?," *supra* note 37, at 10.

certainly civil liabilities in the event that breaking these rules leads to an incident, but generally little effort is made to prevent the activities in advance.

4 Civil Disobedience

Perhaps the most instructive case for the right to break the law comes in the form of civil disobedience, as explained by Dr. Martin Luther King, Jr., in his "Letter from a Birmingham Jail."[57] King lists criteria for challenging the morality of a law: laws imposed on a minority which are (1) not applied to the majority, or (2) created through the exclusion of the minority's participation. But more relevant here, King justifies illegal activities made in furtherance of changing unjust laws:

> "Sometimes a law is just on its face and unjust in its application. For instance, I have been arrested on a charge of parading without a permit. Now, there is nothing wrong in having an ordinance which requires a permit for a parade. But such an ordinance becomes unjust when it is used to maintain segregation and to deny citizens the First-Amendment privilege of peaceful assembly and protest.
>
> I hope you are able to see the distinction I am trying to point out. In no sense do I advocate evading or defying the law, as would the rabid segregationist. That would lead to anarchy. One who breaks an unjust law must do so openly, lovingly, and with a willingness to accept the penalty. I submit that an individual who breaks a law that conscience tells him is unjust, and who willingly accepts the penalty of imprisonment in order to arouse the conscience of the community over its injustice, is in reality expressing the highest respect for law.
>
> Of course, there is nothing new about this kind of civil disobedience. It was evidenced sublimely in the refusal of Shadrach, Meshach and Abednego to obey the laws of Nebuchadnezzar, on the ground that a higher moral law was at stake. It was practiced superbly by the early Christians, who were willing to face hungry lions and the excruciating pain of chopping blocks rather than submit to certain unjust laws of the Roman Empire. To a degree, academic freedom is a reality today because Socrates practiced civil disobedience. In our own nation, the Boston Tea Party represented a massive act of civil disobedience."[58]

In an implementation of the legal system that prevents illegal activity through architecture, what recourse would someone like King have if nonviolent protests were impossible? What does civil disobedience look like online, and do we allow it with the same proportional penalties as we might for sit-ins and other attention-getting protest mechanisms?

5 Implementation of Regulatory Modalities

If we could prevent any illegal behavior, which ones would we want to regulate via deterrence rather than architecture? If there are cases where an ability to break the law is justified, there are certainly cases where it is not. There is also a subjective component to an act; some may feel it is justified, and some may not. This leeway is inherent in the application of punishment, from selective enforcement and prosecutorial discretion to jury nullification.[59] All of

---

[57] Martin Luther King, Jr., "Letter from a Birmingham Jail," April 16, 1963, available at: www.africa.upenn.edu /Articles_Gen/Letter_Birmingham.html.
[58] Ibid.
[59] Jury nullification only applies to the case of a jury believing someone is technically guilty of an act but not wanting to hold them legally liable (e.g., assisting runaway slaves in pre-Civil War America).

the nuance of the application of proportional punishment and its implied tolerance of some forms of illegality are lost through enforcement by architecture.

The question arises as to whether there might be a systematic approach to determining when to facilitate the ability to break the law. Certainly such ability is necessary in order to allow civil disobedience, by definition. In cases of *potential* law breaking, such as copyright infringement, there is a balance between the rights of legal activity and the various types of damage that might occur from illegal activity: lending someone a movie compared to, say, leaking an unreleased Hollywood blockbuster.

Lessig describes some of the interplay between various regulatory modalities in different situations (e.g., preventing theft of firewood, bicycles, cars, park flowers, etc.):

> "Many things protect property against theft—differently. The market protects my firewood (it is cheaper to buy your own than it is to haul mine away); the market is a special threat to my bike (which if taken is easily sold). Norms sometimes protect flowers in a park; sometimes they do not. Nature sometimes conspires with thieves (cars, planes, and boats) and sometimes against them (skyscrapers).
>
> These protections are not fixed. I could lock my bike and thereby use real-space code to make it harder to steal. There could be a shortage of firewood; demand would increase, making it harder to protect. Public campaigns about civic beauty might stop flower theft; selecting a distinctive flower might do the same. Sophisticated locks might make stolen cars useless; sophisticated bank fraud might make skyscrapers vulnerable. The point is not that protections are given, or unchangeable, but that they are multiplied and their modalities different."[60]

Factors in the determination of whether *ex ante* or *ex post* treatment of illegal activity is appropriate include the nature of the planning and execution of the act (e.g., public, private, concealed), the intended beneficiaries, and the nature of the potential harm (e.g., a public march may be annoying and even costly, but a murder is permanent). Perhaps the Bad Man selfishly plans a robbery in secret and hides his identity during the act, the jaywalker is just trying to avoid cars, and the civilly disobedient intentionally plans in public to increase participation and raise awareness. It is, in part, the *ex ante* willingness to accept the *ex post* punishment that serves as the exclamation mark to the protestor's point. But the view that a law is unjust and therefore worthy of being challenged could come from any point on a political spectrum – neo-Nazis and the KKK are well known for public marching. One person's Bad Man is another's civilly disobedient. While it may make sense to preclude reckless driving, disallowing any and all speeding means that a parent may be unable to rush their sick child to the hospital. In many ways, regulation is defined by the (often unanticipated) exceptions.

The secondary rules discussed earlier include the *rule of change* to address dexterity. This rule is procedural in nature, but to be *effective*, it may require tolerating a degree of illegality. Architectural prevention makes it difficult to change the law because it becomes more difficult to challenge or ignore the law (e.g., sit-ins, medical marijuana). This approach makes more difficult the interplay between norms and law to allow the law to change in order to keep pace with changing norms. The implementation of regulations and their transparency, and code in particular, impacts the way that law is allowed, or forced, to change.

---

[60] Lessig, *Code 2.0, supra* note 1, at 170–171.

V CONCLUSION

Technology is increasingly used to implement and reconstruct the legal system. Its characteristics of efficiency and scale promise to apply regulations to more people more often. Its tendency to work in a mechanical or statistical manner threatens to minimize the role of exceptions, exigency, and empathy that are core components of law. The need to balance efficiency, quality, fairness, and access is nothing new. But as is common with technology, the harm caused by getting it wrong increases with each order of magnitude change in implementation. The necessity of the legal technologist to understand both technology and law cannot be overstated.

1.3

The Origins and History of Legal Informatics

Michael J. Bommarito II

Throughout the twentieth and early twenty-first centuries, the world witnessed exponential growth in the amount of information collected, stored, and analyzed. Not unrelatedly, the *cost* of storing, analyzing, and transmitting information has fallen exponentially during the same period, resulting in substantially greater access to and awareness of data. A few hundred years ago, the cost of storing the sum of written human knowledge exceeded the budgets of all but the very wealthiest institutions; today, the body of all written human knowledge can be accessed by a device that nearly half of the world's population carries in their pocket. As a result, people have become somewhat desensitized to the purpose and presence of data in modern society. In order to understand the purpose of the data and knowledge we have accrued and stored – and which is intrinsically linked to informatics – it is useful to look back to a time when knowledge was genuinely scarce and expensive to access. To understand informatics, we must understand the importance of writing and knowledge systems through history.

I EARLY LEGAL CODIFICATION

While scholars often disagree over which system of writing came first, they generally agree that early systems of information storage emerged in response to the need to organize and manage legal and economic systems. In Mesopotamia, Egypt, China, and the Mayan empires, one primary application of writing was to record information related to stocks and flows, or rights and obligations. The recording of stocks and flows allowed institutions like temples to protect early agrarian societies against natural disaster or invasion. Taxes on agricultural output created centralized stores of food, and population censuses could be used to plan consumption and conscription. Rights and obligations flowed from sources like the Code of Hammurabi, or from the documented lineage of royalty. While droughts and disputes clearly existed before and continued after the invention of writing systems, these societies were the first to recognize the existential threat such catastrophes represented, and they invented institutions and invested entire human lives toward combating them.

Tax administrators and temple priests were arguably the first dedicated knowledge workers in human history. While their scope of responsibilities was somewhat broader than today's legal professionals, the similarities are striking across the millennia. From a young age, knowledge workers in Mesopotamia, Egypt, and China were dedicated to regimented study and testing. These individuals had to develop several requisite skills: maximize information recall by memorizing rules and precedents; apply these rules consistently and accurately in forms of logical computation; and perform lengthy arithmetic and transcription operations on ledgers tracking numerical computations. These professions were economically secure unless "disbarred" through a breach of trust. In these and other ways, the lives of a modern juris doctorate (JD) or certified public accountant (CPA) look strikingly similar to those of Egyptian tax collectors or Sumerian priests over 3000 years ago.

No matter the era, today or 3000 years ago, the task of legal professionals and institutions is to design, codify, implement, and interpret the law – a vast web of imagined concepts developed over thousands of years – to shape the behaviors of an increasingly large and complex world. The first step in this process is to design the law around policies that achieve normative goals or requirements. In most cases, these policies are then translated into the written schema of a legal system through the process of codification. Once codified into something like a law or regulation, legal professionals and institutions then coordinate to implement the policy, whether through education or enforcement. In cases where enforcement meets uncertainty, legal professionals and institutions must interpret and clarify the law, often returning to the beginning of this entire process once more.

At each step in this process, knowledge and data play critical roles. For example, a key component of designing any policy is to first model that policy. In order for an Egyptian administrator to protect the kingdom against famine, they first would have had to estimate the stock and flow of people and agriculture. The need for models thus resulted in processes like the census, cattle count, land survey, and flood nilometer tables (Figure 1.3.1), which

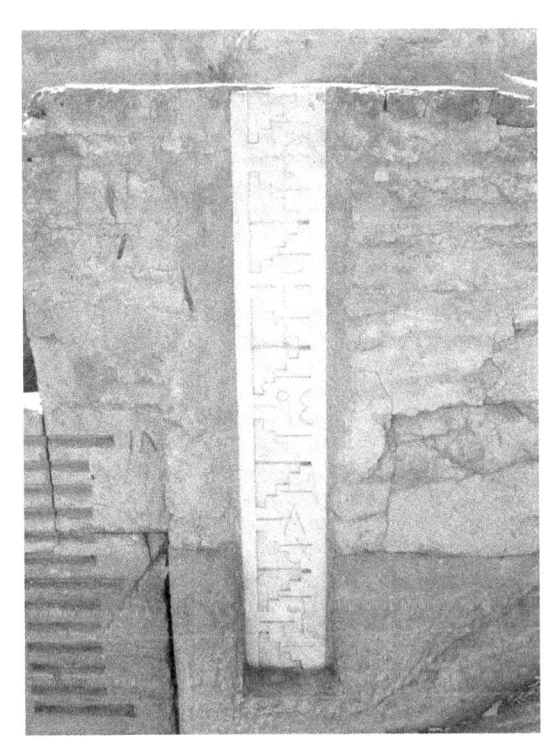

FIGURE 1.3.1 This nilometer on Elephantine Island in Aswan, Egypt is one of the first applications of informatics in the law. The device, which recorded the "inundation" – or flood stage – of the Nile, was used by temples to determine the tax rate.[1]

---

[1] Image from Wikimedia Commons, available at: https://commons.wikimedia.org/wiki/File:Assuan/Elephantine/Nilometer/12.JPG.

recorded population, property, and environmental data. Taken together, these ledgers allowed for the modeling of policy. Would a 5% marginal increase in grain tax have prevented a seven-year famine? Would a subsidy for irrigation improvement have reduced the variation in inundation along the course of the Nile?

II LAW BEFORE LAW

In an informal sense, the "law" predates writing, first originating in the form of norms and customs shared by a group or culture. One of the hallmarks of formal law, as opposed to these older norms and customs, is its codification – norms and customs are transferred into explicit rules and written in a positive or negative form ("shall" or "shall not"). In many historical cases, norms and customs were simple and proscriptive. One of the first and most famous codifications of law that conforms to this description is the Code of Hammurabi, with laws such as:

- "If any man, without the knowledge of the owner of a garden, fell a tree in a garden he shall pay half a mina in money."
- "If any one hire a ferryboat, he shall pay three gerahs in money per day."

Many jurisdictions were once primarily managed by single civil codes such as the Code of Hammurabi, but societies and legal institutions have become more complicated since the time of Babylon. Today, many jurisdictions are managed by increasingly overlapping and hierarchical civil and common law bodies that span national, bilateral, and multilateral international systems. The quantity and character of law has grown well past the bounds of stone tablets.

To be fair to stone, the nature of codification did not really change when paper replaced it. Paper codices, like their stone ancestors, typically enumerated laws as simple lists. Where there was organization, it was limited to single-dimensional categories. As societies and their legal systems accumulated more disparate and historical legal baggage, the need for organization and metadata became more pressing. This tension stretches far back past our modern times; in the fifth century CE, Roman jurists were so overwhelmed by the volume and contradiction of precedent that they required a Law of Citation (*Lex citationum*) to provide guidance. In the following century, jurists addressed the problem again through the development of Roman law's best known product, the Body of Civil Law (*Corpus Juris Civilis* – Figure 1.3.2). The *Corpus* compiled, synthesized, and superseded prior law, but was also notable for including not just law, but also metadata about law, such as its source and date:

> "- **The Same Emperor and Caesar to Florentius, Praetorian Prefect.**
> We order that when pictures or statues are to be erected or publicly placed in Our honor, they shall not be taken from a private collection, in order to prevent the collector of the same from claiming any one of them as his own.
> **Given on the third of the Nones of April, during the Consulate of Theodosius, Consul for the seventeenth time, and Festus, 429.**"[2]

---

[2] Samuel Parson Scott, *The Civil Law: Including the Twelve Tables, the Institutes of Gaius, the Rules of Ulpian, the Opinions of Paulus, the Enactments of Justinian, and the Constitutions of Leo* (Clark, NJ: The Lawbook Exchange, 2001).

FIGURE 1.3.2 *Corpus Juris Civilis*, republished in 1627 with commentary by Johann Fehe.

III MODERN CODIFICATION AND THE WEST REPORTING SYSTEM

Arguably, the next seismic shift in codification didn't occur until the development and adoption of the West Reporting System. At the end of the nineteenth century, the American legal system was facing exactly the same problem that its Roman ancestor had faced in the fifth century. As John B. West detailed in a lengthy complaint titled *Multiplicity of Reports*, the "necessity of index or digest is apparent" and the "only remedy has been recompilation." Where the Romans solved the codification problem by changing the very law itself, the American legal system addressed the problem by changing the way the law was *published* and *accessed*. The West Reporting System, still in use today, uses knowledge management principles to label legal material with topic and key numbers that can be used to develop indices supporting incremental updates. Legal professionals can subsequently use these indices to dramatically improve their knowledge retrieval, increasing breadth of search and reducing the time it takes to search for relevant sources or precedents. West's company dedicated its professional efforts to providing not just a search index, but also to summarizing material in the form of annotations and headnotes. These annotated and indexed systems have subsequently become so popular that they are often cited *de facto* as the law itself. While West still employs human legal professionals in these tasks, automation through informatics has increased notably in the last two decades, as we shall discuss elsewhere in this book.

IV IMPLEMENTATION OF LAW

The design and codification of modern legal systems is only half the battle, though. Once rules are chosen and written down, legal systems must then be executed: implemented and subsequently interpreted. Registers of deeds, patents, and marks must be created. Courts must be built. Judges must be seated. While informatics is important for the design and codification of law in the modern world, it is critical for law's implementation. Unlike the design and codification of law, which continue to this day primarily in the form of natural language, the implementation of law at scale typically requires the development of systems that rely on alternative forms of information representation. For example, while the articles or acts creating American courts may be written in English sentences, the records of these courts are increasingly kept in a much different form. Dockets, the most prevalent of court records, record the actions of the court or the parties before it. When dockets consist of natural English language sentences, they are lengthy, difficult to search, prone to mistakes, and inconsistent across courts, judges, and clerks. When dockets consist of standardized information management systems, however, these problems are partially alleviated (much of the data is still semi-structured).

It is important to note that implementation of law impacts not just public law, but also private law. Interestingly, legal informatics has arguably been applied much more in private law in recent years. Parties and dates are just as important to a corporation searching its contracts as they are to a defendant searching a judge's past docket. Furthermore, many private legal documents, such as contracts, can be *created* and *executed*, not just analyzed *post hoc*, through the application of informatics. The field of document automation is largely concerned with the generation of traditional natural language contracts through automation,[3] and efforts have been made to develop "smart" contracts on so-called "blockchain" or distributed ledger systems. While the term "smart contract" may be somewhat misleading and the field is still nascent, as we will explore throughout this book, such informatics approaches have the potential to be transformative.

V CONCLUSION

Informatics consists of more than just computer science concepts like query languages or proof-of-work systems. Informatics is a broad field with end-to-end scope that not only captures data and knowledge, but also processes, analyzes, and visualizes information. As an ends-focused discipline, informatics is both interdisciplinary and collaborative. Many

---

[3] *See* Lauritsen – Document Automation, *infra*.

successful informatics projects incorporate theory and practice from fields outside of computer science, such as design and UI/UX, behavioral sciences/psychology, business and management/organizational science, engineering, and physics.

More than almost any other human activity, the law has resided mainly in minds and on paper – it is the prototypical *knowledge-based economy*, constrained primarily to analog forms like neurochemical storage. Over the last 50 years, these analog forms have been augmented with digital systems. In some cases, these digital systems are simply more durable, scalable versions of the mental concepts we communicate through oral and written language, such as Word or PDF documents. In other cases, digital systems like court databases or TurboTax are changing the way we encode and interact with the law. Yet even in this digital era, the law still exists *prima facie* as analog concepts. Whether the legal system will continue this progression to adopt a truly computational form – the law as code – is yet to be seen.[4]

While we cannot gaze directly into the future of law, we can use the history of other fields for some guidance. The history of informatics is long, but the most relevant use cases begin with military and governmental applications in the 1940s and 1950s. Such applications gave rise to business computing and companies such as IBM, where informatics was applied to financial, accounting, and human resource processes that were previously manual or completely infeasible. More modern use cases include production and factory management systems, order processing and billing, inventory, logistics and supply chain, more advanced financial and accounting systems, patient records and electronic medical records systems, and, most impactfully, the internet and the omnipresent and expansive information retrieval systems that live within it.

Before providing further detail on how informatics can benefit us, we must first lay a foundation of conceptual and technical understanding. In the chapters in Part II, we provide readers with an overview of material critical for understanding where legal informatics is today and where it can go in the future. Topics include machine learning (ML), natural language processing (NLP), information representation as applied to language and law, information preprocessing, information intermediation and presentation, formal logic, access to justice, expert systems, and quality evaluation. While each of these topics is a field of study unto itself, we have provided several chapters that quickly and clearly introduce the reader to the core concepts of informatics. While those who choose to read only Part II will be prepared to understand all subsequent chapters, additional references to key and related literature are provided for each core concept covered.

---

[4] For an exploration of this idea, *see* Dolin – Technology Issues in Legal Philosophy, *supra*.

PART II

Legal Informatics

Building Blocks and Core Concepts

A.

Information Representation, Preprocessing, and Document Assembly

2.1

Representation of Legal Information

Katie Atkinson

There are a variety of different approaches to representing legal information in order to make that information usable in legal analytics or automated reasoning systems. This variety of approaches stems from the variety of tasks that legal practitioners wish to undertake, and there is no single representation technique that squarely fits all tasks and contexts. This chapter will survey the methods available for representing legal information, and the benefits that each method can bring to the tools used in legal work. This section will also provide a high-level overview of approaches that have been developed to represent laws expressed as statutes, rules, and regulations. It will also survey the standards that have been developed and that are emerging for representing legal information. An overview of methods for representing case law will also be provided, along with a summary of how interpretation of the law can be achieved through automated reasoning mechanisms based on computational models of argument. This chapter will also consider methods of conceptualizing and reasoning about the relations within and between legal documents such as contracts, along with techniques to represent wider networks of information, such as document citations.

Following the high-level overview of the techniques available for representing legal information, I will later offer a case study in Part III of this volume to demonstrate in more detail how one particular technique – computational argumentation – can be used to effectively build automated reasoning tools that provide decision support capabilities for legal practitioners. The case study will demonstrate how legal cases can be represented and interpreted through computational models of arguments, and how this enables software programs to generate and reason about the relevant arguments for deciding a case in a manner akin to human judicial reasoning.

I APPROACHES TO REPRESENTING LEGAL INFORMATION

Just as there are many different kinds of legal information, there are also many different techniques from the fields of AI and legal informatics that can be used to represent legal information for use in computer-support tools for legal practitioners. This section provides an overview of some of the key techniques that have been used for representing legal information. While this survey is not exhaustive – the volume of literature on the topic is vast – it is intended to pick out some representative examples to illustrate how legal information can be captured for use in computerized tools.

A Statutes, Rules, and Regulations

Rules-based approaches to representing domain information have long been used in artificial intelligence (AI). These approaches capture structured information so that it can be reasoned about in a systematic manner. The rules-based approach has particular affinity to the legal domain due to the rules-based expressions of many types of law. A landmark example of early work in the field of AI and law investigated how legislation can be represented in software. *The British Nationality Act as a Logic Program* showed how an Act of the UK Parliament – The British Nationality Act – could be captured in software written in the Prolog programming language.[1]

Prolog is a programming language particularly suitable for AI applications because it is based on formal logic, which is used for knowledge representation and reasoning in AI. This work on the British Nationality Act is an example of an early project that tackled legal information representation, and it is characteristic of a now wider body of work showing how legislation can be captured in software, allowing it to be used in support tools – for example, a tool that advises users on how to meet citizenship criteria.

Many projects have been undertaken to show how civil law can be represented formally so that its reasoning can be automated. Commercial products have been used to address this task. One example of this application is SoftLaw's STATUTE Expert Technology, used to model Italian regulations concerning taxes to be paid to start legal proceedings.[2]

More recent work has considered how to model national-level laws and their interaction with the laws of higher jurisdictions.[3] In this kind of work, formal logic is used to model tiers of institutions such that the norms at each tier are governed by those at the tier above, as reflected, for example, in the way that EU Directives govern member states' legislation. This logical representation enables explicit reasoning concerning the compliance of an institution with the tier above it.

The representation of legal statutes and regulations relates to the access-to-justice agenda and the work aiming to improve the readability of legislation that has been undertaken by AI and law researchers. One study describes how machine learning can predict the readability of sentences from legislation and regulations.[4] This work was applied to a corpus of sentences from the United States Code and US Code of Federal Regulations. The results of the study were fed into proposals for a system that would reduce difficulty with legal language. The

---

[1] Marek J. Sergot, Fariba Sadri, Robert A. Kowalski, Frank Kriwaczek, Peter Hammond, and H. Terese Cory, "The British Nationality Act as a Logic Program," *Communications of the ACM* 29 (5) (1986): 370–386. For an introduction to Prolog, *see, e.g.*, Ivan Bratko, *PROLOG Programming for Artificial Intelligence*, 2nd edition (Boston, MA: Addison-Wesley, 1990).

[2] Giulio Borsari, Claudia Cevenini, Giuseppe Contissa, Stefano Morini, Giovanni Sartor, and Peter Still, "HARE: An Italian Application of Softlaw's STATUTE Expert Technology," in *The Tenth International Conference on Artificial Intelligence and Law, Proceedings of the Conference, Bologna, Italy, June 6–11, 2005*, ed. Giovanni Sartor (New York, NY: ACM, 2005), 225–229.

[3] Thomas Christopher King, Tingting Li, Marina De Vos, Virginia Dignum, Catholijn M. Jonker, Julian Padget, and M. Birna van Riemsdijk, "A Framework for Institutions Governing Institutions," in *Proceedings of the 2015 International Conference on Autonomous Agents and Multiagent Systems, AAMAS 2015, Istanbul, Turkey, May 4–8, 2015*, eds. Gerhard Weiss, Pinar Yolum, Rafael H. Bordini, and Edith Elkind (New York, NY: ACM, 2015), 473–481.

[4] Michael Curtotti, Eric McCreath, Tom Bruce, Sara S. Frug, Wayne Weibel, and Nicolas Ceynowa, "Machine Learning for Readability of Legislative Sentences," in *Proceedings of the 15th International Conference on Artificial Intelligence and Law, ICAIL 2015, San Diego, CA, USA, June 8–12, 2015*, eds. Ted Sichelman and Katie Atkinson (New York, NY: ACM, 2015), 53–62.

results also suggested a set of heuristics for improving the writing of legislation and regulations in order to meet the aim of making the law more accessible to the citizens to whom it applies.

B Legal Work Products

Numerous products are now available that provide support for the legal work carried out daily within law firms. Large, well-known commercial firms such as Thomson Reuters[5] and LexisNexis[6] offer suites of legal solutions that cover e-discovery, intellectual property search, case management, and many other tasks involving legal research and legal workflow management. Another established product, Oracle Policy Automation, offers the ability to "transform legislation and policy and documents into executable and maintainable rules in any language."[7] This product has been developed over a significant period of time, and in its current form the tool enables policies to be modeled, analyzed, and updated for public and private sector users to determine what the obligations of their policies are within the framework of legal compliance.

In addition to the offerings of the large, established firms, several legal tech startups have appeared in the past few years to take advantage of new technological developments that can assist in processing legal work and moving toward automation. The Codex Legal Tech List is a repository that lists these legal technology companies.[8] The list currently divides the listed companies into nine categories: Marketplace, Document Automation, Practice Management, Legal Research, Legal Education, Online Dispute Resolution, E-Discovery, Analytics, and Compliance. The different companies in each category address different tasks, and some are geared toward specific domains. For example, Rocket Lawyer is an established company that provides online legal services both for business use (e.g., contracting work) and for personal use (e.g., estate planning).[9] Document automation services such as those offered by Rocket Lawyer enable clients to create custom legal documents by filling in forms that ensure the data submitted conforms to a particular structure that allows the document to be produced automatically. A key task in a variety of legal work products is identifying the structure common to documents or tasks, and capturing this in a tool that enables automation of these repetitive aspects of the work.[10]

C Networks

Formal models of law can provide insights into complex legislation, both in terms of content and structure. A recent key example of this is the work of Bommarito and Katz.[11] They provide a formal representation of the United States Code in terms of a hierarchical network and a citation network over vertices containing the language of the Code. The representation captures the hierarchical nature of the Code, and the explicit citations between provisions. The formal representation enables measurements to be made between different versions of

---

[5] Thomson Reuters, www.thomsonreuters.com/en/products-services/legal.html.
[6] LexisNexis, www.lexisnexis.co.uk/en-uk/home.page.
[7] "Oracle Policy Automation," Oracle, available at: www.oracle.com/us/products/applications/oracle-policy-automation/policy-automation/overview/index.html.
[8] "Legal Tech List," Stanford CodeX, available at: http://techindex.law.stanford.edu.
[9] Rocket Lawyer, www.rocketlawyer.com.
[10] For more detail and examples, see Lauritsen – Document Automation, *infra*.
[11] Michael J. Bommarito II and Daniel Martin Katz, "A Mathematical Approach to the Study of the United States Code," *Physica A: Statistical Mechanics and its Applications* 389 (19) (2010): 4195–4200.

the code as it changes over time, and these measurements capture how the structure, interdependence, and language of the Code all grow over time.

Citation networks have also been studied in European law – for example, in the citation networks captured for the Italian Constitutional Court.[12] Researchers created a citation network composed of constitutional decisions by the Italian Constitutional Court through identification of the rulings (represented as nodes in the network) and the explicit annotation of the judicial references among them (represented as edges in the network). This kind of representation enables the study of legal relevance, allowing a number of conclusions to be drawn. One remarkable finding is that a large number of cases that are frequently discussed by experts are neither hubs nor authorities in the citation network. Furthermore, cases that *are* relevant in the citation network are scarcely debated by scholars, and sometimes even ignored by them. These conclusions draw attention to the decisions and verdicts that have to be reckoned as most relevant in a given legal system, and they demonstrate the added value of such network representations.

D Standards

A variety of projects have aimed to develop standards for representing legal knowledge. The ESTRELLA project (European project for Standardized Transparent Representations in order to Extend LegaL Accessibility), for example, aims to develop an open, standards-based platform allowing public administrations to develop and deploy comprehensive legal knowledge management solutions. The key technical contribution of the project has been a Legal Knowledge Interchange Format (LKIF) that builds upon XML-based standards.[13]

Work on open standards has recently continued through the MetaLex project, which provides a standard approach to representing sources of law and references to them.[14] The MetaLex project aims to: enable public administrators to link legal information across different countries; enable companies to connect to and use this legal content; provide an open interchange format; and improve accessibility to, and transparency of, the law.

Focusing more specifically on contracts, Stanford CodeX's Computable Contracts project is developing a universal Contract Definition Language to support automated reasoning for contracts.[15] They focus on the representation of terms and conditions in machine-understandable language, based on logic programming.

Rule ML Inc. is a non-profit organization investing in the development and coordination of rule research in order to produce an open standard for business rule technology.[16] The organization aims to bring together academic researchers, industrial collaborators, and standards bodies.

These examples demonstrate recognition of the need for standards to be developed within the legal technology community. As with many such projects, though, widespread adoption of these standards will ultimately determine their success.

[12] Tommaso Agnoloni and Ugo Pagallo, "The Case Law of the Italian Constitutional Court, Its Power Laws, and the Web of Scholarly Opinions," in *Proceedings of the 15th International Conference on Artificial Intelligence and Law, ICAIL 2015, San Diego, CA, USA, June 8–12, 2015*, eds. Ted Sichelman and Katie Atkinson (New York, NY: ACM, 2015), 151–155.
[13] ESTRELLA Project, www.estrellaproject.org. For more information on XML, see Dolin – XML in Law, *infra*.
[14] CEN MetaLex, available at: www.metalex.eu. *See* Alexander Boer, Radboud Winkels, and Fabio Vitali, "Metalex XML and the Legal Knowledge Interchange Format," in *Computable Models of the Law, Languages, Dialogues, Games, Ontologies*, eds. Pompeu Casanovas, Giovanni Sartor, Nuria Casellas, and Rossella Rubino (New York, NY: Springer, 2008), 21–41.
[15] "Computable Contracts," Stanford CodeX, available at: http://compk.stanford.edu.
[16] Rule ML, http://wiki.ruleml.org/index.php/RuleML_Home.

E Argumentation

Arguments are a pervasive feature of legal work, most obviously when they are used in courts to persuade judges and juries to settle legal cases in favor of a particular side. Thus, a longstanding topic of research in the field of AI and law has been computational models of argument, capturing arguments and the interactions between them, and defining methods to reason about arguments and determine the justifiable ones. There is a wide range of literature on argumentation for legal knowledge representation and reasoning.[17]

Two influential systems that have been developed for reasoning with legal cases are CATO[18] and IBP.[19] CATO (Figure 2.1.1) was developed to help law school students form better case-based arguments, with particular emphasis on improving their skills in distinguishing cases, and emphasizing and downplaying distinctions.

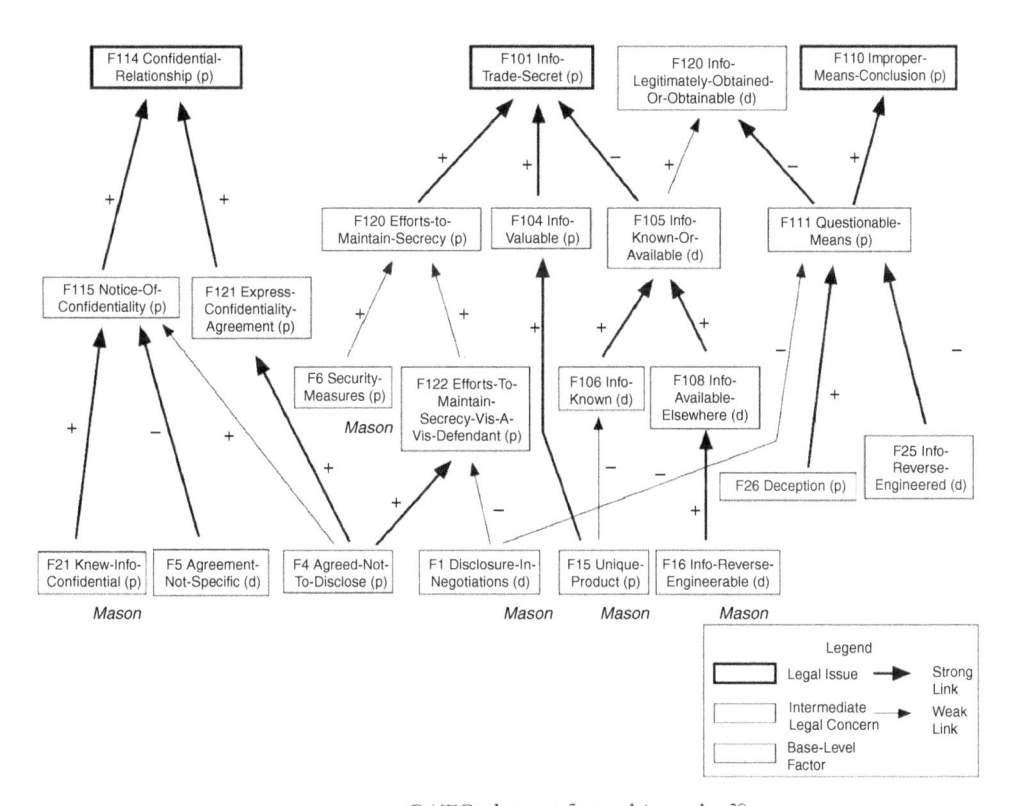

FIGURE 2.1.1 CATO abstract factor hierarchy.[20]

---

[17] For a concise introduction to this topic, see Katie Atkinson, Pietro Baroni, Massimiliano Giacomin, Anthony Hunter, Henry Prakken, Chris Reed, Guillermo Simari, Matthias Thimm, and Serena Villata, "Towards Artificial Argumentation," AI Magazine, March 15, 2017, available at: wwwo.cs.ucl.ac.uk/staff/a.hunter/papers/aimag17.pdf. A more in-depth insight into current work on argumentation in law can be found in Henry Prakken and Giovanni Sartor, "Law and Logic: A Review from an Argumentation Perspective," Artificial Intelligence 227 (2015): 214–245.

[18] Vincent Aleven, "Teaching Case-based Argumentation through a Model and Examples," (PhD thesis, University of Pittsburgh, 1997), available at: https://pdfs.semanticscholar.org/8995/bf5e9d0a686e635d0099976c18cb47f05172.pdf.

[19] Stephanie Bruninghaus and Kevin Ashley, "Predicting Outcomes of Case-based Legal Arguments," in 9th International Conference on Artificial Intelligence and Law (ICAIL), Scotland, UK, June 24–28 (New York, NY: ACM, 2003), 233–242.

[20] Image from Aleven, supra note 18.

CATO describes cases in terms of *factors* – legally significant abstractions of patterns of facts found in a body of cases within a domain. These base-level factors are then built into a hierarchy of increasing abstraction, moving upward through intermediate concerns – called *abstract factors* – then proceeding to issues. Each factor favors either the plaintiff or the defendant, and the CATO program matches precedent cases with a current case to produce arguments suggesting a finding for one side.

In the Issue-Based Prediction (IBP) system – based on CATO – the aim is not simply to discover and present arguments, but to predict the outcomes of cases. To enable this, the issues in CATO's hierarchy are tied together using a logical model derived from law. This strand of work has recently been developed further using a technique from the field of computational models of argument, abstract dialectical frameworks (ADFs).[21] Abstract dialectical frameworks can provide a methodology for reasoning about legal cases. The implementation of ADFs enables any domain of law to be captured, and any relevant cases to be reasoned about.

II CONCLUSION

Representing and interpreting legal cases through computational models of arguments is important for the future of law because it enables software programs to generate and reason about the relevant arguments for deciding a case, akin to human judicial reasoning. For more on CATO, IBP, ADFs, and the application of computational models to arguments, refer to Chapter 3.11, "A Case Study on Representation and Automation of Legal Information." In addition, an extended version of this work can be found in Part III of this volume – "Representation and Automation of Legal Information."

---

[21] Gerhard Brewka and Stefan Woltran, "Abstract Dialectical Frameworks," in *Twelfth International Conference on the Principles of Knowledge Representation and Reasoning, Toronto, ON, Canada, May 9–13* (Menlo Park, CA: AAAI Press, 2010).

2.2

Information Intermediation

Ron Dolin

"Ignorantia juris non excusat"

I INTRODUCTION

The storage, description, collection, organization, and selection of legal information is central to a legal system, whether public or private, professional or lay person, structured or unstructured, textual or non-textual. The ability to get timely information where it is needed is as important to law as it is to any other field, given that law is a system of written rules and procedures. *Ignorantia juris non excusat* – ignorance of the law is no excuse. But where citizens seek to know the law and cannot find it, they have a right to question its legitimacy, at least as applied to them. The function of the reference librarian within a brick and mortar library, while still invaluable, does not scale to the magnitude of the problem. Technological information intermediation, such as a search engine, can thus be increasingly viewed as a necessary component of a modern legal system, and familiarity with the basic concepts is an important tool in the legal technologist's toolkit.

A *Example: Online Dating*

Online dating is an interesting example of matching descriptions of candidates with search criteria. A dating site attempts to find two people who might like each other by matching profiles provided by each user. Each profile can be viewed as both a document and a query, as users describe themselves and what they are looking for in a match. In the case of looking for a document, the document does not need to like the searcher. However, in the case of, say, finding a service provider such as a driver, a lawyer, or a handyman, both the client and the provider must be interested in each other. Since personal interviews, whether romantically or professionally, may take a long time, or simply not scale to the number of candidates, it is more efficient to extract information about both sides and match them. In addition, profiles and search templates may bring out search criteria that the user might not have otherwise considered.

The system stores intermediate information so that the matching does not require interacting with the candidates in real time. Once the information necessary for the matching is gathered, it can be used over and over, quickly and efficiently, to match against any number of queries. This same type of intermediate storage of information is used for document search and knowledge management (e.g., expert systems). Information about something or someone is culled in advance, in a format that can be used to answer questions without having to go back to the original source. If done well, that is, if quality is maintained, orders of magnitude more queries are answered, lawyers are found, and romances are started.

B Overview

Information intermediation is the process of getting information where it is wanted, like a computerized reference librarian. A user may or may not know exactly what they are looking for, and a librarian has an array of techniques at their disposal for locating documents that may fulfill a user's information needs. There are various types of queries: a particular document, an answer to a specific question, general information about a topic, etc.

Document: Information, of course, ranges in size, format, topic, and use, such that generalized information intermediation often involves bringing together a very heterogeneous variety of information types and descriptions, with a potentially complex means of specifying the information requirements.[1] While data or information may reside in a static document, it may also reside in a dynamic format such as an online spreadsheet, a database, or even in an expert's head. The notion of a discrete "document," however, is still quite useful – particularly in law – as it captures a single procedural step that focuses on a particular interaction (e.g., a court opinion, a contract, a patent). Generalized information intermediation includes text, images, video, music, etc. In this chapter, *document* means any single vessel of contained information that is considered an atomic unit for the purposes of storage, search, and retrieval.

Query language: There are several components to the process of accessing information. To start, a person or system that wants information needs a way of specifying exactly what information is required. This request is described in what is called a *query language* or *specification language*, with a range of formalisms: natural language; specific criteria such as creation or expiration dates, geographical regions, sources, and formats; SQL; Boolean expressions; and more.

Metadata extraction: In order to search a collection of documents in an efficient manner, it is impractical, if not intractable, to search through or otherwise analyze documents at the time of the query. Thus, information must be *preprocessed* so that it can be available quickly and effectively.[2] Preprocessing entails the extraction of *metadata* and *indexes*. Metadata describes the context of the information (e.g., author, publication date, format) and can be thought of as "information about information." *Indexes* aggregate and reorder information found in a document collection; they might store, for example, the location of any term or phrase in any document, such that documents could be looked up by the specific terms they use.

Search algorithm: In addition to the specification of the information need and the description of available data, there also needs to be some type of *search algorithm* that calculates which information is likely to be the most *relevant* to a query (varieties include *multifaceted search*, *sorting*, *matching*, and *ranking algorithms*).[3] Furthermore, the selected

---

[1] *Data* is often used to describe lower-level or smaller pieces of *information*, often with a more formal definition (e.g., type, size, etc.). This chapter uses the two terms interchangeably.
[2] See Bommarito – Preprocessing Data, *infra*, for a discussion of preprocessing.
[3] *Relevance* is a term of art for the score assigned to a document by a search algorithm. It may or may not jibe with the user's actual information need, because information retrieval accuracy can be limited by restrictive parameters at any step in the process, including the query language, the preprocessing, and/or the search algorithm.

information needs to be placed in an appropriate location and format for the given use case (e.g., a ranked search result list, a spreadsheet cell, a set of "responsive" discovery documents).

Evaluation: Finally, in order to monitor the effectiveness of the process and to allow for improvements, there needs to be an *evaluation methodology*. This is often defined by standard *quality metrics* (e.g., *precision*, *recall*) to determine the accuracy of search results. The main goal is to determine how closely the relevance scores actually match users' perception of the usefulness of search results.[4]

II TYPICAL SEARCH STEPS

In general, search is composed of two main steps: document preparation and query processing. These steps are handled asynchronously by design.

A *Document Preparation*

Document preparation consists of locating, gathering, and processing documents in order to construct information about each document in a way that can be efficiently used for query matching. This document information is generally referred to as metadata, which is just data about data. As a simple example, imagine trying to find pages in a book that contain an important word or phrase without an index, or trying to find books in a library by a certain author or about a particular topic if all the books were simply randomly placed on shelves. In law, relevant activities might include trying to find information found in, or relevant to, case law, statutes, patents, or contracts.

Simplistically, a book index is constructed by reading a book once and, for each important term or phrase, noting the pages on which it appears. Once the index is built, finding a term is just a matter of looking it up in the index – not looking through the book each time (so long as the book has not changed since the index was built). Similarly, once metadata about a book is constructed, such as topic, author, publication date, and the location of the book, finding a book by author or by those topics in the metadata is easy, and does not require looking through all the books in the library.

For web search, documents are generally online. Gathering the documents generally involves *crawling* – starting off with a set of links, then links of links, etc., until some reasonable set of web pages has been examined, locations recorded, metadata stored, and indexes generated. There are a plethora of details and challenges here, well beyond the scope of this chapter, but it is not hard to imagine some of the difficulties. There are duplicate names for the same site (e.g., unitedairlines.com is united.com, but ua.com is underarmour.com). There are *spam* web servers that change the content of a page if it is being viewed by a web crawler rather than a user. There are link farms that try to trick search engines into assessing that a page is popular even though the links all come from the same company. In fact, the presence of spam creates limitations to the types of search algorithms that can be used effectively.

Most content that involves the law, however, is edited and curated; compared to the general web, it is largely free from spam. That being said, there are still problems with gathering legal information, including fees charged for case law, non-homogeneous document formats, and inconsistency in the use of terms.[5]

---

[4] *See also* Dolin – Measuring Legal Quality, *infra*.
[5] Issues related to case law search are covered more extensively elsewhere in this book. *See, e.g.*, Walters and Asjes – Fastcase, and the Visual Understanding of Judicial Precedents, *infra*.

B Query Processing

In order to find information, we need to describe what we are looking for. Most web search engines have migrated to natural language queries. Natural language is not as precise as a formal query language, however, so many systems have a specific codification for stating queries, such as SQL for databases. Consider, for example, looking for a specific email message. Natural language may help you match certain terms. However, if you want messages that have an attachment, come from a particular person, and were received within some specified date range, natural language queries do not work well. One might use a more advanced query page that allows the user to fill in certain fields with certain types of information (e.g., content terms, dates, and checkbox options). The fact that this information gets transformed into a formal language for processing does not require the user to know the underlying query language.

No matter the format of a query, one is limited to searching only for information (metadata) that the system has extracted about the email. For example, if you want to find an email whose attachment is a photograph of a seagull at sunset, it is unlikely that the system would be able to specify that. The limitation is inherent both in the type of metadata collected and the types of queries that are supported in the query language.

When a query is processed by the system, the matching algorithm is limited to what it has extracted about each document, as well as by the query language. Therefore, the calculation of the similarity between the query and a candidate document in the collection can only be as good as how well the user's information needs can be expressed within the query language and found within the document metadata. A "perfect" numerical relevance score does not mean that the information requirement has been adequately met; it means that the match is as good as the system is able to determine within its limitations. Querying is an iterative process in which a user attempts to modify the query within a given query mechanism in order to improve search results.

C Similarity Matching

Sometimes the best "query" is a document selected from the collection that the user has reviewed and indicated to be a perfect match. Many systems use this type of feedback mechanism to refine search criteria – in particular, systems involving machine learning.[6] In addition to searching documents, *recommender systems* exist for selecting movies, consumer products, and dating partners, all of which provide additional results based on other users' prior selections.[7] The criteria used for searching, based on document metadata, can be used not just to match queries to documents, but also to match documents to other similar documents. This approach is similar to that used to find relevant case law – if your search terms yield results that all cite to a case not in the original search results, there is a good chance that the cited case is also relevant to your search.[8] A common approach in e-discovery and contract analytics, for example, involves *supervised learning*, in which results are tagged

---

[6] See Katz – AI + Law: An Overview, *infra*; Nay – Natural Language Processing for Legal Texts, *infra*.

[7] Note that recommender systems often utilize information about users as an aid (e.g., "users *like you* who liked this product also liked this ..."). Similarity of users might include demographics, search or purchase history, etc. This type of *personalized search* is beyond the scope of this chapter.

[8] For more on the uniqueness of case law search, *see* Walters and Asjes – Fastcase, and the Visual Understanding of Judicial Precedents, *infra*.

as correct or incorrect by the user and that information is used to modify the original query to improve the results.[9]

III DOCUMENT REPRESENTATION

As previously defined, a *document* is a convenient abstraction of an atomic container of information. As such, one can describe both the *internal* information found within the document, and the *external* context or environment in which the document exists. Internally, a document may contain words, images, or data elements, as well as abstract topics and various types of metadata (creator, creation date, format, etc.). External information might include the location of the document in a network graph such as web links or court opinion citations.

When internal information is extracted and compared with similar information across a collection, it becomes contextual. For example, books can be grouped by author or publication date. Similarly, contracts can be grouped by the amount of risk assumed, or patents can be grouped according to their subject area. Of particular importance to law is the notion of the aggregate information embedded within an entire collection of documents.

Law school typically explains the elements of various types of documents such as a contract, a patent, or a court opinion. But corpus analysis allows broader questions to be answered, such as the total amount at risk within a large contract portfolio, or the technical fit in an M&A transaction based on the source and target patent portfolios. Therefore, the extraction and representation of a document's internal information can be transformed into important external information that can address questions about the overall collection. Furthermore, the aggregate information is critical for document retrieval, since the relative importance or ranking of a document is often determined largely by comparing it to the other documents in the collection (e.g., the contract with the biggest risk).

A Internal Information

Perhaps the most intuitive type of internal document information is simply the terms found in a common written document such as a book or contract. As in a book index, terms and their locations within a document are organized by term, rather than by page number, whereby each term is associated with a list of locations (which document, page number, and position on the page) where the term can be found. This allows the search engine to efficiently look up all uses of a term across an entire collection. As discussed later, a term index may be extended to the use of multi-term phrases. Additional information such as metadata may be collected so that documents can be found based on information about the document, such as author or publication date.

Documents as defined here fall on a continuum of structure.[10] One common type of document structure includes the use of tags such as XML that allows for identifying various types of data elements within a document. Such tags may define page layout such as titles or section headers (e.g., contract clauses). In addition, tags may define content (e.g., components of an address or the parties involved in litigation). Whether through direct identification of data via XML, or indirect identification via more complex applications of natural language processing (NLP), extracting specific data elements is often part of the information associated with documents.

---

[9] *See* Kerry-Tyerman and Shankar – The Core Concepts of E-discovery, *infra*; Waisberg – Contract Analytics, *infra*.
[10] *See* Dolin – XML in Law: The Role of Standards in Legal Informatics, *infra*.

Finally, more abstract information such as topics or concepts may be assigned to a document. Some notions of "aboutness" of a document are often derived manually, such as the assignment of a call number within a *library classification system*, or various *subject headings* from a *taxonomy* or *controlled vocabulary*. The terminology of these topics may or may not be used directly in the document itself. Beyond manual assignment of such topics, many *automated classification* systems exist to automatically detect and assign topics to documents, with varying degrees of accuracy.

B External Information

While internal information is derived from content within a document or its metadata, external information is derived by looking at other documents that place a given document in some type of context. A well-known example of such external information is the set of web pages that point to a given page of interest. Google's well-known *PageRank* algorithm seeks to measure the relative importance of a web page based on the number and importance of web pages that link to it.[11] This is obviously applicable to scholarly citation networks and case law citations, as well as to social networks.

C Query-Independent Analysis

At first blush, external information is one measure of the quality of a document, irrespective of the relevance of the document to a given query. A highly cited case or article is important, and a readable contract is less likely to cause ambiguous interpretations, regardless of the degree to which such documents may or may not address a particular issue. Given two cases of equal relevance, a SCOTUS citation is likely to be more important than a non-controlling case from an outside jurisdiction. Thus, a query-independent score of the quality or prominence of a document factors into how the document compares to other documents. As discussed below, ranking algorithms must merge query-dependent and query-independent factors to select documents that are both relevant and of high quality.

External information may be combined with internal information in an attempt to create a query-dependent context. For example, documents may reference other documents for any number of reasons; simply noting that one document cites another does not indicate the reason for that link. Cases may cite to other cases for procedural definitions (e.g., the rules of summary judgment), to overturn prior rules, to discuss the persuasiveness of a non-controlling opinion, or to discuss some type of analogous reasoning and the degree to which such an argument may or may not relate to the case at hand. Thus, the external information may or may not be relevant to a given query. More generally, there are many contexts in which a document resides, only some of which relate to a given information need.

D Spam

Spam denotes unwanted or fake content, usually used by its creators for their personal benefit – financial, political, etc. Spam can take the form of unwanted email or phone calls, but it can also show up as fake content used to get people to view a web page in hopes of

---

[11] Lawrence Page, Sergey Brin, Rajeev Motwani, and Terry Winograd, "The PageRank Citation Ranking: Bringing Order to the Web," Technical Report 1999-66, Stanford InfoLab, Stanford University, 1999.

following ads. Other forms of spam include fake product or service ratings. Spam flourishes in an environment that lacks editing and curation. One impact of spam is that algorithms that might function very well without spam can easily fail when fake content is designed to game those algorithms. For example, if words in document titles were given extra weight, then spam documents might include title words that are more designed to attract users than to describe the content of the page. Most document collections in law, however, are highly edited and curated, such as case law, contracts, patents, or even e-discovery. As a result, search algorithms in the legal context may have more flexibility than in other arenas.

IV RANKING RESULTS

Given a query and a collection of documents, a search algorithm typically assigns a *relevance* score to each document and ranks them.[12] As discussed above, these scores are impacted by factors such as limitations of the query specification mechanism, the document representation, spam, etc. In general, the scores indicate the likelihood that a selected document fulfills the user's information requirement. If the system works reasonably well, then the higher the score, the more worthwhile is the effort to manually inspect the document.

A Approaches

There are many ways in which documents in a collection might be selected with a query that would provide some manner of estimating their usefulness. Suppose, for example, a user wanted to locate a particular email message. She might want to look through messages from a certain person, to her, within some date range, and about a particular topic. Ignoring for the moment the issues around the interaction within the system, the interface of the query input, and the types of metadata known about each message, we can focus on the way that we assign scores to the messages. In particular, for messages that fall within the filtering criteria (e.g., from the correct person, within the specified date range), we want to find messages that focus on the sought-after topic. For general document collections, we may be looking for documents that pertain to an idea, rather than a specific term, and may not know which terms might be used to discuss that idea in particular documents.[13] For example, a patient or client may not know the terminology used among professionals for a given medical or legal concept (e.g. "myocardial infarction" or "rule of perpetuities").

One of the most challenging aspects of scoring the relevance of a document is in deriving some notion of a meaning or topic contained in a document and determining if the subject matter relates to that sought by the user as represented by the query. This is central to informational queries, which are arguably the most common query types within the legal domain. For example, statutes and case law related to IP protection would encompass an array of state and federal law, including trademarks, copyright, patents, trade secrets, and unfair competition. Contracts in a portfolio do not generally use the same format, section headers, or wording to cover similar material.

A common goal of information intermediation is a translation process of sorts – translating the language of a query into the language in a document. This leads to the problem of how to

---

[12] For more details, *see* Dolin – Measuring Legal Quality, *infra*.
[13] *Query classification*: typical classes of queries include navigational (looking for a particular document or website), informational (looking for research or general information), or interactional (looking to order a product or use an online service). Each type of query benefits from different search algorithms and must be evaluated differently.

discover *latent* topics in queries and documents based on the words that appear. The goal is to reduce the importance of the particular words used, and instead try to match the topics sought by the user with the topics contained in a document. A method of addressing this is to represent the documents and the query in some type of *(latent) topic space*. The goal is to find documents that are "near" the query in this space. If done well, the distance metric between two objects in this space correlates to what the user would consider to be topic similarity between them.[14] What might this space look like, and which measure of proximity in the space best matches our notion of topic similarity?

B *Term Vector Space*

A search algorithm must accommodate the high variability found in natural languages and build some type of model to represent both the words and the meanings inherent in various types of documents. Although many such models exist, a helpful starting point is the basic *term vector space* model.[15] This simplistic *bag of words* approach does not attempt to understand or parse the natural language of a document. Instead, it simply counts the number of times each unique word (or phrase) occurs. It ignores document structure, word order, or the presence of multi-word phrases. The model then represents the documents and the query as locations in a multi-dimensional space, where each word found in the collection gets its own dimension. The location of a document in this space is determined simply by the number of times a given word occurs in the document, for each word in the space. Once we have a way of representing queries and documents in the space, we need to measure their proximity to each other. For reasons discussed below, this model uses the angular separation between items rather than their geometrical distance.

Imagine that we have two documents, D_1 and D_2, and a query, Q, as shown in Figure 2.2.1. Suppose that we are trying to figure out which of the two documents is the better result. Suppose for simplicity that each document has just four words. D_1 deals with "pediatrics" and contains the word "child" three times, and the word "nutrition" once. D_2, dealing with "developmental psychology," contains the word "child" twice and the word "Freud" twice. In this case, the words "child," "Freud," and "nutrition" define a three-dimensional space – one dimension for each word, forming the x, y, and z axes, respectively. Finally, suppose that Q is a simple query containing the words "child" and "nutrition" once each, but not "Freud," as shown in Figure 2.2.1a. Since the representation of documents in the space is determined by the number of times each word appears in a document (or query), setting the (x, y, z) coordinate, respectively, D_1 would be represented by the position (3, 0, 1), D_2 by (2, 2, 0), and Q by (1, 0, 1).[16]

We could use geometrical distance as the measure of similarity. However, this would yield unintuitive results based on document lengths since long documents have more words than short documents. Using geometrical distance would mean that long documents might be far away from short documents, and queries, even though they discuss the same topics with the same words. In the approach used here, topics are represented as the ratio of term co-

---

[14] Certainly documents may contain multiple topics at various degrees of granularity. For ease of explanation, we assume a simplistic form of document with a single main topic. Extensions such as working within document sections or multiple overlapping topics are discussed below.

[15] See, *e.g.*, Gerald M. Salton, Andrew Wong, and Chungshu Yang, "A Vector Space Model for Automatic Indexing," *Communications of the ACM* 18 (11) (1975): 613–620.

[16] More specifically, each item in the space is represented as a vector from the origin to the position determined by the word counts.

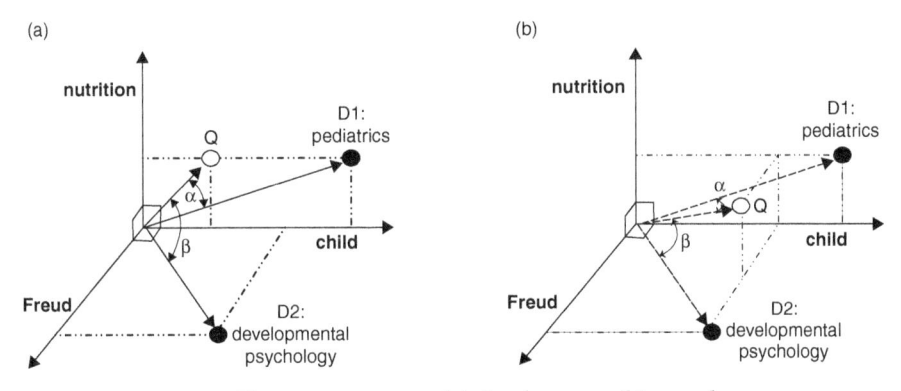

FIGURE 2.2.1 Term vector spaces: (a) simple query; (b) complex query.

occurrences. Imagine that, on average, documents about pediatrics use the word "child" several times more than they use "nutrition," and rarely use the word "Freud." Similarly, suppose that documents about developmental psychology use the words "child" and "Freud" roughly as frequently. In this case, what distinguishes different topics is not the absolute distance between items in the space, but the direction of the item out from the origin. Thus, similar documents can be thought of as pointing in roughly the same direction rather than by how far away they are from each other. This removes the issue of document length, and tends to rate documents as more similar if they have more words in common, in similar proportions.

We can use the *cosine similarity* of the vectors in the space between Q and each document (here, just D1 and D2) to get a value between 0 and 1 that represents the cosine of the angle between the two vectors. A value of 0 means that there are no words in common between Q and the document, while a value of 1 means that all the words are in common, and used in the same proportion. In our example from Figure 2.2.1a, the angle between Q and D1, α, is smaller than the angle between Q and D2, β. Since the smaller angle gives the larger cosine, the relevance score indicates that Q and D1 is a better match than Q and D2 – that is, $\cos(α) > \cos(β)$.

C Extensions

Modern *information retrieval* (IR) systems extend the capabilities of the term vector model. Simple extensions include incorporating document lengths,[17] multi-word phrases, pluralization and *stemming*, and excluding *stop words*.[18] A more sophisticated way of assigning more importance to less frequent, content-rich terms is to assign different weights to terms based on how common they are across all the documents in the collection (e.g., *tf-idf* term weighting[19]). Another common feature of IR systems is to work within documents, which may contain sections of relevance: an article in an encyclopedia, a particular clause in a contract, or a statute within a broad set of regulations. Thus, mapping page structure,

---

[17] While a long document is more likely to contain more terms, where two documents have the same relative term density, the longer one is more likely to give a better treatment of the topic.
[18] Stemming removes word suffixes so that words with the same root are treated as the same word. Stop words are common to almost all documents in a given language and add little to no content value (e.g., "the" and "and" in English).
[19] "tf-idf" (term-frequency/inverse-document-frequency) increases the weight of a term the more times it shows up in a document, but decreases the weight of a term the more it shows up in multiple documents in the collection. Stop words are likely to show up in all/most documents and therefore are given very little weight, obviating the need to use a stop word list.

such as indentations or headers, into logical chunks of meaning may allow the system to find relevant shorter sections within a longer document.

Another feature of modern IR systems involves inferring topics or semantics based on a statistical analysis of term co-occurrences. As the simplistic documents in Figure 2.2.1 demonstrate, combinations of terms in varying frequencies imply a type of topic, such as "child" and "nutrition," co-occurring in a document discussing pediatrics. This is true even if the term pediatrics itself is not used in the document. The identification of a pattern of term co-occurrences can be used as an aid in locating relevant documents without requiring that they contain exact matches of the query terms.[20]

Term co-occurrence analysis is particularly important in finding similar documents, or in incorporating feedback in supervised learning. For example, in e-discovery or contract analytics, the user looks over a set of results and tags them as relevant or irrelevant. Obviously these documents will usually contain terms well beyond the original query terms. Many of these additional terms, occurring in some particular proportion to the occurrence frequency of other terms, may be representative of some of the latent concepts that tend to occur in relevant documents. In contrast, other co-occurrences may indicate topics that are correlated to those documents that the user finds irrelevant.

As a simple example, think of a query such as "jaguar." Suppose a user finds relevant those documents that contain words such as "automobile" and "car," and irrelevant documents with words such as "cat" and "jungle." After the user tags a small set of these results as relevant or not, an IR system would be better able to distinguish appropriate uses of the query term found within a document collection. In this example, cars and cats have very few overlapping terms. But many topics are much more related, such as, say, the *treatment* of cancer compared to the *structure* of cancer. A user may have no idea how these topics are discussed in the literature or which terms might distinguish them. In fact, the user may have no idea that she is looking for one or the other topic until she sees the search results and notices that some seem relevant and some do not. Many shared terms might show up in documents related to either topic, and both topics might show up in some of the same documents. By analyzing how often sets of terms show up and in which proportion, more subtle differences in meaning are decipherable. Thus, the search algorithm works best, at least for informational queries, when it can analyze groups of terms and not rigidly expect that any particular term must or must not be present in a highly relevant document.

The main distinction between a simple query, such as that in Figure 2.2.1a, and a complex query, shown in Figure 2.2.1b, is that the complex query is not only longer, but also contains multiple occurrences of the terms. Once a document is found to be relevant and tagged as such, that document may be incorporated into the query, and the query repositioned in the term/topic space. However, the notion of the metric used (e.g., cosine similarity to determine the angle) remains the same.

---

[20] Prior work in this area involves *latent semantic analysis* (LSA), and more modern approaches extend that to *topic models*. LSA uses a mathematical technique known as *singular value decomposition* (SVD) to assign weighted combinations of terms into a new, smaller, multi-dimensional space. By thinking of each topic as some combination of terms of varying frequencies, the new space could be thought of as a *topic* vector space rather than a *term* vector space. This process also accommodates the goal of stemming, since the same root of a word, used with varying suffixes, all co-occurring with other words in the same proportion, would likely map to the same topic dimension. For example, *puppy* and *puppies* would be handled essentially as the same word via the process of SVD.

Additional techniques include the use of *n-grams* and *NLP* techniques such as *parsing*, *information extraction*, and *question answering*. Beyond analyzing the text of documents, *query log analysis* is very useful in understanding short queries, or in suggesting commonly used extensions to short queries that can help disambiguate otherwise generic search terms. Finally, a lot of information is contained in non-text items such as audio-visual recordings, maps, images, etc. While very different techniques are used on non-text, a similar approach is to create a space in which to represent items being sought, the query, and a metric that correlates to the subjective opinion of relevance.

V RELATED FIELDS

There are several important fields that pertain to information intermediation in general, and legal information in particular.

A *Classification*

"The classification of information-bearing entities is as old as libraries themselves."[21] *Classification* involves the manual development of *taxonomies*, *ontologies*, and other forms of *controlled vocabularies* and *subject headings*.[22] A document is assigned one or more relevant categories or terms from these. For example, a common reference library might use the *Library of Congress Classification* (LCC) system or the *Dewey Decimal System* as a way of identifying the overall topic of a document. Similar systems are common in many fields such as medicine, business, and biology.

The use of classification systems to place physical documents on shelves implies that every time a system is updated, documents might need to be physically regrouped. This creates a disincentive to modernize such systems, or to integrate them into online information systems:

> "Ultimately, all efforts will have to concentrate on the envisioned function of the electronic [classification system] as an online retrieval tool. For online browsing and navigation of electronically stored information, including segregation of whole portions of one class and transfer to another, a knowledge-based, field specific structure of the classification is of utmost importance. So, also, is the separation from the shelving function."[23]

Since ontologies are built around the way that humans characterize knowledge, they are a natural way of grouping and identifying information needs.[24] However, manual classification of documents is time-consuming and can be an insurmountable barrier to a broader use of classification methodologies. This barrier can be overcome, however, through the use of automated classification.

---

[21] Francis L. Miksa, *The DDC, the Universe of Knowledge, and the Post-Modern Library* (Albany, NY: Forest Press, 1998), 33.

[22] General classification is a rather broad topic and may or may not incorporate controlled vocabularies. This chapter focuses on what may be called *document classification* within both library and information science.

[23] J. E. Goldberg, "Library of Congress Classification: Shelving Device for Collections or Organization of Knowledge Fields?" in *Proceedings of the Fourth Conference of the International Society for Knowledge Organization (ISKO)*, Washington, DC, July 15–18, 1996.

[24] A typical difficulty with the use of ontologies for information retrieval is the UI, since users may not know where documents might be located within the classification system. There are many ways to resolve this, however, and the problem is generally with the interface, not necessarily with the structure of the ontology.

Automated classification is the process by which documents are automatically associated with classification categories.[25] For a simple example, a binary classifier may be used to determine whether a document is relevant to a query or not, or responsive to an e-discovery request. As discussed above, as a user tags results as being relevant or not, this additional information can be fed back to the system as an enhanced query, improving result accuracy.

For a more sophisticated classification system such as the LCC, which consists of thousands of hierarchically nested categories, the data used to classify documents comes from *training sets*. Training data generally comes from prior manual classification of thousands or millions of documents. For example, given all the books classified under the LCC at the Library of Congress, one can aggregate that information and come up with some type of representation of each category. Imagine that the documents in Figure 2.2.1b represent classification categories, and the query Q is a new document to be classified. Since Q is more similar to D_1 than D_2, it could be assigned the category D_1.

B Clustering

While classification attempts to place a document within a human-generated knowledge framework, *clustering* attempts to define groupings of documents in a collection that are more like each other in some manner than they are like other documents in the collection. Clusters of documents may or may not be related in a way that is easily discernable by a user. As an example, consider placing documents in the term vector space of Figure 2.2.1. If many documents cluster around the same angle, that means that they share many of the same terms in roughly the same proportion. Thus, there is a good chance that those documents are addressing related topics.

That being said, it is difficult to know in advance, with no prior information, how many clusters are appropriate, or whether they may be distinguished in ways that assist in resolving the information need. As a result, evaluation methodology for clustering algorithms is a challenge due to the fact that for any given mathematical similarity measure, there may or may not be a relationship to a human notion of information clusters for the type of documents involved. For example, two paintings may be very similar from a mathematical model that looks at color distribution, or texture, but may involve completely different styles, content, and meaning.

Clustering movies, music, documents, etc., by several different methods allows a system to learn which combination of those methods provides the best overall similarity match. A recommender system may use both user similarities and content similarities in a hybrid clustering mechanism. For example, music can be compared based on rhythm, harmonies, chord progressions, instruments, lyrics, era, etc. A cluster based on instruments alone might not help a user find what they consider to be "similar" music. But perhaps an appropriately weighted combination of instruments, rhythm, and lyrics would help a user discover a wonderful, previously unknown, collection of music. Similar clusters based on user information such as past behavior, current selections, and demographics can help identify other users with similar tastes. Therefore, while classification has the advantage of placing documents within a human-developed knowledge framework, clusters offer a dynamic

---

[25] For a detailed discussion on the use of automated classification as an aid in general, scalable information intermediation, *see, e.g.*, Ron Dolin, "Pharos: A Scalable Distributed Architecture for Locating Heterogeneous Information Sources," PhD Dissertation, UC Santa Barbara, 1998.

grouping that can be easily adjusted when the reason for document similarity is not particularly important to the user.

Both classification and clustering extend the set of techniques used to intermediate information, far beyond simple word matching. By taking into account the context of documents (and perhaps also the context of users), these approaches allow information needs to be met in ways not possible by non-machine methods alone. Not surprisingly, the re-implementation of prior manual practice with technological approaches increases not only the efficiency of the process, but also the quality of the results.

VI EVALUATION

Regardless of the mechanism used to represent the documents and the query – or the algorithm used to match them – the user is the gold standard for judging the effectiveness of the system. Thus, without an evaluation mechanism, there is no way of tuning or improving a system to better align the results with the actual information need.[26] Not surprisingly, evaluation shows up frequently in this book, including chapters dealing with case law search, e-discovery, contract analytics, and more.

The evaluation of a search system is dependent upon many factors, including an understanding of both the actual meaning of the query and the available documents. Even the presentation of the results is context-dependent. In web search, for example, the order of results for a navigational query is quite important, because users want the correct result in the first position. In contrast, any result that has helpful information is fine for an informational query. For this reason, evaluation metrics for navigational queries heavily weight the top position, while metrics for informational queries might look at how many results among the top ten positions are relevant.

Perhaps the most common metrics used in the field of IR, especially for a fixed collection of documents, are precision and recall.[27] *Precision* is the fraction of documents returned by the system that are actually relevant to the query. *Recall* is the fraction of relevant documents in the entire collection that are returned in the result set. Given a collection of documents and a query, assume that the total number of relevant documents in the collection is N_T, and that the number of documents returned for the query is N_Q. Finally, suppose that the number of *relevant* documents returned is N_R.

$$\text{Precision } P = N_R/N_Q$$

$$\text{Recall } R = N_R/N_T$$

Clearly, $0 \leq P \leq 1$ and $0 \leq R \leq 1$. In general, in IR systems, increasing P tends to decrease R, and vice versa. In order to filter out more irrelevant documents (increasing P), we also filter out more relevant ones (decreasing R). Similarly, increasing the number of relevant documents returned (increasing R) involves broadening the query, resulting in a larger fraction of irrelevant ones (decreasing P).

Ordering a result set requires using a single ranking score, which requires combining precision and recall into a single metric. One common method is the *F-measure* or F_1 score, which is a (harmonic) mean that gives equal weight to both P and R. The intuition behind this score is that

---

[26] The significance of evaluation is explored further in Dolin – Measuring Legal Quality, *infra*.
[27] These concepts have equivalents in other fields, such as *false positives* and *false negatives*, Type I and Type II errors, and specificity vs. sensitivity.

a simple (arithmetic) average of the two values is not as aligned with our intuition as a score that gives higher weight when the values are closer together. This type of averaging is often deemed more intuitive for ratios like P and R than the standard arithmetic average. A common variation of the F-measure, the F_β score, allows for weighting precision or recall. In web search, for example, precision is often more important than recall. On the other hand, recall is often preferred in e-discovery.[28]

Other metrics try to measure efficiency (e.g., how long it takes to find adequate information [*satisficing*], or how many iterations are required to train a machine learning system). Another important class of metrics relates to user satisfaction or user happiness, commonly referred to as *usability*. These metrics relate not only to the relevance of the results and the efficiency of finding them, but also to the overall user experience, the ability to easily and accurately describe an information need, the clarity of the result display, and the suppression of unwanted material (e.g., ads, spam), and more.

VII CONCLUSION

This chapter just scratches the surface of the topics discussed. The goal is to provide a survey of the types of issues that information intermediation addresses. Many conferences and journals provide a deeper perspective.[29] As pointed out in the introduction, information intermediation is central to a legal system. It plays an important role in document management and automation, legal research, contract analytics, e-discovery, patents, and on and on. Whether a builder or user of these systems, a basic understanding of their underlying concepts and the role they play in legal applications are important in the modernization of legal workflow. These systems are integral to the improvement in efficiency, affordability, and quality that a modern legal system requires.

---

[28] The harmonic mean and the geometric mean (the "G-measure") share several properties that make them superior for combined quality metric scoring than the arithmetic mean. The problem of matching subjective notions of quality to various mathematical representations is discussed in Dolin – Measuring Legal Quality, *infra*.

[29] The following are a few examples: The Text REtrieval Conference (TREC), Conference on Information and Knowledge Management (CIKM), the Association for Computing Machinery (ACM) Special Inter Groups (e.g., SIGIR), and the *Journal of the Association for Information Science and Technology* (JASIST).

2.3

Preprocessing Data

Michael J. Bommarito II

I INTRODUCTION

Every once in a while, a ready-to-use data set falls down the chimney like a diamond in a gift box, perfectly suited to the problem at hand. Unfortunately, what we usually have is a pile of coal and a rusty shovel. This is because most data resides in *unstructured* and disparate information systems or data sources. In order to apply most informatics methods, including a markup system like XML, we must first *retrieve* and then *preprocess* data from these sources to produce a *structured*, linked data set. These phases, sometimes colloquially referred to as data scraping, cleaning, wrangling, or "munging," are arguably more important, and typically more time-consuming, than many other tasks in legal informatics.

Retrieving and preprocessing data can be difficult for a number of reasons. First, these tasks can require a wide range of technical skills; for example, interacting with and understanding information systems might require knowledge of technologies like XML, SQL, or JSON. Second, data can take many forms, and preprocessing experience may not translate across all these forms. Those who have primarily worked with numeric or textual data are often ill-prepared to work with audio or visual data, for example.

The last reason, and the most critical, is that retrieval and preprocessing often require specific domain knowledge. Preprocessing is intimately related to data quality and data representation. This poses a problem: how can you assess the quality of a source if you are not already familiar with similar data? Moreover, how can you determine which elements of a source are more or less important without some intuition or experience regarding the problem at hand?

This chapter is not exhaustive; a detailed treatment of the many kinds of human endeavors and data formats would require several volumes by itself. We can, however, provide you with an overview of common problems and a map to help you navigate typical solutions. While data comes in many forms, we will focus on the most common types – numeric, textual, visual, and audio – and the most common approaches to preprocessing them. This chapter focuses primarily on data from the real world, but there are many problems for which simulated or computer-generated data can be useful.[1]

---

[1] For more information about simulation and computational modeling, *see* Joshua M. Epstein, *Generative Social Science: Studies in Agent-Based Computational Modeling* (Princeton, NJ: Princeton University Press, 2006); Allen B. Downey, *Think Complexity: Complexity Science and Computational Modeling* (Sebastopol, CA: O'Reilly Media, 2012).

II RETRIEVING DATA

Before we can preprocess data, we have to obtain it. Figure 2.3.1 provides a simple process flow and decision tree that we can use to help determine the steps necessary to retrieve data. The first step in this process, identifying relevant data, seems simple. Given one or more questions or quantities of interest, what data from the real world would be most relevant? In some cases, we can measure the quantity of interest directly; for example, if we want to know how many cases the Supreme Court decided last term, we can count them directly from the Court's docket. However, for other questions, the quantity of interest may not be directly observable, but might instead be estimated based on a directly observable quantity. For example, if we wanted to estimate how many hours Supreme Court clerks spend researching and drafting, we might use information about the number and length of majority, concurring, or dissenting opinions written by each Justice to estimate this quantity for each clerk. For some problems, approximate or "quick" solutions are adequate, and data source research is less important; for other problems, the quality and comprehensiveness of data sources is critical.

A number of data repositories and information systems come up frequently in legal informatics. In the USA, public repositories like the CourtListener project, RECAP, PACER, and Data.Gov are good sources of information. For private information held inside organizations like law firms or corporate legal departments, data typically resides in a handful of common information systems like matter management, document management, time-keeping, and financial systems. Some common examples of these systems include

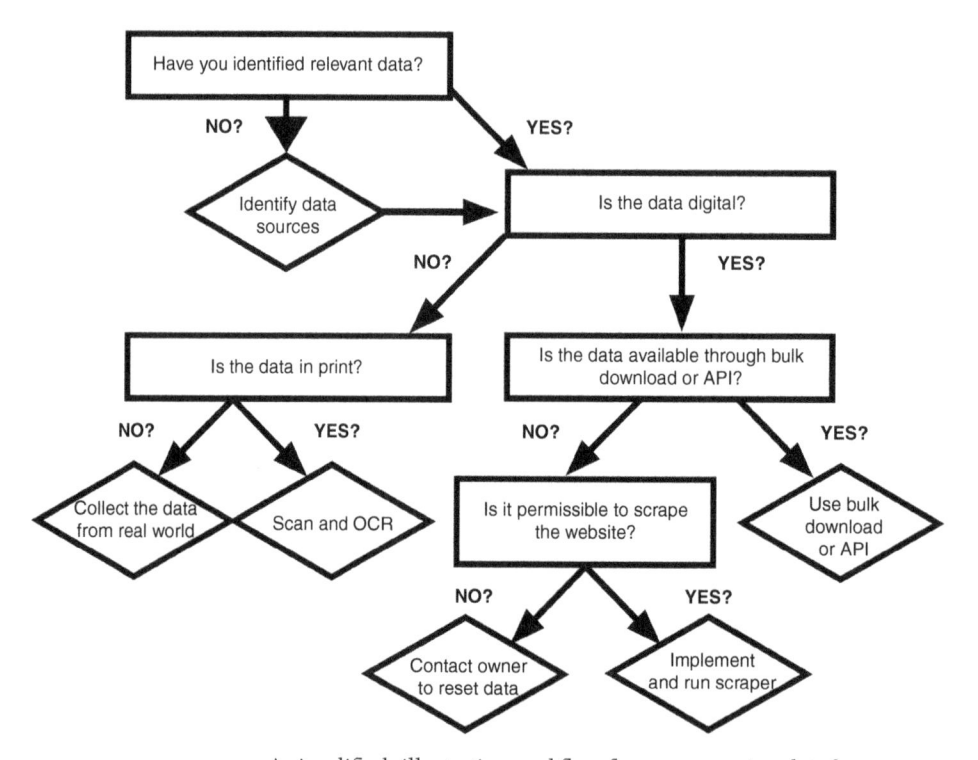

FIGURE 2.3.1 A simplified, illustrative workflow for preprocessing data.[2]

---

[2] Image © Jase Sancrainte, for *Legal Informatics*, 2018. For more on decision trees, *see* Agin – Examining Public Court Data to Understand and Predict Bankruptcy Case Results, *infra*.

MitraTech, TeamConnect, iManage, NetDocuments, Aderant CompuLaw, Thomson Reuters ELITE, and SAP Financials.

Figure 2.3.1 shows another important issue to focus on. In some cases, especially those that involve data retrieved from the internet, you may not be the owner of the data. It is important to carefully review such data sources. If the data source or website has terms of service or license information, you must ensure that your use case is compatible with their terms; for example, some sources may only allow academic or non-commercial usage. Second, once you've determined that the terms of service and licensing are compatible with your use case, then it is important to look for "polite" approaches to retrieving data. For example, if a data source provides a bulk download or API option, then it would be unwise and inefficient to scrape data directly from all those web pages.

III PREPROCESSING DATA

A *Numeric Data*

While data comes in many forms, when most people think of data they think of *numeric data*. Not only that, but the purpose of preprocessing other forms of data like text or images is often to transform them into a numeric representation. When we preprocess image data, for example, we might be looking to identify the number of persons or vehicles in an image. When we preprocess audio data, we may in fact be trying to count the number of speakers or questions asked.

There are a number of common tasks in preprocessing numeric data. Listed below are a few of the most common.[3]

- **Data validation:** Does your preprocessed data seem plausible compared to your raw data? For example, if your data counts the number of people employed in a certain profession in a certain country, does the number wind up negative? Is the number greater than the total population of the country? These may be obvious errors in the collection or retrieval of data.
- **Outlier detection:** Related to validation, are there outliers in the data? Depending on the subsequent visualization or analysis methodology, outliers might need to be removed or modified. For example, if you're analyzing the number of legal matters created per day in a corporate legal department, you might find that a data migration on a certain date creates a large outlier (i.e., matters already handled appear to be "new" because of the file migration from Point A to Point B).
- **Transforming and scaling:** Depending on the visualization or analysis methodology, data might need to be *transformed* or *scaled*. For example, if you are interested in trends in legal expenses, the percentage change in monthly spend is more important than the actual dollar amount. Similarly, if you are asked whether recent increases in budget expenses are significantly large, you might scale your percentages relative to historical minimum and maximum values to show trends.

---

[3] These preprocessing tasks are covered in more detail in Trevor Hastie, Robert Tibshirani, and Jerome Friedman, *The Elements of Statistical Learning: Data Mining, Inference and Prediction* (New York, NY: Springer, 2016).

- **Encoding:** *Encoding* is a technique whereby data in strong form – like "low," "medium," and "high" values for data – is converted into an integer value for easier manipulation. "Low," "medium," and "high" might then be encoded as "1," "2," and "3," for example.

B Textual Data

Relative to other applications of informatics, legal informatics is particularly characterized by its extreme dependence on textual data. More so than most other fields, legal professionals and institutions produce written material. Therefore, in order to answer many questions in law, it's important to understand how to retrieve and preprocess text.

There are a number of common tasks in the preprocessing of textual data, discussed below.[4]

- **Optical Character Recognition (OCR):** OCR converts standard text (sometimes paper-based) into a digitized text format. In many cases, legal documents at some point are rendered in hard copy format, often in order to obtain a signature, and then returned to the digital world as a scanned image file. These document images, commonly stored in TIFF or PDF format, have to be converted back into a structured, text-based representation. Depending on the nature of the documents and the scanning process, OCR can range from trivial to herculean. In some cases, 100% accuracy is possible in OCR conversion, but in many cases a complex figure, or a bad scanner – or even a spilled cup of coffee – can reduce the data quality of a document.
- **Segmentation:** In some cases, documents come in clearly distinct iterations, where each new filing or agreement is saved separately. In many cases, though, a single PDF file might contain one or more distinct units of text. In these cases, it is important to segment text into the relevant unit of analysis. For example, in some contract use cases, it might be important to separate the main agreement from any appendices, annexes, addenda, or amendments, even if they are scanned and saved together. Segmentation can be used at a more granular level, too; we can apply it to more generic units of analysis, such as pages, sections, paragraphs, or sentences. Lastly, segmentation is critical when the source of the text is informal and potentially rife with flaws, like if the document originated in a communication medium like SMS or in an audio transcription.
- **Character encoding:** While a reader of this book is likely most familiar with the 26 letters of the modern English alphabet, there are thousands and thousands of other characters across dozens of languages and writing systems. While the encoding and translation of these characters is generally complicated, it is important that those working with textual data gain an understanding of encoding and character sets, especially if material may come from non-English sources. Even English-language legal sources are full of characters that require additional encoding and translation, such as the section symbol (§), ampersand (&), or left and right quotation marks (" ").

---

[4] These preprocessing methods are covered in greater detail in Christopher D. Manning and Hinrich Schütze, *Foundations of Statistical Natural Language Processing* (Cambridge, MA: MIT Press, 1999).

- **Language model:** Many methods of analyzing textual information are based on models that encode text as mathematical vectors or sequences. Some of these models are inspired by standard linguistics and adhere to formal concepts such as grammar and sentences, while other models are more data-driven, such as N-gram or statistical models. Each type of model has strengths and weaknesses; for example, while formal grammar-based models struggle to handle informal text, they can provide more information for formal text, such as the subject or direct object of a verb. The most common model used to encode documents is the so-called *bag-of-words* model, which represents a unit of text (a sentence, paragraph, or a whole document) as a jumbled bag of words, discarding the order of words and instead relying entirely on frequency information.
- **Stop-wording, stemming, and tagging:** Some languages make heavy use of auxiliary or low-semantic-content words such as "of" or "to." These small function words are commonly referred to as *stop words*. Languages also frequently decline root words that then take on multiple variations that nevertheless have almost the same meaning. These roots can be represented as *lemmas*. One common lemma in English, for example, is *go*. Words lemmatized to the word *go* include *going*, *went*, *gone*, and *goes*. Lemmatization of text can group words that share a root meaning. Similarly, *stemming* is the process of grouping words based on shared morphemes. The words *produce*, *product*, and *production* all share the same stem ("produc"). Unlike lemmatization, stemming does not group words that do not contain the same string of characters (in the above example for lemmatization, *went* would not be correctly stemmed, which is why you need both lemmatization and stemming). Depending on the use case, it can be important to remove stop words or "un-inflect" words through stemming or lemmatizing, returning them to their root or shared morpheme.
- **Named entity recognition and resolution:** Many problems in text analysis involve the identification of so-called *named entities*: people, companies, places, or events. Furthermore, these entities often need to be resolved or normalized against some reference; for example, a country search should return references to both "USA" and "United States of America" in contracts, or a company search should return references to both AMZN and "Amazon, Inc." The reliable recognition and resolution of named entities is a critical step in the preprocessing of textual information.

C Audio Data

Audio data frequently arises in legal informatics in the context of evidence or court records. For example, a large volume of telephone conversations might be requested in discovery or investigation. The preprocessing of this data is key in order for subsequent search and information retrieval. A full treatment of audio data is outside the scope of this book, but common tasks include background noise reduction, speaker identification, anomaly detection, song fingerprinting, and transcription.[5]

---

[5] *See generally* Ben Gold, Nelson Morgan, and Dan Ellis, *Speech and Audio Signal Processing: Processing and Perception of Speech and Music* (Hoboken, NJ: Wiley, 2011).

D Visual Data

Visual data, like audio data, arises in a number of different circumstances in legal informatics. The first and most common source of visual data is scanned documents, already discussed. Images arise in many other contexts as well, such as technical diagrams, maps, and, increasingly, video, such as police bodycams or automobile dashcams. A full treatment of visual data is outside the scope of this book, but common tasks include foreground and background segmentation; edge, shape, object, or scene detection; motion detection; and automated summarization and encoding.[6]

---

[6] *See generally* John C. Russ, *The Image Processing Handbook* (Boca Raton, FL: CRC Press, 2011); Rafael C. Gonzalez and Richard E. Woods, *Digital Image Processing* (London: Pearson, 2007).

2.4

XML in Law

The Role of Standards in Legal Informatics

Ron Dolin[1]

I INTRODUCTION

"To structure or not to structure – that is the question."

Somewhere between sonnets and Beat literature lies the notion of the semi-structured document, in which some type of, if not formalized, than perhaps anticipated, or at least understandable, textual layout, sectioning, and various forms of visual and labeled elements assist the reader in deciphering the document's meaning. In fact, had the publisher been able to accommodate it, Faulkner had hoped to publish his masterpiece, *The Sound and the Fury*, in various colored text, each color denoting a different period of time, in order to assist the reader in making sense of what might otherwise be viewed as incoherent ramblings coming through his severely mentally disabled character's narrative.[2] And such is the current fate and ongoing dilemma facing a legal system that has historically been centered on the static, written document, collecting dust if lucky enough to be on a shelf, rather than buried in a random box under a desk in a remote office, yet all the while holding forth the rules and consequences of not abiding its every word and punctuation mark, scribbler's errors included. This is the glue that holds society together.

For legal information is rarely available in a structured format such as a database. Furthermore, trying to excessively structure legal information could grind the production of new documents, as well as the further development of legal innovation, to a halt. That being said, however, most legal information comes via documents such as statutes, court opinions, contracts, patents, etc. If documents are to be helpful in the twenty-first century, they need to be more than simply electronically produced or scanned in, more than "OCR'ed," more than annotated with various forms of metadata (manual or automated). Documents in law need to be UNLOCKED. They need to be definitively understood (where not intentionally ambiguous) – not just by humans, but by machines. Legal documents store information, and this information is part of the complex processing and integration that is the legal system. We want to know which parties are involved in a lawsuit. We want to know when a contract expires, or the consequences of a breach. We seek to understand how various patents relate to each other. We need to execute a will. To be handed even an electronic version of a document, let alone a portfolio of a million contracts, leaves us (or our future applications) struggling to figure out elements buried within it – if not too slowly by

---

[1] The author would like to thank Thomas Bruce, Director of the Legal Information Institute at Cornell Law School, for his insightful feedback. Space does not allow a full discussion of the issues raised in this brief introductory material, and the reader is encouraged to peruse the Institute's material for further details.

[2] "The_Sound_and_the_Fury," *Wikipedia*, available at: https://en.wikipedia.org/wiki/The_Sound_and_the_Fury (accessed June 9, 2020); "Benjy's Red-Letter Days," *New York Times*, available at: www.nytimes.com/2012/09/16/books/review/the-sound-and-the-fury-in-14-colors.html.

hand, then perhaps by machine – probabilistically assigning names, dates, amounts, clause goals, assigned risks, purposes for various citations, etc.

Parsing an unstructured document has been shown to be possible, with varying degrees of reliability, by the application of various types of NLP and AI. But documents whose elements are already accurately tagged, labeled, identified, or otherwise "marked up" are immediately amenable to complex search and integration with any number of tools, with minimal downstream costs, and with the highest level of accuracy. The trade-off here is between the burden of more difficult initial production, and the ongoing burden of downstream challenges to the usefulness of otherwise latent legal information hiding in a sea of random text. Semi-structured documents allow for free-form where needed, yet also accommodate reliable and straightforward identification of particularly important components. This balance requires a useful and informed set of labels or tags for known classes of legal documents, and a simple-to-use production mechanism so as not to burden document creators.

II MARKUP LANGUAGES, XML, AND SCHEMAS

"If I am only for myself, who will be for me?"

Merriam Webster defines a *markup language* as "a system (such as HTML or SGML) for marking or tagging a document that indicates its logical structure (such as paragraphs) and gives instructions for its layout on the page especially for electronic transmission and display."[3] The tags are not directly visible when viewing the document, but simply inform the rendering system how to layout the various page elements, say for viewing or printing. Beyond page layout, however, markup languages such as XML can identify non-structural information such as the type of data given within enclosing tags.[4] "In computing, Extensible Markup Language (XML) is a markup language that defines a set of rules for encoding documents in a format that is both human-readable and machine-readable."[5]

Though the details of XML are beyond the scope of this chapter, a plethora of information and tutorials about XML is available online.[6] At their simplest, markup languages in general, and XML in particular, are structured like this:

```
<Contact>
  <Name>
    Chris Jones
  </Name>
  <Phone>
    123-456-7890
  </Phone>
</Contact>
```

[3] "Markup language," Merriam-Webster, www.merriam-webster.com/dictionary/markup%20language.
[4] Strictly speaking, HTML is not an XML subset. For example, some HTML tags do not require a closing tag, while all XML tags need to be closed. HTML has a fixed number of pre-defined tags, and is usually used to display information. XML is extensible, and is usually used to store and transmit data. HTML is often generated incorrectly, but since its goal is to be rendered as a web page, errors are generally handled invisibly by the browser. XML is typically handled in a formal manner along the lines of a programming language – poorly formed XML generates an error. For details, *see, e.g.*, "HTML Parser," available at: www.html5rocks.com/en/tutorials/internals/howbrowserswork/#HTML_Parser.
[5] "XML," *Wikipedia*, available at: https://en.wikipedia.org/wiki/XML (accessed June 9, 2020).
[6] *See, e.g.*, "XML," *Wikipedia*, available at: https://en.wikipedia.org/wiki/XML; "XML Tutorial," w3schools, available at: www.w3schools.com/xml; www.xml.com; "Introduction to XML," XML Files, available at: www.xmlfiles.com/xml/xml_intro.asp.

The tags, such as "Contact," "Name," and "Phone," have a start and end tag surrounding the information they are labeling, and they can be nested. The tags themselves are not displayed for rendering purposes. By enabling the ability to add such tags to an otherwise unstructured document, XML allows as much structure as wanted around data elements that might be particularly useful, while allowing the rest of the document to be free-form. As a result of these tags, for example, a program would have no trouble extracting the contact information accurately. In addition to document tagging, however, XML may be used to label data to facilitate general information exchange (not necessarily residing within a human-readable document).[7]

Both the producer and the consumer of an XML-encoded document must understand the same sets of tags (e.g., "Contact," "Name"). Otherwise, unknown tags are simply ignored by the user/reader, and the corresponding data is treated as unstructured free text, defeating the purpose of tagging. There are several ways that the XML tags used in a document may be defined or known to the consumer. For example, HTML (or its XML version, XHTML) is a standard defined by the W3C.[8] The elements are predefined and known to web browsers (i.e., the consumers of HTML pages).

When not predefined, XML elements can be declared through one of many available definition languages or "schema":[9] document type definition (DTD),[10] XML schema definition (XSD),[11] RELAX NG,[12] etc. These declaration languages define which tags are allowed, which attributes they may use, and how complex elements are built (e.g., "Contact" contains "Name" and "Phone"). Some permit defining data types such as "string," "number," "date," etc., as well as the input format (e.g., date defined as YYYY-MM-DD). Declaring the tags allows the XML to be checked for correctness – not only for "well-formed" syntax (e.g., all open tags are closed), but also for "validity" (i.e., tags are defined and used correctly).

XML schemas can be included in an XML document itself (i.e., the DTD's "internal" mechanism), or outside the XML document via a link (i.e., DTD's "external" mechanism). External schemas are useful for sharing XML information, either among a small number of collaborators (e.g., DTD is "private") or among the general public (e.g., DTD is "public"). The benefit of private schemas includes the ease of implementation and experimentation. Alternatively, public schemas encode an XML structure that can be considered stable and therefore useful for a wide range of users and applications. For example, "backend" schemas are used in many word processors and document automation systems to encode documents in XML (e.g., Microsoft's DOCX,[13] OpenOffice's ODF[14]).

Much of the benefit of public XML schemas comes by way of backend use hidden from the user. The end-user is not required to understand the XML component of the documents. This is similarly the case for embedding information within legal documents such as contracts, statutes, and court filings. Hidden or not, however, the greatest benefit from XML derives from the

---

[7] See, e.g., "XML for Data Exchange," *Wikipedia*, available at: https://en.wikipedia.org/wiki/Data_exchange#XML_for_data_exchange (accessed June 9, 2020).
[8] "HTML & CSS," W3C, available at: www.w3.org/standards/webdesign/htmlcss.
[9] "XML Schema," *Wikipedia*, available at: https://en.wikipedia.org/wiki/XML_schema (accessed June 9, 2020).
[10] "Document Type Definition," *Wikipedia*, available at: https://en.wikipedia.org/wiki/Document_type_definition (accessed June 9, 2020).
[11] "XML Schema (W3C)," *Wikipedia*, available at: https://en.wikipedia.org/wiki/XML_Schema_(W3C) (accessed June 9, 2020).
[12] "RELAX NG," *Wikipedia*, available at: https://en.wikipedia.org/wiki/RELAX_NG (accessed June 9, 2020).
[13] "Office Open XML," *Wikipedia*, available at: https://en.wikipedia.org/wiki/Office_Open_XML (accessed June 9, 2020).
[14] "OASIS Open Document Format for Office Applications (OpenDocument) TC," OASIS, available at: www.oasis-open.org/committees/tc_home.php?wg_abbrev=office.

existence of standard schemas so that any information provided by a producer can be utilized by any potential application consumer of that information. Thus, to be truly useful as a tool, specific legal use of XML needs to be standardized and sufficiently adopted in the market.

III FUNCTIONALITY VS. USABILITY

"What if they wrote a standard and nobody came?"

Legal XML[15] is (or was) a non-profit organization developing open standards for legal documents, related applications, and legal information exchange, including electronic contracts, court documents, statutes, citations, transcripts, and more.[16] Such standards generally require a list of requirements and a reference implementation to show proof of concept, usability, and working examples.[17] For example, one of Legal XML's more mature standards is eContracts, with associated requirements[18] (2003) and reference implementation[19] (2007). Additionally, the first version of the LegalDocML standard was finalized in 2017.[20] But widespread use of any of these standards to date seems limited at best.[21]

In the 1990s, before the birth of the World Wide Web, work was proceeding on "digital libraries" and related large-scale information retrieval activities.[22] A component of this effort was defining a small set of metadata elements that could easily be adopted for widespread basic cataloging and retrieval purposes. The result is known as the Dublin Core, a set of a dozen or so attributes such as title, author, creation date, etc.[23] The standard has been widely adopted and is often incorporated into other standards (e.g., Legal XML). The relative simplicity of the standard and the market need facilitated its widespread use.

In contrast, consider the fate of the P3P privacy standard for web browsing.[24] In 1999, there was at least some optimism that P3P would allow wide-scale individualized privacy control.[25] By 2002, criticisms of the complexity and lack of usability by the target market of typical web users appeared.[26] Within a few years, the standard was shown to be inadequate even when

---

[15] www.legalxml.org; "Legal XML," *Wikipedia*, available at: https://en.wikipedia.org/wiki/Legal_XML (accessed June 9, 2020).

[16] "About LegalXML," LegalXML, available at: www.legalxml.org/about.

[17] See, e.g., "Reference Implementation," *Wikipedia*, available at: https://en.wikipedia.org/wiki/Reference_implementation (accessed June 9, 2020).

[18] "OASIS LegalXML eContracts XML Markup Requirements," OASIS, available at: www.oasis-open.org/committees/download.php/4598/eContracts-chambers-requirements-02.xml.

[19] "eContracts Version 1.0," OASIS, available at: http://docs.oasis-open.org/legalxml-econtracts/CS01/legalxml-econtracts-specification-1.0.html.

[20] "Committee Specifications for Akoma Ntoso v1.0 and Akoma Ntoso Naming Convention v1.0 Published by LegalDocML TC," OASIS, available at: www.oasis-open.org/news/announcements/committee-specifications-for-akoma-ntoso-v1-0-and-akoma-ntoso-naming-convention-v; "Akoma Ntoso Version 1.0. Part 1: XML Vocabulary," OASIS, available at: http://docs.oasis-open.org/legaldocml/akn-core/v1.0/cs01/part1-vocabulary/akn-core-v1.0-cs01-part1-vocabulary.html.

[21] See, e.g., Monica Palmirani and Fabio Itali, "Legislative XML: Principles and Technical Tools," May 2012, Inter-American Development Bank, No. IDB-DP-222, available at: https://publications.iadb.org/bitstream/handle/11319/5166/IDB-DP-222_XML%20Toolkit_final_Bologna_ENG.pdf.

[22] "NSF/DARPA/NASA Digital Libraries Initiative," D-Lib Magazine, available at: www.dlib.org/dlib/july98/07grif fin.html.

[23] "Dublin Core," *Wikipedia*, available at: https://en.wikipedia.org/wiki/Dublin_Core; http://dublincore.org (accessed June 9, 2020).

[24] "P3P," *Wikipedia*, available at: https://en.wikipedia.org/wiki/P3P (accessed June 9, 2020); "P3P and Privacy on the Web FAQ," W3C, available at: www.w3.org/P3P/p3pfaq (accessed June 9, 2020).

[25] "P3P: An Emerging Privacy Standard," XML.com, available at: www.xml.com/pub/a/1999/05/p3pdraft.html.

[26] "Criticisms," *Wikipedia*, available at: https://en.wikipedia.org/wiki/P3P#Criticisms (accessed June 9, 2020).

implemented.[27] An article in 2013 refers to the "widely forgotten and ignored" P3P standard causing problems with the Internet Explorer browser.[28] And these days (2018), trying to find an implementation of P3P at Facebook or Google yields an explanation as to P3P's non-use and inadequacy.[29] Arguably the market need was/is there, and the problem seems to be more about complexity; users did not understand how to set up P3P in their browser, and they were not willing to forego the use of desired websites that did not conform to their privacy settings. Instead, most web browsers now allow for a more simplistic set of privacy settings such as blocking third-party cookies.

One might hypothesize that both the complexity of the Legal XML standard and the perceived lack of need among practitioners have limited the adoption of XML use within legal documents. As described in Chapter 2.12, it is often helpful to start with a minimally useful set of features in order to test a design and to start building adoption. That seems to have worked for the Dublin Core standard, and was perhaps one of the main factors that led to the downfall of P3P. A glance through the Legal XML standard seems to indicate a focus on comprehensive functionality rather than ease of use and implementation. That would be consistent with a difficulty gaining widespread adoption (though it may be too soon to say for the recently released standard). While those involved in the modernization of the legal system might see an important role in the adoption of XML standards, there is hardly a cry of demand among most lawyers and other potential users. However, the potential of XML in law is as hidden, yet likely as useful, as HTML is in everyday web browsing – comparable to the difference between interacting with a website versus downloading static files via ftp.

IV PROS AND CONS OF XML

"XML is the new black."

XML provides solutions to some concrete problems, such as locating and identifying named entities within a legal document (e.g., parties, companies, locations). It allows for the embedding of descriptive information and metadata within an online document without intruding on the document's rendering, whether printed or viewed online. In fact, there are many benefits to incorporating XML structure into legal documents:

- accuracy of information identification;
- ease of use by computers (APIs) – XML incorporated into standard SDKs (software development kits) and libraries;[30]
- display/rendering characteristics do not need to be specified in the document (e.g., contact information can be rendered differently on different types of devices);[31]

---

[27] "A Loophole Big Enough for a Cookie to Fit Through," Bits, available at: https://bits.blogs.nytimes.com/2010/09/17/a-loophole-big-enough-for-a-cookie-to-fit-through

[28] "Craft and P3P Policy to Make IE Behave," Tech Republic, available at: www.techrepublic.com/blog/software-engineer/craft-a-p3p-policy-to-make-ie-behave.

[29] "Facebook"s Platform for Privacy Preferences (P3P)," Facebook, available at: www.facebook.com/help/327993273962160; "P3P and Google's Cookies," Google, available at: https://support.google.com/accounts/answer/151657.

[30] See, e.g., Python XML libraries, available at: https://wiki.python.org/moin/PythonXml; "XML Parsers," w3schools, available at: www.w3schools.com/xml/xml_parser.asp; "Comparison of XML Editors," Wikipedia, available at: https://en.wikipedia.org/wiki/Comparison_of_XML_editors (accessed June 9, 2020).

[31] See, e.g., "XSLT," w3schools, available at: www.w3schools.com/xml/xsl_intro.asp; www.w3schools.com/xml/tryxslt.asp?xmlfile=cdcatalog&xsltfile=cdcatalog.

- complex data relationships such as hierarchies can be communicated unambiguously;
- reduced ambiguity;
- harmonizing disparate applications around controlled vocabularies[32] (similar to their substantial use in, for example, medical informatics[33]);
- XML tools can enforce standards to ensure that documents are well-formed and valid;
- enabling more sophisticated, database-like structured queries of the marked-up elements within documents;
- XML is an open "eXtensible" standard, and thus useful between and among any parties that want to use it (e.g., law firms, courts) by using their own set of tags; this allows for immediate use and organically grown standards development, as common elements appear across uses;[34]
- XML can be reliably rendered via the XSLT framework.[35]

As one may expect, of course, there are also drawbacks to using XML:

- ease of use by humans requires a carefully designed UI;
- simplistic document handling is harder (e.g., must incorporate, or at least ignore, XML tags to display);
- XML tags for both display and semantics need to be shared by the producer and consumer to be useful;
- complex standards are difficult to propagate and integrate into otherwise more simple authoring and viewing tools.

Thus, the use of XML involves trade-offs, generally requiring upfront expenditure for long-term payback. That said, many/most word processors are now XML-based, and Adobe enables exporting PDF documents to XML.[36] Most of the drawbacks of XML have workarounds, though arguably not necessarily trivial ones.

Perhaps the biggest challenge in injecting potential XML and related standards in law relate to propagation and integration. There is an intimate relationship between the information that needs to be exchanged in various types of legal activities and the shared, controlled vocabulary used to express details (e.g., contract language, court procedures).[37] In medical informatics, one of the main drivers of such developments is the sheer size and complexity of

---

[32] "Controlled Vocabulary," *Wikipedia*, available at: https://en.wikipedia.org/wiki/Controlled_vocabulary (accessed June 9, 2020).

[33] "Medical Subject Headings," *Wikipedia*, available at: https://en.wikipedia.org/wiki/Medical_Subject_Headings (accessed June 9, 2020).

[34] Examples of bottom-up standards development can be seen, for example, in medicine and information technology: "Harmonizing and Extending Standards from a Domain-Specific and Bottom-Up Approach: An Example from Development Through Use in Clinical Applications," available at: www.ncbi.nlm.nih.gov/pubmed/25670750; "Fast-Moving Technologies Need Bottom-Up Standards," Medium, available at: https://medium.com/foggy-bottom/fast-moving-technologies-need-bottom-up-standards-2f94de9a29a8.

[35] "Associating Style Sheets with XML Documents 1.0 (Second Edition)," W3C, available at: www.w3.org/TR/xml-stylesheet.

[36] "File Format Options for PDF Export," Adobe, available at: https://helpx.adobe.com/acrobat/using/file-format-options-pdf-export.html#file_format_options_for_pdf_export.

[37] "Legal XML," Service Architecture, available at: www.service-architecture.com/articles/xml/legal_xml.html; "Electronic Court Filing Version 4.0," OASIS, available at: http://docs.oasis-open.org/legalxml-courtfiling/specs/ecf/v4.0/ecf-v4.0-spec/ecf-v4.0-spec.html; "eContracts Version 1.0," OASIS, available at: http://docs.oasis-open.org/legalxml-econtracts/CS01/legalxml-econtracts-specification-1.0.html.

the biomedical industry, requiring multiple actors in the delivery of care, payments, insurance, etc.[38] For this system to function, it necessitates a complex set of information exchanges with well-defined descriptions of symptoms, diagnoses, procedures, research topics, and so on. For whatever reason, the legal system has been relatively slow to adopt such standards. However, it is likely that the inevitable migration to a computation-based legal system will necessitate increased use of data description standards, along the lines of UTBMS billing codes,[39] in addition to some standardized methodology for information exchange.

V EVOLVING USES OF XML

"Its future's so bright, it has to wear shades."

XML and related technologies such as standardized information descriptions and exchange protocols enable a wide range of applications seen in other fields with a more mature informatics infrastructure, such as the biomedical industry. The US Congress now uses the USLM XML standard to mark-up US statutes and regulations.[40] Internationally, the Akoma Ntoso legal document XML standards are gaining traction, in part due to their simplicity.[41]

For starters, many legal documents derive from a template "precedent" document library or a document automation system. Thus, by embedding appropriate XML *semantic* structure in the template, newly generated documents will facilitate new computational applications with minimal impact on the document creator.[42] This is as true for court opinions and filings as it is for contracts. Of course, if, for example, LegalZoom were to embed XML in an estate plan, the benefit gets lost if the documents are simply printed (losing the tags) and stored on the proverbial dust-collecting shelf. But that invites the move toward a more dynamic document and document structure that is accessible online (whether for courts, corporations, or consumers), and a corresponding shift in the legal system's infrastructure and attitudes about where legal information should properly reside. This movement would allow for, say, the development of consumer/client "electronic legal records" (ELRs) similar to the pervasive use of electronic health records (EHRs).[43] Many of the benefits derived from EHRs[44] have legal equivalences owing to the ability to track dates of past and upcoming events (e.g., a lease expiration, a relevant change in law), compliance with current best practice (e.g., a recommendation for a change in an estate plan), and the ability to analyze the effectiveness of prior interventions.

---

[38] See, e.g., James J. Cimino, "Desiderata for Controlled Medical Vocabularies in the Twenty-First Century," *Methods of Information in Medicine*, 37(4–5) (1998): 394–403 ("The need for controlled vocabularies for medical computing is almost as old as computing itself"), available at: www.ncbi.nlm.nih.gov/pmc/articles/PMC3415631; Margaret H. Coletti and Howard L. Bleich, "Medical Subject Headings Used to Search the Biomedical Literature," *Journal of the American Medical Informatics Association*, 8 (2001): 317–323 (discussing the history of medical controlled vocabulary going back to the US Civil War), available at: https://academic.oup.com/jamia/article/8/4/317/724351.
[39] http://utbms.com.
[40] https://xml.house.gov.
[41] "What It Is," Akoma Ntoso, available at: www.akomantoso.org/?page_id=25.
[42] As previously noted, there is a distinction between XML display/format tags and semantic tags. Thus, the fact that a legal document may be encoded in XML via DOCX or ODF is insufficient to accurately extract detailed legal information it contains.
[43] "EMR vs EHR – What Is the Difference?" HealthIT.gov, available at: www.healthit.gov/buzz-blog/electronic-health-and-medical-records/emr-vs-ehr-difference.
[44] "Health IT and Health Information Exchange Basics," HealthIT.gov, available at: www.healthit.gov/providers-professionals/electronic-medical-records-emr; "Benefits of EHRs," HealthIT.gov, available at: www.healthit.gov/providers-professionals/benefits-electronic-health-records-ehrs.

In addition to streamlining and expanding current practice, since XML enables generalized information exchange, it opens up the potential for a broad range of applications via a general API.[45] Current APIs in the legal sphere include digital signatures and law firm rates.[46] For legal services to appear within the growing cloud computing infrastructure,[47] APIs using standardized data exchange protocols are imperative. Increasing use of XML may help to facilitate this transformation, allowing law to capitalize on the growing information infrastructure.

VI CONCLUSION

"Anything worth doing is worth doing slowly."

Mae West

"Someone is sitting in the shade today because someone planted a tree a long time ago."

Warren Buffett

HTML is currently on its fifth version.[48] The original HTML standard was minimal and allowed enough capability to make web pages compelling and demonstrate its powerful potential.[49] It started with a dozen or so tags, most of which remain in the current standard. This 30-year development process allowed for a continuing, organic growth of the standard, incorporating more sophisticated extensions over time. The current HTML5 standard even includes the handling of video.[50]

While it may be premature to predict the future of Legal XML in particular, a few points are worth noting. First, the development of European civil code was a multigenerational process.[51] A comprehensive, standardized structure for legal information should be viewed as a long-term proposition, and various fits and starts need not individually succeed to demonstrate forward motion. Second, taking Dublin Core and HTML as successful examples, consistent with the design process, the use of some minimal set of XML tags for legal information exchange is sufficient to gain the foothold necessary for further development. Incorporation of (any) *semantic* XML into patents, contracts, court documents, etc., begins to create the ecosystem required for integration across the legal system. Legal informatics as a field will likely need to incorporate XML within its structure, allowing both legal documents and legal information to become integrated into an online, distributed legal system.

---

[45] See, e.g., "API Economy," Deloitte, available at: http://api.epdb.eu.

[46] For example – DocuSign (www.docusign.com/developer-center/api-overview), HelloSign (www.hellosign.com/api); Attorneyfee.com was quietly acquired by LegalZoom and is now LegalZoom Local (https://us.pycon.org/2016/blog/2016/04/03/2016-startup-row/).

[47] "Service Models," *Wikipedia*, available at: https://en.wikipedia.org/wiki/Cloud_computing#Service_models (accessed June 9, 2020).

[48] "HTML," W3C, available at: www.w3.org/TR/html5.

[49] "Development," *Wikipedia*, available at: https://en.wikipedia.org/wiki/HTML#Development (accessed June 9, 2020).

[50] "4.8.9 The Video Element," W3C, available at: www.w3.org/TR/html5/embedded-content-0.html#the-video-element.

[51] "History," *Wikipedia*, available at: https://en.wikipedia.org/wiki/B%C3%BCrgerliches_Gesetzbuch#History (accessed June 9, 2020); "German Civil Code," Britannica, available at: www.britannica.com/topic/German-Civil-Code; "Napoleonic Code," *Wikipedia*, available at: https://en.wikipedia.org/wiki/Napoleonic_Code (accessed June 9, 2020); "Codex Maximilianeus Bavaricus Civilis," *Wikipedia*, available at: https://en.wikipedia.org/wiki/Codex_Maximilianeus_bavaricus_civilis (accessed June 9, 2020); "Napoleonic Code," Britannica, available at: www.britannica.com/topic/Napoleonic-Code.

2.5

Document Automation

Marc Lauritsen

Document assembly, the computer-assisted generation of texts, is a form of automation with wide applicability in law. Most legal tasks involve document preparation. Drafting effective texts is central to lawyering, judging, legislating, and regulating. The best way to support that work with intelligent tools is an ancient topic in legal informatics circles. This chapter surveys the history and current state of the legal document assembly field and reviews the typical concepts, features, and development processes involved. It describes illustrative applications of document drafting software and the knowledge representations and interfaces they leverage.

I INTRODUCTION

Document automation covers a broad field of functions, some of which are summarized in Figure 2.5.1. Tools and techniques of document production often interoperate with processes and technologies that deal with the raw material for, and outputs of, legal drafting work. Some of these tools and techniques are shown in Figure 2.5.1. In this chapter, we will focus on the first branch of the diagram – creation – where humans and non-biological assistants produce documents.

An important preliminary step in this subject is to consider where the various forms of document automation fit within the broader context of knowledge management (KM) technologies. Figure 2.5.2 portrays KM as an overall discipline of managing professional knowledge, whether "in motion" in human heads and interactions, or reified in various forms of content. Document management forms a subset of content management, and specialized versions of document management deal with contracts as a particular document type, as well as with documents that serve as templates or models for new documents.

A *Varieties of Document Automation*

Table 2.5.1 illustrates the range of functions, features, and software categories (beyond basic word processing, spreadsheets, and email) at play in the document automation field. These may be used by legal and contract professionals, or by business and consumer self-helpers.

B *Notes on Vocabulary*

Readers will note varying terminologies throughout this chapter. *Document assembly* is often used to refer to legal document generation technologies, but that phrase only describes one

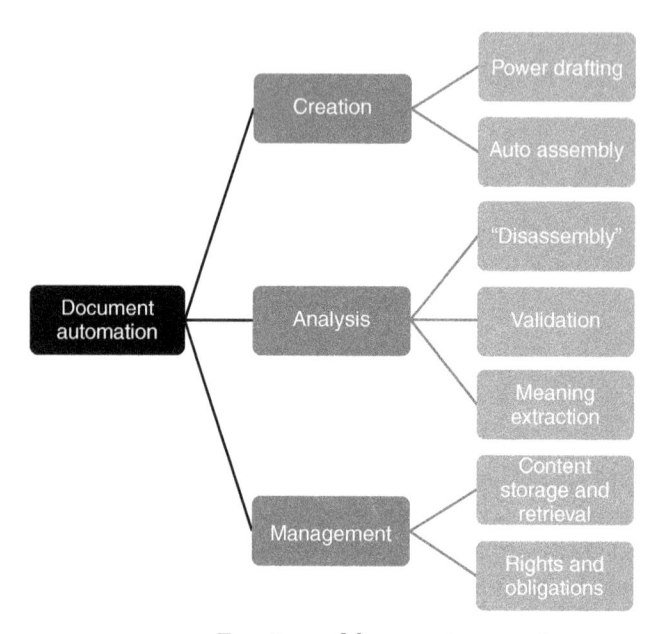

FIGURE 2.5.1 Functions of document automation.

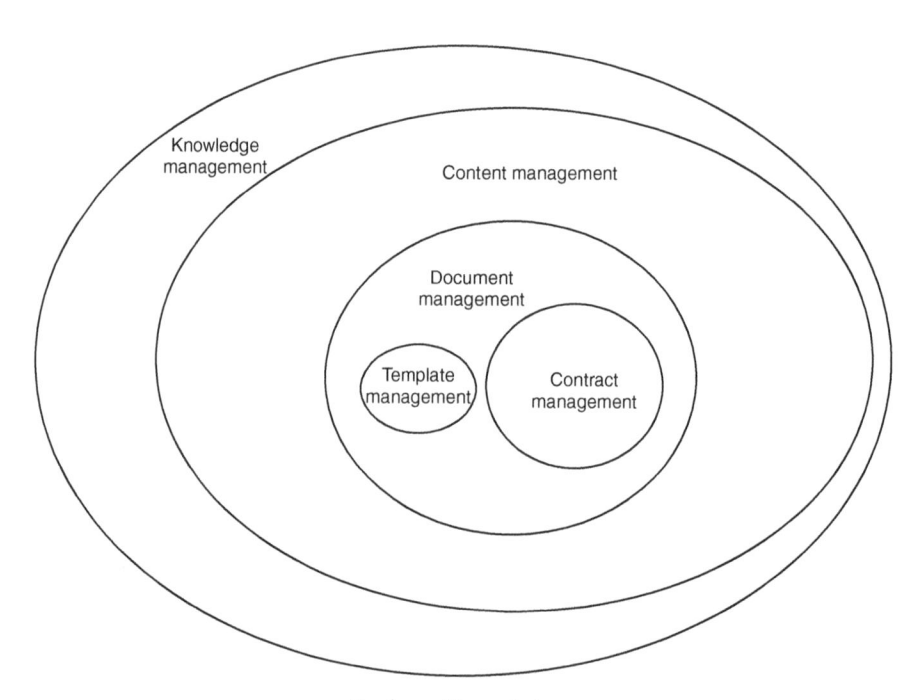

FIGURE 2.5.2 Realms of knowledge management.

particular function that drafting systems can perform. Such systems can and should provide knowledge-based support for organizing facts, research, analysis, and other processes, as well as provide generation of specific documents. *Assembly* also implies a mode of use in which textual components are combined automatically based on user responses to extra-

TABLE 2.5.1 *Document automation range of functions.*

Function/activity	Software categories	Illustrative features	Products and services
Discrete documents			
Creation (authoring, drafting, generation, assembly)	Document assembly expert systems	"Intelligent templates" Dynamic questionnaire Auto assembly	ContractExpress, Exari, HotDocs, Leaflet, KMstandards, Neota Logic
Access (model language and guidance)	Intranets (document assembly and expert systems)	Annotated models Clause libraries	SharePoint
Review/analysis		Disassemble, benchmark a draft against a standard	KMstandards
Negotiation		Collaborative editing	CommonAccord
Execution	eSignature		Docusign, EchoSign
Storage and Retrieval	Document management Enterprise content management	Profiles Search Version control	OpenText, iManage, Worldox
Management (including administration)	Contract life-cycle management (both pre- and post-execution)	Wizards, workflow, triggers, alerts, audit trail, change orders, approvals	Upside, Emptoris, Lawtrac
Collections of documents			
Review/analysis (for compliance monitoring or auditing)			eBrevia, Exemplify, Kira Systems, KMstandards
Extraction/abstraction		Query Report	Brightleaf, Seal
Template and model creation	Authoring systems Development platforms	Author Maintain	Doc assembly engines, KMstandards
Template and model management		Store, profile, share, manage	SharePoint
Standardization		Standardize, define acceptable variations	Contract Standards

documentary queries, whereas other more directly interactive modes are increasingly supported by today's technologies.

Document modeling is a term that fails to capture how models are actually used. *Document automation*, on the other hand, suffers from overbreadth. This term can sometimes refer to complementary technologies: document management, comparison, and analysis tools, and word processing features like automatic numbering and cross-references. Additionally, it implies a degree of automaticity that doesn't reflect the mixed initiative nature of present-day and emergent drafting technologies.

Computer-aided, advanced, or intelligent "drafting" systems (i.e., those that compose texts) probably comes closest to an accurate term. *Computer-aided drafting system* is a term that encompasses both preparation of legislation and legal instruments.

C Basic Concepts

Computer-aided drafting systems are reasonably common in the contemporary legal world. A lawyer, paralegal, secretary, or do-it-yourselfer works through a series of question-and-answer dialogs, perhaps laced with reference material, and the system assembles a draft document. Alternatively, the user may pick forms, clauses, and other components as needed from libraries of options.

Sometimes such an application is obtained from a legal publisher or software vendor. TurboTax from Intuit, for example, is a familiar consumer example in the USA. Such applications afford the benefits of automation, but with little effort and expense on the part of the user. Alternatively, sometimes an organization develops a custom system with a document assembly "engine" that uses its own forms and experience. This can require a fair amount of upfront time thinking through and handling many possible scenarios, but it can result in excellent leverage of practical legal knowledge.

Such systems capture the regularities that underlie the documents – where different sections, paragraphs, sentences, and words go, and under what circumstances. The software prompts a user to make choices and specify details like names, numbers, dates, and phrases. Instead of cutting and pasting, one picks the desired options or alternatives from lists. Instead of searching for phrases like "lender's name" and replacing them with a client's name, a user responds to questions and lets the computer do the needed work. And as far as keying in lots of text and manually fussing with formats, the application handles all predictable variations, boilerplates, and layouts.

Terminology varies among programs. There is usually a *template* that models a particular kind of document, with variables and instructions placed at locations that must change from case to case. A user answers questions in a series of interview-style dialogs, the responses are stored in an answer file, and the desired document is generated in a common format like Word, WordPerfect, RTF, or PDF. Typically, each answer file stores all the data relevant to a single client or matter, and thus can be used to generate more than one document or form (e.g., a complaint for divorce, a financial statement, and various motions in a family-law system). When answers are changed, the documents can be instantly re-generated.

In addition to basic point-and-shoot clause selection and fill-in-the-blanks variable replacement, these systems can store drafting rules and practitioner know-how that guide the hands of novices and experts alike. For example, a divorce system may ask about the client's state of residence, financial situation, and number of children. Based on answers to these and other follow-up questions, the system will insert appropriate material in the complaint and in any associated motions.

II A BRIEF HISTORY OF DOCUMENT ASSEMBLY

A Word Processing Beginnings

The origin of document assembly systems can be found in search-and-replace, macro, merge, and related features of word processing programs.

Search-and-replace functions allow users to locate all instances of a given word, phrase, or string of characters and replace them with another word, phrase, or string. A boilerplate document with placeholders like [plaintiff], [defendant], [court], and [attorney for plaintiff] can thus be tailored for a given case by replacing those phrases with matter-specific information. These replacements are ordinarily done one at a time, although they can also be put under the control of a macro. A *macro* is a series of recorded commands that can be played back when desired. Macros can retrieve documents, pause for user input, call other macros, and do anything a computer user can do from the keyboard.

A *merge* involves the combination of text from multiple files. An elementary use is the so-called *mail merge*, in which a series of customized letters is created by inserting addresses, salutations, and other information about different people (contained in a secondary merge file) into a boilerplate form (the primary merge file). Merge routines in modern word processors can prompt the user for data and launch macros.

Most word processing programs have long supported explicit programming with conditional branching. Conditional branching is the inclusion of decision points at which alternative procedures can be followed, depending upon information entered up to that point, using IF, THEN, and ELSE commands and logical operators like AND, OR, and NOT.

By chaining together macros and merges, and taking advantage of common word processing features like automatic paragraph numbering, it is possible to construct satisfactory systems for the automatic assembly of moderately complex documents. However, if one is not careful, this can lead to a confusing spaghetti of code that is hard to maintain.

B Specialized Programs

Specialized programs for legal document assembly emerged in the late 1970s and early 1980s. The ABF Processor and CAPS were two of the earliest research efforts. Commercial products like Document Modeler, WorkForm, Work Engine, DocuMentor, FlexPractice, ExperText, and Scrivener soon followed. These applications offered several advantages over word processors: (1) they made it much easier to author, maintain, and distribute models; (2) they had nicer interfaces for data entry and user guidance; (3) they supported graphical forms; and (4) they made it easy to reuse data across sessions and templates.

The same automation of routine text editing processes that made word processing so pervasive thus became attainable on the conceptual level of document assembly. Current document assembly programs use a wide spectrum of approaches and boast an impressive array of innovative features. They excel in the richness of their user interfaces and the sophistication of documentary output. If word processors can be thought of as helping to edit text with power steering, advanced drafting tools are like being driven in a robotically chauffeured limousine. As this chapter progresses, you will see many different choices and considerations available with these powerful new tools.

C Important Differences between Word Processing and Document Automation

The first major difference between word processing and document automation is the latter's use of graphical forms. Document assembly generally encompasses both freely editable word processing documents and fixed-format "graphical" forms, where the background is static and information can only be placed in pre-designated fields.

Second, in most document assembly applications the users provide information and make drafting decisions through questionnaire-like screen dialogs that are outside of a target document; there is an interface through which questions can be asked and guidance given. But many document assembly tools can in fact be used to produce information-gathering modules, advisory systems, and intelligent checklists that needn't result in any document at all.

Third, document assembly technology can be used, and is being used, both by professionals serving clients and by individuals doing work for themselves. There are even some hybrid scenarios in which a client completes a computer-based questionnaire on their own, and the answer file goes to the legal professional for further review, revision, and document drafting.

D Online Document Assembly

The internet has opened up new opportunities for organizing and delivering document assembly applications. Any or all of the major components – the engine, templates, answers, documents, help material – can be accessed from a web server. This provides location independence, multi-user access, client access, ease of use, and other benefits. For law office staff, a big advantage of web-based implementation is the centralization and instant updating of template collections. Robust document automation can be delivered without having to purchase, install, configure, and maintain special-purpose locally installed software. Often, the application only requires a browser, an internet connection, and a printer. For IT professionals (and budget-conscious managers), a single centralized server and staff can economically provide document assembly capabilities to hundreds or thousands of users.

Nevertheless, full local processing modes (desktops) retain some advantages. Built-in library interfaces can be used to choose templates; data entry and revision can be done in context on graphical forms; *ad hoc* combinations of documents can be assembled; database connectivity can be done out-of-the-box; and clause libraries and local customizations of templates can be easily used. And of course, local processing modes can still function while disconnected from the internet.

E Varieties and Venues

Document assembly technology has been applied to everything from simple thank-you letters to elaborate expert systems that advise on the laws of many jurisdictions and generate document sets reaching into hundreds of pages. There is a vast range of application types. The main polarities include: off-the-shelf vs. custom-built; in-house vs. client-facing; textual vs. graphical; question-driven vs. clause-selection; desktop vs. online; and document-oriented vs. interview-focused. The possible combinations of these dualities are numerous, and there is a great variety of different contexts in which these document assembly types can be used.

Small law firms and legal departments most commonly use document assembly for routine or high-volume paperwork, purchasing pre-written template sets when possible. Larger firms and departments are more likely to develop custom in-house applications, drawing upon their own precedents and integrating with KM efforts. Practitioners in both settings are increasingly interested in sophisticated drafting applications that combine advanced models of complex documents with rich layers of annotational guidance. And firms of all sizes are experimenting with outward-facing applications aimed at clients and customers.

Corporate law departments are starting to show great interest in document automation for client self-service as well. Cisco and Microsoft, for example, provide do-it-yourself sales contracts, non-disclosure agreements, and software licenses to their business users. Law departments can offload routine work and delight their clients with rapid turnaround, while retaining control of transactions that deviate from pre-approved "safe" terms.

Non-profit legal services have long used both online and offline initiatives, some even developing their own systems and making them available to fellow programs. Family law and eviction defense systems are quite common, for example, and the California-based I-CAN!™ project serves interactive forms to thousands of lay users. LawHelp Interactive is a related effort, funded by grants from the federal Legal Services Corporation, the State Justice Center, and software donations from the HotDocs Corporation.[1]

Courts have also taken a strong interest in automated forms as a response to the deluge of self-represented litigants. Many state court systems have made their standard forms available as fillable PDFs. Several states – including California, Idaho, and Utah – have mounted much more sophisticated, interactive applications. The integration of document automation and e-filing raises especially interesting possibilities.

Commercial players have also seen the value of targeting the consumer marketplace. There are now many fee-for-service providers of prefabricated forms aimed at self-helpers, such as USLegal,[2] SmartLegalForms,[3] and LegalZoom.[4] There is also a growing universe of non-lawyer "legal document preparers." These private sector developments are helping to expand consumer choice – and shake up a complacent legal profession – but may pose questions of second-class quality, especially for disadvantaged citizens. They also do not provide the insurance function of a lawyer – an individual you can sue if things go wrong.

With so many varieties, document assembly and automation applications have gone beyond mere specialized tools held only by skilled professionals. Increasingly, these applications are being used directly by consumers. People have long used off-the-shelf packages for their own wills and taxes, but now large international law firms sell subscriptions to online expert systems that deliver sophisticated legal analyses without direct human involvement; corporate law departments equip field personnel with do-it-yourself contract assemblers; courts and legal aid programs provide intelligent forms for unrepresented litigants; and lawyer-less entities vend interactive documents and automated legal assistance over the web.

Document automation has steadily gained traction in law, and we are entering a period of even faster growth. There is vigorous competition between excellent vendors and products, a large community of qualified consultants, rising client expectations, aggressive new competitors giving consumers alternatives to the profession, and huge latent opportunities for process improvement in legal work.

---

[1] LawHelp, https://lawhelpinteractive.org.
[2] USLegal, www.uslegalforms.com.
[3] SmartLegalForms, www.smartlegalforms.com.
[4] LegalZoom, www.legalzoom.com.

F Commercial Engines

Since the late 1970s, a dizzying variety of technologies, vendors, and approaches have emerged in the legal document assembly universe. In one exercise, this author was able to list 65 discrete engines aimed at lawyers that have been commercially available at some point. At present, most of these are long gone. Table 2.5.2 presents only a partial list of specialized document generation products that have been marketed to lawyers over the years. Some of these are still in use, but their vendors have disappeared, moved on, or withdrawn their products from general availability. Even though they are no longer marketed or supported, some offices still use old programs like CAPS and PowerTxt, or have converted from them to contemporary platforms.

Today's well-established applications include the following: ActiveDocs Opus, ContractExpress DealBuilder, Exari, HotDocs, Innova, Leaflet, MacPac, Pathagoras, Rapidocs, TheFormTool, and XpressDox. Newer applications like CaseRails, DraftOnce, Drawloop, Legal Nature, and WeAgree have emerged in just the last few years.

Clearly there has been a lot of churn in the document automation business, but this has led to productive innovation as vendors attempt to leapfrog each other. ContractExpress, for example, is purely web-based on the user end and offers an AI-based authoring environment that reduces the need for traditional template programming; precedents marked up in ways intelligible to substantive experts can often be converted automatically into interactive "masters."[5] Business Integrity originally developed ContractExpress as a beachhead in the London Magic Circle firms, and made major inroads into top law departments there and in the USA, building on the self-service themes mentioned above. Rapidocs, also originating from the UK, includes innovative features to optimize it for e-commerce applications, and is also active in the "virtual law practice" space.[6] Exari is a web-based solution with a strong commitment to open systems and standards, especially XML.[7] HotDocs has the biggest market presence and most developed ecosystem, with an excellent online knowledge base, email discussion list, and consultant community.[8] HotDocs offers the best tools for automating graphical forms, and has a full-featured web implementation. The company continues to periodically release significant new versions. It was owned for many years by LexisNexis, but is now in private hands.

G Professional Reception

The act of drafting legal documents does not seem to inherently make use of advanced technology necessary. Drafters today appreciate the power-steering aspects of modern word processors, such as cut-and-paste, spell check, search-and-replace, and auto-numbering. The power to revise drafts on the fly, insert extended passages with a couple keystrokes, and quickly manipulate format and structure are now largely taken for granted. These features of word processing are straightforward power tools, ultimately used by an expert person. Technologies that involve more autonomous software behavior, however, are unsettling to many.

---

[5] Thomson Reuters Contract Express, www.contractexpress.com.
[6] "About Rapidocs," DirectLaw, available at: www.directlaw.com/rapidocs.asp.
[7] Exari, www.exari.com.
[8] HotDocs, www.hotdocs.com.

TABLE 2.5.2 *Document assembly products, past and present.*

- ABF Processor
- Agility
- Ajlsoft
- AmazingDocs
- Atlis
- BizDocs
- Black Letter
- Blankity-Blank
- Boilerplate
- Brentmark Document Assembler
- CAPS
- Cetara WordShare
- Chameleon
- Clause-It
- D3
- DAS@H
- DataPrompter
- DocBuilder
- DocCon
- Docdolittle
- DocFire
- DocRite
- Documaker (Ducucorp)
- Document Modeler (LegalWare)
- DocuMENTOR
- Docuscribe
- EasyDocs
- eDrafter
- ExperText
- FastDraft
- First Draft
- FlexPractice
- Form Bank
- General Counsel
- GhostFill
- Grantha
- GroupDocs
- ILS Techniques
- IQDocs
- JumpStart
- KillerDocs
- LincDocs
- Masterdraft
- Masterform
- Memba Genesis
- Millrace
- NovaDocs
- Oban
- Overdrive
- Perfectus
- PowerTxt
- Precedent
- Qshift
- SansWrite
- Scrivener
- smart-DOCS
- Structure (Attenex)
- Supra II
- Synthesis Publishing Architecture
- ThinkDocs
- WinDraft
- Work Engine (Anselm)
- WorkForm
- WriteSpeed
- XpertDoc

Documents that automatically complete themselves or populate themselves with relevant provisions as users interact with them can be downright scary. Lawyers may not be accustomed to working at such speeds. And the whole concept of interacting with a document under draft via an extrinsic "interview" can seem an unwelcome distancing of the drafter from their work.

In part, this is about getting used to a new method of wordsmithing. Once understood, intelligent document assembly can be just as much of an expert's tool as a word processor. The drafter makes decisions and specifies information in an interface that lives above and apart from the words themselves, with confidence that the right stuff is going in the right place, and great freedom to recast large segments of the draft by simply toggling switches. Lawyers who understand the general operations of a document assembly program, and the specific logic embedded in a particular model, can achieve both high efficiency and good professional satisfaction.

New pressures for document quality and auditability arising from regulatory compliance and ethical concerns will drive legal and business professionals away from today's artisanal drafting approaches and toward document assembly and automation. The change management challenges involved with this transition will be daunting for many organizations, but ultimately very rewarding once complete.

III ILLUSTRATIVE SCENARIOS

The following imaginary scenarios, taken from this author's *Lawyer's Guide to Working Smarter with Knowledge Tools*, illustrate practical uses and benefits of document automation.[9]

> It's Monday morning. You're a mid-level associate at a large firm, coffee in hand, about to settle into work after a rare weekend of relaxation. A fax is sitting on your chair. It seems that the town of Wellville has finally decided to float that bond for the new school building. Market conditions are such that time is of the essence. Several hundred pages of documents may need to be completed. A few days' delay could cost the town tens of thousands of dollars if interest rates rise as many predict. Missing sections or inappropriate phrases could spell embarrassment at best, and costly malpractice at worst.
>
> Last year these kinds of transactions typically took a small team of lawyers, paralegals, and secretaries two days of feverish work. Examples were found of similar transactions in the firm's document collection, and copied into a new draft. Then the parts that obviously didn't apply were deleted, and parts that were obviously missing, but needed for the peculiarities of the current deal, were found in yet other old documents. Names were adjusted by global search and replace. Dates and numbers were individually edited to reflect the terms of the current deal. Everything was proofed, then sent to the associate in charge, who still found dozens of little errors, and inappropriate and missing passages. This cycle continued a few times until the documents were sent for "final" review by the partner, who discovered a major inconsistency between two sections, requiring yet another round of editing and proofing. After nearly 36 hours, a finished package could be sent to the client, who not uncommonly would decide to change a few details at the last minute to reflect negotiations with the funding bank.
>
> This year, fortunately, the firm's new automated practice system for municipal finance documents is in place. You enter details from the term sheet faxed by the client on a series of screens that adjust to present only those questions that must be answered for the situation described. All the basic legal and strategic choices needed to draft documents are presented for your point-and-shoot disposition. Since this is a kind of transaction the system has been programmed to handle, you quickly review your answers, click a button, and smile as 120 pages of customized documents appear on the screen. You're confident that 95% of the grunt work has been done, and that the drafts will contain few if any of the picky little mistakes so common last year. And if the client needs a change at the last minute, you know you can accommodate it without panic. The coffee is still warm.

> It's Christmas Eve. Horace Witherspoon is unexpectedly in the waiting room. It seems that he and his wife are off to Venice for the holidays, and he's picked this time to make

---

[9] Marc Lauritsen, *Lawyer's Guide to Working Smarter with Knowledge Tools* (Lanham, MD: ABA, 2010).

> a long-planned revision to his will. It involves a complicated restructuring of the trusts into which most of the estate pours. Your efforts to discourage his last-minute revisions are unavailing.
>
> Ordinarily you would be uncomfortable drafting the necessary instruments and having them executed without careful proofreading and a colleague's review. But your estate planning system has been in regular use for several years now, and routinely produces flawless documents now that a dozen lawyers have used it extensively and participated in its refinement. You bring up Horace's previous information, specify the desired changes, and assemble the needed paperwork. An alert reminds you to check an obscure possibility that turns out not to be problematic. Two late-working staff members serve as witnesses. The Witherspoons are on their way, and so are you.

IV THEORETICAL FRONTIERS

A *Theory in Practice*

Many people have pondered legal document automation over the past several decades, and have built sophisticated software to embody their ideas. Their collective work represents a huge knowledge pool, albeit largely uncharted and inaccessible except in the scattered files and memories of experts. Few vendors or developers have had time or interest to consider, let alone document, the theoretical angles. As a result, it's not uncommon to encounter those who believe they have "discovered" techniques that have actually been extant for 20 years. This produces great redundancy in document automation engine implementations, but also fruitful innovation and learning.

B *Academic and Research Attention*

Thomas Gordon pointed out as early as 1989 that most commercial products lack the advantages of declarative knowledge representations, such as automated explanation, and thus do not handle defaults and exceptions very well, and provide no support for reasoning in multiple interpretative contexts.[10] Many products still follow the procedural markup paradigm associated with Sprowl, wherein master documents are expressed in terms of if–then structures, repeat loops, and variables.[11] Neither the documents nor the legal-factual circumstances occasioning their particular configurations are explicitly modeled.

Karl Branting was among the earliest to examine the notion of self-describing documents and their potential role in new modes of expressing and delivering knowledge pertinent to legal drafting.[12] His DocuPlanner system used models of illocutionary and rhetorical

---

[10] Thomas F. Gordon, "A Theory Construction Approach to Legal Document Assembly," in *Expert Systems in Law*, ed. Antonio A. Martino (Amsterdam: Elsevier Science Ltd., 1992), 211–225.

[11] James A. Sprowl, "Automating the Legal Reasoning Process: A Computer That Uses Regulations and Statutes to Draft Legal Documents," *American Bar Foundation Research Journal* 1 (1979): 1–8.

[12] L. Karl Branting, James C. Lester, and Charles B. Callaway, "Automating Judicial Document Drafting: A Discourse-Based Approach," *Artificial Intelligence and Law*, 6 (2–4) (1998): 105–110; L. Karl Branting, Charles B. Callaway, Bradford W. Mott, and James C. Lester, "Integrating Discourse and Domain Knowledge for Document Drafting," in *ICAIL '99 Proceedings of the Seventh International Conference on Artificial Intelligence and Law*, Oslo, Norway, July 14–17, 1999 (New York, NY: ACM, 1999); L. Karl Branting, James C. Lester, and Charles B. Callaway, "Automated Drafting of Self-Explaining Legal Documents," in *Proceedings*

structures to make goals and stylistic conventions explicit, so that documents become queryable.[13] The operators involved in expressing these structures constitute a grammar that can be used to generate new documents.

Another similar strand of work is found in the legislative and regulatory drafting area. A goal in this area is to produce texts that can be easily searched or automatically reasoned against, like in question-answering systems. But drafting support tools also assist in automating the construction of legal sources, as when they ensure stylistic and content requirements and improve formal representations.[14] Other researchers have used an XML framework to introduce first-order predicate calculus models into the text of regulations.[15] Meanwhile, the Italian "Norme in Rete" project has shown how document type definitions (DTDs) can guide the drafting of legislation,[16] and the European ESTRELLA project has a "workpackage" on managing legislative texts and other sources.[17]

C New Theoretical Directions

Many theoretical frontiers remain unexplored, and the legal document automation field has lacked a universal model of computer-aided drafting. Such a model could supply a means for all of a system's knowledge and behavior to be explicitly declared. A conceptualization that is sufficiently rich and general to comprehend both present and foreseeable functionality would be an important step forward.[18]

V PRACTICAL CONSIDERATIONS FOR PRACTITIONERS

Many legal documents, even quite complex ones, can be reliably drafted by intelligent software when it is supplied with appropriate inputs. Consumers and businesses have become accustomed to preparing their own documents with software tools, and they expect their service providers to have even better tools in place. As a practitioner, there are several questions to ask yourself about the tools you use.

A Should You Choose a Document Automation System?

This first question is a no-brainer. Basic word processing is a thing of the past. Drafting documents and preparing forms is a cornerstone of just about every kind of practice, and

---

of the Sixth International Conference on Artificial Intelligence and Law, Melbourne, Australia, June 30–July 3, 1997 (New York, NY: ACM, 1997).

[13] L. Karl Branting, "Techniques for Automated Judicial Document Drafting," International Journal of Law & Information Technology 6 (2) (1998): 214–229.

[14] Marie-Francine Moens, "Improving Access to Legal Information: How Drafting Systems Help," in Information Technology & Lawyers: Advanced Technology in the Legal Domain, from Challenges to Daily Routines, eds. Arno R. Lodder and Anja Oskamp (New York, NY: Springer, 2006), 119–136.

[15] Shawn Kerrigan and Kincho H. Law, "Logic-Based Regulation Compliance-Assistance," in Proceedings of the Ninth International Conference on Artificial Intelligence and Law, Scotland, June 24–28, 2003 (New York, NY: ACM, 2003): 126–135.

[16] Carlo Biagioli, Enrico Francesconi, PierLuigi Spinosa, and M. Taddei, "A Legal Drafting Environment Based on Formal and Semantic XML Standards," in Proceedings of the Tenth International Conference on Artificial Intelligence and Law, Bologna, Italy, June 6–11, 2005 (New York, NY: ACM, 2005): 244–245.

[17] See the ESTRELLA Project, www.estrellaproject.org.

[18] See generally, Marc Lauritsen, "Current Frontiers in Legal Drafting Systems," working paper for a tutorial at the Eleventh International Conference on Artificial Intelligence and Law, Palo Alto, California, June 4–8, 2007, available at: www.researchgate.net/publication/228376699_Current_Frontiers_in_Legal_Drafting_Systems.

many lawyers now have a recognized obligation to keep up with the benefits and risks of relevant technology. Even if you don't get the final word on technology decisions in your practice environment, you should seek to influence them.

B Which Document Automation System Should You Choose?

Choosing an optimal document automation solution is more complicated. Newcomers are understandably perplexed because it's hard to know what you want until you know what's possible and what it costs. Making matters more complicated, the picture is constantly changing. Products evolve, new vendors enter the market, and the broader technology context morphs. A careful choice you made two years ago could well become less than ideal today.

This author has had 30 years of hands-on experience with a couple dozen software packages and their comparative assessment. My colleagues and I have worked with organizations that have devoted hundreds of hours to product selection. They've converted applications from and to a variety of platforms, and have wrestled with their differences and quirks. Even so, sometimes the selection process remains bewildering.

C Clear Goals

Every good document automation system will respond to the very specific needs of its users. Imagine one system that would significantly improve your work environment. Before worrying about technicalities, start by getting a clear idea of what you would ideally like to accomplish. Table 2.5.3 presents a handy worksheet.

Your answers to the questions presented in Table 2.5.3 will evolve as you learn more about the functional possibilities and cost/effort/benefit trade-offs of candidate solutions, especially if this is your first effort of this kind. There is little point in setting off on a journey without at least a general sense of your destination, and these questions can begin that process.

D Preliminary Steps

Before deciding which document assembly and automation platform to use, it's important to understand your economic case for doing so. Assuming you select a platform and deploy applications, what benefits do you anticipate? Will they outweigh the effort and expense? This requires a preliminary approximation of the bundle of functions you hope to secure, and how you expect to deploy those functions in productive work. You should have at least a preliminary sense of who will exercise what functions where, when, how, and how often. You can't gauge the cost or benefit of a system in the abstract.

E Buy or Build

Any technology procurement presents choices about how much to buy "off the shelf" and how much to cobble together yourself. In the case of document drafting tools, there are three choices to make.

The first choice is whether or not to use an existing software platform or *shell*, or to instead build the technology yourself. For most uses, many existing platforms will serve admirably, but a surprising number of organizations still like to create their own underlying document automation tools. Reinvention can be wasteful or empowering.

The second choice is whether you should create your own content (templates) or acquire access to content that someone else has prefabricated. There is a growing market for the latter. Some examples include Blumberg's DL Libraries, DirectLaw, HotDocs Market, Smokeball, WealthCounsel, and VentureDocs. If you're lucky enough to find content that meets your needs, this will generally also settle your first choice, as your work will already be in a particular platform's framework. In some cases, you can have the best of both worlds by customizing such content, but that can raise complications when the vendor releases an update.

Third, ask yourself if you should do the associated work with your own personnel, or engage an outside consultant. For most organizations not already active in this kind of work, outsourcing makes the most sense. However, be prepared for the likelihood that the choice of consultant may tie you to a particular platform already in use by them.

VI CONCLUSION: OPTIONS ABOUND

A wealth of choices awaits those who want to kick the tires of document automation systems. Be prepared for a blizzard of options. But while a lot of attention is given to pure-play products, it is important to know that substantial document automation functionality can be found in products in other categories, such as Contract Logix for case management systems, and Neota Logic for expert systems. Both of these options have especially robust

TABLE 2.5.3 *Worksheet for document automation goals.*

	Your possible solution
Purposes – What are the driving goals of the system? Speed up processing? Improve quality or consistency? Achieve greater capacity? Allow work to be delegated to more efficient staffing levels? Assist in training?	
Users – Who are the intended users? Lawyers, paralegals, secretaries, students, clients? Are they experts in the area in question, or novices? Are they a few, or many? Do they work in proximity, or are they spread among floors, offices, or cities?	
Documents – What documents is the system designed to produce? Short and simple, long and complex, or somewhere in between? Are they typically first-draft -final, or do they require lots of post-assembly editing? Are official, graphical forms involved? Are the documents produced individually, or in related sets? Can they be neatly handled with fill-in-the-blank variables and alternative/additional passages, or do they involve lots of material that doesn't lend itself to straightforward rules?	
Scope – What range of fact scenarios is the system intended to support? How deep do you intend to go in modeling the variations from scenario to scenario? Is the system designed only to produce first drafts, or guide users through several stages of revision and negotiation? Should it offer project management and decision support features?	
Staffing – Will the project be done entirely with in-house personnel, by an outside consultant, or by some blend? Is it conceived of as a project by lawyers in a practice group, aided by others; or as an initiative by IT professionals, aided by lawyers?	

document automation feature sets. There are also dramatically new approaches, such as KM Standards and CommonAccord, that do not quite fit into any existing category.

In sum, there are many document automation systems in the market. One of the most difficult, but less obvious, challenges for legal professionals is *which* system to use, not whether to use one. Legal informatics is a vast field that continues to grow, and document automation represents a subfield that is all but mandatory for any firm or in-house department hoping to compete in today's market.

B.

Artificial Intelligence, Machine Learning, Natural Language Processing, and Blockchain

2.6

AI + Law

An Overview

Daniel Martin Katz

There are a variety of informatics-centric tasks for which the goal is to predict something or extract some kind of signal. In this section, we consider artificial intelligence broadly, artificial intelligence applied to law, and the very fruitful fields of machine learning (ML) and natural language processing (NLP).

Each of these topics is worthy of its own book, and there are many high-quality treatments already available. Our goal here is to place particular emphasis on lawyers, legal technologists, and academic legal researchers, and spur further inquiry by introducing these readers to the core ideas and terminology in these somewhat overlapping fields.

I THE AI + LAW RENAISSANCE

Over the past several years, artificial intelligence (AI) has experienced a renaissance within law.[1] While the field of AI and law is at least three decades old,[2] the majority of the legal industry has historically paid scant attention to work undertaken within the field. Following the 2008 financial crisis, the demand among enterprise clients (i.e., Fortune 1000 companies and the like) for better, faster, and cheaper legal services has driven an increased interest among legal service providers in tools and methods that can facilitate the innovation imperative. Times have changed and there is now significant interest in AI among law firms, corporate counsel, and within the academy.[3]

In fields outside of law, there has been a much deeper incursion of AI-enabled technology. White-collar fields such as medicine, finance, and accounting provide instructive examples.[4] Finance, in particular, has seen, over the past few decades, a sea change from human-driven trading activity to algorithm-driven trading.[5]

As of the time of this writing, there is still significant confusion in the legal market regarding what AI is, what it is not, what is technically possible, what is economically feasible,

---

[1] "Why Artificial Intelligence Is Enjoying a Renaissance," *The Economist*, July 15, 2016, available at: www.economist.com/the-economist-explains/2016/07/15/why-artificial-intelligence-is-enjoying-a-renaissance.

[2] Trevor Bench-Capon, Michał Araszkiewicz, Kevin Ashley, et al., "A History of AI and Law in 50 Papers: 25 Years of the International Conference on AI and Law," *Artificial Intelligence and Law* 20 (3) (2012): 215–319.

[3] *See, e.g.*, Lauri Donahue, "A Primer on Using Artificial Intelligence in the Legal Profession," *Harvard Journal of Law and Technology*, January 3, 2018, available at: https://jolt.law.harvard.edu/digest/a-primer-on-using-artificial-intelligence-in-the-legal-profession.

[4] European Society for Medical Oncology, "Man Against Machine: AI Is Better Than Dermatologists at Diagnosing Skin Cancer," *Science Daily*, May 28, 2018, available at: www.sciencedaily.com/releases/2018/05/180528190839.htm.

[5] *See, e.g.*, Daniel Faggella, "Machine Learning in Finance: Present and Future Applications," *Tech Emergence*, June 1, 2018, available at: www.techemergence.com/machine-learning-in-finance.

and what the rise of AI implies for the future of the legal industry. These are problems that require a detailed treatment and it is not possible to do complete justice within this book, but we can offer a historical overview of the field of AI, a description of the major subfields and methods, and an enumeration of a handful of use cases in which AI might be fruitfully deployed within the legal industry.

Given all the past mistakes regarding declarations of AI ascendancy, it is important to be cautious about any strong pronouncements; the so-called "robot lawyers" are far off on the horizon, if they ever come at all. Nevertheless, significant levels of automation are very much underway. The market for legal services has already felt meaningful impact from AI, but the real prize is the movement toward greater levels of automation and the substitution of labor for technology, which will provide a generally positive outcome for clients and society as a whole.

II THE HISTORY OF AI, AND AI WINTERS

The history of AI is replete with false starts, bold pronouncements, spectacular failures, and yet, significant promise. Starting in the middle of the 1950s and well into the 1960s, early leaders in the field made a series of public and private statements regarding AI's future.[6] Herbert Simon, a 1978 Nobel Prize winner, is said to have argued in 1965 that "machines will be capable, within twenty years, of doing any work a man can do."[7] In 1967, Marvin Minsky, a leading AI researcher of his age, stated that "within a generation – the problem of creating 'artificial intelligence' will substantially be solved."[8] In hindsight, these statements were obviously inaccurate. Indeed, the dramatic failure to deliver on these and other such promises is what led to the first of a few "AI winters." These winter periods of the latter half of the twentieth century were defined by scarce funding for AI development, and the future of the field in general appearing bleak.

But after every winter freeze, there is a thaw. A variety of driving forces have fueled the current AI summer in which we find ourselves. These include the ongoing march of exponentially increasing processor speed (Moore's Law),[9] exponentially decreasing data storage costs (Kryder's Law),[10] and other important factors that augment these trends. The visibility of AlphaGo's tournament wins, IBM Watson's victories on *Jeopardy!*, the rollout of driverless cars, and a range of other high-salience use cases make this current time period one of significant importance and interest for AI.

Despite the warmth of the current AI summer, its applications are more specific than media narratives would have you believe. What the wider public is slowly learning is what a small subset of academics and other professionals have known for some time: AI is designed to solve specific problems, like driving a car, retrieving a relevant document based on user criteria, detecting a particular image, or playing certain games. But the somewhat widespread

[6] *See generally*, Alan Turing, "Computing Machinery and Intelligence," *Mind* 59 (236) (1950): 433–460; Vannevar Bush, "As We May Think," *The Atlantic*, July 1945, available at: www.theatlantic.com/magazine/archive/1945/07/as-we-may-think/303881.
[7] Raymond Kurzweil, "What Is Artificial Intelligence Anyway? As the Techniques of Computing Grow More Sophisticated, Machines Are Beginning to Appear Intelligent – But Can They Actually Think?," *American Scientist* 73 (3) (1985): 258–264.
[8] Quote appears in: Daniel Crevier, *AI: The Tumultuous Search for Artificial Intelligence* (New York, NY: Basic Books, 1993).
[9] Gordon E. Moore, "Cramming More Components onto Integrated Circuits," *Electronics* 38 (8) (1965): 114ff.
[10] Chip Walter, "Kryder's Law," *Scientific American*, August 1, 2005, available at: www.scientificamerican.com/article/kryders-law.

concern that *artificial general intelligence* (AGI) will appear in the near term is significantly off-base.[11]

III THE SUBFIELDS OF AI

Artificial intelligence is a broad field with a wide range of use cases and methods that are both useful for automation and that reimagine the value proposition associated with the work lawyers currently undertake. Figure 2.6.1 offers a classic representation of the subfields within AI. While there is some debate regarding the exact contours of these subfields and whether an alternative division might be more accurate, this figure offers a reasonable segmentation of the various kinds of work undertaken within the overall field. Of particular relevance to this book are the three subfields of machine learning (ML), natural language processing (NLP), and expert systems.

Machine learning is a field of AI largely devoted to the task of prediction or characterization of some class of data. The field further subdivides into the fields of supervised learning and unsupervised learning.[12] In *supervised learning*, a machine is exposed to a range of labeled training examples, from which it attempts to learn which function performs the best, and then uses that function to predict future examples. In *unsupervised learning*, no labels are provided on data, which leaves algorithms to group like items together as best they can, often uncovering previously hidden patterns in the data.[13]

Natural language processing software tools focus on ingesting and extracting meaning from a set of linguistic inputs. Models built by NLP leverage statistical patterns within syntax in the hopes of providing insights that might be of use to end-users. Real-world implementations include language identification, information retrieval, machine translation, automated essay scoring, machine summarization, and sentiment analysis. These applications can leverage either syntactic or semantic understanding or a combination of the two, depending on the application's particular emphasis.[14]

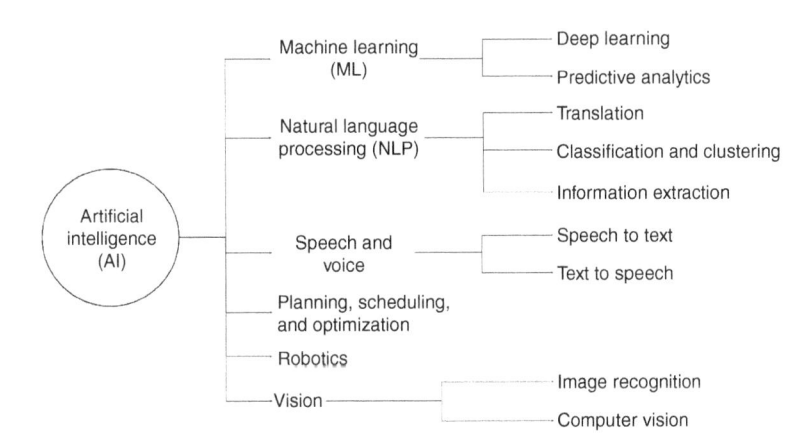

FIGURE 2.6.1 Subfields within artificial intelligence.[15]

---

[11] As with teleportation or faster-than-light (FTL) travel, artificial general intelligence remains beyond the scope of this book.
[12] A third subdivision within ML, *reinforcement learning*, is beyond the scope of this inquiry.
[13] Supervised and unsupervised learning both have pros and cons. For more detailed definition and analysis of these two forms of machine learning, *see* Katz and Nay – Machine Learning and Law, *infra*.
[14] For more on NLP, *see* Nay – Natural Language Processing for Legal Texts, *infra*.
[15] If anything, this figure vastly understates the size of the field.

Expert systems, meanwhile, are computer systems "that emulat[e] the decision-making ability of a human expert. Expert systems are designed to solve complex problems by reasoning about knowledge, represented mainly as if–then rules."[16] Expert systems require an expert to address how some class of decision making is undertaken. This can prove challenging, and in some cases is impossible, because subject-matter experts sometimes have difficultly formalizing the basis of their decision making. Despite this potential problem, there exist a range of use cases for expert systems, including tax preparation, medical diagnoses, planning, scheduling, and troubleshooting.[17]

The development of a specific solution to a specific problem may necessitate a combination of a range of AI methods and models. For example, it is possible to use NLP tools to extract information from text and then feed that information into a broader ML model. It is also possible to use ML or NLP to help inform the composition or refinement of an expert system.

IV AI MEETS LAW

There are a range of use cases in which AI has been fruitfully applied to the work of lawyers.[18] Here, we offer just a high-level treatment of some problems lawyers currently confront that could feasibly be automated or augmented using AI.

A E-Discovery

Electronic discovery (e-discovery) is the most mature incursion of informatics technology into law. While many other technologies lawyers may use (e.g., telephones, word processors, copy machines, computers) were designed for a more general business user, the various e-discovery tools and platforms on the market were all specifically designed for tasks that lawyers undertake. E-discovery is a relatively straightforward concept – identify and produce all information relevant to a particular litigation matter.[19] In the modern era, e-discovery has understandably become more and more focused on sifting through increasingly large bodies of email communications. Artificial intelligence, particularly binary and multiclass classification,[20] has been central to the automation of this type of lawyer activity, and has significantly reduced (though will likely never eliminate) the need for human experts in the review and production of ever-widening corpora of documents in discovery.

B Contract Analytics[21]

From a technical standpoint, the analysis of contracts for due diligence and other related tasks bears substantial similarity to the e-discovery problem. The analysis of contract information is typically part of larger efforts, such as M&A, benefits standardization, revenue recognition,

---

[16] Peter Jackson, *Introduction To Expert Systems*, 3rd ed. (Boston, MA: Addison-Wesley Longman Publishing, 1998), 2.
[17] *See generally*, Paul Harmon, Rex Maus, and William Morrissey, *Expert Systems: Tools and Applications* (Hoboken, NJ: Wiley, 1988).
[18] A range of use cases, many of which directly involve AI and ML, can be found in Part III.
[19] *See generally*, Fed. R. Civ. P. 26. Duty to Disclose; General Provisions Governing Discovery, available at: www.law.cornell.edu/rules/frcp/rule_26.
[20] For a more complete definition and discussion of classification, *see* Dolin – Information Intermediation, *supra*.
[21] In-depth treatments of multiple aspects of contract analytics can be found in Waisberg – Contract Analytics, *infra*.

supply chain risk, policy and procedure consolidation, and lease abstraction. In examples such as these, the analysis of contractual information is merely an element of a broader set of legal tasks.

The goal of contract analytics is to analyze the content of one or several contracts in order to identify certain information contained therein. While this identification step has become more and more the province of computation, the requirement of deeper analysis of relevant contract clauses and their legal import means that this task still remains largely human-centric. Over time, the standardization of clauses and the training of contract analytic systems should allow for greater levels of automation (through perhaps not complete automation). The challenge today, and one major reason why contract analytics remains human-centric, is because contracts are still largely unstructured or semi-structured data objects.[22] The ultimate arc of this field will one day lead to contracts being born computational. In the meantime, there are real challenges associated with building efficiency in contract analytics, but several important strides have already been taken.[23]

C Legal Expert Systems

The construction of expert systems, as discussed above, typically requires experts to attempt to articulate the step-by-step processes they follow to reach their conclusions, so that each of those paths can be codified in software (typically as a set of "if–then" conditionals).

The first known expert system in law was developed by Richard Susskind and Phillip Capper, and was applied to a provision of UK law called the Latent Damage Act.[24] Although this effort was met with real interest, such efforts have been difficult to scale to the broader industry.[25] Expert systems applied to law lay somewhat dormant as interest turned to the world wide web and other technological innovations around the turn of the last century. Recent years have seen expert systems used for discrete problems, though. For example, in the legal aid community, A2J Author – developed by CALI and Chicago-Kent College of Law – has provided support to nearly four million individuals.[26] In the commercial sphere, Neota Logic has developed a series of discrete applications designed to assist lawyers and other allied professionals.[27]

Perhaps the most well-known and commercially successful expert system of all time is TurboTax. TurboTax transforms the process of completing various tax forms into a step-by-step software experience. For more than 30 million users per year, this software experience has reduced the complexity of filing taxes to merely answering a set of structured questions. The answers provided by the user traverse a decision tree and systematically populate one or more IRS forms.[28] The tax code is in a constant state of flux; however, given the number of

---

[22] For further elaboration on the evolution of contracts from analog to structured data objects, *see* Dolin – XML in Law. The Role of Standards in Legal Informatics, *supra*.
[23] *See, e.g.*, ContraxSuite by LexPredict, an open-source contract analytics platform, https://contraxsuite.com.
[24] Phillip Capper and Richard E. Susskind, *Latent Damage Law: The Expert System* (London: Butterworths Law, 1988).
[25] *See generally*, Philip Leith, "The Rise and Fall of the Legal Expert System," *European Journal of Law and Technology* 1 (1) (2010); *see also*, Richard Susskind, "Future of Artificial Intelligence and Law," March 22, 2014, video available at: https://vimeo.com/89806445.
[26] For more on A2J Author, *see* Staudt and Rabanal – Access to Justice and Technology: Reaching a Greater Future for Legal Aid, *infra*.
[27] *See*, "Expert Advisors," Neota Logic, available at: www.neotalogic.com/solution/expert-advisors.
[28] For more on decision trees, *see* Ashley – Mining Information from Statutory Texts in a Public Health Domain, *infra*.

users involved, it is possible for TurboTax to finance its software updates as quickly as the law changes.[29]

Despite some success, expert systems have not achieved what many had expected. The ability of TurboTax to dynamically update is an impressive exception to an otherwise fairly consistent rule: Updates to expert systems are expensive and time-consuming. This inability of expert systems to dynamically update has, among other reasons, stymied their broader commercial success.[30] In addition to the challenge of updating expert systems and setting bounds on their knowledge, there is also the challenge of extracting expertise from the experts themselves. For problems that have medium to high levels of complexity, the set of possible decision paths within a system can become quite large. Experts are not always very good at articulating the basis for their expert decisions, and this makes it challenging both to populate decision paths and to break down expert processes into discrete steps. The most successful efforts thus far have been directed toward either low-complexity tasks whose contours do not change very often, or to problems of immense scale where it is economically feasible to update the system as relevant rules and laws change, as TurboTax has demonstrated.

Chatbots represent a resurrection of that stagnating field of expert systems. They hold immense promise because they are a data-structuring exercise in which a set of question-and-answer interactions can be tracked and fine-tuned as a function over time. One of the largest challenges with expert systems has been the acquisition of data at scale to demonstrate how an expert might interrogate a particular problem. While much more aggregation and study remains to be done, the two-way interaction between users and chatbots – particularly those that are supervised and tuned by experts – may help ameliorate some of the challenges that have historically plagued expert system development.

D Legal Prediction Models

The use of prediction models is still new to law, but over the past few years has gained substantial ground.[31] Growing access to larger and larger bodies of semi-structured legal information has led to a new disruptive technology known as quantitative legal prediction (QLP). Although multiple variants of QLP exist, the general march of its development will define much of the coming innovation in the legal services industry.[32]

Questions about whether a case should commence, what a party's exposure might be, how much a case will cost, what provisions of which contracts will trigger certain outcomes, and the best ways to staff a particular legal matter, are all areas of concern for everyone from general counsels to the average retail consumer. And all of these concerns can be addressed by QLP.

Whether generated by a mental model or a sophisticated algorithm, prediction has always been a core component of the guidance lawyers provide to their clients. Every single day,

---

[29] See, e.g., David Williams, "2017 Tax Reform Legislation: What You Should Know," Intuit TurboTax blog, available at: https://turbotax.intuit.com/tax-tips/irs-tax-return/2017-tax-reform-legislation-what-you-should-know/L96aFuPhc.

[30] See generally, Leith, "The Rise and Fall of the Legal Expert System," supra note 25.

[31] See, e.g., Daniel Martin Katz, Michael J. Bommarito II, and Joshua M. Blackman, "A General Approach for Predicting the Behavior of the Supreme Court of the United States," PLoS One, April 12, 2017, available at: http://journals.plos.org/plosone/article?id=10.1371/journal.pone.0174698.

[32] Daniel Martin Katz, "Quantitative Legal Prediction, or, How I Learned to Stop Worrying and Start Preparing for the Data-Driven Future of the Legal Services Industry," Emory Law Journal 62 (2013), available at: http://law.emory.edu/elj/_documents/volumes/62/4/contents/katz.pdf.

lawyers and law firms provide predictions to their clients about the likely impact of choices in business planning and transactional structures, as well as predictions about litigation and the costs associated with its pursuit. The method of these predictions has been largely conducted via inference and intuition by the seasoned professional lawyer. But these predictions could be augmented by better data and robust modeling by using data drawn from previous, "similar" instances. Quantitative legal prediction already plays a significant role in certain practice areas, and this role is likely to increase as greater access to appropriate legal data becomes available.[33]

V CONCLUSION

Computational methods are slowly merging with the advanced expertise-driven methodologies that have successfully steered the practice of law for centuries. Machine learning, NLP, expert systems, and the hybridized methods that spring therefrom are in some areas nudging – and in other areas careening – the practice of law toward data-driven systems that are scalable, accurate, and cost-effective. The potential is vast and exciting and, as we shall see throughout the other chapters of this book, eminently adaptable to improvisation and maturation via ever-evolving computational and relational approaches.

---

[33] *Ibid.*

2.7

Machine Learning and Law

Daniel Martin Katz and John J. Nay

As highlighted in Figure 2.6.1, the field of artificial intelligence (AI) is broad and embraces a wide range of approaches. While it is of course possible to imagine the linkages between topics such as machine vision and robotics to the business, practice, and delivery of law, the two most relevant topics within the AI landscape are natural language processing (NLP) (discussed in Chapter 2.8) and machine learning (ML).

One of the defining properties of AI is its ability to make artificial (by means of instantiation through an algorithm) some process that was previously the exclusive province of the human reasoner. Machine learning is one of the branches of AI that is particularly focused upon the cognitive task of processing and interpreting data. More clearly stated, ML is the process of training a computational model to accomplish a task or tasks using data.

While there is a tendency in the layperson to believe in some sort of fanciful version of the artificially omnipotent computational machine, much of the work in data science is the engineering task of applying one or more of the general menu of available algorithms to the specific task in question. Thus, it is important for the reader to think of ML models or algorithms "off-the-shelf" as general recipes from which a more particularized model might be constructed. Under the direction of a data scientist or data engineer, the completion of a given task can thus be accomplished either by deploying an individual algorithm or more typically through the construction of an organized workflow designed to properly sequence the set of necessary algorithms.

I ML: SUPERVISED AND UNSUPERVISED LEARNING

Machine learning models come in a variety of flavors and thus there are a variety of approaches by which one could seek to characterize such models. However, arguably the largest division within ML can be drawn between *supervised learning* and *unsupervised learning* algorithms. This division also embraces the two primary task categories in ML: prediction and data exploration. Prediction is accomplished by a subset of ML called *supervised learning*. In supervised learning, *observations* (e.g., congressional bills) composed of pairs of predictor variables (such as a bill sponsor's political party) and outcome variables (whether the bill was enacted into law) are used to create a model that can take in a new observation's measurements of the same predictor variables (a new bill's sponsor party) and predict its outcome (enactment). If the outcome predicted is a real-valued number (e.g., the number of votes for a bill), then the model is called a *regression model*. If the outcome predicted is a category (e.g., "enacted" or "failed"), the model is called a *classification model*.

The model learning process involves making predictions with the model, measuring the prediction error, adjusting the tunable parameters of the model to reduce prediction error, and repeating this process until the parameter adjustments suggested by the learning algorithm are negligibly small. This process of tuning and repetition is known as *convergence*. The primary goal of supervised learning is to create a model that will generalize from the initial *training data* to new data, known as *testing data*. The model can then be used in real-world situations where the outcome is unknown and the predictor variables are known to forecast the value of the outcome.

A variety of off-the-shelf supervised learning algorithms can be leveraged to support either a binary or multiclass classification task. These include the following methods: random forest, naive Bayes classifier, support vector machines, k-nearest neighbors (KNN), and stochastic gradient descent (SGD) classifier; there are also many others.[1] No approach is dominant for all tasks. Rather, each approach has certain strengths and certain weaknesses that must be considered on a problem-by-problem basis. Among other things, the task of a data scientist or data engineer is to select which model to apply to which problem, to understand how best to obtain improved performance through model tuning, and to know how to best generalize from the training data so as to avoid overfitting.

Data exploration and information retrieval tasks are facilitated by the other category of techniques, *unsupervised learning*. In contrast to supervised learning, unsupervised learning only includes the measured variables. This has the effect of greatly increasing the quantity of data available, because most data is not explicitly labeled with an outcome of interest, known as the *outcome variable*. A legal informatics task suited for unsupervised learning would be, for example, finding any and all congressional bills that have similar textual content to a given congressional bill or obtaining all lawsuits similar to the lawsuit at hand. Of course, this calls for a prediction of a sort, but the key distinction from supervised learning is that the data has not been previously subjected to human supervision or validation.

The challenge in unsupervised learning such as clustering is how precisely to implement the notion of "similarity" in a rigorous and replicable manner. Objects such as documents feature multi-dimensional attributes (text, author, date, other metadata, etc.) whose elements must be quantified and combined in order to group them. For any reasonable sized set of objects, the possible set of groupings is theoretically infinite. Thankfully, many years of academic and industrial research have yielded a series of approaches designed to algorithmically cluster objects based upon different notions of "similarity." These include hierarchical clustering, centroid-based clustering (such as k-means), density-based spatial clustering (DBSCAN), and many others.

Measuring a model's performance on supervised learning tasks is usually more straightforward because there are standard measures of predictive performance, such as accuracy for a classification task, or mean-squared error for a regression task. On the other hand, the tasks of automatically finding similar documents or clustering together documents into coherent groups usually have no objectively correct answers. Even expert human judges can disagree on some of the results. Therefore, validating unsupervised learning systems is more difficult than validating supervised learning systems.

---

[1] The interested reader should consult one of many ML texts such as Peter Flach, *Machine Learning: The Art and Science of Algorithms that Make Sense of Data* (Cambridge: Cambridge University Press, 2012); Tibshirani Hastie, Robert Tibshirani, and Jerome Friedman, *The Elements of Statistical Learning: Data Mining, Inference, and Prediction* (New York, NY: Springer, 2009); Tom M. Mitchell, *Machine Learning* (Burr Ridge, IL: McGraw-Hill, 1997).

II THE RISE OF EMPIRICAL LEGAL STUDIES

Describing the mechanisms and dynamics that operate to produce both stasis and change in the law has been the charge of a diverse set of scholars deploying a diverse set of methods. "From within the legal academy and across allied disciplines such as political science, sociology, anthropology, physics and economics, an extensive set of positive and normative scholarship attempts to characterize legal outputs and the interconnected layer of actors and institutions that collectively generate the canon."[2] Those who are familiar with the majority of existing legal scholarship might be wondering: Where exactly do ML tools fit in?[3] While not part of mainstream legal scholarship, ML could help support the scientific *characterization* of legal systems or components thereof, the *prediction* of legal systems or components thereof, and help *measure* the performance (broadly construed) of legal systems or components thereof.

While legal academics have long been interested in the *characterization* of legal *prediction* and outcome *measurement*, those questions have historically been addressed through either qualitative methods or through approaches such as rhetoric or argumentation. In response to its shortcomings, law has been undergoing a "credibility" revolution where the scholarship of a greater percentage of faculty members (particularly at the more elite institutions) is slowly converging upon the profile of the broader universities where many law schools sit. In particular, the past years have witnessed increasing interest in the empirical evaluation of legal rules and associated outcomes. Namely, although legal scholars commonly posit both "is" and "ought" theories (i.e., claims about how the law worked and how it should work) and had historically failed to actually empirically evaluate or support those claims, the legal academy is on a long arc toward modernization.

The first wave of this empirical scholarship has been aimed at the most traditional of legal questions – the quantitative evaluation of public policy. Whether adopted by legislatures or by courts, legal rules (statutes and regulations) are the means by which policy makers bring their ideas to life. Many legal scholars' self-conception is associated with the critique of public policy (particularly but not exclusively legal policy implemented by appellate courts). Given this, much of the empirical work to date in law has often been focused upon policy evaluation using the tools of causal inference.[4] The actual validity of these approaches is somewhat of an open question. Arguably, legal theories that cannot predict future events are what might otherwise be called "overfit legal theories." As noted by several leading legal commentators discussing theories of judicial behavior, "the best test of an explanatory theory is its ability to predict future events. To the extent that scholars in both disciplines (social science and law) seek to explain court behavior, they ought to test their theories not only against cases already decided, but against future outcomes as well."[5] This maxim arguably applies to all theories not just court decision making.

---

[2] Daniel Martin Katz, Josha R. Gubler, Jon Zelner, and Michael J. Bommarito II, "Reproduction of Hierarchy: A Social Network Analysis of the American Law Professoriate," *Journal of Legal Education* 61 (2011): 76.

[3] For more on ML in the law see Daniel Martin Katz, "Quantitative Legal Prediction: Or How I Learned to Stop Worrying and Start Preparing for the Data-Driven Future of the Legal Services Industry," *Emory Law Journal* 62 (2012): 909; Harry Surden, "Machine Learning and Law," *Washington Law Review* 89 (2014): 87.

[4] For a review of the tools of causal inference see Guido W. Imbens and Donald B. Rubin, *Causal Inference in Statistics, Social, and Biomedical Sciences* (Cambridge: Cambridge University Press, 2015). For Econometric methods more broadly see Damodar N. Gujarati, *Basic Econometrics* (New York, NY: McGraw-Hill Education, 2017).

[5] A. D. Martin, K. M. Quinn, T. W. Ruger, and P. T. Kim, "Competing Approaches to Predicting Supreme Court Decision-Making," *Perspectives on Politics* 2 (4) (2004): 761–767.

A From Empirics to Machine Learning and Law

In societies across the globe, lawyers serve many roles – from policy makers and policy advocates to trusted advisors and navigators of legal complexity. Whether it is an enterprise legal customer, an individual seeking access to justice, or any individual or entity in between, clients often ask their lawyers to cast various types of predictions.[6] Will we win this case? Should I accept the terms in this contract? How much will this legal matter cost? Should I settle this matter? Will this agency adopt this proposed rule? These are just a subset of the questions posed to lawyers on a daily basis.

For most problems, an ML model alone or a technology and human expert ensemble is the proper approach to find an answer. While the volume of academic papers is still small, there is a growing number of technically oriented but otherwise law-focused papers that leverage ML methods. Machine learning methods have been used to forecast decisions of judges,[7] to predict outcomes in tax law,[8] in medical malpractice cases,[9] and in securities fraud class actions.[10] Beyond litigation, ML has been leveraged to explore a variety of transactional questions, including the analysis of choice of law[11] and force majeure clauses.[12]

In many instances within law, the industrial use of AI/ML is actually far in front of its use within the academic environment. Within the legal industry, hundreds if not now thousands of new legal tech companies have been formed over the past decade. Many of these companies purport to have either developed AI/ML products or embedded some form of ML in their broader product offerings. If one also considers law or law-like applications in the RegTech, DealTech, InsurTech, and FinTech spheres, the scale of industrial applications developed over the past decade is fairly staggering.

III MACHINE LEARNING AS A SERVICE (MLAAS) AND THE CHANGING ECONOMICS OF LEGAL INFORMATICS

Programming machine learning models has historically been the exclusive domain of highly trained developers whose craft required many years of dedicated training to hone. While the upper echelon of technical problems will likely still demand the talents of the most technically skilled, there exist many other problems for which ML might be applied with far greater ease. Namely, there is an emerging set of "standardized parts" delivered via cloud computing under what could be characterized as a "machine learning as

---

[6] Katz, "Quantitative legal prediction," *supra* note 3.
[7] Daniel Martin Katz, Michael J. Bommarito II, and Josh Blackman, "A General Approach for Predicting the Behavior of the Supreme Court of the United States," *PLoS One* 12 (4) (2017): e0174698; Theodore W. Ruger, Pauline T. Kim, Andrew D. Martin, and Kevin M. Quinn, "The Supreme Court Forecasting Project: Legal and Political Science Approaches to Predicting Supreme Court Decisionmaking," *Columbia Law Review* 104 (2004): 1150–1210; Nikolaos Aletras, Dimitrios Tsarapatsanis, Daniel Preoţiuc-Pietro, and Vasileios Lampos, "Predicting Judicial Decisions of the European Court of Human Rights: A Natural Language Processing Perspective," *PeerJ Computer Science* 2 (2016): e93.
[8] Benjamin Alarie, Anthony Niblett, and Albert Yoon, "Using Machine Learning to Predict Outcomes in Tax Law" (2017), available at: https://ssrn.com/abstract=2855977.
[9] M. Bonetti, P. Cirillo, P. M. Tanzi, and E. Trinchero, "An Analysis of the Number of Medical Malpractice Claims and Their Amounts," *PLoS One* 11 (4) (2016): e0153362.
[10] Blakeley B. McShane, Oliver P. Watson, Tom Baker, and Sean J. Griffith, "Predicting Securities Fraud Settlements and Amounts: a Hierarchical Bayesian Model of Federal Securities Class Action Lawsuits," *Journal of Empirical Legal Studies* 9(3) (2012): 482–510.
[11] Sarath Sanga, "Choice of Law: an Empirical Analysis," *Journal of Empirical Legal Studies* 11 (4) (2014): 894–928.
[12] Eric Talley and Drew O'Kane, "The Measure of a MAC: A Machine-Learning Protocol for Analyzing Force Majeure Clauses in M&A Agreements," *Journal of Institutional and Theoretical Economics* 168(1) (2012): 181–201.

a service" (MLaaS) offering.[13] After success in its public display on *Jeopardy!*, IBM Watson was arguably first to market with its MLaaS offering. However, other large technology providers soon created competitive offerings. Google's Tensor Flow, Microsoft's Azure, and Amazon's AWS platform sought to match the initial offering created by IBM. The competition between these and other providers is rapidly changing the economics of ML/AI. While we do not endorse any particular provider, we encourage the reader to explore the emerging set of offerings.

In addition to MLaaS, past years have witnessed an increasing number of enterprise-grade open-source tools becoming available for use in the broader developer community. Some of these have been developed from first principles as open-source developer libraries, while others have been developed by large technology companies and later converted to open-source. Either way, the ubiquity of such high-quality libraries has had a profound impact on the developer community. As one leading technology publication noted, "the golden age of open source had arrived."[14]

Taken together, the emergence of enterprise open-source and MLaaS is transforming the economics of ML/AI. This is a particularly important development for legal informatics applications as many problems in law do not scale particularly well. However, with a changing economic landscape, many problems in law for which AI/ML technologies were not previously economically feasible may soon be conquered.

---

[13] Mauro Ribeiro, Katarina Grolinger, and Miriam A. M. Capretz, "MLAAS: Machine Learning as a Service," in *14th International Conference on Machine Learning and Applications (ICMLA)* (New York, NY: IEEE, 2015).

[14] Marius Moscovici, "The Golden Age Of Open Source Has Arrived," Tech Crunch, December 15, 2015, available at: https://techcrunch.com/2015/12/15/the-golden-age-of-open-source-has-arrived.

2.8

Natural Language Processing for Legal Texts

John J. Nay

I INTRODUCTION

Almost all law is expressed in natural language; therefore, natural language processing (NLP) is a key component of understanding and predicting law. Natural language processing converts unstructured text into a formal representation that computers can understand and analyze. This technology has already intersected with law, and is poised to experience rapid innovation and widespread adoption. There are three reasons for this: (1) the number of repositories of digitized machine-readable legal text data is growing; (2) advances in NLP tools are being driven by algorithmic and hardware improvements; and (3) there is great potential to dramatically improve the effectiveness of legal services due to inefficiencies in its current practice.

Natural language processing is a large field, and like many research areas related to computer science, it is rapidly evolving. This chapter focuses primarily on statistical machine learning (ML) techniques with NLP, because they demonstrate significant promise for advancing legal informatics systems and will almost certainly become critical in the foreseeable future.

First, we will provide a brief overview of the different types of legal texts and the different types of ML methods that process these texts. We will then introduce the core idea of representing words and documents as numbers. Next, we will describe NLP tools for leveraging legal text data to accomplish tasks. Along the way, we will define several important NLP terms and show examples to illustrate the utility of each of these tools and concepts. We will describe methods for automatically summarizing content using sentiment analyses, text summaries, topic models, extraction of attributes and relations, and document relevance scoring. We will also describe methods for predicting outcomes and answering questions.

II LEGAL TEXT

Legal texts can be divided into five primary types: constitutional, statutory, administrative, case law, and contracts. The legislative branch of the US government creates statutory law; the executive branch creates administrative rules; the judicial branch creates case law in the form of court case opinions; and private parties create contracts. Laws are found at all levels of government: federal, state, and local.

Different types of laws possess different characteristics that make certain computational methods more relevant. The more uniform the layout and the more predictable the content, the more amenable the documents are to automating their conversion to formal representations. Every kind of law represents a unique set of circumstances, though. For example, there can be large variation in the content of judicial opinions due to their focus on concrete facts in real-world cases. Administrative regulations, on the other hand, implement statutory laws and are thus usually more specific and detailed than the corresponding statutes. In fact, public laws and regulations follow regular patterns and their content is relatively structured. That said, public law does not attempt to cover all the contingencies and possible scenarios that may occur, and statutes must often be interpreted by judges. Private contracts, meanwhile, stand apart from this interconnection, covering a large number of possible outcomes relevant to the relationship being formalized. This suggests that contracts have a higher chance of moving out of the messy ambiguous world of natural language than public law does, and indeed the rise of distributed ledgers and related information technologies may be accelerating this shift.[1]

Law types other than private contracts are curated in advantageous ways as well. Adopted versions of public law are compiled in official bulk data repositories that offer machine-readable formats. Statutory law is integrated into the United States Code. Administrative policies become part of the Code of Federal Regulations (or a state's Code of Regulations), which is organized by subject. Case law, meanwhile, is created by judges writing opinions pertaining to specific court cases. The examples we will explore in this chapter leverage these different kinds of bulk data repositories of law in order to train and test ML NLP models.

III MACHINE LEARNING AND NATURAL LANGUAGE PROCESSING

As noted above, ML is the process of training a computational model to accomplish some kind of task by using data. There are important nuances involved with bringing ML constructs to bear on a set of language-centered inputs. One such process, vital to applying ML, is the conversion of raw unstructured data into a suitable computational representation. In NLP, this process often means creating a numeric representation of text. There are two primary methods used to represent words and documents computationally, and both usually require a dictionary of the vocabulary words that exist in the corpus. This dictionary is a list of words (or, less often, characters) to be analyzed.

The *one-hot-encoding* method is one such form of analysis. One-hot-encoding represents a collection of words (e.g., a sentence) as a list of 1s and 0s the same length as the number of words in the established vocabulary. A number "1" appears in the list if the word in that location appears in the sentence, and a "0" appears if that word does not. For each word, this *indicator variable* denotes whether the word occurs in a sentence. A sentence is thus represented as a long list of 0s, with a few 1s. This is called a *sparse representation*. Instead of indicating the vague presence of a term in a document, we can actually count the number of times the word occurs. This *term frequency* representation is generally more effective for document retrieval tasks, while the presence of words is generally more effective for sentiment analysis.[2]

---

[1] For more on distributed ledgers and blockchain technology, *see* Rosario – Introduction to Blockchain and Cryptography, *infra*; and Kilbride – Distributed Ledgers, Cryptography, and Smart Contracts, *infra*.

[2] Bo Pang, Lillian Lee, and Shivakumar Vaithyanathan, "Thumbs Up? Sentiment Classification Using Machine Learning Techniques," in *Proceedings of the ACL-02 Conference on Empirical Methods in Natural Language Processing – Volume 10* (Stroudsburg, PA: Association for Computational Linguistics, 2002), 79–86, available at:

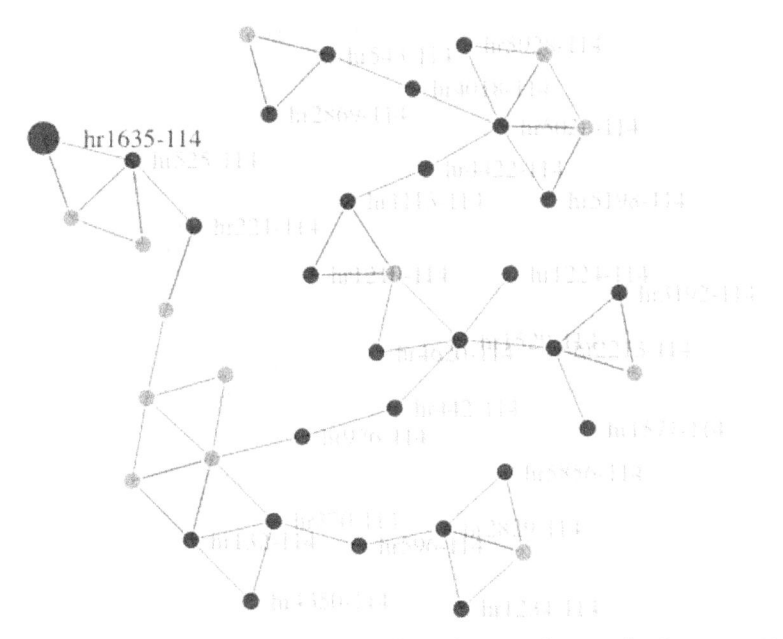

FIGURE 2.8.1 Example of a network of similar bills under consideration by Congress. House bills are dark gray and Senate bills are light gray.[3]

For most ML models, observations need to be represented[3] by the same set of variables. Therefore, if we are modeling phrases, sentences, and documents, we need some way to convert the varying-length strings of words into a fixed number of variables. One approach is to treat a document as a *bag-of-words*, effectively ignoring word order.[4] With one-hot-encodings, a bag-of-words representation of a document means we have a list of which words are in the document and how often each one occurs, but we do not have information about where the words are located *within* the document. Once again, the presence of mostly 0s makes this a sparse representation.

Whatever specific numeric representation technique we use, the same process for obtaining a single representation of a document can be applied to all documents in a corpus so that the final ML system has equal-sized representations. We can then apply further numerical processing techniques to the resulting vectors, including an array of ML models. If we obtain vector representations of a collection of texts, for example, we can apply clustering algorithms directly to these representations to automatically group similar documents together. Figure 2.8.1 shows an example of this kind of visualization.

There are multiple kinds of models that can be applied to text like this. Supervised learning models could even be used to predict an outcome related to the text. The possibilities are almost endless.

IV NLP TASKS AND TOOLS

Let's take a step back and describe the NLP tasks that are most relevant to legal informatics. To do this, we need to divide our discussion of NLP tasks and tools into the following

---

http://doi.org/10.3115/1118693.1118704; Bo Pang and Lillian Lee, "Opinion Mining and Sentiment Analysis," *Foundations and Trends in Information Retrieval* 2 (1–2) (2008): 1–135.

[3] Image by John J. Nay, 2017. For an extended discussion of congressional data and visual representations thereof, see Nay – *Gov2vec*: A Case Study in Text Model Application to Government Data, *infra*.

[4] The word order is ignored when we count only single words (called unigrams), but when we use n-grams where $n > 1$, the local order of the words is at least partially captured.

subcategories: summarizing content, extracting content, retrieving documents, predicting outcomes correlated with text, and answering questions.

A *Summarizing Content*

There are large amounts of text related to law and legal outcomes, and much of that text can relate to the emotion expressed within those outcomes. To utilize NLP effectively, one task that must be undertaken is an estimate of those emotions, so that a short summary of a longer text can be created and, ultimately, the main themes and topics of a corpus can be discovered. These kinds of NLP tools can augment human synthesis abilities and partially automate the process of quickly obtaining insight across large collections of texts.

1 Sentiment Analysis

Sentiment analysis tools attempt to automatically label the subjective emotions or viewpoints expressed by text. For example, the phrase "I really enjoyed the chapter" expresses positive sentiment, whereas the phrase "There were terrible example phrases in the chapter" is negative. This kind of analysis has a lot of practical application in the context of obtaining public comments on bills, rules, and regulations, where scoring such statements with sentiment analysis models can provide lawmakers with the public's reaction to pending law and policy.[5]

Sentiment labels may be on a numeric scale from positive to negative, or they may use more specific emotion classes, such as excitement or pride. On a numeric scale, the scores for all the words in a document can be averaged to assign an overall score for the document.[6] If using categorical emotion labels, the proportion of words assigned to each emotion can summarize the sentiment. Most sentiment analysis techniques can be divided into either dictionary-based or learning-based techniques. *Dictionary-based methods* use a large list of words previously scored by human reviewers for their subjective sentiment. This scoring is usually at the level of individual words (unigrams), because sets of more than one word (bigrams, trigrams, etc.) occur much less often and scoring their sentiment has very little practical value. Dictionary-based methods may work relatively well for tracking public sentiment on, for example, Twitter;[7] however, they can perform poorly if negation or sarcasm are present. Take, for example, the sentence "he is not happy or loved." If we input this sentence into a simple dictionary-based emotion-detection algorithm, it is described as one-third anticipation, one-third joy, and one-third trust.[8] If we input the sentence into

---

[5] Claire Cardie, Cynthia Farina, and Thomas Bruce, "Using Natural Language Processing to Improve eRulemaking: Project Highlight," in *Proceedings of the 2006 International Conference on Digital Government Research* (San Diego, CA: Digital Government Society of North America, 2006), 177–178; Namhee Kwon, Stuart W. Shulman, and Eduard Hovy, "Multidimensional Text Analysis for eRulemaking," in *Proceedings of the 2006 International Conference on Digital Government Research* (San Diego, CA: Digital Government Society of North America, 2006), 157–166.

[6] However, the sentiment is often bi-modal, and in these cases the average can be misleading, *see* Pang and Lee, "Opinion Mining and Sentiment Analysis," *supra* note 2; Giuseppe Carenini, Jackie Chi, Kit Cheung, and Adam Pauls, "Multi Document Summarization of Evaluative Text," *Computational Intelligence* 29 (4) (2013): 545–576.

[7] Peter S. Dodds, Kameron D. Harris, Isabel M. Kloumann, Catherine A. Bliss, and Christopher M. Danforth, "Temporal Patterns of Happiness and Information in a Global Social Network: Hedonometrics and Twitter," *PLoS One* 6 (12) (2011), available at: www.uvm.edu/pdodds/research/papers/files/2011/dodds2011e.pdf.

[8] Saif M. Mohammad and Peter D. Turney, "Emotions Evoked by Common Words and Phrases: Using Mechanical Turk to Create an Emotion Lexicon," in *Proceedings of the NAACL HLT 2010 Workshop on Computational Approaches to Analysis and Generation of Emotion in Text* (Stroudsburg, PA: Association for Computational Linguistics, 2010), 26–34.

a dictionary-based numeric sentiment algorithm, it is scored as moderately positive.[9] See the problem?

To improve a dictionary-based system, sentences can be automatically parsed and the function that a word serves within the sentence can be labeled with separate tools. Then, rules of negation – also known as *valence shifters* – can be added into the computation of sentiment.[10] This is important because dictionary-based approaches may not generalize well to texts in a specialized domain where important words are too rare to be previously scored in a dictionary, or where words that are scored serve different purposes in different contexts. This is important for legal text because most existing sentiment dictionaries are scored by legal non-experts who use the context of more general texts, like news articles.

Machine learning-based sentiment analysis methods can leverage the data within a corpus to build a model that predicts sentiment based on strings of words. The ML model will often take an entire sentence or document as input and predict the sentiment for the whole collection of words. The user must then manually label the sentiment of a sufficient number of documents, use one of the methods described above to map the texts into numeric representations, and then learn a prediction model that outputs a sentiment label for any given text representation input. This prediction model would be trained on the labeled documents and then could be deployed to predict unlabeled, unseen documents. For a practical example, this approach has been applied to predict lawmakers' support or opposition to policy issues by looking at their congressional floor-debate transcripts.[11]

There is a drawback to this approach that is similar to the drawbacks of dictionary-based methods. If an ML model is trained to predict sentiment within one domain, it may not transfer well to a different domain.[12] Most documents with sentiment labels are not legal documents. Context matters. There is a very common instructive example that nearly every native speaker of English can immediately understand that illustrates this sentiment problem rather well: the phrase "go read the book" has a *positive* sentiment in a book review, but a *negative* sentiment in a movie review.[13]

---

[9] Finn A. Nielsen, "A New ANEW: Evaluation of a Word List for Sentiment Analysis in Microblogs," in *Proceedings of the ESWC2011 Workshop on "Making Sense of Microposts: Big Things Come in Small Packages,"* eds. Matthew Rowe, Milan Stankovic, Aba-Sah Dadzie, and Mariann Hardey (Heraklion: CEUR-WS, 2011), 93–98, available at: http://ceur-ws.org/Vol-718/paper_16.pdf.

[10] Alistair Kennedy and Diana Inkpen, "Sentiment Classification of Movie Reviews Using Contextual Valence Shifters," *Computational Intelligence* 22 (2) (2006): 110–125, available at: www.site.uottawa.ca/~diana/publications/ci.pdf.

[11] Matt Thomas, Bo Pang, and Lillian Lee, "Get Out the Vote: Determining Support or Opposition from Congressional Floor-Debate Transcripts," in *Proceedings of the 2006 Conference on Empirical Methods in Natural Language Processing* (Stroudsburg, PA: Association for Computational Linguistics, 2006), 327–335; *see also* the companion case study for this chapter, Nay – Gov2vec: A Case Study in Text Model Application to Government Data, *infra*.

[12] Sara Owsley, Sanjay Sood, and Kristian J. Hammond, "Domain Specific Affective Classification of Documents," in *AAAI Spring Symposium: Computational Approaches to Analyzing Weblogs*, 2006: 181–183; Jonathon Read, "Using Emoticons to Reduce Dependency in Machine Learning Techniques for Sentiment Classification," in *Proceedings of the ACL Student Research Workshop* (Stroudsburg, PA: Association for Computational Linguistics, 2005), 43–48.

[13] Pang and Lee, "Opinion Mining and Sentiment Analysis," *supra* note 2.

2 Textual Summaries

This group of tools includes methods that automatically convert longer texts into shorter texts. This includes converting longer documents into shorter documents or converting entire corpora into an informative summary of all the documents. There are two general approaches to this task. The simpler approach, *extractive summarization*, identifies important portions of a text (words, phrases, or full sentences), extracts them, and combines them into a summary. The more difficult, but potentially more powerful approach, *abstractive summarization*, involves generating entirely new text that was not necessarily found in the text that is being summarized. This requires the algorithm to build a complex representation of the text that captures its essence, conditions on that representation, and generates a grammatically correct smaller block of text that expresses the essence of the larger block.

At this point in time, for texts longer than a paragraph or two, purely abstractive summarization techniques are outperformed by extractive summarization. A widely applied extractive technique is TextRank.[14] TextRank creates a graph structure in which each vertex is a sentence in a document. It determines the similarities between the sentences based on the number of words sentences share, normalized by their lengths. TextRank then uses these similarity relations as edges between the graph vertices in order to apply a graph-based ranking algorithm to score the importance of the sentences. Finally, TextRank includes the most important sentences in a summary.

The most famous graph ranking algorithm is Google's PageRank, which uses links between web pages to form a large graph. Graph ranking algorithms work by determining the number of recommendations for a given vertex, and then determining the value of the recommendation. A vertex with many highly valued recommendations is deemed important. For a web page, page X is recommended by page Y if Y links to X, and the importance of that recommendation depends on how many pages recommend Y, which is recursively computed by running the algorithm repeatedly until importance scores no longer change much. In a text-based example, this process is accomplished by looking at when a sentence recommends another sentence, and whether they contain similar text.

3 Topic Models

An algorithm like TextRank can often provide high-quality summaries of longer texts, but it is only designed to summarize one document at a time. If we have a large collection of documents on a potentially wide range of topics, then an overview of the various topics and how much each document is devoted to each topic will provide a more useful summary. A *topic model* is a mixed-membership probabilistic model of distributions over words for a corpus.[15] In this case, a *topic* is defined as a list of words that describe that topic. For example, an environmental topic may be described by the words *recycle, planet, clean*, and *environment*.

The topic modeling algorithm can be described by a generative process: create topics for an entire corpus, choose a topic distribution for each document, then for each word in each document choose a topic from that document-level distribution of topics and then choose

---

[14] Rada Mihalcea and Paul Tarau, "TextRank: Bringing Order into Texts," in *Proceedings of the Conference on Empirical Methods in Natural Language Processing (EMNLP)* (Barcelona: ACL, 2004), 404–411.

[15] David M. Blei, Andrew Y. Ng, and Michael I. Jordan, "Latent Dirichlet Allocation," *Journal of Machine Learning Research* 3 (2003): 993–1022.

a vocabulary term from the topic, which is a distribution over the terms in that corpus. This process models documents as being composed of multiple topics in various proportions. For a given number of topics, estimating the parameters of the model automatically uncovers the topics spanning the corpus, the per-document topic distributions, and the per-document per-word topic assignments.[16] A *correlated topic model* explicitly represents the variability among topic proportions, allowing the prevalence of topics within documents to exhibit correlation.[17] For example, a climate change topic in a judicial opinion is more likely to co-occur with a high proportion of words from an energy topic than with words from a financial regulation topic.

We often accumulate important data about text, called *metadata*, and a topic model can be extended to incorporate this text metadata about time, location, and author.[18] The *structural topic model* extends the correlated topic model by modeling topical prevalence – the proportion of a document devoted to a topic – as a function of the document-level variables.[19] This allows us to flexibly model the relationship between document characteristics and topic prevalence. The distribution over words – the actual content of the topics – is also modeled as being affected by a combination of three things: the topics, the document metadata, and the interactions between topics and metadata. In this way, both the *prevalence* and the *word content* of topics can be modeled as a function of document metadata, allowing us to test hypotheses about the effects of any metadata (e.g., the author of a document) on the topics expressed.

Let's explore the power of the topic modeling approach with an example. There is controversy over the US president creating law and policy through actions such as executive orders, but there is little rigorous research on the topic that leverages the full texts of presidential actions. Researchers recently applied the structural topic modeling approach to all presidential legal documents to understand which policy topics shift from a statutory type of presidential action (proclamations or determinations) to a more unilateral type of presidential action (memoranda or executive orders), or vice versa. The researchers analyzed whether the language used to describe these topics changes over time from president to president.[20]

The researchers created a text corpus consisting of all documents through which unilateral presidential lawmaking authority had been exercised.[21] They then analyzed the period from

---

[16] David M. Blei, "Probabilistic Topic Models," *Communications of the ACM* 55 (4) (2012): 77–84.

[17] David M. Blei and John D. Lafferty, "A Correlated Topic Model of Science," *The Annals of Applied Statistics* 1 (1) (2007): 17–35.

[18] David M. Blei and John D. Lafferty, "Dynamic Topic Models," in *Proceedings of the 23rd International Conference on Machine Learning* (New York, NY: ACM, 2006), 113–120; Michael Rosen-Zvi, Chaitanya Chemudugunta, Thomas Griffiths, Patrick Smyth, and Mark Steyvers, "Learning Author–Topic Models from Text Corpora," *ACM Transactions on Information Systems* 28 (1) (2010): 1–38; Jacob Eisenstein, Brendan O'Connor, Noah A. Smith, and Eric P. Xing, "A Latent Variable Model for Geographic Lexical Variation," in *Proceedings of the 2010 Conference on Empirical Methods in Natural Language Processing* (Stroudsburg, PA: ACL, 2010), 1277–1287.

[19] Margaret E. Roberts, Brandon M. Stewart, Dustin Tingley, and Edoardo M. Airoldi, "The Structural Topic Model and Applied Social Science," in *Advances in Neural Information Processing Systems Workshop on Topic Models: Computation, Application, and Evaluation*, 2013, available at: https://scholar.princeton.edu/files/bstewart/files/stmnips2013.pdf.

[20] J. B. Ruhl, John J. Nay, and Jonathan M. Gilligan, "Topic Modeling the President: Conventional and Computational Methods," *George Washington Law Review* 86 (1243) (2017), available at: www.ssrn.com/abstract=3086226.

[21] All presidential memoranda (1465), presidential determinations (801), executive orders (5634), and presidential proclamations (7544) available on Gerhard Peters and John T. Woolley's "The American Presidency Project" (www.presidency.ucsb.edu), which is the most comprehensive collection of presidential documents.

early 1929 through 2015 to model how policy topics changed during this time and how the type of presidential action changed. In order to conduct this analysis, the researchers had to use several techniques. A first step of most NLP tasks is *tokenization* of the text. A tokenizer divides a document into its individual words. This can often be accomplished by simply separating words by the white space between them. After tokenization of the text, all letters are converted to lower-case, and numbers, punctuation, stop words, and common words (e.g., "the") are removed. The researchers also *stemmed* all words using the Porter stemmer.[22] A stemmer removes the unneeded morphological endings of many words (e.g., "consolidate," "consolidated," and "consolidating" would all be converted to "consolid"). These are common preprocessing techniques applied to text data before unsupervised modeling, with the goal of reducing the dimensionality and complexity of the text in order to capture the most important parts of words and of the overall document.[23] As a final preprocessing step, the document was converted to a one-hot-encoded bag-of-words representation, an integer vector of frequencies of terms occurring in at least five documents. By using only terms occurring in at least five documents, this removed 16,864 of 25,653 terms. The final corpus had 13,730 documents, 8789 terms, and 1,563,608 tokens (individual words) (Figure 2.8.2).

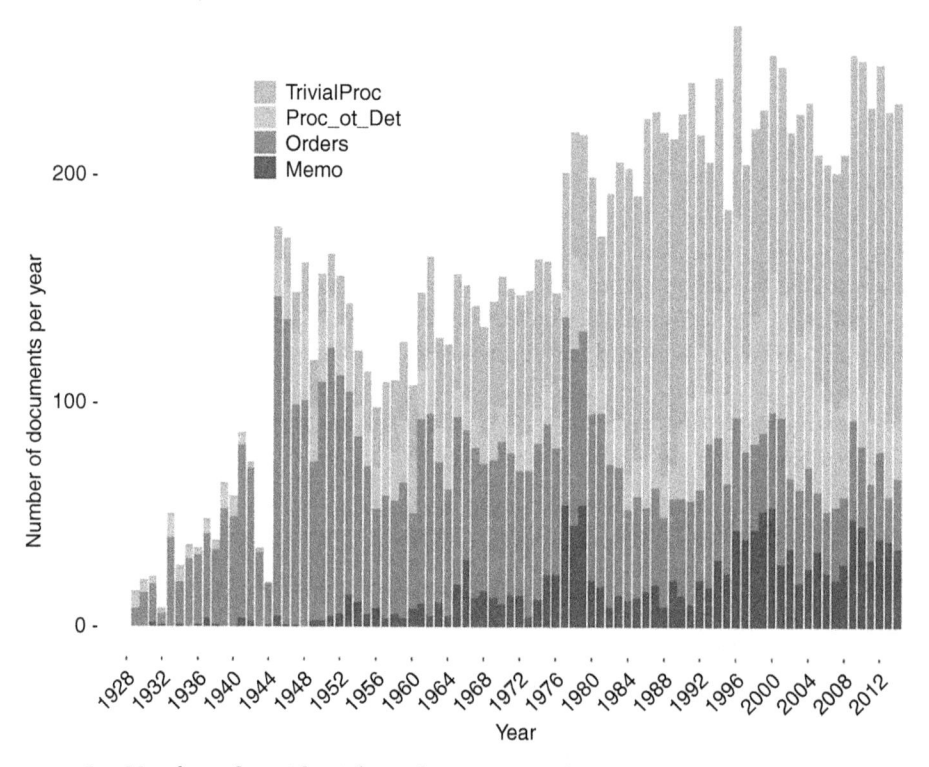

FIGURE 2.8.2 Number of presidential proclamations or determinations, trivial proclamations, memoranda, and executive orders, from 1928 through 2015.[24]

[22] M. F. Porter, "An Algorithm for Suffix Stripping," *Program* 14 (3) (1980): 130–137, available at: http://doi.org/10.1108/eb046814.

[23] For unsupervised tasks, it is usually advisable to apply stemming and removal of stop words; however, if there are a sufficient number of training observations, these techniques can actually degrade the performance of a supervised learning model. *See* Christopher D. Manning, Prabhakar Raghavan, and Hinrich Schütze, *Introduction to Information Retrieval*, 1st ed. (New York, NY: Cambridge University Press, 2008).

[24] Image adapted from Ruhl et al., *supra* note 20.

Each document was either a presidential proclamation, determination, memorandum, or executive order. Most proclamations with substantive weight are authorized by statute requiring presidential issuance of the proclamation to trigger policy programs, such as disaster aid. Executive orders, by contrast, spring from unilateral presidential action. Memoranda, while less attention-grabbing, are legally similar to executive orders; therefore, if a topic shifts from executive orders to memoranda, this may suggest that the president is trying to downplay exercise of power for that topic. Presidential proclamations, meanwhile, are often considered trivial, so the researchers created a separate category ("TrivialProc") for those presidential proclamations with at least one of these terms in the title: *day*, *week*, *month*, or *anniversary*. Because non-trivial proclamations and determinations are similar from a legal perspective, they were grouped into one category. The researchers created a 50-topic model, with the year of effect, the type of presidential action, and the expected proportion of a document that belongs to a given topic.

Because there is an explicit model on between-topic correlation within documents,[25] the researchers were able to discover which topics were likely to occur in the same presidential document as an environmental topic. Figure 2.8.3 shows positive correlations between topics that indicate a likelihood that both topics will be discussed within a given presidential document.

B Extracting Content

Content extraction is similar to summarization, but with some notable differences. While sentiment analyses, text summaries, and topic models seek to obtain a holistic view of a corpus, the primary goal of content extraction is to convert a large amount of text into a formal representation of specific fine-grained facts found in texts. Content extraction is often a lower-level operation within a larger NLP pipeline that uses extraction output as a first step. For example, we may want to automatically extract two types of information from

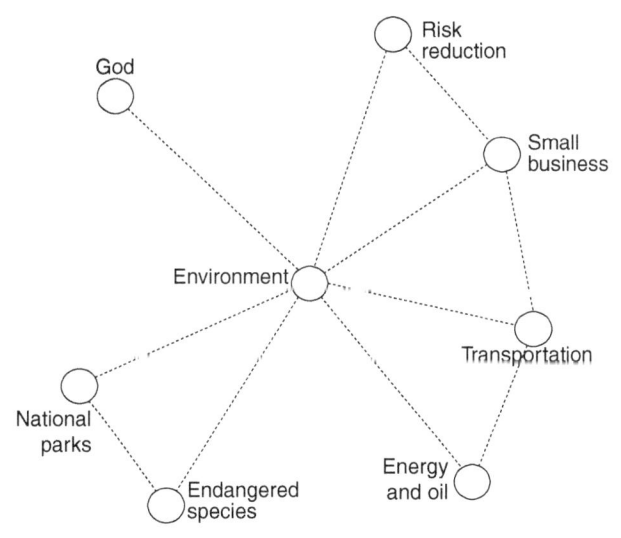

FIGURE 2.8.3 Positive correlations between topics represented as lines.[26]

---

[25] Blei and Lafferty, "A Correlated Topic Model of Science," *supra* note 17.
[26] Image by John J. Nay, 2017.

complex corporate contracts: (1) all pairs of dollar amounts and (2) the description of the expense associated with that dollar amount. We may then want to use this information to compare thousands of contracts to determine what particular language surrounding the expenses led to more or less litigation involving the contract. This analysis of language surrounding a qualified value could inform the drafting of future contracts.

The simplest type of extraction is *attribute extraction*, in which we attempt to extract certain pre-specified attributes from a string of text, such as dollar amounts from a judicial opinion.[27] *Relational extraction*, meanwhile, attempts to extract useful relationships among attributes.[28] So, after determining a dollar amount, the system would determine the object the dollar amount refers to. To demonstrate the output of these techniques, the Stanford Core NLP software toolkit was applied to the following sentence from a Tennessee state bill:

> "Title 68, Chapter 201, Part 1, is amended by adding the following language as a new section: (a) As used in this section: (1) "Covered electric-generating unit" means an existing fossil-fuel-fired electric-generating unit located within this state that is subject to regulation under EPA emission guidelines."

The toolkit tokenized the text, split the sequence of tokens into discrete sentences, predicted the part-of-speech for every token, and determined whether each token was a named entity.[29] The software also identified the syntactic relationships of the words in the sentences and determined whether entity mentions throughout a document are referencing the same entity, referred to as *co-reference resolutions*.

Part-of-speech tagging systems use manually labeled data to train supervised learning models to predict the part-of-speech of a word, given the surrounding words.[30] Part-of-speech (POS) categories can include singular proper nouns (NNP), cardinal numbers

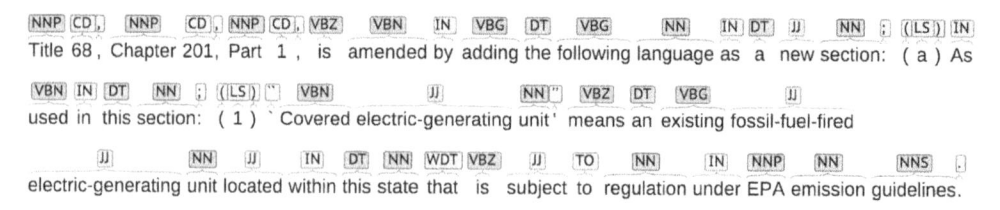

FIGURE 2.8.4 Part-of-speech tagging for a sentence in a state bill.[31]

---

[27] Stuart J. Russell and Peter Norvig, *Artificial Intelligence: A Modern Approach* (3rd ed. (Upper Saddle River, NJ: Prentice Hall, 2009).

[28] *Ibid.*

[29] Christopher D. Manning, Mihai Surdeanu, John Bauer, Jenny Finkel, Steven J. Bethard, and David McClosky, "The Stanford CoreNLP Natural Language Processing Toolkit," in *Proceedings of the 52nd Annual Meeting of the Association for Computational Linguistics: System Demonstrations* (Stroudsburg, PA: Association for Computational Linguistics, 2014), 55–60.

[30] Many state-of-the-art models for predicting syntactic and semantic characteristics of sentences explicitly represent the order of words in a sentence by either representing the one-dimensional structure of the flow of a sentence as it would be read by a human, or by the complex tree-like structure of relations between words. This is accomplished with complex ML models such as recursive and recurrent neural networks, and conditional random fields. See, e.g., Kristina Toutanova, Dan Klein, Christopher D. Manning, and Yoram Singer, "Feature-Rich Part-of-Speech Tagging with a Cyclic Dependency Network," in *Proceedings of the 2003 Conference of the North American Chapter of the Association for Computational Linguistics on Human Language Technology – Volume 1* (Stroudsburg, PA: Association for Computational Linguistics, 2003), 173–180, available at: http://doi.org/10.3115/1073445.1073478.

[31] Figures 2.8.4–2.8.7 were all created using the brat (http://brat.nlplab.org) visualization tool.

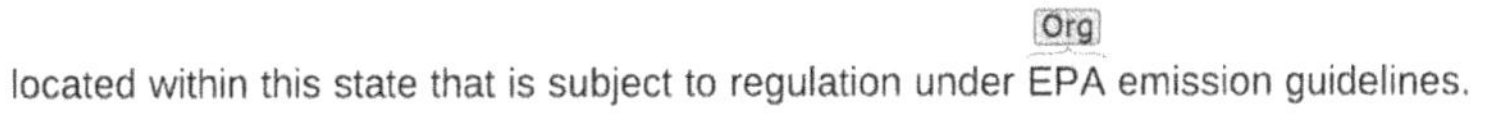

> [Org]
> located within this state that is subject to regulation under EPA emission guidelines.

FIGURE 2.8.5 Named entity recognition for the last part of the bill sentence.

(CD), third-person singular present verbs (VBZ), past-participle verbs (VBN), prepositions (IN), adjectives (JJ), and so on. Figure 2.8.4 demonstrates POS tagging for legislative text.

Named entity recognition predicts whether a token is a named entity (person, location, or organization) or a numerical entity (money, date, time, duration, or set). Named entities are often predicted using supervised learning models trained on texts whose words have been manually categorized into these classes.[32] Numerical entities, meanwhile, are often predicted using simple hand-coded rules; for example, the Environmental Protection Agency (EPA) was identified as an organization in the last part of the bill sentence (Figure 2.8.5).

Syntactic parsing systems predict the functional relationships between words in a sentence. This is a difficult task because of the inherent ambiguity of natural language. Supervised learning models are trained on large labeled corpora, and then state-of-the art systems use neural networks to find the relationships between words.[33] With long sentences, such as the legislative sentence in Figure 2.8.6, there can be multiple syntactic relationships.

The Stanford Core NLP software was also applied to a larger section of a Tennessee bill in order to demonstrate co-reference resolution.[34] For example, Figure 2.8.7 shows mentions of "Subsection (f)" and its linkage to a previous mention, and within the sentence the physical and internet-based notices are predicted to be referring to the same underlying concept of notice.

After NLP has been used to effectively extract content from a corpus of documents, the next step is information retrieval.

C Retrieving Information and Documents

Information retrieval (IR) tasks are characterized by a user's query, a set of documents to search, and the subset of the documents returned by the system.[35] Query results come in the form of a list of documents relevant to that query. The simplest type of system, *Boolean retrieval*, returns documents that simply contain the words found in the query. More complex systems use ML. An advantage of using ML representations over Boolean search is that Boolean search only returns an unranked list of all documents that contain the terms in the query, while the ML approach provides a ranking of the documents based on how relevant they are to the query.[36] If the ML vector representations correctly capture the meaning of the

---

[32] Jenny Rose Finkel, Trond Grenager, and Christopher D. Manning, "Incorporating Non-local Information into Information Extraction Systems by Gibbs Sampling," in *Proceedings of the 43rd Annual Meeting of the Association for Computational Linguistics* (Stroudsburg, PA: Association for Computational Linguistics, 2005), 363–370, available at: http://doi.org/10.3115/1219840.1219885.

[33] Daniel Andor, Chris Alberti, David Weiss, Aliaksei Severyn, Alessandro Presta, Kuzman Ganchev, Slav Petrov, and Michael Collins, "Globally Normalized Transition-Based Neural Networks," *Proceedings of the 54th Annual Meeting of the Association for Computational Linguistics*, Berlin, Germany, August 7–12, 2016, available at: http://arxiv.org/abs/1603.06042.

[34] Heeyoung Lee, Angel Chang, Yves Peirsman, Nathanael Chambers, Mihai Surdeanu, and Dan Jurafsky, "Deterministic Coreference Resolution Based on Entity-Centric, Precision-Ranked Rules," *Computational Linguistics* 39 (4) (2013): 885–916, available at: http://doi.org/10.1162/COLI_a_00152.

[35] Russell and Norvig, *Artificial Intelligence: A Modern Approach*, supra note 27.

[36] Manning et al., *Introduction to Information Retrieval*, supra note 23.

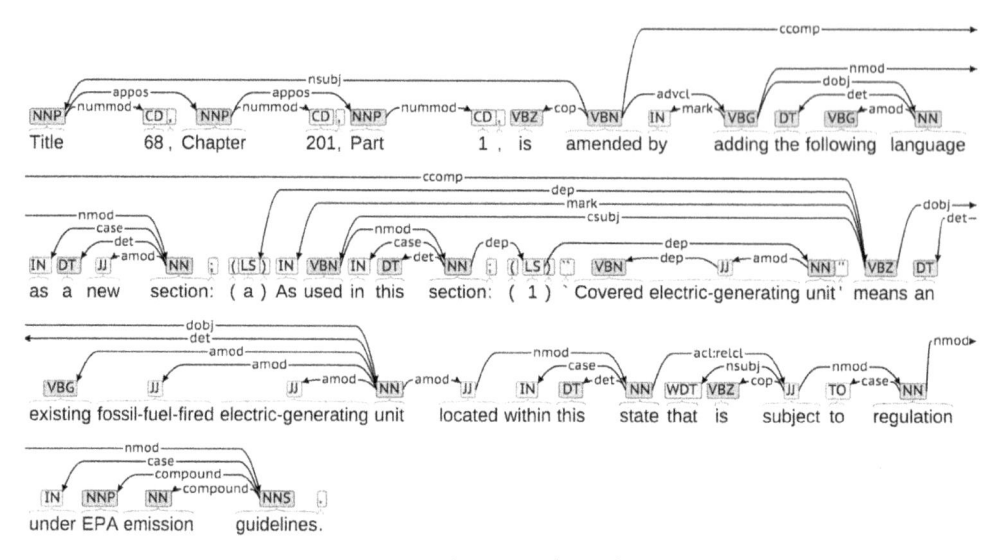

FIGURE 2.8.6 Syntactic dependencies.

FIGURE 2.8.7 Co-reference resolution.

documents and the queries, then they will outperform Boolean retrieval and provide the most relevant documents.

There are two primary measures of the performance of IR systems. *Precision* measures the proportion of the returned documents that are relevant to the user's needs, and *recall* measures the proportion of all the relevant documents in the system that were returned to the user.[37] With a very large corpus where multiple documents may serve a similar purpose for a user (e.g., searching for law review articles on administrative law), one should be more interested in optimizing precision. On the other hand, in situations where it is more important to ensure comprehensive coverage of a search query (e.g., reviewing emails deemed potentially relevant to a court case), recall is probably more important.

When we don't expect the user to manually classify documents as relevant or not to their query, we can utilize unsupervised learning techniques and map the queries and the documents into a shared mathematical space to return documents located near the query. When the user *does* interact with the ML system, providing feedback on the relevance of the documents returned in an iterative process, then this information can be leveraged for supervised learning models tailored to a particular query or set of queries. While this interactive approach with iterative human–computer review requires much more human

[37] For a more detailed discussion of precision, recall, and related measures, see Dolin – Information Intermediation, *supra*, and Waisberg – Contract Analytics, *infra*.

input, it is a superior approach to take when the stakes are high, such as during document review for a court case.

1 Unsupervised Learning

Now let's take a more detailed look at unsupervised learning approaches. One of the simpler transformations from raw text into a mathematical representation is obtained by the *term frequency-inverse document frequency (tf-idf)* technique. The term frequency, *tf*, is how often a term occurs in a document. Inverse document frequency, *idf*, is the logarithm of the total number of documents divided by the number of documents that contain the term in question. It is important to consider the *idf* because some words in some contexts, such as the word "section" in a piece of legislation, will occur very often across all documents in the collection, but their presence adds little or no value in discriminating between documents. The *tf-idf* is computed by multiplying the term frequency by the inverse document frequency, and is therefore high when a term occurs very often in very few documents. In this way, *tf-idf* allows us to map documents and queries into vectors that are useful for discriminating between documents.[38] These vectors are a bag-of-words representation because the order of the words is discarded. This can be problematic for subtle textual differences.[39]

Continuous-space vector representations of words can capture the subtle semantic variations across the dimensions of a vector, and potentially learn more useful representations of texts. One method to learn these representations is to use a neural network model to predict a target word using either the mean, the sum, or another transformation of the representations of the surrounding words (e.g., vectors for the two words on either side of the target word in Figure 2.8.6). The prediction errors are then used to update the representation in order to enhance the probability of observing the target word.[40] After randomly initializing representations and iterating this process, called *word2vec*, over many word pairings, words with similar meanings are placed in similar locations in vector space as a by-product of the prediction task.[41]

Using continuous-space vector representations of words and documents in an IR system may allow a query to return a document that is deemed similar and relevant to the query, even though it may not actually contain any words that were in the query.[42] One of the simplest methods of obtaining a continuous-space representation of a document is to average all the word vectors in the document that were learned with *word2vec* and create a representation that captures the general meaning of the entire document. Figure 2.8.8 demonstrates this visually.

---

[38] Manning et al., *Introduction to Information Retrieval*, supra note 23.
[39] An example of this ambiguity: The phrases "reversed the lower Court" and "the lower Court reversed" are represented by the exact same vector in a bag-of-words model, but the two phrases have very different meanings, and widely divergent legal implications.
[40] Tomas Mikolov, Ilya Sutskever, Kai Chen, Greg S. Corrado, and Jeff Dean, "Distributed Representations of Words and Phrases and their Compositionality," in *Advances in Neural Information Processing Systems 26*, eds. Christopher J. C. Burges, Leon Bottou, M. Welling, Zoubin Ghahramani, and Killian Q. Weinberger (Red Hook, NY: Curran Associates, Inc., 2013), 3111–3119, available at: http://papers.nips.cc/paper/5021-distributed-representations-of-words-and-phrases-and-their-compositionality.pdf; Yoshua Bengio, Réjean Ducharme, Pascal Vincent, and Christian Jauvin, "A Neural Probabilistic Language Model," *Journal of Machine Learning Research* 3 (2003): 1137–1155.
[41] Mikolov et al., "Distributed Representations of Words and Phrases and their Compositionality," supra note 40.
[42] John J. Nay, "Gov2Vec: Learning Distributed Representations of Institutions and Their Legal Text," in *Proceedings of 2016 Empirical Methods in Natural Language Processing Workshop on NLP and Computational Social Science* (Stroudsburg, PA: Association for Computational Linguistics, 2016), 49–54.

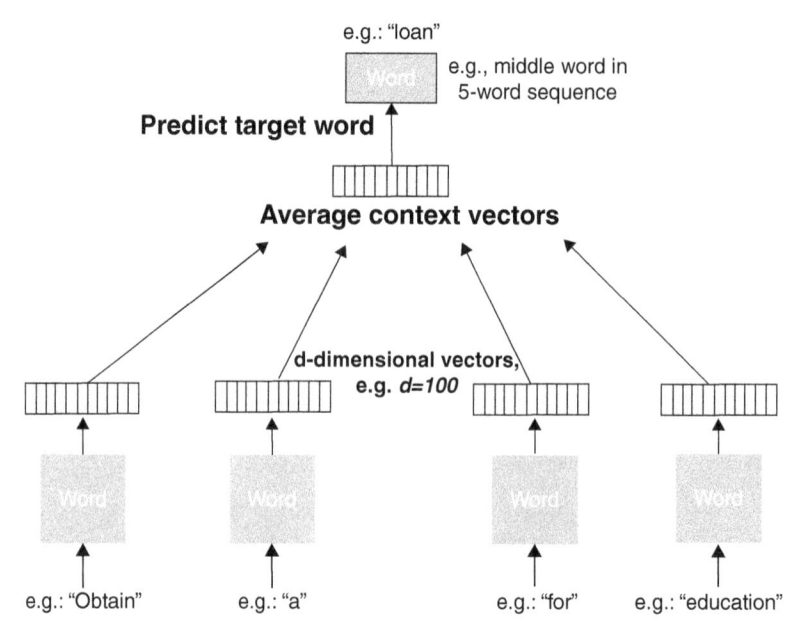

FIGURE 2.8.8 Word2Vec algorithm.[43]

2 Supervised Learning

When the stakes are high, it is worth spending time to manually label documents. During the legal discovery process, there are often hundreds or thousands of documents to review for relevance. Electronic discovery – or *e-discovery* – finds documents relevant to a case. E-discovery is a supervised learning technique in which a user iteratively provides relevant documents, has the machine use those documents to train a model to predict what other documents may be relevant, and from those candidates chooses the most relevant documents.

Document review is an important IR use case. Federal judges have issued opinions permitting,[44] and sometimes requiring,[45] the use of technology to assist lawyers in searching documents for evidence. There are often hundreds, or even thousands, of documents that may be relevant to a court case, and lawyers must find the relevant documents within this set. Manually reviewing every document is not only less efficient than a technology-assisted approach that would rule out many documents, but it is also less effective because humans are more prone to error.[46]

E-discovery and *technology-assisted review* (TAR) use supervised learning to improve the discovery process. An effective TAR technique for discovering nearly all relevant documents in a corpus is *continuous active learning* (CAL).[47] This consists of four primary steps: (1) find

---

[43] Image adapted from John J. Nay, "Predicting and understanding law-making with word vectors and an ensemble model," *PLoS One* 12 (5) (2017), available at: https://doi.org/10.1371/journal.pone.0176999.
[44] *Da Silva Moore v. Publicis Groupe*, 868 F.Supp.2d 137 (2012).
[45] *EORHB, Inc. v. HOA Holdings, LLC*, Civ. Action No. 7409-VCL (Del. Ch. Oct. 15, 2012).
[46] Herbert L. Roitblat, Anne Kershaw, and Patrick Oot, "Document Categorization in Legal Electronic Discovery: Computer Classification vs. Manual Review," *Journal of the American Society for Information Science and Technology* 61 (1) (2010): 70–80.
[47] Gordon V. Cormack and Maura R. Grossman, "Evaluation of Machine-Learning Protocols for Technology-Assisted Review in Electronic Discovery," in *Proceedings of the 37th International ACM SIGIR Conference on Research & Development in Information Retrieval* (New York, NY: ACM, 2014), 153–162.

at least one example of a relevant document; (2) train a supervised learning model to predict relevance to the case using the document(s) from step 1, and use the model to score the remaining documents and return the documents scored as most likely to be relevant; (3) review the documents from step 2, and manually classify each as relevant or not; and (4) repeat the previous two steps until there are no more suggested review documents that are considered relevant.[48]

V CONCLUSION

This chapter provided a high-level overview of NLP tools and techniques applied to legal informatics. Both ML and NLP tools have already provided powerful examples of programs and models that can summarize textual content and predict outcomes correlated with textual data, and the examples provided in this chapter represent just a handful of applications of such tools. There remains significant untapped potential for legal academic studies to use these techniques for summarizing patterns of law across vast amounts of text, and for detecting how laws change over time and jurisdiction. Perhaps more significant than this is the possibility for efficiency gains for those legal services providers who embed these computational techniques in order to augment the synthesizing and reasoning skills of attorneys.

---

[48] Maura R. Grossman and Gordon V. Cormack, "Continuous Active Learning for TAR," *Thomson Reuters E-Discovery Bulletin* April/May (2016), 32–37, available at: http://cormack.uwaterloo.ca/caldemo/AprMay16_EdiscoveryBulletin.pdf.

2.9

Introduction to Blockchain and Cryptography

Nelson M. Rosario

I INTRODUCTION

The blockchain industry has recently broken through into the general public's consciousness. Gone were the days of blockchain projects being solely the interest of computer programmers, libertarians, and anti-government activists. Now, discussion of the industry graced the pages of the *New York Times*[1] and the *Wall Street Journal*,[2] and the nascent industry was regularly covered by television news programs such as CNBC's Fast Money.[3] The majority of this attention was directed to price increases in cryptocurrencies, such as Bitcoin, but a new vehicle for raising capital – known as an initial coin offering, or ICO – also fueled public enthusiasm. All of this excitement and curiosity has made it harder and harder for lawyers to ignore this industry. As such, it is beneficial for lawyers to get a high-level understanding of what the blockchain industry is, and how it makes technologies like cryptocurrencies possible.

Unfortunately, there is no universally agreed-upon definition of what a blockchain is. Definitions of a blockchain include such descriptions as "a communally maintained database,"[4] "global distributed ledgers,"[5] "an inviolable universal ledger,"[6] "a list of validated blocks,"[7] and perhaps most technically, "a linked list using hash pointers."[8]

At a high level, a blockchain is a ledger of information that is shared among a group of participants. The information is typically peer-to-peer transaction information, and the

---

[1] Nathaniel Popper and Steve Lohr, "Blockchain: A Better Way to Track Pork Chops, Bonds, Bad Peanut Butter?" *New York Times*, March 4, 2017, available at: www.nytimes.com/2017/03/04/business/dealbook/blockchain-ibm-bitcoin.html.

[2] Tom Loftus, "Blockchain Will Drive Business Value, Increase CEO Cool Factor – Eventually," October 3, 2017, available at: https://blogs.wsj.com/cio/2017/10/03/blockchain-will-drive-business-value-increase-ceo-cool-factor-eventually.

[3] Angelica LaVito, "'The Sky Is the Limit' for Blockchain Technology in Banking: Credit Suisse Banker," CNBC, October 10, 2017, available at: www.cnbc.com/2017/10/10/the-sky-is-the-limit-for-blockchain-technology-in-banking-credit-suisse-banker.html.

[4] Nathaniel Popper, *Digital Gold* (New York, NY: Harper Paperbacks, 2015), 21.

[5] Alex Tapscott and Don Tapscott, *Blockchain Revolution: How the Technology Behind Bitcoin Is Changing Money, Business, and the World* (London: Portfolio, 2016), 6.

[6] Paul Vigna and Michael J. Casey, *The Age of Cryptocurrency: How Bitcoin and the Blockchain Are Challenging the Global Economic Order* (New York, NY: St. Martin's Press, 2015), 43.

[7] Andreas M. Antonopoulos, *Mastering Bitcoin: Unlocking Digital Cryptocurrencies* (Sebastopol, CA: O'Reilly Media, 2014), xix.

[8] Arvind Narayanan, Joseph Bonneau, Edward Felten, Andrew Miller, and Steven Goldfeder, *Bitcoin and Cryptocurrency Technologies* (Princeton, NJ: Princeton University Press, 2016), 11.

participants are active in maintaining the ledger that the transaction information lives on. This transaction information is gathered together into blocks that are then eventually stored on a shared ledger that is the official record of transactions.

The reason this shared ledger concept is such a big deal is that with the advent of Bitcoin people were finally able to create unique digital property without the use of a central administrator. All blockchain networks achieve this by utilizing core techniques and technologies similar to Bitcoin. Thus, in order to better understand how blockchains work, and the promise they hold, it is necessary to take a brief look at the history of Bitcoin.

II BRIEF HISTORY OF BITCOIN

On October 31, 2008, an unknown person, or persons, going by the name Satoshi Nakamoto posted the following to a cryptography mailing list: "I've been working on a new electronic cash system that's fully peer-to-peer, *with no trusted third party*."[9] This new electronic cash system was designed to solve a very particular problem known as the *double-spend problem*. In the process of doing so, the system also solved another problem known as the *Byzantine generals problem*.

The double-spend problem had plagued electronic currency projects since they were first conceived. The problem is best illustrated by the question "what is to prevent anyone from making several copies of an electronic coin and using them at different shops?"[10] This is a crucial problem, since by definition, any electronic cash system involves digital information that normally can be copied with impunity. What Bitcoin showed was that you can create digital scarcity through the use of a shared ledger where all transactions are public by default. If everyone shares a ledger of all transactions, then everyone knows when "coins" are sent to anyone else on the network. The question then becomes: How do you ensure that everyone has the same copy of the ledger?

The Byzantine generals problem (BGP) is central to the problem of ensuring that everyone has a copy of the same ledger. The BGP[11] is concerned with issues in designing reliable computer systems; specifically, how to ensure that the information in those computer systems is accurate.

The problem is conceptualized as a group of Byzantine generals who need to agree on a plan to attack a city; however, the generals suspect that at least one of their cadre is a traitor. How, then, can the generals be sure that "[a]ll loyal generals decide upon the same plan of action," and "[a] small number of traitors cannot cause the loyal generals to adopt a bad plan?"[12] Put another way, how can you trust information that is sent over an untrusted network if you do not trust all of the other actors on the network? The key is to design a system in which participants sign transactions, broadcast those transactions to everyone on the network they are connected to, and require participants to expend work (known as *proof-of-work*), or in some cases stake resources (known as *proof-of-stake*), to add those transactions to the underlying ledger. Participants are incentivized to perform the proof-of-work or proof-of-stake by

---

[9] Emphasis added. Satoshi Nakamoto, "Bitcoin P2P E-Cash Paper," October 31, 2008, available at: www.metzdowd.com/pipermail/cryptography/2008-October/014810.html.

[10] David Chaum, Amos Fiat, and Moni Naor, "Untraceable Electronic Cash," in *CRYPTO '88 Proceedings on Advances in Cryptology, Santa Barbara, California, USA* (Heidelberg: Springer-Verlag Berlin, 1990), 319–327.

[11] Also known as *Byzantine fault tolerance* (BFT).

[12] Leslie Lamport, Robert Shostak, and Marshall Pease, "The Byzantine Generals Problem," *SRI International, ACM Transactions on Programming Languages and Systems* 4 (3) (1982): 382–401.

the promise of a reward of cryptocurrency if their block is added to the blockchain.[13] Users can verify transaction information, as well as verify that updates on the ledger were added to the ledger by participants who expended work or staked resources, all prior to the information becoming a part of the ledger. This allows participants to trust the information in the blockchain because it has been rigorously vetted.

Blockchain networks, then, deal with trust in two different types of information: trust in the veracity of any one transaction, and trust in the ledger of transactions as a whole. This trust is dependent on the use of tried and true tools that humans have used in many other domains. Namely, all blockchains use ledgers, peer-to-peer networks, cryptography, and some sort of consensus mechanism.

III LEDGERS, PEER-TO-PEER NETWORKS, CRYPTOGRAPHY, AND CONSENSUS MECHANISMS

Like many other inventions, a blockchain is a combination of existing technologies assembled in a novel way that oftentimes looks obvious in hindsight. Here, the technologies are *ledgers*, *peer-to-peer networks*, *cryptography*, and *consensus mechanisms*.

A Ledgers

As long as humans have been keeping records, they have used ledgers to track commercial and other transactions. These systems developed even before writing was invented. The author Jane Gleeson-White tells the story of French archaeologist Denise Schmandt-Besserat, who over the course of twenty-five years discovered proto-accounting systems in Mesopotamia starting in 7000 BCE that utilized clay tokens to track a person's wealth.[14] These systems evolved over several thousand years into larger clay tablets that tracked the same information.[15] These ledgers, and all subsequent ledgers, are "an account book of final entry, in which business transactions are recorded."[16] The difference with blockchain networks is that they use *distributed ledgers* as opposed to the historically more common centralized ledgers.

Traditionally, a financial institution (e.g., a bank, a stock exchange) kept a ledger of all its transactions. This ledger was held centrally by the bank on behalf of its customers. All updates to the ledger had to be run through the bank. Customers trusted the bank to keep an accurate record of the ledger to track the credits and debits to their accounts. If the bank failed, all of its customers would be at risk. This meant the bank would be a single point of failure for the centralized ledger.

Blockchain networks take a different approach because there is no central institution responsible for the ledger. Instead, the ledger is maintained by network participants and each participant in the network may keep a copy of the ledger themselves so that they may verify transactions as they see fit. In this way, the ledger is distributed, replicated across any participating node in the network that wishes to keep a full copy of the ledger. This makes the

---

[13] For more on proof-of-work and proof-of-stake, see Kilbride – Distributed Ledgers, Cryptography, and Smart Contracts, *infra*.

[14] Jane Gleeson-White, *Double Entry: How the Merchants of Venice Created Modern Finance* (New York, NY: W. W. Norton, 2013), 11–14.

[15] Id.

[16] Definition of "Ledger," Dictionary.com, available at: www.dictionary.com/browse/ledger.

ledger more resilient, since there are multiple copies of the ledger on the network and any invalid changes to the ledger would require some level of collusion among participants. The participants in the network communicate with each other directly, which leads to the second building block: peer-to-peer networks.

B Peer-to-Peer Networks

A network may simply be a group of individuals and/or machines connected together to exchange information. Similar to ledgers, networks may be centralized or decentralized. For example, a messaging service such as Apple's iMessage is a centralized network: Apple dictates the maintenance of the network and how participants in the network communicate. A person using iMessage is a client of the network, and Apple runs the servers for the iMessage network.[17]

Conversely, a *peer-to-peer network* does not need a central authority dictating how messages are routed through the system. Instead, in a peer-to-peer network participants can communicate with any other participant in the network with far fewer restrictions. In particular, "clients and servers are not distinguished from one another; instead, all nodes within the system are considered peers."[18] Peer-to-peer networks have a somewhat problematic reputation, given their association with former file-sharing companies such as Napster and issues related to copyright infringement,[19] but peer-to-peer networks are advantageous to blockchain networks because they allow participants to communicate directly with any other participant on the network. How participants in the network verify communications on the network is the subject of the third element common to all blockchain networks: cryptography.

C Cryptography[20]

The goal of *cryptography* is "not to hide the existence of a message, but rather to hide its meaning."[21] Blockchain networks use two types of cryptographic items: digital signatures and hashing. A *digital signature* is intended to function as a physical signature indicating that a particular individual is the one who signed a transaction. These signatures should have two properties: (1) only you can make your signature, but anyone can verify that it is your signature; and (2) the signature should be tied to a particular document.[22] These properties are achieved through the use of what is known as public key cryptography. Public key cryptography uses a pair of keys (the keys are just very large numbers) that are related to each other. One of the keys is held out to the public for anyone to know, and the other key is kept in secret and referred to as the private key.

In some ways, public key cryptography is similar to a person having a locked mailbox. The person who owns the mailbox holds the mailbox out to the world to receive information, but

---

[17] For an interesting discussion of the vulnerabilities associated with iMessage and centralized messaging protocols, see Matthew Green, "Attack of the Week: Apple's iMessage," Personal blog, March 21, 2016, available at: https://blog.cryptographyengineering.com/2016/03/21/attack-of-week-apple-imessage.

[18] Abraham Silberschatz, Peter Baer Galvin, and Greg Gagne, *Operating System Concepts* (Hoboken, NJ: Wiley, 2008), 36.

[19] See, e.g., *A&M Records, Inc. v. Napster, Inc.*, 239 F.3d 1004 (2001).

[20] For more on Cryptography, see Kilbride – Distributed Ledgers, Cryptography, and Smart Contracts, *infra*.

[21] Simon Singh, *The Code Book: The Science of Secrecy from Ancient Egypt to Quantum Cryptography* (London: Fourth Estate, 1999), 6.

[22] Narayanan et al., *Bitcoin and Cryptocurrency Technologies*, supra note 8, at 15.

only they can unlock the information sent to the mailbox. In this example, the mailbox is the public key, and the key used to unlock the mailbox is the private key. If a message is signed with a person's private key, then it is trivially easy for a recipient of the message to verify that the message had to be signed by the holder of the private key using the public key. These keys are used to guarantee that only the holders of private keys are transacting information on the blockchain networks. These transactions are bundled together into blocks of transactions, which leads us to the second cryptographic item: hashing.

Hashing refers to cryptographic hash functions, which are mathematical formulas to create a digital fingerprint for a set of data. Cryptographic hash functions must have six properties: input data can be of any size; the hash function produces a fixed-size output; the hash function is efficient; different data inputs produce different fixed-size outputs; the hash function output cannot feasibly be used to figure out the input; and there exists no solution for solving the hash function that is better than guessing random numbers.[23]

In a blockchain network, hashing is used like a fingerprint for each block of transactions added to the ledger. When a new block of transactions is to be added to a blockchain, a hash of all the information in that block is included in the block itself. This hash functions as a fingerprint for the block. When an additional block is added to the network, that block includes the hash of the previous block in the blockchain. Hashes of blocks are never broadcast alone. They are only ever transmitted to other nodes as part of the transmission of the block. Consequently, the hash of the newly added block is therefore dependent on the hash of the previous block. In this way, the blocks are "chained together" through a sequence of hashes stored in each block in the ledger that point to the previous block in the ledger. How, then, do participants in the network decide which blocks to add to the ledger? To answer this question we have to look at the last building block: consensus.

D Consensus Mechanisms

Human beings have deployed numerous *consensus mechanisms* throughout history. We have relied on experts to arbitrate disputes, authority figures to make decisions, and complex systems of rules for deciding what information is correct. In a blockchain network, consensus must be achieved among parties that do not necessarily know each other or trust each other. At a minimum, to address this issue, blockchain networks allow all participants to independently: verify each transaction; aggregate those transactions into blocks; and verify new blocks and assemble them into a chain.[24] Additionally, blockchain networks may use other heuristics for verification: selecting the chain with the most cumulative proof-of-work as the official chain such that the longest chain wins in the event of two competing chains of blocks; or staking a certain amount of cryptocurrency on a particular block to be added to the chain. These approaches allow for consensus to emerge over time as to what the correct state of the underlying ledger is. Eventually, the underlying transaction data is trustworthy and you have unique digital property created by the community. Once you have unique digital property there are lots of interesting applications for it.

---

[23] Id. at 2–9. For more details and applications of hashing and cryptographic keys, *see* Kilbride – Distributed Ledgers, Cryptography, and Smart Contracts, *infra*.

[24] Antonopoulos, *Mastering Bitcoin*, *supra* note 7, at 177.

IV BLOCKCHAIN APPLICATIONS

Blockchain networks can be used to track all sorts of information, but some of the more interesting use cases are cryptocurrency, hosting and executing smart contracts, and, someday, hosting and executing decentralized autonomous organizations.[25]

The first cryptocurrency was Bitcoin, launched on January 3, 2009. Since that time, thousands of cryptocurrencies have been created because the Bitcoin protocol is open-source and free for anyone to use or modify to create their own coin. Similar to the definition of a blockchain, no universal definition of a cryptocurrency exists; however, a working definition could be "a digitally native censorship-resistant valuable piece of data." Cryptocurrency is censorship-resistant if its underlying blockchain is not controlled by any one entity, and the blockchain network is transacted over the public internet. Cryptocurrency has value for no other reason than that the market values it. This is little different from how traditional fiat currencies issued by governments operate. With cryptocurrencies, people have the opportunity to engage in a variety of economic transactions that may not make sense using traditional financial infrastructure, because cryptocurrencies have fewer middlemen, are far more easily divisible than fiat currency, and can lead to new kinds of payment automation when combined with smart contracts.

Smart contracts were first invented by Nick Szabo in 1994. As defined by Szabo, "[a] smart contract is a computerized transaction protocol that executes the terms of a contract."[26] Smart contracts do not need a blockchain network, but certain blockchain networks, such as the Ethereum network, allow for the storage of computer code at addresses on the blockchain network. Thus, the code representing a contract may be stored all across the network, and executed in a more resilient and guaranteed manner than if it was stored on a single computer.

Lastly, by combining cryptocurrency with smart contracts it is in theory possible to code into a set of smart contracts rules for governing organizations. This would lead to the creation of leaderless organizations that are governed solely by the code in the smart contracts; however, the world's first attempt at this idea of a decentralized autonomous organization failed with the DAO hack in 2016.[27]

V CONCLUSION

Blockchain networks use known techniques such as ledgers, peer-to-peer networking, and cryptography to achieve consensus on unique digital property created by a community without a central administrator. This represents a fundamentally new set of trust technologies, and lawyers – having always acted as trusted advisors for their clients – must educate themselves about blockchain and its potential. As with any new innovation, lawyers are well positioned to capitalize on this technology if they establish a baseline of knowledge.[28]

---

[25] For more on these applications, *see* Kilbride – Distributed Ledgers, Cryptography, and Smart Contracts, *infra*.
[26] Nick Szabo, "Smart Contracts," 1994, available at: www.fon.hum.uva.nl/rob/Courses/InformationInSpeech/CDROM/Literature/LOTwinterschool2006/szabo.best.vwh.net/smart.contracts.html.
[27] For a riveting telling of the DAO hack, *see* Matthew Leising, "The Ether Thief," *Bloomberg*, June 13, 2017, available at: www.bloomberg.com/features/2017-the-ether-thief. For a brief discussion of the DAO, *see* Kilbride – Distributed Ledgers, Cryptography, and Smart Contracts, *infra*.
[28] *See generally*, Part III.

C.

Process Improvement, Gamification, and Design Thinking

2.10

Legal Informatics-Based Technology in Broader Workflows

Kenneth A. Grady

Let me tell you a story, one that may sound familiar to you. Anna is preparing a termination agreement. This task takes her anywhere from one to four hours. That's a lot of time to spend on what should be a simple contract, but each time she is asked to prepare one she runs into the same problems. She starts her work by asking human resources for information about the employee. Then she goes back and forth with emails, trying to track down all the bits and pieces she needs to create the agreement. She also has to contact multiple people: the equity plan administrator to find out if the employee has any stock grants; the safety manager to find out if there are any outstanding claims; and someone in finance to check for any promissory notes the employee has signed. Then, she goes back to HR to clarify all the information before she goes to chase down more.

While gathering the facts, Anna starts drafting the agreement. First, she has to find a template for the state. Then, she must work through the special provisions in the template. Is the employee over age 40? Is this a single termination, or are several employees being terminated at the same time? Does the employee self-identify as male or female?

Anna reaches out to the employee's supervisor while she works on the draft. She discovers that each employee termination is a special case. Although Anna wants to rely on HR, her colleagues are busy and often not in the loop on important details. Anna talks to the supervisor to find out any information she needs that HR might not know.

As emails come in, Anna stores them in an online folder. Using folders makes it much easier to find information about each employee, but it also means going back and forth to store and retrieve information. Once she retrieves new information, she then opens the draft termination agreement and updates it. She sends follow-up emails if necessary. Anna keeps up this iterative process of emails and draft updates until she finally has a complete working draft.

Anna prints the draft agreement and reads it all the way through. She corrects minor errors, tinkers with the wording, and pauses to send out emails with additional questions. If she has time, she updates the document with the changes. If she's too busy, the assistant she shares with three other attorneys makes the changes instead. Depending on the assistant's workload, it might take 1–3 days to get a draft turned around.

Eventually, Anna is satisfied with the draft and emails it to HR for review. After incorporating any appropriate changes from HR, Anna sends the completed agreement to them. Usually, this is the extent of her work. Occasionally, the employee hires an attorney and Anna must discuss the terms of the agreement with the employee's attorney. Sometimes, she makes changes after this discussion. If she does make changes, she then once again sends the final agreement to human resources and the opposing lawyer, and lets them arrange to have it signed.

Anna followed a process to prepare these termination agreements. Like most attorneys, she had tweaked the process to become as efficient for her as possible. Her changes shaved some of the time off the total time it took her to prepare an agreement, but it still took too long and she knew she could do better.

In this chapter, you will learn how to get those better results. You will learn what we mean by *process* in the context of legal services. We will see several examples of process maps, which are used to visualize processes. Anna's termination agreement drafting is a process, but we will see how it could become a *project*, requiring expert leadership and project management tools. We will also cover how Anna could improve her process using *lean thinking*. To get that improvement, she will need to remove the eight types of waste we commonly find in processes.

Processes can be woven together to form workflows, and we will see how these processes and workflows can benefit from the introduction of computers at any step in the process. When we talk about improving legal services, we are talking about this integration of process improvement, project management, and computer technology into our workflows.

I LEGAL SERVICES AS PROCESSES

A *process* is a sequence of operations that leads from a start point to the completion of a goal. A story like the one above can provide a mental image of Anna's process, but the more complex a process gets, the more cumbersome this mental image becomes. If you have a visual image – a map – of a process, it becomes easier to describe and explain the process. You can start by listing the steps in a process. Table 2.10.1 shows Anna's process, recorded in a standard process study sheet. You could create each entry by watching or interviewing Anna. You could then track how long each step took through several cycles (a cycle is a complete run-through of the process).

What Anna does can be transformed from an *ad hoc* series of steps into an efficient and effective process using something like the study sheet in Table 2.10.1. The next step in process improvement is to turn each task in the standard process study sheet into an image of Anna's process for preparing a termination agreement. This is shown in Figure 2.10.1.

Process mapping yields many benefits. For example, members of a practice group or department often look at process maps and find that each person follows a different path to complete a process. By mapping the process, members of the team can find and remove any unnecessary variability among those paths, and then standardize the process and give team members a map to show what should happen and when.

Finding creative legal solutions to client problems adds value. Making processes more efficient and less costly also helps to improve service quality. We will explore improving legal services processes in the next section. Before we get there, though, we should take a more detailed look at our map by breaking down each step in a process into one or more processes. When Anna sent emails, you probably had a mental image of Anna going through several steps. Each of the steps you imagined is a step in the process of "email." We could write those steps in a standard process study sheet, or make a list, as shown in Figure 2.10.2.

Figure 2.10.3, meanwhile, shows an example of an email process in Anna's termination agreement process map, but drawn as a separate process using the steps listed above. This is a map of what Anna might do for steps P2 and P16 from her termination agreement process

TABLE 2.10.1 *Process study sheet.*

Legal Process	Process: Term Agreement	Service: Legal Department	Observer: Sue Smith	Date/Time: 12/2, 9:15 a.m.
Step	Process Element		Time 1	Time 2
P1	Ask HR generalist for information			
P2	Back and forth emails for information			
P3	Contact equity plan administrator			
P4	Contact safety manager			
P5	Contact finance			
P6	Search for template			
P7	Begin modifying template			
P8	Determine if employee is age 40 or over			
P9	Determine if single or multiple terminations			
P10	Determine if employee identifies as male or female			
P11	Contact employee's supervisor			
P12	Store emails in online folder			
P13	Update draft agreement			
P14	Print and review draft agreement			
P15	Correct errors and revise agreement wording			
P16	Send out emails for additional facts			
P17	Update draft with email information			
P18	Email draft to HR for review			
P19	Update draft with changes from HR			
P20	Send final document to HR			
P21	Discuss agreement terms with employee's lawyer			
P22	Update document with changes if appropriate			
P23	Send signature copies to HR			

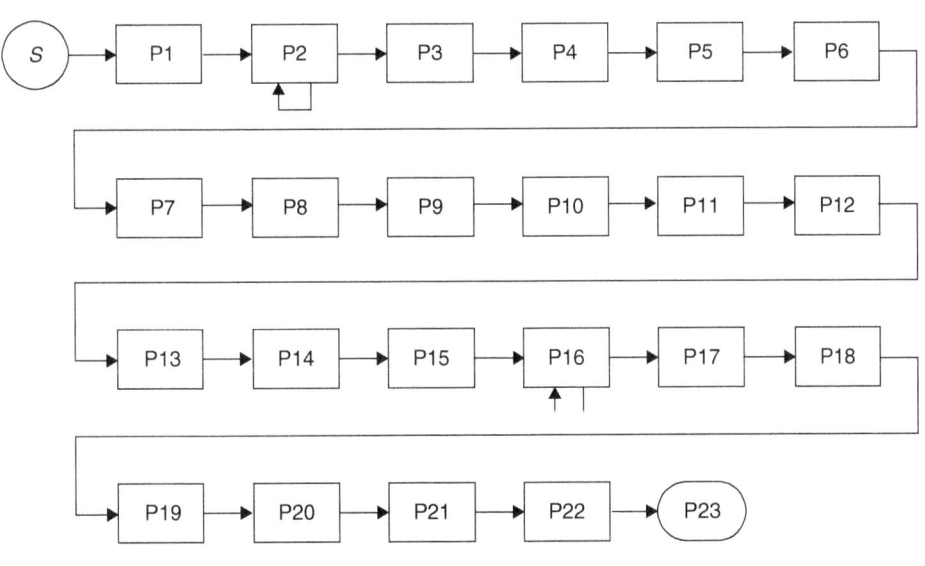

FIGURE 2.10.1 Anna's process.

Step	Process
P1	Boot computer
P2	Open email application
P3	Click new email icon
P4	Type email
P5	Type subject
P6	Select recipient
P7	If another recipient
P8	Select recipient
P9	Otherwise, click send email icon
P10	If another email, go back to new email icon step
P11	Otherwise, terminate email process

FIGURE 2.10.2 Chart of email steps.

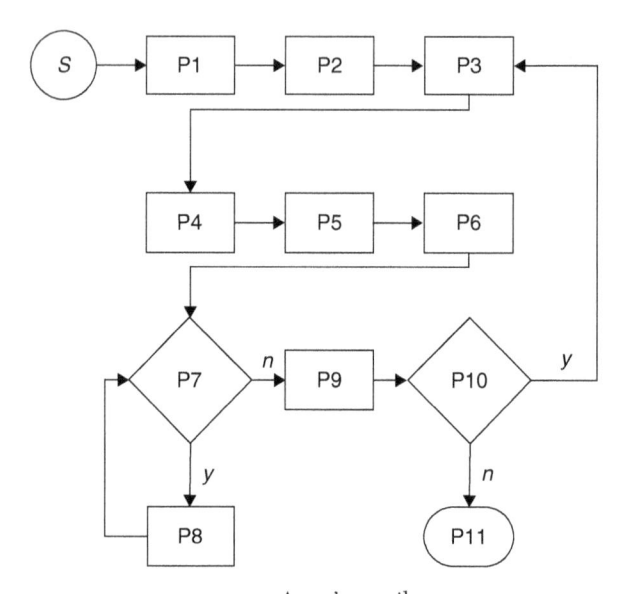

FIGURE 2.10.3 Anna's email process.

from Table 2.10.1 (P18, another email step, requires adding an attachment, a step not included in this process).

This is a very granular map for a legal process, but it shows how we can take the process map tool and use it to paint a detailed picture of what lawyers do to deliver legal services.

Let's get back to Anna's challenge. Anna follows a process to prepare each termination agreement. Although the facts change for each agreement, we've seen how to identify the steps she follows, put them in sequence, and create a process map for Anna to follow when preparing agreements. This is part of the standardization of the process. Our standard process study sheet (Table 2.10.1) and process map (Figure 2.10.1) are the first steps.

Lawyers often shudder when someone talks about standardizing a legal service process. They have a nightmare vision of a legal services production line where they perform a routine step, akin to the automobile assembly line workers in old movies who installed one wheel on each automobile as it came down the assembly line. Lawyers see standardization as robbing them of creativity, and they view creativity as something that sets them apart and defines their approach to solving client problems. But standardization doesn't inhibit creativity; it actually enables it. Clients want lawyers who can find creative solutions to their problems; they know that creativity adds value, and they will pay for that value. But clients also want lawyers who are very efficient when it comes to executing solutions. Inefficient execution costs a lot and does not add value. Clients do not want to pay for that kind of inefficiency. In the end, inefficiency robs lawyers of time they could spend putting their minds to work building creative solutions. Standardization of processes takes inefficiency and cost out of legal services, and frees up time for those more creative forms of work.

We will see later how a detailed process map can help us identify which steps in Anna's termination agreement process we can turn over to a computer. We will want to make sure that any process map we create includes enough detail to make it easy to find and remove waste from each process.

A Projects versus Processes

So far, we have discussed processes as though there is only one type. There are actually two major categories of processes in legal service delivery. The first category is *projects*. A project is any process that does not repeat, like a lawsuit. A lawyer might interject here to say that because lawsuits happen frequently, lawsuits do not qualify as projects. That's not quite accurate. In legal services, we think of each lawsuit as a separate, unique project. One may litigate many lawsuits, and they may very well all be of the same type, but each lawsuit is only litigated once. That makes each lawsuit a unique project.

The second category of processes doesn't have a name. These are the day-to-day processes that explain how we do all the things that get us through life. Unlike projects, these processes repeat. For example, Anna sends many emails each day. Each time she does, she invokes the email process.

At first, it may be difficult to understand which processes are projects and which aren't. Sometimes it will feel like a process should be a project, and sometimes it will feel like a process is so routine it should not be called a project. Think of it this way: All projects are processes, but not all processes are projects. Do not obsess over which processes are projects. The key lies in understanding how often you do something, and whether the effort to gain more control over a process exceeds the value of spending the time to get that control. We focus process improvement efforts on repeated processes. We leave project managers to handle processes that do not repeat.[1]

Let's get back to Anna. Last year, Anna's company had to reduce its workforce when a customer did not renew a contract. Anna worked with teams in HR, finance, operations, and several other areas to handle the termination of 60 employees. In addition to preparing 60 termination agreements, Anna and the team had to coordinate press releases, benefits packages, communications with all employees, and many other tasks.

The reduction in force was a project that included many processes. Anna did many things in addition to drafting termination agreements. That is, there were many other aspects of the project outside the termination process. Those other things, combined with the termination agreement drafting process that Anna repeated 60 times, comprised the reduction-in-force project. When you consider doing 60 termination agreements, you can see how efficiency benefits everyone.

---

[1] Professionals with the title "project manager" may lead both process improvement and project management activities. But, as we shall see in a moment, what we do to improve processes is different than what we do to manage projects.

Usually, separating processes from projects in legal services is not difficult. We did it in the previous paragraph. A lawsuit, a corporate acquisition or divestiture, any real estate transaction, an environmental clean-up; those are all projects. Within those projects are processes that lawyers repeat many times, sometimes within a project and sometimes across projects. Some of these processes within projects include drafting interrogatories, preparing new corporate bylaws, writing deeds, and drafting stock acquisition agreements. The facts will differ each time a lawyer iterates the process, but we can define the process that should be followed each time.

As with Anna's reduction-in-force project, legal projects are often very complicated and bring processes together in unique ways. We rely on project managers to keep all the tasks and processes happening at the right time and in the correct order. Lawyers typically act as project managers or as providers of legal services, but very few lawyers have training in project management, a complex discipline by itself. As a result, most legal services projects are not well managed and lawyers spend valuable time – and client money – muddling through project management.

Professional project managers can manage projects better and at lower cost. Because projects only happen once, project managers usually do not spend a lot of time improving the flow of tasks and processes within a specific project. The investment is not worth the return. Instead, the project manager uses a special set of tools to keep the project on track. Legal project managers talk about two types of project management: waterfall and agile. Legal project management is complex, requiring knowledge of change management and legal processes, as well as the methodologies of project management. But, it helps everyone involved in legal services to know the differences between the two types of project management.

Waterfall project management is the oldest of the two types and represents a traditional, linear approach. At the project's outset, the project manager and team spend significant time planning the project and each step. This style gets its name because each step must be completed before the project cascades to the next step, like water falling down stairs. It is most effective when the team has a lot of control over the project and does not expect many significant changes during implementation.

Agile project management, on the other hand, is very young and comes out of a lean-thinking approach to managing IT projects. Agile may have begun in IT, but it has spread far beyond and is now used for a wide variety of projects, including legal projects. Agile projects may last months or years, but the work is done in short bursts of fewer than 30 days. The goals and tasks get updated frequently to meet the project's needs. Agile project managers hold back work until the team is certain it will be needed. This avoids spending resources on work that isn't needed. The name comes from this flexible approach. Agile involves much less initial planning than waterfall management, and the team shifts quickly as the project refocuses resources on what needs to be done.

Legal project management helps knit together the many processes within a project. Think of Anna's reduction-in-force project. Anna's termination agreements had to come together with the work done by human resources on benefits packages, by operations staff on shifting responsibilities of departing employees to other employees, by communications staff who had to explain the reasons for the terminations, and by the work of several other teams. The project manager leads all of these disparate groups; she uses her tools to make sure the project is completed professionally, on time, and within budget.

B Workflow

Our goal is to improve the sequence of operations in a process that by definition repeats, and the coordination of processes that are part of delivering legal services to our client. We talk about this sequenced set of processes using the phrase *workflow*. A workflow describes the movement of inputs to outputs through many processes. Figure 2.10.4 is an example of how the workflow might look for termination agreements at Anna's company.

Although it sounds a bit New Age, the easiest way to describe workflow is the state an organization achieves when its processes work together fluidly, with minimal waste, to achieve the clients' goals on time. An organization that has achieved flow does not provide services early or late, it does not over- or under-produce, it minimizes transport and motion waste, eliminates defects, and uses employees and computers at their optimum skill levels. If this sounds like an organization you have never seen and cannot imagine, you have good reason to be skeptical. Waste-free workflow is a lean-thinking state that organizations want to achieve, yet never do. They keep trying, though, through a method of continuous improvement.

Even simple legal service providers have hundreds or thousands of processes. Those processes weave together in complex ways. As computers enter the fray, legal service providers feel the urge to rip out entire processes and replace them with computers. While that may ultimately be a good decision, starting with process mapping and process improvement gives the provider a better shot at making any software implementation successful. Once you know your processes and have removed significant amounts of waste, you can focus your technology efforts on improving the efficiency of value-added processes. If you skip process mapping and process improvement and go directly to installing complex computer systems, you will find you have merely automated the waste. Done correctly, your system will avoid waste, and cover value-added *and* non-value-added steps. These steps require training and maintenance that

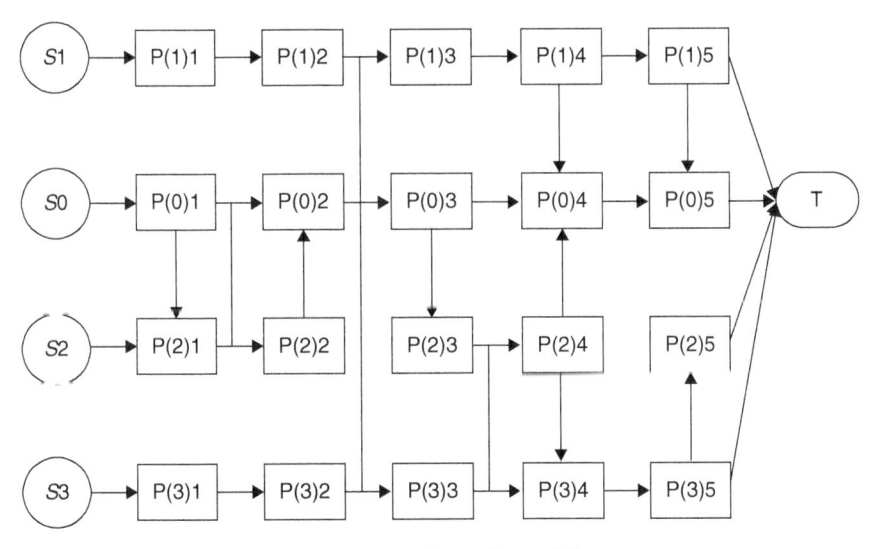

FIGURE 2.10.4 Example workflow.

will be difficult to change quickly, so don't rush to implement automation until you have everything the way you want it.

There are ways to eliminate, or at least automate, entire processes. For example, you can use predictive analytics to identify the reasons for lawsuits and use that information to change the process that results in lawsuits. Eliminating lawsuits means you eliminate litigation processes. If you can't eliminate a process (e.g., reviewing documents in discovery) you can consider whether to automate it (e.g., technology-assisted document review[2]). As we simplify workflows, we move closer to the lean-thinking ideal of perfection, a state in which processes do not include any waste; humans perform steps appropriate for their training, skill, and experience, and technology handles the rest.

II IMPROVING PROCESS IN LEGAL SERVICES

If a client asks Anna what to do to protect the company when terminating an employee, Anna might suggest asking the employee to sign a termination agreement. After Anna learns more about the employee being terminated and the circumstances of the termination, she might suggest including particular clauses in the termination agreement. Anna has focused on the skills lawyers learn in school, such as critical thinking.

To solve her client's problem, though, Anna must execute her idea. This is where she adds legal services to legal analysis. Neither Anna nor her client benefit from taking more time or adding more steps than are necessary to complete the agreement. Doing so would be wasteful of Anna's time and her client's money. When we first met Anna, she complained about the inefficiency of the termination agreement process. Anna can avoid some of those problems by using process improvement.

Process improvement is part of a broader area called *operational excellence*. Corporations use operational excellence to accomplish many things, such as increasing quality, productivity, and consistency. A manufacturer may use operational excellence to reduce the time and cost of producing products, a retailer can use it to improve store operations, and a financial services company can use it to decrease the time and effort of answering customer questions (or even find ways to stop the questions from arising). For lawyers, operational excellence means finding ways to use fewer resources (inputs) to achieve what the client wants (outputs), while reducing the time it takes to get there and improving the quality of the outcome. We will look briefly at Six Sigma and lean thinking, two methodologies lawyers use to improve processes.

A Six Sigma

Six Sigma, developed at Motorola in the 1980s, focuses on improving the quality of products and services. It started when Motorola decided it wanted to significantly reduce the number of defective products made during manufacturing, and so created a methodology built on various statistical techniques for monitoring and measuring improvement. The name *Six Sigma* comes from a statistical measure: *sigma* refers to standard deviation, which measures the dispersion of measurements around their mean. For example, a bell curve with a broad bell shape shows a large dispersion of scores and has a high standard deviation. A bell curve

---

[2] For more discussion of technology-assisted review (TAR), *see* Tyerman and Shankar – The Core Concepts of E-Discovery, *infra*; and Matveeva – Predictive Coding in E-Discovery and The NexLP Story Engine, *infra*.

with a narrow bell shape shows a small dispersion of scores and has a low standard deviation. When a process reaches six sigma – that is, six standard deviations – that means that 99.99966% of all products or services are error-free. At that level, no more than 3.4 defects occur for every million iterations of a process.

Six Sigma works well when you have an opportunity to collect significant measurements about a task or process. Because it relies on statistical analysis, you get the most benefit from it if you can measure the task or process through many cycles. It also works well when your principal concern is measuring and improving quality in a task or process. However, because of the strong math orientation, the need for significant data, and the challenges of learning Six Sigma tools, many in the legal industry have turned their attention to lean thinking.

B Lean Thinking

Lean thinking, developed at the Toyota Motor Company in the 1940s, focuses on removing waste to improve processes and workflows. It builds on two pillars: continuous improvement and respect for humanity. By following lean principles and using lean tools, practitioners analyze a process, remove waste, and then measure improvements in the process. *Continuous improvement* refers to repeating this cycle again and again to maintain and improve efficiency.

The easiest way to think about waste is to think from a client's perspective. Ask this question: "If I were a client, would I pay my lawyer to do this task?" If the answer is "no," then you should find a way to eliminate or at least minimize the task in question. You can eliminate tasks by making improvements, and improvements come in infinite forms. The key is not in *how* you make the improvement, but rather the improvement's impact on waste and value. If the improvement reduces waste in a process, then it is a good improvement. If you are concerned about the cure costing more than the disease, then you need to refocus on waste. Develop an approach that quickly recovers the cost of the new way of doing things. Otherwise, your new approach is just another form of waste.

Computers can help us improve processes in many ways. Often, lawyers bring in expensive and complicated computer systems to improve efficiency, but instead of achieving the desired effect, the expensive and complicated system adds cost, complexity, and risk. In these situations, focusing on process improvement and selective automation are simpler steps with much better outcomes.

Waste in a process shows up as variability. If every time you run through a process the amount of time it takes varies significantly, the process probably has a lot of waste in it. Lean thinkers have identified at least eight categories of waste. We will go over these eight categories of waste, and look at some examples in legal processes.

Lean thinkers use a short acronym to remember the eight wastes: "TIM WOODS." If you hear a lean thinker ask if you have seen TIM WOODS, they are asking whether you have seen one or more of the following types of waste in a process:

- **Transport:** Time spent moving things around. When we carry a document from one office to another, email a document to another person, or retrieve and return files, we are performing transport waste.
- **Inventory:** Storing more of something than is needed to meet customer demand. Many law firms run into this problem when they have too many associates or other

lawyers for a given volume of work from clients. Lawyers with too little to do are a form of excess inventory waste.
- **Motion:** Moving around more than necessary. If you have to twist around at your desk to get files, reach your computer, answer the phone, or walk across the hall to retrieve other materials, you are performing motion waste.
- **Waiting:** You are ready to move to the next step, but you do not have everything you need so you have to wait until everything arrives. When you are waiting for information from a client, from opposing counsel, from a court acting on a motion, or just from a co-worker, you are performing waiting waste.
- **Over-production:** You do more of something than is needed to meet the client's needs. If you take more depositions than are needed, prepare a complex contract when a simple one would do, or add unnecessary clauses to a contract, you are performing over-production waste.
- **Over-processing:** You work something more than is necessary to meet the needs of the client. When a client talks about getting a Cadillac when all they needed was a Chevrolet, that's over-processing waste. If you conduct excessive due diligence, or research remote legal theories when the matter is low risk, you are performing over-processing waste.
- **Defects:** Changing something because of a mistake, an omission, or some other quality or service error problem. When you read a brief to fix typos or rewrite what someone else wrote, you are performing defect waste.
- **Skills:** When someone does tasks well below their skill or experience level, or does tasks for which they are inadequately trained. When you have a partner do work an associate or paralegal could do, ask an associate to draft a document that she has never been trained to draft, or have lawyers do project management, you are[3] adding skill waste.

As you can see from these examples, legal service processes are filled with waste. One way to visualize the amount of waste in a process is to draw a process stick (Figure 2.10.5). This

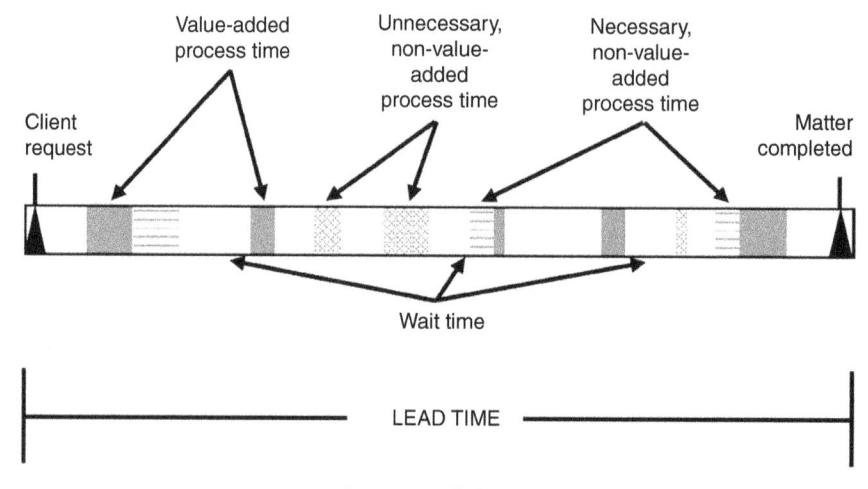

FIGURE 2.10.5 Process stick for Anna's activities.[3]

---

[3] *See, e.g.,* Karen Martin and Mike Osterling, *Value Stream Mapping* (New York, NY: McGraw Hill Education, 2014), 71.

process stick should show four things: (1) the total time to complete a process, called "lead time"; (2) the portion of time spent on value-added activities (necessary and value-adding process time), called "process time"; (3) the portion of time spent on necessary, non-value-added processing time; and (4) the portion of time spent on unnecessary, non-value-added processing time.

Using metrics like this can provide a quantitative feel for the status of our process. There are many ways to measure process performance. We will look at four ways commonly used in lean thinking.

First, we can measure *lead time*. This is the total elapsed time for the process (often called "cycle time"). For Anna's termination agreement process, the lead time starts when she is asked to prepare a termination agreement, and it ends when she delivers the final agreement to human resources for the employee to sign.

Second, we can measure *process time*. Process time is the amount of the total lead time when tasks are being done that add value. When a process has not been improved, process time usually is very small compared to lead time.

Third, we can construct an *activity ratio*. An activity ratio is the total process time divided by the total lead time. Ratios can be helpful in many situations where raw numbers provide limited value. For example, the total process time for drafting an email might be 3 minutes, and the total process time for drafting (actually writing) a termination agreement might be 60 minutes. Comparing 3 minutes to 60 minutes does not tell us much, because the tasks are very different. But if the activity ratio for email drafting is 0.5 and the activity ratio for agreement writing is 0.2, we know Anna is more efficient at drafting emails than writing agreements.

Finally, we can measure percent-complete-and-accurate, often written as "%C&A." Each time Anna delivers an agreement to HR, she can record whether HR comes back to her with errors or requests for clarification. She can count the number of times HR came back to her, divide by the number of agreements she has delivered to them, subtract that number from 1, and multiply the result by 100. This number is the percentage of times she has delivered a complete and accurate agreement to human resources.

C Computers

As legal service providers improve processes by removing waste, they spark a new question: Should the remaining value-added steps be performed by humans or computers? Until recently, this was not a significant question; computers were not able to perform many of the tasks needed in the legal industry, and so legal services were labor-centric. Whether lawyers, paralegals, or staff performed the work, it was done by hand and computers were seldom used except as fancy typewriters. In recent years, the number of alternative ways to perform many tasks has increased. Computers offer a cost-effective, often higher-quality alternative to humans for some tasks in legal services. As computers and the software they use become more powerful, the need to understand and manipulate processes increases. To understand this relationship, we will go back to process maps.

Think of process maps as flowcharts. Flowcharts are already used in computer programming, so this provides a natural link between process improvement and computers. As we map a legal process, we "modularize" it. Each step in the process (each box on the flowchart) becomes a module with its own process. We can look at each module and ask whether it could be performed better by a computer or a human. By mapping, we visualize the structure of a process in order to find which tasks can migrate from human to computer.

This relationship is easy to see if we go back to Anna and her termination agreement assignment (Table 2.10.1). The second step in Anna's process, P2, involves Anna going back and forth with HR to gather information about the employee. In steps P8, P9, P10, and P16 she gathers more information. In step P7, Anna begins modifying her template agreement to cover the specific facts involving the employee being terminated. She updates the agreement in step P13 and again in steps P17 and P19.

We can and should look at all these steps and ask whether computers could automate some or even all of what Anna does. For example, using software that focuses on rules-based functions, complex reasoning, and document logic, we could replace Anna's emails with a system that gathers the information for Anna. When the company wants to terminate an employee, the human resources person logs on to the system and completes an interactive questionnaire. Throughout the process (similar to tax return completion software), the user enters information in response to questions and the software takes the user to the next appropriate question, depending on the response.

If the user does not have the answer to one or more questions, she can log off the system, gather the information, and go back on the system when she is ready. Anna is removed from gathering the information and, as the user learns what information the software needs – which could be signaled in advance by using a checklist – the user becomes more proficient at having the information available to answer the questions. The process of getting information to draft the termination agreement becomes more efficient.

Once the software has gathered all the information, it can provide that information to another software program that uses templates to create draft documents. Anna prepares the template using her form termination agreement. She leaves coded blanks where she needs information specific to each employee. She can also give the template options, such as language specific to each state, a provision to include whether the employee has stock grants, or additional language if the employee is over age 40. The software uses the information supplied by HR to complete the template, sends an email to Anna, and Anna opens the document to look at a draft based on her template with the added information highlighted.

Combining these programs streamlines Anna's process. Anna spends less time drafting the document and more of her time focusing on specific questions. We didn't use software to replace the entire process, but we did use software to replace many steps. Software could easily replace other similar steps in other processes as well. In fact, it shouldn't be hard to imagine HR opening a software package, checking a "termination" box and entering an employee's name. Rather than asking a person to complete the questionnaire, the software goes directly to the HR information system and queries it for the necessary information. By looking for iterative improvements and implementing each when appropriate, Anna's company would be engaging in continuous improvement.

No amount of process improvement will elevate humans to machine performance levels. We cannot teach a person to search for words in text as quickly or as accurately as a computer. Computers may outperform humans, but we do not always make that substitution. Sometimes this is cost-related; a computer process that costs ten times what it costs to use humans, with only marginal quality improvements, would not make sense unless we could use the computer process enough times to recover the cost. Other times, we do not make the substitution because we lack an understanding of the best ways to improve our processes.

III CONCLUSION

Although times are changing, the legal profession still delivers most legal services using a labor-centric model that does not focus on process. The recent introduction of a process-driven approach, through project management and operational excellence methodologies such as Six Sigma and lean thinking, is changing how lawyers think about what they do. The first step is understanding the processes you use today. Once you have an understanding of those processes by using tools such as standard process study sheets and process mapping, you can look for opportunities to improve processes. Six Sigma and lean thinking offer ways to focus on improving quality and taking waste out of processes. Project managers and tools can help smooth workflow. Computers also play an important role, offering ways to replace some steps in processes, further increasing the efficiency, cost effectiveness, and quality of legal service delivery processes.

2.11

Gamification of Work and Feedback Systems

Stephanie Kimbro

I INTRODUCTION

Gamification refers to the use of game mechanics merged with behavioral analytics in a non-game setting.[1] Gamification is used to improve production and performance in the workplace by engaging the user to behave in a way that is aligned with the goals of the business. Gamification occurs when a process, such as entering billable hours into the firm's software or filling out an online client intake form, is mixed with game elements in such a way that firm members are motivated to complete tasks in a more desirable way. Businesses have used gamification strategies, with differing levels of sophistication, on issues including customer relationship management, training, market research, business intelligence, and education. Other professions, many in health care, are now also turning to gamification to increase engagement in a number of workplace processes for both their staff, and the clients they serve.

Several years ago, gamification made its way into the workflow of companies. A report by Gartner Inc., an international IT research and advisory company, predicted 25% of workplace processes would be redesigned to include some form of gamification.[2] The market for gamification was expected to grow to over $2.8 billion by 2016, and continues to grow at present.[3] In the workplace, the number of employees who are so-called "digital natives" is increasing. *Digital natives* are accustomed to receiving real-time feedback and communicating online, and they also prefer more engaging methods of communication, many of which incorporate game mechanics.

But the ascendancy of digital natives has not occurred in a vacuum. The use of gamification has increased because the use of technology has increased. More of our workplace productivity has become automated; human and technology interaction have become more commonplace, and workers now spend more time communicating online via technology

---

[1] There are many definitions of gamification, and some controversy over the term as it relates to games. This chapter does not enter this debate, and will use the definition most useful in this context. For a definition of gamification, *see* Sebastian Deterding, Dan Dixon, Rilla Khaled, and Lennart E. Nacke, "Gamification: Toward a Definition," in *CHI 2011 Gamification Workshop Proceedings* (2011), available at: http://gamification-research.org/wp-content/uploads/2011/04/CHI_2011_Gamification_Workshop.pdf. The term gamification is sometimes considered a buzzword, but empirical data continue to show positive results from strategic gamification methods, *see* Gabe Zichermann, "Gamification: From Buzzword to Strategic Imperative," *Wall Street Journal*, May 15, 2013, available at: http://deloitte.wsj.com/cio/2013/05/15/gamification-from-buzzword-to-strategic-imperative.

[2] Brian Burke, "Gartner Says By 2015, More Than 50 Percent of Organizations That Manage Innovation Processes Will Gamify Those Processes," *Gartner, Inc.*, April 12, 2011, available at: www.gartner.com/newsroom/id/1629214.

[3] "Gartner Reveals Top Predictions for IT Organizations and Users for 2013 and Beyond," *Gartner, Inc.*, October 24, 2012, available at: www.gartner.com/newsroom/id/2211115.

than they do in meetings and working with people face-to-face. This creates a work environment that is less human-centered, which can make employees disengage from their work and feel no psychological connection to their company. This makes it a challenge to build a company culture that fosters collaboration and human communication and interaction, all of which are factors essential to innovation.

Law firms are not immune to this sea change in the workplace environment, and they face the same challenges to their growth and success. As law firms evolve, they need to foster a positive organizational culture that supports the growth and morale of their associates. Without injecting challenges into the daily operations of a law firm, it is difficult to create and maintain the right balance of work and socialization that motivates employees to continue to grow as individuals and to seek out innovation in their work for the benefit of the law firm and its clients. When corporations focus on building this form of workplace culture, they often focus on team-building corporate events. Law firms often attempt the same kind of culture building, with law firm charity events, nights at a sporting event, or annual parties. These efforts may all help, but what really motivates and brings out the best in people is when they feel they are a part of a firm's culture, and this type of feeling simply cannot be created by a single event or a one-time incentive. Motivation needs to be integrated into the daily workflow of a law firm's business. This is where gamification can have an impact.

Law firms face problems with employee motivation and with building a law firm culture that fosters innovation. The law firm organizational culture is largely built upon the reputation of the law firm with its clients and the public. New associates already know the "personality" of each different law firm: how many billable hours a week it takes to survive on the partnership track; which firms are family-friendly; and which firms provide flexible hours and time away from the office. Associates may take pride in working for a firm with a more prestigious "personality," but by itself this provides little to ensure the growth of the law firm in the long run. This is especially the case now, as a large population of lawyers in partnership and mentorship positions move steadily toward retirement. Most law firms lack innovative thinking and tend to follow the traditional law firm hierarchy in terms of training, mentorship, and production of work. With the older population of lawyers about to retire, many law firms are about to lose not only mentors for younger lawyers, but the traditions and culture of the firm as well. Clinging to these traditional organizational cultures and relying on annual events and one-time, pay-based incentives is not a sustainable long-term strategy for the growth of a law firm, especially as the legal marketplace continues to change rapidly amid increasing competition for top associates.

New law firm associates are sometimes not even interested in the traditional partnership track, so existing pay-based work incentives lose appeal. As these associates take up a greater share of a firm's workforce, the partners who have worked at a firm since they graduated law school pose a different problem: many of them are not open to learning new technologies, despite evidence that new technology tools can increase a firm's efficiency. Law firms have various cultural and social issues to address in order to maintain growth. Gamification can benefit these firms by helping to create a coherent firm culture and to increase cooperation, mentorship, and collaboration among law firm members.

Law firms should care about increasing engagement through gamification because their employees increasingly expect to interact with technology at work in the same way that they interact with it at home with their friends and family. When people communicate online in social applications, the user interface and user design and experience (UI and UX) of the application facilitates the interaction to make it more enjoyable. Law firm gamification systems need to have the same level of intuitive design in order for firm employees to be similarly engaged at work. In addition, the new generation of law firm employees have grown up playing games and working with other gamified technology applications. These young firm members already communicate and collaborate using interfaces with game mechanics, and there is already evidence of the potential of these systems.[4] Furthermore, millennials are not the only generation used to gaming: the average age of a game player is 31, significantly older than most new law firm associates.[5] Law firms that can adapt to these new realities will succeed at engaging and retaining talent in the long run.

Though demographics are slowly changing, in many firms there still exists a wide generation gap between the firm's partners and its associates. Games can be used not only to motivate desired behaviors for increased productivity, but may also help bridge the generational gap by incorporating friendly competition, positive peer pressure, and an added measure of accountability. If implemented at all levels of a firm, gamification can be used to foster collaboration among the disparate generations and help younger associates stay engaged.

Even if these reasons are not enough to convince law firms to explore gamification for the benefit of increasing productivity and retention of law firm associates, another reality may ultimately compel them: client bases are also changing with the times. Law firms cannot ignore the growing demand for access to legal services online, and even if a firm works primarily with corporate and business clients or in-house counsel and company general counsel (GC), these clients are also looking for ways to use technology to make legal services more cost-effective, and to find ways to unbundle legal services with alternative fee arrangements (AFAs). Elements of gamification can be added to processes that help a firm deliver legal services to different types of clients in whatever way those clients prefer. Quite simply, gamification can maintain or strengthen a firm's competitive edge.

This chapter will look at the ways companies are using gamification, and how these techniques can be adopted by law firms. Methods of gamification will necessarily differ based on the make-up of the law firm and its goals for increasing engagement. For that reason, this chapter will not provide a complete gamification model for a law firm. Instead, it will provide the basics for understanding how gamification can be applied to a law firm, and provide some sample applications and a basic guide for moving forward with gamification. Some of the objectives of gamification in law firms might include:

- increased associate retention rates;
- efficient and effective training of new technologies and processes, including methods to improve associate recording of billable hours;
- human resources productivity, such as onboarding new associates, training new hires, collecting associate reviews, etc.;
- increased communication between members of the firm;
- encouragement of inter-generational mentorship;
- increased participation in pro bono activities;
- training and education on use of firm resources; and

[4] Lawyers and law students have been learning the law and improving their courtroom and procedural skills using games for over ten years, *see, e.g.,* TransMedia's *Objection!*, www.objection.com/company.html; and LawDojo, www.lawschooldojo.com, designed to help law students learn better.

[5] *See* Entertainment Software Association (ESA), "2014 Sales, Demographic, and Usage Data: Essential Facts About the Computer and Video Game Industry," 2014, available at: www.theesa.com/wp-content/uploads/2014/10/ESA_EF_2014.pdf.

- encouragement for individual law firm members to innovate for the benefit of the firm.

II BACKGROUND ON GAMIFICATION: THE SCIENCE BEFORE THE ART

In order to understand how gamification works, one must first look at the psychology behind the process. There are multiple different perspectives on gamification, with a range of topics being explored: entrepreneurs and innovators looking at forms of persuasive technology; marketing companies focused on customer loyalty and retention; corporations wanting to train and incentivize employees; psychologists and neurologists interested in the effects on users; and non-profit organizations creating "games for change" or meaningful play. From this research, this chapter's author has compiled the key points from each of these perspectives, and how they might be useful for law firms seeking to implement gamification techniques into their existing systems. At the time of this writing, several industries have implemented forms of gamification into their work processes. Their efforts and results provide clear evidence of, and in several cases actual scientific studies in support of, the validity of gamification. The next step is to use these findings to determine how best to apply gamification to law firms and the legal profession.

Gamification is different than playing a game, even a "serious" game designed to educate the player. Gamification does, however, still have similar elements of fun and motivation that can provoke a psychological reaction that leads to a desired behavior change. One of the reasons gamification can be so successful in the workplace is that many processes in companies are streamlined for efficiency and focused on final production. In a law firm, these processes include the focus on the billable hour, or the use of technology to complete legal work. The focus on production often removes self-motivation for the people involved in that process, but gamifying the process can add back the intrinsic motivation otherwise lost. Accordingly, in order to design gamification for law firms, it is necessary to first identify the intrinsic and extrinsic motivations related to the tasks to be gamified. Once sources of motivation are identified, the firm can turn to which business functions it wants to gamify.[6]

A Intrinsic Motivation

Jane McGonigal, game designer and author of *Reality is Broken: Why Games Make Us Better and How They Can Change the World*, identifies four essential human cravings that game designers attempt to address when they build a game. If all four of these cravings are satisfied, people become more engaged and can actually have fun accomplishing work. These four cravings are: (1) satisfying work; (2) the hope or experience of achieving success; (3) connecting socially; and (4) meaningful work that allows us to be a part of something larger than ourselves.[7] When there is a way to address each of these cravings in the workflow of the business day, the employee has increased motivation to engage in the process and do the work on a level that encourages them to fulfill their maximum potential.

---

[6] For a general discussion of design methodology applied to law, *see* Hagan – Introduction to Design Thinking for Law, *infra*.

[7] Jane McGonigal, *Reality is Broken: Why Games Make Us Better and How They Can Change the World* (London: Penguin, 2011), 49.

Another way of looking at motivational behavior has been identified by behavioral neuroscientist Dr. Amy Jo Kim, who works with companies on gamification.[8] She identifies several behaviors that may be used to create intrinsic motivation. These include: (1) self-expression, or the desire to show off creativity; (2) competition, both with others and to improve oneself through mastery; (3) exploration, which can encompass content, tools, people, and worlds, as long as a player is accumulating access and knowledge to new stimuli; and (4) collaboration, which includes socialization and being a part of a team or collective.

There is a lot of overlap between Dr. Kim's elements of motivation for gamification and those discussed by McGonigal. These various elements reflect the fact that there are different forms of intrinsic motivation.[9] For some lawyers, learning something new while completing work is intrinsic motivation for completing the work product. For others, pure rewards and reputation-based motivation, such as leaderboards or badges, may not be enough. There needs to be connection to a personal goal and for some useful, meaningful benefit as a reward. How does this translate to the law firm work environment and the expectations of associates and law firm members? What kinds of players should gamification systems be designed for?

B *Player Types*

Different types of motivation appeal to different types of people. The game industry has known this for a long time, and has identified four major player personalities, of which a single player may actually embody more than one. High-budget video games are often successful when they incorporate the needs of each personality type into a single game. Understanding these four types of gamer personalities will reveal which gamification mechanics will work best to motivate the greatest number of firm members.

The Bartle Test of Gamer Psychology identifies four types of gamers: achievers, explorers, socializers, and killers. Professor and game designer Dr. Richard Bartle, one of the earliest developers of massively multiplayer online games (MMOs), defined these types of players and their needs in 1996, while working on the design of one of the earliest MMOs:[10]

- **Achievers:** Value achievement, self-expression, the desire to show creativity, and the hope or experience of achieving success.
- **Explorers**: Value exploration and finding meaningful work that allows them to be part of something larger than themselves.
- **Socializers**: Value socialization, connecting and collaborating with others.
- **Killers**: Value competition and satisfying work.

Most players will embody more than one of the four personalities, and often embody elements of all four. If one matches these four types with the four descriptions of intrinsic

---

[8] *See* Amy Jo Kim, "Tapping the Trinity of Intrinsic Motivation," personal web page, March 12, 2014, available at: http://amyjokim.com/blog/2014/03/12/tapping-the-trinity-of-instrinsic-motivation.

[9] *See generally*, Daniel Pink, *Drive: The Surprising Truth About What Motivates Us* (New York, NY: Riverhead Books, 2011).

[10] *See* Richard Bartle, "Hearts, Clubs, Diamonds, Spades: Players Who Suit Muds," 1996, available at: http://mud.co.uk/richard/hcds.htm. This article provides a detailed taxonomy of gamer types and how game mechanics can be developed to appeal to each, and how the different types interact with each other in a game environment. *See also* Doug Palmer, Steve Lunceford, and Aaron J. Patton, "The Engagement Economy: How Gamification Is Reshaping Businesses," Deloitte University Press, July 1, 2012, available at: http://dupress.com/articles/the-engagement-economy-how-gamification-is-reshaping-businesses.

motivation described by McGonigal and Kim, one can clearly see a valuable framework for looking at how to implement a successful gamification project.

C The Fun of Mastery

Learning is fun because we acquire new skills or mastery of old skills. Because the desire for mastery is self-motivated, it results in a psychological phenomenon called *flow*. Flow is "the satisfying, exhilarating feeling of creative accomplishment and heightened functioning."[11] Flow occurs when something is done for fun rather than for money, status, or obligation. In order to experience that rewarding feeling that comes with mastery, the puzzle solved or the information acquired must have been challenging enough in the first place to provide the sense of accomplishment and pride in the resulting mastery. If the game mechanics used in a gamification system are too simple, or not connected to the learning process – such as clicking on X number of buttons, or going to Y number of websites, or giving ratings on Z number of posts – they will not be enough to motivate behavior and may in fact deter the use of the system because of the lack of a challenge within the game mechanic.

When the goal of the gamification system is clear, then the addition of rules into the game will direct the user to the end goal. Rules are added to create the necessary challenge that will lead to the feeling of mastery over the goal. Well-structured goals are set out so that each time the user comes back to the system, their progress is noted and the goal is presented again. Setting up the user for small feats of mastery by breaking down the overall goal into multiple difficulty levels and mini-goals serves two purposes: (1) it moves the user further toward the complete overall goal; and (2) it provides more moments of mastery that motivate the user to continue.

The goals themselves need not only be challenging, but also differ in degree of difficulty so that the user masters one set of skills while still feeling motivated toward the next goal because they see that the next goal is going to challenge them yet further. Simply repeating the same level of mastery over and over will not encourage the user to continue because they will not feel the flow described above. Likewise, the challenges set out in the game mechanics need to include failure. This enables the user to learn from their mistakes, but also motivates them to try again, which can increase the effect of flow when they finally achieve mastery. Winning on your first try every time you set out to achieve something is not fun, and will not work as a form of gamification. Rather, the quality and the quantity of challenges both need to increase. For example, if a challenge involves generating X number of billable hours in Y number of weeks, merely increasing the goal of X for the next challenge level is not really a different challenge. That particular skill has already been learned – how to increase X. Adding another skill to this task will work better: instead of only generating X number of billable hours in Y number of weeks, one may have to also complete Z hours of CLE training, or Z hours of pro bono work, or train a colleague in the use of a feature on the platform. In using gamification to train law firm members on the use of a technology platform, a goal might also be that they use a different feature of the technology each time. Rather than focusing on how many hours are logged in a single task, the challenge needs to progress in order to provide opportunities for new mastery.

---

[11] Mihaly Csikszentmihalyi, *Flow: The Psychology of Optimal Experience* (New York, NY: Harper, 2008).

D Juicy Feedback

Even though the mastery of a new skill provides the desired flow sensations, the cues that the user receives when he or she masters something need to be adequate to convey the accomplishment of the goal. Game designers must provide feedback on accomplishments, which can include loud celebratory noises, slow-motion victory cut-scenes, dramatic level-up notifications, etc. This is called *juicy feedback*, and it serves the purpose of letting the player experience the sense of flow that comes from mastery. While this type of display might not be appropriate in some forms of gamification, the idea of providing frequent acknowledgments of both success and failure on the road to progress is important for keeping the user engaged. Where rewards are associated with the accomplishment of business objectives, it is best that feedback is as close to real-time as possible. If the reward system comprises a leaderboard or other scoring system where members of the firm are competing, then the feedback needs to be kept current to ensure fair score-keeping and more immediate acknowledgments and rewards for the player.

E Clear Goals

The lawyer engaged in the gamification task needs to see that task completion is increasing their abilities, that they are gaining useful skills, and that they are not only achieving rewards but also that those rewards are a result of their mastery of the desired skills. A leaderboard or other rankings system only works if the users actually care enough about getting recognition for their accomplishments from the other lawyers in the firm. To this end, allowing lawyers in a firm to brainstorm the ultimate rewards or the collective goals of the gamified system ensures that the meaning in those forms of reward acknowledgment will have value for the lawyers.

Creating a storyline around the entire gamification process might help create connection between the users' actions, the game's rewards, and the end goal. Visual aids make a huge difference in helping to facilitate a story. Filling up bar graphics or displaying badges without a common graphical theme or storyline is not enough to maintain user interest. This is why successful video games grab our interest by being so abstract and separate from our reality. If there is a common theme, within a visual context, and all of the users' actions and rewards are wrapped up in that theme, then it will lead them more naturally to their end goal.

F Meaning in the Goal

In order for gamification to work for lawyers, the design should focus on the meaning in the process. While flashy game mechanics may attract users' attention at first, in a vacuum these tactics are too shallow to keep players engaged, and the gamified system would not have the desired long-term effect and would not produce a return on the firm's investment. A game has to establish meaning behind the goals it sets for its users.

An example of instilling meaning into the goal set by gamification can be seen in Nike's Nike+ app.[12] The app encourages individuals to set and accomplish fitness goals, and by using game mechanics that include a social networking aspect it challenges the user to exercise and to join in with friends in setting and accomplishing goals. The meaning of this goal is that the user wants to live a healthier lifestyle and improve their health. Without this underlying

---

[12] www.nike.com/us/en_us/c/nike-plus.

personal meaning behind the goals the user sets in the application, it is unlikely that the app would be so popular and effective.

For law firms, the meaning behind a goal is often tied to learning. Learning might be in the form of increasing knowledge of a specific practice area through legal research or discovery of new case law, or it might be the acquisition of creative thinking and analytical skills involved in drafting a plea and thinking through new approaches to a legal outcome for a client. Tapping into a lawyer's passion for different parts of the legal process, and making the gamification feed into a lawyer's personal passion or the collective goals for the firm, will result in meaning for firm members. For example, a lawyer might be passionate about volunteering on pro bono cases for the firm or collaborating with other associates to increase the firm's overall pro bono hours. By creating a system that pools these associates' work into a common output that encourages and produces this valuable pro bono work, a single associate can find positive, prosocial meaning. He or she may not be able to complete a legal project for a pro bono client alone, but contributing to a system where other associates are also volunteering can feed his or her passion for the work, and also create a sense of community and collaboration around that goal.

Depending on a firm's culture, a common goal might be focused on the number of hours billed per week, the number of new clients retained by the firm, or the number of cases closed or cases won. Many of these goals depend on the nature of the work that the firm produces. For example, a firm that handles patent filings might be able to attribute a point and reward system to the number of patents filed and successfully obtained by each associate, but this type of point system would not work where the speed and efficiency of the work product, such as complex litigation, is not within an associate's control, or where it's not necessarily in the client's best interest to focus on speed over the end result of winning the case favorably for the client. Developing the meaning for a game may thus be the most difficult process for law firms considering gamification.

G Let Them Play

Similar to how a gamification system can fail if it lacks meaning in its goals, gamification can also fail when the method feels imposed on the user. A method's design needs to give the user a sense of autonomy so that they feel like they have the ability to play with the system, explore it, learn with it, and obtain skills their own way without a quota or expectation that must be met. Intrinsic motivation, as discussed above, is of paramount importance. Thus, creating a sense of autonomy for users is critical to a gamification method's success.

If a gamification activity is monitored by a supervisor, or includes quotas that will be reflected in an associate's annual review, this can remove a user's feeling of autonomy over the process. Such oversight of a system cannot achieve the desired effect of teaching a user or increasing productivity if the user feels burdened by the system. There are ways to provide firm members with the kind of autonomy that will encourage use of the system, while still creating common goals within the system. An effective system will give users free rein to be creative in choosing how they accomplish whatever goals their firm has set. This will play out differently depending on what the goal is. For example, if the goal is for law firm associates to complete X hours of technology training, it's a good idea to provide associates with choices of how to complete that training: watching a video that can be started and stopped and watched from anywhere; listening to a podcast; attending a related event or continuing legal education (CLE); attending a computer science course at a local college; working with a hands-on mentor, etc. The goal will be accomplished, but the associate has the freedom to choose *how* it is accomplished. A key component of a method that effectively induces autonomy is that when an associate must complete a worksheet or quiz about their understanding of the technology, the system asks for more than just a pass-or-fail indication. A system should provide more detailed feedback, and give associates personalized information that they can use to improve. Areas of improvement may include an assessment of how far they are from completing a goal, or other areas in which they may need further training. Similarly, positive feedback should be more than just a congratulations; the system needs to give empowering feedback that will entice users toward the next goal by analyzing how their choice for accomplishing the task actually played out. This sense of autonomy over the learning process and final mastery of a skill is key to making gamification work successfully.

H Watching Out for Social Contexts

Gamification may not work for some law firm goals. For example, many lawyers who volunteer their time to provide pro bono legal services are motivated by a desire to help and to serve the public. Thus, trying to encourage lawyers in a firm to increase volunteer hours by gamifying the process may backfire if set up incorrectly. The reward for pro bono work is already in place: the feeling the individual receives from assisting those who need legal services. Therefore, there needs to be a different sort of challenge associated with pro bono work that might encourage more lawyers to increase their hours of pro bono work, or the way that they deliver those services. One way to do this might be to create a reward system around the use of a new technology tool to work with pro bono clients, such as the use of a document automation and assembly program.[13] This might motivate lawyers to use the gamification system in order to learn how to use a beneficial technology tool, while also maintaining the original meaning behind the goal of helping pro bono clients. The reward would then be acknowledgment not of the pro bono service itself, but of the completion of new training skills that improve workflow.

III BEYOND SCORES, BADGES, AND LEADERBOARDS

Typical gamification involves rewarding the user with points as a way to encourage them to complete a specific behavior. The more the user does the desired behavior, the more points they earn. Points serve as a form of feedback on the behavior, as well as a reward. Badges are a frequent next step. A badge is awarded every time a user amasses a set amount of points. These badges serve as goals for the user to achieve within the game. Leaderboards are another very common gaming tool. A leaderboard can showcase a user's progress against other users, creating a form of competition.

A basic example of how these tools work in a game can be found in the application Foursquare. The app rewards users with points for checking into locations on the app. Players are awarded points for check-ins, are rewarded with badges for a certain number of check-ins, and then are ranked with other visitors checking into those same sites. However, though the number of Foursquare profiles has increased over the past few years, the number of check-ins has actually decreased.[14] This is likely because there is not enough re-

---

[13] For more on document automation and assembly, *see* Lauritsen – Document Automation, *supra*.

[14] *See* Will Francis, "Foursquare's Relaunch Has Only Temporarily Recaptured the Public," *Guardian*, August 18, 2014, available at: www.theguardian.com/media-network/media-network-blog/2014/aug/18/foursquare-relaunch-mobile-app-advertising.

engagement and feedback looping built into the application. This form of gamification triggers initial involvement, but can't sustain itself because there is a lack of motivation. This lack of motivation comes from a dearth of new challenges and *feedback loops*.

Why is a feedback loop more important than separate game elements like point systems, badge rewards, and leaderboards? A system with multiple feedback loops must include what is called a *core loop*, centered around the primary goal of the system. An effective system will also include mini-loops and nested loops within other goals, and these provide opportunities for feedback on different levels of mastery. The core loop, though, is what entices the user to continue to use the system, because the feedback continues to move them toward the next challenge and greater goals.[15] The most popular free-to-play games make use of this concept in order to increase retention. Individuals might participate in a basic challenge for the purpose of moving up on a leaderboard or acquiring high scores and badges, but without a core loop this will not motivate them for long.

There are several companies that provide easy-to-implement gamification solutions.[16] Many of these companies offer turnkey solutions to apply gamification to the workplace environment, but turnkey solutions will not work for law firms. Some of these solutions do include features that could be added to existing systems, but again the focus for gamification needs to be on setting goals, creating mastery, and ensuring autonomy. This kind of system design has to involve user-centric design, and not simply an application of generic gimmicks to existing processes. The personality and background of users is vital to the success or failure of game mechanics, so the use of generic solutions designed for the average employee at the average company will not work when used by lawyers working in firms that each have their own unique culture. In addition, it's common knowledge that most lawyers are "Type A" personalities, which operate with different mechanisms of internal motivation.[17]

Some law firms have attempted to implement gamification with employees only for it to backfire. These companies used gamification to simply highlight the top performers in the law firm, which created a hostile work environment that pitted employees against each other. While the intent was to foster a sense of healthy competition to increase productivity, what happened instead was panic: Employees focused on their ranking on the leaderboard, fearing layoff for whoever ended up at the bottom of the list. These systems often feel like a form of hyper-monitoring of employee productivity, which can make a workplace uncomfortable and competitive, instead of collaborative and productive. In this vein, the practice of rewarding badges for daily activity can feel demeaning to employees who would rather take personal pride in doing their work and focusing on the quality of the end product, and not focus on receiving a cute digital badge. This friction between intrinsic motivation and rewards of dubious usefulness is even more acute for lawyers, who often already feel a very high intrinsic motivation to do their work. A better system would look like this: Imagine a law firm that provides corporate law services, or that works with clients in industries that require clients to maintain compliance with federal and state regulatory requirements. Imagine this firm uses a gamification platform that assists the firm's clients in obtaining and maintaining regular compliance. The platform's data could be monitored by the law firm, and advice and preemptory guidance could be given based on this data collection. Game mechanics in the

---

[15] See Michail Katkoff, "Mid-Core Success Part 1: Core Loops," Gamasutra, October 24, 2013, available at: www.gamasutra.com/blogs/MichailKatkoff/20131024/203142/MidCore_Success_Part_1_Core_Loops.php#comments.

[16] See, e.g., Bunchball, www.bunchball.com.

[17] See generally, Saul A. McLeod, "Type A Personality," SimplyPsychology, 2017, available at: www.simplypsychology.org/personality-a.html.

platform could encourage clients to provide compliance information on a regular basis, and keep them engaged in communicating with the law firm. The service itself could be a competitive advantage that the firm provides free to clients, or it could be an annual subscription service bundled with the firm's legal services, designed to help the firm stay current on compliance by keeping everyone apprised of changes in laws and regulations. In any event, this hypothetical system certainly involves more layers of motivation and autonomy than a system that awards a lawyer a shiny new badge for a job well done.

In sum, a design that fails to account for intrinsic motivation will never work. Simply awarding badges or posting accomplishments on a leaderboard does not motivate long-term behavioral change. Whether the firm is intending the gamification to change social behavior or to increase productivity, more is required.

IV TESTING

To avoid a gamification system backfiring, it should be rigorously tested. Most likely, the lawyers at the firm who are attempting to add gamification to an existing system, or any programmer hired by the firm to accomplish this task, will already possess a natural preference and affinity for games. This lawyer, programmer, or team of individuals implementing a gamification system may thus approach the task from a different perspective than an associate or partner in the firm who lacks such a propensity for games. For this reason, it is critical that any ideas the law firm develops be tested on the average law firm user for early and frequent feedback. What may be enjoyed by one geek lawyer in the firm might be completely uncomfortable for the majority of the lawyers that the firm wants to use the system.

Additionally, the system should be deliberately hacked. Users should be asked to use the system in a way that does not follow the provided instructions or rules for the gamification. By doing this, the designer or designers will be able to get a clear picture of how users may at some point "game" the system, and thus discover all of the round-about ways users might use the system to accomplish the set goals without actually doing the work or the processes behind those goals. This behavior is common among players and happens naturally with the development of any system. Knowing these weaknesses in a gamification method ahead of time will allow the designers to circumvent those behaviors, or even build them into the rules or game mechanics for that goal. After assessing these weaknesses, the designers should prototype frequently early on in the game's development, generating iterations that take into consideration the ways users are playing the game. Early and frequent iteration will result in a more successful gamification method.

V TECHNICAL LIMITATIONS

Game design will be limited by the platform or system a law firm wants to gamify. There may be technical limitations resulting from a lack of data on individual firm members, as opposed to data collected from the firm as a whole. This will make a difference in determining what resources will be needed, or what will have to be built from scratch, for the development of a gamification project.[18]

---

[18] See Christopher Cunningham and Gabe Zichermann, *Gamification by Design: Implementing Game mechanics in Web and Mobile Apps* (Sebastopol, CA: O'Reilly Media, Inc., 2011).

Imagine a game strategy where points are awarded based on the number of pro bono hours an associate logs. If the collection of this data does not already exist in the law firm's technology solutions, then the firm will have to build a more complex tool that captures real-time data and reports it to a point system and leaderboard. The data the firm collects must also be collected for each individual user, not for the firm as a whole, if the game wants to use data collection to determine points awarded to individual users. On the other hand, if the strategy is based on team efforts and collaborative work, then the collection of that data must be aggregated. The game could thus be designed on transactional systems so that users get real-time feedback on where they stand in relation to other users.[19] As discussed above, this form of feedback is necessary for the game to seem fair to players.

VI STARTING THE DEVELOPMENT PROCESS

A law firm seeking to set up a gamification system should develop a team of two or three individuals to be the primary developers. These individuals should be firm members who are skilled at listening and who others will easily work with and open up to. They will also need to have the leadership skills to coordinate and get cooperation from a number of different individuals in the firm, everyone from partners to entry-level associates and paralegals. If a firm knows ahead of time that the implementation of a gamification method will most likely include the firm's technology or knowledge management systems, then recruiting a member from this department with some technical knowledge may be helpful in understanding the initial issues and behavior to change, in analyzing feasible implementation methods in the firm's technology and resources, and in setting up the final game mechanics within any existing system.

A *Identifying Issues for Gamification to Address*

To help identify the issue or issues that the law firm would like to address, the first step is to understand the goals of the firm, both in financial and reputational terms. Without the support of the business goals behind the gamification plan, it will be difficult to get support for funding, developing, and maintaining any gamification method put in place.

It is also important to know what kind of law firm culture exists: its traditions, the social behaviors of firm members, whether the firm tends to be more conservative or innovative, and the basic demographics that might create more than one law firm identity within the larger firm culture. Are members flexible, or set in their ways and resistant to change? Does the firm have more of a culture of cooperation, or a culture of competition? Whose behavior is involved in the potential issues that the firm wants to address, and how might that behavior need to be changed?

Understanding a firm's culture and its business goals is a good starting point for a development team to then go to the members of the firm and learn their daily routine. This is where the development team needs to take on the role of an ethnographer. Developers should conduct interviews of firm members whose behavior might need to be changed. An informal interview may work better with certain firm members who might otherwise feel pressured under the circumstances, or who may not answer fully, depending on their place in

---

[19] See Henry Lowood, "Real-Time Performance: Machinima and Games Studies," *International Digital Media and Arts Journal* 2 (1) (2005): 10–17.

the law firm hierarchy. Questionnaires or surveys can be a useful way of gathering this data in general, but these will not be as effective as interviews that can identify the specific issues to be addressed. Finding a neutral party within the law firm to handle this interview process is critical for gathering accurate data about firm members' daily routines and thoughts.

There are some useful tips for interviewing firm members on what issues might need to be addressed. First, avoid "yes or no" questions. Ask questions that start with *how* or *why*; asking *how* or *why* helps developers to understand firm members' motivations. Second, focus on listening, and not interrupting or interjecting during the interview. In order to receive helpful information from firm members, they have to feel comfortable in the interview setting. Finally, ask for stories that are related to the law firm and the potential issues. Storytelling is far more useful and edifying than asking abstract questions that only have abstract answers.

In addition to the interview process, the development team may carry out unobtrusive observation of firm members. Many firm members might resent having their daily actions observed, even for the purposes of identifying processes or efficiencies within the law firm. Sometimes, employers install software that records the websites and online habits of employees, but this is not the most effective tactic; many law firm associates and partners dislike this form of employer spyware, and in this case especially, usage of such monitoring devices might not yield the most useful data for understanding the workflow of firm members. Some of this data might already be gathered in the law firm's technology anyway, such as with firm-wide records of time sheet submission. The firm's technology might also record how often and to what extent firm members use different software features. An example of this might be an HR director who has a library of video tutorials and learning materials for firm associates and new hires to use, and who keeps track of how often the materials are used and whether employees retain the information in those materials to a sufficient degree.

Yet another way to gather useful data for developing a gamification system is for firm members to keep a daily journal that essentially tells the story of their day. Ask them to write down their habits and routines; this is the kind of behavior that the team may design the gamification system to modify. Even if a firm member does not label their behaviors as routine, asking them to keep a journal may help to identify an action as routine. Gathering similar routines that show up in multiple firm members' journals can provide telling data for the gamification team to analyze.

Another method of data gathering involves the actual physical paths a firm member takes in a single day. When an associate sits down in the break room, what are they sitting on, what do they see on the walls, what are they doing in this space, and who and what do they interact with in that environment? When an associate sits at their desk, what is the main screen on the computer where they spend the bulk of their time? Do they spend more time drafting in Word, or on the firm's matter management system, or on the firm's legal research tool? Are they spending the bulk of their time on the phone in individual calls or conference calls? How often does another individual interrupt that firm member's environment, and in what manner does the interruption occur? Break down this daily path of physical interaction with items and spaces in the firm, reactions to these elements of the environment, and what the pinch points might be as firm members go about their day. A development team should track what firm members need, how they feel, and what they want to accomplish throughout their workday. The team must have a clear, empathetic understanding of the individuals in the firm in order to tease out the issues that firm members themselves might not otherwise have ever noticed.

Gathering this data will provide a fuller picture of any issues a firm may wish to address through gamification. The next step, once data has been gathered, is to identify all of the stakeholders involved in the issues to be addressed. A good way to do this is to start with one law firm member or department, and then add other members whose interactions affect that initial group. These are the individuals who will be asked to buy into any gamification strategy, so creating a mind map of stakeholders can be useful for seeing the larger picture of how individual firm members interact with each other on a daily and weekly basis. Beginning with one individual in the firm, the mind map will address how these other parties group themselves together, and how parties interact within those groups. Do group members collaborate, or are there frequent disagreements in the group dynamic? Who do group members answer to, and what is the relationship among all the parties in the group?

After conducting this research, the gamification team can narrow down the issues the firm will address:

- **Business goals:** These might include associates failing to record accurate billable hours in the firm's billing software; lack of collaboration and communication between partners and younger associates; associates spending excessive time using a specific software program or failing to use the firm's desired data entry methods; or fewer recorded pro bono hours than the firm's desired output.
- **Specific behaviors:** Who is doing this behavior? Who is impacted by the behavior as it is done now, and how does this compare to the desired behavior? How can each person engaged in the behavior or affected by it benefit from a change in this behavior? The method by which the behaviors are targeted should be in furtherance of the firm's business goals.
- **Environment:** What environment will this behavior change occur in? Examples might include a practice management or other technology solution the firm uses; a physical space, such as a room, or in the firm's office; online or offline, in-person or in remote environments; different groups of firm members and the relationships between and among them. Are there any rules or limitations in these environments that would impact the desired behavior change?
- **Platform:** A gamification method needs an appropriate platform. Some platforms will work better than others, depending on the other aspects of the gamification. These platforms may include mobile applications; games embedded within the law firm's technology solutions; paper-based or board games; and physical games that take place in different environments throughout the firm.

B Understanding the Players in the Firm

In order for a gamification method to work, developers must understand all the different individuals who will play the game. To do this, developers should gather the basic demographics of players, such as gender, age, professional experience, and education level. Based on the user types discussed previously, developers can use this demographic information to identify potential players as Killers, Achievers, Socializers, or Explorers. It will also be advantageous for developers to consider how many of each type of player there is (e.g., a law firm may have more Killers and Achievers than Explorers); whether players are individual- or team-oriented; whether they are part of an older generation unaccustomed to the internet or a younger generation that grew up with it; and what types of behaviors the players typically exhibit in social settings versus professional settings. With this data, the developers can step back and identify the characteristics of the people who will play the game, and thus design a more effective and engaging gamification strategy.

C Establishing a Gamification Strategy

After identifying the issues to be addressed, and coming to an understanding of the players who will play the game, the developers should next reaffirm the primary goal of the gamification project and begin to build a strategy. At this stage, the law firm and the development team need to have a clear principle goal in mind, not just in terms of a final deliverable like increased productivity and revenue, but in terms of how the gamification will impact the firm members themselves. For example, does the firm want to modify associate behavior, increase cooperation, foster competition, have firm members learn a new skill while accomplishing a task, or some combination of these? The gamification project needs its *raison d'être*. Here is an example of what this strategy might entail:

- **The design principle:** Our principle is to foster collaboration among associates while they improve their skills at using the firm's matter management software.
- **The goal of the gamification project:** Our goal is for associates to more consistently and correctly use the matter management software, which will decrease error and increase efficiency of law firm workflow and productivity.

Firm leaders and the game developers should check back to make sure that both the design principle and the goal of the project are in line with the firm's larger business goals. The game's mission should be clearly stated, tracked, monitored, and recorded so that results can be analyzed by the firm. Without the ability to clearly state goals and track the game's success, the gamification method has a much lower chance of success, and may not get full buy-in from the law firm's partners and associates.

D Game Development and Game Mechanics

The next step in the design process involves brainstorming ideas on every aspect of the game, from the general theme to the aesthetics, taking the players and their dispositions into consideration along the way. This process requires broad thinking, and developers need to keep an open mind, laying out all possible ideas, even ones that seem like they won't work. This non-judgmental component of the development process may be uncomfortable to lawyers unfamiliar with creative and design thinking, but it is vital to have as much material to work with as possible. After all ideas are on the table, the developers can begin the process of drilling down to specific game mechanics and measurable goals.

Games need to be clearly defined so that players know what the *objectives* are, and when those objectives are met or when they will reset. Depending on the goals of the firm, the game can last for a day, a week, a year, or continue indefinitely. The point of a gamification design is to engage the player and maintain that engagement for however long the game lasts.

If a game does continue indefinitely, it can serve as a recurring form of motivation for firm members to play. Here the objectives of the game would still track specific measurable goals with "ends" leading to other goals, but these goals might also be reinforced with new levels and challenges, or with new rewards that players can obtain. This tactic allows the game to "reset," so that if the game is score-based with a leaderboard, players who stay at the lower end of the scale do not become discouraged. This also encourages others who have not played the game before to enter in at any level and to have the same chance to achieve among those who have been playing for a while.

To this end, the process or the technology platform that the firm wants to gamify needs to have a *storyline*. If developers view a player's interaction with a game as a kind of story, then they can more easily see whether a player's interaction with the process or platform is increasing in frequency, keeping them tuned in to the game, and whether the game mechanics are building that rollercoaster feeling of actions, payoffs, and new actions that successful games instill in their players. To create this sense of storyline, it is critical for developers to find the right game mechanics. Based on the profile of the project's primary gamer, the development team can select from a number of potential game mechanics that might engage players. Game mechanics include such elements as: a progress bar used to indicate a player's progress toward the desired behavior; achievements that give a score for positive behaviors (e.g., badges, certificates, rewards, awards, raw scores); and punishment mechanics that cause players to lose points when they engage in undesirable behaviors. Game mechanics can also incorporate social elements, such as comments, ratings, reviews, and followers. When implemented successfully, these game mechanics can contribute to the creation of that narrative story-like feeling that keeps players engaged.

To make a truly effective game, the mechanics discussed above should be paired with motivators. *Motivators* are the fun elements of a game that keep players hooked and engaged. Again, the motivators that would work best for a firm's players are going to differ from firm to firm, but this is where the development team needs to take the lead and try to identify what the key motivation would be for the majority of the player types that will ultimately play the game. More than one motivator can be utilized in a single game. Some examples of motivators include: collecting objects or points, or collecting knowledge about a specific topic; creating custom worlds or environments; exploring new worlds or environments; role-playing; betting; competing with others; and self-improvement.

After the objectives and storyline are determined, and the game mechanics to be used are paired with the motivators that will work best for the game's primary players, the development team should consider the *scoring system* for the game. Players need to know that the score is recorded fairly, and that rewards they receive, and losses they suffer, will be a relevant part of the game-playing experience. In most gamification scenarios, it cannot be overstated how important fairness is to the scoring process. If a scoring system is fair, players will generally be satisfied. For this reason, it is important for the scoring system to award points at select intervals, and to have a system of punishments where scores are lowered after failure, instead of a frustrating "game over" screen. As discussed earlier with respect to the psychology behind games, it is important that rewards do not interfere with a player's intrinsic motivation; games are always more effective when a player's primary motivation is internal.

E Development Testing

Once the development team has created a rough idea for a game, their next step is to create *prototypes*. Prototypes can be initially formed with storyboards or with a paper-based board game until the details of the game are fleshed out. These simple, straightforward methods are superior to spending time and funds on building a game into a technology platform, because adequate testing and iteration of the design is needed to prevent sinking money into a poor investment. Starting with inexpensive paper-based prototypes and testing them early in the process is a better way to ensure a finalized design has gone through a rigorous evolutionary process and had all its kinks worked out. *Volumetric modeling* – where designers actually build out models of the user interface – is far more costly, and should be saved for the end of the testing process.

To accomplish a low-tech test of game mechanics in a technology platform, a design team can create a board that looks like the dashboard of the platform. When players in the real world take a desired action, they manually add their action to this physical board, testing the game by playing it next to the actual platform to be gamified. To test out other concepts related to the platform, the design team can print out different pages – such as a leaderboard, badges, or certificates – and test players' reactions to the paper prototypes. This process will give the development team valuable feedback from law firm players, and allow the team to assess the level of engagement from players in the current prototype in order to make improvements and changes to the system. As with the initial interviews of players about their daily interactions with the system to be gamified, this is a time when developers and firm leaders can find out whether players feel the scoring system is fair, and whether the rewards and motivations of the system are working well. Are the players engaged, and are they having fun?

F Monitoring and Metrics

After the development team has designed and implemented well-tested game mechanics into the process or platform, firm members must be carefully brought into the use of the system. Some users may be more familiar with gamification methods than others, so it is critical to a game's success to monitor the way the users play the game. Different kinds of users will experience different learning curves as they begin to engage with the game mechanics. As players gradually familiarize themselves with the game, law firm leaders may want to use metrics to measure how well and in what ways the method is succeeding. *Measurement metrics* can look at the actions, motivations, and engagement levels of players and provide firm leaders with helpful data about the game. To measure engagement over time, for example, a firm can look at the average number of actions a player takes that involve the desired behavior, the number of players who take those desired actions, how often they return to do the same action, and their level of satisfaction with the gamified platform. A firm may also want to know if the productivity of players has increased, if the workflow streamlined by the gamified system has reduced the firm's costs, and whether revenues have increased due to an increase in desired behaviors among employees.

Some problems may arise after firm leaders and the development team have begun monitoring the use of the gamification method and the metrics recorded. One such problem is that a game design may appear to have fallen short of return on investment (ROI) expectations. The gamification goals chosen may not have been in line with the law firm's business goals after all. Or maybe the game is not working within the law firm's culture, or it only worked within a segment of the firm's culture and never adequately engaged other segments of the firm. It is also possible that messages between the players and the parties implementing the game were not clear, such that players did not know what was expected of them, nor what the rewards or benefits would be for them as individuals, or for the firm more generally.

Lastly, lack of long-term engagement can also be a serious issue. As discussed above, players might start strong with a gamification method at the beginning of implementation, but interest may flag if challenges and motivations in the game do not increase over time.

While adequate testing might help to determine short-term engagement success, longer-term engagement is more a factor of monitoring and adjusting the game as needed based on feedback along the way.

VII CASE STUDY 1: PAPER-BASED GAMES AT FENWICK & WEST, PALO ALTO, CA

Human resources director Cheri Vaillancour at Fenwick & West shared details of some of her department's successful experiments in paper-based gamification.[20] One such method involved encouraging firm partners to turn in associate reviews on time. The game was simple: Lawyers who turned in their reviews by a fixed deadline received a gold star on their door. As other partners responsible for their sections saw the stars appear, the completion of the reviews became competitive. Don't have a gold star on your door? Then you haven't completed and returned your reviews. Simple peer pressure and accountability accomplished the firm's goals of getting in reviews on time.

Another gamification method involved reworking the game of *Jeopardy!* to incorporate facts about the law firm. The goal of this game was to provide a crash course on the firm's culture and an introduction to the firm's history during training of new associates and hires. This paper-based method worked well at engaging new hires and getting them to socialize with each other.

VIII CASE STUDY 2: GAMIFICATION OF SUMMER ASSOCIATES AT CADWALADER

Cadwalader, Wickersham & Taft LLP, an international law firm, added several simple games to their website to advertise summer associate programs at the firm.[21] The games are all intended to be fun ways to teach the history and culture of the firm to prospective associates. One game involves matching images; as images are matched, a paragraph appears explaining the relationship between the matching images and how they relate to the firm's history. Another game uses a version of *Jeopardy!*, with answers related to some aspect of the law firm or its work. The final game is a rebus game, which tests a player's creativity by showing images of objects that, when combined, sound out a word or phrase with a relationship to the firm's work.

IX CASE STUDY 3: FUTURELAWFIRM2030 SAMPLE INNOVATION GAME

During a summit in 2011, MJV, a technology and innovation company, designed a game for 200 CEOs of influential Brazilian companies.[22] Since CEOs are typically difficult to engage, the goal of this game was to get a group of them to actively learn and think about the country's economic future while also gathering valuable data from the other participants. This data was later used to inform the group about the perspectives and priorities of the players. This game was highly successful, and has been adapted to engage partners and associates of law firms in

---

[20] This chapter's author, Stephanie Kimbro, interviewed Cheri Vaillancour, HR Director at Fenwick & West, on November 25, 2014.

[21] See Cadwalader's website: www.cadwalader.com/makehistory/makehistory.php?page_id=5.

[22] See Ysmar Vianna, Mauricio Vianna, Bruno Medina, and Samara Tanaka, *Gamification, Inc.: Recreating Companies Through Games* (London: MJV Press, 2014), 74–76. *See also* Macroplan Perspective Strategy and Management, the consulting company that worked with MJV to design the economic scenarios for this game, at www.macroplan.com.br.

thinking about the growth and development of their firm. What obstacles might prevent the firm from growing to its greatest potential over the next decade or two? How might these obstacles be overcome?

The game starts with players receiving a kit that contains four cards depicting macroeconomic scenarios that could affect the growth of their law firm. Each kit also has a blank card so that the player can add a specific scenario that interests them or that they believe might occur before the year 2030. Each kit is worth the same amount of points; this ensures that the game always starts out on a level playing field regardless of the cards in each kit. Play begins when players choose their favorite scenario from the cards. The players don't know the value of each individual card. Fictional news reports are delivered throughout the game, and these reports might affect the probability of specific scenarios happening. It is possible throughout the game to obtain other cards to acquire more points, and this is done by exchanging cards with other players. Another way to earn points is to complete a chart where the player guesses about specific aspects of the economy and legal marketplace that would affect the law firm. For each group of three opinions placed on the chart, a player receives three cards with random point values that correspond to their favorite scenario. Players also interact with NPCs (non-player characters – other staff members of the firm), who introduce new cards with new scores and points. These NPC interactions make exchanges between players more dynamic. The NPCs are responsible for collecting the players' impressions about the scenarios as the game progresses, noting appreciation or disdain of certain scenarios that may impact the choice of cards by other players. At the end of the game, all players count their points. Scenarios that were selected by the majority of players earn their card holder a score bonus of 25%. After the game, players are shown the data collected in the process, and how the opinions of scenarios evolved as the game fluctuated.

This game engages players because they have to think about scenarios and try to understand each scenario's implications for their firm. In addition, players have to place a value on each scenario, and think about how that scenario applies to them professionally and to the firm as a whole.

X CONCLUSION

Gamification in law firms is still far from being ubiquitous. In general, law firms are not willing to invest in innovation, and this includes gamification methods. Oftentimes, spending a small portion of the law firm budget needed to maintain existing technology infrastructures is considered innovation enough. Unfortunately, this means that the use of gamification to increase productivity and efficiency is something only the most forward-thinking firms will be able to grasp. The gamification studies described above are just a few examples, and while it is important to remember that gamification remains a relatively new practice, law firms that emphasize innovation and gamification will continue to find new and improved ways to enhance the way they do business externally, and the way they operate internally.

2.12

Introduction to Design Thinking for Law

Margaret Hagan

I INTRODUCTION

The past decade has seen an increase in conversations about innovation in law, with a focus on how new technology can make the legal system more efficient and effective. Legal technology, in the form of artificial intelligence (AI), data analytics, and mobile applications, has been heralded as bringing a new era of legal services. This chapter advocates for a distinct but complementary approach to legal innovation, based in human-centered design, which can create new non-technological innovations and improve how lawyers and laypeople engage with legal technology. If a technology-driven approach focuses on how to make systems more intelligent and more efficient, a design-driven approach focuses on how to make systems that people want to use, are able to use, and that give them value.

Human-centered design is the practice of building things that are useful, usable, and engaging to people. It is based on the notion that products, services, organizations, and systems should be built for the people who will use them. This method can both evaluate current offerings and generate new ones, with the goal of creating solutions that people actually want to use, that they intuitively know how to use, and that help them accomplish something they need. A design approach is unique because it focuses on user needs, preferences, and behaviors, and its process prioritizes agility and experimentation.

A human-centered design approach holds great promise for improving the legal system and the delivery of legal services. For technologists, policy makers, and professionals working in the legal system, design can flip their view of the system from the default lawyer perspective to the perspective of a layperson. Rather than accept the status quo as a given, design asks how things can be made better, particularly for end-users. A design approach can identify key failure points and frustrations where the legal system does not work, and can help innovators generate new concepts for how to improve the system for both users and professionals, testing and scaling those interventions that hold the most promise.

This chapter presents an overview of how a design approach can be a force for both incremental improvements and large-scale innovation in the legal system. We will consider cases of design used to make legal professionals' work easier and more effective, and cases where design can be used to make the legal system more navigable and understandable for laypeople. In surveying design-driven initiatives among legal organizations, this chapter presents how the field of legal design provides a useful set of structures, methods, and mindsets to guide those working in legal innovation. It also contributes to the definition of *legal design* itself by identifying a typology of problems that legal design is suited to solve, as well as guiding principles for effective legal design work.

This chapter will first explain the relevance of design to law and define the legal design approach. Then, it will examine how design approaches are being brought to law in distinct areas, namely in the creation of new legal communications, products, services, and systems. Next, it will present an initial legal design framework that can capture key learnings and principles of the design approach to legal problems. Finally, this chapter identifies future directions for legal design work, and explains the need for more rigorous and extensive research about this approach to innovation.

Legal professionals should be conscious of tools, processes, and principles from human-centered design that could improve their work, because design-driven approaches have vast potential for legal services. The examples of design-driven legal projects in this chapter give concrete inspiration for how lawyers can adopt more creative, visual, and user-centered approaches. The legal design framework supplies guiding principles, coherent categories, and possible targets for lawyers to use in their own work in order to complement a technology-driven approach to innovation.

II THE INTERSECTION OF LAW AND DESIGN

Several scholars have observed the overlap of legal practice and design practice. Lawyers often act as designers – creating systems, relationships, codes of action – that establish how humans interact with each other. Some have even argued that lawyers inhabit similar professional service roles as engineers and designers;[1] clients come to such professionals with problems they cannot solve themselves, and the professional then provides expert advice and guidance to help the client solve their problem. Lawyers, designers, and engineers are in the business of creating useful devices for clients. Devices created by lawyers usually take the form of documents, and the lawyer's process is legal drafting, but these are not the only forms of solutions that lawyers can design.[2] The key overlap between practitioners of law and design is that both types of professionals aim to solve others' problems by tailor-making solutions for the client's situation.

James M. Cooper observes that lawyers must play more roles than merely the typical "advocate" role associated with lawyers.[3] Lawyers play the role of designers, creating strategies, legislation, and other systems in addition to serving a single client's needs. They also have to craft solutions and solve problems. In these ways, lawyers are the architects of better relationships and positions for their clients and for themselves, and this process is the way in which they cross over into the world of design. Given these overlaps between the role of lawyers and that of designers, it is valuable for the legal profession to more explicitly consider how designers approach problem solving, and what value this approach could hold in the parallel service profession of law.

A What Is Human-Centered Design?

Human-centered design is the practice of building things that are useful for, usable by, and engaging for people.[4] It is based on the notion that products and services should be built in

---

[1] David Howarth, *Law as Engineering: Thinking About What Lawyers Do* (Cheltenham: Edward Elgar, 2014), 67.
[2] *Id.* at 31.
[3] James Michael Cooper, "A Window Opens: Importing Horizontal Systems of Justice during a Time of Judicial Reform," Proyecto Acceso, 2002, available at: www.proyectoacceso.com/CCPS/publications.htm.
[4] Richard Buchanan, "Design Research and the New Learning," *Design Issues* 17 (4) (2001): 14–15.

response to the needs, preferences, and behaviors of the people who will be using them. Innovative solutions aren't created by professionals working on their own, but instead by collaborative and participatory processes in which designers engage with other professionals to gather insights into their users' needs, brainstorm a wide variety of solutions, then prototype, test, and iterate upon a handful of those proposed solutions.[5]

The design process has been developed over the past decades in many creative and technology-driven domains, including industrial design, software development, and consumer product design. Now it is being adopted in more social and service-driven professions, including legal and government services, finance, management, and health care.[6] The term *design thinking* refers to the use of the professional designers' approach in other domains, often by those who are not formally trained or employed as designers. Design thinking brings the processes, mindsets, and tools of the designer into other areas, like law, in order to solve vexing challenges.

The design approach is focused on creating and improving the product offered to the target audience. The design approach gets the audience's voice into the process, brainstorms a wide variety of solutions, and then quickly prototypes and tests these ideas with users and experts to find the most promising and valuable ideas to develop. To understand this approach and its value, it is useful to think of design as a combination of core processes and mindsets. Human-centered design is not a strictly defined process, but it does have a relatively stable set of steps and priorities.

B The Essential Design Process

Rather than a traditional waterfall method of creating new technology or service offerings – in which a group of professionals scope out a project that they think will be successful, plan it out in full detail, and then try to implement this plan over a long period of time – the design-driven approach spends more time investing in understanding the perspectives of the intended users, experimenting with possible solutions, building and testing them quickly with stakeholders, and then gradually refining the design through quick cycles while scaling it up. It allows for more user input, more creativity, and more agility. A human-centered design process is not a rigidly defined structure, but it generally consists of five core stages.[7]

The first stage of the design process is called *discovery and understanding*. In this stage, designers frame the challenge and its context by gathering input from stakeholders, with a deep empathy for their perspective. They conduct empirical research through competitive analyses, discussions with domain experts, and qualitative research with target audiences, in order to ascertain the status quo situation and what might be possible. After this, designers *synthesize and scope* their plan, making sense of the information gathered, and then recognizing key insights and patterns in order to define who the key stakeholders are, and what their essential needs, values, and interests are in the given challenge area.

The third stage is the *create and build* stage, where designers brainstorm and prototype solutions to the challenges that would match the identified requirements and serve the needs of the stakeholders. Once a prototype is ready, designers *test and refine* their design, piloting

---

[5] IDEO, *Human Centered Design Toolkit*, 2nd edition (Palo Alto, CA: IDEO, 2011), 6, available at: www.ideo.com/work/human-centered-design-toolkit.
[6] Tim Brown, "Design Thinking," *Harvard Business Review*, June 2008.
[7] *Ibid.* For more on the waterfall method versus the agile/lean method, *see* Grady – Legal Informatics-Based Technology in Broader Workflows, *supra*.

and evaluating the prototypes with domain experts and target users in order to iterate and find the most ideal outcomes. Testing and refining continues until a workable version emerges.

Finally, the fifth stage is the *evolution* stage. In this stage, designers measure the performance of the prototypes according to their use by stakeholders, their resolution of the stated challenge, and other outcomes that have resulted. They then may scale the early prototypes up from a pilot into a full, public version.

Human-centered design provides a rich set of methods for carrying out each of these five stages, which manuals and websites from design organizations flesh out in detail.[8] This core design process offers a practical, flexible, empirically grounded approach to tackling problems. Design methodology promises to deliver effective solutions because it puts a central emphasis on understanding user needs, questioning the status quo, and developing and testing new prototypes quickly.

C Design Mindsets

Good design does not simply follow a standard process, though. While going through the design cycle, there are a handful of mindsets that can guide a team to better outcomes, and this design-oriented approach means prioritizing the following mindsets:

- **End-user focus:** When developing a new solution or reviewing a current offering, the goal should be to know who the user is, to understand what their needs and values are, and to ensure that the solution fits this user.
- **Experimentation:** Before rushing to the single perfect solution, or before doing what is typically done in a similar situation, a team should play with what is possible. This means a willingness to try many different types of solutions before settling on one, with an eye toward taking new approaches and testing them, and drawing on analogous situations outside of the given domain.
- **Prototyping and early testing:** When trying to create a new thing, build rough and sketchy versions first, and do so quickly. Prototyping means creating quick approximations of a new idea so that it can be understood and tested immediately, and then improved upon. This is in contrast to an approach in which a team delays producing anything until all plans are finalized, and in which they don't seek out feedback on early prototypes, opting instead to wait until a thing is complete and "perfect" before testing it.
- **Interdisciplinary teams:** Better solutions can be developed by working with professionals with varying expertise. Though it is often more comfortable to build a team of people who think and speak in the same way, richer solutions emerge when disciplines mix. For example, to solve a legal challenge, there is value in having people who are not lawyers – including technologists, businesspeople, and designers – work with lawyers to create solutions.
- **Intentionality with process:** A team should be thoughtful about what stages and techniques it uses to solve a problem. Consciously following the core steps of the design process can give structure to a team, with important benchmarks and metrics. Without this, innovation initiatives often fail due to lack of direction, or

---

[8] *See generally* IDEO, *Human Centered Design Toolkit*, supra note 5; Luma Institute, *Innovating for People: Handbook of Human-Centered Design Methods* (Pittsburgh, PA: Luma Institute, 2012).

because they become more about the team members' preferences than about the needs of the target users.

These mindsets need not only be practiced when a team is explicitly following a design process. Taken independently, each of these mindsets can improve how lawyers, and other service professionals, operate effectively in general.

D What Design Offers Service Professionals

The power of design thinking lies in its ability to go beyond analysis and into creation: "[I]n a world with growing problems that desperately need understanding and insight, there is also great need for ideas that can blend that understanding and insight in creative new solutions. Implicit in this notion is the belief that design thinking can make special, valuable contributions to decision making."[9] What does design have to offer service professionals, bureaucrats, and social service providers? There are six main points of value for improving the practice of law and the way the legal system operates.[10]

The first main point is that design helps us understand service offerings better, and helps us be more innovative in creating better ones. This is because design is human-centered. The values, organization, and mechanics embedded into any design solution will respond to all the involved parties' interests, practices, and constraints. Design may prioritize some stakeholders' interests over others, but it researches all of them in order to find the best workable balance.

The design approach is grounded in research about all stakeholders, and because of this, we can find a fuller understanding of who we are working for and what we can do to serve them. A central tenet of design is to gather qualitative data from all user groups *before* laying out a possible resolution. The design approach resists the temptation to gather experts together, roundtable ideas, and choose to pursue the most popular one. Instead, the design process is participatory and based not on assumptions but on data. It allows for a systemic vision of a domain.

The third main point is that the design approach helps us create breakthrough ideas that disrupt the inertia of the status quo by tapping into the design team's creative leaps. Ideally, the design process will be carried out by an interdisciplinary team collaborating at each stage. Each team member can be a designer; there is no special requirement to qualify. A designer works by always asking questions to probe into the future. This means she uses her informed intuition to develop concepts. Here lies the potential for new innovations and for finding new ways to address gaps.

The fourth point is that the design approach also leads to actual innovations, rather than just ideas or concepts for innovation, because it is product-driven. Design, like the social sciences, attempts to understand and analyze complicated social problems. But it differs from the social sciences with its insistent focus on how to resolve such problems. Its aim is not just to consider *who*, *what*, or *why*, but also *how*. Design considers how a product, service, or entire system could serve the needs of the situation. The design process learns due to its bias for action. By placing prototypes in the field, gathering feedback, and iterating quickly, design does more than just hypothesize and write about problems; it's an action-driven process.

---

[9] Charles Owen, "Design Thinking: Notes on Its Nature and Use," *Design Research Quarterly* 1 (2) (2006): 17.
[10] Many of these points of value are adapted from Charles Owen's essay discussing fundamental characteristics and advantages of design thinking (*Id.* at 23–25).

The fifth main point is that design is agile, quick, and iterative rather than conclusory. A design approach arrives at successful interventions sooner, because it is built with the expectation that its first proposed solutions will fail. It intends its mechanisms to be prototyped, piloted, and tested with stakeholders before it is embraced as *the* solution. The process uses the pilot – and its likely failure – as an opportunity to witness what underlying dynamics are at work in the situation. Before major resources are devoted to a solution, that potential solution must go through user testing and feedback cycles. This process allows for iterations from the prototype so that it can evolve. Multiple iterations then respond to feedback from previous ones, and this evolution produces a useful and usable mechanism for the stakeholders.

Lastly, the design approach helps to break from the status quo in the ways it solves problems, by forcing a team to reconsider what can be done better. Just because something has always been done a certain way, that doesn't mean it should continue to be.

E *The Four Orders of Design*

The design approach can be applied at many different levels to solve many different types of creative challenges, from fashionable clothing and addictive games to city planning and efficient transportation systems. A useful scheme to make sense of these many types of design comes from Richard Buchanan, who proposed that there are essentially four orders of design.[11] Each of these orders contains many different kinds of domain applications of design, but they are unified by a fundamentally similar type of challenge they are trying to solve.

First-order design is in graphic, visual, and communication design – where there are simple, relatively concrete units of work product. *Second-order design* is the creation of products and industrial objects, where there are concrete work products being designed, but where these products involve greater complexity and interactions. *Third-order design* focuses on process, interactions, and services – the deliverables are more abstract and also involve more people, interactions, and objects. Finally, *fourth-order design* concerns the creation of systems, culture, and organizations, with lots of complex factors and people, and with very abstract deliverables. The first and second orders produce more concrete things and have more discrete work product. The third and fourth orders, meanwhile, result in more intangible deliverables and have a larger scale of things being designed.

Most people, including those in law, tend to think of design in terms of first- and second-order designs; for example, the crafting of communication networks or the building of software. These orders have great potential to help legal professionals work better and serve their clients in better ways, but third- and fourth-order designs also have great promise. At a more ambitious level, they can help craft a radically different kind of legal service, legal organization, or legal system.

III LEGAL DESIGN IN PRACTICE

A growing number of legal professionals and researchers have championed design thinking as a way to improve their practice, and as a method to innovate in the creation of new kinds of legal tools, services, and systems. There are design thinking classes and ongoing design-driven

---

[11] Richard Buchanan, "Wicked Problems in Design Thinking," *Design Issues* 8 (2) (1992): 7–9.

research and development efforts at Stanford Law School,[12] Northeastern Law School,[13] and Michigan State University's Law School.[14] The design thinking consultancy IDEO has recently begun to work with law firms and courts to bring its design approach to their challenges.[15] The architectural design consultancy Gensler works with law firms to bring design to their organizations.[16] Legal OnRamp also champions design thinking in its approach to bringing better technologies and analytics to law firms.[17] Conferences run by courts,[18] legal aid groups,[19] and law firms have all spotlighted design as a new toolset that law professionals should learn. A research project on the near-future trends of innovation in law reinforced this trend: legal organizations will have to invest in a deeper understanding of users' experiences, and then use data and design to deliver better products and services to their users.[20]

This initial wave of legal design work is best understood through the lens of Buchanan's four orders of design, which provides the essential categories of design work being undertaken to improve law. Adapting Buchanan's scheme to the legal domain, we can consider three essential types of design-driven approaches to legal innovation: legal communication design, legal product and service design, and legal system design. Like Buchanan's four orders, these groupings proceed from the most concrete, discrete work products that rely mainly on visual design, to much more complex and abstract solutions that involve a wider array of design tools.

This section considers prominent examples of human-centered design used in the three areas of communication, product and service development, and systems and organizational redesign. It profiles how legal professionals have employed design to solve specific challenges, and what insights and solutions have emerged from their work. Section IV will then propose an initial legal design framework to make sense of these various cases and identify best practices and principles that future design-driven efforts can use.

A Legal Communication Design: Policies, Contracts, and Business Documents

One of the most active areas of legal design is centered around improving the presentation of legal information in both physical and digital documents. Lawyers have used design, particularly the principles of visual design, to lay out legal information in ways that make legal

---

[12] A fuller description of Stanford Law School's Legal Design Lab can be found at: http://legaltechdesign.com.
[13] Northeastern University's NuLawLab embraces a design thinking approach to legal services. More information is available on the project pages at: http://nulawlab.org.
[14] Michigan State University's LegalRnD, the Center for Legal Services Innovation. More information is available at: http://legalrnd.org/.
[15] Sean Hewens, "Designing the Future of Legal Practice and Technology," webinar, Ravel Law, 2016, available at: http://info.ravellaw.com/ravel-law-webinar-ideo-designing-the-future-of-legal-practice-and-technology.
[16] Marilyn Archer, "Business as Unusual: Gensler's Legal Innovation Lab and the Law Firm of the Future," GenslerOnWork, February 12, 2015, available at: www.gensleron.com/work/2015/2/12/business-as-unusual-genslers-legal-innovation-lab-and-the-la.html.
[17] Paul Lippe, "Do Lawyers Have the 'Design Mojo' Needed to Re-Think the Delivery of Legal Services?" ABA Journal, December 31, 2013, available at: www.abajournal.com/legalrebels/article/legal_by_design.
[18] See Judicial Council of California, "Beyond the Bench 2015 Conference: User Experience," which had user experience as its focus; available at: www.courts.ca.gov/btb2015.htm.
[19] The plenary session of the Legal Service Corporation's Technology Innovation Grant conference in January 2016 centered on user experience design for access to justice. Legal Services Corporation, "LSC Technology Initiative Grant Conference 2016," 2016, available at: www.lsc.gov/meetings-and-events/calendar/technology-initiative-grant-conference-2016.
[20] Jeff Leitner, "Law 2023," Insight Labs, April 8, 2014, available at: https://issuu.com/jeffleitner/docs/law_2023_manifesto_final.

documents better products for their intended audience to use. As Canadian lawyer Mark Szabo proposes, design thinking can help lawyers be more persuasive and coherent communicators, taking complex information and presenting it in more intuitive and usable ways that more effectively reach their audience.[21] Lawyers have already taken a design approach when remaking all kinds of documents, from the bill they present to their clients, to the way trial presentations are crafted to tell a narrative,[22] to how access-to-justice materials are distributed to laypeople.[23] Colette Brunschwig has collected examples of legal communication design in the legislative process, court public relations, legal education, litigation, and attorney–client communications.[24] There has been particularly robust legal design work on corporate documents and contracts, which the following subsections profile in detail.

1 Graphic Design for Corporate Work Product

Jay Mitchell, the director of the Organizations and Transactions Clinic at Stanford Law School, has pioneered the use of visual design in the creation of corporate documents. He works with non-profit partners and students at the Clinic to create versions of contracts, policies, organizational charts, and other types of legal documents that differ from the typical visual design of corporate documents.[25] Mitchell's design approach does not involve heavy use of graphics or technology; rather, it focuses on better composition of information on a page, stronger use of font and sizing of text, and an emphasis on stronger hierarchies and more white space to give greater guidance to the user of the document. Some of the work product created in this way includes poster-sized organization maps and flowcharts, and governance documents like bylaws and policies that have new visual design and content.[26]

Mitchell's work is a good example of a user-centered design approach making meaningful, but not radical, improvements to legal work product. The Clinic's work, in the practices that it uses or the products that it delivers, does not dramatically depart from the status quo. Rather, it bolsters current practices of lawyers – such as speaking with clients to understand what kind of deliverable would best serve them, and crafting a document to capture the lawyer's knowledge and transfer it to the client. As Mitchell explains, the design approach helps him and his Clinic team to reorient the document away from the status quo design, and focus it on the "reader and actual user experience," thinking of the legal document as a tool that people will have to use. From his experiments, Mitchell concludes that lawyers should "experiment, prototype, and test new executions of core legal products" by looking more

---

[21] Mark Szabo, "Design Thinking in Legal Practice Management," *Design Management Review* 21 (3) (2010): 44–46.
[22] Paul Roberts, "In Practice: Bring Your Trial Ideas to Life," *The Recorder*, November 14, 2013, available at: https://static1.squarespace.com/static/54fdfd67e4b0b18bd95dea63/t/58c1f283e3df28a52ab9f79f/1489116964895/In+Practice.pdf.
[23] *See* Center for Urban Pedagogy, a nonprofit based in New York that has many visual legal education projects that pair designers with domain experts to create community education in visual ways. More information is available at: www.welcometocup.org.
[24] Colette R. Brunschwig, "On Visual Law: Visual Legal Communication Practices and Their Scholarly Exploration," in *Zeichen Und Zauber Des Rechts: Festschrift Für Friedrich Lachmayer*, ed. Erich Schweihofer, Meinrad Handstanger, Hofmann Harald, et al. (Bern: Editions Weblaw, 2014), 899–933.
[25] Jay A. Mitchell, "Putting Some Product into Work-Product: Corporate Lawyers Learning from Designers," *Berkeley Business Law Journal* 12 (1) (2015).
[26] Mitchell gives examples of these new work product designs (*Id.*). *See also*, Jay A. Mitchell, *Picturing Corporate Practice* (Eagan, MN: West Academic Publishing, 2016) for more examples of diagrams, timelines, and other document designs to inspire better legal document design.

closely to designers' methods and tuning in to how these products can best serve their audience.[27]

2 User-Centered Contracts

Similar to Mitchell's design approach to corporate legal work product, there is a growing group of lawyers and designers creating new types of contracts. A movement toward more user-centered contracts means using the design approach to consider how various stakeholders will be using a contract, and then changing how the contract is composed, visualized, and distributed based on this.

For example, Finnish lawyer Helena Haapio has advocated a design thinking approach to creating contracts. She proposes that lawyers draw "from the designer's toolkit" to bring "a new, more user-centered mindset" to contract drafting that will result in "better contract design, considering not only content but also the way in which it is presented."[28] Some of the design methods that Haapio advocates alongside designer Stefania Passera are the concepts of usability – "the extent to which a contract can be used by a specified user to achieve specified goals with effectiveness, efficiency, and satisfaction in a specified context of use" – and of user experience – "how the different users feel before, during, and after using the contract."[29]

They target lawyers' design illiteracy, which they have observed in corporate lawyers' "lack of models and grammar to obey when designing contract documents; a lack of understanding of affordance and gestalt; and a lack of empathy with the user."[30] Haapio and Passera propose that design can address one of the fundamental failures of contracts, that drafters lack understanding of how information should be communicated and how people interact with and interpret information, which can result in costly litigation about how to interpret a contract.[31]

Based on her own work in creating more visual and user-friendly business contracts, Haapio encourages lawyers to embrace information design principles because they generate work product. She suggests that lawyers familiarize themselves with graphic design principles so they are able to identify, select, organize, compose, and present information to an audience in a way that will effectively achieve a specific purpose.[32] This may include incorporating more tables, charts, images, and visualizations that explain the clauses in better ways than text descriptions can, and that may illustrate the terms and objects that comprise the subject matter of the contract, providing greater guidance as to how the contract should be interpreted.

Taking a design approach can help define what a "good" document is. With this metric, a lawyer can transform their document's content, structure, layout, design process, and user experience accordingly.[33] To do this, Passera and Haapio suggest considering the possible

---

[27] See Mitchell, "Putting Some Product into Work-Product," *supra* note 25, at 42.
[28] Helena Haapio, "Bringing Design Thinking to Contract Design: Visual Tools for Better Contracting," in *IACCM Thought Leadership Webinar*, 2014.
[29] Ibid. For a high-level introduction to the work of Haapio and Passera, look no further than their contribution to this volume, Haapio and Passera – Contracts as Interfaces: Visual Representation Patterns in Contract Design, *infra*.
[30] Stefania Passera and Helena Haapio, "Transforming Contracts from Legal Rules to User-Centered Communication Tools: A Human–Information Interaction Challenge," *Communication Design Quarterly Review* 1 (3) (2013): 38–45.
[31] Ibid.
[32] Ibid.
[33] Ibid.

specific use cases for those dealing with contracts. Who will the contract's primary users be, and what value do they need to derive from it? Are they using a document for decision making, as a reference point, to resolve disputes, to manage legal risk, to create a business link, to enhance corporate image, or to improve usability of a service?[34] If the lawyer engages in this user research and prioritization before drafting the document, she will be able to set the metric for what makes a good document in that particular situation, and then generate a more focused and usable communication for that document's users.

B Legal Product and Service Models

Aside from documents, legal professionals have also begun to use design approaches to create new software products and new types of service offerings. Law firms have been particularly interested in design as a method for developing new offerings for potential clients. These include technology products, as well as services that are more accessible and comprehensive. The Chicago-based firm Seyfarth Shaw has embraced design thinking, among other innovation strategies, to create new tech products and new business offerings. Its online publication "Rethink the Practice" has a section on design thinking that profiles these efforts.[35] The firm Davis Wright Tremaine has launched a design-driven consulting team for innovation, DWT De Novo, inspired by human-centered design to create new kinds of software and services for clients.[36]

In addition to firms, courts have similarly explored user-centered design to offer new kinds of services to litigants. A new crop of design-oriented law labs at various schools have become a home for firms, courts, legal aid groups, and others to research and develop new ways to serve people in the legal system. These university labs have become sandboxes for other legal organizations to learn design, and to identify new products they can develop. The following subsections dive into specific examples of how design has been used to craft new products and services.

1 Service Design for Self-Represented Litigants

One of the most extensive and substantial legal design projects came out of a collaboration between the Illinois Institute of Technology and Chicago-Kent College of Law, with a partnership with the National Center for State Courts, conducted between 1999 and 2001. Called "Meeting the Needs of Self-Represented Litigants: A Consumer Based Approach," the project focused on how courts could be made more user-friendly for self-represented litigants. Over the course of several years, many different interdisciplinary teams of law students, designers, and technologists worked through human-centered design cycles to identify the needs of people without lawyers, and to test out new ideas to serve them. The teams followed core design principles of interdisciplinary work, cycling through many different rounds of prototyping and testing and doing extensive user research to guide their output.[37]

---

[34] Ibid.
[35] See generally Seyfarth Shaw, "Rethink the Practice: Essays on Change in the Legal Industry from Seyfarth Shaw," available at: https://web.archive.org/web/20181005144515/https://medium.com/rethink-the-practice.
[36] DWT De Novo, http://denovo.dwt.com.
[37] Charles L. Owen, Ronald W. Staudt, and Edward B. Pedwell, *Access to Justice: Meeting the Needs of Self-Represented Litigants* (Chicago, IL: Pearson Custom Publishing, 2001), available at: www.kentlaw.iit.edu/Documents/Institutes and Centers/CAJT/access-to-justice-meeting-the-needs.pdf.

The project resulted in dozens of concept designs for new products and services the courts could offer to litigants in order to improve the user experience. One of these proposals, A2J Author and its Guided Interviews, has become a prominent product used by hundreds of courts and legal aid groups. A2J Author allows domain experts to create an interactive, visual software guide to put on top of forms that need to be filled out.[38] These guides help make forms easier to complete for any person who is not a legal expert, and who may be intimidated by lots of forms.

2 User-Friendly State Court Services

Two officers in the Los Angeles Superior Court have adopted a design approach centered around user experience and usability, in order to reconsider what the future of their state court should be.

John Clarke and Bryan Borys publicly decried that courts are currently "not designed for the convenience of end users," and they call on court officials to reimagine the system from the litigant's point of view.[39] Their focus on design comes in part from a concern over resources. As they consider the last two decades' worth of ideas about improving court experiences – many around providing more services, intermediaries, and coordinators – they point to the feasibility concern: these solutions tend to require more staff, which raises several flags for them. First, staff cost more money, something that many courts do not have much of. Second, the more staff that are added to the court, the more bureaucracy and systems will grow, leading to a more complicated and heavy experience. These additional services can also end up as "sidecars" outside the main system, and thus remain segmented without clear integration.[40]

The authors instead advocate a design approach with a focus on usability and disintermediation. This means replacing points of friction with court staff members, using technology and other self-help products with great attention paid to how the user will get a customized, intuitive, and friendly experience with the new service design. Clarke and Borys argue that it is not sufficient to simply patch technology onto existing services like the phone or the internet. Rather, they advocate for a court-wide design process that changes the mindsets of court managers and other staff members, and taps into the unique needs and ideas of the court.

Using a design approach, the authors found ways to provide more user-friendly services without simply adding more staff. For example, in the self-help centers that exist to support people without lawyers, the LA Superior Court devised a usability-based system that encourages collaboration between litigants and court staff, with litigants getting tailored workshops and support for their situation so that they can complete some parts of the service themselves. The designed service also eased barriers within the system with a redesign that included changing the language used in the courtrooms to be more common and simple; changing the office locations of clerks to put them into the self-help center to ease the filing process; and replacing complex instructions with checklists that highlight common failure points and warn litigants on how to avoid them.[41] These changes to the service flow were combined with

---

[38] A2J Author can be found at its website, www.a2jauthor.org.
[39] John A. Clarke and Bryan D. Borys, "Usability Is Free: Improving Efficiency by Making the Court More User Friendly," *Future Trends in State Courts*, 2011 (2011): 76–81.
[40] *Id.* at 77–78.
[41] *Id.* at 78.

larger shifts in the court staff's approach to service delivery. Rather than having the courtroom and clerk's office as the center of the court universe, the self-help center instead becomes the center – where resources, staff, and support are concentrated.[42]

The LA jury management system used another usability-centered design process. The court staff shifted from treating "prospective jurors like cattle: roping them in, penning them up, and sending them off in small groups" to an approach that was more respectful, collaborative, and efficient.[43] They provided online orientation and tools to jurors to allow them to get through basic requirements on their own time, in more comfortable locations, rather than having to come into courts. They used the power of technology for user customization, developing an online system to postpone their service date and have some control over when they could come into the courts. The design also used space, eliminating the jury assembly room and instead having a direct summoning system that let the jurors be where they liked until they were called. The court officers point to the design approach as a key way to develop more efficient, cost-effective, and satisfying services, but they also warn against some of the more tempting default approaches that legal organizations tend to use in order to make improvements, such as "simply dumping tasks online" or hiring more staff to fill in the usability gaps.[44] These two defaults are lacking, and a user-centered design approach is more productive.

3 Law School Design Labs

Law schools have also begun to invest in establishing laboratories that teach a design approach to future lawyers, and that act as a sandbox for other legal organizations to use design on challenges they are facing. Northeastern Law School has the NuLawLab, founded and directed by Dan Jackson. Stanford Law School and Institute of Design has the Legal Design Lab, founded and directed by the author of this chapter, Margaret Hagan. These labs both take an explicit design thinking approach, in which students are led through the human-centered design cycle while partnered with a legal organization that is reviewing its current services or creating new ones. These labs, in addition to providing training in legal design to students and professionals, also produce concept designs and working pilots of new legal products and services.

The NuLawLab has been developing RePresent, an online game for self-represented litigants.[45] The team of students at NuLawLab has worked with Statewide Legal Services of Connecticut and New Haven Legal Assistance to research what issues litigants face when navigating the legal process and preparing for court hearings. They have used design to create video games that capture common scenarios, address typical failure points and frustrations, and test users on what they've learned. The team works in an interdisciplinary way, with a mix of legal aid lawyers, technologists, game designers, students, and artists collaborating to make the game. Using a similar process, the NuLawLab team has created a new mobile software tool for female veterans to access legal services. Working with a legal services partner, Pine Tree Legal Assistance

---

[42] *Id.* at 78.
[43] *Id.* at 79.
[44] *Id.* at 79.
[45] The RePresent game has a project page available at: http://nulawlab.org/view/online-simulation-for-self-represented-parties.

in Maine, the lab team has helped create a resource bank with forms, letters, and social service referrals for women from the military service.[46]

The Legal Design Lab has similarly partnered with various legal organizations, including firms, corporate legal departments, courts, and legal aid groups, to create new product and service designs. One such effort is Navocado, an online tool to guide pro bono attorneys through the process of representing unaccompanied minors through state and immigration legal procedures.[47] It was built using human-centered design, with an interdisciplinary core team and an iterative, prototype-driven approach.[48] The Legal Design Lab's teams have also worked with groups like California's Judicial Council, the California Department of Justice, and the Financial Industry Regulatory Authority to run exploratory workshops and develop design recommendations for them to implement as new products and services. The university lab trains these organizations in the design approach, and then crafts implementation plans for them to develop new products and services inside their own organizations.

C System and Organizational Designs

Far larger than the redesign of discrete services and products is the legal design work that considers new system and organization design. This involves many different stakeholders, as well as a series of products, services, and communications. Law firms have begun to consider how to use design as a way to develop new business models and organizational structures. Seyfarth Shaw, for example, has used design for new kinds of organizations a law firm could spin out to build a more sustainable business, and has also considered a design approach to how it hires and staff engagements.[49]

For the most part, though, these larger-scale efforts have been used by courts and government agencies to redesign their entire systems of operation. In the UK, the RSA worked with Cisco Systems to run design thinking sessions about how courts of the future would operate, with more technology and virtual services.[50] The Design Council in the UK had a project between 2004 and 2006, called Touching the State, that employed user-centered design to understand how laypeople experienced government services (including legal ones) and to reimagine how these systems could operate.[51] This initiative included extensive user experience research of how people do jury duty, and proposed new ways this system could operate.[52]

In Canada, government agencies have partnered with a law school, Osgoode Hall, to bring design to their intellectual property systems. In the past two years, Osgoode has hosted two different multi-day design hackathons, bringing together government officials, designers, lawyers, law students, and engineers to design new ways the patent system could be made

---

[46] The project page describing this effort is available at: http://nulawlab.org/view/women-veterans-outreach-tool. The tool is available at: http://women.statesidelegal.org.
[47] The tool is available at: http://navocado.org.
[48] The project write-up is available at: http://legaltechdesign.com/legalnavigators.
[49] Josh Kubicki, "An Open Letter from Seyfarth's New Chief Strategy Officer," Rethink the Practice, June 2015, available at: https://medium.com/rethink-the-practice/an-open-letter-from-seyfarth-s-new-chief-strategy-officer-91a88f8d41e9#.cb5588iba.
[50] Jamie Young, "A Virtual Day in Court: Design Thinking and Virtual Courts," RSA Projects, December 2011.
[51] "Design Council Tackles Rift between State and Public," Design Week, October 21, 2004, www.designweek.co.uk/issues/21-october-2004/design-council-tackles-rift-between-state-and-public.
[52] Ben Rogers and Hilary Cottam, Touching the State: What Does It Mean to be a Citizen in the 21st Century? (London: Institute for Public Policy Research, 2005).

more user-friendly to inventors,[53] and to design a new system for orphan works to be dealt with.[54] Like these efforts, most system and organization redesign efforts in law are still in the beginning stages. The next sections profile some of the more robust legal system design projects within this small but growing area.

1 Midtown Community Court Redesign

New York's Midtown Community Court was an experiment in using design and technology to transform how court staff processed litigants' cases. Launched in New York in 1993, its goal was to improve the efficiency and quality of the services courts provided to criminal defendants, and to improve the work experiences of the judges and court staff. This effort led to a range of system redesign proposals in order to improve the different stakeholders' ability to act in the system. One set of design proposals was for judicial tools to give judges and clerks richer and more visual sets of information to help them track cases, see patterns, and efficiently process them.[55] Other proposals were designed for laypeople, to provide greater transparency of the court process and of their own data, using more graphics and contextual information.

Those on the design team for the Midtown Community Court redesign discovered some trends in the ways court systems could be improved through design. One lesson was that design needs to give users of the legal system more information, and more ways to use that information intelligently.[56] Another lesson was that court professionals need more process-based views of the systems, in order for them to work efficiently and more collaboratively with the other employees, and with the litigants or defendants.[57] Finally, this initiative found that visuals and user-friendly graphical interfaces must be a priority for the software and the physical documents that the system uses.[58] They see great potential in the use of more visual design to increase stakeholders' capacity to make smart decisions and work quicker.

2 Australia Tax Office Redesigns the Tax System

From the early 1990s to the early 2000s, the senior management of the Australian Tax Office (ATO) collaborated with design academics and consultants to redesign their entire tax system.[59] The ATO adopted a design approach for how to restructure their system, as well as how they could create more user-friendly interfaces. The head of the ATO was involved, as

---

[53] Meenakshi Lakhanpal, "The First Ever IP Hackathon Took Place at Osgoode Hall Law School," IP Osgoode, November 5, 2014, available at: www.iposgoode.ca/2014/11/the-first-ever-ip-hackathon-took-place-at-osgoode-hall-law-school.

[54] Giuseppina D'Agostino and Margaret Hagan, "IP Osgoode Orphan Works Hackathon: Final Report of the Concepts, Process and Insights," IP Osgoode, March 31, 2016, available at: www.iposgoode.ca/wp-content/uploads/2016/06/Orphan-Works-Hackathon-Final-Report-Posted-14-June-2016.pdf.

[55] Robert G. M. Keating and Richard Zorza, "The Ten Commandments of Electronic Courthouse Design, Planning, and Implementation: The Lessons of the Midtown Community Court," in *Fourth National Court Technology Conference, Nashville, Tennessee*, 1994.

[56] *Id.* at 3.

[57] *Id.* at 3.

[58] *Id.* at 2.

[59] Alan Preston, "Designing the Australian Tax System," in *Managing as Designing*, eds. Richard J. Boland, Jr. and Fred Collopy (Stanford, CA: Stanford University Press, 2004), 208–214; Nina Terrey, "Managing by Design: A Case Study of the Australian Taxation Office," PhD dissertation, University of Canberra, 2012.

well as the top three levels of management below him.[60] The ATO undertook a human-centered design process with the expectation that it would make the ATO more innovative and citizen-centered. Several leaders within the ATO consciously decided to refocus the ATO's tax design practice from a technical exercise in writing tax laws and establishing administrative roles toward a process with an intentional focus on design. This change was prompted by a need to transform the model from a centralized processing house of all returns – which required a huge amount of resources to process and control the materials – to a self-assessment model that was easy for the taxpaying community to use.[61] The design-driven change to the ATO took place over a decade and went through several different individual initiatives: sessions about possible changes; communication design through the Tax Law Improvement Project; and administrative system design through an initiative called "A New Tax System."

The ATO leadership desired to be market-facing, and to use innovative problem solving tools.[62] Beginning in December 1999, the ATO convened a series of design trainings and conferences for its staff, and gradually began to win over their employees, many of whom were skeptical of design as a passing fad. The ATO employees became more design-driven in their work, and helped contribute to a system-wide redesign. The facilitators trained the leadership to adopt design mindsets in order to teach them two main lessons: to have comfort with ambiguity regarding the exact right way to do something, and to design the organization from the customer backward rather than from the status quo or the tax professionals' perspective.[63]

Along with these "strategic conversation" workshops, the designers also used tools like protocol analysis to map out how a layperson could understand and process complex information about tax law. This was used to redesign tax legislation in ways that people could understand more intuitively – with simpler grammar, more scenarios, and more examples. It also led to more user-friendly changes to the architecture of the information, the navigation between sections, and the categories and concepts of the information systems. The designers created visual diagrams and purpose clauses to make the legislation more usable and comprehensible.[64] Beyond the design of the legislation, the ATO design team also tackled the challenge of how the ATO administrative system could be redesigned to make the laws work. The team created a Corporate Design Forum in which possible changes were workshopped during a series of one-day sessions held over two years. These sessions were facilitated using a design thinking approach, in which possible changes were visualized, prototyped, and assessed.[65]

A public outcry occurred after a particular tax law was misunderstood by the public and led to many people facing penalties. In order to correct this, more design work followed. The ATO had the design team diagnose what the customer's user experience was, as well as the organization's protocol that led to the mistakes. This led to a departure from the ATO's typical approach of market research – asking target users for their opinions – and instead using design research of observations, user testing, usability exercises, and other hands-on testing to assess the system. The designers had ATO officials try to fill in the tax forms, only to realize they themselves were unable to. This helped them realize that the system they were building was

[60] Second Road, "Introducing 'Design Thinking' to the Australian Tax Office," available at: www.secondroad.com.au/portfolio-item/introducing-design-thinking-to-the-australian-tax-office.
[61] Ibid.
[62] Ibid.
[63] Ibid.
[64] Ibid.
[65] Ibid.

profoundly unfriendly to users. These exercises helped the design team build institutional support and train more of the administrators to be designers.[66]

This system redesign has been one of the most substantial efforts in legal design, in terms of the scope of the redesign targets, and the investment of the organization in experimenting, piloting, and establishing the design efforts. The ATO example presents a rich case study for any other legal organization interested in using design to change not only documents, products, or services, but also to change how an organization operates, and how the entire user experience functions.

IV A FRAMEWORK FOR LEGAL DESIGN WORK

Out of this survey of legal design work, there are several ways in which a design approach can serve lawyers and the legal system. First, the design process helps to encourage lawyers to appreciate research and development. This approach helps lawyers develop promising new concepts for software, services, organizations, and communications, by giving them a clear process and core principles with which to do this work. Even if lawyers otherwise feel as if they are not creative or technology-literate, design gives them a clear and flexible way to work on innovation.

Second, a design approach can transform legal professionals' relationships with their clients, and with each other. Because design involves so much empathy-driven conversation and collaborative work, going through the process strengthens lawyers' understanding of how they can better serve their clients. The design process goes beyond thinking only of what services a lawyer has been trained to provide, and instead sees the situation from a client's point of view. Even if no new product or service comes out of the process, it's an effective tool for connecting with a client.

Finally, design can help build new leadership and interdisciplinary skills among lawyers and law students in order to help shape the next generation of lawyers. Those who go through the design process learn to be more creative problem solvers who can work collaboratively with other professionals and who have a strong orientation toward serving clients and identifying new revenue sources. These types of hybrid lawyers will be better managers of existing organizations, and the founders of brand new types of organizations that know how to adapt to the changing legal market.

Given that a design approach holds many points of value for the legal system, it is necessary to think more systematically about how legal professionals can best integrate design into their work. This section accordingly presents an initial framework of insights, guidelines, and targets for legal design work.

To begin with, it is useful to categorize legal innovation work according to the three orders laid out earlier – legal communication design; legal product and service design; and legal system design. This scheme creates clearer ways to evaluate projects and to review legal organizations in order to find out what types of changes they might need. Each of these orders may have its own particular best practices and guiding principles, as the core design process for creating a user-friendly governance document and a user-friendly self-help station at a court may be similar but ultimately based on detailed mechanics from diverging methods of design. This section will begin to identify some of these best practices for good design work for the different challenge areas.

[66] Ibid.

A Visual and Product Design Principles for Legal Innovation

From the previous surveys, as well as this author's own work running workshops, classes, and design projects at the intersection of law and design, some principles have emerged that are specific to user-friendly legal service design. These include trends in what good solutions look like, and guidelines that can help a team create well-designed documents and products. These principles can be useful for teams that are explicitly taking a human-centered design approach to solving a challenge, but they can also be useful heuristics for any legal professional trying to create better work product.

1 Principles for Visual Legal Design

Here is a short list of design principles for document creation, presentation, and other forms of communicating legal information. These lessons in particular derive from the projects of Mitchell, Haapio, Passera, and the Legal Design Lab mentioned earlier.

- **Clean composition:** Use large fonts, uncluttered text, tables, and generous white space to keep material highly readable.
- **Strong hierarchy and digestible structure:** Structure materials with clear priorities and messages. Keep one topic per page to make the entire document more scannable and quickly digestible to a reader who may be intimidated or emotional while dealing with legal matters. Label and tag materials extensively.
- **Visualization:** Integrate graphics, tables, charts, and other visuals that capture information in a more structured and direct way than textual descriptions. Visuals engage users more than text does, and they have the potential for more intuitive and meaningful communication.
- **Layers and stages:** Provide relatively simple overviews of the information being communicated, and then layer more details, references, and examples underneath these essential points. Let the more casual or lay user understand the key points quickly, and then selectively dig into complexities.
- **Wayfinders and easy action paths:** Put clear links to actions for the user to take, so they can see clearly how to use the information provided to them. Give them clear options and scenarios, so they know what they should be doing with the information they are receiving. Frame the document as a wayfinder tool for the audience to use to achieve something.
- **Plain and simple:** Separate highly technical information or jargon, and provide as much plain language as possible. Cut as much material out as you can, keeping only what is necessary.

2 Principles for the Design of Legal Products and Services

Many guiding insights have emerged for better legal products (particularly software applications) and better legal services. These complement the above visual design principles, focusing more on how to make tools and interactions more user-friendly.

- **Empower users:** Significant numbers of users of legal services can participate more and make the relationship between legal professionals and laypeople more collaborative. Tools should give users more strategic information, and support their intelligent use of this information. Users want and need more tools to parse legal information, assess it, and see scenarios that may result from it. These tools can also serve lawyers, judges, and court administrators.

- **Provide process-based views of legal work.** It's important to make sense of complex legal information and trajectories and render them as step-by-step, branching processes. A clear process with discrete steps and a well-mapped journey from beginning to end resonates with laypeople and professionals alike. Products and services that clearly delineate the process for a user's situation are extremely effective. A process-based approach makes it easier for users to comprehend what is happening and what they might do, and can also let the user feel like the process is "theirs."
- **Bird's eye view:** The user should have a broad overview of where they are in a process, service, or system. A design approach should have something like an interactive map, where a user can zoom out to see the broader system that they are a part of, and zoom in to see the particulars of where they are now, where they have come from, and where they are going. Oftentimes, users of the legal system – and sometimes the professionals within it – do not have a strong conception of why they are doing what they are doing, or what their overall journey will be. Tools and services must provide this perspective and transparency, because it is essential to user empowerment and engagement.
- **Provide opportunities to interact as equals:** Users of the legal system often feel deprived of agency when interacting with lawyers, the courts, and government actors, as they do not know enough to behave strategically or to assert themselves. The power balance feels stacked against them. To be user-friendly, legal tools and services must address this problem by giving people more opportunities to respond and to have two-way conversations.
- **Simple front, smart back:** Give a user a limited menu of options that prevents information and choice overload. The front end of a legal product or service should be intuitive, clean, and supportive. This can be accomplished with more intelligence on the backend of the system. Use data, technology, and research to know what information and options are of highest priority, and which are most likely to be relevant to the user. Similarly, automate tasks where possible to cut back the number of tasks the user – whether lay client or legal professional – has to do.
- **Multiple modes provide user customization:** Even if the law is the same for all people, different people want to understand and use it in distinct ways. Well-designed legal services let users customize their experiences to their preferred style, technology channel, and level of participation. There is a spectrum of user types, from those who want to self-serve, to those who want full service with significant human interaction, to those who want a mix of the two. Legal service providers must shift their perspective from maintaining control over users, to finding the right type of service model for the right user. This means giving more autonomy and flexibility to some.[67]

---

[67] See Clarke and Borys, *supra* note 39. They speak about this principle at length in their article, explaining that this is a break from the typical approach of court staff to litigants, but that it helps to identify key new ways to improve court services.

Introduction to Design Thinking for Law 173

Inherent in all of these guiding principles for quality legal design is an investment in the core design process and its mindsets, outlined earlier in this chapter. Legal organizations should invest in understanding the needs, desires, and behaviors of their users in order to effectively revise current service offerings and implement these principles in the best possible way.

B An Agenda for Legal Design Work

The legal system could benefit from design-driven innovation projects at many levels (Figure 2.12.1). Based on the trends of legal design initiatives, this chapter proposes a six-level typology of innovation work in order to make the legal system more user-friendly. This typology concerns projects primarily aimed at the layperson as the target user, but this typology could also benefit lawyers, court staff, and corporate clients as users. These orders range from the most incremental to the most ambitious.

At the lower levels, legal organizations can reconsider how information is communicated by focusing on the language used and how information is composed in documents and presentations. From there, organizations can consider new tools they could build to help users interact with legal processes, and to give them intelligent predictions and strategies to

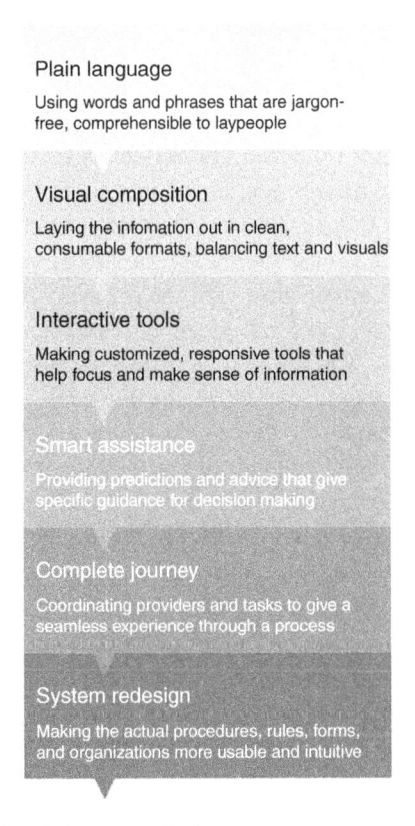

Plain language
Using words and phrases that are jargon-free, comprehensible to laypeople

Visual composition
Laying the infomation out in clean, consumable formats, balancing text and visuals

Interactive tools
Making customized, responsive tools that help focus and make sense of information

Smart assistance
Providing predictions and advice that give specific guidance for decision making

Complete journey
Coordinating providers and tasks to give a seamless experience through a process

System redesign
Making the actual procedures, rules, forms, and organizations more usable and intuitive

FIGURE 2.12.1 Six levels of legal design work that can improve users' experience with the legal system, from least ambitious to most.[68]

---

[68] Figure 2.12.1 © Margaret Hagan 2015.

use while navigating the system. Finally, innovation efforts can aim to change the legal system at more profound levels, making it a more fluid and intuitive journey for a user by changing how services are provided. Design work can also be aimed at the rules, organization, business models, and culture of the system itself, changing these fundamental parts of the system in order to transform it into something that more effectively serves target users.

This scheme of possible legal design work is presented as a set of targets for courts, legal aid groups, self-help centers, government agencies, and others interested in developing a more user-friendly legal system. The more ambitious projects are needed in many areas, but the more incremental ones can also provide significant benefits to laypeople, and they do not require significant budgets or long timelines to implement. The case studies presented in this chapter provide some examples of how a design approach can spur user-centered innovation, and these can provide more inspiration for what legal organizations can do to create better experiences for their users and their staff.

V THE FUTURE OF LEGAL DESIGN

Over the past several years, the use of human-centered design has moved from software development, industrial products, and other technologies into more complex service domains like personal finance, health care, and government services. Professionals in these domains have launched laboratories, hackathons, startup incubators, and funding sources to tackle core challenges in creative and user-centered ways. The same trend is now catching on in the legal system. Professionals working in courts, law firms, corporate legal departments, and law schools have trained themselves in design in order to understand who their users are and how to create new communications, products, and services that better serve them. These projects show that design can be a powerful driver of innovation in legal services. It is also an approach that is easy to learn, yet profoundly transformative in its focus on human needs, analogous thinking, and agile prototyping and testing.

This survey of the initial wave of legal design work indicates several points of value for human-centered design in the world of law. Design's greatest potential is in fundamentally improving the legal system so that it better serves the ultimate end-user, the person who needs the law's help in solving a problem. Design can also transform how lawyers and courts communicate, giving them a more robust and visual toolset to engage people with legal materials, persuade them on an argument, and empower them to understand and act on legal information. A design approach can help lawyers create improved work product that engages their target audience better, including with contracts, policies, corporate documents, and software. Additionally, design has the potential to help lawyers improve their own organizations, such as helping them devise new business models to sustain their organization, and helping them develop and retain talent in their organizations.

Now that there are numerous examples of legal professionals taking a design approach to innovation, there is a new research opportunity to document and evaluate these projects as case studies. This means providing resources for these teams to administer self-evaluations, and also having teams of researchers from universities conduct unbiased evaluations of projects. We should invest in more rigorous analysis of these initiatives so we can begin learning how best to utilize design within a legal environment. We should resist the temptation to celebrate projects for simply existing, or to ignore them and refrain from any evaluation if a project seems like it did not produce the intended results. With more rigorous and public discussion about the outcome of design-driven innovation projects, we can identify specific design methods that work in the legal system, as well as more guiding principles to support lawyers as they integrate design into their practice.

The challenge that awaits is one of metrics. There is a need to both define what the key markers of "success" and "quality" are in legal innovation work, and to find tools to measure initiatives on these lines. Thorough case studies can develop these metrics, and these metrics can then be used as guides for future groups who want to use design to improve their work. As more law firms, courts, and other organizations face greater pressure to make their offerings user-friendly, efficient, and intelligent, they will be able to follow best practices established by these initial waves of legal design initiatives.

D.

Evaluation

2.13

Measuring Legal Quality

Ron Dolin

I INTRODUCTION

The General Counsel of a Fortune 100 company was recently asked if he measured ROI (return on investment) on his legal spend. "No," he said, "I can't. I can't measure quality."

At various conference panels, several of the largest firms claim they are revamping the way they handle their legal spend to be more in line with other cost centers.[1] The rise of "Legal Operations" in corporate legal departments is leading the way in the use of legal metrics.[2] These standard business metrics include performance, efficiency, and value. ROI means measuring return, and return requires estimating value. Value can be defined as quality divided by cost. Therefore, measuring quality is key to the modernization of legal departments, as well as their external legal service providers.

Measuring quality is not as simple as developing one's own metric, nor is it solely for quality control purposes within, say, a Six Sigma manufacturing process. As discussed below, quality serves a market purpose – an apples-to-apples *comparison*. As an example, Figure 2.13.1 shows what one reputable litigation law firm advertised as their strength: some notion of winning 88.4% of *something*. However, the details can be challenged. A competitor might argue with the fine (tiny) print, "Our partners have won 88.4% of the cases they have tried in their careers, as of May 2014."

Perhaps they could argue that this could or should be interpreted as an over-abundance of going to trial when the firm should have settled more of the losing cases. Without a broad agreement on standard quality benchmarks, each provider is free to highlight values that might be meaningless to clients, or challengeable – whether rightly or wrongly – by competitors or a professional guild wary of technological progress.

Quality metrics serve to incentivize market behavior. As discussed below, selecting such metrics is a design process that seeks to understand how a product or service is used by a majority of the market. It is also a value that must be amenable to formalization and transparent testing. Legal work product is increasingly subject to a more rigorous standard than simply asking someone if they like an attorney, or if they felt that they got their money's worth. Increasingly, the issue is *why* a client subjectively liked the work. Equally important is

---

[1] *See, e.g.*, Corporate Legal Operations Consortium (CLOC), www.cloc.org; Association of Corporate Counsel (ACC), www.acc.com/legalops.

[2] Susan Hansen, "The Rise of In-House Legal Operations," Bloomberg Law, February 24, 2015, available at: https://bol.bna.com/the-rise-of-in-house-legal-ops. *See also* O'Carroll and Kimbro – Legal Operations at Google, *infra*.

FIGURE 2.13.1 88.4% of what? Failed to settle on 11.6% of losing cases?

the extraction of objective, measurable characteristics of legal work product that help facilitate automation, quality control, and continued improvement of the field.

This chapter first discusses current practice for quality metrics in Section II. It then describes the purposes and benefits of using quality benchmarks in Section III. Section IV presents a brief example of a quality metric. In Section V, we view the development of legal quality metrics within a design framework and lay out some principles necessary for quality metrics within a legal setting. In Section VI, we present an initial formalism, including desirable mathematical properties, procedures for developing metrics, and some interesting textbook-style problems for more sophisticated analysis. In Section VII, we discuss the relationship between quality metrics and statistical analysis. Finally, Section VIII discusses the impact of a lack of quality metrics on the legal system, and the natural evolution of their use within a growing data-driven empirical field of law.

II CURRENT STATE OF THE ART

One of the best-known resources for in-house counsel is the Association of Corporate Counsel.[3] In 2011, they published a 50+ page guide to value-based management of outside counsel,[4] as well as many follow-on guides. There and elsewhere, some common performance metrics in legal services include the accuracy of cost and time estimates, "efficiency,"

---

[3] www.acc.com.
[4] ACC, "Guide to Managing Outside Counsel," 2011, available at: www.accvaluechallenge-digital.com/accvaluechallenge/acc-guide-to-managing-outside-counsel.

"responsiveness," etc. Increasingly, there is also a "big data" approach to metrics, from companies such as Lex Machina[5] and Ravel Law,[6] that seeks to predict outcome probabilities using data aggregated from many prior cases.

The accuracy of outcome predictions is suspect if there are no accompanying confidence levels, or if there are unknown differences between prior examples and the case at hand. That is, are the cases that led to a prediction sufficiently similar to a current case, or are there some material, distinguishing issues in the present case that might render those predictions erroneous? Moreover, the level of granularity is too coarse; it would be helpful to measure quality throughout the entire process. For example, in terms of transactional work, it is too late to know if an estate plan has errors after the testator has died, necessitating a complex legal process to address problems that might easily have been prevented if caught earlier.

Outcome-dependent payment adjustments such as "holdback bucket payments"[7] also miss the mark in terms of measuring work product throughout the process, possibly signaling a mid-course correction. Conversely, a well-written brief that furthers a client's intent is amenable to valuation, and may be high quality even if the client loses a lawsuit for other reasons. Metrics based solely on outcome too easily incorporate factors outside a lawyer's control, and therefore make it difficult to reward work based on its intrinsic value. Similarly, while a lawyer may want to measure repeat business and customer satisfaction as a quality metric, this is also quite coarse-grained, and insufficient to distinguish between objective and subjective measures of quality.

One Sloan article from 2012 discusses the importance of quality standards for patents, but does not list a single measurable quantity.[8] Quality metrics work best when applied industry-wide in order to avoid apples-to-oranges comparisons. Where ViewABill, for example, discusses the importance of quality metrics but does not actually list any specific ones, it is impossible to use their framework to compare legal service providers.[9] Similarly, in one law firm consultant's write-up about useful law firm metrics, nothing is given as a specific, measurable, quality metric; a 2016 article from Bloomberg Law discusses the need to measure the quality of legal work, listing areas such as attorney and client retention, collaboration, billing flexibility, and innovation.[10] However, most of the suggestions do not address quality directly, and no actual metrics are given.

For corporations with a large litigation profile, a risk portfolio is possible and metrics related to outcome goals can be correlated to process milestones. For example, DuPont came up with several factors involving early case assessment where outcome goals included not only final payout but also other characteristics important to management, such as how much time was taken by managers involved in the litigation. Factors even included early assessment of potential jury reaction. As DuPont highlights, measurement is key to improving both internal and external legal work:

> "Determining what to measure is a delicate balance between having a thorough metrics system and being overwhelmed by too much data. DuPont looks to metrics as an

---

[5] Lex Machina (acquired by LexisNexis in 2015), www.lexmachina.com.
[6] Ravel Law (acquired by LexisNexis in 2017), www.ravellaw.com.
[7] See ACC, *supra* note 4, at 25.
[8] David J. Kappos and Stuart Graham, "The Case for Standard Measures of Patent Quality," *MIT Sloan Management Review* 53 (3) (2012): 19.
[9] ViewABill, "Measuring Firm Quality with Client Value Initiatives," June 4, 2014, available at: www.viewabill.com/assets/graphics/press/VAB_Article_4June2014.pdf.
[10] Mark Cohen, "A New Metric to Evaluate Law Firm Quality," Big Law Business, January 6, 2016, available at: https://biglawbusiness.com/a-new-metric-to-evaluate-law-firm-quality/.

informational tool to measure performance in cost efficiency (the business of law) and quality and results (the practice of law). Our approach is unusual because it is used by case teams and primary law firms (or PLFs: firms with whom DuPont established exclusive relationships after its convergence process), not just by upper management, to continuously improve performance ...

Metrics are an integral part of the continuous improvement process, helping ensure that objectives are being met and that the organization is succeeding, and, just as importantly, identifying which programs are not working and where changes should be made. The DuPont metrics tell us more than the cost of improvements to a process or product. They tell us where to focus resources and help us discover the best practices that drive quality and results."[11]

However, it seems this work did not include a more comprehensive analysis to discover possible correlations between outcomes and various discrete, measurable aspects of work product. And while litigation may have measurable outcomes like final payout, it is not as obvious which outcomes might apply to transactional work. A comprehensive, standardized set of metrics would allow us to maintain quality throughout a process, apply appropriate components or "unbundled" services along the way, and accurately weigh cost/benefit trade-offs in purchasing legal services.

III PURPOSES OF QUALITY METRICS

A *Innovation*

In product valuation, there are many kinds of quality metrics and standardized benchmarks. As described by Clayton Christensen in *The Innovator's Dilemma*[12] and his related writings, market maturity is measured in part by a move from all-encompassing integrated solutions to componentized, modular ones (in law, "unbundled" services[13]). The ability to plug in components facilitates finer-grain competition via interface standards. Benchmarks are important because they allow an apples-to-apples comparison of these components. When different quality metrics are used by different suppliers, there is simply no straightforward way to compare components.

With standardized quality metrics in place, components can be used based on a value curve, allowing someone to piece together an appropriate level of quality within a given cost framework. This is why, for example, we see benchmarks for computer components, such as CPU floating-point operations per second (FLOPS), or mean time between failures (MTBF) for memory and hard drives. Competition at the component level allows us to buy commodity products of varying capabilities and price points, while the quality benchmarks help guarantee that the overall system will function correctly.

Several *MIT Sloan Management Review* articles over the years have looked at quality within the technology sector. The question is whether there is anything inherent in technology that might preclude the same approach to measuring the quality of legal products and

---

[11] Thomas L. Sager and Gerard G. Boccuti, "Achieving the Common Goal: DuPont's Performance Metrics," in *Representing the Corporation: Strategies for Legal Counsel*, 2nd ed., ed. Richard H. Weise (New York, NY: Aspen Publishers, 2006).

[12] Clayton M. Christensen, *The Innovator's Dilemma: When New Technologies Cause Great Firms to Fail* (Boston, MA: Harvard Business Review Press, 2013).

[13] Stephanie L. Kimbro, *Limited Scope Legal Services: Unbundling and the Self-Help Client* (Chicago, IL: American Bar Association, 2012).

services. For example, in 2005, one article, "What Quality Means Today," discussed the role of quality in the internet marketplace:

> "Today's highly competitive worldwide marketplace and advances in information technology have created greater customer demand for quality than ever before. The Internet, for example, has made the quality of a company's products and services transparent to customers. As a result, new offerings not perceived as being of high quality are increasingly likely to fail or become quickly commoditized. What's more, consumers now view quality as a fundamental measure of their total perception of the product or service as well as of the company, delivery and maintenance network that provides and supports it – a kind of unified "quality–value" metric."[14]

Another *Sloan* article from 2011, "How Quality Drives the Rise and Fall of High-Tech Products," describes how quality trumps having an established user base:

> "In our study, we defined quality as a composite of the brand attributes (such as reliability, performance and convenience) that customers valued. We then derived our measure of quality from the reviews in four of the most respected and widely circulated computer magazines of the time. We selected the personal computer products and services markets because these markets are supposed to exhibit strong network effects. Yet we found that not only did quality prevail in these markets, but network effects enhanced the role of quality. In other words, network effects drove customers to quality and superior brands."[15]

Isn't this trend inevitable? Could legal services avoid these types of metrics? So far, perhaps – consider the ROI dilemma of the general counsel mentioned above. However, given the market changes happening in legal services and the shift from a producer-driven market to a consumer-driven market, corporate counsel is pushing the field forward.[16] Standardized quality metrics are key.

A typical pattern in the rollout of legal technology is exemplified by e-discovery.[17] An existing, human-based system is assumed "good." A new technology-based process is triggered for whatever reason (e.g., new technology, scalability issues, cost issues). The quality of the new process is questioned, and shown to be imperfect. This then forces an analysis, long-overdue, of the prior process, using quality metrics such as precision and recall.[18] The new process is shown to be higher quality, less expensive, and faster. Thus, in the face of the vast inefficiencies inherent in legal practice, the usual project management mantra of "pick any two" does not apply.[19] A simple question remains: *How much quality is efficiency worth?* Since, in law, gains in efficiency frequently correspond with gains in quality (e.g., document automation), the only way to determine if quality is negatively impacted at all, let alone by how much, is to measure it.

---

[14] Armand V. Feigenbaum and Donald S. Feigenbaum, "What Quality Means Today," *MIT Sloan Management Review* 46 (2) (2005): 96.
[15] Gerard Tellis, Eden Yin, and Rakesh Niraj, "How Quality Drives the Rise and Fall of High-Tech Products," *MIT Sloan Management Review* 52 (4) (2011): 14.
[16] See, e.g., Dolin and Buley – Adaptive Innovation: The Innovator's Dilemma in Big Law, *infra*.
[17] See, e.g., the EDRM model (www.edrm.net/frameworks-and-standards/edrm-model), Figure 3.5.1, *infra*; The Sedona Conference, www.thesedonaconference.org; and *Rio Tinto PLC v. Vale SA*, 306 F.R.D. 125 (2015).
[18] Herbert L. Roitblat, Anne Kershaw, and Patrick Oot, "Document Categorization in Legal Electronic Discovery: Computer Classification vs. Manual Review," *Journal of the American Society for Information Science and Technology* 61 (1) (2010): 70–80.
[19] The trade-offs are between some form of cost, time, and quality. See, e.g., "Project Management Triangle," *Wikipedia*, available at: https://en.wikipedia.org/wiki/Project_management_triangle (accessed June 9, 2020).

B Access to Justice: UPL vs. Technology

There is ongoing debate in the USA about whether or when the use of technology constitutes unauthorized practice of law (UPL). One panel at the ABA's Center for Professional Responsibility's Second UPL School (2015) was entitled, "The Users and Abusers: Technology and the Unauthorized Practice of Law."[20] Part of the discussion extended prior work[21] that questioned whether document automation should be considered UPL. Depending on the particular implementation, if the software simply instantiates what a lawyer would produce anyway, should it be considered "unauthorized"? The ABA panel yielded a heated debate among panelists and attendees, which included state bar executives, ABA ethics experts, and even the GC of LegalZoom.

1 Comparisons between which Lawyers and which Software

A lot of the discussion around UPL and technology seems to boil down to the assumption that software produces lower-quality work product than lawyers do. Depending on the audience, it might seem outright offensive to even raise the issue. But before we can rationally object to the putative lower quality of technology, we need to examine the quality of lawyer-produced work product. Lawyers and law firms often argue or advertise that they produce the highest-quality work, as compared to other lawyers. In other words, by lawyers' own account, lawyers do not think that all lawyers produce the same quality of work. If some work is better, some must be worse. In an objection to the relative quality of technology as compared to lawyers, which lawyers are being compared? The quality threshold for lawyers is usually malpractice, based mainly on standards for competence and negligence. In criminal procedure, merely poor work is insufficient for a criminal defendant to receive a new trial. There is a range of allowable quality of legal work performed by licensed attorneys. Should technology have to perform better than the worst allowable lawyer?

One complaint that came up at the ABA panel discussion was that judges and lawyers have seen poor results from software – usually related to estate plans or bankruptcy. Even assuming that those complaints are valid, does it imply that we should throw out the baby with the bath water? Perhaps software produces at least "good enough" work product in areas such as eviction, uncontested divorces, or debt collection, such that consumers are better off with, rather than without, the software. If any restrictions are necessary, would it be better to limit software by practice area than to claim UPL for all of it? Moreover, many lawyers complain about new clients coming in with poorly structured incorporation documents created by other lawyers. Why would we tolerate poor work product from some lawyers but not argue for shutting them all down, and then turn around and make that argument about software?

2 Realistic Minimal Standards

Assume for argument's sake that we compare technology to the "reasonable" attorney, however reasonableness might be determined, and find the technology to be lower quality. Should the technology standard be "as good as the reasonable lawyer" in order for it to leave clients better off

---

[20] More information is available at: www.americanbar.org/groups/professional_responsibility/events_cle/2015abauplschool/uplschoolcoursematerials/breakout2.html.

[21] Ron Dolin, "Using A Document Automation System: Authorized Practice of Law?" mycase.com, August 28, 2013, available at: www.mycase.com/blog/2013/08/guest-post-using-a-document-automation-system-authorized-practice-of-law.

than the real-world alternatives they face? The American access-to-justice (A2J) crisis is so severe (as has been broadly discussed by the ABA,[22] LSC,[23] etc.) that it is unconscionable to ignore that millions of people are representing themselves and failing miserably in the process. The issue is not whether technology can compare with a given attorney, or even the worst allowable one. The issue is whether technology leaves the client better off than viable alternatives. *If individuals are unable to work with an attorney due to a lack of personal or societal resources, are they better off using technology or not, regardless of whether the technology is as good as an unavailable attorney?* No other comparison is rational. Even if we were to compare technology with lawyers, how do we measure the quality of lawyers to make the comparison? Having no data is not an excuse to block technology that can help people who have no other choices.

3 Advantages of Technology

There are several advantages of software-based legal help. The first is how inexpensive it is. Fees for common work product from LegalZoom and other technology-based for-profit legal service providers are generally substantially less than one-on-one lawyer fees.[24] Non-profit technology solutions are even less expensive. Another benefit is the ability to correct software when problems are found; problems are more likely to be discovered with software than with humans, since interactions can be logged and analyzed. Moreover, software can be certified just like people, but, once certified, software's behavior is predictable.

Software can also be classified, so that some, like "yes/no" decision trees, can be highly predictable and tailored to specific cases (e.g., types of eviction, bankruptcy, divorce, incorporation). Other technology that is more fuzzy might be available only if accompanied by lawyer review, thus allowing a gain in efficiency while bypassing any UPL issues. In addition, quality control is at least as available for software as it is for people. Just because a professional might be personable does not mean the work product is good. For software, we are more likely to measure the work product than simply the interface – the interface is more of a market issue, while the work product is more of a licensing issue. Finally, and most importantly, there is no other option that can scale up to the level of the problem *except* technology. There are simply not enough lawyers or resources to fund a person-to-person oriented solution to the A2J problem.[25]

4 Quality Standards Enable Actual Solutions

In computer science, the Turing Test is a way of gauging the level of intelligence in a software system.[26] Software passes the Turing Test if a person interacting with it cannot determine if the software is a person or not. In a similar vein, if software-generated legal work product is

---

[22] ABA, "ATJ Assessment Materials," available at: www.americanbar.org/groups/legal_aid_indigent_defendants/initiatives/resource_center_for_access_to_justice/atj-commissions/atj_commission_self-assessment_materials1.html.

[23] Helaine M. Barnett, *Documenting the Justice Gap in America: The Current Unmet Civil Legal Needs of Low-Income Americans* (Washington, DC: Legal Services Corporation, 2005), available at: www.lsc.gov/sites/default/files/LSC/images/justicegap.pdf.

[24] *See, e.g.*, Benjamin Barton, "The Fall and Rise of Lawyers," CNN, May 23, 2015; available at: www.cnn.com/2015/05/22/opinions/barton-rise-and-fall-of-lawyers/index.html.

[25] For more on A2J, *see* Staudt and Rabanal – Access to Justice and Technology: Reaching a Greater Future for Legal Aid, *infra*; and Bulinski and Prescott – Designing Legal Experiences: Online Communication and Resolution in Courts, *infra*.

[26] Alan Turing, "Computing Machinery and Intelligence," *Mind* 49 (1950): 433–460; available at: www.csee.umbc.edu/courses/471/papers/turing.pdf.

indistinguishable from human-generated work product, how bad could the software be? Most importantly, how is the client worse off? The goal of UPL is to protect clients, not to prevent them from getting help. Compare this goal with the fact that most UPL formal complaints in the USA are brought by protectionist lawyers rather than by "wronged" consumers.[27] A focus on measuring the quality of work product, rather than the process used to generate it, stands to help a lot of people who really need it.

C Machine Learning Evaluation

A lot of machine learning (ML) development requires human-generated test/training data. Similarity matching, ranking, and general relevance (e.g., e-discovery "responsiveness") are subject to interpretation. Even binary classification requires human-generated test data.[28] Research has indicated that there is a dearth of human-generated training data.[29]

Even if more data were available, however, the assumption that it is consistent is questionable:

> "Part of what a human indexer does is to interpret the text (understand the message). Human indexers do this in the context of their cultures and their personal experiences, including their prejudices, as well as taking into consideration user needs and desires. Consequently, an index based on human indexing may not travel well between cultures. A freedom fighter in one culture may be a terrorist in another ...
>
> One conclusion that must be drawn from this survey of expert commentary on human intellectual analysis of messages is this: the one thing we definitely do know about human indexers is that they rarely agree on what is important in a message, or what to call it."[30]

Asking an expert whether something is in or out of a set, or should be tagged a certain way, etc., is prone to error and uncertainty. Automated evaluation techniques such as BLEU and ROUGE extend human-evaluated training data by identifying objective aspects of "good" work that correlate to subjective analysis.[31] To the degree that the objective measures are "good enough" to facilitate, at a minimum, coarse tuning (and often better than that), they can greatly impact the development of ML systems. A quality formalism presents a framework that facilitates more of a direct mapping from the reasons behind expert analysis to a model that is extensible and directly useful to automation. Instead of simply asking experts for their scores, this methodology seeks to uncover the reasons for their scores and model them

---

[27] Deborah L. Rhode and Lucy B. Ricca, "Protecting the Profession or the Public: Rethinking Unauthorized-Practice Enforcement," *Fordham Law Review* 82 (2013): 2587.

[28] Ron Kohavi, "A Study of Cross-Validation and Bootstrap for Accuracy Estimation and Model Selection," in *International Joint Conference on Artificial Intelligence (IJCAI), Volume 14* (San Francisco, CA: Morgan Kaufmann, 1995), 1137–1145.

[29] Kishore Papineni, Salim Roukos, Todd Ward, and Wei-Jing Zhu, "BLEU: a Method for Automatic Evaluation of Machine Translation," in *Proceedings of the 40th Annual Meeting on Association for Computational Linguistics* (Stroudsburg, PA: Association for Computational Linguistics, 2002), 311–318; Chin-Yew Lin, "ROUGE: A Package for Automatic Evaluation of Summaries," in *Text Summarization Branches Out: Proceedings of the ACL-04 Workshop, Volume 8*, Barcelona, Spain, 2004, available at: http://anthology.aclweb.org/W/W04/W04-1013.pdf.

[30] James D. Anderson and José Pérez-Carballo, "The Nature of Indexing: How Humans and Machines Analyze Messages and Texts for Retrieval. Part I: Research, and the Nature of Human Indexing," *Information Processing & Management* 37 (2) (2001): 231–254.

[31] Papineni et al., *supra* note 29; Lin, *supra* note 29. One substitute for a well-translated text might involve, for example, translating from one language to another and then back to the original, and counting the number of longer phrases that are identical. This is a reasonable approach for certain types of testing, but it does not get to the heart of whether or why a translation is high quality when read by a native speaker.

accordingly. In the legal realm, uncovering what makes work product high-quality, such as a patent, a court brief, a contract, etc., can serve to facilitate a more robust, larger, and more consistent collection of test and training data.

IV EXAMPLE: DEPOSITION WITNESS FILES

Suppose that a new legal service provider produces "witness files" that include documents used for depositions. How might they measure the quality of their work in a way that would allow them to compete with similarly situated companies?

In information retrieval (IR), documents are deemed "relevant" when they relate to a given query. We measure the quality (Q) of a query result set with the notions of precision (P) and recall (R). Precision is the fraction of documents in a result set that are relevant. Recall is the fraction of relevant documents from the entire collection that are contained in the result set. Clearly, both P and R range in value from 0 to 1. Thus, by setting $Q = P \times R$, the highest quality result set, $Q = 1.0$, would be one in which every document in it is relevant, and which also contains all the relevant documents from the entire collection. We can use this metric to measure the quality of a witness file.[32]

Define *relevant* in this case as those documents put in front of a witness by opposing counsel during a deposition. The highest-quality witness file would consist of all and only such documents with a quality score of 1.0. Suppose that the witness is too busy to have time to be prepped for all the documents in the witness file. We would like to order the documents in the witness file in some efficient manner so that the witness is prepped for the most important documents. How might we assign weights to the documents?

Assume that any document used by a judge in a court opinion is really important – assign it a weight of 3 out of 3. Documents that are not used in opinions but are used as evidence in trial will receive a weight of 2. Finally, documents that are used in neither opinions nor evidence, but are used by opposing counsel during deposition, are given a weight of 1. All other documents get weight 0. Define the efficiency score, E, as the total of the weights used in witness prep divided by the optimal.[33] For example, suppose that a witness was prepped on ten documents, of which three were 3s, four were 2s, and three were 1s. However, the witness file contained five 3s and five 2s. Thus, the efficiency score would be 20/25, or 0.8.

The perfect witness file and prep would have a quality–efficiency (QE) score of $Q \times E = 1.0 \times 1.0 = 1.0$. This score entails a set of documents that were all brought up by opposing counsel in deposition. Moreover, the most important documents in the witness file that were used in the case were discussed with the witness, given the amount of time the witness had for prep.

Even though a QE score of 1.0 is improbable, the point is to set a metric that creates a competitive landscape based on a desired goal. In this case, companies wanting to do the best trial prep work, based on this metric, would be arguing that they can effectively anticipate opposing counsel well by selecting documents of interest to them. Furthermore, they can anticipate which documents are most likely to be used in court and by a judge, and efficiently work with busy clients. In addition, a high score means that the amount of time being spent on non-relevant documents is minimized. This is good for clients under a billable-hour

---

[32] For an introduction to precision and recall, *see* Dolin – Information Intermediation, *supra*.
[33] Obviously the weights cannot be assigned until after the case has resolved, so the efficiency score cannot be calculated at the time the witness is prepped.

model, and this is good for service providers under a flat-fee model. A good metric incentivizes competition based on desirable market goals.

V PRINCIPLES AND THE DESIGN PROCESS

A Goals

There are many reasons to pursue legal quality benchmarks, beyond the previously discussed goal of allowing consumers of legal services to make apples-to-apples comparisons of various service providers. Such benchmarks also, for example, provide a common framework for data-driven assessment of legal spend (i.e., ROI). They allow for the stratification of service quality so that consumers can buy the appropriate level of service to match the importance or complexity of a given problem, paying only as much as is warranted. This overcomes the problem, detailed by Christensen in *Innovator's Dilemma*, of driving the market toward the highest-end customers with features not needed by most consumers.[34] Another important reason to develop benchmarks is to focus on what, not how, legal work is produced (e.g., licensing of both people and software), which supports increasing efficiency without degrading quality. In addition, benchmarks provide a framework for continual quality improvement. Finally, benchmarks allow for the prevention and discovery of problems with continuous measurement, especially where such assessment is automated.

B Evaluation as Design Process

Imagine that we ask a technician in an electronics lab what he might consider to be a key quality aspect of memory chips. Suppose his work entails constantly swapping memory chips on boards, and he says that he needs chips with strong pins. From his perspective, he might want pins made from a certain material, and not care how long the chips last. His needs are legitimate, but uncommon, and are unhelpful for the vast majority of users. Alternatively, consider two benchmarks for computer components – FLOPS and MTBF. These common industry benchmarks are likely consistent with the use patterns of most users, who care much more about the robustness of their computers, which are left unchanged once acquired. Quality benchmarks are derived by ethnographic analysis that investigates common use patterns and pain points. These types of analyses are a normal component of the design process.[35] Legal quality benchmarks are no different; they are derivable only by uncovering the needs of typical legal consumers, and then designing metrics that meet the quality requirements and principles unique to the legal market.

C Legal Quality Metric Principles

One of the most important principles of legal quality metrics, discussed in Section IV, is that the metric should *incentivize desired market behavior*. As with FLOPS and MTBF, the behavior should be agreeable to both producers and consumers of the product or service – a marketable quantity. Second, the metric needs to be *neutral* to any particular interest or stakeholder. Thus, a litigation benchmark must be viewed as reasonable to both sides and be

---

[34] Christensen, *The Innovator's Dilemma*, *supra* note 12; For more details, *see* Dolin and Buley – Adaptive Innovation: The Innovator's Dilemma in Big Law, *infra*.

[35] *See, e.g.*, Hagan – Introduction to Design Thinking for Law, *supra*.

helpful to the process. For example, if both sides in litigation have high confidence in the likely damages award ranges assessed by their own experts, and the two ranges sufficiently overlap, then further litigation, and additional consumer costs, are disincentivized. A quality metric that gives such confidence is helpful to both sides. Third, as stated above, metrics need to address core use patterns – they need to be *based on consumer needs*. Fourth, since law includes human-to-human activities requiring agreement by more than one party (e.g., negotiation, dispute resolution, agency approval), quality measurements often need to *account for the input complexity* of the work. For example, some patent subject matter has a much lower acceptance rate than others. Similarly, some negotiating parties are known to be challenging, and thus the expected complexity of a contract is greater. Fifth, quality metrics must be *practical and implementable* to parties expected to produce them. Sixth, discussed in Section VI, a quality metric needs to *correlate to a consumer's subjective interpretation* of quality. Finally, quality metrics need to be *objective, transparent, mathematical measurements*.

VI MATHEMATICAL FORMALISM

A What's in a Number?

An engineering perspective on quality is described succinctly in an IEEE article that states that in most (image) quality assessment approaches, "the main objective is to develop measures that are consistent with the subjective evaluation."[36] Section IV presented an example using deposition witness files to describe what this might look like, focusing on showing how a *QE* score might encourage competition of desirable characteristics of a particular legal product or service. In this section, we examine how to select numerical values that correlate with our subjective notion of quality.[37] The mathematics presented here is straightforward – a weighted normalized geometric mean.[38] The point is to closely associate the formalism with our intuition.

B Example: Selecting an Attorney

Selecting an attorney is in many ways similar to selecting an online date.[39] We care about several factors and have to combine them to get a ranked list of candidates. Matching algorithms are similar to how we measure general search results. In search, we may want to factor in topic, author, date, or even geographic region. Similarly, as we consider measuring something like *QE*, we have to combine several factors to come up with a set of selection criteria – which provider should we use?

---

[36] Gabriel Dauphin and P. Viaris de Lesegno, "Analysis and Comparison of Quality Metrics with Reference Based on Uniform Colour Spaces," in *2nd European Workshop on Visual Information Processing (EUVIP)*, Paris, France (Piscataway, NJ: IEEE, 2010), 23–28.

[37] Nothing in this approach is inherently specific to law.

[38] Computationally, a geometric mean is often performed in log space, but that makes the mapping from subjective to objective less intuitive. As previously discussed in Section III.C, BLEU used a simpler version of geometric mean, *supra* note 29. See the section *infra* about statistical metrics regarding the use of geometric vs. harmonic mean.

[39] See, e.g., Eli J. Finkel, Paul W. Eastwick, Benjamin R. Karney, Harry T. Reis, and Susan Sprecher, "Online Dating: A Critical Analysis from the Perspective of Psychological Science," *Psychological Science in the Public Interest* 13 (1) (2012): 3–66, available at: http://journals.sagepub.com/doi/full/10.1177/1529100612436522. This article discusses, in part, the limitations of current dating algorithms, which raises more questions than it answers.

How we incorporate factors is an individualized choice. A good result for one person is not necessarily a good result for someone else. Moreover, what matters to us is impacted by what is available. If we do not find what we are looking for (search results, vendors, online dates, whatever), we have to adjust our criteria. We are looking for the best from a pool of potential candidates, and that pool may vary from region to region or from day to day. The example of selecting an attorney highlights how we combine characteristics in general.

C Step One: Combining Normalized Scores

Suppose I want to select an attorney to help me with a legal issue. The most simple case would be one in which I care only about a single factor – say, cost. Suppose there are a set of attorneys whose only distinguishable difference is how much they charge for handling my issue. I can just rank them based on who is the least expensive. Of course, I am likely to care about other factors, too. Suppose I also care about distance. If I cared only about distance, I could do the same with distance as I did with cost and just rank the attorneys by proximity. But I need to combine both cost and distance to get a single ranked list (i.e., reduce two dimensions to one). This will be the order in which I look through the results in more detail to make a final selection.

Imagine two hypothetical cases. Suppose that for Case 1, one attorney, A_1, would charge $1000 and is 20 miles away, and that a second attorney, A_2, would charge $2000 and is 10 miles away. We can represent this as A_1 = ($1000, 20 mi) and A_2 = ($2000, 10 mi). I might prefer driving the extra 10 miles to save $1000. I could score the attorneys by simply adding the cost and distance values: score(A_1) = 1020; score(A_2) = 2010. In this case, I would select the attorney with the smaller score. But what if, in Case 2, the less expensive attorney is 100 miles away, A_1' = ($1000, 100 mi) and I do not want to drive that far? The numbers do not work: score (A_1') = 1100, which is still smaller than score(A_2) = 2010. In this case, the smaller score is no longer my preference.

Another approach might be to derive the score by multiplying cost and distance. For Case 1, that would yield equal scores, even though I prefer the less expensive attorney: score (A_1) = score (A_2) = 20,000. This sets each mile of distance equal to $100 in fees, which does not fit what I want. Case 2 works a bit better: score(A_1') = 100,000 > score(A_2). So my preference of A_2 is again the lower score. However, an attorney A_1'' who is only 21 miles away, an acceptable distance for the reduced cost, would get a higher score than the more expensive attorney, A_2: score(A_1'') = 21,000 > score(A_2). This still does not fit what I want.

To reconcile this, we first derive a new score for each factor (e.g., cost, distance) before combining them together. The new scores are *normalized* – a range from 0 to 1 – such that a score of 0 is completely unacceptable, and a score of 1 is perfect. We can then multiply the normalized values to arrive at a new combined score whose range is also 0–1, where 0 means completely unacceptable and 1 means perfect. The higher the score, the better the candidate.

To get the values for each factor, we define ranges (there are many ways to accomplish this). Suppose that for distance, we define three levels: very close, close enough, and too far. Very close, say anything within 10 miles, will get a 1. A distance of 50 miles or greater is unacceptably far, so we give that a 0. Finally, a distance between 11 and 49 miles will get 0.5. We can similarly stratify cost: 1 ($0–$999); 0.75 ($1000–$1999); 0.5 ($2000–$2999); 0.25 ($3000–$3999); and 0 ($4000+).

Using this scoring system, Case 1 yields score(A_1) = (0.75 × 0.5) = 0.375, and score (A_2) = (0.5 × 0.5) = 0.25. For this type of scoring, since the larger number is better, we would select the less expensive attorney (who happens to be within our acceptable driving distance). Case 2, however, yields score(A1´) = (0.75 × 0) = 0 for the less expensive but very distant attorney. We would thus select the more expensive attorney – the only one within our distance limits. These values are closer to what we wanted.

D Properties

At this point, we have a ranked list based on a "cost–distance" score with some intuitive characteristics. What are a minimal set of properties required from a mathematical framework that would allow us to adequately quantify the characteristics that lead to our subjective assessment of relative quality among a set of candidates?[40]

Property 1: First and foremost, we need an *ordered ranking* that correlates to our intuitive notion of how to balance the trade-offs between various criteria (e.g., cost and distance). This only needs to be a *non-strict total order*, in which we can assign a score to each candidate, but multiple candidates can get the same score. For example, if one lawyer is farther away but less expensive, and another lawyer is closer but more expensive, the two might be equally desirable. We are effectively assigning an equivalency relationship between the various characteristics (e.g., a certain change in distance is equivalent to a certain change in cost, though not necessarily linearly).

Property 2: The scoring approach needs to be *heterogeneous* – it has to be able to accommodate and combine any type of data. So far, we have described distance and cost, which are one-dimensional. Section VI.G shows an example of extending this to other types of (multidimensional) data.

Property 3: We need a *filter* that excludes all unacceptable candidates. In this case, we exclude any attorney that is either too far or too expensive, regardless of how good that attorney might be in any other way. We can get this property, for example, by multiplying values, and assigning 0 for any unacceptable characteristic. If a candidate is unacceptable in any one of its characteristics, the final score will be 0, and thus excluded from the result set.

This is an important property. If we have any hard limits for any characteristic (too far, too expensive, wrong city, etc.), then it simply does not matter if a candidate fits all the other characteristics perfectly. The flip side of this, however, is to use filtering judiciously. For example, if we set a hard limit at 50 miles, but an otherwise perfect lawyer is 51 miles away, did we really want to exclude her? Furthermore, since we need to adjust our scoring based on the candidate set, we may need to set our exclusion limit differently on a case-by-case basis. If we are looking for a lawyer in an urban area, we might be able to justify a shorter limit on distance than if we are in a rural area – and perhaps the inverse on cost for the same reason (density of lawyers). Filtering is more appropriate for, say, excluding a lawyer who works in an unrelated practice area.

Property 4: We need *normalized scoring*: All characteristics are assigned a value within a range from 0 to 1, inclusive. This is an extension of Boolean scoring, which is either 0 (exclude) or 1 (include). But while Boolean scoring also has the filtering property, it does not have the ranking property – all acceptable candidates get the same score: 1. With normalized scoring, any characteristic treated as a Boolean can be included in a multiplicative combination of scores and the product will still function properly.

Property 5: We would like to incorporate a *hierarchy* (or *nesting*) property. Hierarchical scoring allows us to derive sub-scores and treat them as atomic scores, or take an atomic score

---

[40] Other (non-essential) desirable properties are listed later in this chapter. A *recursive* property is discussed in Problem 1 in Section VI.H. A *similarity metric* property is discussed in note 48, *infra*.

and decompose it into smaller elements without impacting the way that characteristic is used. For example, in Section IV, QE scoring was derived by first combining precision and recall. That combination was then merged with an efficiency score. If we want to derive efficiency by incorporating additional characteristics, we can do so without having to modify the quality component. This property is important for easily accommodating different weighting schemes, described below.

Property 6: Combining different types of data and their corresponding quality metrics is more intuitive with *averaging* the (normalized) sub-scores.[41] Suppose that we assign a value of 0.5 to the midpoint between unacceptable and perfect for all the characteristics we care about – say, a cost of $2500 and a distance of 30 miles for an attorney candidate. If we just multiply the respective scores, we get 0.25 (0.5 × 0.5). On the other hand, if we take the square root after we multiply, we get back to 0.5. That is, if we multiply the scores of n characteristics that all have the same value, and then take the nth root, the final score is the same as the value of all the individual characteristics. This property should also hold under weighting.

Property 7: Finally, we need a scoring mechanism that is *weightable* – that is, one in which we can accommodate making some characteristics (or sub-characteristics) more or less important relative to other ones (further discussed in Section VI.F).

E Formalism: Capturing Our Intuition

First, define relevance, *Rel*, as the total generalized quality score (extending the more limited notion of a quality score used previously for QE). There are several reasons that multiplying sub-scores works better than adding them. As pointed out above, it is difficult to get the various characteristics to take on appropriate relative values without normalizing them within a 0–1 range. Once normalized, however, addition is still problematic. Consider two examples in which we combine two different characteristics, say cost and distance. In Case 3, let cost and distance both have a score of 0.5. In Case 4, though, let cost be a perfect 1, and distance be an unacceptable 0. If we take the additive mean, both cases would give us a final score of 0.5. Case 3 would be (0.5 + 0.5) / 2, and Case 4 would be (1 + 0) / 2. If we use multiplicative scoring with averaging (geometric mean), it turns out differently. Case 3 would still be 0.5 ($\sqrt{(0.5 \times 0.5)}$), but Case 4 would end up with a score of 0 ($\sqrt{(1 \times 0)}$). Since we want to filter out candidates for which any characteristic has a score of 0, the additive method is completely inadequate, and the multiplicative method is closer to our subjective perspective.

This is easier to understand visually. Additive scoring is shown in Figure 2.13.2a, which shows the total score along the z-axis, by averaging (additively) the individual scores along the x (cost) and y (distance) axes. In Case 3, the total score at (0.5, 0.5) is 0.5, which is fine. However, everything along that contour line, from (0, 1) to (1, 0) is also 0.5, including Case 4 at (1, 0). This is erroneous – Case 4 should get a score of 0 due to the unacceptable distance, regardless of cost. In fact, we need everything along the x and y axes (where x or y are 0) to yield a total score of 0 – the filtering property.

---

[41] For the mathematically oriented reader, the most basic property of averages is that the average of a list of identical elements is that element itself. Another important property is that the average is bound by the minimum and maximum of the elements. Beyond that, there is extensive literature on various types of averages and means, and several of their relevant properties and individual differences (*see, e.g.,* topics such as "average," "mean," "generalized f-mean," "Fréchet mean," etc.). The selection in this chapter of the weighted geometric mean as the most appropriate formalism is discussed throughout, with the main alternative being the harmonic mean.

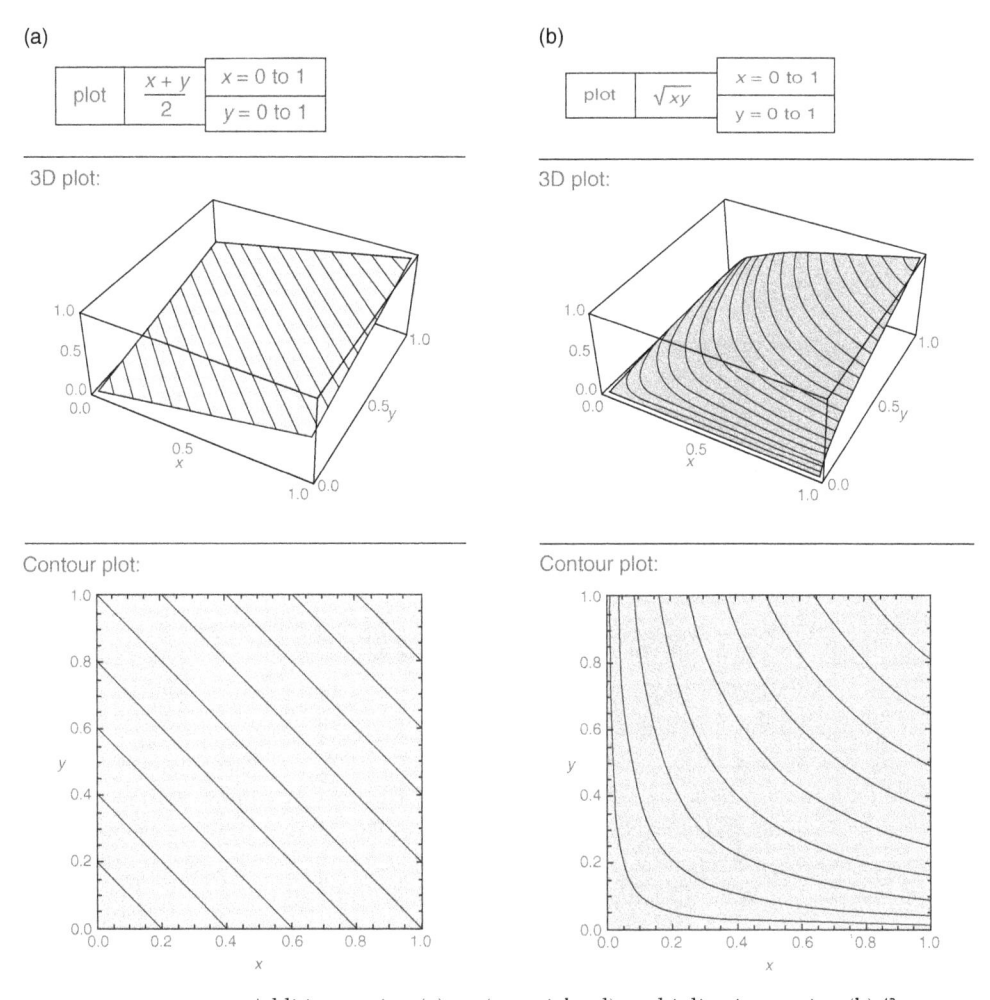

FIGURE 2.13.2 Additive scoring (a) vs. (unweighted) multiplicative scoring (b).[42]

Compare this to (unweighted) multiplicative scoring, shown in Figure 2.13.2b. The relevance formula for unweighted multiplicative scoring is shown in Equation 2.13.1, where Rel is the total relevance score, and n is the number of factors, F_i.

$$Rel = \sqrt[n]{\prod_{i=1}^{n} F_i} \qquad (2.13.1)$$

With this scoring method, Case 3, at (0.5, 0.5) also gets a score of 0.5, as desired. Case 4, however, at (1, 0), gets the requisite score of 0 (the filtering property). In addition, the score for any point along the diagonal from (0, 0) to (1, 1) is equal to the value of x and y.

F Step Two: Hierarchical Weighting

Consider the example from Section IV, assigning a QE score to deposition witness files. Suppose that for some bet-the-company lawsuit, quality may be a lot more important than cost. We would

---

[42] Figures 2.13.2 and 2.13.3 were created using Wolfram Alpha, www.wolframalpha.com.

like to weigh quality much more than efficiency in the QE score. Efficiency, however, still matters. If two vendors are able to supply roughly the same quality work, but one can do it much more inexpensively, the scoring algorithm should favor the less expensive vendor.

QE was composed of three separate characteristics. First, the quality score, Q, was derived from precision, P, times recall, R. We then multiplied Q times an efficiency value, E, to arrive at a final score in the 0–1 range. In that case, we were multiplying all the values: $QE = P \times R \times E$. In order to simplify that example, we did not adjust the scoring to get an average value, which would entail taking the cube root. Since we want to tweak Q, we can view QE as $Q \times E$, or $(P \times R) \times E$. In order to give more weight to quality, we can raise its value with an exponent greater than 1, depending on how much we want to emphasize it.[43] Then, in order to retain the averaging property, we take the associated root. Suppose, for example, we have two characteristics, x and y, and we consider the y criteria much more important (though x still matters). We could adjust the score by raising the y value to, say, the fourth power, and then take the fifth root of the combined score, as shown in Figure 2.13.3.

This approach (i.e., weighted geometric mean) provides all the desired properties discussed in Section VI.D. We maintain averaging – for example, where $x = y$, $z = x$ (or y); also, the final score falls between the minimum and maximum of the sub-scores. Furthermore, by using multiplicative scoring, we maintain the filtering property under weighting. Both 0 and 1 remain unchanged when raised to any non-zero power, so an unacceptable sub-score of 0 remains 0 under weighting; thus the total score will stay 0, excluding that candidate. Furthermore, something that is perfect for a given characteristic remains perfect under weighting. The difference in applying the weighting, though, is that the more heavily weighted term has a greater impact on the final score. Figure 2.13.3 shows that, for most of the values over x and y, the final score z is mainly determined by the y value (except where x is close to 0, which we expect and want). Thus, under the weighted geometric mean approach, we enable weighting without losing the other required properties.

In general, the relevance formula for weighted multiplicative scoring is shown in Equation 2.13.2, where Rel is the total relevance score, n is the number of factors, F_i, and W_i is the per-factor weight. Since $0 \leq F_i \leq 1$, Rel will also be in that range. In general, $W_i \geq 0$ (see below).

$$Rel = \sqrt[\sum_{j=1}^{n} W_j]{\prod_{i=1}^{n} F_i^{W_i}} \qquad (2.13.2)$$

Returning to QE, we can increase the importance of quality in our final score by raising Q to some appropriate power. But, more importantly, since we have the hierarchy property, we can also examine the Q score and adjust the individual weightings of its elements. Suppose that it is more important that the witness is prepped on all relevant documents than it is that the witness potentially wastes time on irrelevant ones. In that case, we can increase the weight of R over P, and calculate Q prior to combining it with E. By doing this hierarchically, we do not have to figure out the relative weights of P or R to E. We are also free to decompose E into separate elements and weightings, without having to relate them back to any of the Q sub-components. In this case, we would first set Q as, say, $Q = (P \times R^3)^{1/4}$, emphasizing R over P. Then, to emphasize Q over E, we could set $QE = (Q^5 \times E)^{1/6}$.[44]

---

[43] The selection of appropriate weights depends on the combination of individual goals, availability pool, and the set of evaluative criteria being used.

[44] This reduces to $QE = P^{(5/24)} \times R^{(15/24)} \times E^{(4/24)}$. Simplifying nested weighting is arguably more straightforward and intuitive using the basic laws of exponents via geometric means than the use of reciprocals under a harmonic mean model.

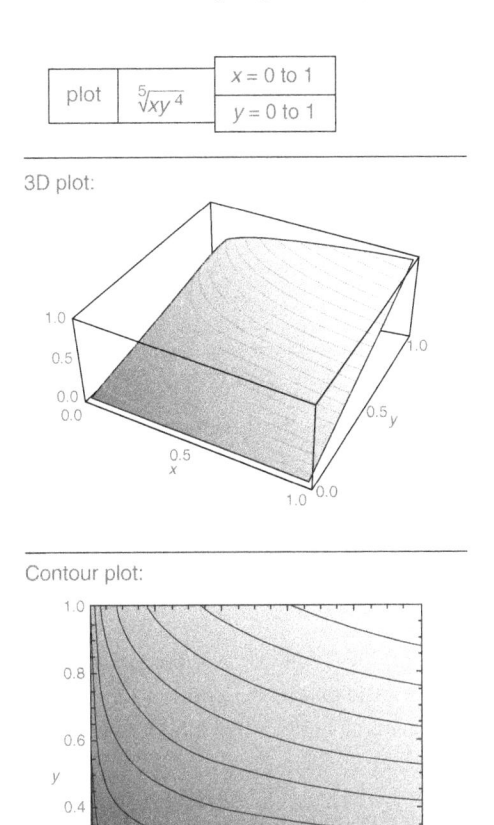

FIGURE 2.13.3 Weighted multiplicative scoring.

As another example, consider how we used "cost" earlier. Suppose that we now want to decompose the cost value into three criteria: flat fee (F), contingency (C), and hourly (H): score (cost) = $F \times C \times H$. Suppose that, for a particular case, we prefer to work under a flat-fee model, are willing to work under a contingency arrangement, and are not willing to pay hourly. We can increase the weight of the F component of the cost score, and give a zero weight to the H component. Since raising anything to the power of 0 is equal to 1, no matter how good or bad the hourly rate may be, it will have no influence on our cost analysis. For example, score (cost) = $F^2 \times C \times H^0$. For any candidate that allows only hourly billing, score (cost) = 0 × 0 × 1 = 0, and the candidate is excluded.

G Example: Multidimensional (Geographical) Data

Geographical information involves regions of interest, and is generally multidimensional. This is not the same as a distance metric, perhaps centered around a particular point. Suppose, for example, we want environmental information regarding part of a country, including aerial photographs or satellite images. We might also care about the content,

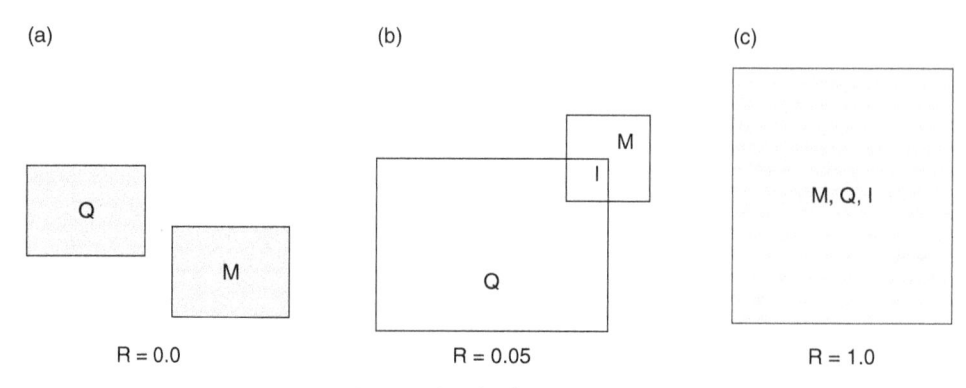

FIGURE 2.13.4 Geographical relevance of 0, 0.05, and 1.[45]

date, format, resolution, labeling, etc., of the information. If all other information about a particular document is "perfect," but it does not cover our area of interest, it is useless. If it does cover our area of interest, but at the wrong scale (e.g., zoomed in too much or too little), it is less useful but still relevant.

A natural measure for geographical relevance is the percentage of overlap of the area of interest, or spatial query Q, with the candidate information or document, say map M. Both Q and M are defined by their spatial locations and total areas. The overlap, or intersection I, is also measured in area. The relevance Rel is then calculated as $(2 \times I)/(Q + M)$. For example, suppose that Q and M do not overlap at all, so that $I = 0$, and thus $Rel = 0$, as depicted in Figure 2.13.4a.

Another example, Figure 2.13.4b, is where Q and M only minimally overlap, and $Rel = 0.05$. A final example is where Q and M cover the exact same region, in which case $I = Q = M$, and $Rel = 1$, shown in Figure 2.13.4c.

By selecting a normalized score that jibes with our notion of regional relevance, we can then combine this value with other metrics, as we did with cost, topic, date, etc. So long as we can define a reasonably intuitive value, we can incorporate it in the quality score.

H Further Considerations

1. The output of the relevance equation is intentionally in the same scale and range as the inputs. One might consider the impact of continually recalculating the relevance score, but with the output of the scoring function fed back to itself as an additional input parameter (i.e., a *recursive* property via a feedback loop). This is the case by default, if one assumes a weight of 0. As the weight of the output-as-input is increased, it becomes harder to modify the value of the output. What if we were measuring the ongoing quality of a dynamic entity, rather than a one-off measure of a static artifact, and wanted to balance prior output and current output? We can represent the components that make up the Rel score in a graph structure, where atomic scores (e.g., P and R) are children of their parent (e.g., Q). In general, what are the pros and cons of a quality metric graph being a directed acyclic graph (DAG) or other graph structure? If there are cycles, but fixed external inputs, would the outputs be stable and/or converge?

---

[45] Figure 2.13.4 images copyright Ron Dolin. Used with permission.

2. With unweighted additive scoring, calculating the equivalent values between two factors is pretty straightforward. For example, in Section VI.C we set $1 equal to 1 mile in Case 1. With unweighted multiplicative scoring, it is harder to determine the equivalences, especially if we use non-linear mappings to derive a characteristic's normalized value. For example, suppose we use a logarithmic scale to get to a distance score. If we use a linear scale for cost, how much money is a mile worth? Is it the same for each distance interval? What if we add weights?
3. In weighted multiplicative scoring, how large should the exponent be to get an intuitive boost in relative importance? What happens with weights between 0 and 1?
4. How would the non-hierarchical relevance formula change if we incorporated sub-components into a single grand weighted formula (e.g., separate weightings for precision and recall to derive our quality score)? Assume, say, m levels of nesting. Would we be able to do this in closed form if we had any feedback or cycles in the relevance network graph? (See Problem #1)
5. What type of user interface would allow a user to modify the various weights used to calculate a final score? For example, you could use a set of sliders to adjust weights as the ranked list changes in real time. You could display candidates on a map, color-coded to their relevance score. You could enable a rollover of candidates to see which factors led to their ranking.

VII STATISTICAL ANALYSIS AND SELECTING A FORMALISM

Statistical scoring measures, such as precision and recall, quantifies the *accuracy* of classification systems, which are used, for example, in contract analytics, e-discovery, and legal research.[46] These measures are also components of the overall quality of these systems since, not surprisingly, accuracy is among the most important factors of such a system's usefulness.

There are several types of tests that are commonly used to evaluate statistical results, depending on the type of issue being addressed. "Whereas descriptive statistics describe a sample, inferential statistics infer predictions about a larger population that the sample represents."[47] Statistical inferences (e.g., Bayesian, frequentist) yield a probability that a hypothesis derived from a set of data is true, as determined from a sample of the data population.[48] For example, precision and recall are often estimated based on sampled results. Another example is estimating the outcome of litigation based on prior cases. Yet another example is the integration of feedback in supervised learning (e.g., e-discovery, contract analytics). This leads to evaluative criteria such as statistical significance and a confidence level via a "p-value," all based on various expected probability distributions (e.g., t-test, chi-squared test). However, the fact that a result is statistically significant does not mean that the result is subjectively interesting. Testing for the degree of impact involves the notion of "effect size," typically summarized as small, medium, or large (though with no lack of rigor).

Although there is a difference between evaluating the overall quality of (legal) work product and the accuracy of an automated system, the two are intertwined. As mentioned,

---

[46] *See*, respectively, Waisberg – Contract Analytics, *infra*; Tyerman and Shankar – The Core Concepts of E-Discovery, *infra*; and Dolin – Information Intermediation, *supra*.
[47] "Mathematical Statistics," *Wikipedia*, available at: https://en.wikipedia.org/wiki/Mathematical_statistics (accessed June 9, 2020).
[48] *See, e.g.*, "Statistical Inference," *Wikipedia*, available at: https://en.wikipedia.org/wiki/Statistical_inference (accessed June 9, 2020).

values such as precision and recall measure the accuracy of classification systems and are an integral component of their quality. In addition, statistical scoring is often associated with probabilities, ranging from 0 to 1, with interpretations along a continuum from useless/impossible to perfect/certain. The framework for quantifying quality, described *supra*, is intentionally similar to the statistical framework – statistical analysis can and must be integrated into legal quality metrics. As a result, there is some overlap in combining statistical tests with combining components of a quality score.

The chapter in this book on information intermediation mentions an "F-measure" for combining precision and recall that uses a weighted *harmonic* mean, while this chapter combines them using a "G-measure," or weighted *geometric* mean. What are the pros and cons of potential formalisms? Both the harmonic and geometric mean are characterized by many of the same properties described *supra* (e.g., filtering and averaging), while the arithmetic mean clearly lacks important ones (e.g., filtering). So while not all formalisms are adequate, more than one may suffice.

Of the available formalisms, it is challenging to argue that one or another produces values that best fulfill the ultimate goal of operationalizing and formalizing our subjective notions of quality. For example, assigning weights is fraught with subjectivity, and there is arguably more variability caused by differences in the underlying data than by which type of mean is used. In selecting one over another, issues such as *intuitivity* and ease of application are at least as important a consideration as the derived score, so long as the required properties are maintained. The geometric mean is quite straightforward and intuitive, and therefore a good candidate. At the end of the day, if a better result has a higher score than a worse result, something is working right.[49]

VIII CONCLUSION: FUTURE DIRECTIONS

As demonstrated by the ROI discussion in the Introduction, quality metrics are financial metrics. Certainly, in the push to increase efficiency of legal services, quality is part of the equation, explicitly or not. Otherwise, for example, we could resolve disputes by a simple coin toss, or use the monkey approach to writing legal memos.[50] *Efficiency without quality is useless.*

How does the lack of *standardized* quality metrics hurt the field? As one legal tech startup CEO said, it can be insufficient to show a prospective client quality data for his company's service if a competitor can be dismissive of the meaning of the metrics, arguing, for example, that other factors are more important. Without standardization, quality metrics become an apples-to-oranges comparison.

---

[49] For the mathematically oriented reader, there are several factors to consider. For example, Property 1 requires simply a non-strict total order. We avoided trying to correlate degrees of subjective similarity with some type of distance metric, such that scores would be closer to each other the more similar two candidates are in the desired characteristics. Such a *similarity metric* property would include such a measure (*see, e.g.*, Dolin – Information Intermediation, and its discussion of cosine similarity, *supra*). Instead, we simply required that the better candidate should receive a higher score than a worse candidate, by any amount. The difference between harmonic mean and geometric mean is evident when viewing Figure 2.13.2b with its equivalent for harmonic mean side-by-side. However, it is not clear which might yield the best approximation to our subjective notion of quality on a case-by-case basis. As mentioned in note 41, it is arguably easier to accommodate Properties 5 and 7 – nested weighting – under the geometric mean model than with the harmonic mean. The weights also seem more intuitive.

[50] The Infinite Monkey Theorem is an oft-cited theorem in probability studies that states that a monkey sitting at a typewriter with an infinite amount of time could produce any functional document.

Quality metrics come in several flavors. For example, many companies that work with document review establish a human-to-human quality evaluation built into the system in a way that tracks, aggregates, and automatically analyzes each reviewer. A single poor performer, for example, is relatively easy to identify. But systematic problems can occur if several people make the same mistake. Statistical sampling of reviews, or selectively duplicating reviews, is sufficient to guarantee high-quality output without necessitating human oversight of each individual review. Once quality is compared to efficiency, one can arrive at high-*value* work. This is especially important within a non-billable-hour framework where performance is measured by work output per hour rather than by the number of hours billed per employee.

While aggregated human-to-human evaluation is important, it is not the only type of quality metric that matters. The ability to do some type of automated quality control is also important. We can start with simple quantities and migrate to more complicated ones. Thus, the ability to discern simply if various clauses exist in contracts is easy in a framework of, say, an XML-encoded document within a known markup standard.[51] More sophisticated document automation systems allow for pre-drafting error minimization as well as post-drafting analysis.

But the real issue is how to automatically measure the quality of the bulk of legal work going forward – the consumer reports or UL of law. With commodity products, we look for standard benchmarks (e.g., FLOPS, MTBF). We also look for some type of certification (e.g., Good Housekeeping). But for legal work, what should we measure?

What might we expect in a high-quality estate plan, for example? Are there common elements in an IP license agreement that we could use to measure quality – say, checking for common phrases that have been shown in case law to be problematic? What about the number of citations per 1000 words, or the ratio of controlling to persuasive citations, or the number of Supreme Court cases cited? What about the level of argument nesting? Beyond these static factors, there are contextual elements, such as the number of citations to opinions written by the judge hearing the case, or cases that that judge commonly references. How might we measure the quality of dispute resolution systems?[52]

As we inevitably increase the role of automation in the legal system, building in quality metrics and automated evaluation guarantees that increasing efficiency does not come at the cost of decreasing quality.[53] This is as important for large corporate clients managing their Big Law providers as it is for middle-class consumers using an automated online document delivery system, not to mention those who simply cannot afford an attorney at all.

Law seems to be moving toward more empirical work, as seen, for example, in the journal and conferences of the Society for Empirical Legal Studies (SELS).[54] However, a cursory examination of such work yields little in terms of the quantification and measurement of quality. The development of standardized quality metrics via the application of quantitative techniques and empirical analysis is an important component of unlocking the efficiency gains in law that technology has provided in other industries. Quality benchmarks guarantee the preservation, or even improvement, of the quality required for removing existing barriers to the adoption of technology and the further injection of efficiency into legal practice.

[51] For more on XML, *see* Dolin – XML in Law: The Role of Standards in Legal Informatics, *supra*.
[52] For more on dispute resolution specifically, *see* Bulinski and Prescott – Designing Legal Experiences: Online Communication and Resolution in Courts, *infra*.
[53] For a discussion of the trade-offs between legal quality and efficiency, *see* Dolin – Technology Issues in Legal Philosophy, *supra*.
[54] *See* Cornell Law School Society for Empirical Law Studies (SELS), www.lawschool.cornell.edu/sels.

PART III

Use Cases in Legal Informatics

A.

Contracts and Patents

3.1

Contract Analytics

Noah Waisberg

I INTRODUCTION

Companies, and the professionals who serve them, spend vast amounts of time extracting data from contracts. This work is done in areas including M&A due diligence and integration, corporate contract management, lease abstraction, auditing, and others. In recent years, software has come to market that helps users review contracts faster and more accurately, and that also helps to better organize the process and understand its results.

Currently, most contract review is done by human reviewers without the aid of dedicated software tools to assist with the analytical parts of the work. These reviewers are often lawyers, but they are sometimes other experienced individuals. Their task is to read agreements and look for specified information (e.g., in an M&A transaction, what happens on assignment and change of control under a target company's agreements) and put their findings into summary charts. These summary charts take different forms, including organized lists of verbatim clauses, summarized provisions, and answers to questions. More senior people in an organization – such as mid-level partners at large law firms – often spot-check these first-level reviews. In the case of due diligence contract review, results are sometimes further refined into high-level summaries, descriptive reports, and disclosure schedules.

Human-driven contract review has the conditions for a perfect storm of risk: by most accounts the work is achingly tedious, but at the same time serious consequences can result from errors. This calls for extreme attention to detail.[1] Stories abound of missed provisions that were only found at the eleventh hour – or worse, *after* a deal was completed. The status quo contract review process is slow, costly, prone to human error, and can also generate initial results that are not as useful as they might appear.[2] Contract review software can help change all that.

Many companies could benefit from a much better understanding of their contracts, but the current status quo of contract review usage does not often meet this goal of understanding. The reason contract review software is so vital is because it can encourage a broader understanding of what a company's contracts actually say. Technology has significantly improved the contract

---

[1] There is significant research on the negative impact – in terms of both work quality and job satisfaction – of performing repetitive, mechanical tasks in the legal environment. *See*, *e.g.*, Maura R. Grossman and Gordon V. Cormack, "Technology-Assisted Review in E-Discovery Can be More Effective and More Efficient than Exhaustive Manual Review," *Richmond Journal of Law & Technology* 17 (1) (2011); Jerome M. Organ, "What do We Know About the Satisfaction/Dissatisfaction of Lawyers? A Meta-Analysis of Research on Lawyer Satisfaction and Well-Being," *University of St. Thomas Law Journal* 8 (225) (2011).

[2] Paul Lippe, Daniel Martin Katz, and Dan Jackson, "Legal by Design: A New Paradigm for Handling Complexity in Banking Regulation and Elsewhere in Law," *Oregon Law Review* 93 (4) (2015): 831.

review process before, and the latest developments in machine learning will fundamentally transform contract review again. This chapter surveys how software is changing the contract review process, and offers insight into how companies and law firms are simplifying and expediting contract review by taking advantage of new technologies.

A central aspect of contract review software is that it automatically finds instances of contract provisions. It is easy to get software to do this, but hard to have it work accurately. There are three ways that systems can find provisions: rules-based approaches, comparison methods, and machine learning. This chapter will describe the advantages and disadvantages of these three approaches as applied to finding contract provisions. We will also include case studies on law firms that use machine learning contract review software in their work.

II CONTRACT REVIEW SOFTWARE SYSTEMS

Contract review software helps users review contracts faster and more accurately, and improves organization and results. Early contract review systems focused on streamlining the categorization process by providing questionnaires that prompted users to input values on specific contractual issues (e.g., title, assignment, term). These systems collected reviewer responses into queryable databases, and tracked reviewer progress. Notably, several of these efforts were homegrown at top law firms to help with legal due diligence.

The current state of the art for contract review systems includes features that automatically locate user-specified information in contracts and put findings into summary charts. Some systems also include interface features to help users refine or organize results. This author co-founded and is CEO of Kira Systems, a company that provides this kind of software. Kira Systems' technology automatically reads contracts for user-specified provisions (e.g., change of control, assignment, term), puts its findings into summary charts, and includes workflow tools to help users refine results.[3]

Companies offering automated contract abstraction systems base their extraction systems on one of two very different technologies: keyword searches and machine learning approaches. Each technology has particular trade-offs: keyword search systems are easier to set up but have significant performance limitations, while machine learning-based systems are very hard to build well, but can be powerful once up and running. Comparison methods provide yet another possible tactic, and they can also be used to identify contract provisions for extraction. All three are discussed below at greater length.

In order to compare different types of contract review software, a common set of performance metrics are used to define the software's accuracy in classifying unfamiliar documents.[4] A system's *accuracy* is a function of its recall rate and its precision rate. *Recall* measures the extent to which relevant results are found. For example, in a set of documents with 50 assignment provisions, if a search system found 48 of the 50, the recall rate would be 96%. *Precision*, meanwhile, measures the extent to which irrelevant results are mixed in with relevant ones. For example, if the same system returned 300 provisions as assignment hits when there were only 48 actual assignment provisions, the precision rate would be 16%.[5]

---

[3] *See, e.g.*, Kira Systems, https://kirasystems.com; Victor Li, "Contracts 2.0: Technology Rewires the Drafting and Reviewing of Contracts," *ABA Journal* November (2014), available at: www.abajournal.com/magazine/article/contracts_2.0_technology_rewires_the_drafting_and_reviewing_of_contracts.

[4] Christopher D. Manning, Prabhakar Raghavan, and Hinrich Schütze, *Introduction to Information Retrieval* (Cambridge: Cambridge University Press, 2008), available at: http://nlp.stanford.edu/IR-book/html/htmledition/irbook.html.

[5] For a more detailed explanation of precision and recall, *see* Dolin – Information Intermediation, *supra*.

There is generally a trade-off between recall and precision. Given the problem of trying to find assignment provisions in a contract, one way to get perfect recall would be to return *all* of the contract's provisions – that way the system would be certain that no assignment provisions were missed. Conversely, trying to obtain perfect precision could come at the expense of missing some (perhaps atypical) provisions. As a result, a system's accuracy is measured by its ability to find relevant provisions and *only* relevant provisions. Users often prioritize recall when using contract review software in their practices, because it is generally more important to find *all* relevant results, even if some false positives show up in the mix. Contract review systems therefore tend to skew their results by favoring completeness over strict accuracy, and try to employ intuitive user interfaces for eliminating undesired results.

Contract review software is also measured by its accuracy when tested against unfamiliar documents. Some contracts are automatically generated using a predefined form, such as a template used by a landlord to generate rental agreements so that they always read "tenant will pay $[xxx] monthly." This kind of contract would be considered a *known document*; the only feature that changes between contracts is the specific amount of rent. It is relatively easy to write rules or train models to extract data from known documents where the majority of content is invariable. By contrast, in an unfamiliar document the form and wording is typically not known in advance. Accurately extracting information from these *unknown documents* – and doing so in a reasonable amount of time – is ultimately what defines an effective piece of contract review software.

Conceptually, contract provision extraction systems are relatively simple. Most systems start with a provision model that is either preloaded or available on request or with some customization.[6] Documents under review are converted to machine-readable text if necessary.[7] This text is then scanned by the system's provision models and hits are extracted. Despite this apparent simplicity, though, two issues determine the extraction models' success, and ultimately the overall complexity of the provision extraction process: (1) which technology is used to build the provision extraction models; and (2) who is involved in teaching the system what a "correct" hit looks like.

A *Manual Rules, Comparison Systems, and Machine Learning*

1 Manual Rules Systems

The quick-and-easy way to generate provision models is to write manual rules that describe provisions (e.g., Boolean search strings). While this approach is reasonably simple to set up and easy to understand, it has significant drawbacks. Most notably, the resulting models are unlikely to be especially accurate on unfamiliar documents.[8] It also becomes hard to measure system accuracy on unfamiliar documents. Comparison systems and machine learning-based

---

[6] Ben Klaber, "Artificial Intelligence and Transactional Law: Automated M&A Due Diligence," paper presented at *ICAIL 2013 Workshop on Standards for Using Predictive Coding, Machine Learning, and Other Advanced Search and Review Methods in E-Discovery (DESI V Workshop)*, Rome, Italy, June 14, 2013, available at: www.umiacs.umd.edu/~oard/desi5/additional/Klaber.pdf.

[7] E. L. Mencía and J. Fürnkranz, "Efficient Multilabel Classification Algorithms for Large-Scale Problems in the Legal Domain," in *Semantic Processing of Legal Texts*, eds. Enrico Francesconi, S. Montemagni, W. Peters, and D. Tiscornia (Berlin: Springer, 2010).

[8] *See* David C. Blair and M. E. Maron, "An Evaluation of Retrieval Effectiveness for a Full-Text Document-Retrieval System," *Communications of the ACM* 28 (3) (1985): 289, available at: http://yunus.hacettepe.edu.tr/~tonta/courses/spring2008/bby703/blair-maron-evaluation.pdf.

technology can help correct these shortcomings with more accurate provision models, but these alternatives are more difficult to build.

2 Comparison Systems

A comparison-based contract provision extraction system uses a database of provision examples and compares all new text against the database with respect to a predetermined similarity threshold. The software powering this comparison can be based on the *diff utility*, a common tool for comparing strings of text that can also be used to power other programs.[9] For example, any new provision whose text is ≥70% similar to a provision in the database of amendments will be determined to be an amendment provision.

Comparison-based systems run into trouble when provisions in agreements for review differ from ones in the provision database. This can occur when agreements are drafted differently, which often happens in common commercial agreements such as supply and distribution contracts. Trouble can also arise due to poor-quality scans, leading to inexact agreement transcriptions. Comparison-based systems can cope with dissimilar agreements or difficult-to-OCR text by relaxing their comparison threshold, but this increases the odds of finding false positives. Comparison-based provision detection could work with a provision database covering all examples of how the provision is drafted, assuming no poor-quality scans are reviewed, but it takes considerable effort to build a good provision database and it is hard to ensure the database is actually comprehensive.

3 Machine Learning Systems

Machine learning-based contract extraction systems use both supervised and unsupervised techniques to build extraction models.[10] In supervised learning, provisions from real contracts that have been categorized by an experienced lawyer are fed into a training system, which considers the examples. The system takes this data and learns the language that is relevant to a given provision concept, and the language that is not. On the basis of this classification, the system generates probabilistic provision models, then the models are tested against a large pool of annotated agreements with which the system is unfamiliar. This last step measures how far the system has successfully learned the lessons it has been taught, and also measures its readiness to be used against unfamiliar documents in the real world.[11]

Machine learning comes with some drawbacks. Its accuracy depends on the representativeness of the training data it is exposed to, and not only is it sometimes difficult or impossible to obtain appropriate training data, but it is also time-consuming to manually feed the system

---

[9] Free Software Foundation, "GNU diffutils: Comparing and Merging Files," August 20, 2016, available at: www.gnu.org/software/diffutils/manual.

[10] Other chapters in this book deal more thoroughly with the mechanics of machine learning and its various techniques. For a discussion of the machine learning pipeline in the document review and classification context, see Kartik Asooja, Georgeta Bordea, Gabriela Vulcu, Leona O'Brien, Angelina Espinoza, Elie Abi-Lahoud, Paul Buitelaar, and Tom Butler, "Semantic Annotation of Finance Regulatory Text Using Multilabel Classification," paper presented at *2015 International Workshop on Legal Domain and Semantic Web Applications (LeDA-SWAn 2015)*, Portoroz, Slovenia, June 1, 2015, available at: http://cs.unibo.it/ledaswan2015/papers/asooja-et-al-ledaswan2015.pdf; Gary King, Patrick Lam, and Margaret Roberts, "Computer-Assisted Keyword and Document Set Discovery from Unstructured Text," *American Journal of Political Science* (2017), available at: http://gking.harvard.edu/files/gking/files/keywordalgorithm.pdf; see also Klaber, supra note 6.

[11] Kira Systems (www.kirasystems.com), a major player in this space, is discussed in Section III.

examples to learn from.[12] That said, the benefits of using machine learning techniques to build contract provision models are significant. With appropriate algorithms and good training data, models can be surprisingly accurate, even on unfamiliar documents, and can remain accurate even on poor-quality scans. And the fact that the system is designed to yield a quantifiable level of accuracy against unknown agreements helps manage expectations among users and purchasers.

B Who Teaches the System?

Contract provision extraction systems that rely on supervised machine learning apply the judgment of the person who instructed them to decide whether new text is a certain contract provision. As a result, the adage "garbage in, garbage out" applies: A contract provision extraction system's accuracy and quality can only be as high as the experience level of the human contract reviewers who train it. For example, a 2013 study compared the performance of human- and technology-assisted teams against a standardized benchmark – a previously settled matter between Sun Microsystems and Oracle, where outside counsel had supervised a rigorous document review process "that included a thorough review with multiple quality checks."[13] The study found that a single senior-level attorney produced better results than a team of low-cost temporary attorneys, concluding that "software is only as good as its operators."

The real promise of automated contract provision extraction software is its ability to support tired, overworked, and novice reviewers working on unfamiliar text, giving those workers the benefit of an experienced reviewer's guidance via software. But we must be careful. Without appropriate human expertise as a foundation, these systems will struggle to perform at a level at which quality-obsessed users can come to trust the results.

III CASE STUDIES IN CONTRACT REVIEW SOFTWARE

Machine learning remains the leading technology behind software-aided contract review systems. The following two case studies draw on the experiences of law firms that have used Kira Systems,[14] a major player in the contract review space that leverages machine learning techniques to support and supplement human reviewers.

A DLA Piper: Improved Fee Predictability Through Software–Associate Interaction

DLA Piper, an international law firm with locations in more than 30 countries, provides a useful case study on the performance and quality benefits that can be realized from injecting machine learning processes into existing workflows. DLA Piper uses Kira Systems'

---

[12] Harry Surden, "Machine Learning and Law," *Washington Law Review* 89 (1) (2014): 105.
[13] Gordon V. Cormack and Maura R. Grossman, "Evaluation of Machine-Learning Protocols for Technology-Assisted Review in Electronic Discovery," in *Proceedings of the 37th International ACM SIGIR Conference on Research & Development in Information Retrieval* (New York, NY: ACM, 2014); Steven C. Bennett, "E-discovery: Reasonable Search, Proportionality, Cooperation, and Advancing Technology," *John Marshall Journal of Information Technology & Privacy Law* 30 (2013): 433; Lewis Carroll, "The Grossman-Cormack Glossary of Technology-Assisted Review," *Federal Courts Law Review* 7 (1) (2013).
[14] These case studies are based on interviews with representatives of each of the two featured law firms, with additional data and cooperation from representatives of Kira Systems.

platform as part of its M&A practice, conducting due diligence exercises for its clients in connection with acquisitions and dispositions of various targets.

DLA Piper adopted Kira with the main goal of improving the efficiency of its due diligence workflows and providing greater cost certainty to its clients. Due diligence is an area particularly suitable for technologies that offer predictability with respect to costs: If a deal is successful, the cost of due diligence is negligible in the overall context, but if the deal fails to close, then due diligence represents a significant sunk cost. Particularly in an active deal market, DLA Piper's clients wish to know that their counsel can conduct due diligence quickly, efficiently, and with a relatively defined cost structure. To address these concerns, DLA Piper adopted Kira, a contract analysis technology platform that can be utilized in combination with human resources to enable better handling of costs associated with large-scale due diligence projects.

Replacing lawyers (or the professional thought that goes into their analysis) was not DLA Piper's intention in adopting Kira Systems' technology. Rather, DLA Piper saw Kira and related technologies as tools that its professionals could leverage to increase their proficiency and accuracy on contract review and analysis projects. For that reason, an important consideration for selecting Kira Systems' platform was its integration into existing workflows at DLA Piper. In the past, DLA Piper has used software-aided review tools to remove bottlenecks and associated unpredictability in the due diligence workflow, without affecting the rigor with which the review is conducted. In a typical due diligence workflow, a cost-sensitive client asks DLA Piper to review a set of contracts, with the scope limited to a specific set of clauses – for example, change-of-control and assignment provisions. Very often, however, due diligence exercises like these reveal additional issues and clauses to be identified and reviewed. As a result, a set of documents may potentially be reviewed many times over.

When conducted without software-assisted review tools, bottlenecks and unpredictability arise in the due diligence workflow in two ways. First, each pass over a set of documents takes the same amount of time, and so whenever additional issues are spotted, the cumulative time required to complete the due diligence process varies directly with the number of follow-up reviews required. Second, in order to keep costs down, due diligence work is usually done by the youngest, most inexperienced people in the firm, who take longer to identify relevant clauses than more senior – and more expensive – lawyers. It is nearly impossible to correct due diligence mistakes in a cost-effective way, since doing so requires effectively redoing the entire review process.

Kira has helped DLA Piper remove these bottlenecks in two ways: (1) offering workflow tools that make it faster and easier to read and review individual documents and clauses; and (2) automatically identifying and extracting clauses so that additional terms are faster and easier to find on subsequent reviews. The platform's ability to recognize and classify clauses matches and often exceeds that of a junior associate; when DLA Piper conducted a formal comparison, the firm found that Kira was no less accurate than their lawyers. Also, the platform made it easier to escalate complex or ambiguous clauses to senior lawyers for review, which made it possible to review or correct errors without needing to redo the entire workflow. The end product for DLA Piper has been the ability to provide clients with greater certainty on fees, and often a reduction in the fees themselves.

The increase in value DLA Piper has been able to deliver by using Kira is substantial in three ways. First, Kira has accelerated and improved the accuracy of the due diligence process. Second, through the time savings provided, Kira has reduced the overall time required to complete the deal, reducing risks and cost for the client. And third, Kira has also empowered DLA Piper to carry out due diligence exercises on additional provisions requested by its client in a faster and more cost-effective manner.

DLA Piper's M&A group was the first in the firm to rollout Kira, and to date it makes up 90% of Kira's usage across the firm. The remaining users are found in DLA Piper's technology group, but in addition to this DLA Piper says that since its initial implementation of Kira, other practice groups within the firm – such as the real estate group and employment practice group – have shown significant interest in utilizing Kira to help produce higher-quality deliverables for their clients.

B *Freshfields Bruckhaus Deringer LLP: Beyond English-Language Documents*

Software-aided contract review systems offer dramatic improvements in efficiencies when used in conjunction with human experts, and they demonstrate how machine learning techniques are a powerful and flexible technology that can be extended beyond traditional usage scenarios such as due diligence. The following case study reveals this flexibility. Freshfields Bruckhaus Deringer LLP ("Freshfields"), a Magic Circle law firm headquartered in London, UK with 27 worldwide offices, successfully trained machine learning models within the Kira platform to conduct a large-scale review of non-English contracts in a regulatory context.

Freshfields' task arose when a German client in the healthcare sector required an assessment of its potential exposure following a change in German anti-bribery and corruption law. The client asked Freshfields to review a large number of its agreements with third-party healthcare providers. The deadline was tight, and the client needed Freshfields to review a set of 11,500 documents as quickly and cost-effectively as possible. All documents were in German and were organized by counterparty name rather than by contract type.

The senior associate on the matter, in consultation with Freshfields' Innovation Team of lawyers, legal technologists, continuous improvement professionals, and project management resources, selected Kira to assist with the contract review. Freshfields had not used Kira to undertake this kind of review in the past, and the software had not been pre-taught any specialized provisions relating to the specific anti-bribery and corruption laws in question. In addition, Kira could only read contract texts in English unless trained otherwise. After much consideration, Freshfields' Berlin office decided to teach Kira to review documents in German; the scale of the project would provide a sufficiently large training set to apply learnings to the balance of documents.

Despite the promise of machine learning-assisted contract review, the task was an unusual one for several reasons: the application of contract analysis software would be applied in a regulatory context rather than for M&A due diligence; the platform would need to be trained to recognize provisions in a language that it had not previously been taught (German); and Kira would be required to recognize and extract highly specialized provisions.

The associates in Berlin worked with Freshfields' Legal Services Centre to coordinate teaching efforts. The work effort was divided as follows. Using a training set, the associates taught Kira: (1) to recognize six boilerplate German provisions; (2) to identify the titles and types of the contracts (ranging from loan agreements, to maintenance and service agreements); and (3) to recognize certain provisions that might trigger a breach in law. Once the teaching was completed, the legal support assistants in Freshfields' Legal Services Centre applied Kira to the balance of the documents, extracted problematic provisions for review by lawyers, and helped provide analytics on the client's potential exposure.

Freshfields found the use of Kira on this project to be a significant success. The client benefited from a quick and efficient review that adhered to very high standards of quality, and the lawyers were able to organize a chaotic data set very quickly, allocate contracts to the appropriate reviewers, and run real-time analytics to provide the client with a clear picture of its exposure, allowing for consistent reporting. Additionally, through its analysis of the documents, Freshfields was able to provide better support to their client in contract lifecycle management on an ongoing basis.

Most importantly, the knowledge and experience gained from this exercise – with regard to both language and legal expertise – was now captured within Freshfields' instance of Kira, and going forward could be used for the benefit of clients undertaking similar exercises. Following the initial review, the client in fact extended the scope of the review, engaging Freshfields to review a further 5000 documents in Germany and 800 documents in Latin America. Leveraging the firm's international network, Freshfields took the approach used for teaching Kira to recognize German provisions and applied that approach to teach Kira to perform extraction in Spanish. An associate in Freshfields' Madrid office and two Spanish-speaking members of the Legal Services Centre, working with Freshfields' Berlin and Hamburg offices, taught the engine to recognize ten Spanish provisions. Freshfields now expects the scope of work to extend to further jurisdictions and to expand Kira's capabilities accordingly.

IV CONCLUSION

The full potential of software-aided contract review technology to shape the legal profession is only beginning to be realized. As the DLA Piper case study demonstrates, machine learning platforms like Kira are able to bring down the cost and complexity of traditional document review tasks, making it possible for law firms to remain competitive and profitable even in a challenging legal economy that demands efficiency. Moreover, as Freshfields' experience with applying Kira Systems' platform to non-English documents shows, machine learning approaches can yield a system flexible enough to be extended beyond what it was initially trained to do. Much work remains in remaking contract review through use of technology, but the results so far are impressive.

3.2

Contracts as Interfaces

Visual Representation Patterns in Contract Design

Helena Haapio and Stefania Passera

I INTRODUCTION

The world of contracts is undergoing fundamental changes. This is partly due to technology: there can be tremendous benefits from self-enforcing, machine-readable contracts. But these technologies are not used everywhere. Many contracts continue to be performed by people. In the context of commercial deals and relationships,[1] a vast number of contracts still need to be planned, understood, approved, implemented, and monitored by people.[2] Initiatives across the world seek to innovate contracting processes and documents and develop more effective, engaging ways for people to work with them. This chapter focuses on these initiatives and the need to make contracts truly human-readable.

Today's contracts do not work as well as they should. Surveys by the International Association for Contract and Commercial Management (IACCM) reveal that the vast majority of businesspeople find contracts hard to read or understand, and that current contracts are of little practical use to delivery teams and project managers.[3] When it comes to usability and user experience, contracts are well below the standard people have come to expect from anything else they work with. In terms of style, the complexity of contracts is not advantageous for cognitively overloaded readers trying to search, integrate, and understand the information contracts contain.[4] In terms of content, contracts are written with litigation in mind rather than day-to-day business support. Their focus is on creating legally enforceable promises and causes of claims against the other party, rather than on helping both parties to deliver on their promises.

---

[1] This chapter focuses on business-to-business (B2B) contracts that anticipate ongoing relationships over time. Apart from some examples in Section VI, we do not address consumer contracts or public procurement contracts. Still, many of the issues discussed here may also apply to such contracts. In B2B contracting, the parties' freedom of contract is at its widest. Legislators have taken steps to promote the writing of consumer contracts in plain language, to protect consumers from making contracts they do not understand, and to help consumers to better know their rights and duties under those contracts. See Christopher Williams, "Legal English and Plain Language: An Update," *ESP Across Cultures* 8 (2011): 139–151.

[2] "The results are not always as spectacular as one might wish," *id.* at 144; "the general situation is that contracts still tend to be plagued with old-fashioned forms of legalese," *id.* at 146.

[3] IACCM, *Attitudes to Contracting* (Ridgefield, CT: International Association for Contract and Commercial Management, 2015); IACCM, *Commercial Excellence: Ten Pitfalls to Avoid in Contracting* (Ridgefield, CT: International Association for Contract and Commercial Management, 2015).

[4] Stefania Passera, Anne Kankaanranta, and Leena Louhiala-Salminen, "Diagrams in Contracts: Fostering Understanding in Global Business Communication," *IEEE Transactions on Professional Communication* 99 (2017).

While contracts can serve as a means to sanction breach and provide a winning argument in court, we believe that they should not be seen "primarily as a source of trouble and disputation," but rather as a way of getting things done.[5] This is a fundamental premise of the work of Louis M. Brown, known as the father of preventive law.[6] While in curative law it is essential for lawyers to predict what a *court* will do, in preventive law it is essential to predict what *people* will do. This chapter's focus is on people: those in charge of planning, negotiating, implementing, or monitoring contracts (e.g., proposal, contract, commercial, sales, procurement, and project managers). We look specifically at the PPL approach, which stands for proactive/preventive law. *Proactive* focuses on achieving positive goals and adding value. *Preventive* focuses on the future and on using the law and legal skills to prevent disputes and eliminate causes of problems.[7] Taken together, the PPL approach can harness tools to promote smoother operations and more successful outcomes.

One of the ways contracts can improve how they help people achieve their business goals and prevent unnecessary problems is through *information design*. Information design is a discipline concerned with displaying information in ways that support effective and efficient understanding by the intended audience, in the expected context of use. In order to work well, contracts can no longer simply be drafted *by* lawyers *for* lawyers. Instead, the concept of *contract drafting* should be replaced by that of *contract design*, where strategic choices about the drivers and goals of collaboration merge with business and legal knowledge about how to maximize the chances of success and minimize risks and disputes, all wrapped up in people-centered communications that ensure the contract can actually be implemented within the allotted time, with the resources that have been allocated, and within budget.

Contract design is not only a matter of selecting the right content, words, or clauses. It is also a matter of making sure the message is understood. In this chapter, we concentrate on the communicative aspects of contracts, particularly on the relatively new stream of research and practice that proposes visual communication as a way to enhance contract clarity and ease of use.[8,9] To understand the diverse visual practices and approaches in this emerging field, we propose a categorization based on *design patterns*. Patterns can be defined as reusable models of a solution to frequently occurring problems in a domain.[10] Each pattern solves a specific

---

[5] Ian Macneil and Paul Gudel, *Contracts: Exchange Transactions and Relations* (New York, NY: Foundation Press, 2001).

[6] Louis M. Brown, *Preventive Law* (New York, NY: Prentice-Hall, Inc., 1950).

[7] *See generally*, Thomas D. Barton, "Three Modes of Legal Problem Solving – and What to Do About Them in Legal Education," *California Western Law Review* 43 (2007): 389–416, available at: www.works.bepress.com/thomas_barton/10; Helena Haapio and Thomas D. Barton, "Business-Friendly Contracting: How Simplification and Visualization Can Help Bring It to Practice," in *Liquid Legal: Transforming Legal into a Business Savvy, Information Enabled and Performance Driven Industry*, eds. Kai Jacob, Dierk Schindler, and Roger Strathausen (New York, NY: Springer International, 2017).

[8] The IACCM Contract Design Award Program and the IACCM Contract Design Assessment Program promote the creation of clear and easy-to-use contracts and the use of contract visualization; see www.iaccm.com/iaccm-awards, www.iaccm.com/iaccm-assessments.

[9] Helena Haapio, "Good Contracts: Bringing Design Thinking into Contract Design," in *Proceedings of the 2013 IACCM Academic Forum*, ed. J. Chittenden (Ridgefield, CT: International Association for Contract and Commercial Management, 2013), 95–136, available at: www.iaccm.com/resources/?id=4958; Helena Haapio, *Next Generation Contracts: A Paradigm Shift* (Helsinki: Lexpert Ltd., 2013); Stefania Passera and Helena Haapio, "Facilitating Collaboration through Contract Visualization and Modularization," in *Proceedings of the 29th Annual European Conference on Cognitive Ergonomics (ECCE '11)* (New York, NY: Association of Computing Machinery, 2011), 57–60, available at: dx.doi.org/10.1145/2074712.2074724.

[10] Helena Haapio and Margaret Hagan, "Design Patterns for Contracts," in *Networks: Proceedings of the 19th International Legal Informatics Symposium IRIS 2016*, eds. E. Schweighofer, F. Kummer, W. Hötzendorfer, and G. Borges (Vienna: Österreichische Computer Gesellschaft, 2016), 381–388.

problem, just like how different tools in a toolbox have unique functions. While the exact implementation of a pattern may vary, each pattern will retain distinguishing features that allow it to be recognized and recreated.[11] Framing visualizations into patterns like this can help avoid an overly prescriptive approach to contract design, an approach of which we are wary. For us, designing contracts means making highly contextual strategic choices. What constitutes a "good" solution will depend on the users' characteristics (e.g., literacy levels), information needs and goals (e.g., what they need to know to perform their job), and overall business strategy (e.g., whether the transaction or relationship is short term or long term).

Our particular focus is on diagrams, icons, and other visual representations that can be used to explain and disambiguate contract text. These patterns can be used in actual contracts, contract briefs, or guidance, and as thinking tools during negotiations. Following the design pattern approach, we describe the benefits of these visual solutions by illustrating the problems they address. Each pattern is explained through actual examples encountered in our research and practice.

To legal informatics scholars and practitioners, our approach may seem handcrafted and very non-computational. This is a valid concern, but it is important to recognize that our brains are information processing systems that should not be forgotten in the pursuit of the exciting possibilities of technology. In a sociotechnical system composed of people, computers, and business and legal information, we need to ensure that people do not become the weak link. While a contract can be easily and automatically assembled by dedicated software relying on clause libraries, those clauses still need to be of good quality and intelligible to end-users. Our approach is a useful complement to the field of informatics because it helps to address the problem of "garbage in, garbage out." In addition, the process of visualization can help contract authors to plan, clarify, and test the logical correctness of the text they create.[12] Visual design patterns can then be used to present the content to contract users in simpler, more transparent ways.

This chapter is structured as follows: First, we address some unwarranted assumptions about the purpose and functions of contracts. We then propose the need for new, people-centered approaches, focusing on the paradigm shift from contract drafting to contract design as envisioned in PPL. We then introduce the concept of design patterns, the repeatable best-practice solutions to communication problems in contracts. We go on to examine three families of contract visualization patterns that can be used to make contracts more readable, understandable, and engaging. Finally, we show examples of six kinds of visual representations which, we believe, offer repeatable solutions to recurring contract communication problems.

II THE CHALLENGE: DYSFUNCTIONAL CONTRACTS AND THE NEED FOR A PARADIGM SHIFT

The IACCM's *Attitudes to Contracting* study reveals that weaknesses in contract terms and negotiations are a frequent source of cost overruns and project delays. The use of traditional,

---

[11] Pramod Khambete, "A Pattern Language for Touch Point Ecosystem User Experience: A Proposal," in *Proceedings of the 3rd International Conference on Human Computer Interaction (IndiaHCI '11)* (New York, NY: Association for Computing Machinery, 2011), 68–74, available at: doi.acm.org/10.1145/2407796.2407805.
[12] Australian Office of Parliamentary Counsel, *Plain English Manual*, December 19, 2013, available at: www.opc.gov.au/about/docs/Plain_English.pdf; David Berman, "Toward a New Format for Canadian Legislation: Using Graphic Design Principles and Methods to Improve Public Access to the Law," Human Resources Development Canada and Justice Canada, November 30, 2000, available at: www.davidberman.com/NewFormatForCanadianLegislation.pdf.

legally driven forms renders most contracts of little practical use to delivery teams and project managers, undermining their primary value as instruments of communication and understanding.[13] More than 90% of businesspeople find contracts hard to read or understand. This results in users seeing contracts as irrelevant to business needs.

Furthermore, in more than 90% of organizations, contracts are viewed primarily as instruments for control and compliance rather than business enablers and tools for improved communication and understanding.[14] One reason for this is that lawyers have monopolized contract drafting, even in countries where there are no regulatory requirements for such monopolizing. As a result, contracts look like legal documents, not business documents. Their look and feel reinforces the view of contracts as purely legal tools, something to be left to lawyers.[15] Unfortunately, when it comes to content, lawyer-drafters pay more attention to legal functionality than business functionality. Their aim is to draft content in a way that is precise, accurate, unambiguous, enforceable, legally binding, and interpreted in a way that favors the party drafting it. Legal drafting anticipates hostile readers reading the document through the eyes of bad faith.[16] IACCM's *Top Negotiated Terms* confirms that, year after year, negotiators continue to focus on terms that deal with the consequences of failure and neglect the terms that are most important for guiding the relationship.[17]

The backbone of a contract is rarely drafted from scratch. Any given business deal resembles previous deals, so most law firms and corporate legal departments reuse templates and clause libraries to be as efficient as possible when preparing new contracts. There is a downside to this, however: If archaic language and style are used in the original, repeating and automating those templates easily becomes "an exercise in garbage in, garbage out."[18] Whether the process is based on copy-and-pasting or automation, contracts are compiled using templates put together by lawyers driven by the goal of minimizing legal risk in court, often at the cost of clarity and understanding.[19] Using such templates can mean that even a great deal ends up with a terrible contract.[20] How do we move beyond this vicious circle?

Contract drafters imagine courtroom settings, their attention focused on whether a contract's language will prevail in court if its meaning is disputed by other lawyers. The needs of delivery teams and project managers, who need documents they can work with and act upon easily, are ignored.[21] When this happens, contract implementers may create their own

---

[13] See IACCM, *Attitudes to Contracting*, supra note 3.
[14] Id. at 6.
[15] See Haapio and Barton, "Business-Friendly Contracting," *supra* note 7.
[16] "Some day someone will read what you have written, trying to find something wrong with it. This is the special burden of legal writing, and the special incentive to be as precise as you can," David Mellinkoff, *Legal Writing: Sense & Nonsense* (St. Paul, MN: West Publishing, 1982), 15.
[17] IACCM, "2015 Top Terms in Negotiation; No News Is Bad News," International Association for Contract and Commercial Management, 2015, available at: www2.iaccm.com/resources/?id=8930.
[18] Kenneth A. Adams, "Dysfunctional Drafting," *National Law Journal*, September 8, 2008, available at: www.adamsdrafting.com/wp/wp-content/uploads/2014/06/NLJ-Dysfunctional-Drafting.pdf; Kenneth A. Adams and Tim Allen, "The Illusion of Quality in Contract Drafting," *New York Law Journal*, 248 (11) (2012), available at: www.koncision.com/wp-content/uploads/2012/07/Illusion-of-Quality-NYLJ.pdf.
[19] See Haapio, *Next Generation Contracts*, supra note 9, at 50.
[20] Deepak Malhotra, "Great Deal, Terrible Contract: The Case for Negotiator Involvement in the Contracting Phase," in *The Psychology of Negotiations in the 21st Century Workplace: New Challenges and New Solutions*, eds. Barry M. Goldman and Debra L. Shapiro (New York, NY: Routledge, 2012), 363–398.
[21] Haapio and Barton, "Business-Friendly Contracting," *supra* note 7.

translations of the contract, thus widening the gap between what Macaulay calls the "paper deal" and the "real deal."[22]

The underlying assumption of legal drafters seems to be that meaning and control are in the words; if the content and wording are right, the appropriate behaviors will follow.[23] However, it is not realistic to assume that once something is in a contract, compliance will automatically follow. Experience and research in fact suggest otherwise: controlling content does not necessarily control people's behavior, nor guarantee the desired outcome. People may choose not to read what they are supposed to. Or they may try to read it, but not understand it. If we want to make our contracts work, we need to make it easier for people to read, understand, and comply with them. This is where PPL and information design come in.

If we are to break the vicious circle, we need to make the current paradigm explicit and challenge it. We can begin with the basic truth that a judge is not a frequent contract user, but that the people in charge of negotiation and implementation are. PPL invites us to think of contracts as business tools. They are shared, visible scripts that support communication and collaboration and empower parties to understand their commitments, show them what they can expect from each other, and demonstrate how to work together to create, share, and protect value.[24] To fulfill this role appropriately, contracts need to be designed, not just drafted. Figure 3.2.1 shows how PPL can facilitate a paradigm shift from current contract

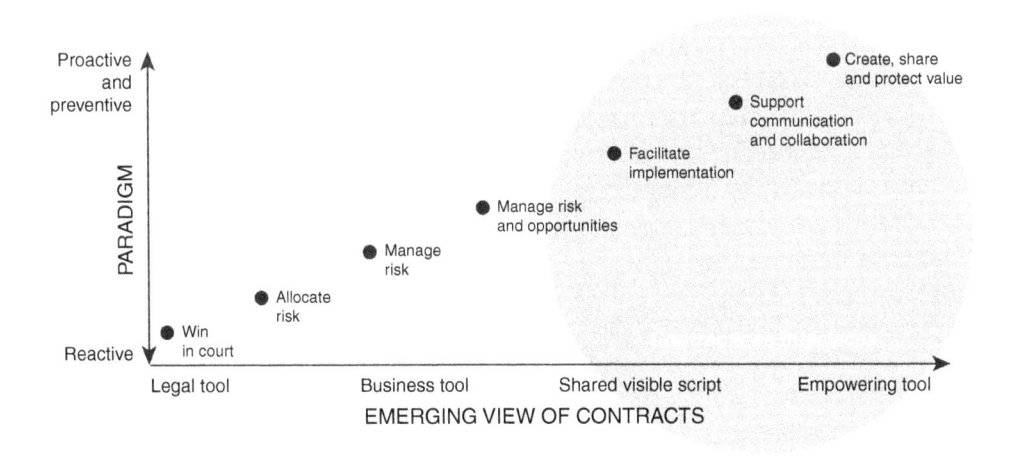

FIGURE 3.2.1 The emerging view of the purpose and functions of contracts.[25]

---

[22] Stewart Macaulay, "The Real and the Paper Deal: Empirical Pictures of Relationships, Complexity and the Urge for Transparent Simple Rules," *The Modern Law Review* 66 (1) (2003): 44–79, available at: www.law.wisc.edu/facstaff/macaulay/papers/real_paper.pdf.

[23] David Sless, "Regulating Information for People: How Information Design Has Made a Difference in the Ways in which Governments and Industry Regulate Information," in *Information Design as Principled Action: Making Information Accessible, Relevant, Understandable, and Usable*, ed. Jorge Frascara (Champaign, IL: Common Ground Publishing LLC, 2015), 190–209.

[24] Helena Haapio and Vaula Haavisto, "Sopimusosaaminen: tulevaisuuden kilpailutekijä ja strateginen voimavara. [Contracting Capabilities: Emerging Source of Competitive Advantage and a Strategic Resource]," *Yritystalous – Leader's Magazine* 2 (2005): 7–15; IACCM, *Commercial Excellence*, supra note 3.

[25] Helena Haapio, "Contract Design Manifesto," proposal accepted for presentation at the IACCM Academic Forum, San Diego, California, October 24, 2016. Helena Haapio and Stefania Passera. Used with permission.

drafting practices to contract design. This has implications for both the process and the outcome, for contract development and implementation, and for the contract as a whole document. Contract content should be front and center. First impressions, tone of voice, look and feel, structure, layout, and text navigation tools are all crucial. By paying attention to these things, contracts can become more engaging, useful, and usable. This allows them to become powerful business tools or, as we will argue later in this chapter, *interfaces*.

We are not alone in calling for a paradigm shift to remedy the current challenges facing contracts. Earlier research has explored, for example, the simplification of contract language and of design, visualization, and collaborative contracting.[26] Taken together, these efforts form an important part of the move toward PPL and next-generation contracts.[27] However, research on these possibilities is still in its infancy.

III RESPONDING TO THE CHALLENGE: CONTRACT DESIGN

In order to create contracts that work as useful and usable business tools, we need to bring business-specific knowledge, along with effective communication strategies, into contracts. Contract design is like a jigsaw puzzle that brings together technical, operational, financial, legal, and communications expertise.[28] From this perspective, legal expertise is just one piece of the contract puzzle.

Argyres and Mayer have demonstrated that contract design is a potential source of competitive advantage, but to develop this capability, design must become multidisciplinary.[29] Managers and engineers, for example, are key repositories of deal-specific knowledge about roles, responsibilities, operations, and collaboration practices, and should be in charge of designing the relevant contract clauses. Lawyers, in turn, are best equipped to take care of contingency planning, dispute resolution, indemnities, and similar legal protections.

In order to orchestrate cross-professional contributions to a contract, we first need an *information architecture* to bring a consistent logic to the whole.[30] We then need to ensure that the content is presented in a logical, understandable, and functional way. For example, it might be best to structure a contract thematically so that different interest groups (e.g., human resources, finance, or production) can easily find the parts that are relevant for them. Then there are questions about how to make the content clear within each section. What is the best way to communicate, say, shipping quantities and schedules to production? Or the best way to communicate agreed KPIs and service levels to an implementation team and its manager?

In contrast to the idea of contracts as legal tools, we prefer the metaphor of contracts as *interfaces*. One set of interfaces is between organizations, allowing coordinated action and exchange[31] and

---

[26] Joseph Kimble, "The Elements of Plain Language," *Michigan Bar Journal* 81 (10) (2002): 44–45; H. W. Jones and M. Oswald, "Doing Deals with Flowcharts," *ACCA Docket*, 19 (9) (2001): 94–108; Thomas D. Barton, "Collaborative Contracting as Preventive/Proactive Law," in *Proactive Law in a Business Environment*, eds. Gerlinde Berger-Walliser and Kim Østergaard (Copenhagen: DJOF Publishing, 2012), 107–127.

[27] Haapio, "Good Contracts," *supra* note 9; Haapio, *Next Generation Contracts*, *supra* note 9; Haapio and Barton, "Business-Friendly Contracting," *supra* note 7.

[28] Haapio, *Next Generation Contracts*, *supra* note 9, at 37.

[29] Nicholas Argyres and Kyle J. Mayer, "Contract Design as a Firm Capability: An Integration of Learning and Transaction Cost Perspectives," *Academy of Management Review* 32 (4) (2007): 1060–1077.

[30] Haapio and Hagan, "Design Patterns for Contracts," *supra* note 10.

[31] Kaj U. Koskinen and Seppo Mäkinen, "Role of Boundary Objects in Negotiations of Project Contracts," *International Journal of Project Management* 27 (1) (2009): 31–38; Donald J. Schepker, Won-Yong Oh, Aleksey Martynov, and Laura Poppo, "The Many Futures of Contracts: Moving Beyond Structure and Safeguarding to Coordination and Adaptation," *Journal of Management* 40 (1) (2014): 193–225.

influencing the nature of the ongoing relationship.[32] Other sets of interfaces are between users and the information they need to do their jobs. This is called the *human–contract interaction*.[33] Our guiding questions are: What methods can facilitate the interaction between people and contracts? How can we express the affordances of contracts through contract design?[34]

Pursuing the idea of contracts as interfaces, we need to look at how designers, engineers, and others have learned to identify, collect, and share best practices to produce effective, usable, and intuitive information.

IV A DESIGN PATTERNS APPROACH FOR CONTRACTS

Experienced professionals draw upon a number of solutions to problems they meet in their work, yet they do not necessarily have names for the solutions. Without names, solutions can be hard to discuss or teach.[35] By using what are called *design patterns* – reusable models of solutions to commonly occurring problems – we can alleviate this difficulty.

Design theorist Christopher Alexander and his colleagues first used the concept of design patterns in architecture to create a common language for recurring sets of experiences and insights. They then codified them all into a standardized collection of patterns.[36] Each pattern describes a problem that occurs repeatedly, and then provides the core of a solution that the designer can use over and over again, without repeating it precisely.[37] These patterns offer model solutions without dictating exactly how they should be implemented, providing a shared toolbox of robust, tested practices that improve communication between people working together on a project. For this reason, these *pattern languages* are easy to use for both experts and laypeople.

Inspired by Alexander's initial work, *pattern libraries* have become a way to share solutions, not only for architects but also for interaction designers, software engineers, and information designers.[38] Borrowing tools from these professions seems a natural continuation of the idea of contracts as interfaces mentioned earlier. These tools allow contracts to become informa-

---

[32] Lilly Weber and Kyle J. Mayer, "Designing Effective Contracts: Exploring the Influence of Framing and Expectations," *Academy of Management Review* 36 (1) (2011): 53–75.

[33] Stefania Passera and Helena Haapio, "Transforming Contracts from Legal Rules to User-Centered Communication Tools: A Human–Information Interaction Challenge," *Communication Design Quarterly* 1 (3) (2013): 38–45, available at: www.sigdoc.acm.org/wp-content/uploads/2012/09/CDQ-April-1-3-FINAL.pdf.

[34] The concept of affordance – first introduced by Gibson in the field of ecological psychology, and then popularized by Norman in the field of design and human–computer interaction – indicates the possibilities of action and use that an object affords to its users. Norman in particular focused on perceived affordances; that is, how well an object intuitively communicates its functions; see James J. Gibson, "The Theory of Affordances," in *Perceiving, Acting, and Knowing*, eds. Robert Shaw and John D. Bransford (Hillsdale, NJ: Lawrence Erlbaum Associates, 1977); see also Donald A. Norman, *The Design of Everyday Things*, revised and expanded edition (New York, NY: Basic Books, 2013).

[35] Robert Waller, Judy Delin, and Martin Thomas, "Towards a Pattern Language Approach to Document Description," *Discours* 10 (2012), available at: https://journals.openedition.org/discours/8673.

[36] Christopher Alexander, Sara Ishikawa, Murray Silverstein, Max Jacobson, Ingrid Fiksdahl-King, and Shlomo Angel, *A Pattern Language: Towns, Buildings, Construction* (New York, NY: Oxford University Press, 1977).

[37] *Id.* at ix; see also Christopher Alexander, *The Timeless Way of Building* (New York, NY: Oxford University Press, 1979).

[38] See generally, Waller, Delin, and Thomas, "Towards a Pattern Language Approach to Document Description" *supra* note 35; Jenifer Tidwell, *Designing Interfaces*, 2nd ed. (Sebastopol, CA: O'Reilly Media, 2014); Yue Pan and Erik Stolterman, "Pattern Language and HCI: Expectations and Experiences," in *CHI 2013 Extended Abstracts on Human Factors in Computing Systems* (New York, NY: Association of Computing Machinery, 2013), 1989–1998.

tion products, and so their crafter's work can be viewed as information design.[39] In a number of contexts, the work of lawyers has many similarities with the work of designers, architects, or engineers.[40] In this vein, law has been compared to engineering and lawyers referred to as legal architects, with a number of observers also noting similarities between contract drafting and computer programming.[41]

We are not the first to use design patterns in this context. Gerding examined how Alexander's pattern language framework provides a unique lens to look at how transactional attorneys draft contracts.[42] He explored the various functions contract patterns can perform, like helping to deconstruct complex problems and bargains by breaking them into components, allowing teams of lawyers to work on different aspects of a contract or transaction simultaneously; or providing lawyers with devices they can use repeatedly to quickly estimate whether particular contract language solves certain bargaining problems, meets client objectives, and will be interpreted by courts in an anticipated manner.[43]

In 2008, researchers at Harvard proposed a Contracts Wiki.[44] The online platform provided modular contract terms through an online community, creating new contract modules to solve problems arising from changes in regulation or the business environment. While its creators did not use the term *pattern language*, the idea was similar: to provide a resource to bring together good-practice solutions to particular contracting problems, and to promote efficiency and standardization by disseminating these solutions.[45]

More recently, similar ideas have been implemented by a number of web-based resources that provide reusable contract forms, samples, and clause libraries for both

---

[39] Haapio, "Good Contracts," *supra* note 9; Bruce H. Kobayashi and Larry E. Ribstein, "Law's Information Revolution," *Arizona Law Review* 53 (4) (2011): 1169–1220, available at: www.arizonalawreview.org/pdf/53-4/53arizlrev1169.pdf; Elizabeth Orna, *Making Knowledge Visible: Communication Knowledge Through Information Products* (Aldershot: Gower Publishing, 2005).

[40] Howarth sees the work of lawyers as designing useful devices for clients. Lawyers can become more innovative and effective as designers of new devices by using the methods of engineers. Mitchell, meanwhile, explores how lawyers can make their work product a better product. David Howarth, *Law as Engineering: Thinking About What Lawyers Do* (Cheltenham: Edward Elgar, 2014); Jay A. Mitchell, "Putting Some Product into Work-Product: Corporate Lawyers Learning from Designers," *Berkeley Business Law Journal*, 12 (1) (2015): 1–44, available at: www.scholarship.law.berkeley.edu/bblj/vol12/iss1/1.

[41] See Lon L. Fuller, "The Lawyer as an Architect of Social Structures," in *The Principles of Social Order: Selected Essays of Lon L. Fuller*, ed. Kenneth I. Winston (Durham, NC: Duke University Press, 1981), 264–270; Erik F. Gerding, "Contract as Pattern Language," *Washington Law Review* 88 (4) (2013): 1323–1356, available at: www.ssrn.com/abstract=2371097; Helena Haapio, "Lawyers as Designers, Engineers and Innovators: Better Legal Documents through Information Design and Visualization," in *Transparency: Proceedings of the 17th International Legal Informatics Symposium IRIS 2014*, eds. E. Schweighofer, F. Kummer, and W. Hötzendorfer (Vienna: Österreichische Computer Gesellschaft, 2014), 451–458; Helena Haapio and Stefania Passera, "Visual Law: What Lawyers Need to Learn from Information Designers," blog post, VoxPopuLII, Cornell University Law School, May 15, 2013, available at: www.blog.law.cornell.edu/voxpop/2013/05/15/visual-law-what-lawyers-need-to-learn-from-information-designers; Tobias Mahler, "A Graphical User-Interface for Legal Texts?" in *Internationalisation of Law in the Digital Information Society: Nordic Yearbook of Law and Informatics 2010–2012*, eds. Dan Jerker B. Svantesson and Stanley Greenstein (Copenhagen: Ex Tuto Publishing, 2013): 311–327.

[42] Gerding, "Contract as Pattern Language," *supra* note 41.

[43] *Id.* at 1328, 1346.

[44] The Wiki was established with the sponsorship of Harvard Law School and the Berkman Center for Internet and Society; see "System Shocks and Collaborative Contract Innovation," Harvard Law School Contracts Wiki, last accessed May 30, 2017, available at: http://ackwiki.com/drupal/about.

[45] The Contracts Wiki did not succeed as a platform. Its webpage is still online, but it is not being actively maintained.

lawyers and non-lawyers. Docracy hosts a crowdsourced library of contracts that allows people to upload and share contracts on the platform; Legal Robot and ContractStandards, meanwhile, aim to improve the contracting process by comparing current documents to standards and metrics.[46]

Haapio and Hagan have gone further than these early proposals of patterns only related to content, clauses, and language.[47] They stress the need for patterns that present and communicate contracts and make them function properly. Their Contract Design Pattern Library website suggests four main categories of patterns: composition, visualization, process, and text.[48] *Composition patterns* highlight the importance of functional document elements that help navigate contracts: tables of contents, checklists, and summary pages, to name a few elements. The *visualization patterns* use visual elements to help users find, understand, and experience the content in easier and more congenial ways. *Process patterns*, meanwhile, offer patterns of "actions that people involved in crafting, finalizing, and implementing a contract take in order to make it more useful and to accomplish the ends that it intends to," such as creating a contract briefing document and holding a meeting to discuss it.[49]

Other pattern approaches go beyond language, offering solutions in terms of layered layout, providing compositional and functional elements like checklists, and explanatory visualizations like timelines and icons.[50] These patterns are categorized according to their functions: supporting strategic reading, explanations, user response, and reader engagement.

These research approaches are the first in the contracting field to explicitly organize and structure design patterns around a combination of problem, solution, and rationale.[51] A coherent and expandable organization is necessary for creating pattern libraries, even though the way the patterns are structured usually depends on the field of application. Detailing the several different research approaches is beyond the scope of this book. Table 3.2.1 shows five different structuring approaches, from three different fields.[52] For the remainder of this chapter, we will focus on one of the pattern categories proposed by Haapio and Hagan: visualization patterns.

V CONTRACT VISUALIZATION PATTERNS: PROPOSING A CATEGORIZATION

The idea of using visual communication in the world of contracts is not new. Despite ample interest in this idea, however, the approaches described in the literature have so far varied a lot in terms of style, basic assumptions, and goals. The various names for these approaches

---

[46] Docracy, www.docracy.com; Legal Robot, www.legalrobot.com; ContractStandards, www.contractstandards.com.
[47] Haapio and Hagan, "Design Patterns for Contracts," *supra* note 10.
[48] The Contract Design Pattern Library, www.contractpatterns.design, is an early-stage prototype of what such a library may look like. It currently has a limited number of patterns, but welcomes suggestions and entries.
[49] For the difference between contract design patterns and contract templates, models, and standards, see www.contractpatterns.design/patterns; *see also* Haapio and Hagan, "Design Patterns for Contracts," *supra* note 10.
[50] Robert Waller, Jenny Waller, Helena Haapio, Gary Crag, and Sandi Morrisseau, "Cooperation Through Clarity: Designing Simplified Contracts," *Journal of Strategic Contracting and Negotiation* 2 (1–2) (2016).
[51] Haapio and Hagan, "Design Patterns for Contracts," *supra* note 10.
[52] Waller et al., "Towards a Pattern Language Approach to Document Description," *supra* note 35.

TABLE 3.2.1 *Examples of pattern structures.*[53]

Alexander	Tidwell	Yahoo	Waller et al.	Haapio and Hagan
Architecture	Interface design	Interface design	Contract design	Contract design
Number and name	Name	Name	Name	Name
Photograph	Illustration	Illustration	Challenge	Illustration
Upward links	What	What problem does this solve?	Typical solution	What
Problem statement	Use when	When to use this pattern?	Typical issues	When
Explanation	Why	What's the solution?	Example	Why
Sketch/diagram	How	Why use this pattern?		How
Solution summary	Examples	Accessibility		Examples
Downward links	In other libraries			

include: diagramming transactions,[54] graphical user interfaces for legal texts,[55] visual interfaces for deal-making,[56] and contract visualization.[57] Haapio and Hagan have developed a pattern library in order to bring together all these disparate visualization patterns.[58] Table 3.2.2 offers a categorization of these approaches and a common language to describe them.

Our first category of contract visualization patterns, *visual organization and structuring patterns*, is the least obviously visual. These patterns organize and structure texts visually, using layout, page design, and typography to increase readability and legibility and to support strategic reading activities such as searching, skimming, and selecting relevant content. Page layout is particularly important for effective reading and writing because it provides a hierarchy and the visual cues necessary to navigate information on the page.[59] Contracts are highly textual documents, so organizing and structuring the text is the first step toward making the content accessible and usable to readers. A key reference for this approach is Butterick's *Typography for Lawyers*, a concise compendium on why typography, fonts, and page design matter, and how they contribute to polished, legible, and clear legal

---

[53] Structuring approaches gathered from: Alexander, *The Timeless Way of Building, supra* note 37; Alexander et al., *A Pattern Language, supra* note 36; Haapio and Hagan, "Design Patterns for Contracts," *supra* note 10; Tidwell, *Designing Interfaces, supra* note 38; Waller et al., "Cooperation Through Clarity," *supra* note 50; and Yahoo (n.d.), "Yahoo Design Pattern Library," available at: www.developer.yahoo.com/ypatterns.

[54] Kevin Conboy, "Diagramming Transactions: Some Modest Proposals and a Few Suggested Rules," *Transactions: Tennessee Journal of Business Law* 16 (2014): 91–108.

[55] Mahler, "A Graphical User-Interface for Legal Texts?" *supra* note 41.

[56] Daniela-Alina Plewe, "A Visual Interface for Deal Making," in *Evolving Ambient Intelligence – AmI 2013 Workshops, Dublin, Ireland, December 3–5, 2013, Revised Selected Papers*, eds. Michael O'Grady, Hamed Vahdat-Nejad, Klaus-Hendrik Wolf, Mauro Dragone, Juan Ye, Carsten Röcker, and Gregory O'Hare (Cham: Springer International, 2013), 205–512.

[57] Passera and Haapio, "Transforming Contracts from Legal Rules to User-Centered Communication Tools," *supra* note 33.

[58] Haapio and Hagan, "Design Patterns for Contracts," *supra* note 10.

[59] Robert Waller, "Graphic Literacies for a Digital Age: The Survival of Layout," *The Information Society* 28 (4) (2012): 236–252.

TABLE 3.2.2 *Categorization of contract visualization patterns.*

Categories of visualization pattern	Examples
Visual organization and structuring patterns	• Searchable headings • Layered layouts • Typographic highlighting • Bulleted and numbered lists
Multimodal document patterns	• Comic-based contracts • Visual contract guides
Visual representation patterns	• Timelines • Tables • Flowcharts • Swimlanes • Companion icons • Delivery diagrams

documents.[60] Typography and page design are important, as are effective layout patterns that use, for example, left-handed headings to facilitate skimming, thematic color-coding to signal different parts of the document, and multi-column layered layouts to accommodate explanations, examples, and definitions.[61] Another effective method is to highlight key parts of text using italics, boldface, or color to capture attention.[62] Bulleted and numbered lists are also helpful for communicating things like hierarchies, steps, or a family of items. In general, these tactics help ameliorate the pervasive problem of contracts appearing too cluttered and dense to their readers.

Though useful, the conservative nature of typographic and layout patterns often suggests that contract designers do not have the will, time, tools, or skills to explore more visual solutions, or that they feel the time taken to produce them is unreasonable. If the status quo of contract-as-text is not challenged, however, other communication possibilities will be missed that could ensure substantially better understanding and engagement.

To this end, the second category from Table 3.2.2, *multimodal document patterns*, challenges the idea of contracts as something only *textual*. Multimodal document solutions transform contracts into more dynamic documents that fully integrate text and images. Fully integrated visualizations can be used not only *in* contracts but also *as* contracts or *about* contracts. Comic-based contracts are one such example. In comic-based contracts, meaning arises when text and visuals come together to create a narrative. The visual aid cannot be separated from the text: The comic *is* the contract. Robert de Rooy has successfully applied this *visualization as contract* approach to employment contracts for low-literacy audiences in South Africa, and this approach has also been used for experimenting with

---

[60] Matthew Butterick, *Typography for Lawyers*, 2nd ed. (Houston, TX: O'Connors, 2015).
[61] Waller et al., "Cooperation Through Clarity," *supra* note 50.
[62] Tetiana Tsygankova, "Design for Good Commercial Contracts: Practical Tools for Contract Drafters," in *Networks: Proceedings of the 19th International Legal Informatics Symposium IRIS 2016*, eds. E. Schweighofer, F. Kummer, W. Hötzendorfer, and G. Borges (Vienna: Österreichische Computer Gesellschaft, 2016), 407–414.

non-disclosure agreements for researchers at a university engineering school in Australia.[63] *Visualizations about contracts*, meanwhile, are exemplified by a visual contract guide, which is a full collection of visual and multimodal explanations of a textual contract. This application first appeared in the guidance notes and flowcharts for the New Engineering Contract (NEC) family of contracts, which is used in the construction industry and for other large projects.[64] Each page of a visual contract guide features one flowchart about a specific contract topic, with cross-references to the relevant contract clauses. To test the rigor of visual contract guides, Passera et al. created and tested a visual contract guide for public procurement of services in Finland in order to demonstrate how this format made the meaning of the contract's terms more accurate, and made the contract easier to understand.[65]

Lastly, the third category, *visual representation patterns*, focuses on representing the logic, content, or prerequisites of contracts through a diagrammatic or pictorial representation. Visual communication is used to explain the text, with the goal of making the abstract relationships within contracts visible. This can be done with sequences, transitions, interactions, or hierarchies, to name a few examples. Importantly, the visual representations do *not* substitute for text; instead, they complement and disambiguate the text. After all, textual elements are a key component of diagrams, providing necessary conceptual labels and meaning. Combining text with visuals that show the relationships between concepts constrains possible interpretations of a contract, guiding readers toward the right inferences and aiding comprehension.[66] The cognitive cost of comprehension is also reduced, since the external representation pre-processes and integrates the information in a meaningful model, instead of readers having to create their own associations in their mind's eye from scratch.[67] Compared to pure text, the presence of visual representations significantly improves comprehension accuracy and speed.[68]

---

[63] Helena Haapio, Daniela Alina Plewe, and Robert de Rooy, "Next Generation Deal Design: Comics and Visual Platforms for Contracting," in *Networks: Proceedings of the 19th International Legal Informatics Symposium IRIS 2016*, eds. E. Schweighofer, F. Kummer, W. Hötzendorfer, and G. Borges (Vienna: Österreichische Computer Gesellschaft, 2016), 373–380; Adrian Keating and Camilla B. Andersen, "A Graphic Contract: Taking Visualisation in Contracting a Step Further," *Journal of Strategic Contracting and Negotiation*, 2 (1–2) (2016): 10–18; Daniela Alina Plewe and Robert de Rooy, "Integrative Deal-Design: Cascading from Goal-hierarchies to Negotiations and Contracting," *Journal of Strategic Contracting and Negotiation*, 2 (1–2) (2016).

[64] NEC, *NEC3 Engineering and Construction Contract Flow Charts* (London: Thomas Telford, 2013); NEC, *NEC3 Professional Services Contract Guidance Notes and Flow Charts* (London: Thomas Telford, 2013).

[65] Stefania Passera, Soile Pohjonen, Katja Koskelainen, and Suvi Anttila, "User-Friendly Contracting Tools: A Visual Guide to Facilitate Public Procurement Contracting," in *Proceedings of the 2013 IACCM Academic Forum for Integrating Law and Contract Management: Proactive, Preventive and Strategic Approaches*, ed. J. Chittenden (Ridgefield, CT: International Association for Contract and Commercial Management, 2013), 74–94; "JYSEn käyttämisopas: JYSE 2009 PALVELUT," Julkisten hankintojen yleiset sopimusehdot palveluhankinnoissa 21.10.2010, 2013, Aalto University/SimLab & Association of Finnish Local and Regional Authorities, available at: http://goo.gl/MXx6u5.

[66] Keith Stenning and Jon Oberlander, "A Cognitive Theory of Graphical and Linguistic Reasoning: Logic and Implementation," *Cognitive Science* 19 (1) (1995): 97–140.

[67] Mike Scaife and Yvonne Rogers, "External Cognition: How Do Graphical Representations Work?" *International Journal of Human–Computer Studies* 45 (2) (1996): 185–213.

[68] *See generally*, T. Mamula and U. Hagel, "The Design of Commercial Conditions: Layout, Visualization, Language," in *Co-operation: Proceedings of the 18th International Legal Informatics Symposium IRIS 2015*, eds. E. Schweighofer, F. Kummer, W. Hötzendorfer, and G. Borges (Vienna: Österreichische Computer Gesellschaft, 2015), 471–478; Stefania Passera, "Beyond the Wall of Text: How Information Design Can Make Contracts User-Friendly," in *Design, User Experience, and Usability: Users and Interactions*, ed. Aaron Marcus (Cham: Springer International, 2015), 341–352; Passera et al., "Diagrams in Contracts," *supra* note 4; Passera et al., "User-Friendly Contracting Tools," *supra* note 65.

While there are many different representation techniques, there are six that seem to recur frequently in contract research and practice.[69] These six key visual representation patterns are: (1) timelines, (2) flowcharts, (3) tables,[70] (4) swimlanes,[71] (5) companion icons,[72] and (6) delivery diagrams.[73] All of these different visual representation patterns are flexible and can be used for different purposes: *in* contracts, as explanatory complements;[74] *about* contracts, as the building blocks of visual contract guides;[75] and *for* contracts, as templates and tools used in negotiations to support thinking, promote understanding, and generate content for an agreement.[76]

VI VISUAL REPRESENTATION PATTERNS

The idea of contracts as interfaces has guided the development of six visual representation patterns.[77] We include the name of each pattern, and a short description of its essence. We then provide examples of communication problems in contracts and how the pattern offers a solution, and end with visual examples of the pattern in action in the context of contracts. In essence, we identify a useful, repeatable solution to a common contract-related problem, and then give it a name and a description so that it can join a future contract designer's repertoire of potential solutions to similar problems.[78]

[69] See Ralph Lengler and Martin J. Eppler, "Towards a Periodic Table of Visualization Methods of Management," in *Proceedings of the IASTED International Conference on Graphics and Visualization in Engineering, GVE '07* (Anaheim, CA: ACTA Press, 2007), 83–88, available at: http://dl.acm.org/citation.cfm?id=1712936.1712954; Isabel Meirelles, *Design for Information: An Introduction to the Histories, Theories, and Best Practices Behind Effective Information Visualizations* (Beverly, MA: Rockport Publishers, 2013).

[70] Our references suggest the use of tables in legal documents generally. The examples in this paper show their application to contracts; see Australian Office of Parliamentary Counsel, *Plain English Manual*, supra note 12; Kimble, "The Elements of Plain Language," supra note 26; Plain Language Action and Information Network, "Federal Plain Language Guidelines, Revision 1," May 1, 2011, available at: www.plainlanguage.gov/howto/guidelines/FederalPLGuidelines/FederalPLGuidelines.pdf; John Strylowski, "Using Tables to Present Complex Ideas," *Michigan Bar Journal* 92 (2) (2013): 44–47.

[71] Passera et al., "User-Friendly Contracting Tools," supra note 65; Stefania Passera, Anssi Smedlund, and Marja Liinasuo, "Exploring Contract Visualization: Clarification and Framing Strategies to Shape Collaborative Business Relationships," *Journal of Strategic Contracting and Negotiation* 2 (1–2) (2016).

[72] Haapio and Hagan, "Design Patterns for Contracts," supra note 10; Passera, "Beyond the Wall of Text," supra note 68; Waller et al., "Cooperation Through Clarity," supra note 50.

[73] Information designers and lawyers created a prototype booklet as part of a collaboration during the Information Design Summer School 2013 in Syros, Greece. The Contracts for the International Sale of Goods (CISG) is the uniform international sales law of countries, and accounts for most of world trade; see Stefania Passera, Helena Haapio, Robert Waller, Oliver Tomlinson, Christopher Edwards, Olivia Zarcate, Gonzalo Arellano, and Julia Mariani, "Visual CISG: A Prototype of Legal Information Design," Draft 10.10.2013, CISG Legal Design Jam Group @ Syros 2013, available at: http://legaldesignjam.com/wp-content/uploads/2016/03/visualCISG_booklet.pdf; Helena Haapio, "Using the CISG Proactively," in *International Sales Law: A Global Challenge*, ed. Larry A. DiMatteo (New York, NY: Cambridge University Press, 2014), 704–723; Incoterms 2010 Wallchart, International Chamber of Commerce ICC, ICC publication No. 716E, 2010.

[74] Mamula and Hagel, "The Design of Commercial Conditions" supra note 68; Passera et al., "Diagrams in Contracts," supra note 4; Haapio et al., "Next Generation Deal Design," supra note 63.

[75] Passera, et al., "User Friendly Contracting Tools," supra note 65.

[76] Passera et al., "Exploring Contract Visualization," supra note 71; Plewe and de Rooy, "Integrative Deal-Design," supra note 63; Plewe, "A Visual Interface for Deal Making," supra note 56; Haapio et al., "Next Generation Deal Design," supra note 63; George J. Siedel, *The Three Pillar Model for Business Decisions: Strategy, Law & Ethics* (Ann Arbor, MI: Van Rye Publishing, 2016).

[77] *See generally*, Tidwell, *Designing Interfaces*, supra note 38; Waller et al., "Cooperation Through Clarity," supra note 50; Haapio and Hagan, "Design Patterns for Contracts," supra note 10.

[78] While a number of design tools and software are available to create visual representations, we have chosen not to mention them here. The essence of design patterns is technology-independent, and specific tools or software may become obsolete.

A Timeline Pattern

Timelines represent time or duration, a series of steps or processes taking place within a given time frame, or a sequence of events. Timelines are useful for clauses that specify duration (e.g., contract term, or notice or warranty period); that list milestones, to-do items, and deadlines (e.g., payment or reporting schedules); or that describe steps or processes (e.g., agreement termination, giving notice, or audits).

The rationale for using timelines is that they provide an explicit and concrete representation of time and the order of steps to be taken, elements that are often abstract and hidden in the text or appendices of a document. Timelines help to explain complex processes by illustrating which steps need to be taken, when they need to be taken, and in what order. Presenting actions, requirements, or deadlines in chronological order makes sense to readers, as it mirrors their lived experience: They can see at a glance what will happen in the future, and what course of action to take.

Time can be represented as a straight or circular line.[79] Straight lines are suitable for representing progress, sequences, and procedures. Figure 3.2.2 shows examples of *linear* timelines, representing different types of term and termination provisions. Time is shown

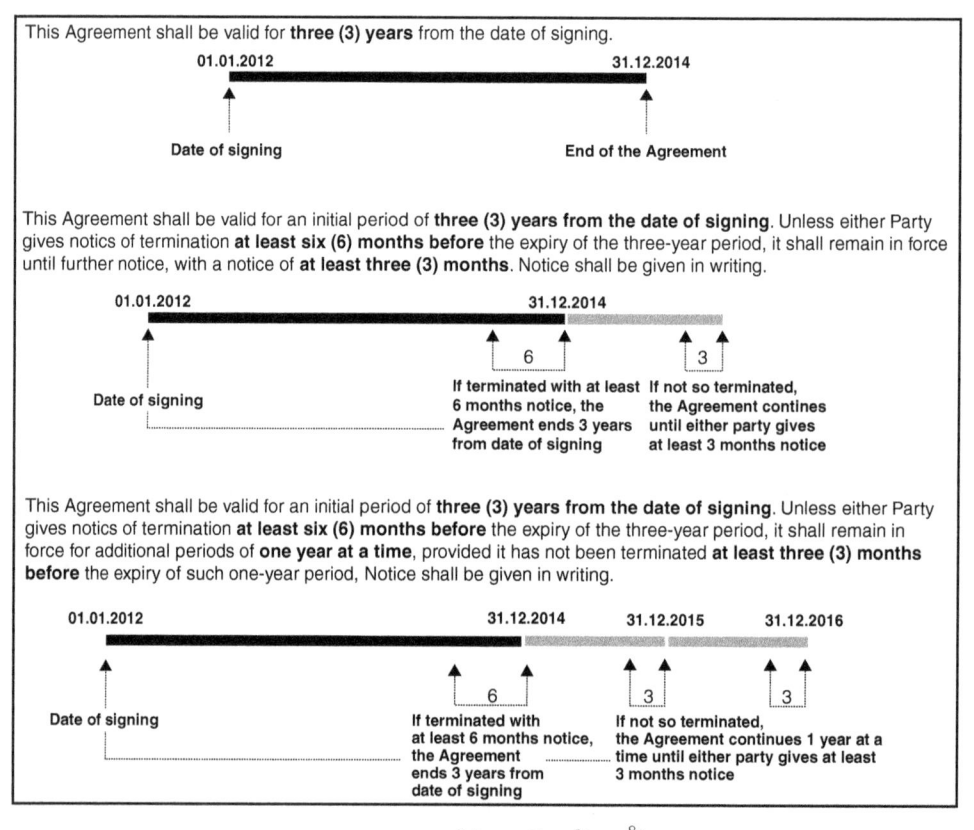

FIGURE 3.2.2 Linear timelines.[80]

---

[79] Meirelles, *Design for Information*, supra note 69.
[80] © 2012 Stefania Passera and Helena Haapio. Used with permission.

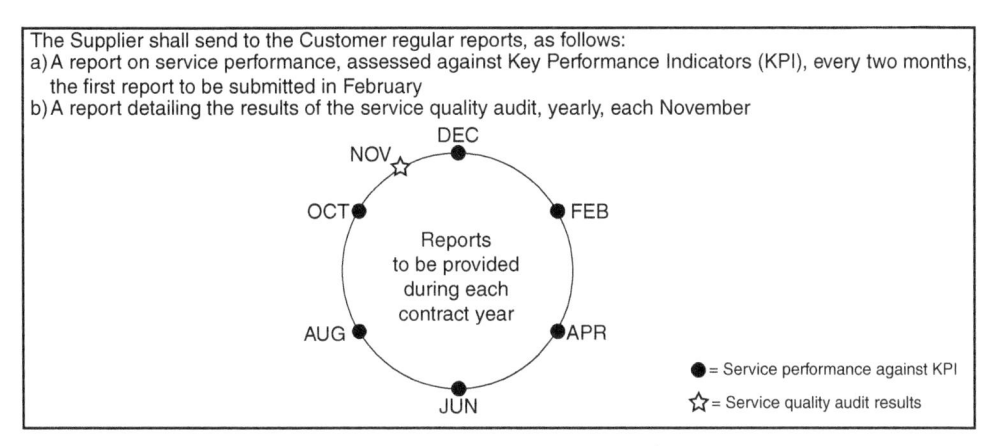

> The Supplier shall send to the Customer regular reports, as follows:
> a) A report on service performance, assessed against Key Performance Indicators (KPI), every two months, the first report to be submitted in February
> b) A report detailing the results of the service quality audit, yearly, each November

FIGURE 3.2.3 Circular timeline.[81]

as a straight line, and key events are marked. Color or shading can be used to distinguish between fixed and optional contract periods, among other things.

Time can also be represented using circular lines. Circular lines are particularly useful when representing recurring events or deadlines on a weekly, monthly, quarterly, or yearly basis. An example of a circular timeline is shown in Figure 3.2.3, illustrating when a supplier needs to submit periodic reports to a customer.

Time is represented as a circle to indicate that the same events repeat each year. Different colors and shapes can help distinguish between different types of reports to be submitted. Milestones, deadlines, and actions are marked on the timeline as dots, tacks, shapes, or call-out boxes. Textual elements can be used to clarify and label the key parts of the timeline.

These basic patterns can be applied to create more complex time-related representations, such as processes that take different paths; variables that change over time; or the synchronous progress of multiple processes or events. Figure 3.2.4 shows processes that take different paths.

This timeline represents the test run process in an equipment sale and purchase agreement. Test runs are usually part of the acceptance process: Equipment needs to perform to specifications in a series of tests before the purchaser will accept it. If the equipment does not perform as promised, the supplier needs to remedy the deficiencies and try to pass the test again. Since the test can be passed or failed, the timeline bifurcates, showing both scenarios.

One can also make a hybrid between a timeline and a bar chart. Figure 3.2.5 shows a representation of liquidated damages for delayed delivery in an equipment sale and purchase agreement. The horizontal axis represents weeks, the vertical axis the liquidated damages to be paid by the supplier. The bar chart is positioned within the axes and shows the liquidated damages rate for each commencing week of delay, capped at 10% of the purchase price.

Finally, Figure 3.2.6 shows synchronous progress of multiple processes or events. As the figure shows, multiple timelines can be stacked and presented together to show how important events take place in time. This example illustrates how title, risk, and responsibility for a piece of equipment pass from the supplier to the purchaser, showing how the "moment of passage" is different for different types of risks and responsibilities.

---

[81] © 2016 Stefania Passera and Helena Haapio. Used with permission.

In the event that the Equipment does not fulfill some of the guarantee values specified in Appendix 1 during the Test Run(s), the Supplier shall **as soon as possible and not later than within one (1) month**, at its own expense and at a time convenient to the Purchaser, remedy the deficiencies noted, after which a new Test Run shall be carried out. If the guarantee values are still not attained in this renewed Test Run, the Supplier shall, at its own expense, **without delay and within a maximum period of two (2) months**, effect the necessary improvements and modifications to the Equipment. If the guarantee values are not attained in the subsequent Test Run, the Purchaser is **entitled to liquidated damages** in accordance with Appendix 8.

Test runs process

1. Test run
   - Successful test run
   - Failed test run
     Supplier has to remedy the deficiencies in the Equipment, at its own expense, **within 1 month**
2. New test run
   - Successful test run
   - Failed test run
     Supplier has to effect improvements and modifications to the Equipment, at its own expense, **within 2 months**
3. New test run
   - Successful test run
   - Failed test run
     The Purchaser is entitled to liquidated damages in accordance with Appendix 8

FIGURE 3.2.4 Processes with different paths.[82]

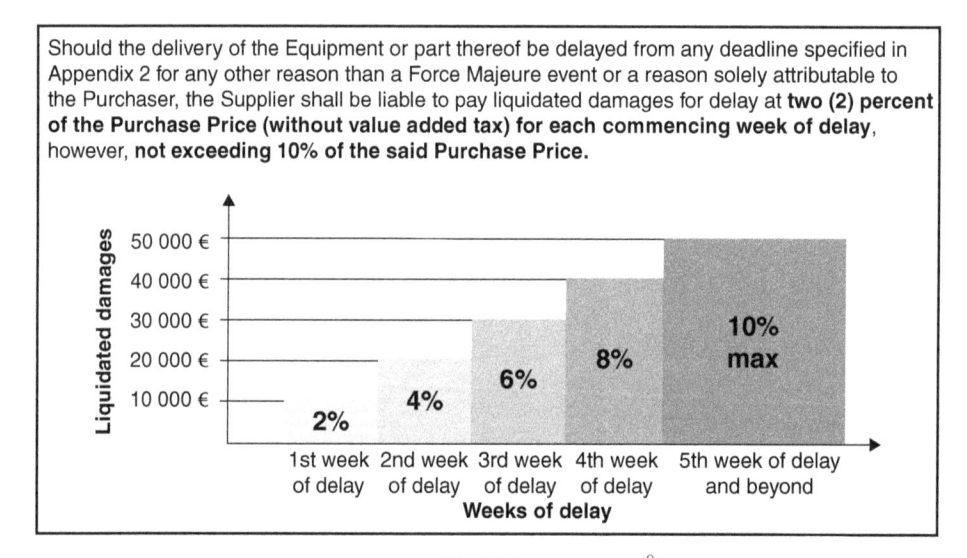

Should the delivery of the Equipment or part thereof be delayed from any deadline specified in Appendix 2 for any other reason than a Force Majeure event or a reason solely attributable to the Purchaser, the Supplier shall be liable to pay liquidated damages for delay at **two (2) percent of the Purchase Price (without value added tax) for each commencing week of delay**, however, **not exceeding 10% of the said Purchase Price.**

Liquidated damages:
- 1st week of delay: 2%
- 2nd week of delay: 4%
- 3rd week of delay: 6%
- 4th week of delay: 8%
- 5th week of delay and beyond: 10% max

FIGURE 3.2.5 Variables over time.[83]

B Flowchart Pattern

Most contract readers are busy people and need quick, clear answers from a contract in order to inform their actions. There are two typical features in contracts, however, that can hinder

---

[82] © 2012 Stefania Passera. Used with permission.
[83] © 2012 Stefania Passera. Used with permission.

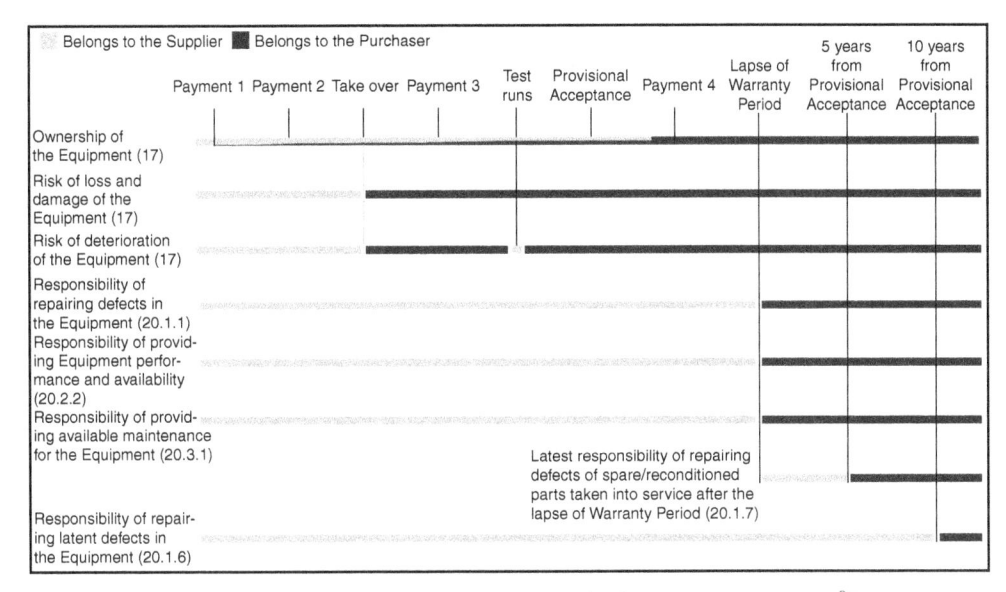

FIGURE 3.2.6 Synchronous progress of multiple processes or events.[84]

straightforward answers. Contracts usually describe many contingencies, and are full of conjunctions that indicate conditional information (e.g., "if ... /then ..."; "in case of ... /NN shall ... "), exceptions (e.g., "notwithstanding," "unless", etc.), and alternatives (e.g., "either/or," "whichever the earliest/highest"). Additionally, cross-references are another typical feature of contracts, forcing readers to divert their attention to other clauses, appendices, or defined terms. These features make contracts hard to understand because they require readers to perform cognitively demanding operations: splitting their attention, keeping several chunks of information in mind, and integrating everything into something meaningful. *Flowcharts* represent a workflow or process in a step-by-step fashion. They are tools to support decision making and problem solving, and they also allow us to identify the actual flow or sequence of events in a process, thus clarifying the myriad pathways of a contract.

Flowcharts offer a step-by-step approach to solving complex problems and making decisions. They present simple, straightforward actions so users do not need to keep all the information they need in mind; instead, they can consider one step at a time. With flowcharts, it is easy to present all relevant information on a single page in an integrated, accessible way. Decision points, alternative paths, and possible outcomes are all visible at a glance.

Flowcharts consist of a series of blocks of text connected by arrows.[85] The text in the blocks is often in the form of a simple yes-or-no question with two arrows – one marked "yes" and the other marked "no" – pointing outward from each block. Depending on their response, users follow the appropriate arrow to the next question and answer each question until they finish.

---

[84] © 2012 Stefania Passera. Used with permission.
[85] Since our interest is on design patterns as model solutions to problems, we do not introduce formal representation methods for flowcharts here. Such techniques have been standardized, for example, in the field of information technology, where there are precise representation rules – e.g., a diamond shape indicates a decision point, a rectangle indicates a process, and so on. See ISO 5807:1985, Information Processing, Documentation Symbols and Conventions for Data, Program and System Flowcharts, Program Network Charts and System Resources Charts.

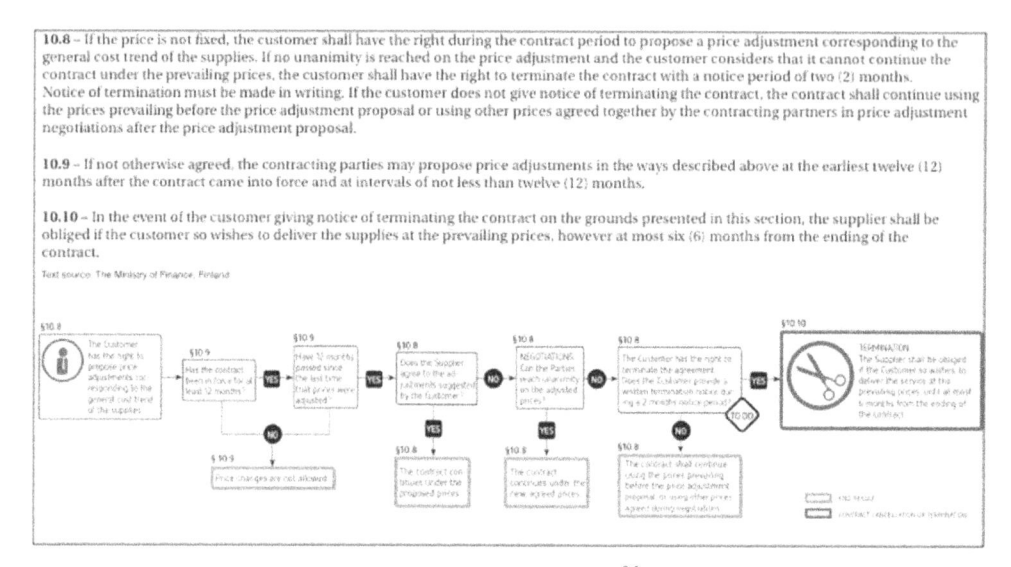

FIGURE 3.2.7 Flowchart.[86]

Figure 3.2.7 shows a flowchart used in a visual guide for public procurement terms.[87] It illustrates a price change procedure and the preconditions for requesting a price change. Different outcomes are set out, and color-coding can indicate whether disagreements may escalate into contract termination. Each block of text in the flowchart cross-references the contract clauses, so that the diagram and text can be used together to further understanding.

C Table Pattern

Dense, long texts can make it difficult for readers to discern key points. Readers may want to compare information in order to make correct choices. They may, for example, need to understand how a provision applies to different actors or in different circumstances, or what the rights and obligations of different parties are in relation to an issue like IP rights. *Tables* can help facilitate these comparisons in order to enhance understanding.

Tables provide a way of structuring information in order to help readers skim and process a lot of information at a glance. A table's systematic arrangement of facts and figures into rows and columns makes it easy to read, and also helps to facilitate comparison and choice between different elements. Like flowcharts, tables compile information that may be on different pages; however, tables are not suitable for conveying complex processes or contingencies. Rather, tables are most effective in simpler tasks that can be performed quickly, such as finding relevant information from a long list, or comparing and choosing alternatives. Another advantage of tables is that people are generally familiar with their structure and have few problems understanding how they work.[88]

All tables consist of rows and columns of cells, each cell containing unique content. Clear, informative headings are important to specify how content is categorized in the columns and

---

[86] © 2013 Aalto University and Suomen Kuntaliitto ry (The Association of Finnish Local and Regional Authorities).
[87] "JYSEn käyttämisopas," *supra* note 65.
[88] Tables are ubiquitous in organizational life. Readers with a background in project or risk management may be familiar, for example, with RACI charts, various types of matrices, and risk registers.

10.1   Ownership of Foreground Information shall belong to Inventing Party.

10.2   Inventing Party may transfer Ownership of Foreground Information to a third party. Prior to the transfer of Ownership of Foreground Information to any third party during Programme and within twenty four months from the end of Programme the other Parties shall be offered Ownership of Foreground Information on the same terms and conditions as agreed with the third party. Party transferring its Ownership to Foreground Information is obliged to transfer its rights and obligations arising from this Agreement.

10.3   Party having Ownership of Foreground Information has the right to grant third parties licences to Foreground Information. However, Party having Ownership is obliged to inform during Programme the other Parties about such grant of licence within 30 days from the execution of license. For the avoidance of doubt, such obligation to inform is not applicable to licensing of a Party's product or services in the ordinary course of business.

10.4   Each Party shall be granted a royalty-free Access Right to Foreground Information.

10.5   Notwithstanding anything to the contrary under this Agreement, Access Right includes a right to sublicense Foreground Information solely to 1) a Party's subcontractors and even then, only for Party's own research or development work or business operations, and 2) the users of a Party's end product or service, particularly in case of software, if elements for Foreground Information are included in a Party's product or distributed appended to it.

10.6   Each Subcontractor shall be granted a royalty-free Limited Access Right to Foreground Information. Subcontractors shall not have Ownership of Foreground Information they have invented, created or generated under Programme. Ownership of such Foreground Information shall belong to Party/Parties that have engaged Subcontractor, and such Party/Parties shall ensure the assignment of Ownership of Foreground Information from its Subcontractor to Party/Parties concerned.

WHO	RIGHT TO FOREGROUND INFORMATION (FI)	RIGHT TO TRANSFER OWNERSHIP	RIGHT TO LICENCE	RIGHT TO SUBLICENCE	DURATION OF THE RIGHTS
INVENTING PARTY & THEIR GROUP ENTITIES	Ownership (10.1)	Yes, as long as (10.3): - Rights and obligations arising from this Agreement are transferred as well - Other Parties have priority over third parties and they have the right to be offered Ownership on the same terms agreed with third parties until 24 months from the end of Programme.	Yes, but (10.4): - Not exclusively; - There is an obligation to inform the other Parties during the Programme within 30 days from the execution of license.	N/A	No time limit, unless Ownership is transferred
OTHER PARTIES & THEIR GROUP ENTITIES	Royalty-free Access Right (non-exclusive, irrevocable and perpetual licence and right to use FI in R&D work and business operations) (10.4)	No	No	Only in these cases (10.7): - To subcontractors for Party's own research or development work or business operations - To users of a Party's end product or service, if elements of FI are included in a Party's product or distributed appended to it	No time limit. Note however that a license to Background Information may be needed.
SUBCONTRACTORS	Royalty-free Limited Access Right (non-exclusive right to use FI to the extend it is necessary for carrying out work within the Programme) (10.6)	No	No	No	For as long as Access Right to FI is necessary for carrying out work within Programme.

FIGURE 3.2.8 Table with bulleted lists.[89]

rows. The information hierarchy can be communicated by font size, boldface, color, and table lines of differing thickness (e.g., a thicker line between two rows can indicate a separation between different categories; thinner lines can indicate a separation between sub-categories within the same category). Bulleted lists can be used within cells to further chunk content. Color-coding and icons can also be included in tables to signal, at a glance, key differences among the cells. Figure 3.2.8 features bulleted lists within cells that chunk content for easy comprehension.

---

[89] © 2016 DIMECC Ltd. Used with permission.

20.1 Each Party shall be liable under this Agreement to the other Party, for all damages, losses, claims, liabilities and expenditures (including all reasonable legal costs) caused to the other Party by the acts and omissions of the Party itself or its employees, Group Entities, agents and Subcontractors. Each Party shall use all reasonable efforts to mitigate its losses. 20.2 No Party shall be liable to another for indirect or consequential loss or damages such as but not limited to loss of profit, loss of revenue or loss of contracts except for breach of confidentiality obligations defined in Section 18 and with the exception of loss or damage caused by a wilful or gross negligent act or omission. 20.3 The total accumulated liability of a Party towards other Parties under this Agreement for each Funding Period shall be limited under all circumstances to the amount of 100,000 euro with the exception of loss or damage caused by a wilful or gross negligent act or omission.	Liability of a Party towards other Parties		
		NOT LIABLE	LIABLE
	20.1, 20.3 Direct damages, losses, claims, liabilities and expenditures		● Limited to 100000 € per funding period *
	20.2 Indirect or consequential damages or loss caused unintentionally or by other breach than breach of confidentiality	●	
	20.2 Direct and indirect or consequential damages or loss caused by breach of confidentiality		● Limited to 100000 € per funding period *
	20.2, 20.3 Direct and indirect or consequential damages or loss caused by a wilful or gross negligent act or omissoiion		● Unlimited liability
	*Unless loss or damages are caused by a wilful or gross negligent act or omission.		

FIGURE 3.2.9 Table with color-coding and icons to show key differences. 2016 DIMECC Ltd. Used with permission.

The table is an excerpt from the FIMECC (now DIMECC) Consortium Agreement.[90] It compares and contrasts the intellectual property rights that different parties have in relation to the IP created during the project (known as *foreground information*, or FI). While this table could work with textual content only, icons are used to indicate the parties. These elements are functional, not decorative; they are used consistently throughout the agreement, and thus aid in complete understanding of the contract.

The table in Figure 3.2.9 uses structure and color-coding (not visible in this greyscale reproduction) to communicate the parties' liability, and whether there is a limit to it. The salient colored elements signal at a glance that there is a difference, even before one reads the specific content of the cells.[91]

D Swimlane Pattern

A *swimlane* is a diagram that shows how roles, rights, tasks, responsibilities, obligations, liabilities, or remedies are distributed between different actors. Every contract concerns the assignment of rights, obligations, and responsibilities to the various parties. When contracts are long and complex, users may struggle to keep track of every assignment, especially since each aspect may need to be recovered from different clauses, often even different documents. During the contract creation stage, this may lead the parties to forget to agree on some of the rights, obligations, or responsibilities, or to believe that they have already been assigned when in fact they have not.

[90] DIMECC, www.dimecc.com, is an open-innovation community facilitating joint R&D between Finnish companies. Access to IP is thus an important issue for its participating organizations, and tables like the one in Figure 3.2.8 greatly aid the community's work.

[91] It is also worth noting that this table uses yes/no logic (i.e., "liable" or "not liable"), a Boolean value that operates in a similar way to decision trees, covered elsewhere in this volume; *see* Ashley – Mining Information from Statutory Texts in a Public Health Domain, *infra*.

During the contract implementation stage, all parties need to have quick and easy access to their share of the promises they have made, in order for them to deliver on those promises. Swimlanes can promote collaboration between the parties by clarifying who needs to do what, and whether a responsibility is shared. Swimlanes provide a concise summary to help people understand their roles and responsibilities, align their expectations, and monitor the contract. They allow the parties to spot whether the contract is balanced and collaborative, or whether most of the responsibilities fall to just one party. They can also be used to make the parties aware of areas where the contract remains silent.

A swimlane works by representing each party with a lane, drawn horizontally or vertically. Responsibilities are represented as blocks of text, and are "assigned" to a party by positioning them in the appropriate lane, with shared items placed between lanes. If the tasks are part of a process, a flowchart can be superimposed over the swimlanes so that the parties can be clear about any possible interdependencies between their actions, all while knowing what is required from either or both of them, and when.

The swimlane in Figure 3.2.10 is used in a visual guide for public procurement terms and illustrates how intellectual property rights are allocated between the parties.[92] Different icons and different colors or shadings can help to distinguish each of the two lanes from its

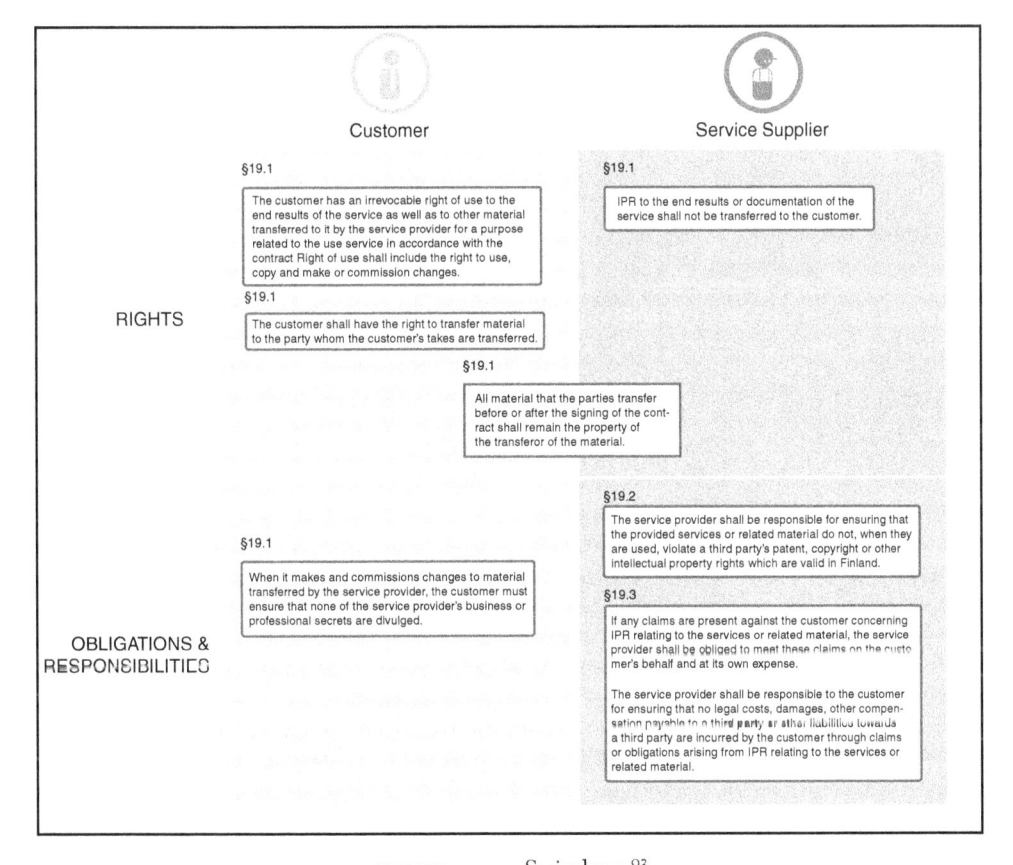

FIGURE 3.2.10 Swimlane.[93]

---

[92] "JYSEn käyttämisopas," *supra* note 65.
[93] © 2013 Aalto University and Suomen Kuntaliitto ry (The Association of Finnish Local and Regional Authorities).

neighbor. Extra textual labels on the left of the swimlanes help distinguish further between rights, responsibilities, and obligations. Clauses and excerpts from clauses are placed verbatim in the swimlane, so as to avoid discrepancies between the original terms and the visual guide.

E Companion Icon Pattern

Companion icons are crisp graphic symbols that represent the meaning or function of the textual element they accompany. A typical contract is long and presented in an undifferentiated way. The visual cues to help skim and search the document are often limited to headings and clause numbers, and they are often not very informative at a first glance. Meaning may remain hidden in the text, not accessible to busy or distracted readers who are not reading the contract line by line. Icons act as visual cues to capture and hold readers' attention. With icons, salient content has a salient appearance, and readers can search and identify relevant information quickly. Icons may not provide sophisticated explanations of the terms, but they do bring the general meaning to the surface. When the same icons are used consistently throughout one or more documents, their meaning becomes more and more familiar to users, who can then identify recurrent topics and terms at a glance. Some examples include the "inventing party," "other parties," and "subcontractor" icons in Figure 3.2.8, and the "customer" and "service supplier" icons in Figure 3.2.10.

In order to avoid misunderstanding, icons in contracts should only be used as a complement to, and not as a substitute for, the text of the contract. Companion icons in contracts are often highly symbolic and metaphorical. They may refer to abstract concepts and terms that are not self-evident, and this is why it is recommended that they be used in tandem with text or close to headings. Wherever possible, use well-known icons that users are likely to interpret correctly as soon as they see them (e.g., a shopping cart to indicate a purchase; a triangle sign with an exclamation mark to indicate a warning; currency symbols to indicate payments), and make sure the icons are relatively simple in shape and have a crisp outline so that they can be recognizable on a smaller scale. In addition, chosen icons should account for the audience's previous knowledge, cultural background, and professional background, and be user-tested to avoid misunderstandings and diplomatic blunders (e.g., a thumbs-up is a sign of approval in the USA, but can be offensive in the Middle East).

Figure 3.2.11 is an excerpt from a prototype tenancy agreement for university students. It uses several icons to easily denote contract topics, and it also provides a more friendly impression of the document. The readers of this particular contract are younger, and for many of them this is the first tenancy agreement they have ever signed.

F Delivery Diagram Pattern

When parties entering a contract for the sale and purchase of goods need to choose their terms for delivery, a *delivery diagram* works best. It can indicate, for example, when and where delivery takes place and when the cost and risk are transferred. But "delivery" may mean many things, not just shipment or arrival; it can also concern placing goods onboard a carrier, for example. Cost, risk, loading and unloading, customs duties, taxes – all of these things and more need to be divided between the parties in a delivery agreement. In order to avoid misunderstandings and simplify choice, the International Chamber of Commerce publishes

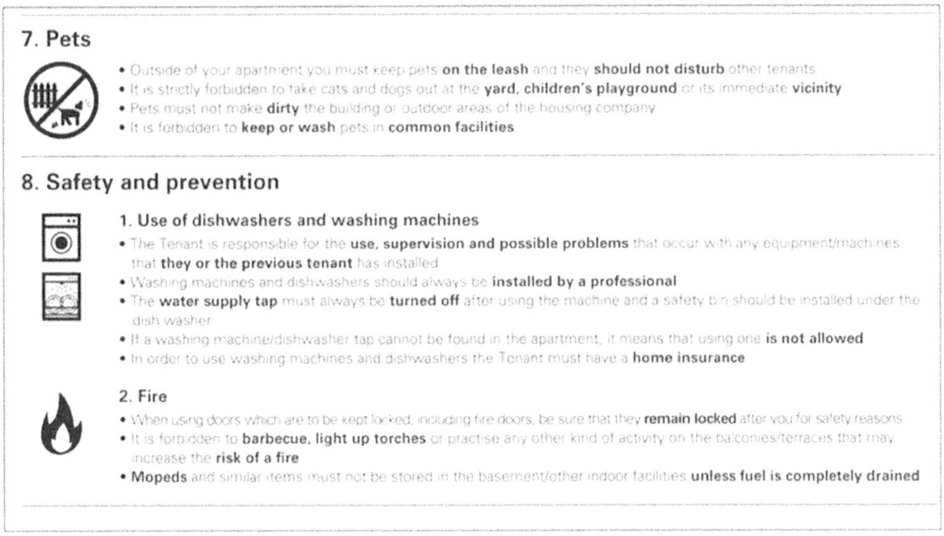

7. Pets

- Outside of your apartment you must keep pets **on the leash** and they **should not disturb** other tenants
- It is strictly forbidden to take cats and dogs out at the **yard, children's playground** or its immediate **vicinity**
- Pets must not make **dirty** the building or outdoor areas of the housing company
- It is forbidden to **keep or wash** pets in **common facilities**

8. Safety and prevention

1. Use of dishwashers and washing machines

- The Tenant is responsible for the **use, supervision and possible problems** that occur with any equipment/machines that **they or the previous tenant** has installed
- Washing machines and dishwashers should always be **installed by a professional**
- The **water supply tap** must always be **turned off** after using the machine and a safety bin should be installed under the dishwasher
- If a washing machine/dishwasher tap cannot be found in the apartment, it means that using one **is not allowed**
- In order to use washing machines and dishwashers the Tenant must have a **home insurance**

2. Fire

- When using doors which are to be kept locked, including fire doors, be sure that they **remain locked** after you for safety reasons
- It is forbidden to **barbecue, light up torches** or practise any other kind of activity on the balconies/terraces that may increase the **risk of a fire**
- **Mopeds** and similar items must not be stored in the basement/other indoor facilities **unless fuel is completely drained**

FIGURE 3.2.11 Icons in a tenancy agreement.[94]

the Incoterms rules, a set of trade terms widely used in international trade.[95] These rules contain a number of alternatives, however; parties often need support in comparing them and making a choice.

A delivery diagram illustrates precisely where delivery happens, how it happens, and at which moment in time and space various responsibilities are transferred. Delivery diagrams have been widely used in connection with the Incoterms rules, in order to explain the various trade terms in a simple way that allows for easy comparison. A quick Google image search shows the popularity of the format – many versions of the diagrams can be found. The diagram can also be used to describe non-standard delivery terms, since its familiar format can be adapted flexibly to a variety of situations. Figure 3.2.12 illustrates this.

The top part of the diagram presents, from left to right, representations of possible places of delivery: the supplier's premises; on board a carrier; at the departure shipping terminal; on board a vessel at the departure terminal; at the arrival terminal; or at the buyer's warehouse. If the goal of the diagram is to compare different delivery terms, it will include many places of delivery. Alternatively, if the diagram seeks to clarify one specific term, then it may only use the one specific delivery place in question. Text labels can be added to provide more details about where the goods are actually delivered (e.g., if they need to be unloaded from the carrier and placed in a certain spot, like in Figure 3.2.12). Below these representations, there are usually color-coded lines (one color for the buyer, one for the supplier) that indicate the division and point of transfer of cost and risk, as well as other obligations (e.g., to clear for customs or to insure).

Figure 3.2.12 features an example of a delivery chart in a framework agreement for the purchase of goods. The clause modifies the DDP (delivered duty paid) trade term as included in the Incoterms 2010 rules by requiring the supplier to unload the goods at the destination. The diagram seeks to underline this crucial difference and help avoid problems.

[94] © 2013 Stefania Passera. Used with permission.
[95] "Incoterms" is a trademark of the International Chamber of Commerce (ICC).

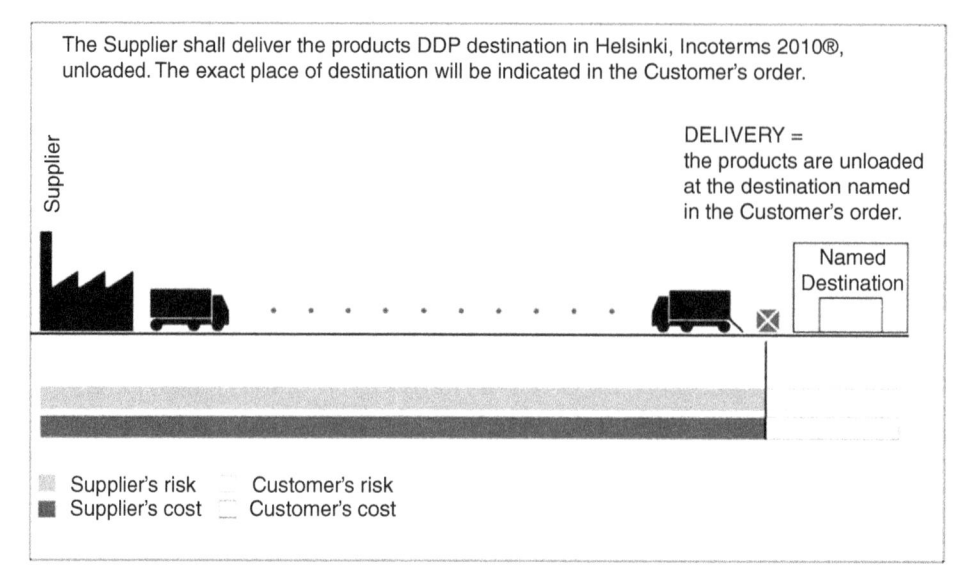

FIGURE 3.2.12 Delivery diagram.[96]

VII CONTRACT VISUALIZATIONS: SAVING MONEY AND MAKING BETTER DECISIONS

In the previous section, we showed how patterns can provide clarity at the implementation stage – *in* and *about* contracts. They can also be helpful PPL tools at the planning and negotiation stage. At times, the interests of the parties to a contract negotiation are widely misaligned. For example, one party may wish to have a long-term commitment, while the other wishes to be able to walk away from the deal on short notice. In the following example from Canada, a termination clause was interpreted differently by the parties, and led to a less than amicable end to the contract.

In the spring of 2002, Rogers Communications Inc., a Canadian telecom company, entered into a contract with Aliant Inc. (Bell Aliant), in which Aliant agreed to string Rogers' cable lines across roughly 91,000 utility poles for an annual fee of CA$9.60 per pole. Early in 2005, Aliant informed Rogers that it was terminating the contract with one year's notice and increasing its rates. Rogers objected, on the grounds that the contract could not be terminated until the spring of 2007.

It would have been best for the parties to have discovered their different views of the contract at the negotiation stage. But they did not. In this case, the misaligned expectations and lack of clarity led to a costly 18-month dispute over the meaning of a single clause. The clause read as follows:

> "This agreement shall be effective from the date it is made and shall continue in force for a period of five (5) years from the date it is made, and thereafter for successive five (5) year terms, unless and until terminated by one year prior notice in writing by either party."[97]

---

[96] 2016 Stefania Passera and Helena Haapio. Used with permission.
[97] Telecom Decision CRTC 2006-45, Ottawa, Canada, July 28, 2006, available at: www.crtc.gc.ca/eng/archive/2006/dt2006-45.htm; Telecom Decision CRTC 2007-75, Ottawa, Canada, August 20, 2007, available at: www.crtc.gc.ca/eng/archive/2007/dt2007-75.htm; *see also*, e.g., Helena Haapio and George J. Siedel, *A Short Guide to Contract Risk* (Farnham: Gower, 2013), 164–167.

This clause was interpreted differently by the two parties. As regards the initial term of the agreement, one party (Rogers) thought that it had a five-year deal. The other party (Aliant) believed that even within this initial term, the agreement could be terminated at any time with one year's notice. In hindsight, it is easy to say that the parties and their lawyers should have had a closer look at the clause before signing the agreement, but neither party had a hand in crafting the text; it was imposed by Canadian telecom regulators. The drafters of the model form used in this case could have used clearer language, of course. Breaking the clause into two sentences might have been a way to avoid the ambiguity. Removing the second comma could have been another.[98] Yet if the parties had merely sketched simple pictures, as in Figure 3.2.13, they would have easily seen their different interpretations laid out before them. This would have allowed them, during the negotiations, to come to a mutual understanding – or to see that they had no deal and walk away. In the words of Louis M. Brown: "It usually costs less to avoid getting into trouble than to pay for getting out of trouble."[99]

Siedel illustrates another way of clearing up situations in which parties have wildly different interpretations of contracts: One can use decision trees to help clarify negotiation decisions and depict the estimated costs and risks of alternatives.[100] One application of decision trees is whether to retain, soften, or eliminate controversial clauses that could result in long and expensive negotiations. For example, insisting on negotiating a pricey indemnity for low-probability risks may in fact create a loss, since it requires management time to negotiate, and the lengthy negotiation delays profits. A decision tree can reveal the average expected value of alternative decisions, based on assumed values and event probabilities.

In the case that follows, this in fact occurs. Figure 3.2.14 shows that the benefits of negotiating the clause are minimal (200 K) when compared to the high costs incurred to negotiate the clause in the first place (1 M). One can also see from the diagram that if the cost of the indemnity were to rise, or if the probability were to change, parties might want to reconsider whether to forego the indemnity clause.

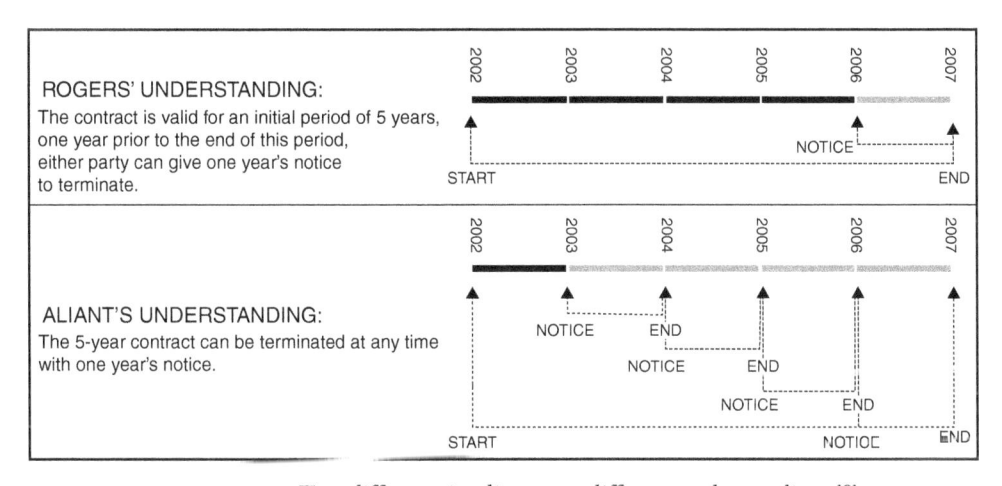

FIGURE 3.2.13 Two different timelines, two different understandings.[101]

---

[98] See Ian Austen, "The Comma that Costs 1 Million Dollars (Canadian)," *New York Times*, October 25, 2006, available at: www.nytimes.com/2006/10/25/business/worldbusiness/25comma.html.
[99] Brown, *Preventive Law, supra* note 6, at 3.
[100] Siedel, *The Three Pillar Model for Business Decisions, supra* note 76, at 177–178.
[101] Passera and Haapio, "Facilitating Collaboration through Contract Visualization and Modularization," *supra* note 9. 2011 Stefania Passera and Helena Haapio. Used with permission.

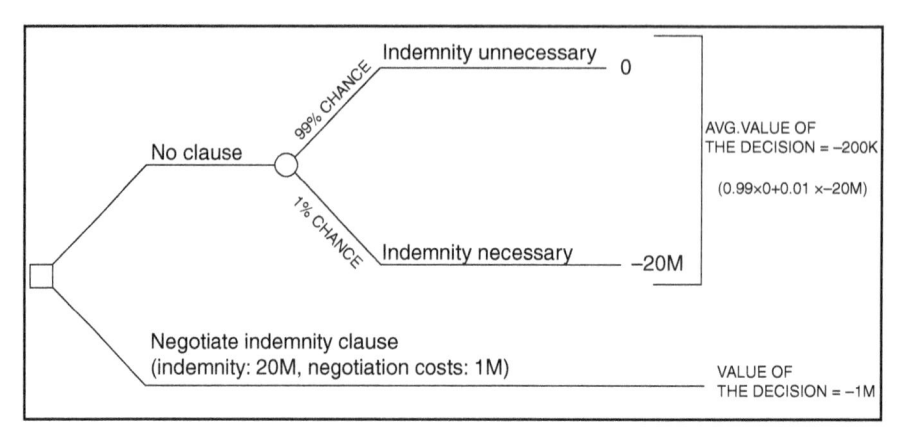

FIGURE 3.2.14 Decision tree evaluating average expected value of alternative decisions.[102]

VIII CONCLUSION

Preventive law and information design share the same goal: empowering people and businesses to attain their goals. Both are results-oriented and centered on users' needs. When written and designed well, contracts can work as interfaces between businesses, helping them attain the greatest benefits of their collaboration. Contract design in general, and design patterns in particular, can provide repeatable and flexible best-practice solutions to current contracting challenges in order to improve business collaboration. These solutions can contribute to the transformation of contracts from dysfunctional legal documents to functional communication tools that are both useful and usable for business. There are many different kinds of contract visualization patterns, and each one possesses unique strengths for developing communicative solutions in a visual way.

Visual representations play a functional and explanatory role, remedying many of the typical shortcomings of contract text. A pattern approach enables practitioners and researchers alike to identify and share effective solutions for planning, negotiating, and communicating contracts. Patterns offer flexibility in contract design: Unlike rigid formalized rules, patterns can be mixed, modified, and adapted to fit specific contracting situations and user needs. The goal is to design contracts that work as effective interfaces, not only between businesses and functions, but also between individuals and the information they require to successfully do their jobs.

Evidence shows that parties' perception of their agreement may vary greatly from the terms that appear in their contracts.[103] Not only that, but evidence shows that most businesspeople find contracts hard or impossible to read.[104] We believe that it is time for change. When contract design succeeds, contracts can reach their full potential, matching the parties' business needs, reflecting their true goals, and supporting implementation. By meeting users' needs, well-designed contracts can strengthen business by helping to maintain sustainable, successful business deals and relationships, and by preventing unnecessary problems.

---

[102] Id. at 177. For more on decision trees, see Agin – Examining Public Court Data to Understand and Predict Bankruptcy Case Results, infra. 2016 George Siedel. Adapted and used with permission.

[103] See generally, Brian H. Bix, "The Role of Contract: Stewart Macaulay's Lessons from Practice," in Revisiting the Contracts Scholarship of Stewart Macaulay: On the Empirical and the Lyrical, eds. Jean Braucher, John Kidwell, and William Whitford (Oxford: Hart Publishing, 2013), 241–255; Macaulay, "The Real and the Paper Deal," supra note 22.

[104] IACCM, Attitudes to Contracting; IACCM, Commercial Excellence, supra note 3.

3.3

Distributed Ledgers, Cryptography, and Smart Contracts

Nina Gunther Kilbride

I INTRODUCTION TO BLOCKCHAIN TECHNOLOGY

The advent of distributed ledger technology has challenged the legal community to learn how technology will change law, finance, and commerce in coming years. Blockchain technology, a method for storing data in cryptographically secure distributed ledgers, has spread all over the world and into nearly every vertical as global commerce searches for secure tools that support ecosystem-wide growth. The World Economic Forum estimates that by 2026, 10% of global commerce will be conducted on blockchain systems.[1] Blockchain technology promises to bring more legal relationships into the realm of data and code, so there is a clear need for legal minds to help guide this development.

A Decentralization

The internet has enabled distribution of data systems among multiple network participants, allowing us to make increasingly distributed applications across a network of *nodes*, or local program installations. This increasing distribution of data leads to decentralized systems in which networked entities share records in order to create security reliability. *Decentralized systems* are a subset of distributed systems in which not only data is shared among the network, but also decision making as well. Decentralization makes data more physically secure, since destruction or corruption of one node on a network cannot destroy valuable data. Decentralized networks of individual nodes also have the ability to conduct operations outside of established control systems, creating potential for large, geographically diverse, interoperable systems.[2] Bitcoin was the first such global, sustained application, but more blockchain use cases gain traction every day.

B The Cryptographic Hash

Decentralization enables new ways of creating, storing, and using data. Cryptography adds security and certainty to decentralized reliability by the process of *hashing*. Any kind of

---

[1] World Economic Forum, "The Future of Financial Infrastructure: An Ambitious Look at How Blockchain Technology Can Change the Future," August 2016, available at: www3.weforum.org/docs/WEF_The_future_of_financial_infrastructure.pdf.

[2] Satoshi Nakamoto, "Bitcoin: A Peer-to-peer Electronic Cash Network," Bitcoin.org, 2009, available at: https://bitcoin.org/bitcoin.pdf.

3J98t1WpEZ73CNmQviecrnyiWrnqRhWNLy

FIGURE 3.3.1 A cryptographic hash.

information can be transformed into a string of 0s and 1s called binary code. Once data has been reduced to binary code, computers can apply mathematical operations to it to produce reliable results. Cryptography involves passing the binary code of a piece of data through a series of arithmetic operations to produce a hash, an encoded string of letters and numbers that represents the data.

Hashing is a one-way operation: While a certain data set will always produce the same unique identifier (the *hash*; Figure 3.3.1), it is effectively impossible to do the math in reverse to decode the data from just the hash. One must have a key to access cryptographically stored information, which in blockchain storage becomes tamper-evident.

In hashing, data is passed through a series of equations in order to create a *digest hash*, a string of characters that represents the data and hides it from those without a key. An effective hash algorithm must produce unique results (called "collision-resistant") for unique data. A hash function is said to be collision-resistant if it is infeasible to find two values, x and y, such that $x \neq y$, yet $H(x) = H(y)$.[3] What this means is that the functions that create the hash must produce different results for every potential input. It should be extremely unlikely that two differing data sets produce the same hash digest.

Additionally, the hash should effectively hide the encrypted information; it should be infeasible to perform the hashing function in reverse. Cryptographic hashing accomplishes this by adding complexity and randomness to the hashing functions. For example, a hash function H is considered hiding if, when a secret value r is chosen from a probability distribution that has high minimum entropy, then given $H(r \| x)$, it is infeasible to find x.[4] But what does this function mean?

Computational power makes it possible to decode a set of deterministic (non-random) functions. In order to add cryptographic complexity to hashing algorithms, message data is *concatenated*, or combined with, a randomly generated 256-bit hash value. This renders the chance of collision or decoding without a key to an infinitesimal probability of $1/2^{256}$. The odds of guessing the correct value of r from the function in the previous paragraph become astronomical.

Hashing and decentralized distributed data structures can be combined with business logic to make many kinds of applications. Value tokens like Ethereum are one such example.[5] Value tokens are just one way of using blockchain technology, though, as the hash can be associated with many different kinds of transactions and data. Cognizable legal documents can also be created with blockchain technology, such as electronic chattel paper, securities, and derivatives.[6]

---

[3] Aravind Narayanan, Joseph Bonneau, Edward Felten, Andrew Miller, and Steven Goldfeder, *The Princeton Bitcoin Book* (Princeton, NJ: Princeton University Press, 2016), 24, available at: https://d28rh4a8wqoiu5.cloudfront.net/bitcointech/readings/princeton_bitcoin_book.pdf?a=1.

[4] *Id.* at 27.

[5] *See* Ethereum Project, www.ethereum.org.

[6] Nina Kilbride, "Monax Commercial Paper Bundles: Toolkit for Financial Engineering," Monax, available at: https://monax.io/2016/03/31/commercial-paper-intro.

C Timestamped Ledger and the Finding of Fact

The result of blockchain technology is a tamper-proof, permanent ledger of transactions. This brings a new level of certainty to the process of legal fact-finding. The underlying proposition of fact-finding is fundamental for legal applications. For one quick example, a core function of the judicial system is the determination of who performed what act at what time in an alleged breach of contract.

Over the course of many years of litigation, lawyers and judges have learned that solving questions of "who did what when" via legal fact-finding (judges and juries) is inefficient and adds no value to the system if the effective acts can be determined by reliable outside evidence. Additionally, lawyers and judges have recognized that a set of freely available rules guiding the interpretation of this evidence would allow parties to predict the outcome of a result and resolve their own disputes accordingly.

Enter the *mailbox rule*, altering the traditional negotiation structure for contracting via post. An offer made by mail is not effective until received by the offeree, and acceptance of the offer is effective as soon as it is placed in the mailbox by the offeree. Thus, for revocation of an offer to be effective, it must be received by the offerer before they mail back a letter of acceptance.[7]

The mailbox rule arose at a time when contract negotiations were often conducted by mail and it was not necessarily possible to determine when the parties had reached mutual assent. Latency – the time the contract messages spent in transit – meant that parties might change their minds about critical terms before the elements of a contract were complete. The mailbox rule used the typical elements of postal timestamp, offer, and acceptance to determine when a contract was effective. The mailbox created predictability. Parties could look at the written evidence before them in terms of timestamps and content and determine when and if the elements for contract formation were present. Predictability obviated the need to bring a fact-finder into the process, and the mailbox rule saved on potential litigation costs.

The mailbox rule, far from being an anachronism of the postal age, scales to electronic commerce. Blockchain timestamps and an immutable datastream are a continuation of the same fundamental ideas behind postal stamps and sworn statements, and are even more effective at proving when a legally significant communication took place. Blockchains and smart contracts provide certain evidence of timing, decision making, and authenticity. The mailbox rule has thus expanded to guide blockchain commerce, even as the latency that necessitated it decreases.

D Data Storage and Management Structures

When collecting data for future use, it is important to save information so that it may be easily located and accessed. In blockchain architecture, hashes are collected over time and stored in groups called *blocks*. The blocks are then hashed and stored into the chain of hashes, and also linked and timestamped (Figure 3.3.2).

The tree structure in Figures 3.3.2 and 3.3.3 is reminiscent of the US court reporter system. Each jurisdiction has a chain of legal precedent composed of court decisions that are given citation addresses and placed in immutable, open storage. This creates a permanent record of the law. The contents of a legal volume, once codified, do not change. If the effects of the

---

[7] See, e.g., Tyrrell Williams, "Restatement of the Law of Contracts of the American Law Institute, Sections 52–74, with Missouri Annotations," *Washington University Law Review* 16 (4) (1931).

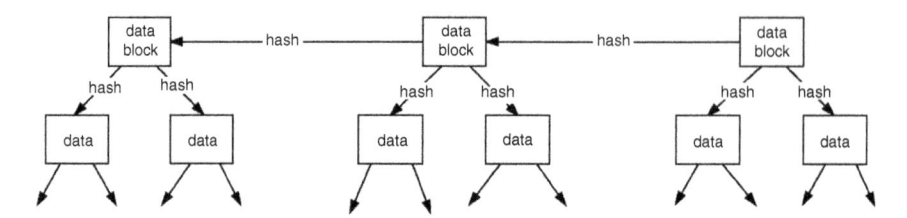

FIGURE 3.3.2 Linked timestamping storage in hash trees (Merkle trees).

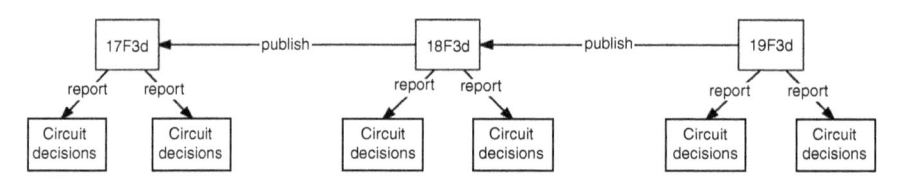

FIGURE 3.3.3 Linked timestamping of case law.

contents change, like when a case is overruled, those changes are recorded in subsequent cases and linked to the prior citation.

E Evidence and Trust

One of the key features of blockchain technology is *trustlessness*, the ability to risk entering into a transaction with an unknown entity because that network guarantees integrity of operative information.[8] Critical to such "trust" is the confidence that courts of law will enforce contractual promises. The key to this inquiry is evidence.

Choosing what data to consider authentic when making decisions is a critical question for legal proceedings.[9] Historically, common law courts have relied on sworn statements from people to establish significant facts. The rules of evidence provide a detailed rubric for the circumstances under which a fact may be admitted into evidence as potentially true and worthy of consideration by the legal fact-finder, the judge or jury. Any out-of-court statements offered to prove the facts asserted are considered hearsay and may not be used to prove a legal case unless the evidence qualifies for special treatment under an exception. Business records receive special treatment under the hearsay rules, which enables large-scale automation of electronic contracts. In practice, this means an employee of a plaintiff can print a copy of a document from a computer and swear to the truth of the information on the page.[10]

Large-scale failures of the current authentication-by-affidavit protocol for financial documents can have disastrous effects. For example, the ability to hide bad loans and produce bogus affidavits were important elements in the financial crisis of 2008 and the subsequent foreclosure crisis of 2010.[11] Smart contracts verify information in documentary transactions

---

[8] "The Great Chain of Being Sure about Things," *The Economist*, October 31, 2015, available at: www.economist.com/news/briefing/21677228-technology-behind-bitcoin-lets-people-who-do-not-know-or-trust-each-other-build-dependable.

[9] *See generally*, Federal Rules of Evidence (FRE), www.rulesofevidence.org.

[10] FRE 803(6), www.rulesofevidence.org/article-viii/rule-803.

[11] *See* "2010 United States Foreclosure Crisis," *Wikipedia*, accessed December 15, 2016, https://en.wikipedia.org/wiki/2010_United_States_foreclosure_crisis.

more reliably than humans, and they allow a window into commerce for businesspeople and regulators.[12]

F Consensus Mechanisms

In a distributed system in which multiple actors have the authority to write to or change the ledger, how do we know the data is reliable? How do we choose between conflicting versions of the same operative fact? How does the structure that houses the electronic records maintain integrity? Chain of custody and vaulting are two critical components of data certainty. They both work toward the ideal of the "trustless" blockchain application: delivering data certainty without having to rely on a controlling central authority that might have an incentive to alter information provided to the network. Automated systems must have a method for determining "truth" of facts contained within the system. This is not a new problem in commerce – this is why the cashier has to call the manager to reset an error at the grocery checkout.

In blockchain architecture, the method we use to establish fact is called the *consensus mechanism*. Bitcoin solved the consensus mechanism problem with a completely open, decentralized network via a *proof-of-work* (POW) algorithm.[13] This is a process by which *miners* (Bitcoin nodes) compete to solve mathematical puzzles that validate Bitcoin transactions. These transactions are then stored to the blockchain. For this work, the miners are paid in Bitcoin. In the Bitcoin consensus engine, a transaction is presumed valid if 51% of miners agree on its validity. This consensus mechanism is necessary to prevent "double spending" of the same token; that is, giving the same coin for value to two or more different parties. This concept is analogous to adverse claims in secured transactions, such as the UCC-1 filing system, which similarly prevents "double spend" of collateral by way of a public notice mechanism.

Not all applications require the completely open distribution of Bitcoin to ensure "trust." Entities can choose to take advantage of distributed cryptographic data certainty in different verticals, meaning different levels of access to a variety of information. "High-trust" actors like banks, insurers, and large companies with the resources to deploy a distributed, cryptographic blockchain system have different needs than average Bitcoin users. *Proof-of-stake* (POS) is a consensus method that determines truth based on shares, or stake, in a blockchain. Rather than mining value, nodes on a POS consensus chain validate activity on the chain. Many other specialized methods of consensus are developing as programmers alter blockchain structures to suit use-case needs.[14]

Settlement finality becomes a critical legal engineering issue when thinking about financial market infrastructure in the context of public chains with a POW consensus mechanism. In existing public chains, there is a small chance a previously committed settlement will be rolled back due to the network converging on a different branch of the blockchain and the transaction being included in a later block. This results in an indeterminate state at the

---

[12] David Mills, Kathy Wang, Brendan Malone, Anjana Ravi, Jeff Marquardt, Clinton Chen, Anton Badev, Timothy Brezinski, Linda Fahy, Kimberley Liao, Vanessa Kargenian, Max Ellithorpe, Wendy Ng, and Maria Baird, "Distributed Ledger Technology in Payments, Clearing, and Settlement," Finance and Economics Discussion Series 2016-095, Washington, DC: Board of Governors of the Federal Reserve System, available at: www.federalreserve.gov/econresdata/feds/2016/files/2016095pap.pdf.

[13] Nakamoto, *supra* note 2. *See also*, the discussion of blockchain and cryptography in Rosario – Introduction to Blockchain and Cryptography, *supra*.

[14] Sigrid Siebold and George Samman, "Consensus: Immutable Agreement for the Internet of Value," KPMG, 2016, available at: https://assets.kpmg.com/content/dam/kpmg/pdf/2016/07/kpmg-blockchain.pdf.

moment when the system needs to make precise calculations regarding risk and liquidity. The US Federal Reserve underscores the care that must be taken when choosing the right consensus method for the use case:

> "With a probabilistic approach to finality, legal liability may be difficult to assign or be ambiguous in such a network, and the uncertainty has implications for the balance sheets of participants as well as the rights of their customers and creditors."[15]

For financial market infrastructures like central clearing and settlement houses, public POW consensus may be too uncertain to support existing processes, because of uncertainty of the ledger's finality. Clearing and settlement in financial markets depends on settlement happening at a precise moment in time, so that deterministic calculations can be made regarding liquidity and risk.

II SMART CONTRACTS: SECURE COMPUTATION OF CRYPTOGRAPHICALLY CERTAIN DATA

Smart contracts are cryptographically secure computations acting on cryptographically secure information in distributed blockchain architecture.[16] Smart contracts were first notably discussed by computer scientist and lawyer Nick Szabo as early as 1997.[17] In 2014, Ethereum combined smart contracts with a public, POW blockchain for developing and running smart contracts. Interest in smart contracts has grown steadily in both the private sector and the public sector ever since.[18]

Smart contracts add logical manipulation to blockchain data while maintaining a tamper-proof audit trail. This allows us to craft computable relationships based on data. These data-driven relationships mean that once data has been encapsulated in blockchain architecture, it is possible to add computational functions to affect the data. For example, a smart contract token with an address hash of 3J98t1WpEZ73CNmQviecrnyiWrnqRhWNLm might be the storage address of a document establishing title to certain property. The contract is owned by an entity whose control over the ability to transfer that token establishes possession. Another smart contract, 3BvBMSEYstWetqTFn5Au4m4GFg7xJaNVN2, might be a contract for sale of the token's subject property. After verifying that payment terms are met, a smart contract can then transfer ownership of 3J98t1WpEZ73CNmQviecrnyiWrnqRhWNLm from the original owner's address to the buyer's address. The entire transaction history can be audited and proved by legal evidence standards, which means it can be used in many levels of finance, commerce, and government.

Smart contracts, however, are not suitable for *nondeterministic computation*, where the result of a function produces a random result. In legal contracts, nondeterminism frequently occurs when parties want to reserve discretionary judgment over a future event, or they want to create ambiguity in order to gain some advantage. An example of a nondeterministic clause

---

[15] Mills et al., "Distributed Ledger Technology in Payments, Clearing, and Settlement," *supra* note 12, at 31.
[16] There are proposed models of smart contracts that do not use blockchain data, which are outside the scope of this chapter; *see, e.g.*, Richard Gendal Brown, "Introducing R3 Corda™: A Distributed Ledger Designed for Financial Services," R3 CEV, April 5, 2016, available at: www.r3cev.com/blog/2016/4/4/introducing-r3-corda-a-distributed-ledger-designed-for-financial-services; Ian Grigg, "The Ricardian Contract," Iang.org, available at: http://iang.org/papers/ricardian_contract.html.
[17] Nick Szabo, "A Formal Language for Analyzing Contracts," 2002, available at: www.fon.hum.uva.nl/rob/Courses/InformationInSpeech/CDROM/Literature/LOTwinterschool2006/szabo.best.vwh.net/contractlanguage.html.
[18] Scott Morrison, "Australia Leading International Blockchain Standards," September 15, 2016, available at: http://sjm.ministers.treasury.gov.au/media-release/097-2016.

in a legal contract is the qualifier "first class," a common clause in commercial real-estate leases. The landlord may quantify the parameters of a "first class" business, but the term retains the element of ambiguity that supports the landlord's right – at some time in the future and for some unknown reason – to change their mind.

Legally significant smart contracts provide mathematically precise, *deterministic* computation of rights and obligations and the ability to execute the result of the computation, all while building a solid evidence chain. Smart contracts are well-suited to a large swath of commerce built on predictable transactions and documentary conditions. Smart contracts offer a new paradigm wherein legally binding agreements can be built to run within a network of computers that no single party can control or alter once deployed. Operating on decentralized networks enables automated legal contracts, including negotiation, execution, and enforcement.

Because of the ubiquitous need for auditable, secure, distributed data-driven processes, the list of potential applications of blockchain technology is long. This list of applications includes currency, derivatives, securities, trade finance, land and chattel property registries, mortgages, supply chain management, insurance, clinical trials, healthcare management, corporate governance, voting, and more.[19]

III BLOCKCHAIN SMART CONTRACTS ADDRESS DATA CRISIS IN MULTIPLE VERTICALS

As the information age progresses, more and more people are using powerful personal electronic devices, businesses are growing increasingly interconnected, and the amount of data we produce is expanding exponentially. Organizations and individuals need to have methods to manage their data-driven relationships, especially to build global commercial systems. The rules by which those methods are developed will be legal contracts, encapsulated in code to provide maximum data utilization in the digital economy.

Blockchains are finding an eager global market because global markets across all sectors and verticals are in need of interoperable, network-level solutions that enable them to use their data more productively. The open-source nature of blockchains means that global commercial system interoperability is a real possibility. The potential for global money solutions has been demonstrated by the worldwide use of the digital currency Bitcoin, which operates on a decentralized, pseudo-anonymous network that allows transactions directly between address hashes (peer-to-peer). Bitcoin has thus far stayed viable for seven years, and banks, governments, insurance companies, universities, scientists, and industries have worked on multiple "proofs of concept" to establish fitness of purpose for blockchain smart contracts.

A *Interoperability*

One of the most important long-term value propositions for blockchains is the ability to create systems that can communicate with each other and work together in an interoperable fashion. *Interoperability* means frictionless execution of business by various counterparties with different degrees of automation and requirements. Interoperability requires mapping

---

[19] Chamber of Digital Commerce, "Smart Contracts: 12 Use Cases for Business & Beyond," Smart Contracts Alliance, December 5, 2016, available at: www.the-blockchain.com/docs/Smart%20Contracts%20-%2012%20Use%20Cases%20for%20Business%20and%20Beyond%20-%20Chamber%20of%20Digital%20Commerce.pdf.

elements in legal contracts and maintaining consistent tools that transform data from one standard to another.

Interoperability is not a new need for data networks, and several attempts have been made in the past to formalize open-source interoperable schemas for network relations and finance, such as with Extensible Markup Language (XML)[20] and ISO 20022.[21] Unfortunately, these attempts often fragment in implementation as market actors create closed-source versions of "interoperable" languages that cannot communicate seamlessly with other network actors. As the reinsurance industry resource Artemis explains: "[d]eveloping closed or non-compatible systems, could hamper companies with a similar range of problems that many are dealing with from their legacy systems today, including becoming locked-in to vendors and technology stacks."[22] Without a commitment to interoperability, we lose much of the promised benefit of blockchains, and the market impetus to bring solutions to life will weaken.

B Utilization of Data and the Rise of Consortia

Smart contracts enable seamless communication and process automation between parties, reducing expensive friction. Once the communication is established, however, interoperability allows entities to use their data collaboratively to solve problems. When given permissioned access, interoperable systems pave the way for synergistic solutions that combine the data resources and experiences of multiple entities.

One of the most appealing aspects of blockchains is the framework for collaborative consortia. Early blockchain consortia included financial consortium R3 CEV and insurance consortium B3i. Consortia offer the promise of not only a shared, minimized ecosystem process expense, but also of solving complex problems with non-zero-sum solutions, such as end-to-end processes for supply chain, risk, and catastrophe management.

IV EXISTING ELECTRONIC CONTRACTING CONTEXT

Blockchain smart contracts are a breakthrough development in the quest for a secure, interoperable technology to create data-driven solutions and conduct global commerce. Existing contract law provides a beginning, multi-step framework for smart contract enforceability.

A Blockchains for Legally Significant Relationships

By combining certain evidence and a rock-solid audit trail, smart contracts can automate legally significant actions based on if–then/if–else logic, saving significant time and money on everyday, business-as-usual commercial processes. Despite enormous potential benefits, stakeholders are unlikely to transfer their valuable business from legacy infrastructure to blockchain systems without firm assurance they are not sacrificing existing hard-won legal rights in exchange for smart contract efficiency. Legal engineers building blockchain systems

---

[20] "Extensible Markup Language," W3, available at: www.w3.org/XML.
[21] ISO 20022, www.iso20022.org.
[22] "Sompo Japan Trials Blockchain for Catastrophic Bonds & Weather Derivatives," Artemis, September 27, 2016, available at: www.artemis.bm/blog/2016/09/27/sompo-japan-trials-blockchain-for-catastrophe-weather-derivatives.

must carefully consider the pre-existing judicial precedent and regulatory structures that govern potential use cases.

B Judicial Enforcement of Electronic Contracts

While many smart contract applications seem far away, ample authority exists to conceive and build some smart contracts within existing legal principles. For smart contracts, the existing body of electronic signature and records law provides both enabling and regulatory frameworks that give legal engineers a baseline starting point. As a practical matter, legally significant smart contracts must meet or exceed existing standards for electronic contracts in order to gain momentum.

Electronic contracts have been vital parts of international commerce and finance since the end of the twentieth century, when many governments enabled electronic contracting through the authorization of electronic signatures. The e-signature language of the USA's Electronic Signatures In Global and National Commerce Act (E-SIGN) contains typical language:

> "(1) a signature, contract, or other record relating to such transaction may not be denied legal effect, validity, or enforceability solely because it is in electronic form; and (2) a contract relating to such transaction may not be denied legal effect, validity, or enforceability solely because an electronic signature or electronic record was used in its formation."[23]

In other words, if the terms of an electronic contract are otherwise binding, an electronically signed contract meets signature requirements such that legal obligations exist in dematerialized, electronic form. Similar rules were adopted by 47 US states as part of the model law Uniform Electronic Transactions Act (UETA).[24] Across the globe, other jurisdictions wishing to participate in electronic commerce over the internet have enacted laws authorizing e-signatures.

A signature is often a requirement for enforcement of legal contracts, so recognition of e-signatures has created the opportunity to transition many kinds of enforceable legal relationships to electronic format. Enforceable e-signatures enable the creation of many kinds of electronic agreements and the ability to trade them worldwide, including consumer contracts, service agreements, and financial instruments.

While e-signature law is largely uniform, there remains a significant degree of variation at the local jurisdictional level as to what agreements still require a traditional pen-and-paper signature. For example, wills are excluded from most e-signature statutes. Real property records often require signed paper. Local variations are significant but not insurmountable hurdles to automated electronic contracts, underscoring the need for careful examination of specific laws when developing smart contract systems.

Electronic contracts are increasingly important elements in commerce today. Courts regularly enforce electronic agreements. Dematerialization and interoperability of contracts and instruments is encouraged and mandated by regulatory authorities.[25] Thus, the

---

[23] 15 U.S.C. § 7001(a).
[24] Uniform Electronic Transactions Act, National Conference of Commissioners on Uniform State Laws, 1999, available at: www.uniformlaws.org/shared/docs/electronic%20transactions/ueta_final_99.pdf.
[25] See, e.g., Exec. Order No. 13642, 3 C.F.R 13642 (2013), "Making Open and Machine Readable the New Default for Government Information," available at: www.gpo.gov/fdsys/pkg/CFR-2014-title3-vol1/pdf/CFR-2014-title3-vol1-eo13642.pdf.

e-signature laws of the turn of the century have created a foundation for enforceable blockchain smart contracts that is strong, well-placed, and ready to support innovative legal models.

C Blockchain Smart Contracts as Transferable Records

The legal engineering inquiry into smart contract systems does not end at judicial enforceability. Smart contract applications must comply with existing requirements for analogous electronic documents. Specifications and standards for systems that maintain data-driven relationships are produced by multiple actors, such as governments, regulators, and ratings agencies. Read together, these specifications and standards are the framework that allows the transformation of contractual obligations into electronic securities and derivatives. Blockchain smart contract systems can be configured to meet and exceed existing requirements for encryption, data integrity, audit trail, and security, trimming operational costs while enabling new revenue models.

One foreseeable blockchain application is the creation and management of enforceable legal contracts. Enforceable contracts become assets that may be securitized (i.e., treated as collateral and/or traded).[26] This process is a core function of existing electronic contract systems. In the USA, E-SIGN and UETA provide similar standards for creation and storage of transferable electronic documents, while other regulations like the Uniform Commercial Code (UCC) and securities law provide further guidance for specific collateral types. An initial issue is whether blockchains can meet these statutes' general requirements that a "single, authoritative copy of the transferable record exists which is unique, identifiable ... and authentic." While it may at first seem counter-intuitive that a system based on a database existing at multiple nodes on a network creates a "single, authoritative copy" of a legal record, blockchain technology both satisfies and exceeds existing standards.

Blockchain smart contracts meet this standard via cryptographically secure content-addressable storage. By hashing, data is passed through complex equations to produce a unique identifier. The hashing process ensures that no two sets of data produce the same hash, and it is infeasible to decipher a hash to reveal its contents without a key. The distributed ledger provides the requisite immutability and audit trail. This combination produces the unique record of provenance, authority, and control required by existing law, exceeding the capabilities of prior technology.

Blockchain technology fills the express needs for better electronic contract solutions. Both E-SIGN and UETA avoid making specific technological recommendations in order to encourage further innovation. UETA notes in comments to the 1999 model law that the statute:

> "[I]s designed to allow for the development of systems which will provide "control" as defined in Section 16. Such control is necessary as a substitute for the idea of possession which undergirds negotiable instrument law. The technology has yet to be developed which will allow for the possession of a unique electronic token embodying the rights associated with a negotiable promissory note. Section 16's concept of control is intended as a substitute for possession."[27]

---

[26] See, e.g., U.C.C. § 9-105, Control of Electronic Chattel Paper.
[27] Uniform Electronic Transactions Act, *supra* note 24.

Blockchain smart contracts align with commercial needs and are well-suited to bridge the gaps in worldwide data-driven relationships.

D Integrating Legal Smart Contracts: Old Questions, New Tools

The existing body of electronic contracts law establishes a firm foundation for the first step in creating automated legal contracts, combining an integrated electronic agreement with a smart contract, or dual integration.

The goal of smart contracts is to be able to predict rules-based results that allow businesses to create reliable future plans and products.[28] Traditionally, contracts were made in any medium, including oral agreements. Enforcing oral agreements requires testimony of humans, an expensive and unpredictable process. The advent of written contracts eliminated much of the uncertainty about enforcing a contract, because the terms are created at the time the contract is signed, not recreated from witness memory. The higher degree of reliability of paper writing led lawyers to develop a way to ensure that a contract means what it says and that it will be enforced as written. This method is called the *integrated agreement*.

An integrated written agreement embodies the entirety of the parties' contract. If a contract is fully integrated, evidence that would contradict or vary the terms of the written document is inadmissible, and a court is limited to the contract document in determining the intent of the parties.

Drafted properly, fully integrated contracts may be proved solely by documentary evidence – no testimony of humans other than document authentication is required or allowed. Well-drafted contracts contemplate potential disputes and provide evidence for managing those disputes as simply as possible. Cumulative lessons of potential outcomes become the boilerplate fine print that addresses as many "what-ifs" as possible. A tightly drafted, fully integrated contract has no loopholes in its performance and prevents time and money wasted on enforcement. It has a high degree of predictability in its outcome.

To ensure enforceability of legal relationships made in blockchain data relationships, the simplest first step is to combine an integrated, enforceable contract with smart contract functions via dual integration. *Dual integration* links smart contracts and full legal contracts by reference to the contract's storage address on the blockchain. Incorporating documents and objects by reference in legal documents is a familiar process to lawyers and delivers the baseline enforceability that industrial applications will demand.

E Self-Enforcing Smart Contracts

With due diligence of dual integration accomplished, legal engineers are free to explore the next frontier of smart contracts: self-enforcing contracts. Enforceability is the right to apply to an actor with authority over the contracting parties to force the breaching party to pay or act. One limitation of self-enforcing smart contracts is their scope: Smart contracts can only enforce agreements to the extent that assets are known and held within the blockchain system itself. Absent legal enforceability, if a contracting party breaches an agreement, she may simply avoid liability by not placing value into the system against which a promise may be enforced.

---

[28] *See generally*, Lorna E. Gillies, *Electronic Commerce and International Private Law: A Study of Electronic Consumer Contracts* (Farnham: Ashgate, 2016).

In the foreseeable future, though, there may be many situations where on-chain enforcement is a viable and desirable tool, such as in cases where collateral is held in blockchain form, where disputes are primarily documentary, or where broader cross-collateralization exists.

V LEGAL ENGINEERING: DESIGNING SMART CONTRACT SYSTEMS WITH LAWYERS IN MIND

When building legally significant blockchain systems, it is important to think like a lawyer. For example, what happens when a dispute involving the program ends up in litigation? One of the main problems with teaching smart contracts to computer science students is that these types of students often lack a lawyer's adversarial thinking skills – the legal perspective needed to design smart contracts in the blockchain space.[29]

Building a computable contract system that will support legal commerce involves creating frameworks and models that are sound and useful for multiple purposes, just like legal tools. Bringing legal engineering skills to the forefront will make sure that the correct information is in the right place at the right time in order to support processes and decision making. Legal engineers use the tools of commerce to make processes work, and in the new economy many of these engineers will work in code and other technical media.[30]

Legal engineering blockchain systems will dissect, examine, reimagine, and improve existing legal, commercial, financial, and data models. Many participants in the blockchain marketplace, from individuals to large corporations, will seek a degree of jurisdictional autonomy, as well as self-execution of much of the legal process within the smart contract code. However, legal contracts must have frameworks of enforceability in which to operate, as discussed in the previous section. This means that when creating a legally significant system, the question of applicable substantive law must be addressed.

A Daubert and Open Source

When building legally significant software, forensic admissibility of evidence is an important concern to address. How do you prove that the system preserves evidence of rights and obligations such that they may be enforced by a court of law? In answering this question, one must have a proven methodology, as well as content that accords with judicial rules of admissibility for scientific and technical evidence. The USA set this framework generally in *Daubert v. Merrell Dow Pharmaceuticals*.[31] Applied to software, this framework is as follows:

1. Can the program or algorithm be explained? This explanation should be in words, not only in code.
2. Has enough information been provided such that thorough tests can be developed to test the program?
3. Have the error rates been calculated and validated independently?
4. Has the program been studied and peer-reviewed?
5. Has the program been generally accepted by the community?

---

[29] Kevin Delmolino, Mitchell Arnett, Ahmed Kosba, Andrew Miller, and Elaine Shi, "Step-by-Step Toward Creating a Safe Smart Contract: Lessons From the Cryptocurrency Lab," Cryptography ePrint Archive, November 18, 2015, available at: https://eprint.iacr.org/2015/460.pdf.

[30] Stuart Barr, "The Rise of the Legal Engineer," Lexology, July 27, 2016, available at: www.lexology.com/library/detail.aspx?g=f8d9bb92-3779-4bc2-9f1b-7354d416acb1.

[31] *Daubert v. Merrell Dow Pharmaceuticals*, 509 U.S.C. 579 (1993).

In evaluating a given program, it is useful to refer to guidelines for crafting software systems that conform to the evidence principles set out in *Daubert*; for example:

1. definition of the challenge problem;
2. requirements definition;
3. test set development;
4. design alternative and decisions;
5. algorithm description (readable in English);
6. code development and walk-through;
7. test and validation process;
8. error rate calculation;
9. community involvement.[32]

B Blockchain as Common Law

The common law system provides a useful analogy for how blockchain systems work. Common law, the backbone of US and UK law, is the set of rules developed by judges deciding cases over time and recording them for posterity. Legal patterns and rules are discerned and shaped by studying the results of consensus breakdown – lawsuits. The different aspects of private common law are: contracts, the law of voluntary obligation; torts, the law of involuntary obligation; and property, the law of stuff. The three interact in ever more complex ways to create new doctrine, but these three essential aspects remain the same. Evolution of private law follows a regular pattern: new property → new contracts → new torts → new regulation.

The record of the common law is kept in case reporters. In the common law case reporter system, distributed nodes look like courthouses, verifying, bundling, and submitting transactions (cases) to the blockchain. Trusted court reporters package, verify, and bundle cases into a book such as 17 F.3d. The contents of 17 F.3d are never going to change. The effect of the cases in 17 F.3d may change by the addition of subsequent volumes to the chain, but the disputes and decisions in 17 F.3d are recorded for the permanent record, accessible to all across the decentralized web of legal information. Prior to computerized recording of legal materials, lawyers spent a large amount of time updating the daily changing state of the common law.

The common law is decentralized, and yet at the same time hierarchical: the law is everywhere and accessible by everyone. The statements of some nodes are given more authority than others – such as the US Supreme Court – but the law tolerates a level of uncertainty at the transactional level, the trial courts. Trial courts are allowed to have different perspectives on an issue until the difference of opinion becomes a problem for the larger system and a uniform rule becomes necessary. When there is a fork of authority, the law refers the issue up to the next level for resolution.

C Model and Soft Law Tools

The guiding principles of model law and soft legal code provide reference tools to help shape all of these relationships. When faced with doing business in new or lawless territory, modern

---

[32] Chet Hosmer, *Python Forensics: A Workbench for Inventing and Sharing Digital Forensic Technology* (London: Elsevier, 2014), 9.

commerce and governments often turn to soft legal code and relationship-by-contract to provide a minimally restrictive, reliable framework. The blockchain is a new territory for doing business where there is no indigenous existing law. The law has encountered such situations in recent history, however, and has developed instructive tools that can serve as guides.

1 The Restatements

Common law develops at the trial level, through the recording of individual cases built into an ever-growing body of permanent jurisprudence. Over time, the rules of common law transactions have grown so complex that it has become important to write them down in order to use them. The Restatements of the Law, especially the comments to them, are a set of treatises that try to give a consensus of the current state of common law and act as guiding principles.[33] They are a secondary source of law, persuasive but not mandatory authority for judges and lawyers who might face a novel situation in their own jurisdictions.

The Restatements are not without primary authority function. Restatements give territories that need law a place to start. In the twentieth century, the US Virgin Islands and Northern Mariana Islands territories had no legal systems. They both needed a non-restrictive framework from which to start, a flexible common law system that allowed commerce to flow, rather than a rigid regulatory civil code. The answer was to adopt the Restatements as common law and evolve them, case-by-case, to suit the individual territory's needs. A complicating issue for smart contract developers, however, is that the Restatements are not open source.

2 The Uniform Commercial Code

The USA faced commercial expansion issues in the mid-twentieth century. The varying state of contract law across the country made commerce cumbersome and unpredictable and limited the ability of large companies to plan and utilize resources across jurisdictions. At the same time, contract law was growing more complex by the day and the human lawyer's job of anticipating and planning contingencies became difficult. The UCC[34] was the solution – a code that provided for predictability in transacting business.

The UCC gave judges and lawyers a reasonable, predictable decision-making rubric to apply to complex business processes. It was an improvement over the Restatements because the UCC adds functionality. The UCC and contract law emphasize that contracting parties are free to make any agreement they want, but complying with the UCC makes agreements more functional. The UCC acts as a gap-filler and a best-practice guide. For example, if a creditor goes through the steps outlined in UCC Article 9 (Secured Transactions) when repossessing and reselling collateral, the creditor is entitled to a judicial presumption of a commercially reasonable sale, saving litigation costs. The UCC continues to function and change to support US business needs in commercial contracts.

---

[33] *See generally*, "The Restatements of the Law," *Wikipedia*, last accessed December 15, 2016, available at: https://en.wikipedia.org/wiki/Restatements_of_the_Law.

[34] Legal Information Institute, "Uniform Commercial Code," Cornell University Law School, available at: www.law.cornell.edu/ucc.

3 UNIDROIT, UNCITRAL, and International Model Law

As global commerce has grown in volume, complexity, and diversity, businesses and governments have struggled with issues not unlike those faced by blockchain commerce today. One organization that developed out of the early League of Nations was the International Institute for the Unification of Private Law (UNIDROIT).[35] Authority is a complicated issue in international commerce, and when making contracts, parties want to avoid the "home field" advantage of having one jurisdiction's law control a contract. International business law is ideally a voluntary and private law created by contract. It is important for parties to set up their relationships carefully, in a way that models known best practices and fairness, especially because the contract may fail. The UNIDROIT was established as a soft legal code, primarily for international trade. The UNCITRAL Convention, meanwhile, applied soft legal code concepts to a much broader scope of contracts.[36]

International model code is an evolution of secondary sources into a more flexible, less intrusive tool that provides an alternative to territorial legal systems. Soft code gives parties useful alternatives to the laws of one of the parties' home countries by addressing:

> "virtually all the most important topics of general contract law, such as formation, interpretation, validity including illegality, performance, non-performance and remedies, assignment, set-off, plurality of obligors and of obligees, as well as the authority of agents and limitation periods ... designed for use throughout the world irrespective of the legal traditions and the economic and political conditions of the countries in which they are to be applied."[37]

Model clauses are modular and allow parties to craft an agreement that reflects their wishes and provides for as much risk management as practicable. Soft legal tools are about providing voluntary, reasonable, stable, predictable relationships in an otherwise chaotic marketplace. This predictability is desirable enough for many international parties to choose to utilize UNIDROIT/UNCITRAL contract language, which is available in 15 languages in order to enhance this global utility.

D Settlement

Reliable settlement services take friction out of the process of contracting by allowing parties to focus on the substance of the contract rather than how and when the consideration changes hands. Settlement, therefore, is the foundation of the commercial system. Bitcoin, for example, has proven that instant, delivery-versus-payment settlement is feasible. This is important for several reasons. Instant delivery of assets in exchange for value eliminates counterparty risk. Contracting parties who exchange funds typically rely on banks – high-trust actors – to ensure that their payments are made as promised. Bitcoin has shown that settlement has the potential to be as reliable with blockchain technology as with traditional clearing technology, but with a different trust model. However, as noted in Section I.F, the lack of certainty in dealing with public chain governance models means that the groundwork for blockchain settlement services is anything but complete.

---

[35] UNIDROIT, www.unidroit.org.
[36] UNCITRAL, www.uncitral.org.
[37] "Model Clauses for Use by Parties of the UNIDROIT Principles of International Commercial Contracts," UNIDROIT, last updated January 30, 2017, available at: www.unidroit.org/instruments/commercial-contracts/upicc-model-clauses.

E Commercial Paper

In order for commerce to flow, fungibility of value items is critical, as is careful typing and classifying of rights, obligations, and objects. For a value object to function as currency, it must flow through commerce with as few strings attached as possible. Lawyers, businesspeople, and governments have grappled with this issue for centuries. One set of tools that has evolved is *commercial paper*, a type of obligation that specifically mimics the fungibility of fiat currency while giving protection against adverse property claims.[38]

Commercial paper instruments are intended to track documentary conditions only and are an evolution of financial technology that directly relates to cryptocurrency fundamentals of reliability and finality of financial transactions. Commercial paper value is based on a promise and obligation to pay money in the future, and it adds a dimension of time to blockchain asset trades. The flexibility and reliability of commercial paper systems allows businesses to use these tools for growth. The basic unit of commercial paper, the promissory note, may be recombined in infinite ways. For example, notes may be bundled into value pools and issued as shares and derivative instruments and payment streams. The ability to create promissory notes, issue shares, and keep track of assets creates the toolkit for financial engineering: Out of these simple structures flow complex uses such as time notes, demand notes, order paper, bearer paper, corporate bonds, securities, stocks, dividends, debentures, certificates of deposit, drafts, loan originations, repurchase agreements, mutual funds, reinsurance, equity options, and more.

F Collateral, or "Article 9 Makes the World Go Round"

Collateral – identifiable property pledged as security for a debt – is a critical part of commerce. Like evidence law, collateral provides a trust proxy. Contracting parties may not trust each other, but the ability to take possession of valuable property in the event of loan default is a powerful trust-based incentive for the lender. That trust is underpinned by the enforceability of the collateral security interest, and makes this a problem that should be handled by lawyers. Collateralization rules vary between property types and across jurisdictional lines. Blockchain technology may provide the long-awaited means by which global markets may standardize some important collateralization procedures as new, global assets like energy credits become subject to certainty and control within blockchain chains of custody.

To support the process of collateralization, governments often establish registries that give an "official" version of ownership and authenticity for property and relationships that are of public importance. Registries produced by court-trusted actors are entitled to special evidentiary treatment. This reliable version of important facts allows for predictability and growth in commercial relationships. Registry systems are both a necessary utility for perfecting security interests and a natural application for smart contracts, allowing parties to note an interest in property by program action.

The UCC has evolved a more centralized filing system to avoid the problem of creditors having to search in multiple jurisdictions in order to determine whether property was previously given as collateral – analogous to the Bitcoin "double spend." The blockchain has the potential to reverse the registry centralization trend in a shared ecosystem.

Because cryptocurrency tokens may represent items of value (e.g., colored coins) as well as hold value (e.g., Bitcoin), they create interesting challenges for secured transactions. Bitcoin likely fits

---

[38] *See generally*, UCC Article 3.

into the property category "general intangibles." Section 9-315(a)(1) of the UCC provides that a creditor's interest continues in general intangibles even after a debtor sells them to a third party.[39] The security interest continues in the Bitcoin, even through subsequent transfers. This rule does not apply if virtual currency is held to be money under § 9-322.[40] However, it is arguably possible for virtual currencies to be considered "investment instruments" under Article 8, potentially providing an improved legal framework for value tokens.[41] An important consideration is that blockchain tokens may be configured in many ways, and examining a use case for its legal framework involves a functional approach – how a token is used, rather than what it is named. Especially for secured transactions, one size does not fit all.

G Contract Complexity

Contracts are the means by which individuals and entities manage their voluntary obligations. Contract law is created by the accumulated wisdom of millions of lawsuits summing to a living pattern of legal doctrine. This doctrine guides dispute resolution and teaches lawyers about how to make predictions about future events. Providing predictability in planning the future is the primary function of contract drafting.

Contract provisions work together algebraically to govern the prospective consensual relationship between parties, which is what makes contracts easily amenable to coding language. If a contract does not anticipate all foreseeable contingencies, it fails and the parties end up in expensive litigation. A lawyer's job is to foresee the maximum number of contingencies and plan for it in a document. This practice has evolved longer and longer contracts over time as more fact patterns and contingencies are added to conventional contract wisdom. This managing of complicated, algebraic contracts is something a computer is naturally equipped to do, once we teach it how. Eventually, metadata will link contracts and jurisdictions and execute compliant protocols depending on the parameters of the contracts. In the meantime, it is up to legal minds to examine clauses, terms, and conditions, and configure the correct smart contract for a given use case, searching for pain points remediable by cryptographic data certainty.

H Corporate Governance

Corporate governance describes the rules under which a corporation or other legal fiction operates. A smart contract entity similar to a corporation is often called a *decentralized autonomous organization* (DAO). A DAO, like a corporation, is a legal fiction, created by consensus, that allows a group to do more than an individual could do alone. Traditional legal systems provide corporate governance models that give options and predictability to business relationships. As DAOs get more numerous and diverse of purpose, it's a good idea to make deliberate choices about the rules of this type of organization as it relates to traditional law. To be autonomous, an organization must be self-governing. Lawyers have used bars to manage self-governed existence for centuries, for example. As long as a self-governing organization does not merit government expending energy to interfere, it can remain self-governing. Once a self-governing group fails to govern itself, it becomes a subject of regulation.

---

[39] UCC § 9-315(a)(1). The UCC is available to view at: www.law.cornell.edu/ucc.
[40] UCC § 9-322.
[41] UCC Article 8.

Early warning signs of a tendency for blockchain developers to eschew broader legal context were borne out in the disaster of The DAO. The DAO was a fundraising project that purported to run immutable, autonomous code on a public blockchain, Ethereum.[42] Participants purchased "DAO Tokens" with the Ethereum native currency, Ether. The tokens were shares of a project that had a monetary value and a profit motive. Participants voted on the worthiness of projects to fund. The DAO developers observed no apparent securities or contract law formalities, because the participants agreed that the code was "law" and would govern the outcome of the project in its entirety. Despite early warnings of flaws in the code and lack of testing, The DAO deployed to resounding success. It raised over $180 million within two weeks of starting.

Several weeks later, The DAO fund began leaking Ether, with losses quickly totaling approximately $60 million. A flaw in the code, previously publicly identified by the open-source community, allowed a participant "attacker" to create an unbreakable, recursive function call that added funds to the attacker's account. Because of the open nature of the Ethereum blockchain, the attack was witnessed in near real time, as exchanges stopped trading Ether to prevent the thief from converting "stolen" Ether to Bitcoin or fiat. The Ethereum community found itself with no civil or criminal legal framework to anchor its rights, engaging in heated online debate as to how to proceed. In the end, the public, "immutable" blockchain Ethereum reset its ledger with a "hard fork," a refactoring of the blockchain that invalidated the attack on The DAO. Further legal issues remain unresolved. The decision regarding how to remedy The DAO attack exposed the deep need for conscious governance decisions in complex business and financial systems.[43]

VI LAW PRACTICE IN BLOCKCHAIN SPACE: LEGAL ENGINEERING

The mailbox rule and the case reporter system are centuries-old examples of legal engineering, the creation of new rules that build on existing models that evolve to fit current tools and future relationships. Legal engineers make sure that the right information gets to the right people at the right time to make good decisions.[44]

The size of the legal engineer's undertaking is tremendous, but it is proportional to the commercial value of automated contract provisions, decisions, and actions. The ability to apply logical legal processes to evidence using smart contracts opens the door to more complex legal agreements limited only by the ability to define fact patterns and affect assets.

While the need for lawyers to build engineered systems is particularly pressing as we change from one commercial medium to another, the concept of legal engineering is not new. Case law systems, modular statutory code, digest systems, commercial paper, uniform best-practices standards, and computerized legal research are just a few world-changing and prediction-enabling achievements of legal engineers over the years. Blockchain smart contracts bring new tools to the ancient art of legal engineering, and open up new possibilities for fostering development of commercial and human potential.

---

[42] See generally, Usman W. Chohan, "The Decentralized Autonomous Organization and Governance Issues," December 4, 2017, available at: https://papers.ssrn.com/sol3/papers.cfm?abstract_id=3082055.

[43] David Siegel, "Understanding the DAO Attack," Coindesk, June 25, 2016, available at: www.coindesk.com/understanding-dao-hack-journalists.

[44] Richard Susskind, *The End of Lawyers: Rethinking the Nature of the Legal Profession* (Oxford: Oxford University Press, 2008).

3.4

Patent Analytics

Information from Innovation

Andrew W. Torrance[1] *and Jevin D. West*[2]

I INTRODUCTION

A Born to be Analyzed

There are many categories of information that defy easy systematic computational analysis. Patents are not one of them. Ever since the earliest *litterae patentes* were granted by host countries to foreigners willing to share their knowledge with their hosts, the monopoly rights granted by governments have been meticulously documented. The richness of data detailing both the monopoly right to exclude – granted to a patent's owner – and the patent document's informational disclosure of how to make and use a claimed invention – intended to enrich the metaphorical storehouse of knowledge – has accumulated at an accelerating pace since the days of the first letters patent. So rapidly has the information embodied in patents grown that analytical techniques for sorting and computationally evaluating that information have always lagged far behind the deluge of accumulating data. In lieu of precise algorithmic methods for understanding the contents of patents, a specialized guild of patent attorneys has evolved to sell their largely subjective interpretations of what patents disclose, cover, and are worth. Since patent attorneys must pass a challenging patent bar exam, in addition to a state bar exam, their numbers are controlled, allowing their fees to be high. However, recent years have seen the inexorable rise of more objective, falsifiable, mathematical, and computational methods for analyzing patents. Progress in patent analytics has accelerated rapidly in recent years, democratizing, elucidating, and making more rigorous the interpretation of patent data.

Patent analytics is the systematic computational analysis of patent data or statistics. Because patents and their ancillary documentation are rich in text, charts, diagrams, citations, and other data; because much of this information is densely interconnected, there is an abundance of patent data and statistics available to be analyzed. A growing repertoire of powerful patent analytics methods capable of discovering, interpreting, communicating, and visualizing patterns in these data and statistics has begun to shift patent analysis from art into science.

---

[1] Andrew Torrance thanks research assistant, Patrick Sullivan, for his excellent research assistance, especially in preparation of a detailed outline of patent analytics. Conflict of interest disclosure: early investor in PatentCore, but sold his entire interest to LexisNexis in 2015; owns shares in PatentVector LLC.

[2] Conflict of interest disclosure: owns shares in PatentVector LLC.

B Patent Harmonization

A modern patent has a formal structure that varies only slightly from technology to technology and country to country. There are a number of reasons for this regularity. Perhaps the most significant is the strong role international treaties have played for more than a century in specifying the requirements of patents. In addition, national and regional patent statutes, such as the US Patent Act, have established legal requirements for written disclosure of a claimed invention that correspond rather naturally to distinct, regular sections in any patent document.

The first major treaty among patenting nations was the Paris Convention for the Protection of Industrial Property (Paris Convention), which was signed in Paris, France on March 20, 1883.[3] With 177 contracting parties,[4] the Paris Convention covers patents, patent-like protections (e.g., industrial designs and utility models), and other intellectual property such as trademarks and geographical indications. The Paris Convention has three primary foci: national treatment, right of priority, and common rules. By emphasizing the need for common rules, the Paris Convention encourages member countries to harmonize the required contents of a patent application. This harmonization has evolved into a standard patent format, including sections summarizing the invention, a detailed description of the invention, and figures and claims.

The trend toward standardization of patent documents was reinforced and accelerated by the Patent Cooperation Treaty (PCT), which has 152 contracting parties, and was first signed in Washington, DC, on June 19, 1970.[5] The PCT makes it fairly uncomplicated for a patent applicant to file a patent application in her own country, and then, after about two and a half years, to extend the geographical reach of that application by using its text as the basis for derivative patent applications in any or all PCT member states. Because the original patent application forms the basis for subsequent foreign patent applications, its document format must be compatible with the formal and substantive requirements of all countries to which it is extended, though many countries do, in addition, require a translation into their local languages.

C Patent Anatomy

A patent application tends to be written in a format so predictable as to be mechanical. The front page of a patent document illustrates this (Figure 3.4.1). A patent usually displays a title on its front page, though the information content of titles is not uniformly rich. For example, while US Patent No. 6,164,870 is entitled "Portable dike having air inflatable reinforcement," US Patent No. D533,480 is sparely named "Vehicle." The front page of a patent usually also lists the identities of the inventors, assignees (i.e., the owner), patent examiners, attorneys, and law firms involved in inventing and patenting. Information is also listed about any patent documents, including foreign ones, to which the patent is related or claims priority. Dates of filing, publication, and issuance are listed. Technology categories in which a claimed invention is classified by a patent office, or in which an examiner searched in order to locate prior art relevant to the patentability of a claimed

---

[3] WIPO, "Summary of the Paris Convention for the Protection of Industrial Property (1883)," available at: www.wipo.int/treaties/en/ip/paris/summary_paris.html.
[4] WIP, "WIPO-Administered Treaties," available at: www.wipo.int/treaties/en/ShowResults.jsp?lang=en&treaty_id=2.
[5] WIPO, "PCT: The International Patent System," available at: www.wipo.int/pct/en/; www.wipo.int/treaties/en/ShowResults.jsp?lang=en&treaty_id=6.

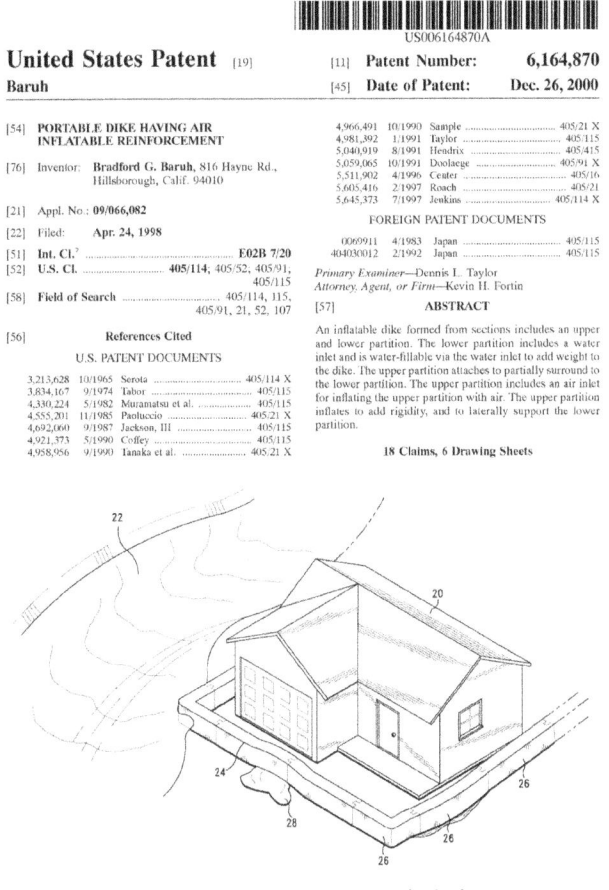

FIGURE 3.4.1 US Patent No. 6,164,870.

invention, are specified.[6] Disclosure is often made about any governmental rights there may be to a claimed invention. Patent documents may also specify an additional patent term during which a patent may be enforceable. The front page often also contains an abstract of the invention and a drawing or figure representative of the claimed invention.

After the front page, there are often diagrams included in the patent. Next comes the main body of written disclosure, often organized into sections with standard headings. The first of these headings tends to be a short section sometimes entitled "Technical Field of the Invention," in which the patent applicant attempts to place her invention within the taxonomy of technology.[7] A section often called "Background of the Invention" tends to identify any problems the claimed invention is meant to solve and, sometimes, this section also describes how the claimed invention differs from existing technologies or solutions. What follows is typically a "Summary of the Invention" that briefly describes the claimed invention, and explains what the claims to the underlying inventions are meant to cover. This is usually followed by a "Detailed Description of the Invention" that provides more

---

[6] A variety of patent technology classification systems have been used around the world, including, recently, the International Patent Classification (IPC – see www.wipo.int/classifications/ipc/en) and Cooperative Patent Classification (CPC – see www.uspto.gov/web/patents/classification/cpc.html).

[7] The sections described pertain specifically to US patent documents, though most patent documents originating in other countries or regions contain similar sections.

comprehensive information about what the invention does, how it works, and what different embodiments of the invention there are. The patent document usually concludes "with one or more claims particularly pointing out and distinctly claiming the subject matter which the inventor or a joint inventor regards as the invention."[8] At times, there may be additional specialized content, such as listings of specific DNA or polypeptide sequences. Thus, a patent contains a large amount of data conveniently arranged in a fairly standard format, facilitating direct comparisons between multiple patent documents, whether they come from the same or different jurisdictions.

D Patent Prehistory

Much of the information disclosed in a patent document originates during the process of preparing a patent application, the filing of the application with a patent office, and then the complex negotiation that takes place between patent applicant and patent office. This process is called *prosecution*, and the entirety of the documentary record generated during the process that leads up to the issuance of a patent is called the *prosecution history*.

It has been difficult, until recently, to gain easy access to the mountains of useful data generated in the prosecution of a patent.[9] Prosecution history provides valuable perspective on the evolution of a patent application, including a detailed record of the back-and-forth discussion between patent examiner and applicant (often via patent attorney) as they negotiate precisely how broad the patent's claims are warranted to be.

Prosecution history provides a necessary lens through which to interpret the legal scope and meaning of issued claims. As discussed in Section II.B, the United States Patent and Trademark Office (USPTO) made prosecution history data freely available to the public in 2012, and, since then, there has been considerable analysis of this data, both by academics and commercial firms.[10] One such patent prosecution data company, PatentCore, has pioneered the computational analysis of prosecution histories to provide profound insights into that process.[11] Scholars have also used this prosecution data to explore many patent issues, such as the productivity of patent examiners over the course of each quarter of the year.[12]

E Patent Ownership

Determining who owns a patent provides crucial information for potential infringers, licensees, and buyers. Countries often require owners of patents or patent applications to record their patent ownership with their relevant national patent offices, which often maintain assignment databases accessible by the public. The PCT also collects such ownership

---

[8]   35 U.S.C. § 112(b).
[9]   Deborah E. Bouchoux, *Patent Law For Paralegals* (Boston, MA: Cengage Learning, 2008), 326.
[10] Michael Frakes and Melissa F. Wasserman, "Empirical Scholarship on the Prosecution Process at the Patent Office," in *Research Handbook on Economics of Intellectual Property Law*, eds. Peter S. Menell and David L. Schwartz (Aldershot: Edgar Elgar, 2017).
[11] The company originally named PatentCore was acquired by LexisNexis on July 1, 2014, and was subsequently renamed Reed PatentAdvisor (see www.ipwatchdog.com/2014/07/02/lexisnexis-acquires-patent-data-analytics-innovator-patentcore/id=50271/#targetText=HORSHAM%2C%20Pa.%2C%20July%201,%C2%AE%20PatentAdvisorSM%20solution%20suite). One of the authors was an early investor in PatentCore, but, at the time of writing, neither author has any financial interest in the company.
[12] Michael Frakes and Melissa F. Wasserman, "Is the Time Allocated to Review Patent Applications Inducing Examiners to Grant Invalid Patents? Evidence from Micro-Level Application Data," *Review of Economics and Statistics* 99 (3) (2017): 550–563.

information. Despite these efforts, assignment databases are often riddled with inaccuracies or contain out-of-date information, lessening their value to those wishing to determine ownership.

There are a number of reasons why assignment databases may not be accurate. Even where there is a legal requirement for patent owners to register their ownership interests, patents are frequently bought and sold. Unless subsequent owners update the records in an assignment database, the value of assignment information tends to degrade over the lifetime of a patent. Though it may sometimes be in the interests of patent acquirers to ensure the accuracy of information held within an assignment database, it is often not worth the effort. Patent assignee databases tend to be rife with inaccuracies.

Even good faith efforts to maintain the integrity of assignment databases can fail. Sometimes this is due to simple transcription errors made by either the owner or the patent office. Companies often list their names in different ways, or attribute their patents to particular subsidiaries.[13] It is also not uncommon for companies to change their legal names for business reasons, such as acquisition or merger (e.g., Google changed to Alphabet in 2015).[14] Patent owners sometimes deliberately create legally separate business entities to hold the patent assets of parent companies. This latter practice is quite common among non-practicing entities (NPEs). For example, Acacia Research Corporation has been associated with multiple patent-holding companies, including Acacia Patent Acquisition Corporation, Saint Lawrence Communications LLC, American Vehicular Sciences LLC, and Battle Toys LLC, to name but a few.[15]

It is something of a puzzle why patent assignment databases often contain unreliable ownership information. Like registering legal interests in land, there can be strong legal incentives for patent owners to ensure accuracy of their legal patent rights in order to prove their ownership in the face of other potential claimants. In addition, governments and other third parties have interests in being able to locate owners of intellectual property rights. Nevertheless, neither patent owners nor patent offices tend to be under strong legal obligations to update assignment databases. Commercial databases of patent ownership do tend to be more accurate, but access to such databases is usually quite expensive. The US federal government has suggested the idea of imposing a legal obligation on patent owners to update the USPTO assignment database of their property interests in patents.[16] In the meantime, the USPTO has released a raw data version of its assignment database for use and further analysis by anyone.[17]

Partial ownership interests in patents present another complication in determining accurate assignment information because such interests – arising from licenses, liens, and other legal obligations – are difficult to discover. Although there are probably many millions of patent licenses in effect around the world, contracting parties often keep the terms, and even the existence, of such licenses confidential. Sometimes, details of patent licenses come to

---

[13] IBM, for example, has 15 different names in the USPTO Assignment Database, as found using PatentVector, www.patentvector.com.
[14] Adam Lashinsky, "Why Google Changed its Name to Alphabet," *Fortune*, August 11, 2015, available at: http://fortune.com/2015/08/11/google-alphabet-why.
[15] These subsidiaries of Acacia Research Corporation were located by performing a simple Google search for "Acacia Research Corporation subsidiaries."
[16] Dennis Crouch, "Whither the USPTO's Authority to Require Ownership Recordation," Patently-O, February 10, 2014, available at: http://patentlyo.com/patent/2014/02/authority-ownership-recordation.html.
[17] Alan C. Marco, Amanda F. Myers, Stuart Graham, Paul D'Agostino, and Kirsten Apple, "The USPTO Patent Assignment Dataset: Descriptions and Analysis," USPTO Economic Working Paper 2015-2, July 2015, available at: www.uspto.gov/sites/default/files/documents/USPTO_Patents_Assignment_Dataset_WP.pdf.

light during litigation, or are required by law to be disclosed to public securities regulators (e.g., SEC [Securities and Exchange Commission] filings in the USA). However, these events are exceptions. Data on patent licenses tends to be scarce and woefully incomplete.

F Patent Litigation

A patent confers on its owner a key legal right: to sue infringers in court for damages and injunctive relief. Only a minority of patents end up being subjects of litigation, but rich information is available about those that do. Trials are conducted by the judicial branch of government, and government involvement often ensures that at least some information about patent trials will be published and accessible to the public. It is usually possible to determine who the parties are to a patent dispute, what the causes of action are, which attorneys represent the parties, the court in which the proceedings take place, and what the procedural and substantive outcomes are. If cases are settled, information may be less available, since final settlement agreements are often kept confidential. Litigation that takes place in the USA can be investigated through services like Public Access to Court Electronic Records (PACER),[18] a fee-based service of the federal judiciary, or through commercial services such as LexisNexis,[19] WestLaw,[20] and Bloomberg Law.[21] Some legal data companies offer specialized information about patent litigations, including LexMachina[22] in the USA and Darts-ip[23] for international cases.

Scholarship suggests that litigated patents are generally more valuable than patents that have never been litigated.[24] Research has suggested that: (1) litigated patents tend to be considerably more valuable than non-litigated patents; and (2) the higher the court in which a patent is litigated (that is, federal district court, Court of Appeals for the Federal Circuit, and/or the US Supreme Court), the higher the value of that patent tends to be.[25] Patent litigation tends to be quite expensive, so it would appear to be rational for patent owners to tend to assert high-quality and high-value patents in litigation; in this case, it should be unsurprising that litigated patents tend to be disproportionately valuable. Consequently, patent litigation data may be biased toward disproportionately valuable patents.

G Patents Grow Bigger

Over the past several decades, both the size and quantity of patents have increased markedly. This should not be surprising; the knowledge that patents embody is largely embedded in the wider world of scientific and technological information, a world that grows rapidly with each

---

[18] www.pacer.org.
[19] www.lexisnexis.com/en-us/home.page.
[20] www.westlaw.com.
[21] www.bloomberglaw.com.
[22] https://lexmachina.com.
[23] www.darts-ip.com.
[24] *See* Dietmar Harhoff, Frederic M. Scherer, and Katrin Vopel, "Family Size, Opposition and the Value of Patent Rights," *Research Policy* 33 (2) (2004): 363–364; John R. Allison, Mark A. Lemley, Kimberley A. Moore, and R. Derek Trunkey, "Valuable Patents," *Georgetown Law Journal* 92 (2004): 435–479; John R. Allison, Mark A. Lemley, and Joshua Walker, "Extreme Value or Trolls on Top? The Characteristics of the Most-Litigated Patents," *University of Pennsylvania Law Review* 158 (1) (2009).
[25] Andrew W. Torrance and Jevin D. West, "All Patents Great and Small: A Big Data Network Approach to Valuation," *Virginia Journal of Law and Technology* 20 (3) (2017): 466–504. This study uses patent importance, calculated using eigenvector centrality, as an indication of patent value.

passing day. Even so, recent growth in patents and their claims is remarkable. According to an empirical study of US patent document size, from 1987 to 2007, total word count increased from about 3600 to about 7000.[26] Thus, the length of a patent almost doubled in two decades. Another study, measuring the size of patent applications published from 2005 to 2010, showed growth in the number of characters in patent applications over this period.[27] Such prodigious growth in patent document size suggests similar growth in information content.

Patent claims have shown a similarly rapid growth trend in recent years. A study that sampled 28,000 US patents issued from 1997 to 2005 found increases in both the total number of claims per patent, and in independent claims per patent.[28] In this period, the total number of issued claims almost doubled, from approximately 10 claims per patent to just under 20 per patent. Although the number of independent claims issued per patent did not rise quite as rapidly, even they did show an increase of almost 50% per patent.

Patent documents have always been rich in data conducive to analysis, and, as they have grown in size, it is likely that their analyzable data has grown as well. However, quantity does not equal quality, so it is possible that patents have increased in size *without* providing more valuable information. Understanding the implications of the expanding patent document may be approached using the methods described in this chapter.

II TRENDS IN PATENT ANALYTICS

Ever since the first modern patents were issued in Renaissance Italy,[29] enterprising investors and businesses have attempted to analyze their value, validity, and scope. In this section, we review the five major foci of patent analytics: prosecution, litigation, valuation, landscapes, and patent office data.

A Patent Prosecution Analytics

Data on the patent prosecution process can be useful for making decisions before, during, or after prosecution. Such decisions include whether or not to file a provisional, non-provisional, continuation, or divisional patent application, whether and how to file a reply or request for continued examination (RCE) in response to receiving an Office action, whether to request a telephone or live interview with a patent examiner, whether to file a notice of appeal or appeal brief to contest a rejection of proposed claims, and whether to request an inter partes review (IPR). Patent prosecution analytics can help to estimate and predict the probabilities of success of particular actions taken during any of the phases of prosecution, taking into account variables such as technology classification, art unit, technology center, examiner, and date of application.

Until recently, complete official patent prosecution records were most reliably available only to those who visited a relevant patent office in person. There, one could often obtain

---

[26] Dennis David Crouch, "The Rising Size and Complexity of the Patent Document," University of Missouri School of Law Legal Studies Research Paper No. 2008-04, 2008.
[27] Dennis David Crouch, "Patent Specifications Continue to Rise in Size," Patently-O, April 23, 2012, available at: http://patentlyo.com/patent/2012/04/patent-specifications-continue-to-rise-in-size.html.
[28] Crouch, "The Rising Size and Complexity of the Patent Document," *supra* note 26.
[29] On June 19, 1421, the city state of Florence granted architect Filippo Brunelleschi a patent, formally described in an official government document, covering a boat he had invented for transporting marble intended for the building of *il duomo di Firenze*, the famous dome that sits atop Florence Cathedral. Frank D. Prager, "Brunelleschi's Patent," *Journal of the Patent Office Society* 28 (2) (1946): 109–135.

permission to browse through mountains of prosecution documents dating back many years, and even obtain photocopies of particular prosecution histories. Commercial services arose to conduct such searches for clients willing to pay for the convenience. Gradually, patent offices began to scan prosecution documents into digital files. Eventually, this information became fully digitized in readily searchable file formats, like .csv or .xsl data files, allowing it to be made available as bulk data for download by anyone.[30] For example, since 2012, it has been possible for anyone to download bulk patent prosecution data from the USPTO. The free availability of this bulk data has democratized patent prosecution analysis, and spurred the creation of patent data analytics tools, both free and commercial.

One free patent analytics system is The Lens (formerly "Patent Lens"), an open-source data tool developed by the Australian-based non-profit organization Cambia.[31] The Lens is designed "to make the innovation system more efficient and fair, more transparent and inclusive," and makes available "nearly all of the patent documents in the world as open, annotatable digital public goods that are integrated with scholarly and technical literature along with regulatory and business data."[32] It allows free text search by desired keyword, inventor, applicant, or patent owner, and its search results can be filtered to reveal only the particular data desired by a user. It provides graphical results displaying both categorical and quantitative data. The Lens also contains some prosecution data from many countries, including publication dates of patent applications, names of inventors, owners, and applicants, and technology classifications according to the USPTO and Cooperative Patent Classification (CPC) systems. There are some limitations, though: A user cannot determine the current status of an application, nor view the full prosecution history of a particular patent application. One of The Lens' analytical tools is called PatSeq Finder, and provides access to patents that disclose genetic sequences and offers bulk downloads of patented sequence data based on jurisdiction, document type, and either sequence type or sequence location.[33]

A web-based service provocatively named Examiner Ninja provided analytics on specific patent examiners in the categories of overview, strategy, history, and timing, as well as information about overall allowance rate, allowance rate before first final rejection, likelihood of early allowance, allowance rate after first final rejection, likelihood of allowance after first RCE, comparative allowance rates among examiners, allowance rates before first final rejection, and allowance rate after first final rejection.

A pioneer in patent prosecution analytics, Patent Advisor provides a rich suite of tools that allows a user to investigate detailed statistical profiles of most aspects of the patent prosecution process. These profiles cover such items of interest to patent applicants as individual patent applications, issued patents, examiners, technology groups, and assignees, as well as all major aspects of patent prosecution, including Office actions, replies, and appeals.[34] Patent Advisor was one of the very first companies to use the vast trove of patent prosecution bulk data made available by the USPTO in 2012. It experienced substantial commercial success, eventually being acquired by LexisNexis.

Similar services are offered by Juristat, which sells patent prosecution data analytics tools.[35] A more recent entrant is BigPatentData Inc., which also offers patent analytics tools focused

[30] Bulk data can be downloaded, refined by a variety of characteristics, or all data can be downloaded in one bulk download. See generally PAIR Bulk Data, https://pairbulkdata.uspto.gov.
[31] www.lens.org.
[32] "The Lens," available at: www.lens.org/about/what.
[33] www.lens.org/lens/bio/patseqfinder.
[34] ReedTech Patent Advisor, http://knowledge.reedtech.com/h/c/261237-patent-prosecution.
[35] Juristat, www.juristat.com/about.

on patent prosecution.[36] Clarivate Analytics offers a wide variety of legal data analytics, including some relating to patent prosecution.[37]

Future advances in patent prosecution analytics will depend in large part on improvements in the prosecution practices of, and data availability from, national and international patent offices. The USPTO has even indicated that its future will rely increasingly on big patent data and improved prosecution process metrics rather than on outcome metrics.[38] Currently, the most powerful widely available patent prosecution analytics tools consist of paid services. Without the financial incentive of subscriptions, free and open-source services have developed at a much slower pace.

B Patent Litigation Analytics

Patent litigation analytics use computational approaches to understand, and even to help predict, patent litigation processes and outcomes. Because patent litigation tends to be quite expensive, there is a substantial market for analytical tools that can improve the likelihood of positive outcomes in legal disputes between parties. Prior to commencement of litigation, analytics may be used to identify possible infringers or plaintiffs. Patent litigation analytics may be of particular interest to NPEs, whose business models often depend on identifying sufficient numbers of promising potential targets for infringement litigation to justify the investments financing their activities. Conversely, practicing entities may employ analytics to identify and, if possible, avoid attracting patent infringement lawsuits from potential plaintiffs. Patent litigation analytics may even be used to avoid litigation by encouraging preemptive licensing agreements or patent assignments.[39]

A growing number of patent litigation analytics services have become available, especially over the past decade. Plainsite is a legal data project, which began at Stanford University, that connects data from millions of federal court dockets, records from half a million lawyers, half a million legal entities, thousands of federal judges, and numerous other federal and state statutes and regulations. It uses computation approaches to allow insights and predictions about a variety of legal issues, with particular strength in patent litigation.[40]

The patent risk management company RPX offers a suite of free litigation analytics tools, including its litigation search engine, which allows users to search patent litigation data by categories such as party name, entity (including parent or subsidiary), or specific patent.[41] The company also distributes annual reports detailing patent litigation activity and statistics, particularly regarding the impact of NPEs.[42] These reports provide users with free data and visualizations of NPE litigation, NPE patent ownership trends, and NPE litigation filings. The patent analytics services and reports RPX makes available may act as valuable publicity

---

[36] https://bigpatentdata.com
[37] Clarivate Analytics, http://clarivate.com/about-us/what-we-do.
[38] Richard Seidel, "Quality Metrics," presented at the Patent Public Advisory Committee Quarterly Meeting, February 4, 2016, available at: www.uspto.gov/sites/default/files/documents/20160204_PPAC_Quality_Metrics.pdf; see also David Stein, "Measuring Examination Quality Through Data Mining of Office Actions," USPTO Talk, April 24, 2015, available at: www.usptotalk.com/measuring-examiner-quality-through-data-mining-of-office-actions.
[39] See, e.g., Silicon Graphics, Inc. v. ATI Techs, 569 F.Supp.2d 819 (2008) No. 06-cv-00611-bbc, at *36–37 (W.D. Wis. Jan. 30, 2008).
[40] Stanford Law School – Plainsite, https://law.stanford.edu/projects/plainsite/. See also www.plainsite.org.
[41] RPX Corporation, https://search.rpxcorp.com.
[42] "2015 Report: NPE Litigation, Patent Marketplace, and NPE Cost," RPX, available at: www.rpxcorp.com/wp-content/uploads/sites/2/2016/07/RPX-2015-Report-072616.FinalZ.pdf.

for the company, attracting attention to the commercial patent risk management services (e.g., patent litigation insurance) it sells.

Another major provider of patent litigation analytics is Lex Machina.[43] Founded in 2006 at Stanford Law School as a public interest data project by Professor Mark Lemley and his colleagues, Lex Machina provides analytical data on parties, law firms, attorneys, districts, judges, and patents involved in litigation. For example, its tools allow analysis of how long it takes specific judges or courts to bring litigations to trial or termination, the likelihood of success of particular motions or overall lawsuits, and even elements of successful motions. Lex Machina analyzes such factors as client lists, open cases, and levels of litigation experience of law firms, either generally or in specific courts. Its clients may then use this information to improve litigation outcomes or encourage favorable settlements. Data on parties to lawsuits also allows investigation of historical damages awards for any particular patent or litigation. Lex Machina even offers assessments of patent strength and litigation history, though their methods for doing so remain largely proprietary. Users can also explore findings of invalidity, infringement, and enforceability for particular patents, as well as outcomes of re-examination proceedings.[44] Common motives for subscribing to Lex Machina's services are to use its patent analytics tools to gain a competitive advantage against opposing counsel in a litigation, or litigate more efficiently in order to reduce litigation expenses. For example, knowing that a particular judge never grants motions to transfer, a user might avoid drafting and filing such fruitless motions with that judge, and instead focus on litigation tactics more likely to succeed with that judge.[45]

Serving clients predominantly interested in the biopharma industry, IPD Analytics uses a combination of attorney researchers and data analytics to monitor and evaluate pending patent lawsuits, and then to create reports that often attempt to predict probable outcomes for these lawsuits.[46] Its reports also evaluate the scope, validity, and enforceability of companies' patents and patent portfolios. Clients pay to receive these reports. For more in-depth analysis, clients may order custom analyses from IPD Analytics.[47] Many of the company's clients are managers of hedge funds or mutual funds who rely on patent litigation analysis to assess investment opportunities involving companies whose valuations are based, at least in part, on patents.[48]

C Patent Valuation

Patent valuation involves estimating the economic worth of a patent. A large part of a patent's value derives from the monopoly property right to exclude others from making, using, selling, offering to sell, or importing an invention claimed by the patent, and depends both on the subject matter of, and the scope of the claims covering, the invention.[49] A prediction of the future value of a patent may inform decisions regarding whether or not to continue patent

---

[43] "Patent Litigation," Lex Machina, available at: https://lexmachina.com/patent-litigation.
[44] Ibid.
[45] "Motion Metrics: Legal Analytics for Successful Motion Strategy," Lex Machine, available at: https://lexmachina.com/wp-content/uploads/2014/12/Motion-Metric-Datasheet.pdf.
[46] IPD Analytics, www.ipdanalytics.com.
[47] Ibid.
[48] *Cheney v. IPD Analytics, L.L.C.*, No. 08-23188-CIV, 2009 U.S. Dist. LEXIS 105678, at *3–4 (S.D. Fla. Aug. 28, 2009).
[49] Michael S. Kramer, "Valuation and Assessment of Patents and Patent Portfolios Through Analytical Techniques," *John Marshall Review of Intellectual Property Law* 6 (2007): 463–465.

prosecution, or even to file a patent application at all. Once a patent has been issued, valuation may help an owner decide whether to pay maintenance fees on, enforce, license, or sell the patent.

Traditionally, data such as citations, family size, claim number, and payment of maintenance fees have been used to inform the value of patents.[50] In addition, a number of discrete events may encourage or inform valuation of a patent: a purchase or sale of a patent (e.g., in bankruptcy, at auction), assessment of damages for patent infringement, estate or gift taxation, property distribution or division, a corporate merger or acquisition event, or any other transaction dependent on assigning a discrete monetary value to a patent.[51]

Patent valuation has been an important factor in settling estates since the nineteenth century and valuation questions continued in the years that followed. For example, one litigation from 1981 involved valuing a patent as of a particular date.[52] Here, there was an exploration and analysis of the patented method of production of Electronic Modules Corporation's acquisition, International Technology (IT). The patent was assigned a nominal value of $1 because, despite considerable effort in the development of sales, IT had been unable to generate a profit by selling products covered by the patent. A conclusion was made that the patent could not be used to generate a profit with available technology and materials. As a result of these problems, the patent was deemed worthless as of the date of liquidation of IT, on September 30, 1971.

Challenges to the accuracy of patent valuations have also arisen in the taxation context. For instance, a 1930 court decision assessed whether or not a company had valued its patents correctly for purposes of annual tax deductions. The US Board of Tax Appeals lamented:

"It has long been recognized that questions of value and estimates thereof involve matters of opinion upon which minds are prone to differ ... Confronted with the same identical facts as to conditions existing at March 1, 1913 – the state of the art, the improvements effected by the inventions, the security and comprehensiveness of the patent protection, the economic advantages resulting from the patented inventions, the superiority of the product obtained by use of the patents, and the growth of the patent-protected business to the basic date – the opinions of the two groups of witnesses, as to the fair value of the patents at the basic date, are so substantially different as to seem wholly irreconcilable."[53]

The difficulty of determining accurate patent values has changed surprisingly little despite the passage of time. Some scholars and courts even take the position that patents are "unvaluable." Nigel Swycher has argued that patents have not yet achieved "asset class" status, despite the fact that "intangible assets and IP now account for over 70% of the value of many organizations."[54] There is a clear need for the development of better methods of patent valuation.

A variety of methods have been employed to value patents. The costs of patent assignments or licenses can be useful indicators of patent value, but are often maintained as trade secrets by parties to these transactions. Book values of patent assets have often been used.[55] However,

---

[50] Gaetan de Rassenfosse and Adam B. Jaffe, "Are Patent Fees Effective at Weeding Out Low-Quality Patents?" National Bureau of Economic Research Working Paper 20785, 2014.
[51] Dennis H. Locke, "A Systematic Approach to Patent Valuation," *IDEA* 27 (1) (1987): 1–5, available at: www.ipmall.info/sites/default/files/hosted_resources/IDEA/27_IDEA_1986.pdf.
[52] *Elec. Modules Corp. v. United States*, No. 179-77, 1981 U.S. Ct. Cl. LEXIS 1463, at *76–77 (Ct. Cl. July 29, 1981).
[53] *Syracuse Food Prods. Corp. v. Commissioner*, 21 B.T.A. 865, 881–882 (1930).
[54] Nigel Swycher, "Big Data Solutions to Determining IP Risk and Value," *Intellectual Asset Management* 42 (2014).
[55] See, e.g., *Simmons Co. v. Commissioner*, 8 B.T.A. 631, 642 (1927).

complicated and subjective combinations of factors often inform patent valuation estimates.[56] Adam Bulakowski has suggested that "The most accurate estimates [of patent value] arise from applying some combination of [traditional income-, market-, and cost-based] methodologies, each informed by a critical interpretation of data on the patents' legal, technical and business attributes."[57] The diversity of divergent methods for conducting patent valuation analyses suggests the need for improvements in how value is assigned to information-rich and complex assets like patents. Patent analytics will certainly play a strong role in these improvements.

A number of more modern approaches have been developed to provide more accurate patent valuations. They may be broadly divided into qualitative and quantitative methods.

Qualitative patent valuation can be used to anticipate market size and profitability for goods or services a patent covers, as well as to assess scope and enforceability of the claims.[58] Employing qualitative analysis, patent attorneys or other analysts examine the claim scope of the claims of a patent of interest, determine how such claims might cover particular products or R&D projects, evaluate vulnerability of the patent to invalidity or unenforceability, and suggest a patent value that may then be used to negotiate a license from the patent owner in order to proactively avoid infringement litigation. Joseph Hadzima has outlined a detailed qualitative approach to patent valuation involving a three-step process: (1) determining the quality of an underlying invention covered by a patent; (2) evaluating how well the patent is constructed; and (3) figuring out how to extract value from the patent.[59] The US Internal Revenue Service (IRS) has formulated largely qualitative approaches for estimating the fair market value (FMV) of patents. Calculating FMV involves determining whether a patented technology has been rendered obsolete by subsequent technologies, bearing in mind any restrictions on a patent recipient's use of, or ability to transfer, a patented technology, and then accurately measuring the remaining enforceable patent term.[60] Graphical approaches have also been suggested, such as the use of a claim scope optimality curve for helping to estimate patent value.[61]

Quantitative patent valuation is more amenable to computational methods of analysis. Over the past several decades, quantitative valuation has been increasing in relative importance. This is due to rapid advances in both the availability of data useful for valuation determinations, and improvements in the quality of analytical methods. Royalty rates on patent licenses, for example, can provide useful valuation information, and can be obtained from commercial royalty pricing services. For example, KTmine provides subscribers with access to licensing agreements, and summaries of those agreements, to help clients estimate patent value.[62] Another commercial firm, RoyaltySource, sells clients' data useful in license negotiation, valuation, litigation, infringement damage measurement, and calculating

---

[56] See, e.g., *Smith, Inc. v. Commissioner*, Docket No. 478-74., 1977 Tax Ct. Memo LEXIS 422, at *16 (U.S. T.C. Jan. 31, 1977).

[57] Adam Bulakowski, "Decoding Patent Valuation," *Intellectual Property Magazine*, September (2014): 78–81, www.ipcg.com/thoughtleadership/Decoding_patent_valuation_IPM_September_2014.pdf.

[58] Robert Fish, *Strategic Patenting* (Bloomington, IN: Trafford Publishing, 2007).

[59] Joseph Hadzima, "How to Tell What Patents are Worth," *Forbes*, June 25, 2013, available at: www.forbes.com/sites/forbesleadershipforum/2013/06/25/how-to-tell-what-patents-are-worth/#7b923e986ac7.

[60] IRS, "Determining the Value of Donated Property," Publication 561 (4/2007), 2007, available at: www.irs.gov/publications/p561/ar02.html#doe862.

[61] William J. Murphy, John L. Orcutt, and Paul C. Remus, *Patent Valuation: Improving Decision Making through Analysis* (Hoboken, NJ: Wiley, 2012), 100.

[62] ktMine, www.ktmine.com.

transfer pricing.[63] This service can generate reports germane to patent royalty rates or payments, licensee and licensor information (including industry-specific information), descriptions of patents licensed or sold, non-royalty compensation (such as milestone and upfront payments), transaction terms (such as exclusivity), field and geographical restrictions, arm's length or related party status, and the sources of all information provided (e.g., SEC filings, news articles, company news releases). Yet another company, RoyaltyStat, offers a paid service for estimating patent royalty rates based on its extensive royalties database.[64] Despite the existence of a market for detailed patent license royalties information, and the existence of firms that specialize in gathering and commercially providing such information, the confidential nature of many patent licensing agreements means that even the best patent license databases remain incomplete. In fact, not only are the details of many patent licenses assiduously protected as confidential information, even the existence of such agreements is often kept secret. For these reasons, accurate patent license data remain difficult to obtain.

Other quantitative measures, such as market indicators, can also assist in estimating patent values. Bulakowski suggests a variety of approaches for marrying market indicators to patent analysis.[65] Stock pricing may be capable of elucidating patent value, because the market premium over book value of a publicly traded company may represent investors' perceived value of intangible assets. A weakness of this relatively easy valuation method is that it relies on valuation preferences of investors whose judgments often pertain to combined intangible assets, not just patents in isolation.[66] Court decisions can also inform valuation calculations, especially when specific infringement damages are assessed, or when uncertainty on issues such as claim scope or technology coverage are resolved in a legally binding manner. Perhaps the highest-quality information about patent value involves pure patent sales in which the purchase price of a patent, or group of patents, directly attributes specific monetary value on the market.[67] In that case, a directly valued patent can subsequently be used as a benchmark with which to make comparisons with other patents, with adjustments made for such factors as differences in claims scope and technology coverage. In such direct patent valuations, characteristics like claim strength, breadth, product applicability, and bibliometric data (that is, citations) may often be informative.[68] In conducting market analysis for taxation assessments, the IRS considers a number of factors to be salient, such as past transactions of comparable intangibles, price information for comparable transactions, and arm's length transactions between independent parties.[69]

An important consideration in patent valuation methods is that, for a market valuation to be accurate and meaningful, a healthy and liquid market must exist for the particular patent asset being valued.[70] If there is no real market for the patent asset in question, the valuation tends to be merely a rough estimate.[71] Establishing a thriving market for patents has been challenging. A self-described "intellectual property merchant bank," Ocean Tomo,[72] and its

---

[63] RoyaltySource, www.royaltysource.com.
[64] RoyaltyStat, www.royaltystat.com.
[65] Bulakowski, "Decoding Patent Valuation," *supra* note 57.
[66] Ibid.
[67] Ibid.
[68] Ibid.
[69] IRS, "Internal Revenue Manual," part 4, ch. 48, sec. 5 (4.48.5.2.4), para 10 (July 1, 2006), available at: www.irs.gov/irm/part4/irm_04-048-005.html#doe58.
[70] Fish, *Strategic Patenting*, *supra* note 58.
[71] Ibid.
[72] www.oceantomo.com.

spin-off patent brokerage, ICAP Patent Brokerage,[73] have been pioneers in trying to solve this persistent problem of making patent markets, including by holding public patent auctions.

Scholars in the field of economic research and in the legal community have proposed methods of patent valuation based on statistical analysis of patents. This analytical approach to valuation utilizes readily available information about patents to mathematically model and predict patent value. One collects quantitative information from a sample of patents, like the number of forward and backward citations, the number of claims, the length of claims, and similar metrics. This data is then input into a mathematical model that carries out regressions against a dependent output variable indicative of patent value.[74] This approach to patent analysis is attractive in part because of the overwhelming wealth of patent data generated by patent systems, and the increasing availability of this data.[75]

There are several weaknesses to this method. One is the inability to validate valuations with real-world patent transactions due to the fact that transactional data on direct patent sales is typically kept confidential by all parties to the transaction. In addition, there is considerable variance in value from patent to patent that cannot be captured by merely counting patents issued for a given time period, technology class, or other categorization. However, more informative patent characteristics may offer a rich data resource that can be used to estimate patent value and other phenomena. Citations may provide a promising source of information about patent value, and both forward and backward citations have been suggested as indicative of patent value.[76] Some scholars have found that the value of a patent increases with the frequency that it is cited by subsequent applications and patents. Manuel Trajtenberg has observed that "citations are more informative of the value of innovations per se, rather than of the size of the market for the products embedding those innovations."[77] Despite this, some scholars have argued against assuming a correlation between citations and patent value, urging that "it should be completely obvious that those numbers have little to do with value of a patent."[78]

One of the services RPX offers to clients is mitigation of litigation risks posed by NPE patent infringement lawsuits.[79] The company also provides patent valuation services. When RPX acquires patents, they promise never to assert them against their subscribing clients.[80] As an ancillary benefit of its practice of purchasing many patents, RPX is able to provide direct estimates of the market value of patents based on their actual purchase prices, and then use this data to estimate values of similar patents.

Mathematical valuation methods are also employed in patent analysis, with a variety of models and approaches used to quantify the value of patents. The IRS, for example, instructs its tax examiners to use a variety of approaches, either singly or in combination, to perform patent valuations.[81] One mathematical approach to valuation relies on option pricing models,

---

[73] http://icappatentbrokerage.com.
[74] Kramer, "Valuation and Assessment of Patents and Patent Portfolios Through Analytical Techniques," *supra* note 49, at 463, 466–467.
[75] Ibid.
[76] Id. at 463, 474.
[77] Manuel Trajtenberg, "A Penny for Your Quotes: Patent Citations and the Value of Innovations," *RAND Journal of Economics* 21 (1) (1990): 183.
[78] Fish, *Strategic Patenting*, *supra* note 58.
[79] www.rpxcorp.com.
[80] RPX, "Defensive Acquisitions," available at: www.rpxcorp.com/rpx-services/rpx-defensive-patent-acquisitions.
[81] The IRS guidance on valuing intangible assets, including IP, suggests that examiners use one of the fundamental valuation methods of: market-based, cost-based, income-based, Monte Carlo probabilistic, or option methods. *See* IRS, Internal Revenue Manual, *supra* note 69, paras. 7–9.

such as the Black–Scholes pricing model, one of the most commonly used tools to value patents.[82] This approach of viewing patents as options has gained increasing support among scholars in economics and law.[83] Viewed as an option, a patent confers upon its holder "the right but not the obligation to make further investments at a future date at a specified price."[84] For the cost of procuring a patent (including the research and development expense of the invention), a patent owner can obtain "the right, at various stages, to purchase a stream of expected cash flows associated with excluding others from developing patented subject matter. Patent holders can monetize this right by developing and commercializing the patent and/or by litigating, or threatening to litigate, the patent."[85] The value of the commercialization option depends on the cost of developing the invention, the likelihood that the invention will be successful, and the potential revenues that the invention may generate.[86] The litigation value depends on a different set of variables that relate to the likelihood of success in litigation, and the cost of enforcing the patent in court.[87]

Income approaches may also be used for patent valuation. For instance, the *discounted cash flow model* relies on calculating the discounted cash flow related to a particular patent, and then using future cash flow and an estimated discount rate to arrive at a present value. Free cash flow depends on the context surrounding the patent of interest, including such factors as apportionment estimates, growth assumptions, royalty rates, and other variables.[88] As with other methods of valuation, the IRS has provided guidance for using the income approach to value patents and other intangible property.[89] This lends an official *imprimatur* to the income approach. Some scholars consider the income approach the most accurate approach to arriving at a present value for a patent.[90]

There are several other approaches to patent valuation. The *cost approach* is a valuation method used primarily in real-estate valuation. It relies on a comparison between the value of an asset and the expected cost to develop or create the equivalent of that asset. In this method, a patent's value is equated to the R&D and development costs of arriving at the inventive concepts claimed in the patent.[91] The cost approach focuses on the costs incurred in the R&D that led to a particular technology, and on securing corresponding patent rights. The strength of the cost approach lies in the ease of calculation, as well as the ease with which it can be explained to those not expert in patents, including investors. A weakness in the cost approach is that there is often little relationship between the cost of inventing, developing, and patenting an invention and that patent's market value.[92] In this method:

> "one makes assumptions about the market size, market penetration, cost of entry, cost of production, lifespan, and profitability of the patented product, and then runs a spreadsheet to estimate profit. The value of patent is then taken to be the discounted present value of the estimated marginal profit, i.e., the profit over and above profit that which one would expect to be generated without the patent. Unfortunately, the validity of the . . . , model depends entirely

---

[82] Bulakowski, "Decoding Patent Valuation," *supra* note 57, at 80.
[83] See, e.g., Joseph L. Bower and Clark G. Gilbert, eds., *From Resource Allocation to Strategy* (Oxford. Oxford University Press, 2005), 354.
[84] Ibid.
[85] Michael J. Burstein, "Patent Markets: A Framework for Evaluation," *Arizona State Law Journal* 47 (507) (2015).
[86] Ibid.
[87] Ibid.
[88] Bulakowski, "Decoding Patent Valuation," *supra* note 57, at 80.
[89] See IRS, Internal Revenue Manual, *supra* note 69, para 12.
[90] Murphy et al., *Patent Valuation*, note 61, at 124.
[91] Bulakowski, "Decoding Patent Valuation," *supra* note 57, at 80.
[92] Fish, *Strategic Patenting*, *supra* note 58.

upon the validity of the underlying assumptions, and those assumptions can vary wildly among different analysts."[93]

A new approach to patent valuation involves the application of network science. PatentVector, a patent analytics firm that employs big patent data and network approaches, uses a combination of its eigenvector centrality-based patent importance metric (i.e., the "PatentVector Score") and empirically derived mean estimated values of patents to calculate an estimated PatentVector Value for every patent in the worldwide patent citation network.[94] Every patent in this network possesses a PatentVector (PV) Score that measures its influence in the network, and is directly comparable to the PV Score of every other patent in the network. This allows the valuation estimate of any one patent in the network to be compared directly to that of any other patent in the network. This patent valuation approach has considerable promise because it offers automated, instant, and objective estimates, though it will take time and testing to ensure its accuracy.

D Strategic Patent Analytics

Patent analytics is capable of analyzing broad patterns of patent coverage and patent trends. *Strategic patent analytics* may be loosely divided into patent landscape analysis, competitive patent intelligence analysis, and patent visualization, all of which intergrade into one another, and increasingly rely on the algorithmic analysis of big patent data.

A *patent landscape analysis* determines concentrations of patents selected using specific criteria. Landscapes may be mapped by particular fields of technology (e.g., patent office art units or technology centers, IPC or CPC classifications), country, industry, assignee, licensee, inventor, specified spans of time, or keywords. Using a patent landscape, a company, country, or other entity may identify areas in which it or other patent owners are technologically strong or weak, complementarities between portfolios, and technological areas either crowded with, or empty of, patented inventions. For example, if a television manufacturer were looking for specific technological areas in which it would be most efficient to innovate, it could conduct a landscape analysis of USPTO technology class 348 (i.e., televisions) by searching for patents having relevant keywords (e.g., display, backlight, curvature, image processor, mounts) to determine which areas of television technology might be ripe for innovation. A similar analysis could be used to generate competitive insight regarding in which areas of television technology its competitor manufacturers were actively patenting. Because technological innovation may occur rapidly, the results of patent landscape analyses may rapidly become obsolete, necessitating frequent updates of these analyses to maintain accuracy. Comparing patent landscape analyses over time may also allow insight into trends in invention and patenting, which could be useful for extrapolating future technological directions.

Patent landscapes analyses are often expressed as visualizations. For example, Patent Inspiration offers both free and subscription-based tools for producing a variety of informative graphical representations. A user may conduct a Boolean search for patents using both keywords and categories such as applicant, inventor, technology classification code, or patent

---

[93] Ibid.
[94] https://patentvector.com. This method is based on multiplying a patent's PV Score by an independently derived empirical estimate of mean patent value, and then correcting the product for both inflation and the size of the economy of the country that issued the patent. Different empirical estimates of mean patent value may be used as an input, depending on user preference. The authors were founders of PatentVector LLC, and currently maintain ownership interests in the company.

or application number. Search results may be filtered by such variables as publication date, applicant, assignee, inventor, CPC code, or IPC code. The search results include a timeline that shows dates of priority, application, publication, and issue, and includes invention descriptions, applicant names, inventor names, IPC codes, CPC codes, patent family members, and the full text of the patent itself. Users may then export these search results in a variety of file formats. Search results are also presented as images. For instance, a search on the term "nanotechnology" yields several different visualizations that may show activities, applicants, IPC codes over time, IPC pie charts, contoured landscape maps, charts showing competitors, patent quality, claimed technology, filings by country or region, and materials (e.g., chemical elements) used in claimed inventions.

There is a variety of patent landscape approaches. A patent analytics company named Chipworks allows users to generate patent landscapes focusing primarily on defined segments of particular markets.[95] Another company, Global Patent Solutions, allows clients "to see the IP 'gaps' that your competitors have missed and help you fill those gaps with protected and licensable patents."[96] TeqMine provides a patent landscape service that "augments traditional cognitive IPR and technology mapping processes with powerful statistical, visual and On-Line tools, boosting your business development."[97] Figure 3.4.2 is a patent landscape map illustrating patent families claiming inventions relevant to shale oil and gas exploitation. It was commissioned by the Canadian Intellectual Property Office (CIPO) for inclusion in its 2016 *Patent Landscape Report: Shale Oil and Gas*.[98]

This landscape visualization of patented shale oil and gas technologies shows peaks at high concentrations of patents (here chosen by keyword or technology, such as "Drill Bit Formation," "Drilling Well Formation," and "Catalytic Zeolite Coke"), with white "snow-caps" indicating the highest concentrations of related patents. The landscape is roughly divided between patented inventions related to shale oil and gas "exploration" (i.e., patents to the left of the diagonal line) and "development and production" (i.e., patents to the right of the diagonal line). It also uses the distance between the dark dots to show the relatedness distances between different technologies. Using this visualization, a user can locate an isolated and non-peak dot that represents a particular technology, and determine that research, development, and patenting efforts in the technological area depicted by that dot might afford a competitive opportunity, whereas a dot on a tall peak indicates an area of technology densely populated by patents. One of the key advantages of patent landscape visualizations is the relative ease with which users can identify areas of technology either crowded with, or devoid of, patents.

Competitive patent intelligence analysis refers to methods of situating patents of interest within the context of such factors as technological area, assignees, licensees, inventors, and competitors. Innography, a company acquired by CPA Global in 2015, offers a wide array of patent analytics aimed at helping users determine competitive patent information. It describes one of its services as discovering "new and emerging competitors, their latest innovations, key markets, and IP litigation activities."[99] A similar company, IFI Claims,

---

[95] TechInsights (formerly Chipworks), http://techinsights.com.
[96] Global Patent Solutions, www.globalpatentsolutions.com/services/other-services.
[97] "Technology Map," Teqmine, available at: http://teqmine.com/technology-map.
[98] Canadian Intellectual Property Office, *Patent Landscape Report: Shale Oil and Gas* (Ottawa: Canadian Intellectual Property Office, 2016), figure 6, p. 10. This figure is reprinted here according to the permission granted on page I of the report.
[99] See "PatentStrength: Patent Value," Innography, available at: www.innography.com/why-innography/patentstrength.

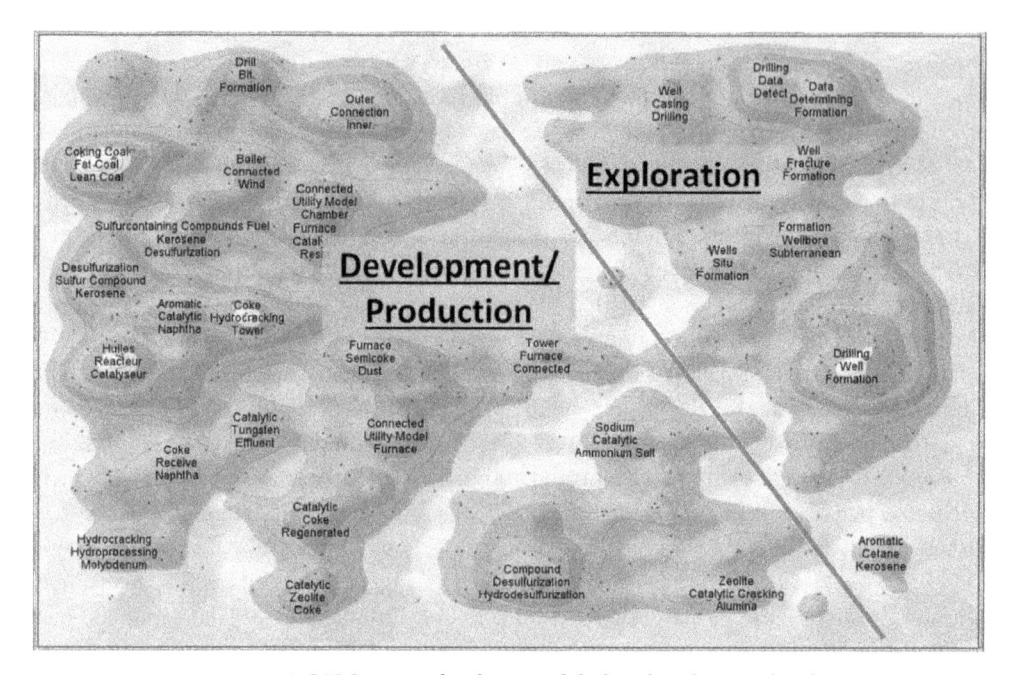

FIGURE 3.4.2 A CIPO patent landscape of shale oil and gas technologies.

helps clients determine which companies possess dominant patent portfolios in particular technologies, or helps them identify potential strategic partners based on patent portfolio overlap and compatibility.[100]

Patent visualization is both an analytics approach and a convenient way of presenting patent data. For example, Innography offers a diverse array of tools that enable a user to view the results of searches and analyses as graphs, charts, trends, or other visual presentations. The explosive growth in big patent data and computational approaches to patent analysis have driven improvements in patent visualizations, which help the human mind – cognitively challenged when attempting to process large numbers of anything – efficiently recognize and derive meaning from patterns. Patent analytics services now offer a wide variety of visualizations derived from patent data. For example, Patent Inspiration, a fee-based subscription service offered by AULIVE Software NV, uses the European Patent Office (EPO) DOCDB patent database in order to offer free language text search of millions of patents from around the world using criteria such as keywords, technology classes, jurisdictions, and important dates.[101] It then filters the results and displays them as graphical representations of the underlying patent search results. Available visualizations include dynamic word clouds, bar graphs, pie charts, data tables, and trend plots. Innography provides one of the leading patent search and data visualization services.[102] It also uses algorithms to generate its own patent metrics, such as PatentStrength®, which the company describes as "a proprietary algorithm that predicts patent value and relevance, by deriving the likelihood that a patent will eventually be litigated."[103]

---

[100] IFI Claims, www.ificlaims.com.
[101] Patent Inspiration, www.patentinspiration.com.
[102] www.cpaglobal.com/ip-intelligence.
[103] "PatentStrength: Patent Value," *supra* note 99.

PatentVector offers a variety of unique visualizations as well.[104] These include diagrams that illustrate how strong an owner's patent portfolio is within each discrete category of technology (see Figure 3.4.5), maps of the worldwide patent citation network that allow users to zoom in on individual patents or zoom out to view larger, increasingly inclusive natural clusters of patents, and flow diagrams illustrating the magnitude and direction of citation behavior among inventors, assignees, or even countries. For example, Torrance and West used PV Scores to illustrate which US federal judicial districts hosted litigation over the most important patents (Figure 3.4.3).[105]

As noted above, patent visualization is not an isolated approach to understanding patents – it is an approach common to every branch of patent analytics.

E Patent Office Analytics

Patent offices around the world are increasingly reliant on patent analytics to measure their own performances as well as the performances of the patent systems they serve.[106] As one of the primary generators of patent data, the USPTO has collected mountains of patent data since the Patent Act of 1790 was signed into law. This data includes the text of patent applications, issued patents, correspondence between applicants and examiners, decisions by USPTO administrative tribunals, and internal communications among USPTO employees. Traditionally, most of this data was used to make internal decisions within the USPTO, such as how to plan and execute the agency budgets, which technology groups and art units required more personnel, and where to devote agency resources to alleviate delays in particular agency services. In 2010, the USPTO created the Office of the Chief Economist, hiring Dr. Stuart Graham to pioneer the position. Of the initiatives Dr. Graham promoted, the public release of huge amounts of patent data was among the most important. Rather than waiting until USPTO patent data had been curated and "cleaned," he championed the release of raw, bulk data, leaving the cleaning and analysis entirely to users.[107] These bulk data releases have enabled anyone interested in patent data, from scholars to companies, to investigate myriad aspects of the US patent system. Although the USPTO had previously analyzed its own data to glean insights, providing public access to this data spurred an explosion of US patent analytics, including both a flurry of academic studies[108] and the founding of many patent analytics companies.

Before the USPTO began to release its data to the public, a different ethos prevailed; patent data was predominantly analyzed to assess agency performance. In fact, "prior to fiscal year

---

[104] https://patentvector.com.
[105] Torrance and West, "All Patents Great and Small," *supra* note 25, at 496, figure 6.
[106] This chapter focuses on the use of patent analytics by the USPTO in order to provide an example. However, other patent offices are increasingly relying on patent analytics too. Notably, the European Patent Office (EPO) has long been at the forefront of collecting big patent data, using that data for internal analyses, and making it available for both research and commercial purposes. Examples of bulk patent data collections made available by the EPO are EBD (European bibliographic data), DOCDB (EPO worldwide bibliographic database), and INPADOC (EPO worldwide legal status database). See "Raw Data," EPO, available at: www.epo.org/searching-for-patents/helpful-resources/raw-data.html.
[107] The terms and conditions of bulk data products (full text available at: www.uspto.gov/learning-and-resources/bulk-data-products) states, in part: "The data is provided 'as is.' Neither the United States Government, nor any agency thereof, nor any of their contractors, subcontractors or employees makes any warranty, expressed or implied, of this data. The USPTO is the data provider only."
[108] See, e.g., Frakes and Wasserman, "Empirical Scholarship on the Prosecution Process at the Patent Office," *supra* note 10, and "Is the Time Allocated to Review Patent Applications Inducing Examiners to Grant Invalid Patents?" *supra* note 12.

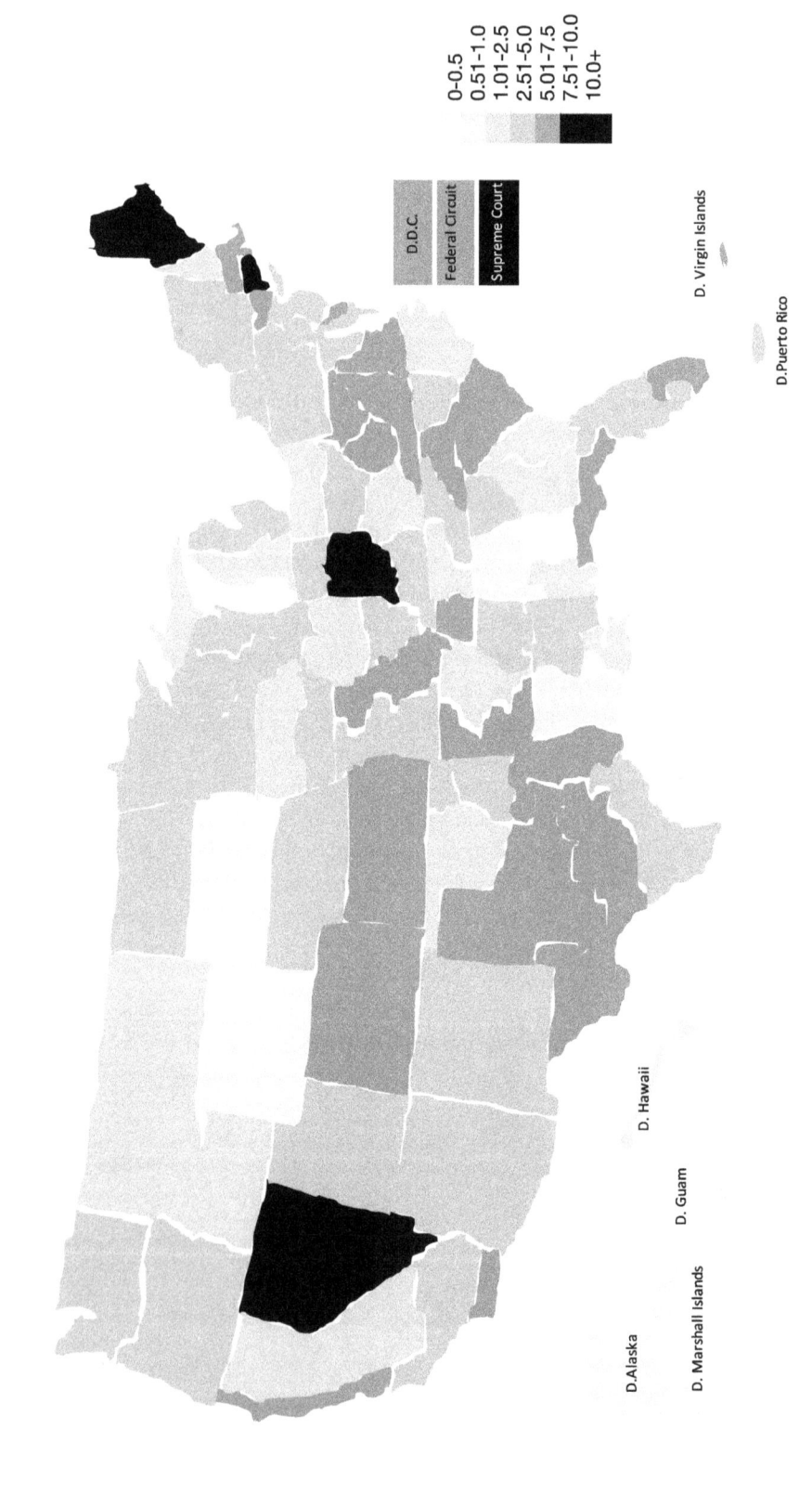

FIGURE 3-4-3 Federal judicial districts by mean importance of patents litigated there.

2005, the USPTO quality metric was solely directed to the correctness of the final output of the examination process that would result in a patent: An allowed application."[109] Efforts at internal performance monitoring and quality control evolved into more detailed analyses of the patent examination process. From 2005 to 2009, an internal USPTO team from the Office of Patent Quality Assurance performed random reviews of examiner performance based on two quality metrics: (1) correctness of allowance decisions, and (2) quality of prosecution decisions.[110] In 2011, the USPTO adopted a new measurement of examination quality called the Composite Quality Metric, made up of seven factors: (1) The final disposition review, (2) the in-process review, (3) the first action on the merits (FAOM) search review, (4) the complete FAOM review, (5) the external quality survey, (6) the internal quality survey, and (7) an aggregation of five factors from the USPTO's Quality Index Report (QIR).[111] In 2015, the USPTO further refined its efforts to improve patent examination quality, notably by closely monitoring individual examiner metrics.[112] Finally, in 2016, the USPTO announced its intention to employ more sophisticated data mining methods during fiscal year 2017 to monitor examination quality during the examination process.[113] Recently, the USPTO released a variety of patent analytics tools on its "Open Data Portal," a beta version of the website they hope to offer in the near future.[114] For example, the agency has made many patent data visualizations available to users, who may customize their searches and visualizations thereof.[115] Although the USPTO has only recently begun to use patent analytics in a systematic way, it is likely to rely more heavily for its own decision making on sophisticated patent analytics in the future, as well as making more patent data open and freely available to the public.

III FRONTIERS OF PATENT ANALYTICS

Big data has captured the imagination of business leaders and researchers from around the world. Improvements in storage, processing, and sharing of large-scale data have led to concomitant changes in machine learning, artificial intelligence (AI) and data analytics. In 2011, McKinsey & Company predicted massive job demand for skills in computer programming, data engineering, statistics, and machine learning (ML).[116] This prognostication didn't overestimate. If anything, it underestimated. Glassdoor, the well-known job and recruiting website, ranked "data scientist" as the best job in America in 2016.[117] There is hardly any industry untouched by big data, and the patent world is no exception. Over the last ten years,

---

[109] "Patent Quality Metrics for Fiscal Year 2017 and Request for Comments on Improving Patent Quality Measurement," *Federal Register* 81 (58) (2016), available at: www.gpo.gov/fdsys/pkg/FR-2016-03-25/pdf/2016-06851.pdf.
[110] Ibid.
[111] Ibid.
[112] Ibid.
[113] Ibid.
[114] https://developer.uspto.gov/analytics.
[115] https://developer.uspto.gov/visualizations.
[116] This McKinsey & Company report has become an oft-cited report for university leaders, venture capitalists, and entrepreneurs in big data and data science. James Manyika, Michael Chui, Brad Brown, Jacques Bughin, Richard Dobbs, Charles Roxburgh, and Angela Hung Byers, "Big Data: The Next Frontier for Innovation, Competition, and Productivity," McKinsey Global Institute, May 2011, available at: www.mckinsey.com/business-functions/digital-mckinsey/our-insights/big-data-the-next-frontier-for-innovation.
[117] "50 Best Jobs in America," Glassdoor, available at: www.glassdoor.com/List/Best-Jobs-in-America-LST_KQ0,20.htm. Three years later, Glassdoor ranked data scientist as the highest paid entry-level job: https://insights.dice.com/2019/05/21/data-scientist-americas-highest-paying-entry-level-job.

there has been a surge of research papers and academic workshops devoted to new methods in patent analytics. A recent WSDM workshop focused on the difficult but important problem of automatically inferring hierarchical classification systems, like the IPC.[118] The venues for publishing these kinds of papers encompass law, computer science, and business. Over this same ten-year period, there has been a similar growth in patent startups specializing in analytics, including those mentioned earlier in this chapter: PatentVector, Juristat, Ocean Tomo, Lex Machina, Patsnap, LegionPatent, Trea, and others. Larger corporations in this space, such as Thomson Reuters (now Clarivate) and LexisNexis, have been acquiring legal analytics companies that extract value from patents.[119]

Venture capitalist investment and new university degrees and programs are pointing in the direction of continued growth in big data and AI.[120] This will impact the innovation that we will see in patent analytics. Students of patent law are now being introduced to data science concepts and skills.[121] They are learning to code, query databases, and run ML software. This will reduce the accessibility barriers for legal practitioners wanting to analyze, for example, the entirety of a patent portfolio over time or the emerging topics within a new field of technology. Probabilistic topic modeling is a popular technique that data scientists use to automatically extract key terms in a corpus of documents.[122] This kind of analysis used to require years of experience in computer science and natural language programming, but the tools and training of these tools have improved dramatically over the last five years.

Because of the unique features of patent data discussed earlier in this chapter, data science professors often use patents in textbooks and in the classroom. The data is open, well-structured,[123] contains full text, and has linked entities for graph analysis. This is ideal for demonstrating how to calculate network centrality or extracting word-embedding in a corpus of documents. Patents are one of a handful of standardized data sets that students of data science are exposed to in their training. This in turn leads to increased interest and innovation in patent analytics.

Nice, benchmark data for predictive algorithms and visualization techniques is not sufficient, though, for spurring company development in this space. There must also be a need in the market. This need seems to exist. Lawyers, examiners, and inventors spend considerable time and money exploring prior art. Given the exponential growth of patents and the high cost for identifying relevant prior art, there is a demand for solutions that can quickly mine the full patent literature for related claims. Large companies are using AI to access their multi-million-dollar IP portfolios. Small companies need to access the novelty of their claims across the full patent landscape before risking their limited funding. Government agencies need to stay abreast of movements in the patent world in order to better forecast and invest in emerging technology. Patent officers have to stay one step ahead of inventors and companies

---

[118] "Web-Scale Classification: Classifying Big Data from the Web," LSHTC, February 28, 2014, available at: http://lshtc.iit.demokritos.gr/WSDM_WS.

[119] LexisNexis, for example, acquired PatentCore in 2014: www.ipwatchdog.com/2014/07/02/lexisnexis-acquires-patent-data-analytics-innovator-patentcore/id=50271.

[120] Jevin D. West and Jason Portenoy, "The Data Gold Rush in Higher Education," in *Big Data is Not a Monolith*, eds. Cassidy R. Sugimoto, Hamid R. Ekbia, and Michael Mattioli (Cambridge, MA: MIT Press, 2016).

[121] P. Gowder, "Teaching Data Science for Lawyers with Caselaw Access Project Data," 2019, available at: https://lil.law.harvard.edu/blog/2019/07/09/teaching-data-science-for-lawyers-with-caselaw-access-project-data.

[122] Mark Steyvers and Tom Griffiths, "Probabilistic Topic Models," *Handbook of Latent Semantic Analysis* 427 (7) (2007): 424–440.

[123] Well-structured data has consistency across individual entities of a data set. For example, nearly all patents will have the same metadata: titles, abstracts, inventors, examiners, etc. This consistency from one patent to the next, over time, allows data scientists to reliably query and analyze millions of patents at once.

so they can perform their gatekeeper roles of novelty. This becomes increasingly difficult as the patent corpus expands but the patent office budget remains constant.

In our view, the patent analytic world of startups and new methods is a response to all these needs. Lawyers, examiners, governments, and patent-holding companies want to save money and make better decisions on intellectual property. This is big data's big promise. The following subsections explain a few ways in which these tools are being applied to the patent literature in order to fulfill this promise.

A *The Patent Sandbox*

The potential for patent analytics is only as good as the data. There has been substantial research and commercial effort developing new user interfaces and statistical methods for predicting and visualizing patent value. But none of these new applications will be of any use if the raw document data is not consistent, transparent, and available for development. This is not unique to patents. This is the case for nearly any industry touched by big data. In 1998, the Commerce Secretary William Daley announced that they were going to make 20 million patents and trademark documents open free to the public.[124] The goal was to make the government more transparent and responsive to the IP market. This decision to make the patent data available led to a flurry of innovation in both the private and public markets. Since that decision, the patent corpus has grown and the quality of the data has improved. The most current versions are found at the USPTO website and partner organizations.[125] For data scientists and entrepreneurs, the data is machine-readable in well-structured XML data.[126] Compared to similar data sets in research and medicine, patents are remarkably consistent over time and are central to the innovation markets globally. When compared to the scientific literature, it is far more comprehensive and reliable. The scientific literature varies from field to field in terms of availability and metadata. This makes patent data an especially attractive data set for the growing population of data scientists and businesses looking to extract new value out of government-released data sets.

The patent corpus is also manageable. The full corpus, including full text documents, is less than 20 terabytes. It includes granted patents and patent applications back to the eighteenth century up to the current year. That may sound like a lot, but the tools available for handling data at this scale can be used in easy-to-access cloud applications. When compared to something like the Large Hadron Collider, which collects more than 40 terabytes *per second*, the entire patent database is relatively small. However, measuring the number of bytes does not reveal the full story. The bulk download of all patents in the world may be small compared to just one day at the Hadron Collider, but the patent data is rich and complex. It is a large graph at its core and has multiple dimensions for analysis. It can be combined with other data sets, such as scholarly literature, news items, and other non-patent literature through its references, inventors, institutions, and subject areas, which increases its complexity. The small number of terabytes quickly becomes messy and unruly again when one includes these additional dimensions.

---

[124] USPTO, "USPTO to Make Comprehensive Patent and Trademark Data Available Free on the Internet," 1998, available at: www.uspto.gov/about-us/news-updates/uspto-make-comprehensive-patent-and-trademark-data-available-free-internet.

[125] USPTO, "Bulk Data Products," 2015, available at: www.uspto.gov/learning-and-resources/bulk-data-products.

[126] Extensible markup language (XML) is a structured set of rules for storing data that is both human readable, and most importantly, machine-readable. For more details on XML, see Dolin – XML in Law: The Role of Standards in Legal Informatics, *supra*.

In a patent citation graph, patents are nodes and citations are links. This graph property of the patent corpus provides unique opportunities for analysis. From 1976 onwards, there are approximately five million utility patents, half a million design patents, and various other patents including plant patents, reissue patents, statutory invention registration (SIR) patents, and defensive publication (DEF) patents. In sum, there are nearly 100 million patents, with approximately 15 million non-patent citations.[127] Of the 100 million citations, approximately 20% of the patents come directly from the examiners. This makes for an especially interesting feature for analysis when looking at network influence measures (see Section III.C). One can, for example, only view the citation graph from the examiners. This provides an alternative view to the citation graph assembled by inventors and lawyers. One could ask whether examiner networks are more reliable when assessing novelty and influence or whether the examiner graphs provide insight into obfuscation and hidden trends in technology.

As noted throughout this chapter, the patent data is unique in its consistency and availability. Nevertheless, there are many "cleaning" steps that must be taken before it is ready for analysis. Cleaning is a common process in any analytics pipeline, and patent data cleaning is no exception. This includes the identification of data input errors (e.g., missing data, misspelled inventors, dates that include years in the future, etc.). It is this cleaning process that consumes the bulk of the effort. If data is not properly handled, spurious findings will inevitably result. "Garbage in, garbage out … " as the saying goes.

Going forward, we encourage the community of scholars and data scientists working with this data to share these cleaning steps and techniques more broadly.

More specifically, *data cleaning* adds missing data, removes fields that were added in one year but not another, and collates variant data. There are always problems when translating text, names, addresses, etc. to digital form, but even when the translation is perfect, problems can persist. As an example, let's focus on company names. They are just one of the many data features available in the patent data, but they illustrate how difficult this one feature can be. Frustratingly, company names can be listed in numerous different ways, making it difficult to assign ownership. International Business Machines (IBM), for example, is a company name that has been written more than 25 different ways over the last couple decades.[128] This creates a problem called *fuzzy matching*, whereby approximate strings need to be found and incorporated into the data set. There are various tools for solving this problem, including proprietary data sets with pre-cleaned data.[129] Calculating the Levenshtein distance is another common approach to solving this problem, but this method can be computationally expensive.[130] Cleaning can also take considerable time even for small data sets, so approximate solutions have been proposed.[131] Fortunately, the two languages of data science, R and Python, have many different libraries for implementing various forms of this algorithm.

[127] Non-patent citations are citations to publications that are not patents (e.g., scholarly literature, reports, news items, manuals, product catalogues, etc.).
[128] Such names include "IBM," "International Business Machines," "International Business Machines Corporation," and more.
[129] Clarivate, formerly Thomson-Reuters' Intellectual Property and Science division, provides these kinds of data sets. However, even these cleaned data sets include inconsistencies.
[130] Влади́мир И. Левенштейн (1965). Двоичные коды с исправлением выпадений, вставок и замещений символов [Binary Codes Capable of Correcting Deletions, Insertions, and Reversals]. Доклады Академий Наук СССР (in Russian) 163 (4): 845–848. Appeared in English as: Vladimir I. Levenshtein, "Binary Codes Capable of Correcting Deletions, Insertions, and Reversals," *Soviet Physics Doklady* 10 (8) (1966): 707–710.
[131] Robert A. Wagner and Michael J. Fischer, "The String-to-String Correction Problem," *Journal of the ACM* 21 (1) (1974): 168–173, available at: https://dl.acm.org/citation.cfm?id=321811.

The fuzzy matching problem is not unique to company names. Inventors, examiners, lawyers, and law firms can have multiple ways of listing their names. Sometimes middle initials are included. Sometimes not. Sometimes abbreviations are used. Sometimes not. Even when a fairly unique data set has been created, there are issues in knowing who owns what or who invented what. Because there is no law requiring companies to publicly advertise patent ownership, analyses that utilize these attributes are always fraught with uncertainties. In 2013, President Obama attempted to solve this problem by announcing executive actions, including improving attributable patent ownership, that may lead to cleaner, more reliable data sets and analyses.[132]

Another common cleaning task involves matching non-patent citations to their sources. This can be important for analyses that utilize the patent citation network (see Section III.C). As noted, this includes more than 15 million citations from the patent corpus. Scientific journals are written and cited in many different ways (e.g., "Journal of Neuroscience," "J. Neuroscience"). Reconciling these names is a difficult task, because without clarity it becomes difficult to make claims about what is being cited by patents outside the patent literature. This is important for identifying influential works algorithmically, for technology forecasting, and for identifying individuals and institutions contributing to the innovation ecosystem.

In sum, the form and accessibility of the patent data, both in the USA and abroad, has spurred new patent analytic methods and applications. As barriers to this data continue to fall, data scientists will not be the only professionals mapping vector embeddings, performing topic modeling, or visualizing large citation networks.

B Learning in the Patent Sandbox

Few things are hotter in technology than machine learning and its parent field of AI. Journalists report daily on advancements and implications of AI. Businesses now use AI frequently in marketing campaigns and in sales pitches. The patent analytic space is no exception. Many of the companies noted above employ and advertise the application of AI to patents. We tend to think both AI and AI as applied to patents are a little oversold, but what is clear is a flurry of activity in the patent analytic space. This is partly due to genuinely useful applications of ML to patents. It is also driven by the commoditization of ML methods applying AI approaches to patent data. Even just ten years ago, it would be difficult to employ a neural network unless you had an advanced degree or extensive experience in computer science. That is different now, with the surge of new cloud computing tools (AWS, Azure) that allow easy access to ML software packages, GPUs,[133] cheap storage, etc. This will continue to remove the barriers to entry for patent analytics. Before, it would take substantial investment in time and money to create a data environment for analyzing large-scale patent data. Now, it only takes a connection to a cloud computing platform and a little experience with ML. These lowering barriers will accelerate even faster innovation in patent analytics.

Machine learning, at its core, is a rather simple idea. Traditionally, a computer program produces output data when given a computer program and a set of input data. Machine

---

[132] USPTO, "USPTO-Led Executive Actions on High Tech Patent Issues," www.uspto.gov/patent/initiatives/uspto-led-executive-actions-high-tech-patent-issues#heading-2.

[133] GPUs are graphical processing units, often used for those using neural networks to make predictions. Cloud computing services such as Amazon's AWS and Microsoft's Azure platform have made access to these computing resources much more attainable. This in turn has created an environment of ML apps and services.

learning flips this paradigm on its head: the computer program itself is what is produced, using the output and input data for a given problem. This inferred computer program can then be used to make predictions when given a new set of input data.[134] This paradigm switch has created an explosion of innovation in automation and prediction. In the last ten years, there has been a resurgence of neural networks. In fact, there has been a resurgence of AI more broadly. A couple decades ago, AI entered a "winter" phase[135] in which funding and interest in the field waned due to overpromises and setbacks. The resurgence over the last decade has been driven primarily by the availability of massive amounts of data – the fuel for these ML algorithms. Many of the standard ML methods, such as k-nearest neighbors, logistic regression, and naive Bayes, have been around for decades.[136] Neural networks have also been around a long time, but again it is the data that has driven a new phase in AI research. The same methods being applied to self-driving cars, medical diagnoses, and translating foreign languages can also be used on patents for predicting patents likely to garner high license fees, or patent applications likely to make it through examiner gatekeepers.

The research communities in computer science have begun adopting patents as one of their model data sets. This will also facilitate more innovation in patent analytics. Papers at the top ML conferences (ICML, KDD, NIPS) focused on law, intellectual property, and patents are showing up more commonly.[137] Basic prediction tasks are being explored. Instead of just finding all patents with "shoe" in the title, ML could aid in predicting when the next shoe patent will be granted, how influential the patent will be, and which companies will likely have similar patents with different descriptions of shoes. There exist several patent search engines that provide these basic searches. The USPTO hosts their own search engine. LexisNexis offers an array of tools for interrogating the patent corpus and related data sets connected to the patent corpus, such as examiner notes and searches. Google patents offers an interface for looking at prior art or finding non-patent citations using the metadata of a patent.[138] Patent search and the application of ML on patents will continue to grow and become standard in any patent product.

For patents, there are many other tasks than just search that could be good places to apply ML approaches. One may want to predict whether a patent will be litigated, whether certain claims will be invalidated, or whether there are missing citations and prior art. The tasks are innumerable, but the ways of measuring a program's performance are more confined. This is due to well-developed methods for formalizing learning and measuring the performance of learning in ML. These methods can be broken down into two primary classes: supervised and unsupervised learning.[139] For *supervised* methods, the known outcomes have labels, and the output data is provided. For example, when differentiating spam email from non-spam email, supervised ML algorithms require a set of labels denoting emails that are spam, and another set denoting emails that are not spam. For patents, a supervised example might be predicting

---

[134] Pedro Domingos, "A Few Useful Things to Know about Machine Learning," *Communications of the ACM* 55 (10) (2012): 78–87.
[135] "AI Winter," *Wikipedia*, available at: https://en.wikipedia.org/wiki/AI_winter (accessed June 9, 2020).
[136] Ian H. Witten and Eibe Frank, eds., *Data Mining* (San Francisco, CA: Elsevier, 2005).
[137] The top academic conferences in machine learning are Knowledge Discovery and Data Mining (KDD), International Conference on Machine Learning (ICML), and Neural Information Processing Systems (NIPS). The 2016 NIPS conference held a symposium on "Machine Learning and the Law." Surprisingly, there have been few articles on patents within KDD.
[138] Metadata includes things like the title, inventors, lawyers, class codes, etc. It does not include the full text, abstract, claims, figures, or any other content.
[139] Some scholars classify most unsupervised methods as *data mining* techniques rather than ML, but for this chapter, and indeed throughout this whole volume, we simply refer to it as unsupervised ML.

whether a patent will be litigated. To do this, we would need example patents that have been litigated and example patents that have not been litigated. We would then need to identify a set of features of the data set that affect the litigation outcomes. Features for predicting litigation could include patent owner, inventor, industry classification, the number of citations, or type of patent (e.g., utility, design, plant). Techniques for identifying the features with the most predictive power exist. This can be useful when designing new patent interfaces that highlight important elements of a patent for an examiner or inventor in a new field.

Unsupervised ML problems do not involve labels but are also useful in the patent analytic space. There are no preset "labeled" answers for learning in these types of problems. There is no data set that reveals whether a patent has been litigated or not. Automatically identifying subject areas is an example of an unsupervised problem. Although labels do exist for fields identified by the patent office, we know that there exist far more categories for patents than are available for inventors. But we don't have labels for all these additional fields. Computer scientists and data scientists have been working on this problem for decades. Patent clustering using text or citations, principal component analysis (PCA), and topic modeling are examples that have no preset ground truth.[140] The goals of these methods – sometimes referred to as data mining and exploration – are to find groups, or clusters, of related patents. The relatedness of grouped patents is determined using features of the patents or citations, such as text within them, that can link the patents together. In the following subsection, we explain citation methods in greater depth.

C Patent Networks

The network property of patents, where nodes are patents and citations are links, is one of the most beautiful and useful properties of the patent literature. It represents the millions of decisions made by inventors and examiners about identifying prior art. It provides important, contextual information on what patents are important and what patents are related. For patent analytics, it is this network property that holds special promise for future developments.

This network property is a result of the legal duty of inventors, law firms, and examiners to acknowledge prior art. The patent system formalizes these acknowledgments via citations and footnotes. These references can be to other patents within the same country, or to patents in other countries. These citations can also be to non-patent publications, such as academic papers, newspapers, product catalogues, books, blogs, etc. In the period from 1976 to 2016, more than 5.7 million US patents published more than 127 million citations to other patent and non-patent entities – more than 20 citations, on average, per patent. In network science, this number is called the *out-degree*. The average out-degree of patent networks is similar to the out-degree of scholarly citation networks (i.e., the length of the reference list is roughly the same). However, the *in-degree*, the number of incoming citations to each node, is much higher for patents compared to academic citation networks.[141] This is likely due to the requirement that patents cite prior art, in contrast to academic papers, for example, for which this is not a legal requirement. This network property makes it highly attractive for

---

[140] Some studies claim to have ground truth for clustering. For example, Jure Leskovic at Stanford University has several data sets in the Stanford Large Network Dataset Collection (SNAP) with "ground truth" labels; see https://snap.stanford.edu/data.

[141] The in-degree of a node is also a metric for measuring the centrality of a given node. The centrality of a node approximates the influence, or importance, of a given node in the network. For patents, this is one way of measuring the importance of each patent.

assessing the influence of individual nodes (patents) and for automatically detecting communities within the full corpus of patents.

Figure 3.4.4 shows an example citation network.[142] It illustrates how the patent corpus can be viewed and explored, demonstrating the future of patent analytics. The data is a sample of scholarly papers from JSTOR.org. It includes 98 papers (nodes) from climate change research, and 328 citations (links) between those papers. Panel (a) shows papers from the field of economics. The larger circles represent papers that are more influential, determined by the citations to that given paper. Citations from other papers that have also received many citations carry more weight. Panel (b) includes the citation links between the papers. One can see a natural clustering of four groups. These groups are determined by the citations connecting the given papers, and by the layout algorithm employed for this interactive visualization. The particular algorithm used for this visualization arranges nodes directly cited by the paper in question to the left, and nodes directly citing others to the right. These kinds of citation network figures are inspiring similar work using patent data and patent citations.

Citations provide clues to the importance of patents. A patent cited 100 times is likely more valuable than citations cited fewer than 10 times, assuming the two patents are published in the same year in approximately the same category. But we can do better than just count citations. The position of a patent in the citation network can provide additional information. Patents that are cited by other important patents provide an additional signal of importance. The idea of, not just counting citations, but also the source of citations is the idea at the heart of Google's famous PageRank algorithm.[143] This algorithm ranks websites based on the hyperlinks between web pages – similar to the role that references and citations play in the patent literature and scholarly literature. Pages earn a higher influential score when they are linked to by many other websites that are also cited many times. Pages earn lower scores if they are not cited, or when they are cited by less influential pages. The authors of this chapter are involved in a project and company called PatentVector that ranks patents based on an idea similar to PageRank. It ranks patents based on their position in the citation network, with several modifications to correct for the time-directedness of patent citation networks. A random visitor to this network could continue walking backward in time if they followed citation links. This is different than the standard PageRank algorithm, which can cycle through hyperlink pathways. The network-based ranking of PatentVector provides improved accuracy compared to simple citation counts like PageRank.[144] Nevertheless, citation counts have also been shown to correlate with patent influence, and one study shows a relationship between these rankings and the court level of litigation for patents.[145] Patents that litigate at the highest court (the US Supreme Court) tend to have higher PatentVector scores, which suggests a link between patent value and citation-based metrics. In addition to ranking, PatentVector has produced a set of unsupervised ML algorithms for identifying patent communities. This provides needed context when comparing patents across time and across the technology landscape. These methods cluster patents based on their citation profiles. Patents that cite each other and receive citations from similar patents are more likely to be in

---

[142] The visualization was created by Jason Portenoy, a PhD student in the DataLab at the University of Washington. The interactive version is available at: http://students.washington.edu/jporteno/jstor/citation_graph.html.
[143] Lawrence Page, Sergey Brin, Rajeev Motwani, and Terry Winograd, "The PageRank Citation Ranking: Bringing Order to the Web," Technical Report, Stanford InfoLab, 1999.
[144] Ian Wesley-Smith, Carl T. Bergstrom, and Jevin D. West, "Static Ranking of Scholarly Papers using Article-Level Eigenfactor (ALEF)," presented at the WSDM Conference: Entity Ranking Challenge Workshop, 2016.
[145] Torrance and West, "All Patents Great and Small," *supra* note 25.

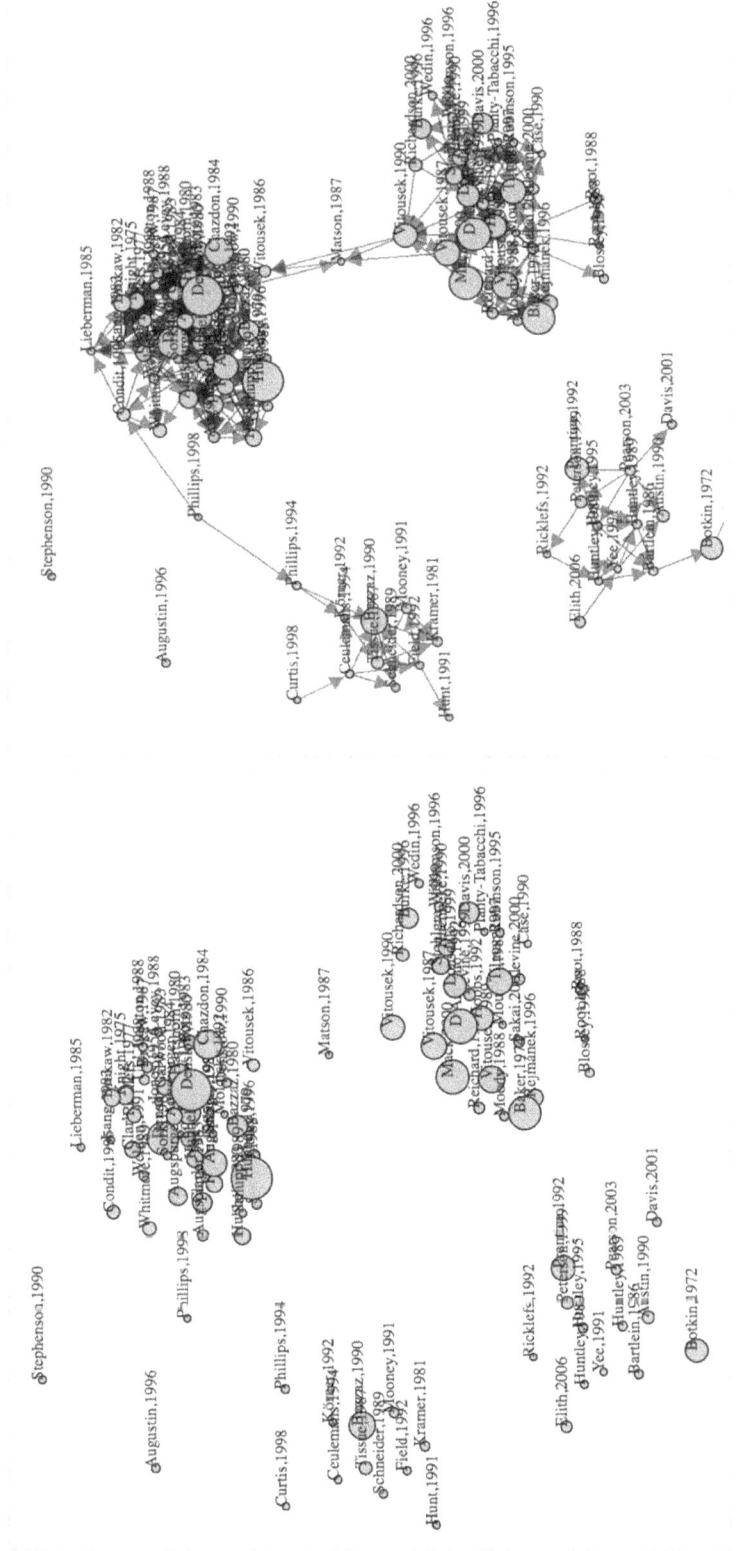

FIGURE 3.4.4 An example citation network.

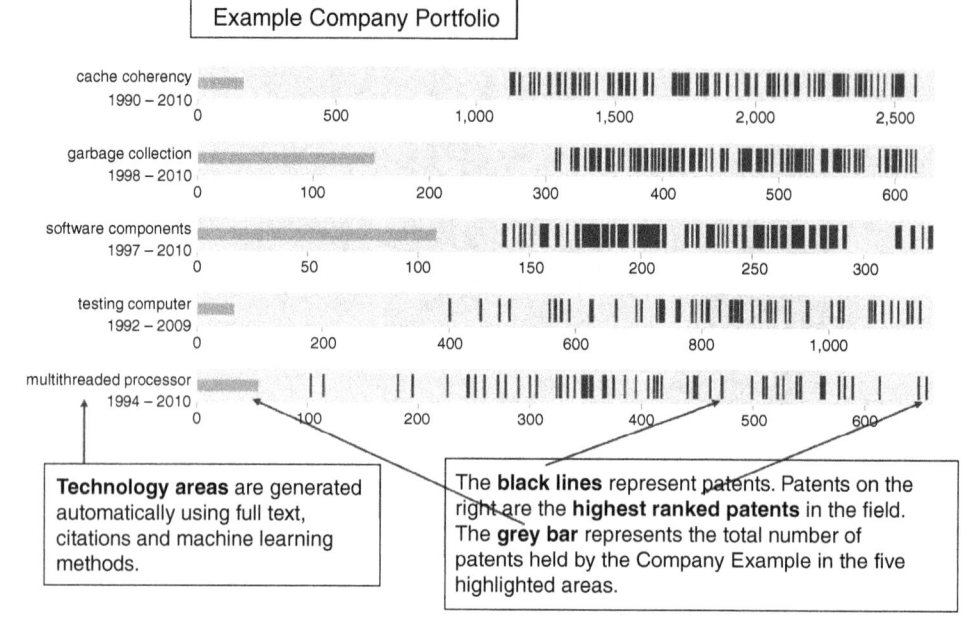

FIGURE 3.4.5 Automatic categorization[146]

the same cluster, or patent community. It can do this hierarchically – top-level fields with sublevels below the top fields – building off the original InfoMap algorithm.[147]

Figure 3.4.5 shows how automatic categorization can be used to analyze portfolios. The five horizontal bars represent a sample of different technology areas for a given company. The fields are determined by using the patent citation network. The field labels are automatically determined using standard *tf-idf* (term frequency – inverse document frequency) methods. This is a common method from the field of information retrieval. A *tf-idf* determines the terms that best describe a set of documents, given the term usage in the given group and the rest of the population. The black lines indicate the ranked list of patents owned by the example company. The patents are in order from most important (right side of horizontal bars) to least important (left side of horizontal bars).[148]

These levels can be used to automatically classify technology areas and recommend similar patents.[149] This is important, especially for fields that change faster than the patent office can create new subject areas. These methods have also been shown to perform well against the multitude of other community detection algorithms.[150] These classifications do not depend on USPTO classifications, or on IPC categories. They are determined by looking at the citations in order to form groups, and then examining the abstract and its claims in order to determine labels for the company. This provides a more objective approach for determining the all-important category for a patent. This allows comparison of patents at a resolution not

---

[146] Image adapted from PatentVector, www.patentvector.com.
[147] Martin Rosvall, Daniel Axelsson, and Carl T. Bergstrom, "The Map Equation," *European Physical Journal Special Topics* 178 (1) (2009): 13–23.
[148] For more on tf-idf, *see* Nay – Natural Language Processing and Machine Learning for Legal Texts, *supra*.
[149] Jevin D. West, Ian Wesley-Smith, and Carl T. Bergstrom, "A Recommendation System Based on Hierarchical Clustering of an Article-Level Citation Network," *IEEE Transactions on Big Data* 2 (2) (2016): 113–123.
[150] Andrea Lancichinetti, Santo Fortunato, and Filippo Radicchi, "Benchmark Graphs for Testing Community Detection Algorithms," *Physical Review E* 78 (4) (2008).

available before. However, there are challenges with the automatic approach: (1) It is difficult to verify at scale; and (2) most automatic categorization methods only allow a patent into one category. Methods are currently being developed for allowing multiple designations.

In addition to auto-categorization, visualization tools have been developed for viewing the patent landscapes generated from this hierarchical clustering map. Other unsupervised methods include mapping patent technology areas using semantic similarity and information-theoretic measures such as KL-divergence. These measures can be used to compare keyword distributions for patents or groups of patents. The next big challenge for this emerging area of patent analytics will be validating these new methods, and helping practitioners use and interpret these techniques in everyday practice.

IV CONCLUSION

Patents are legal documents that, for historical and legal reasons, have a long history of standardized format and richness of informational content. Although mountains of patent data have accumulated over the centuries, until recently the analysis of this data remained the artisanally subjective and qualitative domain of patent attorneys. Improvements in computing power, data analysis, statistical methods, and algorithms in recent years have led directly to the rapid creation of the field of patent analytics. Increasingly, objective data-backed analyses are augmenting, or sometimes replacing, the opinions of patent attorneys and other patent analysts. The more this occurs, the more the speed, cost, and accuracy of patent analysis improves. Patent analytics is transforming a field ripe with data riches, and not a moment too soon.

B.

Litigation and E-discovery

3.5

The Core Concepts of E-discovery

Jonathan Kerry-Tyerman and A. J. Shankar

Electronic discovery (e-discovery) is an integral component of legal informatics, touching on everything from search and artificial intelligence to design and legal services transformation. Any discussion of electronic discovery must begin with an explanation of its relevance to legal work. E-discovery – also known as "ediscovery" or, somewhat datedly, "eDiscovery" – is the discovery in legal proceedings of evidence in an electronic format. Due to the nature of modern technology, e-discovery encompasses an overwhelming majority of evidence, such that e-discovery and other forms of discovery have become virtually synonymous. As such, legal discovery is now fraught with issues concerning how information is stored, retrieved, exchanged, and generally made accessible to parties during legal proceedings.[1] A common challenge for attorneys is what to do with a multi-terabyte collection of evidence that consists of millions of documents across hundreds of file types, with only a matter of months before their first depositions. The best solutions to this kind of increasingly common challenge will include recourse to big data and machine learning, which are discussed in this chapter.

This chapter is divided into four major sections. Section I covers the basics of e-discovery, framed by the ubiquitous Electronic Discovery Reference Model. Section II turns to several of the core technical concepts in the e-discovery process, including text encodings, production protocols, and duplicate definition and detection. This is followed by Section III, an exploration of the relevant technologies central to efficient and effective e-discovery – such as cloud computing, encryption, transcoding, machine translation, and machine learning – and the modern design approaches that make this high-powered technology accessible to busy legal professionals. We close with some thoughts on the future of e-discovery in Section IV.

I E-DISCOVERY BASICS

In nearly any field, there are noble attempts to capture and distill the complexity of the work involved into models, frameworks, templates, guides, or other generalizable representations. While these efforts are never without flaws – they are always short of the full truth – they are nonetheless useful approximations. When used correctly, tools like these create common ground for discussion, analysis, and ultimately improvement of the underlying processes.

In e-discovery, we are fortunate to have the Electronic Discovery Reference Model, commonly referred to as the EDRM. It was first promulgated by a group of e-discovery and legal professionals in 2006 and has been revised several times since then; the latest version, 3.0, was released in 2014. Recently acquired by the Duke University School of Law and

---

[1] For more details on the processing of electronic data, *see* Bommarito – Preprocessing Data, *supra*.

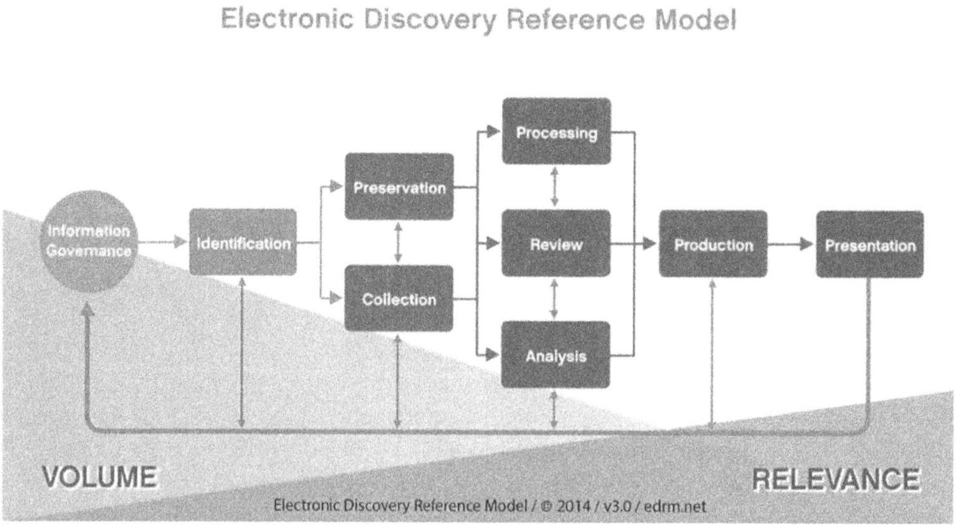

Electronic Discovery Reference Model

FIGURE 3.5.1 The EDRM

integrated into the school's Center for Judicial Studies, EDRM[2] has developed a number of complementary models, frameworks, and standards for everything from metrics to ethical decision making.

Over the years, the EDRM (Figure 3.5.1) has become the standard for understanding the different components of the e-discovery process. It still suffers from the same shortcomings endemic to any model, but it has nonetheless proven relevant enough to real-world practice to stand the test of time.

The EDRM begins with *information governance*, the management of original information within an organization, and it ends with *presentation*, the use of information as evidence in litigation. The EDRM is intended to be descriptive, rather than prescriptive, and is therefore not necessarily to be followed literally in every case; there may be some situations in which a different order of processes is warranted, or where some steps may be skipped altogether. Additionally, the EDRM is designed to reflect the iterative nature of the underlying work; many steps will repeat several times as the approach to a particular matter evolves and refines itself.

In general, the tasks on the left-hand side of the EDRM (i.e., information governance, identification, preservation, and collection) use a technical toolset that remains separate from the toolset used for all the tasks on the right-hand side of the model. Because of this, e-discovery practitioners commonly refer to each side as a distinct unit (e.g., "The left-hand side of the EDRM"). We will also use this shorthand as we discuss the components of the EDRM.

A *The Left-Hand Side of the EDRM*

The left-hand side of the EDRM is, for the most part, the domain of corporations. This is because a corporation in typical US litigation holds the data that the parties want to discover.

---

[2] The parent organization of EDRM is also called EDRM.

The goal of the tasks on this side is to prepare for potential litigation and to quickly respond when litigation arises.

The technological issues for these e-discovery tasks are primarily search-related rather than discovery-related. Search powers data management at its source, the identification and preservation of potentially relevant data within that source environment, and the ultimate retrieval of that information from those sources. The true discovery work – separating the wheat from the chaff using a nuanced understanding of what's actually relevant in the litigation – is the province of the right-hand side of the EDRM.

1 Information Governance

Information governance refers to the process of housing and organizing information within an organization – everything from emails and voicemails to spreadsheets and instant messages – and deciding whether and what to delete over time. This stage is so complex, however, that the EDRM organization created an entirely separate model, the Information Governance Reference Model, to frame the discussion around the activities it contains.[3]

As you might expect, information governance is a collaborative exercise involving close coordination between the people creating and using the data (i.e., business users), the people managing the infrastructure that contains that data (i.e., the IT department), and the people responsible for looking ahead to possible legal or regulatory risks that may involve that data (i.e., the legal and compliance teams). As the EDRM organization itself notes in the annotations to the Information Governance Reference Model, "it takes the coordinated effort of all three groups to defensibly dispose of a piece of information that has outlived its usefulness, and retain what *is* useful in a way that enables accessibility and usability for the business user."[4] In particular, individuals in an organization must work together to ensure that they are not retaining redundant, obsolete, or trivial information that has no business or legal value.[5]

The tools in this space are wide-ranging. End-users will of course use whatever they need to perform their work, from Outlook to AutoCAD, and will store their work product in many different places, from laptops to Dropbox. The IT and legal departments work behind the scenes to tame this wilderness, using technology baked into their document management platforms (e.g., Office 365's Security & Compliance Center; Google Vault) and/or dedicated information governance tools (e.g., Rational Governance; Sherpa Software's Altitude IG). Whatever software is used, the overriding goal is to minimize legal exposure from ROT data by defining defensible retention policies and then automating enforcement of those policies.

2 Identification

The *identification* stage of the EDRM is primarily concerned with determining which sources of information are likely to be relevant to a given matter. In contrast to the more general preparatory work that occurs as part of the information governance stage, what is critical is that by the time the identification stage is reached, there is now a matter at hand and all efforts become focused on the specific, evolving demands of that particular matter.

---

[3] EDRM, "Information Governance Reference Model," available at: www.edrm.net/frameworks-and-standards/information-governance-reference-model.

[4] Ibid.

[5] Redundant, obsolete, and/or trivial information is often referred to by a useful acronym: ROT data.

One cannot identify potentially relevant sources of information without an inventory of those sources, and that is the purpose of a *data map*. The data map provides a comprehensive picture of an organization's data sources – everything from email servers to financial systems to backup tapes – as well as the devices used to access them. It accounts for legacy data from systems no longer in use, and the hardware, software, and technical expertise that may be required to access such data. It also includes an assessment of potential cloud and third-party data sources. Much of the work here is done with the common tools used to create inventories in *any* domain: spreadsheet or project management software may be used to plan and track the interviews of key witnesses and custodians; presentation or mind-mapping software may be used to visualize the data map; email or IM software may be used to communicate about interviews, time frames, and keywords; shared folders may serve as repositories for relevant data retention policies, organization charts, etc.; and the ultimate inventory of identified data sources may be kept in a spreadsheet, database, or simple list.

3 Preservation

Once relevant data sources have been identified, the *preservation* process will hold on to potentially relevant data in a way that is defensible and compliant with legal obligations, without overburdening the custodians of that data or individuals in the wider organization. The ultimate goal of this step is to mitigate risk, and this involves a delicate balance between the organization's legal obligations and its desire for efficiency and minimal legal exposure. A preservation scheme that is disproportionately broad, for example, will not only waste resources both human and otherwise, but may also lead to the unnecessary retention of risky data. This stage is therefore as much about what should be *deleted* as what should be *preserved*, with a bias toward removal whenever it is reasonable, auditable, and legally defensible to do so.

Despite its outsized importance, the most common preservation techniques are relatively unsophisticated. They involve contacting relevant custodians, usually by email, with instructions not to delete certain data from their systems – known as a *legal hold* notice. While there are some simple tools that can automate the legal hold process – such as administrators sending initial and reminder emails to the appropriate people with just a few clicks of the mouse – the task of actually retaining the relevant data falls to the end-user. The information governance tools and business productivity platforms mentioned above offer more advanced integration, not only simplifying the process of issuing legal holds but also managing the actual retention of target data, since they can be preserved "in place" without the need for copying and archiving elsewhere.

4 Collection

Collection is the process of gathering relevant data from everywhere it resides (e.g., corporate servers, employee laptops, phones, etc.) and doing so in a forensically sound manner. Preservation and collection are shown vertically stacked on the EDRM diagram to indicate that they often happen in parallel. It is easy to imagine why: at some point, preserved data will likely need to be collected and made accessible to legal teams for review, and that process itself may alter the assessment formulated in the identification stage, or expand the scope of required preservation.

The key consideration in collection is defensibility. Has the collection process accounted for all data? Has the data been collected in a forensically sound way, properly preserving the original metadata to the fullest extent possible? Can we document the chain of custody? These are serious questions that speak to the very credibility of the data as digital evidence. It is therefore not surprising that collection is the province of an entire field of experts steeped in defensible data retrieval, and that such retrieval is often entrusted only to these experts.

Even collection tools are often highly specialized. Anyone can transfer files from a laptop to a thumb drive using Windows Explorer, or download email from a Gmail account using Google Takeout. But what about collecting this data in a forensically sound manner? To meet this challenge, the digital forensics industry has created an endless array of tools, from general purpose suites like Access Data's Forensic Toolkit (FTK), to specialized software like Elcomsoft Cloud eXplorer, which is focused only on gathering Google account data.

B The Right-Hand Side of the EDRM

The right-hand side of the EDRM is primarily the domain of law firms rather than corporations. Whether it's outside counsel for a corporation, counsel representing plaintiffs in litigation, or any other representation configuration, law firms are typically the entities charged with performing the right-hand side tasks. The goal of these tasks is to quickly determine what is relevant to the case, and to move all relevant documents forward, whether in a production to opposing counsel, a list of deposition exhibits, or some other useful format.

The technology challenges underlying these tasks are inherently more complex, requiring true legal expertise to discover what is important. Software can offer tremendous advantages in that endeavor, from normalizing disparate file types to detecting potential mistakes before they're committed, but it is ultimately legal professionals who shoulder the burden of marshalling the best evidence in service of the best arguments. In light of that, the best technology in this space augments human expertise, helping those humans reach better conclusions at a faster rate.

1 Processing[6]

Processing is a broad term for a set of tasks that ultimately aim to convert collected data into a format suitable for review. Processing is the task that brings order to chaos: input is typically unstructured, collected from a variety of systems, in a dizzying array of formats. The data output from the processing stage is clean, normalized, searchable, enhanced data that facilitate rapid and accurate review.

Processing begins with original data as collected in its native format (emails, spreadsheets, calendar appointments, meeting notes, etc.). Steps in the processing task often include:

- unpacking containers, such as forensic disk images, PST mailbox exports, or ZIP files;
- extracting text, including using optical character recognition (OCR) to recognize text as necessary;[7]
- extracting and normalizing metadata;

---

[6] For more details on the processing of electronic data, *see* Bommarito – Preprocessing Data, *supra*.
[7] For more detail on OCR, see Section III.G.

- generating images – typically in TIFF format, but increasingly in PDF – so file contents may be viewed across devices and without native software;
- extracting embedded documents (e.g., email attachments, files inserted into Office documents); and
- detecting foreign languages.

There can also be several additional steps added alongside these, depending on the processing system and the source data. The tools used in processing are as old as e-discovery, and some that are still prevalent today (e.g., LexisNexis LAW PreDiscovery) trace their roots back to the earliest days of e-discovery. Some of these applications are freestanding and flexible (e.g., Nuix; LexisNexis LAW PreDiscovery), whereas others are relatively well integrated into larger suites (e.g., kCura's Relativity Processing; Ipro Tech's eCapture; Everlaw's processing engine). In all cases, the computing horsepower required is fairly substantial, and high throughput is often cited as the chief concern; however, recent advances in cloud-based processing have greatly eased that concern.

2 Review

Review is the heart of the right-hand side of the EDRM, and may be the heart of all of e-discovery. In the review stage the data is examined – often document by document – to determine whether and how it relates to the matter at hand. Compared to the other phases of the process, this stage has yielded very little to automation, and remains the most labor-intensive part of e-discovery, if not of litigation overall. Nevertheless, technology plays a major role in streamlining and enhancing this critical task.

In the context of a party reviewing documents for potential production (e.g., defense counsel, or a government responding to a FOIA request), there are two primary goals. First, the producing party seeks to identify data that must be produced because it is responsive to the requests made. Second, the producing party looks to ferret out any data within the set of responsive data that should be withheld because it is privileged or subject to other protections. Most commonly, the producing party attempts to withhold data subject to one or several of the following:

- **attorney–client privilege:** confidential communications between a person seeking legal advice from a professional legal advisor;
- **work-product doctrine:** materials prepared in anticipation of litigation or for trial;
- **trade secret protection:** confidential information whose value depends upon it remaining secret, and which the owner has taken reasonable measures to protect;
- **privacy law:** information protected by a right to privacy (e.g., financial information about employees and stockholders; personal financial information).[8]

The process of removing this protected information is called *redaction*, and redaction may take the form of entirely withheld documents, redacted pages or sections of documents, or specifically redacted words, phrases, or other elements within a given document.

Requesting parties, or those receiving data from producing parties, approach the review stage from a different perspective. Rather than responsiveness or privilege, receiving parties are primarily concerned with *relevance*. This does not only mean relevance in a broad sense,

---

[8] While there are several other potential privileges and protections, ranging from spousal privilege to the deliberative process privilege, the vast majority of data successfully withheld falls into these four categories.

but also typically means relevance to the particular set of facts and issues that form the basis of their complaint. Thus, the effort here often involves meticulous review and hand-coding to complex classification schemes, all to aid in the downstream preparation of compelling arguments by the litigation team.

The process is daunting for both the producing and requesting parties. Timelines and budgets are tight, the volume and variety of data is overwhelming, and mistakes can be incredibly costly. In this environment, every technical advantage helps, no matter how large or small. Fast system response times – whether to a search query or to a command to load the next document – can shave hundreds of hours off the cumulative review time. This means that intuitive interface design can mean the difference between continual fumbling and focused progress. Smart defaults and configurable shortcuts can replace halting progress with smooth sailing.

There are hundreds of programs that address this stage of the EDRM, but they can generally be grouped into three generations that have evolved over time. The first-generation tools, which first took hold in the 1990s, attempted to move what was previously a largely paper-based process into the digital era. These tools were thus primarily focused on presenting a familiar workflow to practitioners, just in electronic form. LexisNexis Concordance is a prime example of this first-generation tool. Second-generation tools appeared in the 2000s, and sprang out of a recognition that natively digital data is inherently different from its paper predecessors. These tools sought to tame the growing wilderness of file types and proliferation of data with more robust backend databases and enterprise-grade user experiences. A prime example in this class is kCura Relativity. The third-generation tools, established in the 2010s, are primarily products of the cloud. They capitalize on cloud scalability and efficiency to offer the same level of utility – and in some cases vastly superior utility – with much more intuitive, consumer-grade user experiences.[9] Everlaw is a prime example in this class.[10]

3 Analysis

The *analysis* task involves breaking down the data collection in order to better understand what it contains and to accelerate the process of review. This is undoubtedly the most oversimplified part of the framework; analysis has actually become a component of nearly every other stage of the EDRM, and the approaches and technologies involved are nearly as varied as the file types feeding the e-discovery process. To simplify this discussion, we will refer to these approaches and technologies more broadly as analytics, focus on the analytics used primarily in review, and divide them into two types: *project* analytics and *document* analytics.

Project analytics focuses on monitoring, predicting, and improving review performance. Typically, this takes the form of system-generated reports. These reports focus on one or several aspects of the process: the speed at which individual reviewers move through the review process; the accuracy with which those reviewers classify the data; the overall progress and pace, across all reviewers, including estimates of time and cost of completion of review; and live and historical usage data for each reviewer. Armed with the information from these four measurements, review managers can continually optimize the review process, coaching

---

[9] For more detail on consumer-grade user experience, see Section III.H.
[10] Disclaimer: A. J. Shankar and Jonathan Kerry-Tyerman are the CEO and VP of Business Development, respectively, for Everlaw.

or replacing underperforming reviewers, securing the necessary time and other resources for successful review completion, and otherwise intervening as necessary in the day-to-day review process.

Document analytics, on the other hand, is focused on delivering greater insight about the nature and contents of the data. The toolkit for document analytics is even more varied, ranging from straightforward approaches like email threading, duplicate detection, search term reporting, and coding trend analysis, to more sophisticated techniques. These powerful technologies can greatly accelerate the review process, while simultaneously improving the quality of the output. Some techniques include the following:

- **Data visualization:** the graphical representation of aggregate statistical data about sets of documents, which aids in providing an initial understanding of what kinds of documents are in a particular collection.
- **Entity extraction:** the identification of named entities in the data (e.g., people, places, organizations), which aids in the retrieval of information relating to those specific entities, even where they may be referred to by different names.
- **Concept searching:** the organization of data around key themes in a matter, which improves understanding of the topics covered in the data, and aids in the retrieval of data related to those specific topics.
- **Communication mapping:** the visualization of communication patterns between people in the matter in order to illuminate relationships and anomalous behaviors.
- **Predictive coding:** the use of machine learning to teach the system to automatically identify potentially interesting information, which focuses limited review resources on the most promising data, avoids the unnecessary review of uninteresting data, and ensures that nothing is misclassified along the way.[11]

While project analytics developed more or less organically into existing review platforms, document analytics first rose to prominence in separate applications, offering varying levels of integration into mainstream review platforms. Equivio and Content Analyst, for example, were both market-leading independent companies with proprietary document analytics offerings for e-discovery (Zoom and CAAT, respectively), and their products were offered alongside dozens of review platforms, delivering bolt-on, on-demand analytics to systems otherwise lacking such tools. Both platforms have been acquired by larger organizations looking to integrate those analytics into their e-discovery suites (Equivio by Microsoft, and Content Analyst by kCura).[12] Today, these analytics programs are increasingly viewed as table stakes, and many e-discovery platforms have at least modest capability in this realm.

4 Production

Production is the act of handing the responsive and non-privileged data over to the other side, ideally in a format they can easily use for their own review. By this stage, the set of responsive, non-privileged data has been defined, so the challenges here revolve primarily around the

---

[11] For more details on predictive coding or machine learning, see Section III.C. For more on visualization of legal data, *see* Atkinson – Representation of Legal Information, *supra*.

[12] Frederic Lardinois, "Microsoft Acquires Text Analysis Service Equivio," TechCrunch, January 20, 2015, available at: https://techcrunch.com/2015/01/20/microsoft-acquires-text-analysis-service-equivio; Zach Abramowitz, "Like Peanut Butter and Jelly: Why kCura Bought Content Analyst," Above The Law, March 16, 2016, available at: https://abovethelaw.com/2016/03/like-peanut-butter-and-jelly-why-kcura-bought-content-analyst.

efficient and effective packaging of that data for transfer to opposing counsel. Not surprisingly, the standards in this space are constantly evolving, and are subject to some of the most intense negotiation in the e-discovery process.

A standard production is relatively structured when compared to the unstructured source data from which it is derived. It typically contains the following elements:

- a set of images for each document, most commonly in TIFF format, but increasingly as PDFs;[13]
- a set of text files containing the text extracted from the source documents or generated with OCR software;[14]
- the native source files, at least for those document types for which native files were agreed upon (e.g., spreadsheets); and
- a load file of tabular data that correlates all of the other files and includes any metadata extracted from the native source files, all following an agreed-upon order and labeling convention.

The precise parameters of the production – native file production, metadata production, image file formats, load file formats, appearance of redactions, etc. – are intensely negotiated and recorded in the form of a production protocol. Over the years, litigants looking to simplify this process have settled on several protocols or protocol components that have become *de facto* industry standards (e.g., a Concordance-style load file). Government bodies with significant litigation loads and leverage have also established their own standards. The SEC, for example, has their own standard production protocol for data they request.

All of the data to be produced are typically packaged into an encrypted file or onto physical media and delivered to opposing counsel as circumstances and mutual agreements dictate (e.g., secure file transfer protocol, cloud file repository, courier, etc.). The receiving party then uploads the packaged data into their e-discovery platform to begin their own review. Most of the work of the production task revolves around the transformation of data, so it is not surprising that many of the same tools used in the processing stage are also used in the production stage. As with processing, one has a choice between freestanding applications such as LexisNexis LAW PreDiscovery, or those built into review platforms like Everlaw's production tools. Though throughput continues to be a major challenge, recent advances in cloud-based production tools have alleviated that problem.

5 Presentation

Presentation concerns the curation and use of the most relevant data to help make your case, both at trial and in the steps leading up to trial. This is a fairly broad definition, because the EDRM drafters were more concerned with the actual rendering of exhibits in the real world than with fact development or case strategy. Development and strategy, however, are what bridge the gap between the process of finding relevant data and the act of presenting that data as evidence before a judge or jury.

The approaches to developing a case are as varied as the cases themselves, but there are nonetheless several common techniques that provide great benefit at the presentation stage. The first technique is to assemble a database of facts, usually with extensive cross-references to

---

[13] This set of images may not include those documents that are not reasonably imaged, such as spreadsheets.
[14] For more detail on OCR, see Section III.G.

the relevant people, places, organizations, and events in the case, and with annotations as to which facts favor which party, which facts are contested, and which facts remain unsupported by evidence. Another technique is to build a case timeline, or chronology, to understand the temporal order of the data – preferably through visualization – and to illuminate gaps, patterns, and hot spots. One can also create an outline of the key points to make in a deposition, hearing, or motion, with extensive cross-references to the entities involved and the relevant data discovered during review. Another important technique to consider is to review and organize the output from depositions, including audio, video, transcripts, and exhibits, with an emphasis on incorporating newly discovered information into the overall case strategy.

From a technology or marketing perspective, the tools at this far end of the EDRM are not always connected to e-discovery. Rather, they are positioned as case management tools, and are designed to ingest data from various sources, including e-discovery software. Some software is integrated, to varying degrees, into a suite of tools that ultimately cover most of the EDRM (e.g., LexisNexis' CaseMap case management and Sanction trial presentation software). Other e-discovery systems offer this functionality as part of one tightly integrated package, such as Everlaw's StoryBuilder features.

II TECHNICAL CONCEPTS IN E-DISCOVERY

Even a cursory overview of the e-discovery process through the simplified lens of the EDRM reveals the depth and complexity of the technical issues that pervade this process. Indeed, from the time of the first combination of "electronic" with "discovery" and on into the era of big data, the technological challenges have only grown. Fortunately, many of these challenges are shared with non-legal domains, and have thus benefited from solutions developed elsewhere.[15] There are several technological challenges, however, that are felt particularly acutely in e-discovery.

A *Text Encodings*

By convention, when you type the letter "a" on your keyboard, a particular bit sequence is transmitted to your computer. Historically, each character you could type was represented by a single byte. Since each byte has 8 bits, 256 possible characters could be represented. Early on, one bit was reserved for error checking, which left 128 different character values that could be encoded in the seven remaining bits. In the 1960s, an American standards committee decided exactly which 128 characters could be represented: upper- and lower-case letters, numbers, special characters, line feeds, control characters, and others. This committee also decided exactly which bit configuration mapped to each character. This first *character encoding* is known as ASCII.

ASCII made perfect sense to computer users operating *inside* the USA, but posed a problem for computer users operating *outside* the USA. Many of the symbols needed by other languages were not included in the 128 ASCII characters. Speakers of various European languages could not represent accents properly; users of the Cyrillic or Greek alphabets could hardly express any of the letters they used; and writers using logographic scripts like Chinese *hanzi* or Japanese *kanji* didn't even know where to begin.

---

[15] This issue is covered more extensively in Section III.

Luckily, like all character encodings, ASCII is merely a convention, not an ironclad immutable system. The convention says, "when you press this key, send these bits; and when you read these bits from a file, display this character." The bits themselves have no special meaning, so computer users from around the world created their own character encodings to represent their native tongues. Latin-1 was a natural extension of ASCII that used the eighth bit to add another 128 characters, mostly letters with accents and other diacritics, to provide partial or complete coverage for dozens of written scripts. Microsoft Windows included a handful of different encodings for Cyrillic, Greek, Hebrew, Arabic, and more. By and large, these encodings stuck to a single byte per character, but some, like *kanji* encodings, used two bytes, allowing for 65,536 different characters.

Different parts of the world thus developed their own encoding conventions, and these conventions sometimes even differed in how many bytes they would allocate to each character. To reiterate, the bits themselves did not contain any information about *what* encoding convention they manifested: If one person opened a text file, her screen would display the characters the bits mapped to in her *local* encoding, and if another person opened the same text file across the world, he would see a completely different set of characters based on *his* local encoding. As computers became more connected in the early 1980s and data needed to be shared more universally, these conflicting character encodings became a big problem. How could people share data if they couldn't even agree on what the bits meant? To make sense of the madness, a solution was proposed: What if we could devise a character encoding that encompassed *all* written characters?

Thus Unicode was born.[16] Instead of trying to cram a subset of characters into a small table with 256 entries, Unicode defines a massive table of over 128,000 entries that covers virtually every modern and historic script and thousands of additional symbols. Computer enthusiasts rejoiced.

Though Unicode is staggeringly complex and difficult to implement, its status as the lingua franca of character encodings is invaluable. It provides a single sane medium with which to exchange data in a variety of languages. This value manifests itself in two principle decision points. First, when receiving data from another party, the textual component of the data is required to be represented in Unicode. Failure to do so may result in receiving data that is an uninterpretable bag of bits, unless you happen to know what specific encodings were used and where. Even then, you would have to convert all the data yourself, because most software cannot automatically differentiate between different languages' encoding schemes. Second, when choosing a discovery vendor, the software must have end-to-end Unicode support. Because encodings are so fragile, a single step that does not support Unicode can permanently alter the output. Does the software accurately ingest and display foreign-language Unicode characters? Can you name folders and search using these characters? And can you produce these characters to a load file, knowing the whole time that any tech-savvy opposing party will request productions to be in Unicode?

B Defining and Identifying Duplicates

Any sufficiently large corpus drawn from a single organizational entity is bound to contain duplicate documents. For example, two different employees may have the same Word

---

[16] Strictly speaking, Unicode is a standard that itself has multiple encodings. The most common of these is UTF-8; for simplicity, we will use the word Unicode to mean specifically Unicode with UTF-8 encoding.

document on their hard drives, or an email appears in one employee's sent messages folder and in the inbox of the other. During the review portion of e-discovery, it is often beneficial to identify and then either hide or delete these duplicate files, in an effort referred to as *deduplication*. Deduplication is necessary so that the review effort does not waste time and resources on redundant annotations of the same document.

But beyond this common-sense motivation lies considerable ambiguity. What determines whether multiple documents are identical? Can two documents be considered duplicates by themselves, or does context matter? There is no single agreed-upon answer to these questions, and your position may vary depending on whether you are on the plaintiff's side or the defense's side in a case. The bottom line is that you should know enough about common practices to understand whether your discovery solution's chosen deduplication strategy works for you.

1 Comparing Documents in Isolation

It is prohibitively expensive to compare one document's contents against the contents of all others within a large corpus.[17] A much more efficient method involves the usage of hashes. A *hash* is like a signature, and is computed based on a document's contents. A hash algorithm assigns a string of letters and numbers to each document in a corpus. These strings are small in size: one standard length for hashes is only 128 bits. Hash computation is deterministic, which means that if you feed the same contents to the same hashing algorithm, it will yield exactly the same hash value every time. This means that if a hashing algorithm is used on a corpus of documents, and two documents have the same hash value, they are almost certainly duplicates.[18]

Thus, implementing a hashing algorithm – provided you use the same one consistently – means that only the hash values of documents, not their actual contents, need to be compared. This creates incredible efficiency for deduplication tasks.[19]

For an example of what hashes look like, Table 3.5.1 shows hash values for the text of the Gettysburg Address, obtained by using two common hashing algorithms, MD5 and SHA-1.

There are two important takeaways from Table 3.5.1. The first is that hashing algorithms consume *all* text uniformly. This includes the particular white spaces that appear, and any and all punctuation. Our choice of text for the Gettysburg Address included particular spaces and paragraph breaks; another transcription of the Address that uses different spacing, or one that has even a single extra space, would yield a completely different hash value.[20] Another important takeaway from Table 3.5.1 is that different hashing algorithms yield different values for the same data; thus, it is critical to choose one algorithm and stick with it.

In many common matters this simple strategy runs into snags. Hashing requires a native source file, but if part of your data set is a production from some other party, they may not

---

[17] If a corpus contained one million documents, then roughly one trillion file comparisons would have to be made to identify all duplicates.

[18] Though it is theoretically possible for two different documents to have the same hash value, the way hashing functions are constructed means that it is incredibly rare for two different documents to have the same hash value: you would have to hash one million documents per day for a hundred billion years to have a one-in-a-billion chance of two different documents having the same SHA-1 hash value.

[19] For applications of hashing in cryptography, *see* Kilbride – Distributed Ledgers, Cryptography and Smart Contracts, *supra*.

[20] Later in this section we will discuss near-duplicate detection, which is meant to ameliorate this issue.

TABLE 3.5.1 *Hash values for the Gettysburg Address.*

Hashing algorithm	Hash value
MD5	753c1493597oee423ddeob86b9777513
SHA-1	2c548cf6foe826d3827b66608boc85b26dobf772

have provided the native files corresponding to each document that are needed to compute hashes. It is thus necessary to require outside parties to include specific hash values in their document metadata load files. Furthermore, some documents, such as emails, do not have a standard native representation; their representation is dependent on the email client database in which they reside. These files' native representation cannot be compared, because if one employee uses Gmail but another uses Outlook this discrepancy is sufficient to make identical emails look different. To work around this issue, vendors often create a custom hash for emails that is independent of how they are stored (e.g., by extracting sender, recipient, date, and body information as text and feeding those values into the hashing algorithm). This means that a single vendor can compare duplicates across all the emails it has processed, regardless of the email program they originated from. If you are receiving data from multiple vendors, however, each may hash emails in a different way, rendering useless even the provided hash values in their document metadata load files.

When basic hashing fails, as in the examples in the previous paragraph, a much more aggressive hashing approach can be used in which only the textual content of documents is hashed and compared. This may seem like an inconsequential difference, but hashing only the textual content of documents eliminates all of the software-specific data encoded in a native file. For example, a Word file that contains only the word "deduplication" would be marked as a duplicate of a WordPerfect file that also contains only that exact word, and a PowerPoint document containing that same single word would also be marked as a duplicate. Thus, this text-only approach can find duplicates that a simple comparison of native hashes may miss, even those files that are not true duplicates but just happen to have the same textual content. In certain cases, this approach can be tremendously valuable, but it helps to know what specific needs the corpus in question may have.

2 Comparing Documents in Context

Occasionally, two documents with the same hash value are not, strictly speaking, duplicates. Consider a Word document that exists in two places: one place as a standalone file in a user's "Downloads" directory, and in another place as an email attachment. These two documents may be perfectly identical, but they exist in different contexts. In many cases, especially if you are the producing party, this additional context is worth preserving: eliminate the standalone file, and a receiving party may never know that a user had downloaded the file; eliminate the email attachment, and suddenly an email that refers to a specific attachment in its headers and body is rendered incomplete.

To preserve the context of documents, a simple rule is typically followed: two documents are duplicates if either (1) they are both standalone documents with the same hash value; or

(2) they are both attachments to emails, and the documents, the containing emails, and all other attachments to the emails have the same respective hash values. In other words, email families (emails and their attachments) are either deduplicated wholesale, or not at all. In the very common situation of both a sender and a recipient being custodians on a matter, this strategy will correctly mark emails as duplicates. But in another common situation – where an email attachment is saved somewhere else, or an attachment is sent back and forth between parties – the algorithm will not identify the documents as duplicates.

In certain cases, you might prefer to eliminate this email-family definition of duplicates in favor of the simpler per-document comparison. For certain kinds of review, often found on the plaintiff side, a document's relevance is largely dependent on its contents, and less on its context. In these cases, you might want to review that Word document exactly once, regardless of the differing contexts in which it occurs.

3 Near-Deduplication

Hashes are brittle. As discussed above, documents that differ by only a single character will nevertheless have completely different hash values. This is a useful, conservative trait if a primary concern is to avoid accidentally marking different documents as duplicative. However, sometimes it is appropriate to cast a wider net in order to find all the documents that are merely *similar* to a particular document. This process of identification is called *near-deduplication*. Typically, a specialized hashing algorithm maps similar documents to similar hash values, and a threshold for nearness is established.[21] Because the varied binary formats of native documents are not amenable to such an analysis, near-deduplication is performed on text-only documents. As discussed above, there are trade-offs to this approach.

C Production Formats

There is no standard format for the exchange of data in a litigation. Each matter may result in a bespoke production protocol that defines the format in which documents must be provided. The producing side's primary concerns are typically cost and information exposure. On the receiving side, meanwhile, you are not guaranteed access to the source data, so ensuring a proper format can be essential to getting the most out of the received data. The following list contains some best practices useful for negotiating a protocol on the receiving end:

- Request all textual data in UTF-8 Unicode encoding.[22] Require that extracted text contains page break characters so that searches on the text can be synchronized to the respective image pages.
- Request PDFs instead of TIFFs for image format. PDFs are typically higher fidelity, natively in color, and smaller in size.
- Request native files to accompany as many documents as possible (at a minimum, request native files for spreadsheets and presentations). These formats typically have data (formulas, notes, animations) that do not translate well to a printed format.

---

[21] This nearness threshold is determined by how widely the hashes or document contents should differ before they are not considered near.
[22] See note 16, *supra*.

- In addition to standard fields, request metadata fields that provide valuable context, including: Message-ID and In-Reply-To header fields to enable reconstruction of email threads;[23] SHA-1 *and* MD5 hashes so that multiple hash values are available to compare against other productions; and time zone information to accompany time fields.
- Request top-shelf OCR solutions like ABBYY and Nuance, or cloud providers like Google's Vision API. OCR software varies widely in quality, with some programs providing poor solutions that yield unintelligible and unsearchable text. Open-source software, such as Tesseract, is often used by vendors because it is free, but it performs considerably worse than commercial solutions and may render much of the received data undiscoverable. As of now, you should require top-shelf commercial OCR solutions.[24]

III TECHNOLOGIES POWERING MODERN E-DISCOVERY

Modern technology drives e-discovery. When you are immersed in a field, it is easy to believe that you and your colleagues are the only ones facing the particular challenges before you, and to thus conclude that the solutions must be similarly unique. As with many other fields, however, the challenges in e-discovery are actually rather common. Too much information, too many formats, too little time, and too few people to properly analyze the data; these are perennial problems for e-discovery, just as they are in many other fields. And, in much the same way as in other fields, e-discovery has benefited from enormous advances in the technologies used to address common challenges. These advances have transformed e-discovery, making what was once a dreaded, esoteric workflow into a pursuit that is at once both accessible and cutting-edge.

A Cloud Computing

Cloud computing is the practice of storing, managing, and processing data using a network of remote servers hosted on the internet, rather than using a local server or a personal computer. Cloud computing is the driving force behind companies like Facebook, Netflix, YouTube, and Skype. The advantages are so compelling that even desktop-based stalwarts like Adobe Photoshop and Microsoft Office have transitioned to cloud-based delivery models.

But *cloud computing* is actually a broad term that can encompass many different cloud-provisioned services. The most familiar of these is cloud storage, the provisioning of storage space through the internet, accessible from anywhere and scalable to any size. Dropbox, Google Drive, and Box are examples of services built primarily around the storage aspect of cloud computing. Cloud computing, however, can also involve the provisioning of processing power, memory space, and other server components via the internet. The result of this form of cloud computing is software-as-a-service (SaaS), entire applications that are delivered exclusively through the cloud. Salesforce, Gmail, and Slack are all examples of SaaS software products that offer the full functionality of local desktop- or server-based products, but through the usage of cloud computing.

---

[23] Some platforms, like Everlaw, can reconstruct email threads without this information.
[24] For more detail on OCR, see Section III.G.

The advantages of cloud computing cut across every aspect of how software is made, delivered, and used. By using a cloud provider of storage and computing horsepower, software developers can focus on functionality and user experience instead of infrastructure setup, maintenance, security, redundancy, or scalability. This drastically reduces the barriers to entry, making it possible for any talented engineer with a good idea to spin up fully functional, secure, scalable software with minimal expense. This also makes it much easier for users of the software to collaborate in a way that traditional software never really allowed, because a SaaS application is designed so that users are always connected to the cloud servers.

With a common infrastructure underpinning the software, developers can also build around those capabilities rather than having to accommodate the myriad potential configurations of end-user systems. Developers can also call on special services built by cloud computing providers – such as the transcoding tools available on Amazon Web Services, or the machine translation tools provided as part of the Google Cloud Platform – to seamlessly incorporate those technologies into their offering without having to build them from scratch. All of this makes for a far more efficient development process.

Once a SaaS application is built, it can be deployed to end-users through the most ubiquitous software of all: a web browser. That browser might be on a desktop, laptop, tablet, or smartphone, and it can be accessed from anywhere on the planet. This simplicity and flexibility makes SaaS far more accessible than traditional software. In addition, cloud computing resources are designed to scale up and down, seamlessly and efficiently, as demand dictates. This frees both developers and end-users from worrying about whether and when they might reach the limits of the hardware they are using, or whether they're paying for more than they need (e.g., paying for idle servers).

The massive economies of scale enjoyed by cloud computing providers allow for greater investment in both physical and logical security, creating environments that are far more secure than what a single application developer would be able to achieve with only their own resources. On the customer side, because all patches and upgrades are managed by the SaaS application provider, end-users enjoy a maintenance-free experience while also knowing that they are always using the latest and greatest version. This is a boon to developers as well, since they no longer have to contemplate how a potential change will affect users clinging to older versions of the software, or even how to deliver updates to those users. Managing one codebase, in one cloud location, lets developers use their resources much more efficiently. Moreover, since they call on resources that are shared, distributed, and available on demand, SaaS applications reach economies of scale far faster than traditional software. This means that they can provide cost-effective solutions to even the lowest-value problems.

In e-discovery, this revolution in cloud computing has completely changed the software landscape. The boom-or-bust nature of litigation – in which a single matter can balloon from a few gigabytes to a few terabytes overnight after receiving new production, and then disappear again overnight following a settlement – makes the cloud's scalability and lack of advance hardware commitment that much more appealing. All of the most cutting-edge e-discovery technology is exclusively cloud-based, taking full advantage of the increased efficiency, scalability, simplicity, and connectivity to tackle everything from processing to analytics to collaborative case building. In particular, cloud computing has made it possible to take the most powerful tools and make them accessible to any litigant, on matters of any size, from small-scale investigations to complex multi-district litigation.

B Encryption

Encryption is the process of converting information into a form that is unreadable by anyone not authorized to do so. Historians have traced the origins of encryption as far back as secrets go, with the first recorded use of encryption occurring nearly 3500 years ago in ancient Mesopotamia. Back then, encryption was used to keep the recipe for a particular pottery glaze a closely guarded secret. Not much has changed; present-day encryption is still used to keep important information away from prying eyes. The technology has improved since ancient times, though, and it has also become more widespread. In just the last few decades, truly secure encryption technology has become accessible to the public, where before it had been the exclusive domain of governments and militaries.

Modern e-discovery would be impossibly burdensome without encryption. Encryption allows organizations to securely share highly sensitive internal information with outside counsel for review, even from remote locations. Encryption also makes it possible to send a relevant subset of sensitive information to opposing counsel with reasonable certainty that it will not be intercepted or stolen along the way.

When it comes to applications hosted remotely, it is common to distinguish data that is encrypted *in transit* from data encrypted *at rest*. The distinction matters because – unlike paper, for example – digital information is often not transmitted on the same medium on which it is stored. Data may therefore be encrypted for transmission between two machines (e.g., from a website on a cloud-based server to a web browser on a remote client computer), regardless of whether it is encrypted when stored at either the source or destination. Ideally, you want your data encrypted both where it is stored and while it is being transmitted, and encryption in transit is essential to protect against third-party attacks, such as eavesdropping. Without encryption in transit, someone on the same network as you could in theory listen in on your communication and expose any sensitive documents being transmitted. When data is encrypted, though, the interloper has a much harder time viewing the data without proper decryption keys.

Encryption at rest is just as important. Even though your data may be stored in the cloud, it still physically resides somewhere, usually in a hosting provider's data center. Encryption at rest is the final step in providing physical security: even if an attacker manages to bypass the surveillance equipment, armed guards, authentication mechanisms, and secure environments to find the server hosting your cloud data, they would be unable to do anything sensible with it without the proper decryption keys. Encryption at rest also protects against accidental data exposure. For an example of the necessity of this extra layer of protection, think about if you or someone you know has ever left a thumb drive sitting out unattended.

There are two primary types of encryption, *symmetric* (also known as *private key*) and *asymmetric* (also known as *public key*). In both types, a specific algorithm encodes the original data – or plaintext – into ciphertext. This ciphertext is incredibly difficult to decode without the encryption key.[25] In symmetric encryption, the same key is used both to encrypt and decrypt the data, so the ciphertext and key are both transmitted to the recipient (albeit separately), and the recipient uses both to convert the data back to plaintext. In asymmetric encryption, the encryption and decryption keys are different: the public encryption key is

---

[25] Note that it is only incredibly difficult, *not impossible*, to decrypt encrypted data without the key. Modern encryption relies on the fact that it would take an unreasonable (and usually unattainable) amount of computing power to successfully attack encrypted data. Encrypted data is therefore only secure as long as that assumption remains true.

published for anyone to use to create ciphertext, which can then only be turned back into plaintext by the holder of the secret decryption key.

Asymmetric encryption has the advantage of not requiring that the sender and recipient exchange secret keys, but it does not encrypt and decrypt data as quickly or securely as symmetric encryption. These different advantages help explain why both types of encryption are often used together, to maximize convenience and speed. When you point your browser to a secure website (i.e., any website with a URL beginning with "https"), your browser and the website's server first use the more convenient asymmetric encryption to authenticate that the website is indeed the one you intended to visit. They then share the secret keys for subsequent communication via symmetric encryption. After authentication, the rest of the session is conducted via the more efficient symmetric encryption.

C Machine Learning

Machine learning (ML) is a type of artificial intelligence (AI) that provides computers with the ability to learn without being explicitly programmed. Machine learning is the foundation of the predictive coding technology that has transformed e-discovery, reducing the amount of data that needs to be reviewed by upwards of 80% in some matters.

Machine learning has disrupted many fields, and e-discovery is no exception. Many of the services you use every day incorporate this technology. Any time you give a song a thumbs-up on Pandora with the goal of receiving better recommendations for additional music, you are taking advantage of ML. The recommendations you receive on Netflix or Amazon are also driven by ML. Even your search results on Google are informed by an ML algorithm that examines and learns from your past search and browsing behavior.

In most cases, the ML process follows a few basic steps. First, an algorithm catalogs the features of each object in the corpus (e.g., each song, movie, product, website). Second, a human classifies some objects as relevant or irrelevant. In the Pandora example, this is the stage where the user gives a song a thumbs-up or thumbs-down. Next, the ML system analyzes the human input to determine which features affect relevance, and how. There are at least a dozen different algorithmic approaches for calculating relevance. Finally, the ML system uses this information to classify the remaining objects as relevant or irrelevant.

In e-discovery, ML for document classification goes by many names.[26] The two most common names, *technology-assisted review* (TAR) and *predictive coding*, are used more or less interchangeably. Regardless of what they are called, these methods generally fall into one of two categories. *Simple passive learning* (or TAR 1.0) is a subject-matter expert that classifies some documents to be used for training, which the system then uses to test the reliability of predictions as more and more documents are classified later on. Once performance has reached acceptable levels of accuracy, the prediction model is rolled out to all remaining documents. In *continuous active learning* (or TAR 2.0), all review decisions automatically train the system, and the system continually updates predictions as new human classifications are made. TAR 1.0 requires experts to do the initial training, and this makes it less effective than TAR 2.0 because it cannot learn from subsequent decisions. TAR 1.0 also cannot handle

---

[26] Other names include suggested coding, predictive tagging, meaning based coding, dynamic review, automatic coding, predictive priority, computer assisted coding, predictive ranking, predictive intelligence, suggestive coding, automatic classification, intelligent prioritization, adaptive coding, and automated predictive review.

rolling productions without having to start over. Furthermore, TAR 1.0 doesn't work well when the proportion of relevant documents is low.[27]

As with any specialized domain, there is some jargon with which it helps to be familiar:

- **Richness (a.k.a. prevalence):** The percentage of documents in a data set that are relevant. If a data set contains 100 documents, and only 10 are found to be relevant, then the richness is 10%.
- **Recall:** The percentage of relevant documents retrieved. If there are ten relevant documents in the data set, and the system correctly identified six of them, then the system's recall is 60%. This is a measure of the completeness of the results.
- **Precision:** The percentage of retrieved documents that are relevant. So, if the system correctly identified 10 relevant documents, but incorrectly identified another 40 as relevant, then precision is 20%. This is a measure of the purity of the results.

Precision and recall are often used together as closely related measures of a predictive coding model's performance. There is an inherent trade-off between the two: You can maximize recall by simply classifying everything as relevant, but that would minimize precision because your set of relevant documents would include many irrelevant documents as well. Similarly, classifying only one document as relevant might maximize precision (assuming this one document is indeed relevant), but it would minimize recall if there were in fact other relevant documents. The ideal predictive coding model seeks to optimize this trade-off, although there are some situations in which one metric is more important than another (e.g., recall is more important when hunting for a "smoking gun" document).

The predictions generated by a predictive coding model can be enormously powerful, allowing users to avoid the manual review of documents that are almost certain to be uninteresting, thus saving potentially thousands or even millions of dollars in review time. Predictive coding models can also be used to prioritize documents for relevance review in order to make the review process much more efficient; to identify potentially privileged documents in order to reduce the chance of a costly or damaging clawback; or to double-check review work between humans and machines to improve the accuracy of the review process. With these benefits, it is not surprising that the vast majority of corporate counsel are using predictive coding on their cases,[28] nor that courts are routinely approving the use of predictive coding in the cases before them.[29]

D Machine Translation

Machine translation is when a computer translates a document from one human language to another. This idea is quite old, but only very recently have we begun to enjoy the benefits of

---

[27] For more discussion of TAR, see Nay – Natural Language Processing for Legal Texts, *supra*; Katz and Nay – Machine Learning, *supra*; and Waisberg – Contract Analytics, *supra*.
[28] Norton Rose Fulbright, "2016 Litigation Trends Annual Survey: Perspectives from Corporate Counsel," September 2016, available at: www.nortonrosefulbright.com/files/20160915–2016-litigation-trends-annual-survey-142485.pdf. According to this survey, 71% of corporate counsel reported that they are using predictive coding on at least a minority of their cases.
[29] See, e.g., Magistrate Judge Andrew Peck, of New York's Southern District, who declared that "the case law has developed to the point that it is now black letter law that where the producing party wants to utilize TAR for document review, courts will permit it" (*Rio Tinto PLC v. Vale SA*, 306 F.R.D. 125 (S.D.N.Y. 2015)).

machine translation that can approximate the quality of human translation and make it far more efficient to review foreign-language content.

In its most basic form, machine translation works by substituting each word in the source document with the equivalent word in the target language. This can yield comically poor results, however, because this rudimentary translation does not take into account different grammatical structures of different languages, nor does it account for the context of each word's connotation within a wider phrase or sentence. There are several techniques for producing a more nuanced translation, ranging from rules-based (carefully parsing the structure of each sentence, based on the linguistic rules of the source and target languages) to statistical (making informed guesses based on an analysis of massive databases of previously translated documents). Most recently, however, the industry has begun a shift to *neural machine translation*. This technique is based on *neural networks*, whose base unit of artificial intelligence is modeled on the biological neuron. Neural networks have experienced a rapid rise in the last decade, pushing to the forefront of AI techniques and reaching new levels of accuracy in previously stagnant areas of AI research.

Neural network research stalled about half a century ago, and one primary driver of the recent resurgence of this technology in the past decade is the relatively new technique of combining multiple layers of neurons to create more sophisticated analyses. This technique of *deep learning* has recently become more tenable for three main reasons: improved algorithms for training complicated networks; the existence of very large data sets, often acquired by leading consumer cloud companies (e.g., Google) who train them; and, finally, the repurposing of graphical processing units, or GPUs – historically used for video gaming and graphics applications – to speed up the training process by several orders of magnitude.

One use of deep learning's layered approach is to identify the relevant features of the data at ever greater levels of abstraction. Instead of looking at text as words or phrases, as a human would, a deep learning algorithm might first interpret the text as a series of characters, then look at the text as a series of syllables, then look at the words, and so on until it has developed a sense for both the features of a language and the relevance of each feature. Compared to statistical machine translation models, neural machine translation is both more efficient and more accurate.

In our increasingly globalized economy, the likelihood of encountering foreign-language content in e-discovery continues to grow. The cost of paying humans to translate all of that content can be enormous, sometimes prohibitively so, and this cost is particularly difficult to bear when it is obvious that much, if not most, of the translated content will turn out to be irrelevant, if not completely worthless. Machine translation changes the equation by making it possible to quickly and accurately determine whether foreign-language content is likely to be relevant to the matter at hand. It is important to bear in mind that machine translation is currently not a substitute for certified human translators required to generate translations suitable for use in court. Rather, machine translation is a powerful tool that allows those valuable human translators to focus only on those documents that matter.

E Transcoding

From YouTube to Vine to police body cameras and smartphones, the sources and varieties of recorded audio and video content continue to proliferate at an incredible rate. The good news for anyone tasked with reviewing this information is that encoding standards for media content are undergoing the opposite trend: they are coalescing around a handful of formats reinforced by operating system and hardware defaults popular in the consumer world writ large. Despite this standardization, it would still be an enormous challenge to consume the wide variety of media types available, were it not for transcoding.

Transcoding is the process of converting information from one format to another. It relies on specialized software, as well as specialized GPU components, to execute the relatively complex algorithms involved. Amazon and other cloud computing providers offer highly scalable transcoding services as part of their cloud service portfolio (e.g., Amazon Elastic Transcoder, part of Amazon Web Services). This makes it easier and more cost effective for businesses and developers to transcode media on demand.

Transcoding yields two primary benefits: normalization and optimization. *Normalization* reduces complexity by converting media files from several different formats into one common format, making it easier to consume that media through a single playback application, rather than having to use several. *Optimization* increases efficiency by ensuring that the stored media takes up no more room than necessary and, in a streaming context, by maximizing quality within the bandwidth and computing power available for streaming.

The benefits of transcoding make it possible to visit a free website like YouTube from an array of devices and over many types of connections, and to view content originally recorded in a wide variety of formats. Transcoding has a similar impact on e-discovery. It allows litigation teams to store, organize, and review media in a normalized, optimized fashion, making the process more efficient and straightforward. In the face of rapidly rising volumes of media in litigation, these efficiency gains will only become more important as time goes on.

F Machine Transcription

While technology like transcoding might make media files more accessible, it still does not unlock what is often the most valuable content within them: human speech. Enter machine transcription. This technology converts spoken words in audio or video files into written text, converting human speech into searchable, easily accessible documents.

Like translation, transcription is a task once exclusively performed by humans. Also like translation, humans remain the gold standard when it comes to the quality of transcription. Machine transcription has introduced new levels of efficiency, however, that humans simply cannot match, which has opened up affordable transcription at scale with relatively minimal sacrifice in quality.

The latest machine transcription approaches are also based on deep learning through neural networks. Both Google's Cloud Speech API and Microsoft's Bing Speech API use deep learning to deliver more accurate results. Many of these services can also deliver additional information, such as time codes, speaker identification, and speaker sentiment analysis.

In e-discovery, it is ultimately searchability that matters most. Since the volume of data in a litigation today makes it increasingly infeasible to manually review each document, it has become even more important to ensure that all content is indexed and searchable. Only with machine transcription does rendering audio and video files into text documents become cost effective enough to meet that need in even the largest of matters.

G Optical Character Recognition

Even more basic than recognizing text in audio and video files is the task of recognizing text in documents that are ostensibly text-based, but have somehow lost their embedded text. It's not unheard of for emails to be produced in e-discovery as TIFF files, without either embedded text or accompanying text files. In those situations, making the text searchable with accurate *optical character recognition* (OCR) is the only solution.

Optical character recognition is a complex process. Because OCR engines must deal with a wide variety of inputs – everything from scanned receipts to photos of book pages – they commonly perform a number of preprocessing steps to normalize inbound data. This includes removal of lines and spots; analysis of page layout and the structure of the text; and a process known as *deskewing*, aligning a page to a perfectly vertical or horizontal plane.

After these preprocessing steps are complete, the task of recognizing characters begins. There are two primary approaches to OCR: pattern matching and feature extraction. *Pattern matching* compares each character, pixel by pixel, with a library of stored character images to look for a match. *Feature extraction* is more modern and, predictably, uses ML to develop a more nuanced understanding of the features defining the text and the wider document. Feature extraction techniques yield accuracy rates of up to 99%.

Over time, it is likely that these two OCR tools will merge with those used for machine translation and transcription, as providers aim to consolidate and harmonize their ML approaches in order to stay competitive in the market. Microsoft and Google both already offer on-demand OCR services for recognizing people, places, objects, and other elements beyond merely the text within a given image. Regardless of how it is packaged, however, OCR is likely to decline in importance over time as written materials make up less of the data used in litigation, and materials originally produced in electronic form continue their ascendancy.

H Consumer-Grade User Experience

Enterprise software is a phrase that can conjure memories of being saddled with a tool that is overly complicated, poorly documented, error prone, and expensive. These are experiences we might have tolerated back when there was little overlap between the tools we used for work and those we used for play, but advances in mobile, social, and cloud technology have blurred those lines. Today, we use phrases like *consumer-grade user experience* as shorthand for the much *higher* design quality we have come to expect from applications developed for the consumer market, and the notion that we increasingly expect *all* software to meet these standards.

These heightened expectations have transformed the software we use at work. On the whole, pursuing a consumer-grade user experience (UX) makes software simpler, more visually appealing, more naturally intuitive, more flexible, and more accessible. Perhaps more importantly, a superior UX doesn't end at the software's user interface; a truly consumer-grade UX involves software that is easier to evaluate, purchase, deploy, maintain, and, if necessary, replace. Ideally, it also involves no compromise in utility; the software should be just as powerful as traditional enterprise software. The net result of a well-made UX is users who are more relaxed, comfortable, confident, and capable with the software.

Law is a relatively niche market for technology, and it is often one of the last sectors to enjoy the latest advances. UX is no exception, and due to these factors, legal professionals have taken on an unjustified reputation as technophobes, when in reality they have simply been resisting the inferior UX that other professionals have long since abandoned.[30] The good news

---

[30] For an example of this phenomenon, consider the ubiquitous adoption of the smartphone, a pinnacle of modern-day consumer-grade user experience, as evidence that legal professionals do truly appreciate great UX.

is that the adoption of cloud computing in legal has opened the floodgates to consumer-grade user experiences. From legal research to practice management to e-discovery, legal professionals now have software options that deliver enterprise-grade utility with consumer-grade usability.

IV THE FUTURE OF E-DISCOVERY

By its nature, e-discovery will continue to experience innovation in three critical areas: data formats and storage continue to change; computer science tactics continue to evolve; and users increasingly demand efficiency and design improvements in the software they use.

A Changes in Data Formats and Storage

Discovery must necessarily stay current with corporate trends and best practices for data formats and storage. As discoverable evidence has spread from papers in filing cabinets to word processor documents to emails to chats, electronic discovery has had to remain in lockstep. The cloud and other modern collaboration tools have vastly increased the palette of communication options corporations may use, and all of these options must ultimately be supported during the process of discovery. If, for example, the future of technological development produces viable holographic displays for communication, then electronic discovery vendors must find ways to add hologram support to their processing tools.

Furthermore, we expect cloud storage to alter the collection process. Collection tools today are complicated beasts that must effectively curate data stored in a broad array of on-site and remote locations. As cloud computing and storage become increasingly pervasive across industries, the process of collection will actually become simpler. In a decade, forward-thinking companies might simply connect their cloud storage repositories directly to the processing pipelines of their discovery vendor of choice, and be off to the races.

B Increased Adoption of Cutting-Edge Computer Science

Discovery review and analysis will continue to track the cutting edge of computer science to find the best ways to make sense of the massive, ever increasing volumes of incoming data in the world. Electronic communication is easier to create than ever before, and with voice input, videoconferencing, and chat continuing to pick up steam, it will only get easier as time goes on. Telecommuting and social network use will continue to broaden the opportunities for digital content creation. All of this data will be discoverable in the right context. The end result: corpus size in e-discovery will continue to grow larger and larger.

While corpora will inexorably grow, we do not expect the court system's timelines to lengthen proportionately. Discovery software will have to do more with less,[31] and it easily can by leaning more heavily on computer science. Discovery is a deep, multidisciplinary problem that draws from a rich range of computer sciences, often at the very limits of scale. Discovery will therefore benefit from advances in artificial intelligence, storage, search, distributed systems, data visualization, and human–computer interaction. All of these are areas of active

---

[31] In fact, the complexity of a corpus increases superlinearly as it grows: each additional document must be evaluated on its own, *as well as in the context of its sibling documents*. Corpus size continues to grow, and with it, complexity increases exponentially. This problem is much harder than merely keeping up with the increasing size of corpora.

research at universities today, and discovery vendors will increasingly find themselves reading the latest academic papers to get an edge on the competition. This bodes well for the state of the industry.

C Improved User Experience

Some enterprise tools become more esoteric as they grow more specialized, requiring deep domain expertise and training to use. The entire e-discovery process, on the other hand, continues to become more user-friendly. Discovery is such a bedrock-level aspect of law that accessibility must naturally increase. It is essential to litigation, investigation, M&A due diligence, and more; it simply cannot be relegated to the domain of a few experts.

The modern trend toward more user-friendly e-discovery systems is already underway, potentially exposing tiers of complexity tailored for a user's comfort level, the use case, and the volume of data. Increasing competition on user-friendliness can only aid in access to justice, and it will also lower the blood pressure of lawyers and litigation support staff everywhere.

3.6

Predictive Coding in E-discovery and the NexLP Story Engine

Irina Matveeva

I BRIEF OVERVIEW OF E-DISCOVERY

Changes in the US Federal Rules of Civil Procedure in 2006 made electronic documents part of the evidence material for a case.[1] This led to an "e-discovery revolution," and natural language processing (NLP) technologies became standard tools in the document review process in civil litigation.[2] This was welcome news for investigators and litigators, since nowadays the most interesting and substantial pieces of evidence are often contained in electronic documents, particularly email conversations. However, these legal changes coincided with the explosion of available data, and the sheer volume of electronic information has made it necessary to search for new ways to handle and review electronic information.[3]

The use of electronic media in business has led to a massive explosion of digital documents, especially email. In 2015, the number of emails sent and received per day totaled over 205 billion.[4] That number included business and private emails. This figure was then expected to grow at an average annual rate of 3% ever since, reaching over 246 billion by the end of 2019.[5] One reason for the growing volume of stored email is the steady decline in the cost of digital storage, thanks to commoditization and lower-priced, high-capacity drives now on the market. The price per megabyte of storage in 1980 was $193; in 2014 it was less than $0.01.[6]

The exponential growth of digital information directly effects the amount of data e-discovery systems need to process. A typical e-discovery case circa 2010 included 1–2 million documents; in 2015, that number increased to 5–10 million documents.[7] The traditional methods of e-discovery have rapidly become unsuited to handling this growing volume of

---

[1] Judicial Conference of the United States, "Report of the Civil Rules Advisory Committee," May 27, 2005 (rev. July 25, 2005), available at: www.uscourts.gov/sites/default/files/fr_import/CV5-2005.pdf.

[2] The Sedona Conference, "The Sedona Conference Best Practices Commentary on the Use of Search & Information Retrieval Methods in E-Discovery," *Sedona Conference Journal* 217 (2014).

[3] Jason R. Baron, "Law in the Age of Exabytes: Some Further Thoughts on 'Information Inflation' and Current Issues in E-Discovery Search," *Richmond Journal of Law & Technology* 17(3) (2011), available at: http://jolt.richmond.edu/v17i3/article9.pdf.

[4] The RADICATI Group, "Email Statistics Report," 2015.

[5] Ibid.

[6] Matthew Komorowski, "A History of Storage Cost," personal web page, September 8, 2009, available at: www.mkomo.com/cost-per-gigabyte.

[7] kCura Corporation, "Workflow for Computer-Assisted Review in Relativity: Understanding the Components of Computer-Assisted Review and the Workflow that Ties Them Together," July 2012, available at: www.edrm.net/papers/workflow-for-computer-assisted-review-in-relativity.

data. Machine learning (ML) and NLP technologies are part of the solution to this problem, and have become widely accepted in the past few years.

Volume is not the only challenge for e-discovery. Quality of data is also an important factor, and ML and NLP are often the only means to address quality concerns. An effective e-discovery approach must be able to separate the wheat from the chaff as early in the process as possible in order to avoid incurring exorbitant costs. Deduplication, for example, was one of the earliest issues against which ML and NLP were used. These approaches must also be used to process and analyze data because of another immutable aspect: There is a high volume of unstructured digital data, particularly in email format.

II PREDICTIVE CODING AND ACTIVE LEARNING: PROCESS AND CLASSIFICATION ALGORITHMS

The e-discovery predictive coding workflow, also called technology-assisted review (TAR), was developed as a response to the explosive growth in the amount of data.[8] It aids human reviewers in quickly and effectively finding those documents that are the most relevant to a case. Following is a summary of the steps in the predictive coding process.

A Machine Learning in Predictive Coding

The core of predictive coding consists of ML classifiers that are trained to distinguish between responsive and non-responsive documents. Classifiers are trained in a supervised learning procedure, where the classifier is presented with examples of responsive and non-responsive documents and then builds a model that distinguishes between the two.[9] Users of a supervised learning system have to provide the classifier with examples of both responsive and non-responsive documents in order to build a functional set of labeled training data. After the classifier is trained, it uses its model to assign a score to each document in a case. The score a document receives reflects the probability that that document is responsive.

Many systems use the Support Vector Machine classifier, one of the most effective algorithms for text classification.[10] The choice of which classifier to use for predictive coding is important, but only to a certain degree; the accuracy of a classifier largely depends on the quantity and quality of the manually labeled documents used as training data. To improve the quality of training data, various NLP technologies can be deployed. These include deduplication, as well as identification and removal of repeated content and of metadata information. These processes are discussed in more detail later in this section.

During the e-discovery process, multiple reviewers may be working and tagging documents over a period of time, so it is desirable for a classifier to incorporate the feedback of those users and learn from the tags they create. This process of training the classifier using feedback from the human reviewers is called active learning.[11] The advantage of using active learning is that

---

[8] Maura Grossman and Gordon Cormack, "The Grossman–Cormack Glossary of Technology-Assisted Review," *Federal Courts Law Review* 7 (1) (2013): 4.

[9] Richard O. Duda, Peter E. Hart, and David G. Stork, *Pattern Classification*, 2nd ed. (New York: Wiley-Interscience, 2001).

[10] Thorsten Joachims, "Text Categorization with Support Vector Machines: Learning with Many Relevant Features," in *ECML 1998: Machine Learning: ECML-98* (New York: Springer, 1998), 137–142; Corinna Cortes and Vladimir Vapnik, "Support-Vector Networks," *Machine Learning* 20 (3) (1995): 273–297.

[11] David Cohn, Les Atlas, and Richard Ladner, "Improving Generalization with Active Learning," *Machine Learning* 15 (2) (1994): 201–221.

only a few labeled training documents are needed to start training the classifier, with any additional labels coming from the actual reviewing process. This saves time and effort otherwise spent fully labeling training data beforehand, removes the difficult step of creating a good training set, and also allows the classifier to learn as documents are being reviewed and tagged.

B Document Classification

The basic task of document classification is to build a model of the data and use that model to assign each document in a collection to one of two classes.[12] Different ML algorithms can be used to build the model, but they all require some labeled documents from each of the same classes as the training data. After the model is trained, it is used to assign new documents to one of the two classes. In e-discovery, these classes are called responsive (R) and non-responsive (NR).

Spam filters are a good example of a binary document classifier. The two classes used are "Spam" and "Not spam," and the model is trained using emails that are spam, and emails that are not spam. After the model is deployed on an email server, each incoming email passes through the classifier and emails that are assigned to the class "Spam" end up in the spam folder.

The standard output of a classifier is simply the class assignment (e.g., "Spam" or "Not spam"). This kind of classification is useful in many contexts, but has proven untenable for e-discovery. In predictive coding, the classifier output is instead based on the classifier score, with actual class assignment performed later. This is because classifier score by itself is difficult to interpret directly in most cases. It makes more sense to scale the classifier's scores so that they correspond to probability values. A user sets a threshold, such as 60% probability. Any documents that receive a classifier/probability score above 60% are then deemed responsive and classified accordingly.[13]

C Classification Accuracy

It is almost impossible to build a model that performs class label assignment with 100% accuracy. Though they may be less than perfectly accurate, modern document classifiers still achieve very high accuracy rates and are very helpful in a large number of applications. One does need to understand, though, that a classifier will make mistakes and that human reviewers must prepare to handle these mistakes. To aid this process of error correction, predictive coding solutions typically include a framework for evaluating accuracy. The following terminology is used for classifier evaluation.[14] Here, we assume that the classifier has to assign one of the two labels "R" or "NR":

- **False positives:** documents that are "NR" but the classifier assigns as "R."
- **False negatives:** documents that are "R" but the classifier assigns as "NR."
- **True positives:** documents that are "R" and the classifier correctly assigns as "R."
- **True negatives:** documents that are "NR" and the classifier correctly assigns as "NR."

---

[12] One can also generalize this task to classify documents into more than two classes.
[13] John Platt, "Probabilistic Outputs for Support Vector Machines and Comparisons to Regularized Likelihood Methods," in *Advances in Large Margin Classifiers*, eds. Alexander J. Smola and Peter J. Bartlett (Cambridge, MA: MIT Press, 2000), 61–74.
[14] Tom Fawcett, "An Introduction to ROC Analysis," *Pattern Recognition Letters* 27 (8) (2006): 861–862.

The most widely used classifier performance evaluation measures are precision, recall, and F1 score. *Precision* measures the ratio of the true positive documents among the documents that the classifier labeled as "R." *Recall* measures how many out of all responsive documents were correctly classified as "R." The *F1 score* is the harmonic mean between precision and recall. The F1 score will be high if both precision and recall are high. If either precision or recall is low, however, then the F1 score will also be low.

To understand the importance of evaluating classifier performance with F1 scores and not just with either precision or recall, consider the following two extreme cases. First, imagine that a classifier assigned a value of "R" to all documents. Recall will be 100%, but precision will be low because all documents that were non-responsive have been labeled incorrectly. Next, imagine that the classifier labels very few documents as "R." Precision will likely be very high, but recall will probably be extremely low because many actually responsive documents have been mislabeled. The addition of the F1 score's harmonic mean helps in determining whether precision or recall are unsatisfactory for a set of documents.

The issue of classifier performance evaluation is central to predictive coding. While it is important to have an accurate classifier in most applications, different applications may have different levels of tolerance for mistakes. A mistake in a spam filter classifier may be annoying, but it will probably not have any far-reaching consequences. In e-discovery, though, classifier mistakes may mean that responsive documents are missed, and as a consequence a case may be mishandled.

D Defensibility and Control Set

Courts accept certain threshold levels of precision and recall as sufficient when evaluating document review done with predictive coding.[15] This section discusses how to evaluate classifier performance to make sure that the results satisfy legal requirements, and that the results of the predictive coding workflow are defensible in court.

Defensibility begins with a control set. In practice, building a control set is not only expensive, but also prone to error. If a corpus has low richness, a large number of documents may need to be labeled in order to find even a handful of responsive documents for the control set. Without a sizeable number of responsive documents, a control set simply provides a good estimation of confidence for precision or recall. In addition, the process of creating a control set first may be inaccurate because the reviewers don't fully understand the matter yet, and may not know with certainty which documents are responsive and which ones are not.

After a control set is created, the predictive coding workflow begins. As the classifier is being trained, the model is constantly evaluated on the control set.[16] Training can stop once the precision, recall, and F1 scores reach acceptable levels. These acceptable levels are commonly found by calculating the confidence interval. Confidence interval is calculated by finding a range of values that all estimate a particular parameter within a given level of probability. Think of it as an estimate of an estimate. A good rule of thumb for assessing the

---

[15] Andrew Peck, "Search, Forward: Will Manual Document Review and Keyword Searches be Replaced by Computer-Assisted Coding?," *Law Technology News*, October 2011: 25–29, available at: https://law.duke.edu/sites/default/files/centers/judicialstudies/TAR_conference/Panel_1-Background_Paper.pdf.

[16] John Tredennick, "Measuring Recall in E-Discovery Review, Part One: A Tougher Problem Than You Might Realize," Catalyst Blog, October 15, 2014, available at: https://catalystsecure.com/blog/2014/10/measuring-recall-in-e-discovery-review-a-tougher-problem-than-you-might-realize-part-1.

rigor of a control set is a confidence interval of 95%. This does not mean that the classifier reliably finds 95% of responsive documents within a corpus. Rather, the confidence interval tells us that the precision, recall, and F1 scores will fall within an interval of plus or minus 5% of their estimated value 95% of the time. Discussion of confidence interval is beyond the scope of this chapter, but bear in mind that the confidence interval is computed based on the size of the control set and the number of responsive documents in it.[17] Ideally, the bigger the control set, the smaller the confidence interval will be, and the better trained the classifier will be.

1 Training and Test Set

The standard process of training a classifier requires two special subsets of data. One subset is labeled and contains the examples of responsive and non-responsive documents used for training the classifier. The second subset of documents also has manual labels and is called the test set. This test set is not used during training, and it is in fact critical to keep the training and test set documents separate.[18] Usually, the training set and the test set are created and fixed before classifier training starts.

Since the training set in predictive coding is created in an active learning procedure and grows as the review process continues, particular attention must be paid to the creation of the control set. In predictive coding, the control set is the same as the test set used in other ML processes. Just like a test set, the control set is created by taking a random sample of documents from the total set of documents. As with the test set, it is crucial to make sure that none of the control set documents will be reviewed and tagged as part of the training set. One difference between test sets and the control sets used in predictive coding, however, is that particular attention needs to be paid to the issue of reviewer bias.

2 Reviewer Bias

Reviewer bias is a hard problem to solve, but can have a significant effect on the performance evaluation on a control set.[19] All labels for the training set and for the control set are assumed to be "true" and independent of a classifier training procedure. However, a reviewer may assign a certain label to a document based on what she knows about the control set documents, or about the training procedure. Since precision, recall, and F1 are all computed for the control set, the reviewer may, for example, assign a label to a training document that would improve the numbers for those measures, rather than sticking to more objective measurement of its truth. This bias is more likely to happen in predictive coding systems that support creation of the control set during the active learning process, because the same reviewers are likely to label both the training documents and the control set documents.[20]

---

[17] Maura R. Grossman, Gordon V. Cormack, Jim Wagner, and Maureen O'Neill, "A Practitioner's Guide to Statistical Sampling in E-Discovery," DiscoverReady, October 16, 2012, available at: http://discoverready.com/wp-content/uploads/A-Practitioners-Guide-to-Statistical-Sampling-in-E-Discover.pdf.

[18] Pang-Ning Tan, Michael Steinbach, and Vipin Kumar, *Introduction to Data Mining*, 1st ed. (Harlow: Pearson, 2005), 148–149.

[19] William Webber, Mossaab Bagdouri, David D. Lewis, and Douglas W. Oard, "Sequential Testing in Classifier Evaluation Yields Biased Estimates of Effectiveness," in *Proceedings of the 36th international ACM SIGIR Conference on Research and Development in Information Retrieval (SIGIR '13)* (New York, NY: ACM, 2013), 933–936.

[20] Grossman et al., "A Practitioner's Guide to Statistical Sampling in E-Discovery," *supra* note 17.

3 Generalization Error

Once a classifier is trained, it is evaluated on the documents in the control set. The next step is to compute the precision, recall, and the F1 score. It is possible to compute these measures for the training set as well, and this is often done as part of an evaluation, but in any case, the classifier is expected to perform well on the training set, since that data is used to learn and is incorporated into the model. Where a classifier may not perform as well is on new, unseen data. Finding this kind of behavior is crucial for users. When a classifier performs poorly on unseen data, this is called generalization error. Generalization error is a measure of how well a classifier will work with unseen data after learning from its training data.[21]

An extreme example of massive generalization error is when a classifier merely memorizes the labels of its training set of documents, becomes 100% accurate on that set, and then proceeds to score a 0% on any subsequent, new documents presented. Without a measure of generalization error, there will not be any true indicator of the classifier performance.

Generalization error is impossible to measure exactly in practice because users can never foresee the potential labels for all possible unseen documents, let alone ever encounter every single possibility. A test or control set is a means of estimating the generalization error. If the classifier has access to the test documents during training, it will be able to incorporate them into its model and therefore the test set accuracy, or other performance measure, won't be an estimation of the generalization error. This is the reason for the strict separation of the training set from the test (control) set.

4 Stratified Sampling

When using data with low richness, or data that has a very particular distribution of documents, a control set via a random sample of the entire data set may not be representative of the data as a whole. The solution to this problem is to perform stratified sampling. In stratified sampling, the data is divided into groups, with each group sampled according to its size or some other measure of importance. Stratified sampling may be a more precise method of evaluation for precision, recall, and F1, but just as we stressed above, particular attention must be paid to the sample creation process. For a performance evaluation based on a stratified sampling control set to be acceptable, the control set has to be created from a statistically random sample of the data that has no inherent bias.

E Comparison with Human Review

Evaluation of predictive coding performance is one of the central issues in the e-discovery process. How accurate is an ML classifier compared to human reviewers? To begin to address this, it's important to remember that while classifier accuracy may not reach 100%, human reviewers only very rarely reach 100% themselves. There are many reasons humans fall short of perfect performance. One limitation on human reviewers is that they sometimes become fatigued from work and simply lose concentration. If human reviewers classify documents carelessly, then classifier performance will suffer.

Fatigue is not the only factor, though. Classifier performance is evaluated against the manual labels that are assumed to be truth, but these "truth" labels are produced by human reviewers, each of whom may have their own particular mental model of what "truth" is.

---

[21] Tan et al., *Introduction to Data Mining*, supra note 18, at 172–173.

Different reviewers may have different mental models, and even the same reviewer might change their mental model at some point during the review process. A number of studies have analyzed to what extent humans agree on what are true labels. When asking multiple humans to label the same documents, these studies have shown that this inter-annotator agreement is in most cases around 80%.[22] This means that if multiple different reviewers prepare true labels for the same documents in the control set, the evaluation results may be different for each reviewer's labels and perhaps achieve only around 80% accuracy.

III MACHINE LEARNING AND CLASSIFICATION

A *Decision Tree Classifier*

Training the classifier model is the inductive step of the classification process. Assigning labels to the documents is the deductive step. The actual process of training the model will unfold based on the classification algorithm used. There are, however, some underlying principles of the training process that influence the accuracy of the resulting model. A high-level understanding of that process will help in understanding the importance of the quality and quantity of the training data, and also of feature selection.

Figure 3.6.1 is based on R2D3's "A Visual Introduction to Machine Learning," and provides an illustration of how a classifier can be trained.[23] This diagram shows a classifier for a real estate application, with the objective of automatically differentiating between houses in San Francisco (SF) and New York (NYC). The real estate agency has extensive information about each property, including price and location. Even those who are not experts on real estate probably have at least some background knowledge about these two cities to help them start selecting features for the classifier. The first most prominent differentiator between these two cities is elevation. If a house is at a certain higher elevation, we know it is in SF. Houses at a lower elevation can be in either city. Next, another relatively well-known feature is price: We know that houses at a lower elevation, but above a certain price point, are likely to be in NYC.

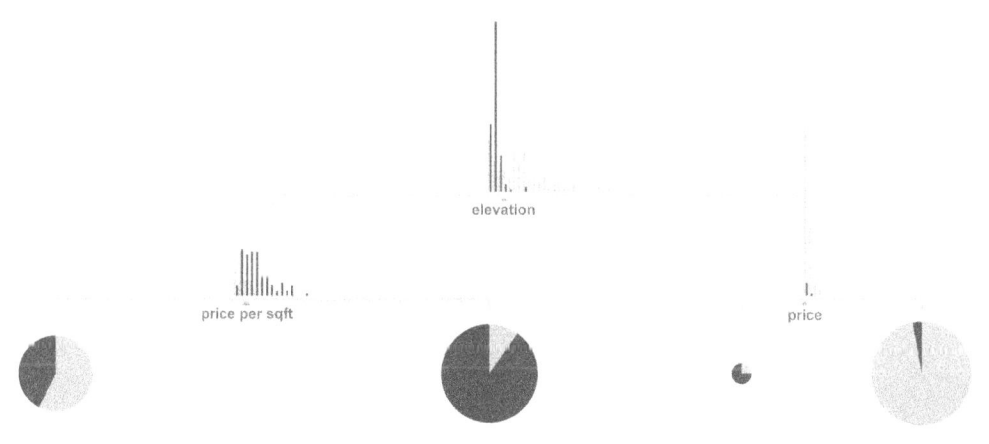

FIGURE 3.6.1 Visualization of the machine learning process.

---

[22] Barbara Di Eugenio and Michael Glass, "The Kappa Statistic: A Second Look," *Computational Linguistics* 30 (1) (2004): 95–101.
[23] R2D3, "Visual Introduction to Machine Learning," available at: www.r2d3.us/visual-intro-to-machine-learning-part-1.

This process of selecting the most prominent features and defining thresholds or other operations on them is the basis of a decision tree classifier.[24] Figure 3.6.1 shows how this may look with the two features already mentioned, with an additional third feature, price per square foot. The actual training procedure is more complex than shown in this example, but the basics are the same. The histograms and pie charts show the number of houses in each city that fit the parameters. Dark gray is used for houses in SF, and light gray is used for houses in NYC. We can see a lot of dark gray on the left-hand side, and mostly light gray on the right-hand side, so a visual inspection seems to point to our initial guesses being valid.

If one is only analyzing a few features, as in this example, it is possible to perform this procedure with just a manual analysis. The more features you add to a model, however, the more complex the classification process becomes, and the harder it will be for unaided humans to comprehend. In e-discovery, the document text comprises the data for the classifier, and the features are a document's individual words. Thus, the number of features in an e-discovery procedure is many hundreds of thousands, even after the standard pre-processing steps that remove stop words and filter by minimum document count.[25] The process of training a classifier for e-discovery is therefore very complex.

B *Support Vector Machines*

The support vector machine (SVM) classifier is comparatively harder to explain than the decision tree classifier.[26] One similarity, though, is that SVM uses words as features and learns how to separate documents into two classes. Since SVM treats documents as mathematical objects, that separation is often depicted as a line on an X–Y plane. This line is called the decision boundary, and it is optimized to find the so-called maximum margin separation between two classes, as shown by the lines in Figure 3.6.2.

The SVM derives its name from the support vectors, the most important training documents from each class. These are depicted as solid circles in Figure 3.6.2. During the label assignment, the SVM computes whether the document is more similar to the responsive or to the non-responsive class support vectors, and assigns each document to whichever class it most corresponds to.

This simple example illustrates a number of critical issues when using ML in any application, and using e-discovery in particular. First, this model illustrates the importance of having a sufficient number of training examples for each class. The exact threshold for sufficiency may depend on the specific problem, but a good rule of thumb is to have a few hundred training documents in order to produce reliable classifier performance. The classifier will stop improving after a certain very large number of training examples, but that number is usually high, with many thousands of examples from each class.[27]

In addition to a good quantity of training examples, it is critical to have good-quality data. Data quality directly translates into the quality of the classifier. In the example previously discussed in Figure 3.6.1, if many of the houses being used as data points either don't have elevation data or don't have price data, then there is no possible way that the classification for every datum will be

---

[24] Tan et al., *Introduction to Data Mining*, *supra* note 18, at 150–155.
[25] Christopher D. Manning and Hinrich Schütze, *Foundations of Statistical Natural Language Processing* (Cambridge, MA: MIT Press, 1999).
[26] Bernhard Schölkopf and Alexander J. Smola, *Learning with Kernels: Support Vector Machines, Regularization, Optimization, and Beyond* (Cambridge, MA: MIT Press, 2001).
[27] Duda et al., *Pattern Classification*, *supra* note 9, at 296–297.

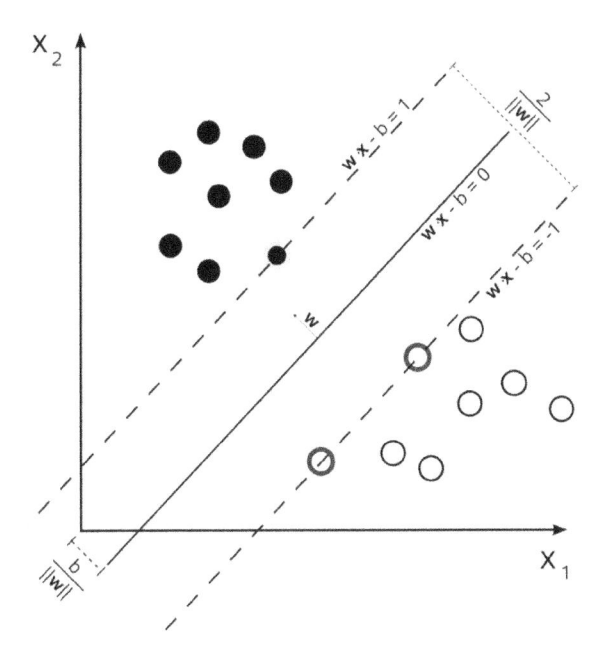

FIGURE 3.6.2 Mathematical objects in SVM with decision boundaries.[28]

correct. In e-discovery, this means that low quality of something like optical character recognition (OCR), for example, will probably result in lower classifier performance.[29]

In addition to quality and quantity concerns, data also needs to be preprocessed and evaluated before classifier training, to make sure there is no noise that may confuse the classifier. If available, one should use prior knowledge or background knowledge when preparing data for the classifier. And, as always, the control set can be used to evaluate the performance of the classifier, bearing in mind that no control set documents can be used for the initial training of the classifier.

IV LATENT SEMANTIC INDEXING AND CLUSTERING

Latent semantic indexing (LSI) and clustering are additional components often used in predictive coding. They can also be used as an alternative to predictive coding that does not require manual labeling and training. Latent semantic indexing uncovers hidden concepts or topics in a document collection, and can find other instances of the concept or topic between documents, going beyond a simple word match from a keyword search.[30] Clustering, meanwhile, is a process of discovering groups of semantically related documents. Both technologies are used to group together similar documents and present groups of related documents to human reviewers. This section explains the basics of LSI and clustering and discusses how they are used in predictive coding.

---

[28] Image sourced from: https://en.wikipedia.org/wiki/File:Svm_max_sep_hyperplane_with_margin.png.
[29] John Tredennick, "Does Bad OCR Make for Good TAR?" Catalyst Blog, July 8, 2013, available at: https://catalystsecure.com/blog/2013/07/does-bad-ocr-make-for-good-tar.
[30] Christos H. Papadimitriou, Hisao Tamaki, Prabhakar Raghavan, and Santosh Vempala, "Latent Semantic Indexing: A Probabilistic Analysis," in *Proceedings of the Seventeenth ACM SIGACT-SIGMOD-SIGART Symposium on Principles of Database Systems (PODS '98)* (New York, NY: ACM, 1998), 159–168.

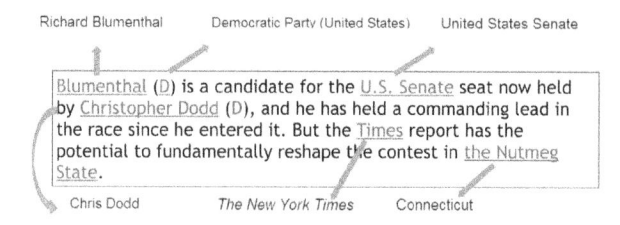

FIGURE 3.6.3 A news article containing last names, nicknames, abbreviations, and metonymy.[31]

A Ambiguity of Natural Language

One of the prominent features of natural language is its variability and ambiguity. People can say the same thing in many different ways, and the same word may have different meanings depending on context. The most famous phenomena of language are synonymy and polysemy. Synonyms are different words with the same meaning (e.g., "car" and "automobile"). Polysemic words are single words that have multiple meanings (e.g., an industrial "plant" versus a house "plant"). Context and life experience provide people with the knowledge they need to disambiguate the meaning of any given word in a document. But without context, it would be incredibly difficult to determine whether the word "bank" refers to the sides of a river ("I walked along the bank"), the movements of an aerial vehicle ("the plane banked left"), or a financial institution ("She deposited her check at the bank").

More complex examples of language ambiguity and variability are illustrated in Figure 3.6.3. In certain writing formats, it is customary to reference only the last name of a person being mentioned, or to use a completely different nickname, instead of referencing a person's full name repeatedly. The upshot of this is that one person can be referred to with multiple different versions of the same name. Organizations do this as well, often using shorter, informal versions of their full name. In addition, metonymy – substitution of well-known descriptive words or phrases in place of a proper noun – is often used to make reference to cities, places, or groups of people via nicknames and shorthand.

B Keyword Search

Keyword search has been a powerful tool in e-discovery for over a decade.[32] At the beginning of the e-discovery process, attorneys compile lists of search terms that they think are contained within potentially responsive documents. Those terms and phrases are subsequently used to find all documents that contain them in order to find responsive documents. Attorneys usually use advanced search technologies such as Boolean search and proximity search, and use search phrases instead of only individual words.

The language phenomena described in Section IV.A pose challenges that are difficult to resolve with keyword search alone. It is certainly possible to handle some of the issues manually. For example, while working on the search terms list, a human reviewer can add all synonyms for a word to the words on the search list. It is also possible to add versions of names, such as nicknames, to a search terms list. A quick example of this would be a reviewer

---

[31] Dan Roth, "Making Sense of Unstructured Data," presentation given at Paul Kantor's Fusion Fest Workshop, 2014, available at: http://l2r.cs.illinois.edu/~danr/Talks/Roth-Andreessen-09-2014.pdf.
[32] EDRM, "Chapter 6: Search Methodologies," EDRM Search Guide, available at: www.edrm.net/resources/project-guides/edrm-search-guide/search-methodologies/.

adding the names William, Will, Willy, Bill, and Billy to their search list. These simple techniques are called query expansion techniques, and they are extremely helpful.[33] The downside, of course, is that these techniques add to the complexity of the search term creation process and extend its duration. And despite these techniques, a search term may still be missed if, for example, the word is simply misspelled at certain points (e.g., Willy spelled Willie).

Another query expansion technique is to add the top responsive documents to a search. With this technique, when one searches a document collection using a search terms list and finds some responsive documents, it becomes possible to add those full documents to the whole query in order to provide more context for the search terms as the search continues. One has to be careful when executing such large queries, though, and evaluate whether this technique will slow down the search process more than is desirable.

A common request for predictive coding solutions is to help users explore the data in a collection to "show me what I don't know." Creation of search terms lists and keyword searches use information that attorneys already have about a case, but these techniques are less effective when trying to discover new information. More advanced ML and NLP techniques are thus required.

C Latent Semantic Indexing

Latent semantic indexing was designed to handle the language phenomena of polysemy and synonymy.[34] Latent semantic indexing uses statistical analysis of the co-occurrence of words within a document collection to discover latent semantic concepts present in the collection. These concepts are latent – they are not explicitly present in the data as either labels or metadata – but they are still powerful concepts existing within the data that LSI has the capability to reveal. For example, the word "accountant" and the phrase "balance sheet" both have similar contexts. Latent semantic indexing would discover this context relationship, and in turn discover a latent concept of "accounting" that is shared between them.

Figures 3.6.4a and 3.6.4b illustrate how LSI uses words that co-occur in the same document, and how it associates different words with larger concepts. Figure 3.6.4a shows an association network for a group of words that might appear in a document. This network reveals that "baseball," "bat," "game," and "ball" often occur in the same documents, and that "stage" and "theater" often occur in the same documents. The word "play" is critical to both concepts, and the context surrounding "play" defines the more specific meaning of this polysemic word. Figure 3.6.4b shows how LSI groups co-occurring words together and computes a latent concept common for all of them (i.e., "play").

After LSI computes latent semantic concepts, it represents each document not as a collection of words, but as a collection of these latent concepts. Consider two documents: the first document contains the word "accountant" and the other contains the phrase "balance sheet." Assume that the case in question concerns accounting. Attorneys will need to search for documents that mention accounting, and so they will probably put the

---

[33] Feng C. Zhao, Douglas W. Oard, and Jason R. Baron, "Improving Search Effectiveness in the Legal E-discovery Process Using Relevance Feedback," in *Proceedings of the Global E-Discovery/E-Disclosure Workshop on Electronically Stored Information in Discovery at the 12th International Conference on Artificial Intelligence and Law (ICAIL '09 DESI Workshop)* (Barcelona: DESI Press, 2009).

[34] Scott Deerwester, Susan T. Dumais, George W. Furnas, Thomas K. Landauer, and Richard Harshman, "Indexing by Latent Semantic Analysis," *Journal of the American Society for Information Science* 41 (6) (1990): 391–407.

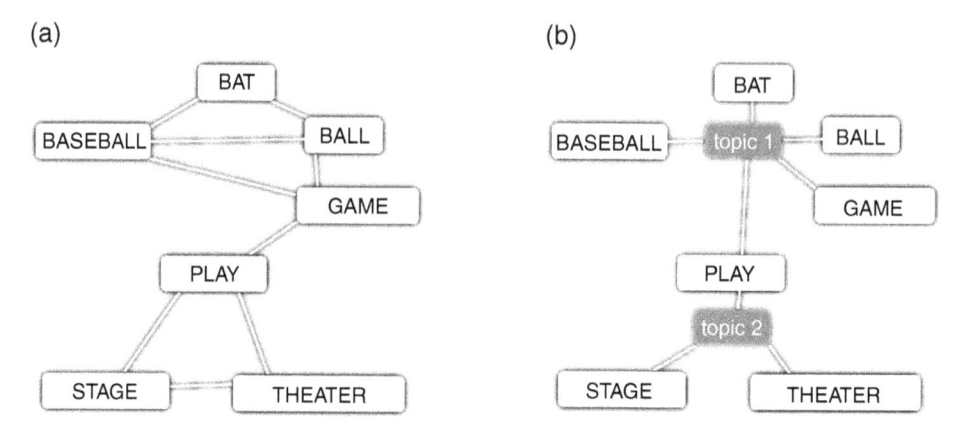

FIGURE 3.6.4 LSI-created word associations.[35]

word "accountant" on the search terms list for a keyword search. However, if the search terms list does not also contain the phrase "balance sheet" as a latent concept associated with "accountant," then documents that mention "balance sheet" without mentioning "accountant" will be missed, despite obvious relevance to the case.

Latent semantic indexing can alleviate this problem by helping to identify all documents that belong to the concept of "accounting." It can compute the latent semantic concepts and discover that the concept "accounting" is expressed not only through words like "accountant," but also through phrases such as "balance sheet," and thus achieve a more thorough search that returns documents related to the wider concept of "accounting."

While LSI can compute the associations between certain concepts, and identify groups of words that occur together and thus describe a common topic, it is important to remember that LSI does not know the actual names of the topics. Latent semantic indexing simply identifies topics with simple names, such as "concept 1," "concept 2," etc. More complete descriptions are assigned to each concept at a later step, achieved using words that are most commonly associated with each concept. One study used a large corpus of emails from the Enron corporation. In this research, shown in Table 3.6.1, LSI analyzed company emails. However, the content of these emails covered a wide range of topics, from work-related topics such as environmental regulations that might impact Enron's business (concept 1), to non-work-related areas of interest to employees, such as fantasy football (concept 2). These concepts can easily be named by human reviewers after LSI has done its job.

Latent semantic indexing is used in multiple steps of the e-discovery process, including as a query expansion technique. A keyword query can be expanded using top words associated with the latent concepts that LSI identifies.[36] Latent semantic indexing can also be used as a data exploration technique, grouping documents by their latent concepts. This can provide an overview and summary of the topics discussed in a document collection.

Latent semantic indexing aids predictive coding workflows by providing options for query expansion, and by expanding the concepts of keyword search terms to include more relevant

---

[35] Thomas K. Landauer and Susan T. Dumais, "A Solution to Plato's Problem: The Latent Semantic Analysis Theory of Acquisition, Induction, and Representation of Knowledge," *Psychological Review* 104 (2) (2007): 211–240.

[36] Andy Garron and April Kontostathis, "Latent Semantic Indexing with Selective Query Expansion," 2017, available at: http://webpages.ursinus.edu/akontostathis/GarronKontostathisTextMining2012.pdf.

TABLE 3.6.1 *LSI-computed areas of interest in Enron emails.*[37]

Concept 1	Concept 2
Environmental	Texans
Air	Win
MTBE	Football
Emissions	Fantasy
Clean	Sportsline
EPA	Play
Pending	Team
Safety	Game
Water	Sports
Gasoline	Games

information beyond the initial keywords. This is valuable for data exploration, and also helps to discover more diverse responsive documents to be used in a training set. Discovering latent concepts, instead of just individual keywords, helps classifiers learn the conceptual model of the set of responsive documents. Predictive coding workflows can also use LSI concepts during the linear review step. If documents are presented to human reviewers in a particular order, then conceptually similar documents can be reviewed together. This helps to improve the efficiency of the review process because a reviewer can create a mental model of the topic in question, and the documents related to that topic, and have an easier time recognizing responsive and non-responsive information.

D Clustering

Clustering is another well-established ML technique for data exploration and summarization.[38] Clustering groups documents that are semantically related, using a different mathematical process than LSI but nevertheless accomplishing a similar goal of organizing and summarizing data. Clustering is a fairly intuitive process: Documents can be clustered into groups so that similar documents are assigned to the same group and dissimilar documents are put into different groups. Clustering is a powerful visual tool, but it is not without its problems. Figure 3.6.5 illustrates some of the potential ambiguity associated with clustering.[39]

The true number of clusters in this data set is not known to the user, and the number may even depend on the level of granularity required by the case. E-discovery solutions don't require the user to specify the number of clusters they would like to compute; instead, they use heuristics to estimate the appropriate number of clusters.

Hierarchical clustering is one possible solution to the issue highlighted in Figure 3.6.5. Instead of deciding how many clusters to compute, one can generate a hierarchy with two clusters on the top level, four clusters on the second level, and six clusters on the third level of

---

[37] Table reproduced from: Michal Rosen-Zvi, Chaitanya Chemudugunta, Thomas Griffiths, Padhraic Smyth, and Mark Steyvers, "Learning Author–Topic Models from Text Corpora," *ACM Transactions on Information Systems* 28 (1) (2010).
[38] Tan et al., *Introduction to Data Mining*, supra note 18.
[39] Ibid.

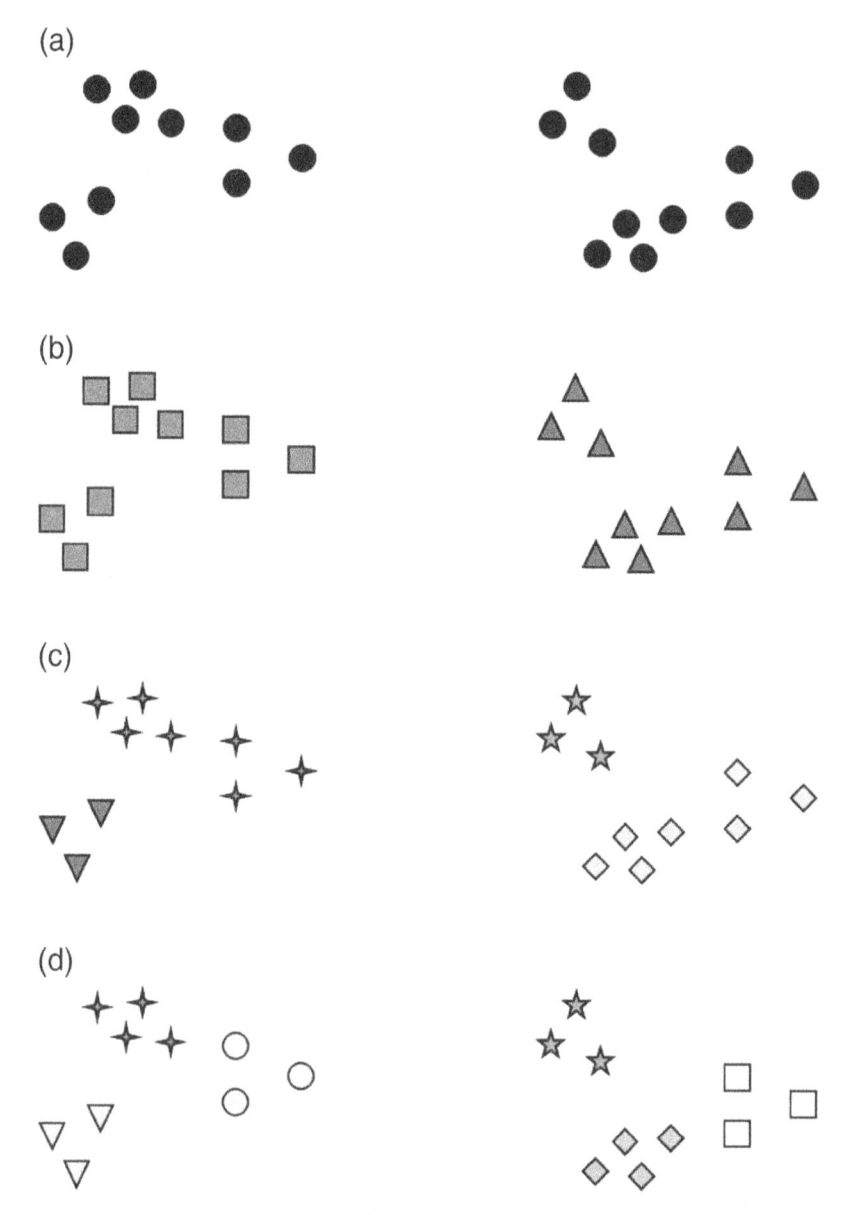

FIGURE 3.6.5 Subdivisions within a cluster.[40]

the hierarchy. Hierarchical clustering is usually visualized with overlapping clusters. Figures 3.6.6 and 3.6.7 show two different methods for illustrating these hierarchies visually.[41]

Hierarchical clustering presents a summary of the topics in the data and it can be explored at different levels of granularity. Some large clusters, for example, may be identified as non-responsive right away, while other clusters will need to be explored across multiple levels of a hierarchy. As discussed above, clustering is used in predictive coding and e-discovery in much the same way that LSI is used; it can create a quick overview of the data, and organize the data for the purposes of early data exploration at the beginning of a case. In predictive

[40] Id. at 491.
[41] Id. at 516.

coding, clusters like these can be used to compute stratified samples for the control set, and also to group documents assigned to a reviewer according to the documents' topics.

V NATURAL LANGUAGE PROCESSING

A Entity Extraction

Recent advances in NLP research and the availability of increasingly powerful computational resources have enabled the introduction of deep language analysis into the e-discovery process. One of the most well-known NLP techniques is extraction of named entities, such as the names of people, organizations, and locations. These are the three most common types of entity extraction, but there are many other types of entities used, such as facilities, vehicles, money, works of art, etc. (Table 3.6.2).

TABLE 3.6.2 *Main named entity types.*[42]

Type	Tag	Sample categories
People	PER	Individuals, fictional characters, small groups
Organization	ORG	Companies, agencies, political parties, religious groups, sports teams
Location	LOC	Physical extents, mountains, lakes, seas
Geo-political entity	GPE	Countries, states, provinces, counties
Facility	FAC	Bridges, buildings, airports
Vehicles	VEH	Planes, trains, and automobiles

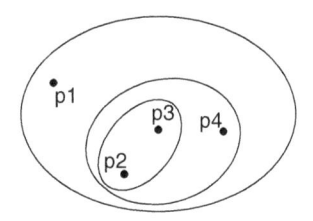

FIGURE 3.6.6 Nested cluster diagram.

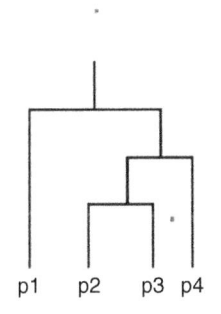

FIGURE 3.6.7 Dendrogram.

---

[42] Table reproduced from: Daniel Jurafsky and James H. Martin, *Speech and Language Processing: An Introduction to Natural Language Processing, Computational Linguistics, and Speech Recognition*, 1st ed. (Upper Saddle River, NJ: Prentice Hall PTR, 2000).

```
CHICAGO (AP) - Citing high fuel prices, United Airlines said Friday it
has increased fares by $6 per round trip on flights to some cities
also served by lower-cost carriers. American Airlines, a unit of AMR,
immediately matched the move, spokesman          said. United, a
unit of UAL, said the increase took effect Thursday night and applies
to most routes where it competes against discount carriers, such as
Chicago to Dallas and Atlanta and Denver to San Francisco, Los
Angeles, and New York.
```

FIGURE 3.6.8 Entities extracted from an article about airline fare increases.[43]

Figure 3.6.8 shows an example of named entities extracted from a news article about airline rate increases. Organization names the NLP program recognizes as primary exemplars of the data being sought are underlined and dark gray. Names of organizations the program thinks might be of secondary importance are shown in lighter gray. Meanwhile, the names of persons are underlined in the lightest gray, and black is used for locations.[44]

This extraction process is an example of how unstructured data – in the form of text – can be turned into structured data using NLP. Knowing the various entities by type makes it possible to more efficiently uncover the story hiding within the data. Extracting entities also makes it possible to extend keyword search and topic exploration and discover, for example, the most discussed locations or organizations in the data, or create a timeline of how often main custodians have discussed competitor companies.

B Sentiment Analysis

Sentiment analysis is another popular NLP technology, used to assign a sentiment score to each document in a collection. A positive sentiment score identifies documents that convey a largely positive opinion of the terms searched for. Similarly, negative scores are assigned to documents that express largely negative opinions. A score of zero means that a document's content has a neutral sentiment. In e-discovery, sentiment analysis adds yet another dimension to data exploration by making it possible, for example, to filter out those documents that discuss certain organizations or people in negative terms. Similar to clustering, the basic explanation of sentiment scores is easy to understand and does not require much training before use. That said, there are two issues that must be considered when using sentiment analysis in e-discovery.

The first issue concerns the level of analysis. Some of the most frequently found examples of sentiment analysis results involve short documents, such as product reviews, that express only one sentiment – positive or negative. The following is an example of a definitely positive document: "I bought an iPhone a few days ago. It is such a nice phone, although a little large. The touch screen is cool. I simply love it!" Things are not always so simple, however. The following product review conveys a much more vague sentiment: "I bought an iPhone a few days ago. It is such a nice phone. The touch screen is really cool . . . However, my mother was mad with me as I did not tell her before I bought the phone. She also thought the phone was too expensive." What to make of this? In this second document, some opinions are positive, while others are negative. State-of-the-art sentiment classifiers are able to take into account the most important language phenomena, such as use of negation, other sentiment shifters ("like" vs. "don't like"), and amplifiers ("extremely

[43] Ibid. (Text reproduced from: Jurafsky and Martin, *Speech and Language Processing*).
[44] Ibid.

positive review"). In this way, a classifier will be able to take the positive data ("The touch screen is really cool"), and separate this from negative data ("She also thought the phone was too expensive").

Most documents processed in e-discovery are more complex than short product reviews. Email documents, in particular, are likely to express both positive and negative sentiment within the same document. In many cases, then, it would be incorrect to simply add up the sentiment for all words and phrases and create the final score from that basic arithmetic. This would result in the scores from the positive parts and the negative parts of the document simply canceling each other out, winding up with a document scored with a sentiment of 0. We need something more. When sentiment analysis is used in e-discovery, it is important to understand how scores from positive and negative opinions are combined so that we reach a correct expectation about the final sentiment score for documents.

Another issue with sentiment analysis is the choice of the sentiment classifier training procedure. One of the main types of classifier used for sentiment analysis uses SVM. This type of classifier manually assigns training documents and trains a model based on those documents. The advantage of this type of classifier is that it uses a training set, and it can learn about how sentiment is expressed in that particular set. The disadvantage is that the classifier will be trained specifically on this data, which may make it difficult for the classifier to analyze data from another case. This problem is referred to as domain adaptation – the specific sentiment data learned from one document set may not be transferable to other cases outside of the training set. Consider once more a sentiment analysis of product reviews. A classifier trained to analyze movie reviews, for example, would have a difficult time handling hotel reviews.

An alternative to training the classifier with labeled data is to use a list-based classifier. This type of sentiment classifier uses a list of all words and expressions that may have a sentiment value. The advantage of this approach is that the list already contains generic sentiment words and thus does not fall prey to domain adaptation. The disadvantage of this approach is that the list of sentiment words and phrases may be incomplete, which could mean that the classifier does not learn from the new examples that are manually labeled.

VI CASE STUDY: NEXLP AND STORY ENGINE

NexLP's Story Engine application is an example of how NLP and ML can be used to solve the *story gap* problem in e-discovery with respect to investigations and information governance. Story Engine allows case teams to efficiently answer basic questions for lawyers and investigators. What actors, places, and things in your data are important? Who was communicating with whom and about what? Why this discussion? When did this discussion take place? Where are the key facts and critical documents hidden? Story Engine asks these questions in order to communicate the narrative that emerges during the course of the review. It uses a variety of NLP tools, including name entity extraction, identification of variations of the same name, topic analysis, and sentiment analysis. After data is processed and converted into structured data, Story Engine builds a communication graph on top of that data. This communication graph encodes and displays who was talking to whom, what entities were discussed, the time frame of the discussion, and other relevant points of data. Figure 3.6.9 shows a "baseball card"-type summary of emails that discuss Enron, extracted from the Enron email corpus.

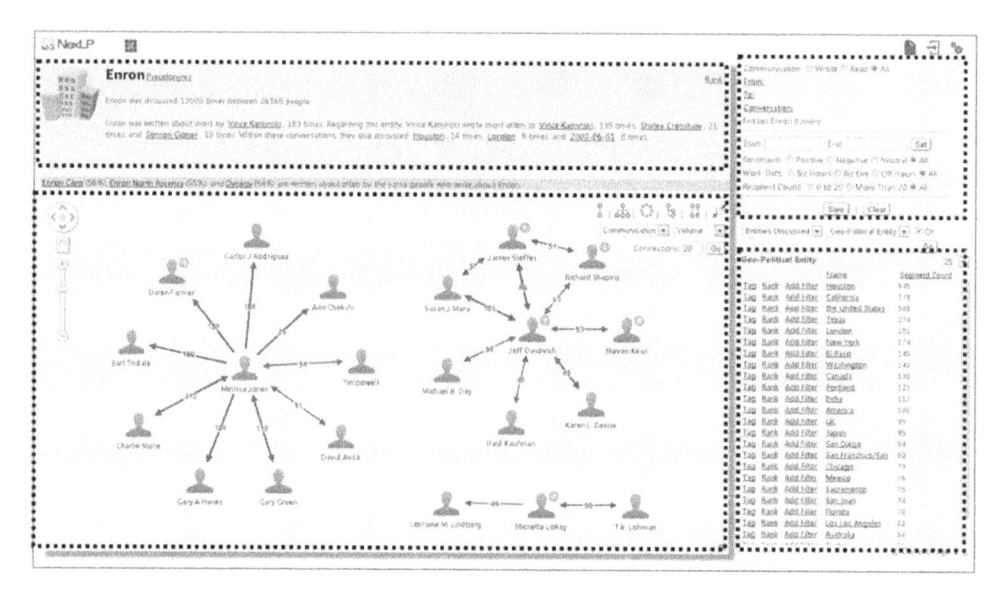

FIGURE 3.6.9 NexLP Enron email communication network and content summary for emails discussing Enron.[45]

Documents that discuss Enron are summarized according to several types of data: geopolitical entity (e.g., Houston, TX; London, UK), sentiment, and work shift. Communication analysis based on extracted entities reveals which custodians have similar communication patterns. The visual summary of the most important communication patterns among Enron employees helps to identify smaller communities within the larger network of that organization.

NexLP can also be used for anomaly detection analysis. Anomaly detection can find sudden changes in communication behavior that might be an indication of wrong-doing. For example, anomaly detection analysis may identify an individual who suddenly started sending an unusual number of emails late at night with negative sentiment. Those factors represent a significant anomaly, one that is a good place to begin an investigation into that person's emails.

COSMIC is NexLP's predictive coding module. It supports active learning for training a classifier, and also supports the creation of a control set during the classifier's training. The classifier can be enhanced with metadata features that Story Engine extracts from each email and that include the communicator information in addition to information about discussed entities and sentiment.

Figures 3.6.10–3.6.12 highlight how NexLP's use of NLP analysis allows the Story Engine application to reach beyond keyword-based searches.

VII CONCLUSION

Natural language processing and ML techniques have become increasingly integral to the function of e-discovery. Predictive coding algorithms, and NLP processing techniques such as LSI, are leading the way toward more efficient e-discovery systems that can shoulder the

---

[45] Data originally from Rosen-Zvi et al., "Learning Author–Topic Models from Text Corpora," *supra* note 37.

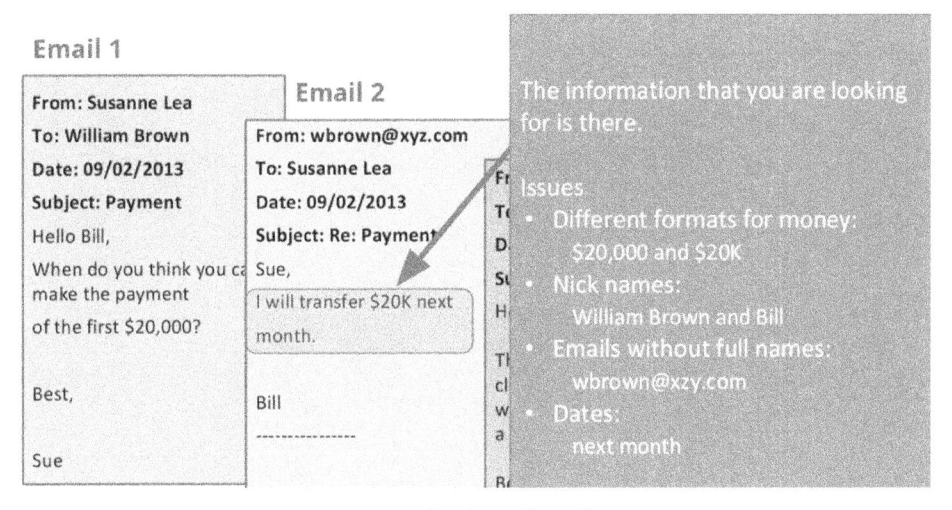

FIGURE 3.6.10 Example of emails under investigation.

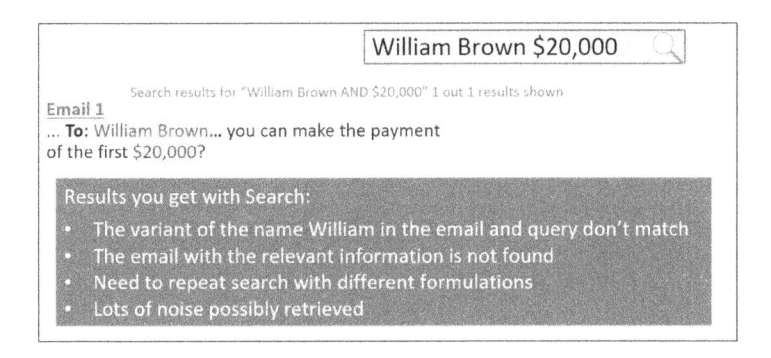

FIGURE 3.6.11 Failure of simple keyword search for "William Brown."

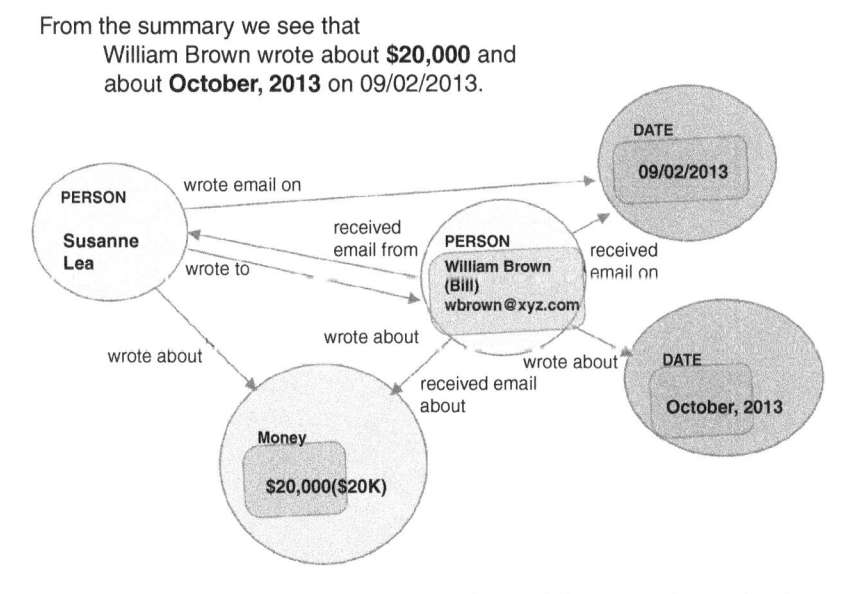

FIGURE 3.6.12 Story Engine summarizes data and discovers relevant details.

burden of work that was once performed by lawyers and other legal professionals in a time-consuming and tedious way.

Though there are many reasons for optimism about these techniques, some challenges still lie ahead. One of the biggest challenges for ML and NLP in e-discovery concerns the evaluation and review of these techniques. A continuous process of feedback and evolution can maintain and improve the consistency of results across the various methods outlined in this chapter.

3.7

Examining Public Court Data to Understand and Predict Bankruptcy Case Results

Warren E. Agin

I INTRODUCTION

Understanding what happens at scale in our judicial systems seems a relatively simple problem, but has proved difficult in the past due to the inability of practitioners to access the needed information. In this chapter, we examine bankruptcy case information made available by the Federal Judicial Center in 2017 and use that data to understand the difficulty Chapter 13 bankruptcy filers have in obtaining their bankruptcy discharge, the potential factors that correlate with obtaining a discharge, and to predict how likely a specific case is to succeed. We discuss a project conducted using data from over 700,000 cases, as well as examine much smaller data sets suitable for manipulation using Excel.

The US Bankruptcy Code provides a number of options that allow both businesses and individuals to obtain financial relief. This case study examines Chapter 13 cases, which allow individuals the opportunity to resolve their financial problems by making payments over a 3–5-year period. When a debtor completes their required payments, they obtain a *discharge*; essentially a court order relieving them from having to pay the remaining debt. The Chapter 13 debtor's goal is to complete the payments and obtain the discharge; however, obtaining a Chapter 13 bankruptcy discharge is notoriously difficult. Prior research shows that only one-third of Chapter 13 debtors complete their obligations under their plans and obtain a Chapter 13 discharge.[1] Usually, the bankruptcy case ends up dismissed, or converted to a case under Chapter 7.[2] Ten years of bankruptcy case data made available by the Federal Judicial Center in 2017 shows that from 2008 through 2017 only 39% of Chapter 13 filers successfully obtained their Chapter 13 discharges.[3]

In "Using Machine Learning to Predict Success or Failure in Chapter 13 Bankruptcy Cases," I describe in detail the process of applying machine learning algorithms to two years of data on Chapter 13 cases to predict, based only on information provided in the initial petition and summary of schedules, whether a specific debtor would successfully obtain a Chapter 13 discharge.[4] A number of techniques were examined, including regression

---

[1] Sarah Greene, Parina Patel, and Katherine Porter, "Cracking the Code: An Empirical Analysis of Consumer Bankruptcy Options," *Minnesota Law Review* 101 (2017): 1031.
[2] In a Chapter 7 case, the debtor still obtains a discharge of debts, but loses the ability to cure past payment deficiencies on loans secured by a house mortgage or car lien. As a result, the debtor might lose their house to foreclosure or have their car repossessed.
[3] Ed Flynn, "By the Numbers: Dead on Arrival Cases (at Bankruptcy Court)," *ABI Journal* 58 (2018).
[4] Warren E. Agin, "Using Machine Learning to Predict Success or Failure in Chapter 13 Bankruptcy Cases," in *Norton Annual Survey of Bankruptcy Law* (St. Paul, MN: Thomson Reuters, 2018).

systems and neural networks. The selected model, a random forest decision tree model, was able to predict case results with 70% accuracy overall – and for about 25% of cases, the model could predict results with more than 90% accuracy. This article also describes how, when case predictions were cross-referenced against actual case results, the model could assign to specific cases a highly accurate probability of success.[5]

This case study summarizes much of the ground covered by that article. It starts by providing a little context about the Chapter 13 process. It then describes some of the prior research by others on the linkages between a debtor's prior financial condition and the likelihood of obtaining a Chapter 13 discharge. After describing generally the information available from the Federal Judicial Center's Integrated Database, and exploring that data, this case study provides some basic information about random forest decision trees, the process used to review, select, and prepare the data set for the machine learning systems, and the results. Two truncated data sets are provided for use – a data set extracted directly from the bankruptcy Integrated Database (IDB), and a second data set organized for use by machine learning systems. Two sample Python scripts are provided in a Jupyter Notebook to facilitate experimentation in or out of the classroom. Finally, this case study presents a number of questions for consideration and class discussion.

II AN INTRODUCTION TO THE CHAPTER 13 PROCESS

The Chapter 13 process provides individual debtors with a mechanism for paying some amount of their debts over three to five years, while obtaining relief from the debts remaining at the end of the payment period. Contained within Title 11 of the US Code, the Chapter 13 provisions require that debtors contribute their excess income to making creditor payments for the term of the Chapter 13 plan.[6] At the beginning of the case, the debtor will file with the court a petition document that contains basic information about the debtor, along with schedules and a statement of financial affairs that provide detailed information about the debtor's financial condition. With these schedules, the debtor will file a "summary of schedules," which summarizes the financial information contained in the full set of schedules.[7] The debtor will also file a plan that describes how the debtor intends to repay a portion of his or her debts, including details on how the payment amounts are calculated. Typically, the debtor makes monthly payments to a Chapter 13 trustee, who then distributes the funds to creditors. The plan is filed with the court, creditors have an opportunity to object to the plan, and the court will confirm the plan if it meets statutory requirements.[8] Assuming the debtor obtains plan confirmation and completes the required payments, the debtor will obtain a discharge of the remaining debt.[9] Through this process, the Chapter 13 debtor obtains the benefits of a Chapter 13 case, namely a discharge from the debts that are beyond the debtor's ability to pay while retaining control over his or her assets.

The Chapter 13 provisions contrast with the Chapter 7 liquidation process, which allows a debtor to obtain a prompt discharge of debts without having to make monthly payments. For many debtors, the Chapter 7 process has many advantages over the Chapter 13 process. In

---

[5] Ibid.
[6] 11 U.S.C. § 1322(a)(1).
[7] The interested student can peruse the official bankruptcy forms at www.uscourts.gov/forms/bankruptcy-forms. The petition is form B 101, and the forms that comprise the schedules commence with form number B 106.
[8] 11 U.S.C. §§ 1322, 1325.
[9] 11 U.S.C. § 1328.

Chapter 7, a debtor keeps property with values under certain statutory amounts – referred to as exemptions – and obtains a discharge of most debts about 90 days after filing the bankruptcy petition. However, the Chapter 7 process has some drawbacks that Chapter 13 plans can address. First, in a Chapter 7 case the debtor must surrender property with a value above the exemption amounts. In a Chapter 13 case, the debtor may keep that property so long as the payments being made during the Chapter 13 plan are sufficient to pay creditors what they would have received in the Chapter 7 case. Second, in a Chapter 7 case the debtor who is behind on house or car loan payments will likely lose the property, which will be foreclosed or repossessed. In a Chapter 13 case, the debtor can keep such properties as long as the loan deficiency is cured during the Chapter 13 case. A number of other special situations exist in which a debtor's goals can be achieved through the Chapter 13 process but not the Chapter 7 process.

For debtors who file a Chapter 13 petition, real benefits accrue from finishing the plan payments successfully and obtaining a discharge. However, only a minority of Chapter 13 filers achieve this goal. Some cases are dismissed. In other cases, the Chapter 13 case is converted to a Chapter 7 case – sometimes voluntarily by the debtor who realizes that he or she cannot maintain the required payments. When a case is converted to a Chapter 7 case, the debtor will likely obtain a discharge of debts, but will also lose the house, car, or other property the Chapter 13 case was filed to protect.

To be successful in a Chapter 13 case, a debtor must be able to meet a number of conditions. First, because a Chapter 13 plan requires that a debtor contribute excess income to pay creditors, the debtor must have a monthly income that exceeds his or her monthly expenses. A debtor whose expenses exceed income, or who has no income, cannot obtain confirmation of a Chapter 13 plan. A debtor also needs to have a steady income for the 3–5 years of the plan. A debtor whose income is uncertain, or who is unable to maintain steady employment, will most likely fail to make the payments at some point during the plan period. Finally, the debtor must be responsible enough to budget for the plan payments, and make them regularly along with monthly house and car payments.

A debtor can suffer real harm from filing an unsuccessful Chapter 13 case. In many cases, the debtor's inability to meet needed conditions is self-evident, yet a Chapter 13 petition is still filed instead of a Chapter 7 petition. This can negatively impact the debtor in a number of ways. First, the legal fees charged for a Chapter 13 case are typically higher than those charged for a Chapter 7 case. The debtor who files a hopeless Chapter 13 case, which soon converts to a Chapter 7 case, might be overcharged for the service provided. Second, if a debtor has his or her plan confirmed, makes payments for a period of time, and then has his case converted to a Chapter 7 case, the debtor loses the money paid to the Chapter 13 trustee. With proper guidance the debtor could have filed a Chapter 7 case in the first place and avoided making what might be several years of payments on debts that would have been discharged completely in a Chapter 7 case. Finally, a debtor who is counseled to pursue Chapter 13 relief when they are unlikely to complete the plan payments might have unrealistic expectations about the final outcomes. The debtor might spend years trying hard to keep up the payments, delaying the point in time when they truly get a "fresh start" and can begin the process of rebuilding their financial future.

As a result, understanding the starting conditions that differentiate successful Chapter 13 cases from unsuccessful Chapter 13 cases can help attorneys better advise their consumer bankruptcy clients. Some differences are obvious. A client without income, or with expenses substantially above their income, will not succeed in a Chapter 13 case (although the data shows that many such cases are filed). Other factors are not immediately obvious, but can be identified by exploring data about Chapter 13 filings.

III PRIOR EXPLORATIONS USING BANKRUPTCY CASE DATA

Domain knowledge – substantive knowledge of the area being examined – is a key element of any data science project. Understanding the relationships between elements plays a role in selecting features for model inclusion, creating useful labels, and selecting algorithms. At the same time, the investigator needs to keep an open mind – even a knowledgeable practitioner might perceive patterns and relationships that don't actually exist in the data, and sophisticated data analysis might uncover surprising correlations in the data, leading to previously undiscovered insights. In addition to preliminary data analysis on the available data sets, the data scientist can increase her domain knowledge through an examination of prior literature.

A substantial body of research exists on the question of why some Chapter 13 cases succeed and some do not. Most of this research focuses on exploring the relationship between a small number of debtor characteristics and case outcomes, generally using standard statistical techniques for conducting empirical research. A small number of papers use more sophisticated regression techniques to correlate debtor characteristics with the likelihood of obtaining a Chapter 13 discharge. These examinations successfully identify key factors underlying case outcomes, and provide information that is useful in building predictive models.

An early study examined a large number of potential features against Chapter 13 outcomes using a relatively small set of cases filed in Utah. In his 2004 master's thesis, David Evans evaluated the predictors for success or failure in Chapter 13 cases.[10] This study was based on a random sampling of 668 cases filed in Utah during 1997, using information obtained from a manual review of PACER information and bankruptcy schedules. A number of potential features were compared with outcomes using logistic regression methods.[11] *Logistic regression* is a linear regression method designed to correlate independent variables with a dependent variable that only has two outcomes. In this example, the dependent variable is whether the debtor obtained a Chapter 13 discharge. The study identified the following as strong predictors of success: whether the debtor filed with a spouse (more likely), had children (less likely), or had filed bankruptcy before (less likely). While the presence of a mortgage correlated with higher success rates, the amount of the mortgage arrears inversely correlated with success rates. Interestingly, the author concluded that case completion was not linked with income or expense numbers, which seems counter-intuitive, given the clear importance of excess income in the Chapter 13 process. However, the regression methods used would have only identified simple linear relationships[12] against variables such as income or expenses. This possibly explains Mr. Evans' failure to find relationships between income, expenses, and case success – relationships which I concluded in my paper were non-linear in nature.

A 2016 paper prepared by the New York Federal Reserve[13] examined Chapter 13 cases filed in the District of Delaware during the 2001 fiscal year. Data was extracted from court

---

[10] David A. Evans, "Predictors of 1997 Chapter 13 Bankruptcy Completion and Dismissal Rates in Utah," *Utah State University, All Graduate Theses and Dissertations*, 2853 (2004), available at: https://digitalcommons.usu.edu/etd/2853.

[11] More on logistic regression can be found in Robert M. Lawless, Jennifer K. Robbennolt, and Thomas S. Ulen, *Empirical Methods in Law*, 2nd ed. (Alphen aan den Rijn: Wolters Kluwer, 2016), 298–304.

[12] That is, a relationship characterized by a straight line.

[13] Hülya Eraslan, Gizem Koşar, Wenli Li, and Pierre-Daniel Sarte, "An Anatomy of U.S. Personal Bankruptcy Under Chapter 13," FRB of NY Staff Report No. 764 (2017), available at: https://ssrn.com/abstract=2726511.

documents. The researchers reviewed 1085 cases, but excluded 134 cases because of data errors, and another 130 due to inconsistent information provided by the debtors. Using a final data set of 821 cases, they compared the case features against outcomes using a logistic linear model similar to that obtained through regression methods. They found that the length of the plan affected case outcomes, while it did not matter whether the filer was above or below median income. The amount of secured debt in arrears and the existence of a prior filing also correlated significantly with case outcomes.

For a 2017 paper, professors Sarah Greene, Parina Patel, and Katherine Porter applied logistic regression techniques to a set of national consumer bankruptcy case data to evaluate the relationships between a large number of variables and obtaining a Chapter 13 discharge.[14] To conduct their study, they used the 2007 Consumer Bankruptcy Project's compilation of information about 770 Chapter 13 cases. This database was previously assembled by academic researchers from bankruptcy case information, written questionnaires, and personal interviews, and contained rich information about family status, demographics, and financial conditions. They identified strong relationships between case success and race, the number of children in a household, availability of medical insurance coverage, whether a debtor filed pro se, and housing costs as a function of income.

IV THE FEDERAL JUDICIAL CENTER'S INTEGRATED DATABASE

For the most part, prior studies about the factors that correlate with Chapter 13 success or failure have had to rely on relatively small data sets. Often the cases are selected from a single judicial district. Since, as it turns out, success rates in Chapter 13 cases vary widely from court to court, results from single court studies can be considered potentially biased, and might not reflect national tendencies. Obtaining data on a national basis has, however, been historically difficult. Although anyone can go to a bankruptcy court clerk's office and review case information manually for free (all bankruptcy courts provide free PACER access terminals in the clerk's office), you have to have a PACER account to access case information over the internet. You have to obtain a separate PACER account for each judicial district – this is a cumbersome process, especially for non-lawyers. Also, the court charges a fee for each docket or document obtained using PACER, making a large-scale exploration expensive.

In 2017, the Federal Judicial Center, in conjunction with the Administrative Office of the US Courts, made data available for almost ten years of bankruptcy case filings through its IDB.[15] The IDB provides, for each individual case, 126 items of information plus a unique case key. A codebook provides details about each item of information in the database. Although the data does not contain debtor names, social security numbers, or other personally identifiable information, each record does include the docket number and district, allowing a researcher to look up a particular case on PACER. Notwithstanding the number of "fields" available for each record, the substantive information provided for each case is actually very limited. The IDB contains information about case opening and closure activity, and final case disposition. For consumer cases, the database provides information from the petition and summary of schedules. However, information from the schedules and statement of financial affairs themselves, and information about activity during the case, is not available.

---

[14] Green et al., "Cracking the Code," *supra* note 1.
[15] Bankruptcy data on cases filed, terminated, and pending from FY 2008 to 2017 is now available from the Federal Judicial Center at www.fjc.gov/research/idb.

In a January 2018 article published in the *American Bankruptcy Institute Journal*, researcher Ed Flynn examined the IDB data to understand how many bankruptcy cases reach successful results, and the relationships between case outcomes and the information the IDB provides.[16] For Chapter 13 cases, he examined a sample of 123,185 cases closed in fiscal years 2010 through 2016. Debtors obtained a Chapter 13 discharge in only 39.1% of cases. About 14% of the cases were dismissed in the first six months. Ed Flynn also identified a number of correlations between the information provided and case results. Filing pro se was possibly the highest predictor of case failure. Pro se cases constituted only 8.7% of all Chapter 13 cases, but almost always failed. Failed cases were also more likely to be filed as a solo case, to be preceded by a prior filing, and to involve missing schedules or unpaid filing fees. In general, in those cases where bankruptcy schedules were filed, the failed cases had lower personal property values, less unsecured debt, and lower income and expense numbers than the successful Chapter 13 cases. Conversely, the median real property values were higher for failed cases than for successful cases. Ed Flynn also noted significant differences based on the court involved. Case failure rates during the first six months ranged from 0.7% in Nebraska to 36.4% in California.

V EXPLORING THE IDB DATA

The analysis project begins with the idea that a debtor's ability to complete her Chapter 13 payments is related to specific characteristics of the bankruptcy case. Thus, if we can discover the nature of these relationships, we can predict outcomes. Some characteristics are unknown at the beginning of the bankruptcy case. For example:

- a debtor loses her job during the case;
- a debtor suffers an illness during the case, causing an unexpected loss of income;
- a debtor obtains a home loan modification, eliminating the need for a Chapter 13 payment plan;
- a debtor receives an inheritance and decides that a Chapter 13 case no longer provides the best result.

Because these characteristics arise *during* the case, we can't use them to predict results at the *start* of a case. Other characteristics that relate to case failure, though, do exist at the beginning of the case. These include:

- filing for bankruptcy without an attorney;
- filing with an income that is too low to maintain a Chapter 13 payment plan despite good intentions;
- having too much debt to qualify for Chapter 13 relief.

Some of these characteristics are easily ascertained from initial case filing information. Other factors, such as having less competent counsel, might be reflected in missing case information or mistakes in petition data.

If the information available at the beginning of the case is sufficiently related to whether or not Chapter 13 cases are successful, a machine learning system should be capable of identifying these relationships and generalizing them into a model that allows us to accurately predict whether an individual bankruptcy case will succeed.

---

[16] Flynn, "By the Numbers," *supra* note 3.

In my paper, I used almost all of the information for Chapter 13 cases filed during fiscal years 2008 and 2009. Because a successful Chapter 13 case will typically run for five years while the debtors make their payments,[17] I needed information for several years after the initial filing in order to see the results for the cases. Given that the available IDB data ended as of September 30, 2017, limiting the analysis to cases filed during fiscal years 2008 and 2009 ensured an eight-year history for every case being analyzed. My initial set of Chapter 13 cases contained information on 746,889 cases, of which only 365 had closed in 2017. This low number suggests that while some of the cases filed in 2008 and 2009 might have remained open at the end of fiscal year 2017, the total number would be very low as a percentage of total cases.

For our case study, I extracted a random sample of 10,000 cases and made them available in the file named *dirty_data.csv*. In this part of the case study, I describe some of the data analysis I performed in preparation for building the machine learning models.

After some preliminary work to remove duplicate case entries, I examined the disposition codes available. The disposition code [D1FDSP] provides information about the final case results – the meaning of each code can be determined by consulting the IDB Codebook. Twenty-two potential case dispositions are coded, covering dismissals for various reasons, discharge status, transfers between judicial districts, and a variety of other potential case outcomes (Figure 3.7.1). Most of these codes apply to a very small set of cases and, unfortunately, the codes do not differentiate between Chapter 13 and Chapter 7 discharges.

The first two codes, A and B, represent cases that received either a regular discharge or a hardship discharge. The other codes all represent cases in which a discharge was denied, or not received, for various reasons. The two most common, K and T, represent dismissal for "other" reasons and dismissal for failure to make plan payments, respectively. Note that the chart uses a logarithmic scale. Another issue concerning disposition codes was the fact that for joint cases, where two spouses file bankruptcy together, the IDB provides a separate disposition for each spouse. Trying to predict for each person would introduce a lot of

Number of cases by disposition code

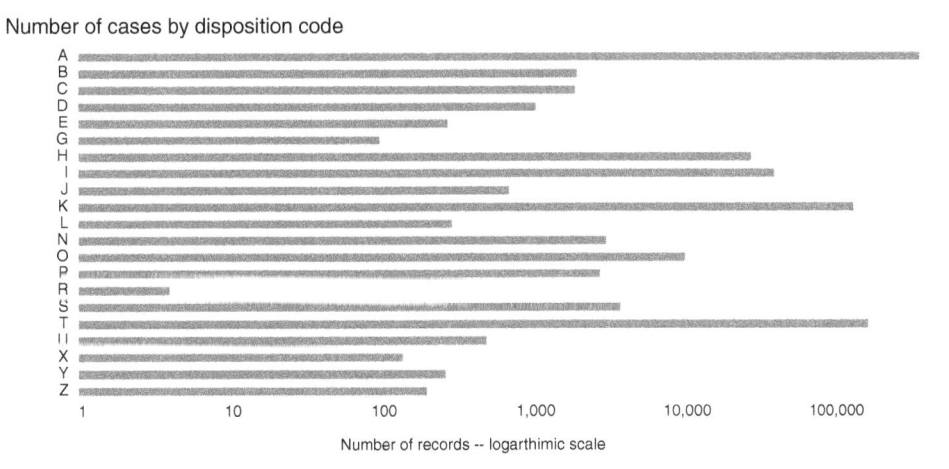

FIGURE 3.7.1 This chart shows the number of cases in the data set for each disposition code. A logarithmic scale is used to make sure the less common codes can be seen. Cases with codes D, L, M, R, X, Y, and Z were excluded from the data set.

---

[17] 11 U.S.C. § 1322(a)(4), (d). Chapter 13 plan periods run between three and five years, depending on household income and whether cause exists for allowing a five-year plan.

complications, and my examination of the data shows that there were only 1578 joint cases in which one debtor obtained a Chapter 13 discharge and the other debtor was denied a discharge or converted his or her case. This was a very small percentage of cases, so I only used the first debtor's case disposition.

I needed a criterion for labeling a case as successful or not. The IDB data provided for each case does not include conversion information, and does not indicate whether the discharge obtained was a Chapter 13 discharge or a Chapter 7 discharge. As a result, the data set did not contain a single data point that I could use as a *label* for my machine learning model. Because the IDB does indicate the case chapter on the disposition date [CLCHPT], I could ascertain whether the case was a Chapter 7 or 13 case when the debtor received a discharge. Based on this, a case was considered to be successful if the disposition code [D1FDSP] indicated that the primary debtor received either a regular discharge or a hardship discharge, and the case was a Chapter 13 case on the disposition date. By this standard, the debtor received a Chapter 13 discharge in 38.4% of cases in the final data set. A new data field was created, called "SUCCESS," for later use as the label for building a machine learning model.

Building a successful model requires both clean and complete data. In addition, not all of the information available in the original data set is necessarily suitable for use in the model. Additional data exploration is needed to identify steps that might need to be taken to clean or transform the data for use by a machine learning model. In this case study, I examined the codes used in the IDB and looked for situations in which data was missing or assigned a null value, and also identified any oddities in the data that might distort or skew machine learning results. Once these situations were identified, strategies needed to be employed to "clean" the data for use by the machine learning systems. In addition, the IDB alternatively uses numerical or alphabetical codes to represent information for various fields. Although some machine learning systems can accept non-numeric codes, others need the data converted into integers in order to process the data. For example "Y" and "N" might have to be converted to "1" and "0" to accommodate data processing limitations.

I also examined a number of variables for relationships between the variable and my new SUCCESS label (Figure 3.7.2). One interesting finding was the relationship between judicial district [DISTRICT] and case outcomes. The success rates for cases varied widely from judicial district to judicial district, ranging from a low of 10.4% in the District of Connecticut to a high of 64.2% in the District of Kansas. I also looked at patterns within judicial circuits, and while there were some substantial variations in success rates between the circuits, a data visualization made clear that there was little uniformity in success rates within a circuit. Within each judicial circuit I found districts with both high and low success rates. Thus, the factors that make success more or less likely are unlikely to be strongly related to case law or procedures established at the Circuit Court level. Later, this insight about variation between districts would play a role in designing the machine learning model.

Some interesting insights arose from examining the data field that indicated whether the case was filed without an attorney, [ORGD1FPRSE] and [ORGD2FPRSE]. Where the primary debtor was filing pro se, only 8.92% of the cases were joint [JOINT] cases. When the primary debtor was represented by counsel [D1FPRSE], 37.51% of the cases were joint cases. This unusual finding suggests either that single debtors are more likely to file pro se than married debtors, or that married debtors who file pro se are more likely to file alone than with their spouse. It also suggests that differences in success rates between solo and joint filers are partially explained by the higher percentage of pro se filings by

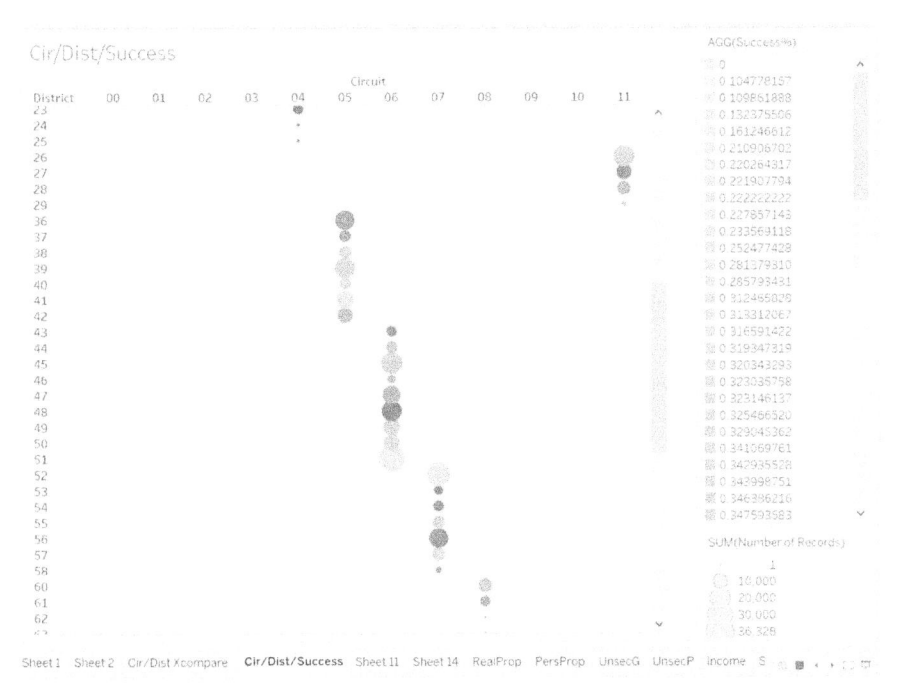

FIGURE 3.7.2 Case volume and success rate by judicial district, grouped vertically by federal circuit. The size of the circle indicates the case volume, and the color indicates the success rates (the darker the circle, the higher the success rate). This image shows a portion of the visualization.

individual debtors.[18] Although a simple data analysis does not provide definitive answers regarding the relationships between filing pro se, filing jointly, and completing a Chapter 13 plan, it does demonstrate how multiple factors work in combination. Machine learning models can build predictions in these situations, where simpler data analysis methods can't.

The IDB also includes average monthly income [AVGMNTHI], average monthly expenses [AVGMNTHE], real property value [REALPROP], personal property value [PERSPROP], secured debt amounts [SECURED], unsecured debt amounts [UNSECNPR], and priority debt [UNSECPR] amounts. These numbers are taken from the summary of schedules that is supposed to be filed with the petition. For all of these data items, about 43,000 records had null values. This could indicate that the summary of schedules was filed with the information missing, was not filed with the original petition, or that the numbers were not entered into the database (which could have occurred with pro se filers). All of these fields showed some extremely large outliers. For example, one case showed real estate worth $140 billion.[19] The highest monthly income shown in the data was $52 million. These, and a few other extreme outliers, were verified as court database data entry errors by looking up the actual cases on the court PACER system. However, their existence called into question the accuracy of the IDB data, particularly where very large numbers were

---

[18] Solo filers had an overall success rate of 32.8%, while the overall success rate for joint filers was 49.7%. When pro se filers were excluded, the success rates were 36.3% and 48.7%, respectively.

[19] Yes, 140 billion, with a B. This case was inspected on PACER and the actual number on the handwritten schedules was $140,800.

reported. Very large outliers can make it difficult for some machine learning models, particularly regression systems, to generate accurate models.

A significant number of cases had zero values for income, expense, debt amounts, and asset values, another apparent anomaly. About 188,000 debtors reported having no real property, and about 11,000 debtors reported having no personal property. No general unsecured debt was reported in 27,579 cases, while about 12,000 debtors reported having no monthly income. Amazingly, more than half of the debtors who reported having zero income were represented by attorneys. This suggests either that the summary of schedules was incompetently completed or that the information in the database does not reflect the information in the schedules.

VI INSIGHTS FROM USING LARGE DATA SETS

This section describes the actual project of examining over three-quarters of a million bankruptcy cases using a random forest decision tree to determine whether the case information available through the IDB can be used to predict Chapter 13 case results. Based on the preliminary analytical work already described, I generated a reduced set of about 743,000 Chapter 13 cases that were originally filed during fiscal years 2008 and 2009.

These records represented substantially all of the Chapter 13 cases filed during those two years. I randomized the cases and extracted training and test sets. From these sets, I engineered "features" suitable for use by machine learning algorithms and tested the data using a random forest decision tree implemented using Scikit-learn.[20] Once the successful model was designed, it was rebuilt and run on three new test sets to validate its effectiveness.

Before going through some of the details of the process, and the results, a short description of a random forest decision tree is warranted. A *decision tree* is a branched structure in which the *branches* are controlled by choices made about the features in our data set. The ends of

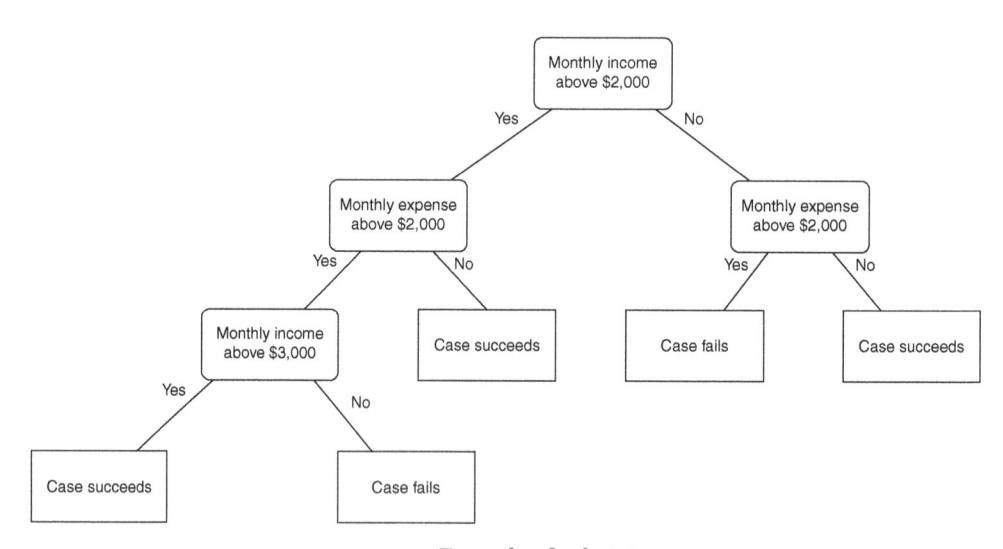

FIGURE 3.7.3 Example of a decision tree.

---

[20] Scikit-learn, available at: http://scikit-learn.org/stable.

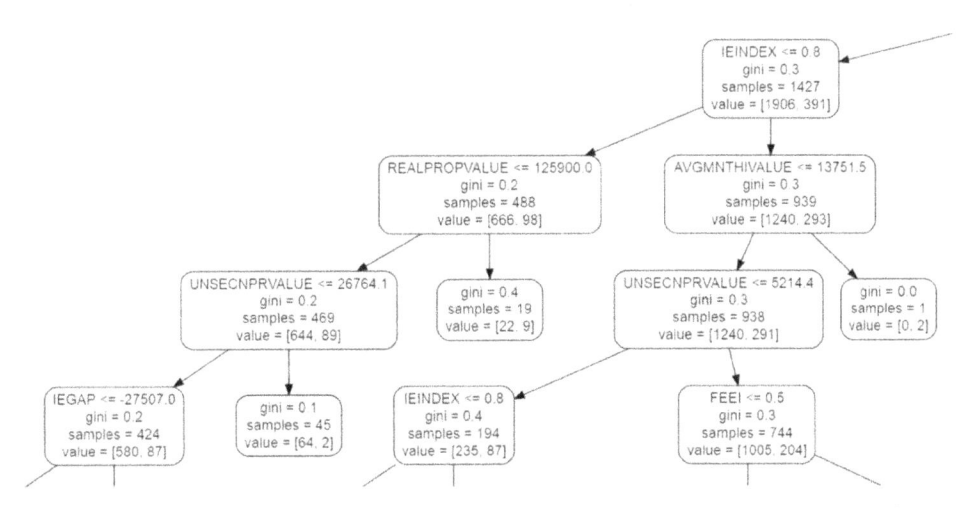

FIGURE 3.7.4 A small section of the final decision tree. The smaller boxes represent "leaves," representing end points to a decision series. The complete tree has over 7000 "nodes" and "leaves."

the branches, called *leaves*, represent the potential outcomes, called *class labels*. The branches themselves represent conjunctions of features that lead to those class labels.[21] A very simple decision tree might look like the one shown in Figure 3.7.3.

The decision tree eventually derived using our machine learning tools was far more complex than this example, with over 7000 decision points (Figure 3.7.4).

At each branch we examine a different feature variable, and make a choice about it, sorting some cases down one branch and the other cases down the other branch. Each data set, representing a separate bankruptcy case, ends up located in a particular leaf at the end of the decision tree, and is assigned a prediction based on the actual results for the majority of the cases that ended up in that leaf. Decision tree algorithms design the tree to generate the best results, using statistical measures of accuracy. The algorithm determines which data feature to examine at each branch, and the rule that sends a case down one branch as opposed to another.

Decision tree algorithms can easily overfit to the training set used. *Overfitting* occurs when an algorithm builds a decision tree that sorts different cases based on unique characteristics of the training set that aren't necessarily related to their label. We address this tendency to overfit by limiting the number of decision points in the tree, and also by using a random forest model – which builds a large number of possibly useful trees and then averages them out into a single model.

For this project, the random forest decision tree model was built using the Scikit-learn RandomForestClassifier function. From our large body of available cases, I took a random 420,000 records to build the actual model. The decision tree itself was limited to 20 branch splits, and configured so that nodes at the end of branches could not split further unless they contained at least 150 cases. These limitations reduced model overfitting, and improved prediction numbers on the test sets. I also used a random forest algorithm set to generate 1000 decision trees, which were used to create the generalized model.

An earlier version of the model, using a large number of available features, was evaluated to determine which features the model found useful. A Scikit-learn function calculated the

---

[21] "Decision Tree Learning," *Wikipedia*, available at: https://en.wikipedia.org/wiki/Decision_tree_learning (accessed June 9, 2020).

Variable	Importance
Variable: UNSECNPRVALUE	Importance:0.14
Variable: IEINDEX	Importance:0.14
Variable: IEGAP	Importance:0.14
Variable: PERSPROPVALUE	Importance:0.13
Variable: DISTSUCCESS	Importance:0.12
Variable: AVGMNTHIVALUE	Importance:0.11
Variable: REALPROPVALUE	Importance:0.09
Variable: UNSECPRVALUE	Importance:0.06
Variable: ORGD1FPRSE	Importance:0.02
Variable: PRFILE	Importance:0.02
Variable: JOINT	Importance:0.01
Variable: FEEI	Importance:0.01
Variable: REALPROPNONE	Importance:0.01
Variable: NTRDBT	Importance:0.0
Variable: FEEP	Importance:0.0
Variable: FEEW	Importance:0.0
Variable: REALPROPNULL	Importance:0.0
Variable: PERSPROPNULL	Importance:0.0
Variable: UNSECNPRNULL	Importance:0.0
Variable: UNSECEXCESS	Importance:0.0
Variable: UNSECPRNULL	Importance:0.0
Variable: AVGMNTHINULL	Importance:0.0

FIGURE 3.7.5 Importance scores for model features.

effect each feature had on the model and assigned each feature an "importance score" (Figure 3.7.5).

As you can see, the model didn't even use a large number of available features. Based on this, the final model was built using just 14 features:

- whether the filing was a joint filing or not [JOINT];
- whether the debtor filed pro se [ORGD1FPRSE];
- whether the debtor had filed previously [PRFILE];
- whether the debtor paid their filing fee in installments [FEEI];
- the success ratio for the judicial district [DISTSUCCESS];
- whether the debtor had real property [REALPROPNONE];
- whether the amount of unsecured debt was missing from the data [PERSPROPNULL];
- the values for real property [REALPROPVALUE], personal property [PERSPROPVALUE], general unsecured debt [UNSECNPRVALUE], priority debt [UNSECPRVALUE], and average monthly income [AVGMNTHIVALUE];
- the gap between average monthly income and average monthly expenses [IEGAP]; and
- the ratio between average monthly income and average monthly expenses [IEINDEX].

Using the information provided by initial random forest decision tree tests, the algorithm was altered to try to reduce overfitting while improving accuracy on the test set. One test set was used to refine the model, which was then rebuilt and tested using a new training set and three new test sets. The results from two regression models were also evaluated to obtain insight into which variables contributed to the results in those models. This methodology protected against what is called "training against the test set," or the risk of creating a model that works well against both the

Combined Confusion Matrix

	Predicted failure	Predicted success
Actual failure	37,185	18,449 false positives
Actual success	8,545 false negatives	25,821

Combined accuracy when predicting failure: 81.31%
Combined accuracy when predicting success: 58.33%

FIGURE 3.7.6 Confusion matrix for the three test sets, combined.

training set and the test set, but won't generalize against new data. During this process the number of features was reduced, and the characteristics of the tree refined to reduce the size of the tree (a process referred to as *pruning*). The final model obtained 0.7417 accuracy on the original 420,000 case training set and 0.7018 accuracy and 0.7115 AUC on the original test set. In other words, it predicted results correctly 70.18% of the time. At that point the model algorithm was finalized and re-run on a new training set and three new test sets to ensure that the model created was capable of generalizing to new data. Accuracy results on these additional test sets were in the 0.69 to 0.70 range. The performance of the model differs depending on the prediction – it is in fact better when it predicts failure than it is when it predicts success (Figure 3.7.6).

A confusion matrix provides a standard method for visualizing a model's ability to correctly predict certain types of results. Out of 90,000 cases (the three test sets), the model predicted 45,730 cases would not receive a Chapter 13 discharge, and it was correct 81.31% of the time. It predicted 44,270 cases would receive a Chapter 13 discharge, and for those cases was correct only 58.33% of the time. Thus, the model is somewhat optimistic – predicting a higher number of successful cases than it should – and more likely to be wrong when it predicts a case will be successful. However, when the model does predict a case will fail, its predictions are very accurate.

Looking at the statistics a little differently, the model predicted success for 25,821 of the 34,366 cases where Chapter 13 discharges issued. Thus, the model was able to correctly identify 75.14% of the successful cases. However, 55,634 cases were disposed of without a Chapter 13 discharge, and the model predicted failure for 37,185 of these cases. Thus, the model was only able to correctly identify 66.84% of the unsuccessful cases.[22]

We compare these accuracy numbers against a baseline of 62%, the accuracy we achieve by assuming that all cases will fail. Although the model already provides an improvement against the baseline numbers, using a decision tree-based model also allows us to predict a likelihood of success for individual cases, and this prediction is highly accurate because it is empirically derived.

---

[22] Precision, recall, and an F-score were not used because they depend on the point of view, i.e., whether you are trying to predict success or failure. However, in predicting failure the model had, on the combined test sets, a recall of 81.3%, precision of 66.8%, and an F-score of 0.733. For more on precision, recall, and F1 score, *see* Dolin – Information Intermediation, *supra*; Nay – Natural Language Processing for Legal Texts, *supra*; and Dolin – Measuring Legal Quality, *supra*.

TABLE 3.7.1 *Prediction accuracy of model for different groupings of probability numbers.*

Success group	Total number of cases in group	Number of successful cases in group	Percentage of cases successful	Prediction accuracy
0	2651	33	1.24	98.76
0.1	2196	166	7.56	92.44
0.2	2688	357	13.28	86.72
0.3	3587	826	23.03	76.97
0.4	4208	1433	34.05	65.95
0.5	4302	1894	44.03	44.03
0.6	4417	2466	55.83	55.83
0.7	3918	2622	66.92	66.92
0.8	1960	1537	78.42	78.42
0.9	73	66	90.41	90.41
Total	30,000	11,400	38	

A decision tree machine learning model essentially predicts case results by outputting, for each case, a "probability number" between 0 and 1. When we evaluate the model's accuracy, the model treats a case as successful if the "probability number" is between 0.5 and 1, and unsuccessful if the "probability" is less than 0.5. The "probability number" is not an actual estimate of a particular case's success, but it does represent the model's estimate of likelihood of success – in other words, when the model outputs a number close to 1, it represents a prediction that success is highly likely, and the obverse is true as well.

These probability numbers allow us to group different case filings based on the probability numbers, and then see, for each group, the percentage of successful cases in that group. Table 3.7.1 shows that the percentage of successful cases is higher when the probability numbers are higher.

We can then convert these numbers to reflect the percentage likelihood that a specific debtor will receive a Chapter 13 discharge. The success rate for each probability group relates exactly to the percentage of cases in that group that succeed or fail, compared to the model's prediction for that group. For example, for the 0.8 group, the model predicts that all of the cases will result in a Chapter 13 discharge. Of the cases in this group, 78.42% of the cases actually received a Chapter 13 discharge. Extrapolating across the group, we can say that the chance of success for cases in the group is shown, empirically, to be 78.42%. When we plot these percentages for each of the ten success groups, we see a clear pattern (Figure 3.7.7).

Using a polynomial regression calculation, we derive an equation for the line that most closely fits the plotted points. This is a third-order polynomial equation, with an R-squared value of 0.9996. This equation is:

$$y = -0.5788*x^3 + 1.2332*x^2 + 0.2982*x$$

where x represents the probability output from the model for a specific case and y represents the percentage chance that that specific debtor will receive a Chapter 13 discharge. Using the model, in conjunction with the conversion equation, allows us to precisely predict the percentage chance of obtaining a Chapter 13 discharge in specific cases.

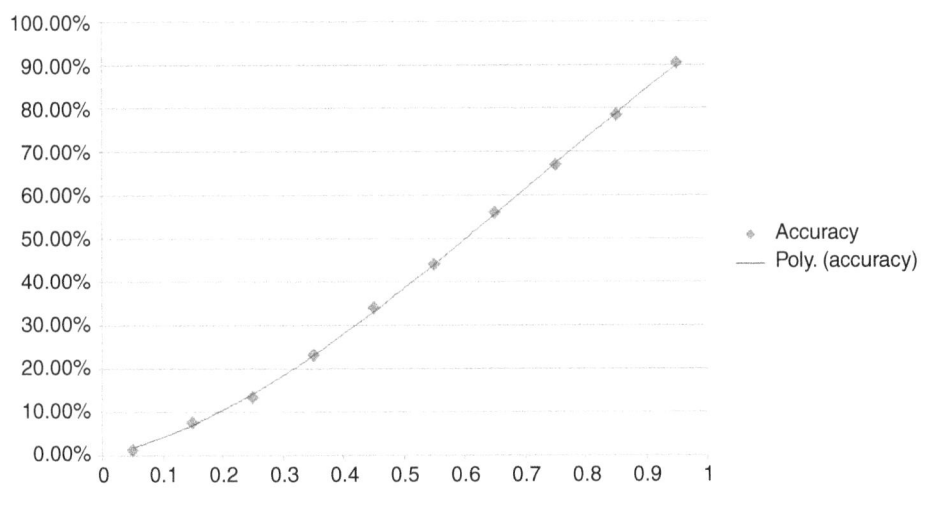

FIGURE 3.7.7 Probability output to percentage conversion graph.

VII USING THE DATA PROVIDED

The Github repository for this project contains two data sets, two Python scripts, and some related files in a Microsoft Azure notebook.[23] The files include:

- *Bankruptcy Codebook 2008 Forward (Rev January 2018).pdf* – this is the bankruptcy IDB codebook. It lists the various data points available in the IDB and provides useful descriptions for the field names used in the *dirty_data.csv* data set.
- *dirty_data.csv* – this is an extract of 10,000 random Chapter 13 cases filed during fiscal years 2008 and 2009. Notwithstanding the name, duplicate entries have been removed and some cases removed to create a usable data set.
- *clean_data.csv* – derived from the *dirty_data.csv* file, this data set contains engineered features built for use by machine learning algorithms.
- *Ch13GenerateMLSets.ipynb* – this Python script is designed to convert the *dirty_data.csv* file into the *clean_data.csv* file. A student with knowledge of Python can revise the code to create additional features for machine learning exploration.
- *Ch13SuccessLearner-RF-Testing Script.ipynb* – this Python script takes the *clean_data.csv* file and applies a random forest decision tree algorithm to the data, testing the resulting model and logging the resulting text files for review. Students can simply run the file to see how it works, run it on their own version of the *clean_data.csv* file, or try applying different machine learning model methods.

VIII EXPLORING THE ORGANIZED DATA

The raw information from the IDB, without changes, was not suitable for building a machine learning model. To actually build a model, I needed to create a label to test my data against, select the information that a machine learning system might find useful, and address outliers and missing data. These transformations were performed using scripts written in Python. The

---

[23] These resources are available at: https://github.com/warrenagin/Ch13Learner and https://notebooks.azure.com/AginW/libraries/Ch13LearnerCaseStudy.

clean_data.csv file contains the transformed data for a random selection of 10,000 bankruptcy cases, and can be used to explore the cleaned data.

Prior to building the cleaned data, I calculated and saved some information about a few variables. First, the software calculated the percentage of successful cases for each judicial district, and saved this information in a file for later use. Second, I calculated a cutoff size for district case volume, below which the data for the success percentage was considered statistically unreliable using a 0.05 *p*-value.[24] Districts with a case volume below the cutoff were assigned a default success rate of 40%. Third, for a number of case data points, such as income, real property value, and amount of unsecured debt, the program calculated the median for the reported values in the data set and an outlier cutoff. The outlier cutoffs would allow the program to exclude from the data the top 0.13% of values,[25] hopefully preventing these unrepresentative outliers from distorting the models. With this information available, the cleaned data set could be prepared.

The cleaned data set includes:

- A SUCCESS field, which has a 1 for a successful case, and the value 0 for an unsuccessful case. This field, used to train the models, is the "label," and the options of 1 or 0 our "classes." For the SUCCESS feature, a case was assigned a 1 if the primary debtor obtained a regular or hardship discharge and the case was a Chapter 13 case at the time of case closure. All other cases were assigned a 0.
- For the fields for whether the case was a consumer or business case (NTRDBT), whether the case was a joint petition (JOINT), whether the debtor originally filed pro se (ORGD1FPRSE), and whether the debtor had filed a prior case (PRFILE), the contents were changed to a "1" or a "0."
- For each case, the judicial district was replaced with a field called DISTSUCCESS, which contained the success rate for cases filed in that district. This was designed to reduce the computational cost of running models.
- I needed to create some new features to communicate filing fee payment status to the models. The IDB included information about payment of filing fees, with five different codes indicating payment, non-payment, waiver, and payment in installments. Instead of using these codes, I created three engineered categorical features to allow the models to assess fee payment status: FEEP, which was assigned a 1 where fees were not paid; FEEI, which was assigned a 1 where fees were set for installment payments; and FEEW, which was assigned a 1 when fees were waived. In all other situations, all three features were assigned a 0, as a default status.
- A number of features – such as the amount of real property value, personal property value, and income – had missing data, zero values where a zero value seemed unlikely, and some large outliers. These features were transformed using median values to replace problem data.

---

[24] Meaning that for those districts there was a 5% or greater chance that the number reported was the result of random variations. This included about one-third of the judicial districts with a training set of 70,000 cases, but only 12 districts were below the cutoff size with a training set of 420,000 cases.

[25] This percentage correlates to the percentage of values that would be more than three standard deviations from the mean in a normal distribution. The actual standard deviations were not used in calculating the cutoffs – a statistical analysis of the distributions for these continuous case fields showed that they were non-normal distributions, primarily due to the large numbers of zero values and excessive outliers (the largest of which were believed to be the result of data entry errors).

- To allow linear regression models to find relationships that were not strictly linear, for each continuous feature I included a feature based on its square and its log value.
- I also wanted the model to recognize cases in which the debtor reported having no real estate, as well as cases with missing data. I created features indicating whether or not a missing entry was found for the value of real property, personal property, unsecured debt, unsecured priority debt, average monthly income and average monthly expenses. In addition, a new categorical feature called REALPROPNONE was set to 1 where the value of real estate was reported as zero, and set to 0 otherwise.
- Finally, I wanted the model to explore the relationship between income and expenses to identify relationship patterns related to plan success. I created two continuous features to explore these relationships. IEINDEX was calculated as income divided by expenses. Thus, IEINDEX would equal 1 when income and expenses were the same. A debtor with high income and very few expenses would have a large IEINDEX, whereas a debtor whose expenses exceeded income would have an IEINDEX between 0 and 1. IEGAP was calculated as income minus expenses, thus allowing a model to consider the amount of excess disposable income available to each debtor.

IX QUESTIONS FOR FURTHER EXAMINATION

The links provided in Section VII allow for user creation of new models and decision trees. Here is a list of questions for further examination. Readers of this chapter can build their own models, using the questions below to help explore on their own.

1. Examine the D1FDSP field in *dirty_data.csv*. How many different codes are represented in the data set? What are the two most frequent codes? The two least frequent codes? Can you recreate a chart similar to the one in the text using Excel or visualization software?
2. In the original project, the SUCCESS field was added using a Python script. Using Excel, add a SUCCESS field to the *dirty_data.csv* file. What percentage of the cases in the sample were successful? How does this compare to the success rate for the 740,000 case sample (38.4%)? What conclusions can you draw from this?
3. Examine the average monthly income field [AVGMNTHI] to identify any unusual characteristics. What is the largest average monthly income in the data set? Do you think outliers are more or less likely to be an issue in working with the smaller data set, compared to the full data set? Why? What do you think might be a useful technique for identifying and dealing with outliers in average monthly income?
4. How many cases are missing an entry for average monthly income [AVGMNTHI]? For the cases where this occurs, can you see patterns in the rest of the data for that case in terms of completeness or possible accuracy problems?
5. Try to build a scatter plot between average monthly income [AVGMNTHI] and average monthly expenses [AVGMNTHE]. Make sure you have a strategy for dealing with missing data points. Can you fit a regression trend line to the data? What is the relationship between the two characteristics? What is the R-squared value for the trend line you made?

6. Can you create a chart or visualization calculating the percentage of successful cases in each judicial district? Why do you think the success rates vary so much from court to court?
7. The preliminary data analysis found data entry errors, and large numbers of cases claiming zero assets, debts, or income. In many cases the debtor had counsel – presumably the summary of schedules document was prepared by an attorney. What do you think might cause these anomalies, and what lessons do you think might be drawn from their existence?
8. Run the testing script using the *clean_data.csv* file provided. What accuracy result did you get on the test set?
9. Using the Python script provided, generate your own version of the *clean_data.csv* file with an additional engineered feature. Describe your feature and why you think that feature might improve the model. Revise the testing script so it works with your additional feature. How do the results compare with those for the original model?
10. Binary features possess only two options, usually a 1 or 0. A *sparse* feature is any feature where almost all of the records have the same information. Can you find any binary features in the *clean_data.csv* file that are sparse? Were these features used in the author's model? Why do you think that was the case? (Hint: When the options are 1 and 0, the sum of the feature column tells you how many records have a 1.)
11. Because a Chapter 13 plan can only succeed when the debtor has excess income, there should be no cases filed when a debtor's expenses exceed his income. How many cases in *clean-data.csv* have a negative number for IEGAP?
12. What are the mean, median, and mode for IEGAP in *clean_data.csv*?
13. Using *clean_data.csv*, prepare a scatter plot to compare the numbers for the value of real property [REALPROPVALUE] and the amount of unsecured non-priority debt [UNSECNPRVALUE]. Use regression to plot a trend line between the numbers. How would you describe the relationship between the value of the real property and the amount of unsecured debt? Determine the R-squared value for the regression line. What does that tell you about the relationship?
14. Do you think better results could have been obtained using different information? Why? What information from the IDB do you think might have been helpful to include or exclude from the project?
15. What data not available in the IDB do you think could have been included in the model to improve it? How do you think you might obtain that data?
16. For about 25% of Chapter 13 cases, the model predicts with confidence that the case will fail – and over 90% of these cases do, in fact, fail. In far more than half of these cases, an attorney was involved, or at least assisted, in the filing. Do you think these attorneys filed all these cases for their clients with the knowledge that the case had a 90% chance of failure? What insights can we derive from this observation?
17. The model's performance was measured against a baseline of 62%, the accuracy of a system that assumes all cases will fail. Is this a reasonable way of evaluating this model? Why or why not? How else might we evaluate the model?
18. This model was built using information from cases filed in 2008 and 2009, during a financial crisis. Do you think it will produce an accurate result for a case filed in 2018? What might cause the model to be less accurate for a case filed in 2018? What changes might be made to build a model that provides useful results for a case filed in 2018?

19. What issues do you think are raised by a bankruptcy judge or Chapter 13 trustee using a model like this in his or her decisions?
20. How might a court respond if a creditor asks the court to grant relief from the automatic stay on the grounds that the debtor's likelihood of completing a Chapter 13 plan is very low based on the model? Do you think a court should allow an attorney to submit model results into evidence? How might this be done?
21. How might someone who represents consumer debtors use a model like this to better assist their clients? What dangers do you see in a debtor's attorney using the model?
22. Can you see ways that the model might inadvertently reflect inappropriate bias against certain races or ethnic groups?

c.

Legal Research, Government Data, and Access to Legal Information

3.8

Fastcase, and the Visual Understanding of Judicial Precedents

Ed Walters and Jeff Asjes

I INTRODUCTION: MAPPING LEGAL RESEARCH AND CITATION RELATIONSHIPS

When arguing before a judicial body, lawyers must support their legal arguments by citing prior court decisions that adopted similar reasoning or reached a similar conclusion. Finding such prior decisions is often a tedious and time-consuming process that requires many hours of reading through judicial opinions to determine if they are actually relevant, and then drawing parallels to those few decisions that are most relevant. Many attorneys employ paralegals and junior associates to conduct legal research on a full-time basis, so any system that makes it quicker and easier for attorneys to locate relevant cases and statutes can save enormous amounts of time and money.

The creation of searchable databases that contain the full text of judicial decisions has gone a long way toward achieving the goal of making legal research faster and easier. By now, this story should be familiar to people from a number of different fields: What used to take hours to do by hand with printed books can now be done almost instantaneously on a computer, without having to maintain large and expensive on-site libraries.

There is room for improvement, though. Traditional legal research is closely tied to a keyword search paradigm, whereby users search for highly relevant keywords in certain configurations. Users create these lists of keywords and use Boolean search operators to filter out a list of documents narrowed down from a universe of several million into a much smaller set of more relevant documents. After this, a sorting algorithm ranks all the filtered documents, with the most relevant documents appearing at the top of the list.

Keyword search is a powerful tool for legal researchers, but the results are often subjective and arbitrary, and a less than ideal way to identify authoritative law. Boolean search is little more than an educated guess about which words courts, legislators, or regulators employ when writing about a topic. Search results are often over-inclusive, including many irrelevant documents, but also under-inclusive, often missing important precedents. A legal researcher reviewing a text-based list of search results has no independent information about when they have identified all important precedents. The process is antiquated, inaccurate, incomplete, and slow.

Citation relationships and data visualizations of search results can improve the accuracy and completeness of legal research. Citations among legal precedents create an information architecture that is rich with meaning for legal researchers, and this architecture can allow for the creation of citation mapping to better identify the most authoritative precedents.

II UNDERSTANDING THE PROBLEMS WITH CURRENT RESEARCH METHODS

Despite the vast potential power that computers bring to the field of legal research, traditional methods of computerized information retrieval have a number of problems that make it extremely difficult for lawyers to quickly find the most relevant and important material. In particular, the results of keyword searches tend to be over-inclusive, under-inclusive, and homogeneous.

A Under-Inclusivity

In the search context, inclusivity refers to the tendency of a given search to include or exclude results. In an ideal world, a "perfect" search would be perfectly inclusive; it would include all of the relevant results, and exclude all of the irrelevant results. Unfortunately, in the real world there are almost no perfectly inclusive searches. Short general searches tend to be more inclusive, whereas longer, more specific searches tend to be less inclusive. Often, the trick to a good keyword search is finding a balance between generality and specificity. However, when a search is so specific that it excludes potentially relevant results, legal researchers call it an under-inclusive search.

Under-inclusivity is a pervasive problem in legal research, because in the legal context the question being asked is often so specific that it becomes esoteric. For example, a lawyer may have a question like, "How is section 3(a)ii of the state tax code applied to building subcontractors with more than two outstanding liens?" Even taking only the keywords from that question, a lawyer might easily miss important cases relevant to their argument, simply because those cases discuss shipping contractors instead of building contractors.

A famous example of under-inclusivity is when a lawyer searches for "*Miranda* warning." The results for that search will include many relevant and important cases, but the seminal case, *Miranda v. Arizona*, will not be among them because the phrase "*Miranda* warning" was coined *after* that case was decided. This is a pervasive and recurring problem in a field in which doctrines are often named after the case that first originated them.

Another reason under-inclusivity is so pervasive is the tendency of judges to find many different ways of saying the same thing. For example, there is a legal rule that in personal injury cases the frailty of the injured person is not relevant to whether or not the defendant is liable. That rule is alternately called the "eggshell skull" rule, the "eggshell plaintiff" rule, the "thin skull" rule, or the rule that "you take your plaintiff as you find him." The problem is immediately apparent; a search for "eggshell plaintiff" will not include cases that discuss the "thin skull" rule, and vice versa. Both searches will be under-inclusive.

Under-inclusivity is arguably the worst problem a search can have. If a search simply fails to include relevant results, then the user has no chance of seeing them. In the legal context, that means potentially missing the one case that might have convinced a judge. Worse, it might mean missing the case the other side will use to convince that judge.

B Over-Inclusivity

Over-inclusivity is the tendency of searches to include irrelevant results. When contrasted with under-inclusivity, over-inclusivity seems like a less severe problem. Better safe than sorry, right? It is a tempting thought that over-inclusive searches and under-inclusive searches are in some sense opposites; that an over-inclusive search may have irrelevant results, but at least it will have the relevant ones as well.

In fact, these two drawbacks are not so much opposites as they are complements: searches are frequently both over-inclusive *and* under-inclusive at the same time. For example, consider the under-inclusive "*Miranda* warning" above. There is a multitude of cases that mention the phrase "*Miranda* warning," only to note that the defendant properly received such a warning. Such cases contain the appropriate phrase, but they do nothing to help define the requirements or discuss the application of *Miranda* warnings. And, as noted above, the actual case that established the *Miranda* warning is still nowhere to be found in the search results.

Examples like this present an enormous problem in the legal research field, because judges frequently mention rules and concepts that may be tangentially relevant, even though they are not particularly important to the case. As a result, relevant or important cases are frequently mixed in with an enormous number of irrelevant results. As of this writing, a search for "*Miranda* warning" on the Fastcase database yields 11,153 results. A lawyer could not possibly read through that many results in a reasonable amount of time, and even if it were possible to do so, it would defeat the entire purpose of using a search engine in the first place.

C *Homogeneity*

Over-inclusivity would not be such a problem if it were easy to tell at a glance which cases are important and which are not. For example, when running a Google search, it is easy enough to scroll quickly through pages of results looking for a title that addresses your issue. By contrast, the "titles" for different judicial opinions are simply the names of the parties; they reveal little or nothing about the issues discussed in the case. This apparent homogeneity makes it impossible for a researcher to separate the wheat from the chaff without some form of assistance. Looking at a list of case names, there is no way to easily figure out which cases are relevant, which are irrelevant, and which ones are simply missing altogether.

III CLASSIC APPROACHES

The combination of these three issues – under-inclusivity, over-inclusivity, and homogeneity – completely undermines the power of a searchable case law database. Without some means of addressing these problems, a researcher is not much better off than when they started. They are left with a set of results that likely includes many irrelevant cases, and is also probably missing a few relevant ones. Worse, they have no easy way of telling which are which. Classic legal search systems do have methods to address these issues, but each approach has some serious drawbacks.

A *Searching Broadly*

As discussed above, under-inclusivity is in many ways the most serious problem one can have with a search, because it means that some relevant results are never even presented to the user. One simple strategy, therefore, is for users to enter more broad or general search queries. Thus, our hypothetical user from above might search for any cases that mention the tax code and liens, rather than only those that mention them alongside building contractors. Similarly, the search engine itself can be made to deliberately interpret searches broadly, or to ignore the most limiting search terms when a search seems too under-inclusive. This is the approach that Google uses for searches that do not return many results: when a search returns few or no results, the engine then begins to ignore the most restrictive search terms in an effort to make the search more inclusive.

The benefit of broadening a search is that it casts a wider net, increasing the likelihood that important or relevant results will be returned. The drawback, of course, is that casting a wider net also means capturing many more irrelevant and unimportant results. Broadening the search necessarily exacerbates the over-inclusivity problem, and can potentially bury the needle in an enormous haystack.

The example in Figure 3.8.1 is admittedly silly, but it demonstrates the point: A user that only wanted to see results with the word "wombat" in them would be sorely disappointed. Thus, despite the tendency to exacerbate the over-inclusivity problem, a broad search that includes all of the relevant results along with many irrelevant ones is still preferable to a narrow search that fails to return relevant results at all.

B Filtering

One common way to address the over-inclusivity problem is to add a filtering function to the results list. This allows users to begin with a broad inclusive search, and then narrow down the list once they already have some idea of what is available. This filtering function also helps to address the homogeneity problem; a well-executed filter presents the user with options for differentiating between otherwise similar results.

One good example of a post-search filter is the one used by Amazon, which allows users to refine broad, inclusive searches by specifying ratings, price ranges, shipping options, and product categories. Fastcase (Figure 3.8.2) works in a similar fashion: It allows users to filter by jurisdiction, court level, and document type. Fastcase also presents the user with a selection of

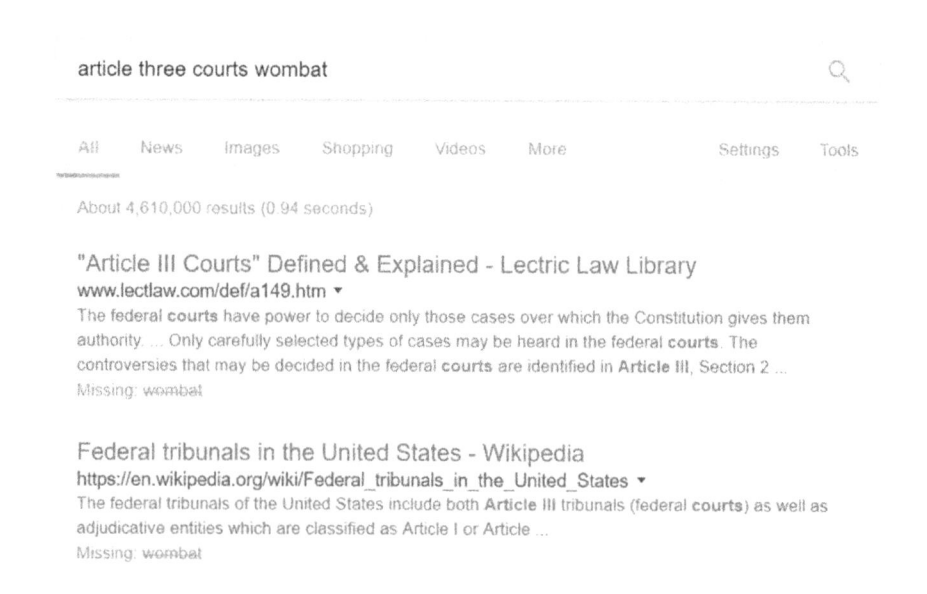

FIGURE 3.8.1 A problem search.

FIGURE 3.8.2 Fastcase search filters.

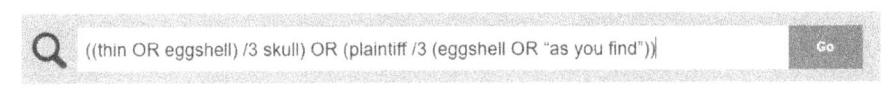

FIGURE 3.8.3 Boolean search.[1]

words and phrases that feature frequently in their search results. This lets a researcher quickly see some options for how to narrow down an otherwise potentially overwhelming list of cases.

The drawback to this approach is that filtering necessarily excludes whole categories of results that otherwise match the search query. Each added filter increases the risk that the search might become under-inclusive, cutting out some relevant or important results. This is an unfortunate fact of search: Almost by definition, approaches meant to address under-inclusivity often increase the risk of over-inclusivity, and vice versa. Knowing this, the tension between inclusion and exclusion of search results begins to seem like a zero-sum game.

C Boolean Search

The traditional way to break out of this zero-sum paradigm is to allow a greater degree of control over exactly how keywords in a search are treated. The most powerful way to do this is the Boolean search. By giving users direct control over the relationships between keywords, Boolean searches avoid the pitfalls of both over- and under-inclusivity. A Boolean search can be hyper-specific about some terms, but flexible about others, and can also account for alternatives. Consider the "eggshell plaintiff" problem discussed above. Rather than conducting four separate under-inclusive searches, an experienced user might enter something like the search shown in Figure 3.8.3.

This single search is broad enough to include most cases that discuss the rule, regardless of which phrasing is used, while still being narrow enough to exclude cases discussing plaintiffs or eggs generally. Because of the power Boolean searches put into users' hands, they have

---

[1] Search example in Figure 3.8.3 taken from Fastcase.

become a staple of the legal research industry. With enough skill, a user fluent in the use of Boolean operators can construct searches that approach the goal of "perfect" inclusiveness. A good Boolean search will include many relevant results and few irrelevant ones.

The problem with Boolean keyword search is that it takes a lot of skill to do well. To construct a Boolean search, users must essentially learn a very simple programming language, and how to use that language to take direct control over the search engine. For a user unfamiliar with Boolean searches, it is easy to make mistakes and end up with even worse results than those a simple additive keyword search would have provided. While Boolean operators represent a powerful toolset for the skilled power user, for less skilled researchers they can be unhelpful or even actively detrimental.

D Natural Language Search

To try to address some of the shortcomings of classic additive keyword searches for less skilled users, Fastcase, as well as many other companies, has implemented a natural language search engine. The goal of natural language search is to try to gain some of the powerful benefits of Boolean search, but in a more intuitive and user-friendly package. Rather than giving users direct control over the way the engine treats each keyword, natural language searches take questions phrased in plain English and attempt to determine programmatically which words are important and how they should be treated.

Every day, computers get better at parsing plain language, and if natural language engines are good enough, they can effectively act as translators – interpreting naturally written queries and forming complex and flexible Boolean searches based off of those queries. For example, a user might directly enter the question used earlier: "How is section 3(a)ii of the state tax code applied to building subcontractors with more than two outstanding liens?" A sophisticated natural language engine might then reinterpret the question as being equivalent to "'3(a)ii' AND 'tax code' AND 'subcontractor' * AND 'lien'*".

Of course, depending on how it is set up, a natural language engine might just as easily prioritize the words "state," "building," and "lien." This illustrates the main drawback of natural language search engines: From the user's perspective, the engine is essentially a black box with no way to tell from the outside what the engine is doing on the inside. Users enter their queries and trust that the system will correctly interpret which words are important and how they relate to one another. Even if the engine isn't exactly "wrong," there is no guarantee that its interpretation will match the researcher's intent. This makes it very difficult for a user to know which results might be missing from their search.[2]

The classic approaches to resolving these issues – complex Boolean queries or natural language search – have offered incremental improvements to problems of over-inclusivity and under-inclusivity of search results. But as we've seen, both remain a problem. Even where these approaches produce a germane set of search results, ranking algorithms still struggle to bring the most important precedents to the top of the list of search results.

IV NEW APPROACHES: CITATION ANALYSIS

One approach for improving on Boolean search operators and natural language search is the use of citation analysis to identify and rank relevant results. As early as 1999, Fastcase began

---

[2] For more detail on natural language processing, see Nay – Natural Language Processing for Legal Texts, supra.

attempting to overcome the shortcomings of traditional legal search methods through the use of data analytics to augment keyword search. In particular, Fastcase has focused on two main methods of improving search results through data analytics: using citation relationships to more effectively sort search results, and expanding the list of search results.

A Doing More with Search Terms

In their basic forms, additive, Boolean, and natural language searches all share something in common. They each consist of a yes-or-no question: "Does this potential search result meet the requirements of the search query?" If the answer is yes, then the case is included in the search results. If the answer is no, then the case is not included in the search results. On their own, none of these methods does anything to differentiate between search results – either the case is included or it is not.

As discussed above, however, not all cases are created equal. Some may discuss the search keywords in depth, while others may only mention them in passing; a case is not necessarily relevant just because it meets all of the criteria for inclusion in the search results. To solve this problem, Fastcase has analyzed various properties of the search terms within each case to determine how likely it is to be relevant for a given search – a way to more effectively sort germane search results to the top of the list. This method is called *enhanced relevance*, and it is based primarily on keyword relevance, maps of citation relationships, and the aggregate history of users of the Fastcase legal research system.

1 Keyword Relevance

Fastcase judges keyword relevance using four factors: the numerosity of keywords, their proximity to each other, their diversity, and their density in the document. *Numerosity* is a simple measure of how many times the various search terms appear in each case result. The more times the search terms are mentioned, the higher Fastcase ranks the case. A case that only contains one reference to the search terms is much less likely to be relevant than a case that references them many times.

Proximity measures how close the search terms appear to each other in each document. Cases in which the search terms appear close together are ranked higher, while cases in which the terms are spread out are ranked lower. This addresses two potential situations. First, this helps ensure that the results Fastcase rates as relevant actually discuss the search terms in combination, rather than separately. Consider a simple search for "building contractor." The intent is to find cases that have the words "building" and "contractor" in the same sentence, but that search will return some documents that mention buildings in one paragraph, and others that do not mention contractors until a completely different paragraph. Proximity can fight this problem by lowering the ranking of those cases. In addition, a case that mentions the search terms frequently in a single paragraph is more likely to be discussing those terms in depth than a case in which the search terms are sprinkled sparsely throughout the document.

To measure *diversity*, Fastcase compares how frequently each of the individual search terms appears. Cases with a more even mix of the various search terms receive a higher rank. Similar to proximity, the purpose of a diversity measure is to prevent returning cases that only discuss a part of a search phrase, rather than the whole thing. Imagine searching for "car chase" and receiving search results that frequently mention "car" in close proximity to itself, but that only mention the word "chase" once in passing. Such cases are less likely to be relevant, and so Fastcase ranks them lower.

Finally, to measure *density*, Fastcase compares the number of terms in the document to the total number of words in the document. Documents for which search terms make up a greater proportion of the total words have greater density. The greater the density, the higher Fastcase ranks the document. In a sense, density is a simple way to measure how important the search terms are to the conclusion of the case in question. For example, a 1000-word case that mentions the search terms 15 times likely revolves heavily around those terms. By contrast, a 100,000-word opinion that mentions the terms 15 times likely doesn't focus very intensely on those terms.

2 Citation Analysis to Rank Results

Keyword ranking of results is pretty standard in legal research. In addition to keyword ranking, though, Fastcase also ranks cases based on the map of citation relationships. Fastcase has indexed every citation in the case law database and created a map of those relationships. Every day, as new cases are added to the database, all additional citations are added to the index. The citation map creates a beautiful information architecture that is rich with meaning for legal researchers. For Fastcase, the citation map helps in ranking the most cited results – and, therefore, the most authoritative – at the top of the list. A case that has been frequently cited is, on balance, more authoritative than one that has never been cited.

Of course, the fact that a document has been cited frequently does not necessarily mean that it is authoritative for the question being researched. An opinion could be cited frequently for a jurisdictional proposition, but a researcher might be seeking guidance on substantive law. To identify cases that are frequently cited for the specific point of law a researcher is focused on, Fastcase also reads the list of search results in real time to see how many times keyword-relevant results cite each other. Documents frequently cited by other documents in the results list are more likely to be germane than those that are frequently cited by the entire database, but infrequently cited by other search results. Users can sort by the number of times each result is "Cited Within" the other search results.

3 Crowdsourced Machine Reinforcement

Finally, Fastcase also ranks results by looking at the aggregate usage history of the database. There are more than one million Fastcase searches per month as of this writing, and the system uses the general usage history to boost germane documents in search results. Precedents that are frequently read, printed, or emailed when users conduct similar queries will be ranked higher in search results.

4 Putting Everything Together

Fastcase's enhanced relevance algorithm uses keyword relevance, citation analysis, and lightweight machine learning to rank the most relevant documents at the top of the search results list. Determining how much weight to give each of these variables is a difficult balancing act, and one that the company continues to refine. In 2017, the company exposed the algorithm to users, allowing them to adjust the relative weight of seven factors that determine the ranking of search results. The end result is a system that helps to quickly sort the wheat from the chaff and bring the cases with the highest relevance to the top of search results lists so that users can conduct broad, inclusive searches, but also spend less time reading through irrelevant results.

B Using Citation Maps to Perfect Keyword Search

Just as the fabric of the internet is woven by links, American common law is held together by citations. For as long as law has been practiced in the USA, legal research has largely revolved around appeals to prior authority. If an issue was decided a particular way in the past by the same court or a higher court in its jurisdiction, then the court must generally decide the issue the same way now. In a very real sense, case citations are the bedrock on which the American legal system is built.

Just as the number and quality of links is a strong indicator of importance for web pages, the number and quality of citations is an excellent indicator of the importance of a case. Seminal cases are cited hundreds or thousands of times by the cases that come after them, while a relatively unimportant case may never be cited at all. Of course, the idea that citations indicate importance is not a new concept: Google's famous PageRank algorithm was itself inspired by the pre-existing field of citation analysis, studying the information that can be derived from citation relationships between pages on the World Wide Web.

Fastcase similarly tracks the number of times each case has been cited somewhere else in the legal research database, and users can sort by this column to bring the most frequently cited cases to the top of the list. As discussed above, Fastcase also lists the number of times each case was cited only by the other documents in the search results. Users can sort the list of results by this value as well, bringing to the top of the list the search results that are most frequently cited by the other germane documents in the results list.

Enhanced Relevance and Cited Within are tools that address the problems of over-inclusivity and homogeneity – they address the sorting function of legal research, and advance the most germane documents to the top of the results list. Both of these tools allow users to quickly identify documents that are more important or relevant than others; however, neither approach addresses the problem of under-inclusivity, which is a filtering problem. If the initial search does not return a seminal result, none of the approaches discussed so far would allow the user to see it.

In fact, the "*Miranda* warning" example discussed above exemplifies one of the thorniest problems in legal research. It is surprisingly common for some of the most important cases on a subject to be excluded from search results. One reason: As with *Miranda*, many legal concepts, rules, and tests generally aren't given a name until well after the case in which they originated. *Brown v. Board of Education* never uses the phrase "school desegregation." "*Terry* stop" is nowhere to be found in *Terry v. Ohio*. *Erie Railroad Co. v. Tompkins* never mentions the "*Erie* doctrine." Another common problem is that the courts of one jurisdiction will sometimes choose to adopt a rule or doctrine from one of their neighbors. Searches limited to a particular jurisdiction will therefore sometimes miss the seminal case, because it was decided in a different jurisdiction entirely.

Thankfully, these seminal cases all have one thing in common. They are the most important case on a given topic, so they are very frequently cited by other cases that discuss that topic. *Miranda v. Arizona* may not come up in a search for "*Miranda* warning," but it is cited by virtually every case that does come up. Fastcase can use that citation data to predict that that case, even though it doesn't technically match the initial search query, is very likely relevant to the user's search. Using these case citation relationships, Fastcase created a tool called Forecite, which uses citation analysis to suggest potentially relevant cases that might have been left out because they didn't meet all of the search criteria or were decided in another jurisdiction. Forecite is one of only a very small number of successful methods for combating under-inclusivity by expanding keyword search results in a focused way.

V DATA VISUALIZATION AS X-RAY VISION FOR RESEARCH

Each of the methods discussed above has helped to improve users' ability to quickly find the most important and relevant cases, either by sorting or expanding the list of cases. Nevertheless, years ago Fastcase discovered that there was still a fundamental problem with search results that no legal research service had come close to solving. This problem was the one-dimensional nature of text-based search results.

As early as 2002, Fastcase created the first set of legal search results that the user could reorder. This system offered 12 different ways of sorting search results, including: relevance score, date, alphabetical order by title, number of times documents are cited somewhere else, number of times documents are cited by other documents in the results, and others.

Users could now sort and re-sort the list according to their needs, but when Fastcase introduced the ability to sort search results in this way, a pattern of usage quickly emerged: Users would sort by relevance, memorize the top ten results, then sort by date and memorize the ten most recent, then sort by citation and attempt to compare where each case fell when sorting by different metrics. Users didn't only need to know either which cases were most relevant or which cases were most recent; they needed to know which cases were the most relevant *and* the most recent.

Essentially, the problem was that Fastcase search results gave users text lists that were only one-dimensional. If a user sorts the most relevant cases to the top, they may simultaneously be sorting the most recent cases to the bottom. If a user sorts the most recent cases to the top, they may be sorting the most cited cases to the bottom, and so on. Lists can only ever sort or display along a single axis: top to bottom. Fastcase needed to create a way to view results multi-dimensionally, so that users could see results that were both authoritative and relevant, or recent and authoritative, or important across every dimension. This realization is where data visualization in legal research was born.

VI DATA VISUALIZATION APPROACH

In 2008, inspired by the work of the late Dr. Hans Rosling, Fastcase attempted to solve the one-dimensional problem by creating the Interactive Timeline (Figure 3.8.4). The Interactive Timeline is a patented visual map of search results that allows users to see where cases fall along all four of the most important metrics, simultaneously, without forcing users to switch views or memorize lists.

A *How the Interactive Timeline Works*

The Interactive Timeline always shows decision dates on the *x*-axis; newer cases appear toward the right of the window, while older cases are positioned farther to the left. In its default configuration, the *y*-axis of the Timeline displays relevance. The higher the relevance score, the higher up a case will be displayed. This means that when a user

FIGURE 3.8.4 Image from Fastcase's Interactive Timeline.

first opens the Timeline, they can see at a glance which cases are the most recent and relevant. These will be the cases closest to the top-right corner. Alternatively, the *y*-axis can be changed to show court levels instead of relevance (Figure 3.8.5). In this configuration, the cases are grouped into lines so that you can see when the issue was addressed at each jurisdictional level.

Each case is represented by two circles. The sizes of the outer circles (lighter grey) represent the total number of citations to that case, while the sizes of the inner, darker grey circles represent the Cited Within number.[3] Cases with very small circles have either never been cited, or have been cited very few times. Cases with a large outer circle and a small dark grey inner circle have been cited frequently in general, but have not been cited by many other cases in the results list. Conversely, cases for which the dark grey inner circle is almost as large as the lighter outer circle have been cited almost exclusively by other cases in the results list. These eclipse-like circles are the prized results: they represent the most significant cases, specific to the subject being researched. The dual-colored circles provide a simple visual indication of how important each case is – both in general (light grey) and for the specific topic being researched (dark grey). The two axes and the two kinds of circles thus combine to allow users to see four separate dimensions simultaneously. This makes it possible to instantly spot key cases, compare them to each other, and even see general legal trends.

---

[3] In the Fastcase Interactive Timeline, inner circles are a bright yellow; they only appear in greyscale in this volume.

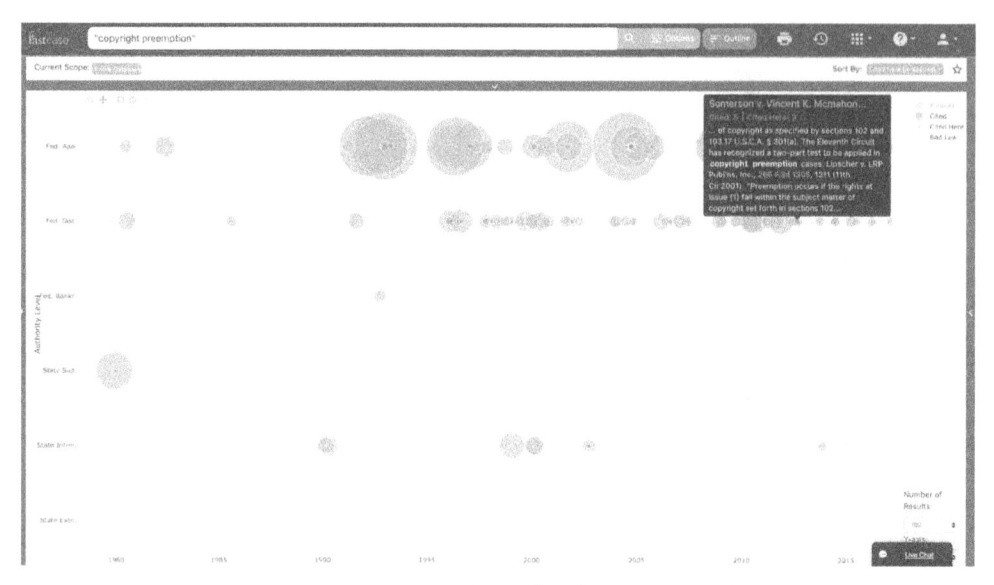

FIGURE 3.8.5 Y-axis changed to show court level.

B How Users Employ Visualization

In general, users look for large, mostly dark grey (yellow[4]) case icons that are located near the upper-right corner of the graph. This means the cases are authoritative (frequently cited), and also that they are likely important for this particular field of research. Picking cases near the top of the window ensures that they are relevant to an in-depth discussion of the search terms, and the farther to the right they are, the more current the case's reasoning is.

For the first time, users can see the usefulness of search results across many dimensions at once. They can filter results, zoom in on a cluster of results, and hover over any case icon to see the name and citation, most relevant paragraph of the case based on the search, and citation statistics that show how authoritative the document is. The Interactive Timeline also includes the Forecite results described above, which expands the list of search results beyond keyword search results and includes seminal results that keyword searches might otherwise miss.

C How Search Visualization Yields Better Results

Sometimes a Timeline map clusters results together, but often the most important results jump out of the pack, hovering above the others, declaring themselves to be the case the user cares about most. If you've ever read hundreds of search results just to find the winning case, this is nothing short of magic. This visualization also has another correlative benefit: For the first time, a user knows when to stop researching. Legal researchers with a visual map can see right away that there are X number of cases they care about, and once they have read those cases, they can stop reading. With prior list-based search methods, one never really knew where to stop unless and until one had read all of the results, in the end leaving a user to wonder if they may have missed the most important precedent.

---

[4] See previous footnote.

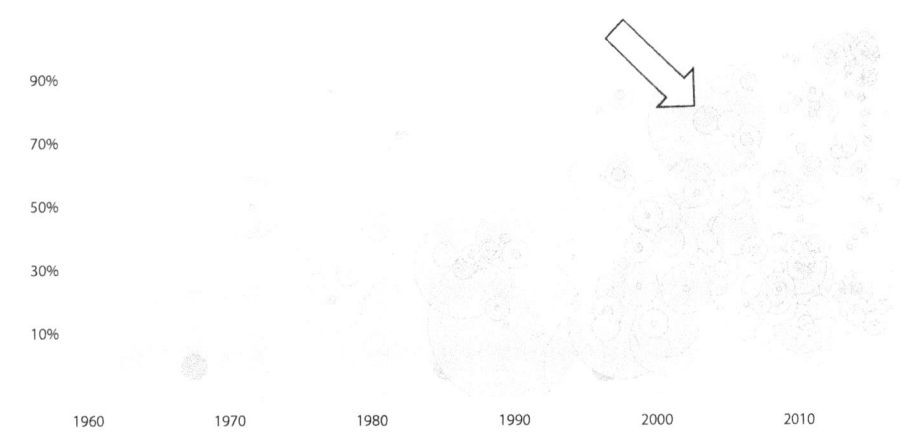

FIGURE 3.8.6 "Same-sex marriage" Interactive Timeline, with arrowing indicating *Lawrence v. Texas*.

Visualization gives users the confidence that they have identified the most important and most precedential cases, as well as any cases they might otherwise have missed. The Interactive Timeline is not just a beautiful rendering of results; it also allows users to understand results better, read more strategically, and gain insights that are impossible to gain from analog, one-dimensional, text-based search results.

D Example

Let's take a look at an example. Figure 3.8.6 shows a search for "same-sex marriage." You can see at a glance how the issue has grown more prominent over time: From 1990 to the present, the number of relevant cases skyrockets, creating a cluster of cases that are both very recent and very relevant. One case immediately jumps out of the pack, though. It is frequently cited, relatively recent, and pretty high up on the relevance scale. This case is *Lawrence v. Texas*, a 2003 Supreme Court decision that ruled sodomy bans unconstitutional.

Zooming in on the cluster of recent, relevant cases in the top-right corner also reveals two 2014 cases rated as 100% relevant and cited somewhat frequently (Figure 3.8.7). These turn out to be *United States v. Windsor* and *Hollingsworth v. Perry*, a pair of high-profile Supreme Court decisions that held that same-sex couples are entitled to federal benefits, and that refused to address a challenge to the overturning of California's controversial Proposition 8, respectively. Finally, clicking on the case that is closest to the upper-right corner reveals *Obergefell v. Hodges*, the case that finally confirmed a constitutional right to same-sex marriage. As a fairly recent decision, it hasn't yet accumulated a large number of citations, but over time its circle can be expected to grow quite large.

VII CONCLUSION

Legal research is a difficult process of sorting and filtering, and text-based legal research exacerbates the process considerably. Boolean keyword searches are clumsy, they are both over-inclusive and under-inclusive, and the lists of text-based search results they return can easily make search more difficult and make all results look the same, with important cases

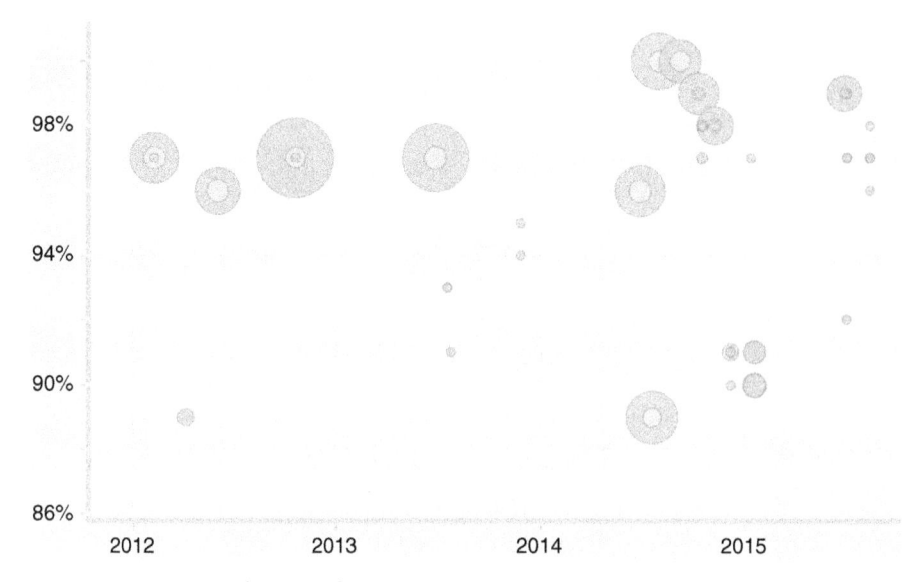

FIGURE 3.8.7 Close-up of Figure 3.8.6, "Same-sex marriage" case relevance.

right alongside completely irrelevant ones. However, by using citation analysis to expand the list of search results, Forecite from Fastcase helps resolve the under-inclusivity problem by finding seminal cases that are frequently cited in search results, but that may not themselves appear in those search results. Fastcase uses citation analysis to sort the top results that are most authoritative, sort the most cited results to the top of the list, and compute the Enhanced Relevance score from the number of citations to a case.

Fastcase's Interactive Timeline helps fight the over-inclusivity problem by creating a visual map of search results so users can instantly see which cases score the highest across five different indices of importance: keyword relevance, date, number of times cited in the database generally, number of times cited by other documents in the search results, and optionally, the seniority of the court deciding the case. Using a timeline, different colors, and different icon sizes to denote cases, users can instantly see the most important cases. They can hover over a document to see a summary of why it's important, including its citation analysis. They can filter the list to see fewer results, or zoom in to get a better look at groups of documents clustered closely together. Citation analysis and data visualization do not solve every problem with legal research, but as this demonstrative example shows, these tools do help to mitigate the classic problems of over-inclusivity and under-inclusivity in search results.

3.9

Mining Information from Statutory Texts in a Public Health Domain

Kevin D. Ashley

I INTRODUCTION

This case study describes how a team of computer scientists assisted a team of public health researchers by applying machine learning to extract information from statutory texts. Researchers at the University of Pittsburgh's Graduate School of Public Health (SPH) had been manually mining specific information from federal, state, and local laws and regulations concerning public health system emergency preparedness and response. The analysts used the information to assess and compare states' regulatory frameworks concerning emergency preparedness. They retrieved candidate legal and regulatory texts from a full-text legal information service, identified relevant spans of text, and systematically categorized the spans in terms of a coding scheme. The SPH's coding scheme captured information about agencies and actors in a state's public health system who were directed by statute to interact with one another in particular ways while dealing with public health emergencies. Based on the coded information, the SPH constructed statutory network diagrams of legally mandated interactions among actors. These network diagrams provide insight into those statutory texts that directed the interactions.

Manually encoding thousands of statutory provisions across 12 states would have been expensive and time-consuming. Instead, a team of computer scientists at Pittsburgh (the machine learning [ML] team) automated the coding task by applying ML to manually encoded provisions to use as training instances. Most of the learned classifiers performed better than baselines, but the scarcity of training instances presented problems. The ML team demonstrated how to improve classification performance on one state's statutory texts by including as training instances other states' annotated statutory texts pertaining to the same general topic. The researchers also adapted e-discovery-style predictive coding methods to improve initial relevance assessment of statutory texts. They showed how to take a classification model trained during one statutory analysis, and reuse it for another related analysis. This case study reveals some missteps, though. The SPH's initial framing of the coding task was problematic, and there are other continuing challenges for attaining a practical solution to the task.

This chapter begins with a survey of related work in statutory legal informatics. It introduces ML concepts and techniques for extracting semantic information from statutes and regulations. Then it illustrates in detail the SPH team's statutory network diagrams. *Network diagrams* are innovative legal informatics tools that graphically represent extracted statutory semantic information. This study presents the ML team's three research projects: (1) applying supervised machine learning to classify statutory provisions; (2) dealing with scarce training instances by using training data from multiple states; and (3) employing interactive machine learning to improve retrieval of relevant statutory texts. The ML team's efforts at times fell short of a practical solution to the SPH's problem, but all three projects demonstrated empirical evidence of some success. The case study concludes by outlining lessons learned and ways to improve performance.

II STATUTORY LEGAL INFORMATICS: RELATED WORK

For the past 15 years, researchers in artificial intelligence (AI) and law have been applying natural language processing (NLP) and ML to classify statutory texts in terms of conceptual labels and network analysis for modeling systems of statutes.

A Applying NLP and ML to Classify Statutory Texts

Natural language processing tools handle parsing, part-of-speech tagging, resolving co-references, and recognizing named entities. Machine learning programs employ statistical analysis to induce a model from a data set of texts, using their models to predict an outcome, such as a classification for a new text.[1]

Important to this case study is that ML programs that have been applied to statutory texts include decision trees, support vector machines (SVM), and naive Bayes models. Given a set of training data, a *decision tree* learns a set of successive questions to test the classification value of a new instance of information (e.g., a text unit). Such a test might be whether a certain feature's weight is greater than a threshold value. If it is, one decision tree branches to the left at that point in the tree; if it is not, the tree branches to the right. Upon reaching a leaf node, all of the questions have been asked and the classification is made. An SVM uses statistical criteria to find boundaries between positive and negative instances of a classification in a multidimensional feature space. The boundary should be maximally distant from all of the instances; ideally, the positive instances all lie on one side of the boundary, and the negative instances all lie on the other. *Naive Bayes* models, meanwhile, calculate the probability of a classification given the feature values, and then select the most likely label. They estimate this probability indirectly by estimating the probability of the classification – and that of the feature values given the classification – and then applying a formula called Bayes' rule.

Researchers in one study used SVM and naive Bayes models to assign 11 labels, including "definition," "permission" ("may"), "obligation" ("must"), or "prohibition" ("must not"), to paragraphs of Italian statutory texts.[2] Another study assigned 13 labels to sentences in a Dutch statute.[3] Francesconi and Peruginelli applied naive Bayes and SVM models to index legal

---

[1] For a comprehensive introduction to NLP and machine learning, *see* Katz and Nay – Machine Learning, *supra*; Nay – Natural Language Processing for Legal Texts, *supra*.

[2] Enrico Francesconi, Simonetta Montemagni, Wim Peters, and Daniela Tiscornia, "Integrating a Bottom-Up and Top-Down Methodology for Building Semantic Resources for the Multilingual Legal Domain," in *Semantic Processing of Legal Texts*, eds. Enrico Francesconi, Simonetta Montemagni, Wim Peters, and Daniela Tiscornia (Berlin: Springer, 2010), 95–121.

[3] Emile de Maat, Kai Krabben, and Radboud Winkels, "Machine Learning versus Knowledge Based Classification of Legal Texts," in *Proceedings of the 2010 Conference on Legal Knowledge and Information Systems: JURIX 2010: The Twenty-Third Annual Conference*, ed. Radboud Winkels (Amsterdam: IOS Press, 2010), 87–96.

literature by assigning topic area labels such as environmental law, European law, and criminal law.[4] A group of researchers has assigned labels to legislative texts from an index tree comprising 230 leaf node topics.[5] Other researchers have used the EuroVoc conceptual thesaurus to assign indexing terms to texts based on the vector similarity among documents represented as bags-of-words, with weights and vectors created for each vocabulary concept.[6] Boella et al. employed an SVM classifier for a similar task.[7] Daudaravicius has worked with multi-jurisdictional and multilingual documents.[8]

Rule-based knowledge engineering approaches and NLP have also been applied to extract information from statutes. Wyner and Peters used manually constructed linguistic rules to extract different types of legal norms (e.g., obligation and permission), as well as antecedents, subject agents, or subject themes.[9] Winkels and Hoekstra focused on identifying concept definitions.[10] Other researchers extracted functional arguments, such as the action or object specified in a statutory provision.[11] Ideally, one could extract logical rules directly from the texts of statutes and regulations, but this has proven difficult to achieve. In general, NLP tools alone do not suffice. On the other hand, researchers who have focused on narrow areas of law and used tailored templates for logical structures have achieved some success.[12]

A different way for a human expert to apply their knowledge is to classify statutory texts in an iterative interaction with an ML *classifier*. The expert user provides feedback to the classifier as the classifier provides the user with suggestions. This works similarly to *relevance feedback*, a technique in which an information retrieval system employs a user's feedback on the relevance of selected documents from the results list.[13] One main difference between the iterative approach and the relevance feedback approach is that, as the name suggests, the

---

[4] Enrico Francesconi and Ginevra Peruginelli, "Integrated Access to Legal Literature through Automated Semantic Classification," *Artificial Intelligence and Law* 17 (1) (2009): 31–49.

[5] Rob Opsomer, Geert De Meyer, Chris Cornelis, and Greet van Eetvelde, "Exploiting Properties of Legislative Texts to Improve Classification Accuracy," in *Proceedings of the 2009 Conference on Legal Knowledge and Information Systems: JURIX 2009: The Twenty-Second Annual Conference*, ed. G. Governatori (Amsterdam: IOS Press, 2009), 136–145.

[6] Bruno Pouliquen, Ralf Steinberger, and Camelia Ignat, "Automatic Annotation of Multilingual Text Collections with a Conceptual Thesaurus," *arXiv preprint* (September 2006), available at: https://arxiv.org/abs/cs/0609059; Ralf Steinberger, Mohamed Ebrahim, and Marco Turchi, "JRC EuroVoc Indexer JEX: A Freely Available Multi-Label Categorisation Tool," *arXiv preprint* (September 2013), available at: https://arxiv.org/abs/1309.5223.

[7] Guido Boella, Luigi Di Caro, Leonardo Lesmo, Daniele Rispoli, and Livio Robaldo, "Multi-Label Classification of Legislative Text into EuroVoc," in *JURIX, Volume 250 of Frontiers in Artificial Intelligence and Applications*, ed. B. Schafer (Amsterdam: IOS Press, 2012), 21–30.

[8] Vidas Daudaravicius, "Automatic Multilingual Annotation of EU Legislation with Eurovoc Descriptors," PowerPoint presentation, *EEOP2012 Workshop Proceedings*, 2012, available at: http://utrecht.elsnet.org/EEOP2012/Daudaravicius-EEOP2012.pdf.

[9] Adam Wyner and Wim Peters, "On Rule Extraction from Regulations," *JURIX, Volume 235 of Frontiers in Artificial Intelligence and Applications* (Amsterdam: IOS Press, 2011), 113–122.

[10] Radboud Winkels and Rinke Hoekstra, "Automatic Extraction of Legal Concepts and Definitions," in *Proceedings of the 2012 Conference on Legal Knowledge and Information Systems: JURIX 2012: The Twenty-Fifth Annual Conference* (Amsterdam: IOS Press, 2012), 157–166.

[11] Francesconi et al., "Integrating a Bottom-Up and Top-Down Methodology for Building Semantic Resources for the Multilingual Legal Domain," *supra* note 2.

[12] For an example dealing with a portion of the Japanese National Pension Law, *see, e.g.*, Ngo Xuan Bach, Nguyen Le Minh, Tran Thi Oanh, and Akira Shimazu, "A Two-Phase Framework for Learning Logical Structures of Paragraphs in Legal Articles," *ACM Transactions on Asian Language Information Processing (TALIP)* 12 (1) (2013): 1–32; for an example that extracts requirements from construction regulations, *see, e.g.*, Jiansong Zhang and Nora M. El-Gohary, "Automated Information Transformation for Automated Regulatory Compliance Checking in Construction," *Journal of Computing in Civil Engineering* 29 (4) (2015).

[13] Christopher D. Manning, Hinrich Schütze, and Prabhakar Raghavan, *Introduction to Information Retrieval* (Cambridge: Cambridge University Press, 2008), 197.

iterative approach involves more iterations of expert user feedback given to the classifier. These forms of interactive ML have previously been applied in e-discovery in predictive coding and technology-assisted review (TAR),[14] but this case study is the first to apply such a framework to homogeneous, structured statutory texts.

B Applying Network Analysis to Statutes

Regulatory systems established by statute can be represented visually as networks or graphs of the relations between different statutes and provisions, all connected in a citation network.

Network analysis involves drawing inferences about the relevance of various objects in the citation network, and using them for conceptual legal information retrieval based on the linkages' relative weights and other properties.

One recommender system applies network analysis to statutes.[15] A program automatically determines the context of laws to display or "recommend" to a user of an online hyperlinked legislative database by measuring their relevance to the particular legal article the user retrieved. Here, relevance is determined based on the network analysis of *context networks* for each article. These context networks consist of a selection of all incoming references to, and all outgoing references from, a retrieved article. The weighting scheme prefers references that are outgoing (i.e., non-internal), that refer to definitions in prior articles, that were recently changed, or that have a high degree of network centrality.

Network analysis can be integrated into legal information retrieval in other ways. A network of special "legal issues" – extracted from a full-text case law corpus – can assist users in retrieving relevant case materials.[16] When cases are connected by citations, these special legal issues represent the propositions for which the case is cited. For example, one system in use retrieves documents based on queries that contain semantic descriptors and indicators of cross-references between documents.[17] Similarly, network analysis can also enable users to draw inferences about a whole corpus of legal regulations, finding the most influential regulations in a corpus of hundreds of legislative documents based on analysis of citation patterns either at the provision level[18] or the

---

[14] Christopher Hogan, Robert Bauer, and Dan Brassil, "Human-Aided Computer Cognition for E-discovery," in *Proceedings of the 12th International Conference on Artificial Intelligence and Law* (New York, NY: ACM, 2009), 194–201; Jianlin Cheng, Amanda Jones, Caroline Privault, and Jean-Michel Renders, "Soft Labeling for Multi-Pass Document Review," in *Proceedings of the ICAIL 2013 International Conference on Artificial Intelligence and Law, Rome, Italy, June 10–14, 2013* (New York, NY: ACM, 2013); Daniel Krasner and Ian Langmore, "Flexible Processing and Classification for eDiscovery," in *Legal Knowledge and Information Systems: JURIX 2013: The Twenty-Sixth Annual Conference*, ed. Kevin D. Ashley (Amsterdam: IOS Press, 2013), 87–96.

[15] Radboud Winkels, Alexander Boer, Bart Vredebregt, and Alexander van Someren, "Towards a Legal Recommender System," in *Legal Knowledge and Information Systems: JURIX 2014: The Twenty-Seventh International Conference*, ed. R. Hoekstra (Amsterdam: IOS Press, 2014), 169–178.

[16] Paul Zhang, Harry R. Silver, Mark Wasson, David Steiner, and Sanjay Sharma, "Knowledge Network Based on Legal Issues," in *Network Analysis in Law*, eds. Radboud Winkels, Lettieri Nicola, and Faro Sebastiano (Naples: Edizioni Scientifiche Italiane, 2013), 23–51.

[17] Nada Mimouni, Meritxell Fernandez, Adeline Nazarenko, Daniele Bourcier, and Sylvie Salotti, "A Relational Approach for Information Retrieval on XML Legal Sources," in *Proceedings of the Fourteenth International Conference on Artificial Intelligence and Law, Rome, Italy, June 10–14, 2013* (New York, NY: ACM Press, 2013), 212–216.

[18] Akos Szőke, Krisztián Mácsár, and György Strausz, "A Text Analysis Framework for Automatic Semantic Knowledge Representation of Legal Documents," in *Network Analysis in Law*, eds. Radboud Winkels, Nicola Lettieri, and Sebastiano Faro (Naples: Edizioni Scientifiche Italiane, 2014), 105–127; Rinke Hoekstra, "A Network Analysis of Dutch Regulations Using the MetaLex Document Server," in *Network Analysis in Law*, eds. Radboud Winkels, Nicola Lettieri, and Sebastiano Faro (Naples: Edizioni Scientifiche Italiane, 2014), 89–105.

paragraph level.[19] This technique has been applied to citation patterns in French[20] and American[21] legal codes, and to email communications in e-discovery.[22]

C How this Case Study Compares to Related Work

In the projects discussed below, this chapter's author and his students developed ML approaches to automatically identify statutory provisions that set up relevant relationships among participants and extracted relevant features to construct and compare statutory network diagrams of multiple states' regulatory systems.[23] Our work integrates network analysis and legal information retrieval in a different way from the above examples, though, by using *statutory network diagrams*. Here, the connected objects in the network are not statutory provisions, but rather a set of reference concepts referred to by, and subject to, regulation across multiple statutes. The links in the networks correspond to statutorily mandated relationships that connect various participants in a system of regulation. As with related work that uses ML to classify statutes, we mine the statutory texts for types of legal norms and the presence of functional rule elements such as acting and receiving agents, type of emergency, or condition. Like the EuroVoc-related work mentioned above, we target similarly purposed legislation from multiple jurisdictions.

III TARGET APP: LENA STATUTORY NETWORK DIAGRAMS

This case study begins with the LENA project (LEgal Network Analyzer) at the University of Pittsburgh SPH. The SPH team had created an online system to generate network diagrams representing statutorily mandated relationships among public health system participants concerning public health emergencies. The nodes in these statutory network diagrams represented agencies and actors in a state's public health system who were directed by statute to interact with one another in particular ways in order to deal with public health emergencies.[24]

---

[19] Dincer Gultemen and Tom van Engers, "Graph-Based Linking and Visualization for Legislation Documents (GLVD)," in *Network Analysis in Law*, eds. Radboud Winkels, Nicola Lettieri, and Sebastiano Faro (Naples: Edizioni Scientifiche Italiane, 2014), 127–145.

[20] Pierre Mazzega, Danièle Bourcier, and Romain Boulet, "The Network of French Legal Codes," in *Proceedings of the 12th International Conference on Artificial Intelligence and Law (ICAIL)* (New York, NY: ACM, 2009), 236–237.

[21] Michael J. Bommarito II and Daniel Martin Katz, "A Mathematical Approach to the Study of the United States Code," *Physica A* 389 (2010): 4195–4200.

[22] Hans Henseler, "Network-Based Filtering for Large Email Collections in E-discovery," *Artificial Intelligence and Law* 18 (4) (2010): 413–430.

[23] Jaromir Savelka and Kevin Ashley, "Transfer of Predictive Models for Classification of Statutory Texts in Multijurisdictional Settings," in *Proceedings of the 15th International Conference on Artificial Intelligence and Law* (New York, NY: ACM, 2015), 216–220; Jaromir Savelka, Gaurov Trivedi, and Kevin Ashley, "Applying an Interactive Machine Learning Approach to Statutory Analysis," in *Proceedings of the 28th Annual Conference on Legal Knowledge and Information Systems (Jurix 2015)*, ed. Antonino Rotolo (Amsterdam: IOS Press, 2015), 133–142; Jaromir Savelka, Kevin Ashley, and Matthias Grabmair, "Mining Information from Statutory Texts in Multi-Jurisdictional Settings," in *Proceedings of the 27th Annual Conference on Legal Knowledge and Information Systems (Jurix 2014)*, ed. Rinke Hoekstra (Amsterdam: IOS Press, 2014), 133–142; Matthias Grabmair, Kevin D. Ashley, Rebecca Hwa, and Patricia M. Sweeney, "Toward Extracting Information from Public Health Statutes Using Text Classification and Machine Learning," in *Proceedings of the 24th Annual Conference on Legal Knowledge and Information Systems (JURIX 2011)*, ed. Katie M. Atkinson (Amsterdam: IOS Press, 2011), 73–82.

[24] Patricia M. Sweeney, Elizabeth F. Bjerke, Margaret A. Potter, Hasan Guclu, Christopher R. Keane, Kevin D. Ashley, Matthias Grabmair, and Rebecca Hwa, "Network Analysis of Manually-Encoded State Laws and Prospects for Automation," in *Network Analysis in Law*, eds. Radboud Winkels, Lettieri Nicola, and Faro Sebastiano (Naples: Edizioni Scientifiche Italiane, 2014), 51–75.

The LENA system assists users who want to determine the mandated reporting relationships between, for example, hospitals and government public health agencies, and it helps those users to determine which particular regulations govern the relationships. A user can satisfy a query like this by using the links in the LENA system's statutory network diagram. The system then retrieves the specific statutory provisions that establish the relationship between the linked participants. In effect, those statutory provisions are the reason why the nodes are linked.

In this way, the statutory network diagram is a kind of visual index into a legal information database. This Emergency Law Database contains the texts of the states' statutes deemed relevant to the project's focus on public health emergencies and response.

A Sample Statutory Network Diagram and Use Case

Figure 3.9.1 shows a screenshot of LENA's statutory network diagram, comparing Texas law to Pennsylvania law on how the agents in the states' respective public health systems deal with epidemic emergencies involving infectious diseases. Circular nodes represent the agents. Where a statute directs two agents to interact, a line connects the nodes in the diagram. The line's thickness represents how many legal directives require an interaction between the connected agents. A node's size reflects the agent's centrality in the network – the smaller the node, the less central the role played by the agent; the larger the node, the more central its role. Centrality of a node is proportional to the number of incoming directives from, and outgoing directives to, other nodes. As the figure indicates, the largest node is labeled as the agent, Governmental Public Health, which represents state and local health departments and boards. Some of the mandated connections appear in both states' laws. Other lines appear only in Pennsylvania law. The line between the Hospitals actor and Governmental Public Health is unidirectional. Other lines are bidirectional, with arrows at both ends, meaning that the interactions may originate with either agent under the statutes.

Visual comparisons in statutory networks can point out inter-jurisdictional differences. These may lead policy analysts to hypothesize about the differences that could be investigated between the retrieved statutory texts. For instance, public health policy makers may find the LENA tool and the Emergency Law Database useful in identifying gaps in a state's regulatory scheme for dealing with public health emergencies and for comparing different states' disease reporting requirements. A Pennsylvania public health agent might be interested in the aftermath of the 2014 Ebola virus events at Texas Presbyterian Hospital, in which it was unclear whether the hospital emergency department staff had been sufficiently alerted to the possibility of seeing an Ebola-exposed patient.[25] The agent might be surprised to learn that, like in Texas law, there appears to be no mandated connection in Pennsylvania law from the Governmental Public Health agency to hospitals. The agent could follow that link to retrieve the texts of the Pennsylvania laws connecting hospitals and Governmental Public Health agencies in order to investigate the mandate. Legally trained personnel would probably have no difficulty researching a question like this using commercial legal information retrieval systems. Non-legally trained personnel, on the other hand, might find it much harder to do so without a tool like LENA to serve as a kind of visual entrée to a legal database.

---

[25] See Kevin Ashley, Elizabeth F. Bjerke, Margaret Potter, Hasan Guclu, Jaromir Savelka, and Matthias Grabmair, "Statutory Network Analysis Plus Information Retrieval," in *Proceedings of the ICAIL 2013 International Conference on Artificial Intelligence and Law, Rome, Italy, June 10–14, 2013* (New York, NY: ACM, 2013); Kevin D. Ashley, *Artificial Intelligence and Legal Analytics: New Tools for Law Practice in the Digital Age* (Cambridge: Cambridge University Press, 2017).

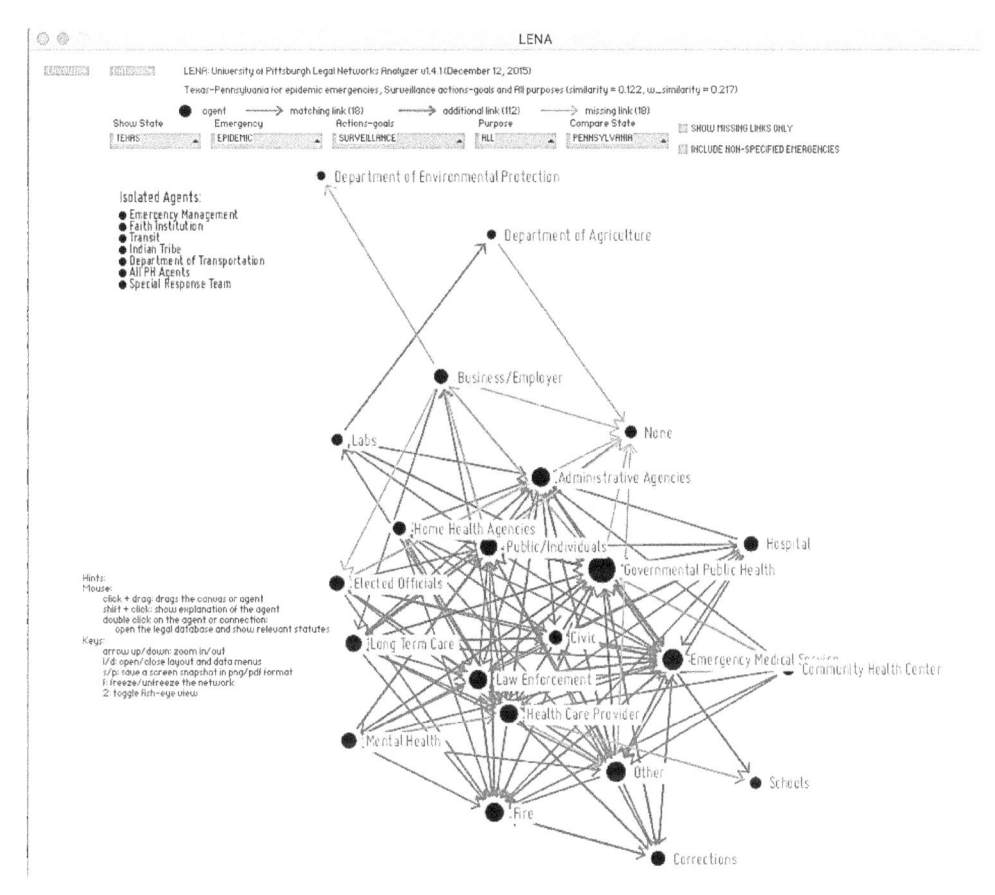

FIGURE 3.9.1 LENA statutory network comparing Texas and Pennsylvania statutes on epidemic emergencies with infectious diseases.

One can apply network analytic metrics – such as centrality or strength – to draw legally interesting inferences. In a weighted network, *strength* is the total weight of incoming and outgoing edge weights for the connections of each agent. The heat map in Figure 3.9.2 shows the strength of 29 public health system (PHS) agents in statutory networks for preparedness, response, recovery, and all purposes. Scaled from minimum frequency (black) to maximum frequency (white), the heat map shows that, with respect to recovery from public health emergencies, statutes in ten states frequently direct interactions between elected officials and other agents. That appears not to be the case in Maryland, however. Conversely, Maryland statutes frequently direct interactions between long-term care (LTC) agents and others, but this is not so in those ten other states.

Public health policy analysts might wish to confirm such information with legal research and, depending on the result, recommend legislative action in the affected states. They should not rely solely on LENA to draw such conclusions, though, because although LENA is a useful tool, legal research with LENA is subject to some limitations. Its statutory network diagrams are based on the statutes and regulations dealing with public health emergency response as of a particular point in time. Such provisions are subject to frequent revision, however, and the Emergency Law Database and LENA resources would have to be updated regularly to reflect these revisions and maintain accuracy. For this reason, it would

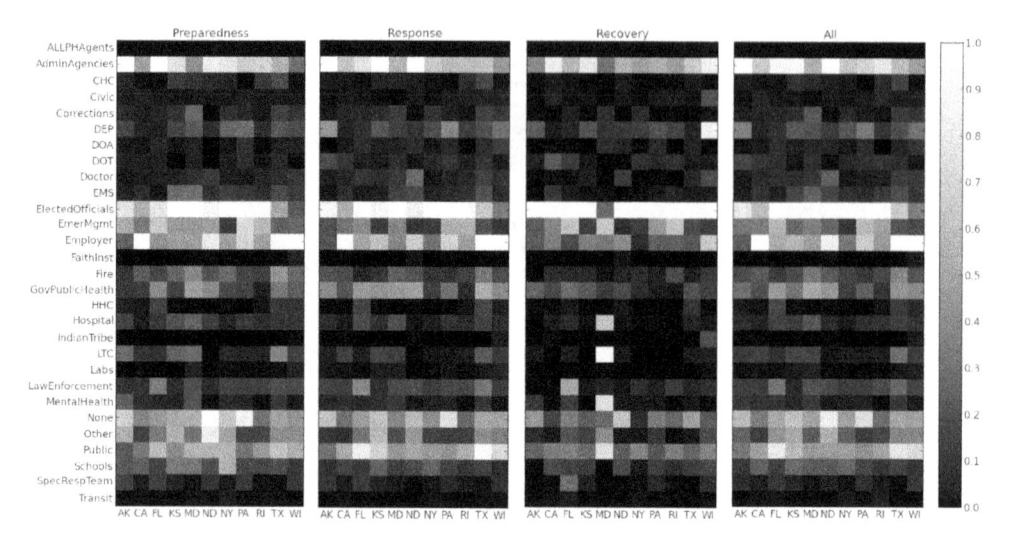

FIGURE 3.9.2 Heat map of agent strength in statutory networks.

be especially useful to apply ML to statutory texts to automatically extract the information needed to construct and maintain contemporaneous statutory network diagrams.

B Statutory Annotation Scheme and Manual Encoding

When the SPH team first developed their approach, they did not have ML in mind. Instead, they retrieved statutory texts from LexisNexis, selected the relevant texts, developed an encoding scheme, and applied it to the selected texts, performing all of these tasks manually. The phases of such a coding process are shown in Figure 3.9.3.

The SPH team selected 11 states from which to obtain statutes and state administrative code regulations. For simplicity, we will refer to both statutes and regulations as "statutes." The states they selected presented a representative range of demographic, climatic, and geographic conditions concerning public health emergencies and risks. They ranged from states that had experienced urban terrorism, like New York on 9/11, to states sitting on earthquake fault lines, like California and Alaska, to Midwestern states lying in "Tornado Alley," such as Kansas and Texas.

The SPH team compiled a listing of standard PHS agent types where "agent" means an organization, government agency, or professional group that contributes to emergency public health within a given jurisdiction. In order to assemble a corpus of statutory texts, the SPH team created Lexis queries involving the various types of public health agents using strings such as "Communicable," "Disaster," "Emergency," "Emergency or Disaster w/p Nuclear or Radi!," "Epidemic," "Food borne," "Hazard!," "Infect!," "Pandemic," "Preparedness," or "Terror!" (see Figure 3.9.3, step 1). An example of such a Lexis query might look like this:

```
(emergency OR disaster OR hazard) AND
(respond OR prepare) AND
(OR fire OR hospital OR medical OR 'Emergency Management
Agency' OR 'community health' OR 'department of health' OR
'environmental protection' OR
(... for each type of institution of interest)
```

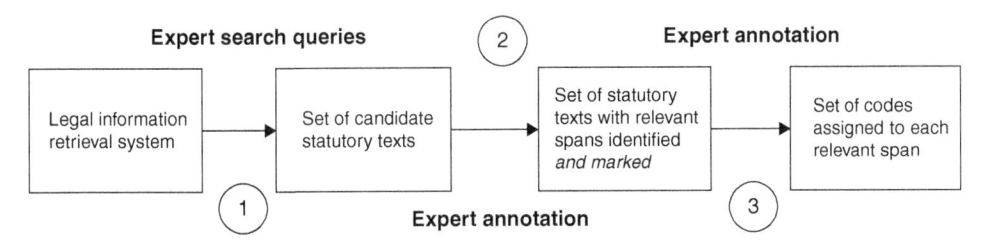

FIGURE 3.9.3 Schematic view of phases of coding text by the SPH team.

These searches of the states' statutory databases yielded more than 33,000 provisions from the 11 states, which the public health team screened manually. The SPH team deemed about 4900 of those provisions to be relevant, and these became the Public Health Emergency (PHE) Corpus, each provision of which had a root-level §-citation (e.g., 4 Pa. Code § 3.24).

The SPH team's scheme for encoding the texts of these state statutory provisions comprised ten classifications: the *acting agents* in the PHS that a *relevant* provision directs with some *level of prescription* to perform a certain *action* with respect to some *receiving agents* under certain *conditions*, with certain *goals* and *purpose* regarding some *type of emergency disaster* in some *time frame*. More specifically, these coding concepts have the following meanings:[26]

- **Relevance:** Whether this provision is relevant to the PHS analysis of public health emergencies and preparedness. This is a binary classification. If "yes," then:
- **Acting PHS agent:** What agent (i.e., organization, group, or individual) does the provision direct to act? This value has 31 codes, such as "hospital," "community health."
- **Action:** What verb best characterizes the action that this provision directs? This value has 82 codes, such as "require," "enact," "establish," and "vaccinate."
- **Receiving PHS agent:** What agent does this provision direct to receive the action from, or to develop a relationship with, the acting agent? This value has 31 codes.
- **Prescription:** With what level of prescription is the action directed? Does it state a mandate, a prohibition, or an option? This value has five possible codes.
- **Goal:** What noun or noun phrase describes the intended product or result of the directed action? This value has 143 codes, such as "establish plan" or "require training program."
- **Purpose:** What phrase or phrases best characterize the reason the action has been directed? This value has four codes, such as "preparing for," "responding to," and "recovering from" emergency.
- **Type of emergency disaster:** In what kind of emergency situation does the legal direction occur? This value has 19 codes, such as "any" or "all" emergencies, or "earthquake," "spill."
- **Time frame:** Over what period of time can/must the action be taken? Is this a one-shot action, or does it recur? This value has 150 codes.
- **Condition:** What event is triggered if the action is to be taken? This value has 172 codes, such as a declaration of emergency or the failure of a plan.

Over a number of time periods, 4–8 human coders manually encoded 4900 statutory provisions in an Excel spreadsheet. They identified the spans that were relevant and could be cited (see Figure 3.9.3, step 2). Each of the provisions corresponded to multiple lines in the coding table. Each line contained a specific reference to the provision and recorded a code label for each of the nine categories other than relevance (see Figure

---

[26] For each category, a comprehensive codebook provides a list of alternative values. Full texts of the provisions are posted at www.phasys.pitt.edu/default.aspx and accessible from the LEgal Network Analyzer (LENA) software (www.phdl.pitt.edu/LENA). The code book is available at: www.phasys.pitt.edu/pdf/Code_Book_Numerical_Defintions.pdf.

> 35 Pa.S. § 521.11. Persons refusing to submit to treatment for venereal diseases, tuberculosis or any other communicable disease
>
> (a.1) If the secretary or any local health officer finds that any person who is infected with venereal disease, tuberculosis or any other communicable disease in a communicable stage refuses to submit to treatment approved by the department or by a local board or department of health, the secretary or his representative or the local medical health officer may cause the person to be isolated in an appropriate institution designated by the department or by the local board or department of health for safekeeping and treatment until the disease has been rendered non-communicable.
>
> Coded as:
> 1. *Citation*: 35 Pa.S. § 521.11(a.1)
> 2. *Public Health Agent (actor)*: 2(12(2)) (state), 2(12(4)) [local governmental public health officer]
> 3. *Prescription*: 3(1) [may]
> 4. *Action*: 4(38) [order]
> 5. *Goal*: 5(48) [isolation]
> 6. *Purpose*: 6(2) [in response]
> 7. *Emergency/Disaster Type*: 7(13) [infectious disease emergency]
> 8. *Public Health Agent (receiver)*: 8(27FN120) [someone who is ill]
> 9. *Conditions*: 9(46) [when the person refuses medical treatment], 9(126) [is suspected of having TB], 9(25) [or a communicable disease]
> 10. *Timeframe*: 10(46) [person can be isolated until the disease is no longer communicable]

FIGURE 3.9.4 Sample public health emergency statutory provision.

3.9.3, step 3). Since some provisions directed more than one task, some provisions had multiple lines for the different tasks. The coding table comprised more than 17,000 lines.

For example, the upper half of Figure 3.9.4 shows a statutory provision that authorizes the quarantine of certain persons with communicable diseases. The lower half of Figure 3.9.4 shows how it is coded. In the actual coding table, only the numerical codes appear. The information in the brackets ("[ ]") is only included here to illustrate what each numerical code represents.

The SPH team did not evaluate the extent to which multiple human coders would agree on the coding assignments across the entire coding process. Instead of evaluating this inter-rater reliability, they identified a sample size sufficient to detect a relative error rate as low as 20%, and drew randomly selected samples that an external analyst reviewed and re-coded. The inter-rater reliability was computed as 68.8%.

IV APPLYING SUPERVISED ML TO CLASSIFY STATUTORY PROVISIONS

The SPH team called upon the author of this chapter and two of his students, Matthias Grabmair and Jaromir Savelka (the ML team), after the full magnitude of the manual classification task became clear and when it was apparent that the funds for manual coding would run out before more than 11 states could be coded. In addition, the SPH team knew that state statutes change over time and that some method would be needed to encode new or modified statutes for inclusion in the LENA database.

The ML team engaged in three successive efforts: (1) an initial foray applying supervised ML with respect to the Pennsylvania coded data; (2) development of an approach to deal with scarce data; and (3) a predictive coding approach to help identify relevant statutory texts. They employed two types of ML programs discussed briefly above: decision trees and SVM.

A Representing Statutory Provisions for ML

The initial task for the first two of these three efforts was to represent the statutory texts for the purposes of supervised ML. The source data, comprising a set of MS Word documents, were first converted into plain text. They were then represented in a tree structure (explained below) and stored in a database.

Each statutory text was divided into spans (text units) whose relevance could be evaluated. Codes were assigned to these spans. The statutory text was represented as a tree with the root corresponding to the title at the beginning of the text. The first level comprised nodes corresponding to each section. The second level comprised nodes corresponding to each subsection of a section. Each span corresponded to a complete branch of the tree from the root to a leaf node. Thus, if the text had five sectional divisions, (1), (1)(a), (1)(b), (1)(c), (2), there would be four spans, one for each unique branch: "(Root)(1)(a)," "(Root)(1)(b)," "(Root)(1)(c)," and "(Root)(2)."

There are other ways to divide a text into non-overlapping units. Some researchers have employed paragraphs or sentences as units.[27] Others have used uniquely citable units.[28] Our representation, however, controls the number of such spans and preserves something of the context of a sectional part along the branch. Although we have assumed that all of the information required to code a provision is contained in the branch, this may not be true. A provision may refer to and incorporate information from other provisions. In addition, proper coding of a subsection may depend on information contained in sibling nodes rather than in parent nodes.

Regular expressions were used to filter words like "TITLE," "PART," or "CHAPTER" away from the title part of each text unit, and Arabic digits were replaced with a token. All letters of the texts were made lowercase. Punctuation and some stop words such as "to" and "for" were removed. Tools from the Stanford CoreNLP library were applied to tokenize and lemmatize all words in the generated text spans; this reduced variant forms of the same words together.[29]

After the text units were allocated to training or test sets for purposes of machine learning, each one was represented as a vector in a multidimensional space in which the number of dimensions corresponded to the number of words in the corpus, and in which the words were arranged in alphabetical order. The length of the vector representing the text unit along each dimension was determined by the number of occurrences in the text unit of the word corresponding to that dimension. If that word did not appear in the text unit, the length was zero. These lengths, in turn, were replaced with a corresponding $weight_{i,j}$, calculated using the tf-idf formula:

$$weight_{i,j} = frequency_{i,j} \times \log_2 (n/document\_frequency_i)$$

In this formula, $frequency_{i,j}$ is the number of times term i appeared in document j, n is the number of documents in the corpus, and $document\_frequency_i$ is the number of documents in which term i appeared. These vectors representing text units were then normalized to their

---

[27] Francesconi et al., "Integrating a Bottom-Up and Top-Down Methodology for Building Semantic Resources for the Multilingual Legal Domain," *supra* note 2; Winkels and Hoekstra, "Automatic Extraction of Legal Concepts and Definitions," *supra* note 10.

[28] Alan Buabuchachart, Katherine Metcalf, Nina Charness, and Leora Morgenstern, "Classification of Regulatory Paragraphs by Discourse Structure, Reference Structure, and Regulation Type," in *Legal Knowledge and Information Systems: JURIX 2013: The Twenty-Sixth Annual Conference*, ed. Kevin Ashley (Amsterdam: IOS Press, 2013), 59–62.

[29] Christopher D. Manning, Mihai Surdeanu, John Bauer, Jenny Finkel, Steven J. Bethard, and David McClosky, "The Stanford CoreNLP Toolkit," in *52nd Annual Meeting of ACL: System Demonstrations, Baltimore, Maryland, USA, June 23–24, 2014* (Baltimore: ACM, 2014), 55–60.

B Supervised ML from Statutes and Initial Results

Deciding whether a statutory provision is relevant is a binary classification. The other classification decisions are multiple-label predictions. According to the SPH team's coding scheme, although each attribute had to be assigned at least one label, most of the attributes could be assigned multiple labels. For example, the goal of an *action* could have up to five of 143 choices; 31 possible codes were associated with *acting PHS agent*.

For these attributes, the prediction task amounted to assigning a number of labels up to the total number of slots specified in the coding sheets and manual. If there were sufficient training data, one could train a binary classifier for each code. In our case, however, there was not sufficient data for that task. In addition, some of the codes appeared only infrequently, which meant that in particular runs of the ML program the training data contained only a comparatively small number of the target codes. The result was that the model could not learn how to predict those codes.

In order to cope with these problems as well as possible, the classifiers were trained with duplicate feature vectors. Where a text unit had been annotated with n codes, the unit was copied into n training instances, and there were n corresponding feature vectors in the training data, each with a different code. This approach did not deal with the problem of data sparseness, which is addressed in Section V. In order to predict a set of n codes for the attribute's value in a test set text unit, the classification model assigned a probability for each possible label. The prediction was based on the top ranked n codes, disregarding any code with a probability less than a static threshold.

The experiment was conducted as a four-fold cross validation, which means that the data comprising 479 provisions was randomly split into four parts so we could conduct four runs of learning and evaluating an ML classification model. During each of the four runs, the classifier was trained on three of the parts and tested on the fourth. The test set was different each time, and the performance statistics were averaged over the four runs. Since some statutory provisions were larger than others, they contained more text units than others. As a result, the splitting process made some parts larger than others.[30]

The experiment included two baselines: most frequent code (MFC), and MFC+/ST (i.e., signal terms). For a given attribute, MFC determines the most frequent code in the training set and predicts that code for test data. For predicting relevance, this amounts to predicting that any text unit is irrelevant since only 22% of the text units in the data set are relevant. Meanwhile, MFC+/ST was "smarter" than MFC; the signal terms comprised the terms from the manual coding dictionary. If the text unit tested contained a term from the ST, then the related code was assigned. Otherwise, the MFC was assigned.

We used the standard evaluation metrics of precision, recall, and F1 score, the harmonic mean between precision and recall. If the set of predicted codes $P = \{p_1, \ldots, p_n\}$ and the set of target predictions $T = \{t_1, \ldots, t_n\}$, then $\text{Precision}_{rank}(P_r) = |P \cap C|/|P|$; $\text{Recall}_{rank}(R_r) = |P \cap T|/|T|$; and $F = (2 \times \text{Aver. } P_r \times \text{Aver. } R_r)/(\text{Aver. } P_r + \text{Aver. } R_r)$.

---

[30] One might attempt to spread a provision's text units across parts to correct this imbalance, but then the provision could be employed in both the training and testing, which would violate an assumption of the cross-validation technique.

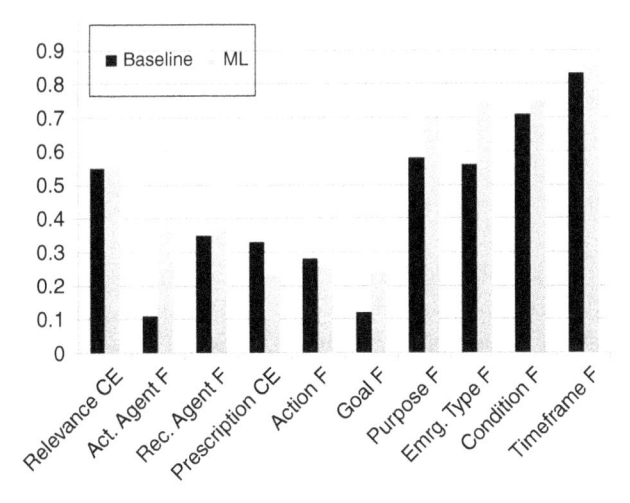

FIGURE 3.9.5 Results of initial machine learning (SVM used for relevance; decision trees used for other values).

The results are shown in Figure 3.9.5. *Classification error* (CE) is shown for the single label classification tasks, relevance and prescription. F1 scores are shown for the classification tasks involving multiple labels.[31] For most of the classification tasks, the ML methods outperformed the baselines, showing higher F1 scores than the baselines in all but one task, *action*. CE for *relevance* was tied, but significantly reduced for *prescription*. Note that a reduction of CE represents an improvement.

Taken together, these results provide preliminary evidence that the text analytic and supervised ML techniques hold promise for this task. These results suggest that ML could supplement the SPH team's efforts at manual coding, but this conclusion is only preliminary. The chief limiting factor on the performance of the ML models was the sparseness of the data. Since the detailed codebook makes many codes available for a given attribute, the number of instances for any given code can be quite small. Our next approach attempted to deal with this problem of scarce training instances.

V DEALING WITH SCARCE TRAINING INSTANCES

While no more data was available from Pennsylvania, the SPH team had coded similar statutes from other states. Could the similarly purposed statutes of other states be used to supplement the scarce training data? Jaromir Savelka empirically assessed this possibility in two successive projects. As a proof of concept, the first project sought evidence that a classifier can improve its performance based on coded statutes from another state.[32] The second project tested a framework for facilitating the transfer of predictive models for classification of statutory texts among multiple state jurisdictions.[33]

---

[31] Grabmair et al., "Toward Extracting Information from Public Health Statutes Using Text Classification and Machine Learning," *supra* note 23.
[32] Savelka et al., "Mining Information from Statutory Texts in Multi-Jurisdictional Settings," *supra* note 23.
[33] Savelka and Ashley, "Transfer of Predictive Models for Classification of Statutory Texts in Multijurisdictional Settings," *supra* note 23.

A Transferring Learning across States to Assign Concepts to Provisions

Although it seems intuitively plausible that a classifier can improve its performance based on similarly purposed coded statutes from another state, it is by no means certain. Here, "similarly purposed" means statutory provisions that are all relevant to the SPH team's project of addressing public health emergency preparation and response.

Despite their common purpose, different states' statutory texts may be quite different both structurally and terminologically. The 784 relevant Pennsylvania (PA) statutes comprised about 3 megabytes (MB) of plain text. The Florida (FL) corpus contained only 462 relevant documents, but with a size of over 4 MB of plain text. Structurally, the Florida statutory texts were longer than those of Pennsylvania, but they also seemed to be more fragmented. The FL corpus yielded over 11,000 text units, while the PA corpus yielded only about 6000. Terminologically, the FL corpus employed more than 6500 unique terms (excluding stop words), while the PA corpus employed fewer than 4800.

For comparison of these differences, Table 3.9.1 illustrates a text unit from a Pennsylvania statute and another from a Florida statute, both of which deal with response to or preparedness for a radiological emergency. The top row shows the citations, the middle row presents the texts, and the bottom row shows the codes assigned by the SPH team. Both provisions require a state agency to develop a plan to deal with a nuclear radiological emergency. Although the Florida provision is shorter, the SPH team's coding of it is more extensive than of the Pennsylvania provision. In light of these differences, it is an empirical question whether including training data from another state can boost the classifier's performance on a given state's test set.

B Proof-of-Concept Experiment

In order to generate some evidence about this empirical question, Savelka tested whether including training data from a second state along with that of a first state improves a classification model's performance on a first state. Given the specialized focus of this experiment, there are some differences between it and the experiment from Section IV. We added two new baselines in which the same type of model was trained on data from only one state, PA or FL. We used only a decision tree classification model for all parts of the experiment. The classifier predicted only one label per attribute. Even though this simplified the multi-label situation, it allowed us to focus directly on the effect of adding the second state's training data.

The experiment proceeded as follows. All text units were first classified for relevance to the SPH team's project. The relevant text units were classified in terms of the nine other attributes. A test set was constructed for each state. Each statutory text had a 20% chance of being assigned to the test set. Training sets were constructed for the intra-jurisdictional (PA → PA and FL → FL), cross-jurisdictional (FL → PA and PA → FL) and multi-jurisdictional (FL + PA → PA and FL + PA → FL) classifications. For each of these classifications, the decision tree model was trained on the corresponding training set and evaluated on the test set.

The results are shown in Table 3.9.2. The relevance metrics are precision (P), recall (R), and F1 score, as previously defined. The metric for the other attributes is accuracy (A), which is inversely related to CE. The boldface measures are the largest. As the table shows, the classification models trained on the combined states' data (right column of each side) performed better than those trained on any single state for most of the tasks. The models

TABLE 3.9.1 *Comparing similarly purposed provisions from Pennsylvania (left) and Florida (right).*

Penn. 35 P.S. § P.S. 7110.502(1)	Fla. Stat. § 262.60(3)
HEALTH AND SAFETY RADIATION PROTECTION ACT RADIATION EMERGENCY RESPONSE PROGRAM Response Program In conjunction with the department, the agency shall develop a Radiation Emergency Response Program for incorporation into the Pennsylvania Emergency Management Plan developed by the agency pursuant to Title 35 of the Pennsylvania Consolidated Statutes (relating to health and safety). Any volunteer organizations which are incorporated into the Radiation Emergency Response Program developed under the authority of this act shall be consulted prior to such incorporation. The Radiation Emergency Response Program shall include an assessment of potential nuclear accidents or incidents, the radiological consequences and necessary protective measures required to mitigate the effects of such accidents or incidents. The program shall include, but not be limited to: Development of a detailed fixed nuclear emergency response plan for areas surrounding each nuclear electrical generation facility; nuclear fuel fabricator and away-from-reactor storage facility The term "areas" shall be deemed to mean the emergency response zone designated by the NRC Emergency Response Plan applicable to each such fixed nuclear facility.	MILITARY AFFAIRS AND RELATED MATTERS EMERGENCY MANAGEMENT GENERAL PROVISIONS Radiological emergency preparedness Emergency response plans. In addition to the other plans required by this chapter, the division shall develop, prepare, test, and implement as needed, in conjunction with the appropriate counties and the affected operator, such radiological emergency response plans and preparedness requirements as may be imposed by the United States Nuclear Regulatory Commission or the Federal Emergency Management Agency as a requirement for obtaining or continuing the appropriate licenses for a commercial nuclear electric generating facility.
Emergency Management [Active agent: 6] of the State [Active agent subset: 2] must [Prescription: 2] prepare [Action: 1] a plan [Goal: 1] for emergency preparedness [Goal: 1] and emergency response [Goal: 2] for an event of nuclear radiological emergency [Emergency type: 7].	Emergency Management [Active agent: 6] of the State [Active agent subset: 2] must [Prescription: 2] prepare [Action: 1], test [Action: 64] and activate [Action: 60] a plan [Goal: 1] and standards [Goal: 124] for emergency preparedness [Goal: 1] and emergency response [Goal: 2] for an event of nuclear radiological emergency [Emergency type: 7] in cooperation with businesses/employers [Passive agent: 1].

trained on the data from the same state (left column of each side) performed better than those trained on the data of the other state (middle column of each side). In other words, the experiment showed that including training data from a second state along with that of a first state can improve a classification model's performance on a first state.

TABLE 3.9.2 *Results of models trained on Florida (FL), Pennsylvania (PA), and combined (FL + PA) data sets applied to PA (left) and FL (right) test sets.*

	PA→PA	FL→PA	FL+PA→PA	FL→FL	PA→FL	FL+PA→FL
Relevance	F: 0.72 P/R: 0.75/0.70	F: 0.54 P/R: 0.62/0.47	F: 0.73 P/R: 0.77/0.69	F: 0.52 P/R: 0.62/0.45	F: 0.35 P/R: 0.27/0.50	F: 0.54 P/R: 0.55/0.52
Act. agent	0.49	0.30	0.52	0.36	0.25	0.44
Prescription	0.76	0.72	0.77	0.77	0.75	0.75
Action	0.29	0.23	0.30	0.23	0.18	0.24
Goal	0.32	0.17	0.32	0.20	0.16	0.25
Purpose	0.59	0.53	0.61	0.58	0.61	0.62
Emrg. type	0.78	0.69	0.80	0.76	0.72	0.77
Rec. agent	0.36	0.25	0.35	0.25	0.25	0.28
Time frame	0.84	0.81	0.85	0.80	0.78	0.80
Condition	0.77	0.68	0.75	0.65	0.65	0.67

C Framework for Transferring Classification Models among Multiple States

How far could one take this? In order to find out, Savelka constructed a framework for transferring classification models learned on other states' data to a target state. For each attribute, we trained one classification model with the target state's training set, as well as additional *auxiliary* models for each of seven other states' training sets. Each of the eight models predicted a label and a probabilistic confidence value in its prediction. We evaluated the first model and each of the seven auxiliary models on the target state's training data to obtain an F1 score indicating how well that auxiliary model worked for the target state's data. Then, for each attribute, we evaluated whether combining the above models resulted in any improvement in classification performance on the target state's test set. In eight successive experiments, we applied the first model plus anywhere from zero to all seven of the auxiliary models. Each model's confidence value was weighted in terms of the F1 score obtained in the training step, and then cumulated. In other words, more weight was given to those predictions of models that had achieved higher F1 scores in the training step while predicting the target state's labels.[34]

Figure 3.9.6 shows the results for Florida (FL) as the target state on the left, and Maryland (MD) as the target state on the right. Each box plot summarizes the results of all the experiments on each of the classification tasks for the target state. Each box plot describes performance in terms of an F1 score within a single experiment. Each cluster of eight box plots depicts a progression of F1 scores on one of the tasks for the given state, from the first experiment to the eighth one. The first box plot from a cluster represents the 100 runs of the experiment when no auxiliary model was used. The second box plot represents the experiment in which one auxiliary model is used. This continues until the eighth boxplot of each cluster, which shows the use of all seven auxiliary models.

One can see that the classifiers' performance tends to increase as more auxiliary models are applied. Each of these models has been trained on the data of a state different from

---

[34] Ibid.

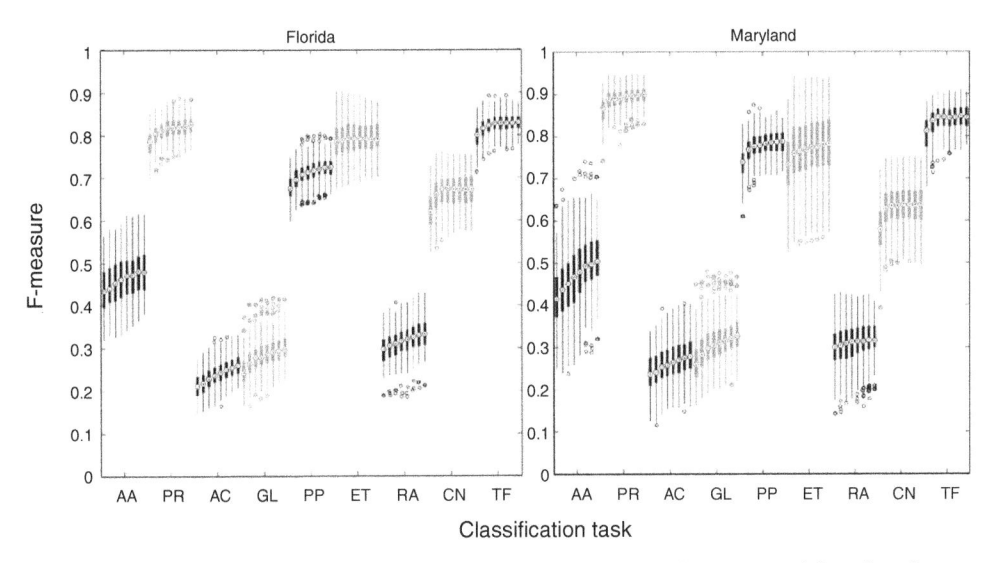

FIGURE 3.9.6 Results of successively applying more states' classification models. Classification tasks include: AA (acting agent), PR (prescription), AC (action), GL (goal), PP (purpose), ET (emergency type), RA (receiving agent), CN (condition), and TF (time frame).

the target state. The improvement is apparent in all of the classification tasks, differing only in the amount of improvement. For example, there was a 9% improvement in performance of the classifier for the active agent (AA) task on the MD data set between the first and last experiments. By contrast, there was only a 2% improvement for the emergency type (ET) task on the FL data set. Significantly, these results indicate that employing additional models does not harm performance. At worst, performance remains constant.

An example of the effect of applying the auxiliary models appears in classifying this MD provision:

"COMAR 01.01.2003.18(D)(2): CODE OF MARYLAND REGULATIONS; TITLE 01. EXECUTIVE DEPARTMENT; SUBTITLE 01. EXECUTIVE ORDERS; Establishment of the Governor's Office Of Homeland Security. The Director shall be responsible for the following activities: Advise the Governor on policies, strategies, and measures to enhance and improve the ability to detect, prevent, prepare for, protect against, respond to, and recover from, man-made emergencies or disasters, including terrorist attacks . . ."

Classifiers trained only on the data coming from FL did not work as well as those employing the auxiliary models, which had been trained on the data sets of other states. The F1 scores increased from 0.56 to 0.86 as more states' data were employed. Using even one auxiliary model boosted the performance. Using all seven models resulted in a substantial improvement. This example, it should be noted, may not be representative of the performance of the classifiers in general.[35]

Nevertheless, the framework for transferring text classification models from different US state jurisdictions goes some way toward dealing with the problem of scarce training data. The available labeled data in each state are limited and sparse, but with this framework, predictive

[35] Ibid.

models trained on data from different states can improve the performance of classifiers on the target state of interest.

This framework's potential has been demonstrated in the public health realm where each state has similarly purposed statutes. This is a fairly common phenomenon in the US context, as well as internationally where states participate in federations or countries participate in international treaties. For example, EU directives establish standards for personal data protection or copyright collection societies, with which member states' national legal regulations must comply. The resulting regulations across the EU states are similarly purposed, but their specific texts and regulatory frameworks may differ. The framework for transferring classification models could be very useful in such contexts. Of course, the multilingual nature of the regulatory texts presents an additional complication.[36]

The ML team has not yet tried other techniques that may improve classification performance by addressing imbalanced and sparse data sets. There are several that exist, though. SMOTE, for example, is a method for creating new "synthetic" instances of a minority class by interpolating between existing minority instances rather than simply duplicating the original ones.[37] The manufactured instances are neighbors of the real instances in the dimensional feature space. Another approach is to enrich the text representation, instead of relying exclusively on a simple *tf-idf* weighted bag-of-words. This includes employing part-of-speech tagging and shallow parsing. One could also apply knowledge such as that from the codebook, the data generated by the network analysis, or the tables of corresponding agents from multiple states. In addition, one could integrate rule-based classifiers and more complex feature generators into the existing framework. If the individual predictive models can be improved, the framework can combine them in ways that will lead to an increase in general performance. The framework is quite general, in that it can be used with any type of classifier or ensemble of classifiers. The only constraint is that the classifiers output a probability distribution over the labels, instead of just predictions. The framework also does not impose any limitations on the kinds of features to use.

VI INTERACTIVE ML TO RETRIEVE RELEVANT STATUTORY TEXTS

Although the last episode in this case study took place at the end of the ML team's efforts, it addressed the first kind of activity the SPH team engaged in: the retrieval of candidate statutory texts from a commercial legal information retrieval system and the assessment of which texts were relevant, all within the domain of a relatively open-ended issue, such as public health emergency preparedness.

This type of task is an iterative process. The legal researcher poses an initial hypothesis concerning the statutory provisions that are relevant, and then constructs a search query to retrieve them from a legal information retrieval system. Typically, this kind of query results in a long list of documents. Upon inspecting this list of documents and examining some of the more promising provisions, the researcher may revise the initial hypothesis and query again for another round. After a series of iterations, the process may then produce a set of relevant provisions.

---

[36] *See, e.g.,* Daudaravicius, "Automatic Multilingual Annotation of EU Legislation with Eurovoc Descriptors," *supra* note 8.
[37] Nitesh Chawla, Kevin W. Bowyer, Lawrence O. Hall, and W. Philip Kegelmeyer, "SMOTE: Synthetic Minority Oversampling Technique," *Journal of Artificial Intelligence Research* 16 (2002): 321–357.

Savelka investigated whether an interactive ML framework could support a more efficient process of compiling a final list of relevant provisions by assisting legal researchers in developing and refining a hypothesis about relevance. Based on a user's selections of relevant examples of statutory provisions, an ML classifier can develop a model of what the user is looking for and provide the user with suggestions backed with explanatory information. This can mean determining whether or not the results of the automatic classification of the statutory texts are relevant, it can involve the model's confidence in its predictions, and it can determine which features are important. The human expert may then provide feedback on the results, confirming that the examples are relevant or not, or suggesting features the user believes to be important. In this way, the framework engages the human expert in an interactive dialogue to refine the model.

According to Savelka's working hypothesis, given a corpus of statutory provisions retrieved from a legal information retrieval system, once a human expert selects as relevant or not a small fraction of the statutory provisions, the interactive framework can provide reasonable suggestions about the relevance of the remaining provisions. As the human expert marks more provisions, the framework's suggestions will become more accurate. Savelka has also hypothesized that a model trained in such a process of statutory analysis can assist in future analyses of a new corpus if it concerns overlapping subject matter, is the same analysis done at a later time, or involves similar statutory provisions in a new jurisdiction.

Savelka examined these hypotheses in the context of two of the SPH team's corpora, the statutory texts originally retrieved with LexisNexis queries for the states of Kansas (KS) and Alaska (AK), using queries like the one shown in Section III.B. These are the documents of which the human coders initially determined the relevance to the SPH team's problem of public emergency response and preparedness, or their lack of relevance. The KS corpus comprised 304 statutory documents, or 4022 individual provisions, of which 802 were deemed relevant. The AK corpus contained 135 statutory documents, or 1564 provisions, of which 474 were relevant.

A sample of two KS state provisions retrieved by the LexisNexis query, shown in Figure 3.9.7, illustrates the kind of decision the human coders needed to make. Both provisions mention fire departments and firefighting, but only the provision on the left was deemed relevant. The provision on the left mentions "emergencies" and specifies an obligation for a PHS agent that concerns preparedness or response to public emergencies. By contrast, the provision on the right does not. The provision on the right specifies an obligation, but of an agent who is *not* a part of the PHS.

In order to assist human coders in classifying provisions for relevance, Savelka adapted an interactive ML tool developed at the University of Pittsburgh for classifying clinical medical texts.[38] As shown in Figure 3.9.8, this tool supports the kind of incremental model and user interactions applied in predictive coding, such as e-discovery, but here it is applied to statutory texts.

With this tool, the user can see five things: (a) a soon-to-be processed example statutory provision; (b) the features and terms that the current learned model treats as most important, and their weights; (c) statistics summarizing how the already processed provisions are currently distributed in terms of relevance; and (d) a list of the previously processed provisions, with labels and confidence scores. This tool suggests to the user: (e) the label for the

---

[38] Gaurav Trivedi, Phuong Pham, Wendy W. Chapman, Rebecca Hwa, Janyce Wiebe, and Harry Hochheiser, "NLPReViz: An Interactive Tool for Natural Language Processing on Clinical Text," *Journal of the American Medical Informatics Association* (2017), available at: https://nlpreviz.github.io.

(i) K.S.A. x 80-1921(a)(1) TOWNSHIP OFFICERS FIRE DEPARTMENT OR COMPANY

The township board of any such township shall have full direction and control over the operation of such township fire department. The board shall have the power to: Provide for the organization of volunteer members of such department and pay compensation to such members for fighting fires, responding to emergencies or attending meetings;

(ii) K.A.R. x 28-29-31(c)(2)(B) SOLID WASTE MANAGEMENT

Each person storing the tires shall meet the requirements of subsection (b) of this regulation and the following requirements: provide access to each storage area for fire-fighting equipment by either of the following means: obtaining certification from the local fire department stating that there is adequate access to each storage area for fire-fighting equipment;

FIGURE 3.9.7 Sample comparison of statutory provision texts.

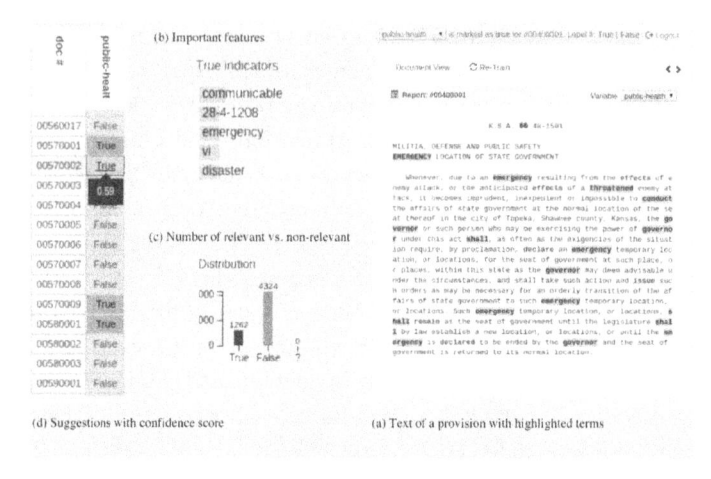

FIGURE 3.9.8 Interactive ML tool screen.

unprocessed provision and the confidence level it has in the suggestion. Prominent features from (b) are highlighted in (a), and in (e) the tool solicits the user's decision and records the user's response. A user may also highlight additional terms in the unprocessed document that they think are important, and then click on them. At the user's direction, the tool retrains its model using an SVM. It learns new features and weights, and takes into account the user's feedback on the example provision.[39]

In an experiment, Savelka analyzed a situation in which an interactive classifier was compared to two baselines, a precision-focused (P-oriented) simulated human classifier that assumed all of the still-unprocessed documents were not relevant, and a recall-focused (R-oriented) simulated human classifier that assumed that all of the still-unprocessed documents were relevant. In the first run, the classifier was trained from a clean slate using 304 KS statutory provisions, and it was tested on a held-out set of 30 randomly selected provisions. Then, in a knowledge-reuse version of the interaction-simulating experiment, Savelka analyzed the situation in which the tool reused the KS-based classifier, learned again on 135 AK provisions, and then was compared to the two human-simulating classifiers. The results are shown in Figure 3.9.9.

In both instances, the "interactive ML" classifier outperformed the simulated human baselines in terms of F1 score ("F measure" in the figure). In the KS results, the "interactive ML" version showed an initially agitated phase; it required the processed data set to be above 25 documents before it could outperform the R-oriented baseline. In the AK results there was

---

[39] Savelka et al., "Applying an Interactive Machine Learning Approach to Statutory Analysis," *supra* note 23.

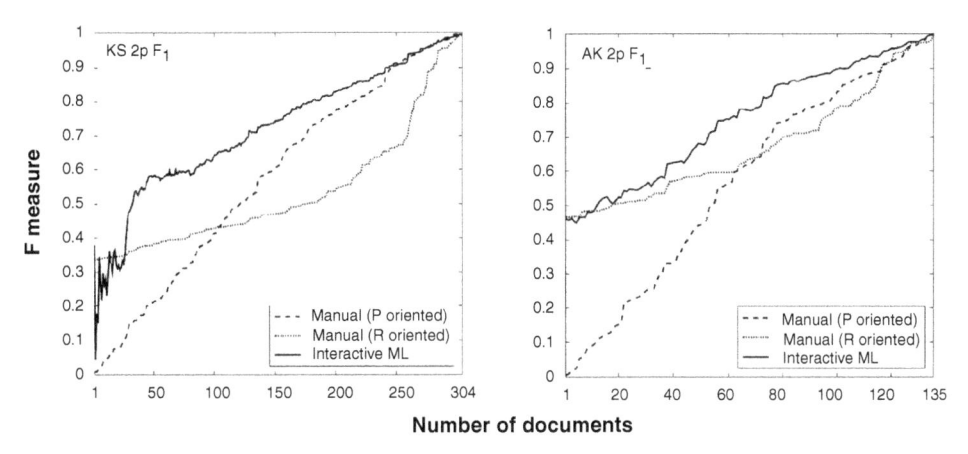

FIGURE 3.9.9 Results of evaluation of the interactive ML approach.

a smoother start; this is attributable to the reuse of the KS-based classifier, which obviated the need for so many documents from the same state to be processed before it became able to outperform the baseline. Again, the classifier improved performance based on data from another state with somewhat different statutory provisions.[40]

VII LESSONS LEARNED

This case study in legal informatics has illustrated some of the challenges of intelligently processing statutory texts, but has also revealed some promising approaches. In particular, the use of statutory networks and the nine agent- and action-oriented attributes can model directives in a statutory system well enough for comparing similarly purposed statutory schemes across jurisdictions, as well as for some useful conceptual information retrieval. Supervised ML achieved some success in automatically classifying provisions in terms of these attributes, but sparse training data limited the results. Using data from other jurisdictions' similarly purposed statutory schemes showed promise as a technique for augmenting sparse data. In addition, an interactive ML approach (Figures 3.9.8 and 3.9.9) showed it could improve the initial task of compiling a set of candidate statutory texts from a legal information retrieval system (Figure 3.9.3, step 1).

The primary lessons to be derived from this case study focus on Figure 3.9.3, step 2. Human coders identified a set of statutory texts with relevant spans, but these spans were *not* marked up and preserved for the purposes of ML in in-line annotations of the statutory texts. One notable shortcoming is that the SPH team computed the reliability of the coding process only rather late in the coding process. Ideally, if resources had allowed, multiple coders would have engaged earlier in the coding process. Multiple coders would have been able to annotate the same texts in parallel, and their reliability could have been monitored systematically. This is important because human coding reliability imposes an upper limit on the accuracy of ML results.

As noted, the SPH team developed and applied a text coding methodology before contacting the ML team. The use of the spreadsheet approach and lack of in-line annotation

---
[40] Ibid.

deprived the ML team of contextual information that could have been used to improve the text representation and the eventual ML results. For a contrasting example, what one would probably do today is introduce a type system for statutory annotation, including general features like logical conditions and consequents, and more domain-specific features like PHS agents. One would then apply a pipeline process to annotate the texts automatically using a combination of ML and rule-based approaches. An ideal conclusion, which will have to wait for another case study, is if hierarchically organized conceptual types and annotated contextual information would improve supervised ML performance.[41] The answer to this question remains elusive, but not far off.

[41] Ashley, *Artificial Intelligence and Legal Analytics, supra* note 25, at 282f.

3.10

Gov2Vec

A Case Study in Text Model Application to Government Data[1]

John J. Nay

1 PREDICTING OUTCOMES FROM TEXT IN CONGRESSIONAL BILLS

If an event of interest is correlated with text data, we can learn models of text that predict the event outcome. For example, researchers have predicted financial risk with regression models that use the text of company financial disclosures.[2] Topic models can predict outcomes as a function of the proportions of a document that are devoted to the automatically discovered topics,[3] and this technique has been used to develop, for example, a topic model that forecasts roll call votes using the text of congressional bills.[4] An advantage of the topic model prediction approach is that the model learns interpretable topics and the relationships between the learned topics and outcomes. A disadvantage of the topic model approach is that other, less interpretable text models often exhibit higher predictive power.

Yano et al. used a logistic regression model to predict whether a bill would survive consideration by US House of Representatives committees.[5] To incorporate the bill texts, the researchers used unigram features to indicate the presence of vocabulary terms. This author, meanwhile, has conducted the most comprehensive lawmaking prediction study to date, which predicted the nearly 70,000 bills introduced in the US Congress from 2001 to 2015.[6] The only preprocessing applied to the text in this study was the removal of HTML and

---

[1] Refer to Nay – Natural Language Processing for Legal Texts, *supra*, for more details on text models and natural language processing.
[2] Shimon Kogan, Dimitry Levin, Bryan R. Routledge, Jacob S. Sagi, and Noah A. Smith, "Predicting Risk from Financial Reports with Regression," in *Proceedings of Human Language Technologies: The 2009 Annual Conference of the North American Chapter of the Association for Computational Linguistics* (Stroudsburg, PA: Association for Computational Linguistics, 2009), 272–280.
[3] Jon D. Mcauliffe and David M. Blei, "Supervised Topic Models," in *Advances in Neural Information Processing Systems 20*, eds. John C. Platt, Daphne Koller, Yoram Singer, and Sam T. Roweis (Red Hook, NY: Curran Associates, Inc., 2008), 121–128, available at: https://arxiv.org/pdf/1003.0783.pdf.
[4] Sean Gerrish and David M. Blei, "Predicting Legislative Roll Calls from Text," in *Proceedings of the 28th International Conference on Machine Learning (ICML)*, Bellevue, Washington, USA, June 28–July 2, 2011.
[5] Tae Yano, Noah A. Smith, and John D. Wilkerson, "Textual Predictors of Bill Survival in Congressional Committees," in *Proceedings of the 2012 Conference of the North American Chapter of the Association for Computational Linguistics: Human Language Technologies* (Stroudsburg, PA: Association for Computational Linguistics, 2012), 793–802, available at: https://projects.iq.harvard.edu/ptr/files/yanosmithwilkersonbillsurvival.pdf.
[6] John J. Nay, "Predicting and Understanding Law-Making with Word Vectors and an Ensemble Model," *PLoS One* 12 (5) (2017), available at: http://journals.plos.org/plosone/article?id=10.1371/journal.pone.0176999.

carriage returns, and conversion to lowercase. Then, inversion of distributed language models was used for classification.[7] Distributed language models were separately fit to the sub-corpora of successful and failed bills from past Congresses by applying the *word2vec* algorithm. Each sentence of a testing bill was scored with each trained language model. Bayes' rule was applied to these scores and to prior probabilities for bill enactment in order to obtain posterior probabilities. The proportions of bills enacted in the same chamber as the predicted bill in all previous Congresses were used as the priors. The probabilities of enactment were then averaged across sentences in a bill to assign an overall probability.

Starting in 2001 with the 107th Congress, we trained models on data from previous Congresses, predicted all bills in the current Congress, and repeated the process for subsequent Congresses. The 113th Congress served as the test. The model successfully forecast bill enactment: The median of the predicted probabilities where the true outcome was failure (0.01) was much lower than the median of the predicted probabilities where the true outcome was enactment (0.71).

With these language models, in addition to prediction, we created *synthetic summaries* of hypothetical bills by providing a set of words that captured any topic of interest. Comparing these synthetic summaries across chamber and across "Enacted" and "Failed" categories uncovered textual patterns in how bill content is associated with enactment. The title summaries were derived from investigating word similarities within *word2vec* models estimated on title texts, and the body summaries were derived from similarities within *word2vec* models estimated on the full bill texts. Distributed representations of the words in the bills captured their meaning in a way that allowed semantically similar words to be discovered. Although bills may not have been devoted to the topic of interest within any of the four training data sub-corpora, these synthetic summaries still yielded useful results because the queried words were embedded within the semantically structured vector space along with all vocabulary in the training bills. For an example, we can look at the words that best summarize the topics of "climate change emissions," "health insurance poverty," and "technology patents" in both the House and Senate (Table 3.10.1). "Impacts," "impact," and "effects" are in House Enacted, while "warming," "global," and "temperature" are in House Failed. This suggests that, for the House climate change topic, highlighting potential future impacts is associated with enactment, while emphasizing increasing global temperatures is associated with failure. For the health insurance poverty topic, "medicaid" and "reinsurance" are in both House Failed and Senate Failed. The Senate shows words related to more specific health topics, such as "immunization" for Failed and "psychiatric" for Enacted. For technology patents, "software" and "computational" are in Failed for the House and Senate, respectively.

The text model provides sentence-level predictions for an overall bill and thus predicts what sections of a bill may be the most important for increasing or decreasing the probability of enactment. Figure 3.10.1 compares patterns of predicted sentence probabilities as they evolve from the beginning of a bill to the end of a bill, across four categories: enacted versus failed, and the first available version (oldest) versus last available version (newest) of the bill text. In the last available (newest) texts of enacted bills, there is much more variation in predicted probabilities within bills.

---

[7] For clarification of this technique, *see* Matt Taddy, "Document Classification by Inversion of Distributed Language Representations," in *Proceedings of the 53rd Annual Meeting of the Association for Computational Linguistics* (Beijing: Association for Computational Linguistics, 2015), 45–49.

TABLE 3.10.1 *Synthetic summary for three topics, "Enacted" or "Failed," in the House or the Senate.*

	House		Senate	
	Enacted	Failed	Enacted	Failed
Topic: climate change emissions				
Title	cosmetic, growth, expansion, additional, administration	suspend, exchange, terminate, products, lending	privacy, programs, authorities, control, pilot	nuclear, recreational, cooperative, area, space
Body	impacts, diversion, potential, nitrogen, impact, effects, wildfires, future, degradation, mitigate, posing, efficiencies	warming, global, leakage, risk, temperature, constraints, bycatch, congestion, variability, mercury, negative, reliability	contamination, mitigating, disruption, flooding, fishery, earth, economy, spills, efficiencies, threat, targets, growth, models	sequestration, mercury, emission, warming, volume, anthropogenic, variability, economy, penetration, temperature, congestion, impacts
Topic: health insurance poverty				
Title	make, deposit, revenue, exclude, trade	medicaid, patient, assure, supplemental, act	spouses, block, needs, efficiency, institutions	adequate, choice, long-term, about, plans
Body	benefits, benefit, quality, catastrophe, employer-sponsored, coverage, welfare, disability, market	pension, reinsurance, medicaid, dental, uninsured, medical, hospital, medicare, child, insurers, uncompensated	defender, hospice, means-tested, long-term, respite, index, institutional, illness, themselves, kinship, psychiatric, imminent, pain	employer-sponsored, reinsurance, health-related, choice, uninsured, elderly, medicaid, welfare, chronic, immunization, hapi, dental
Topic: technology patents				
Title	personal, convicted, basis, enhance, species	commerce, fish, agency, authorities, further	support, with, 2004, mental, delivery	great, marine, commission, restoration, implementation
Body	dissemination, registry, complaint, laboratory, space, reliable, invention, research, petition, registration, corporation	copyright, scientific, sensor, manufacturing, technologies, technique, technological, confidential, software, geospatial	budget, systems, registration, capability, breach, munitions, processes, included, registration, processing, naturalization, processed	patents, copyright, telecommunications, invention, technologies, computational, technological, geospatial, state-of-the-art

II CONCLUSION: ANSWERING QUESTIONS

As natural language processing techniques have evolved, it has become increasingly possible to create programs that can provide answers to questions posed to them. There are two approaches for automatic answering of questions. The first approach is a relatively simple

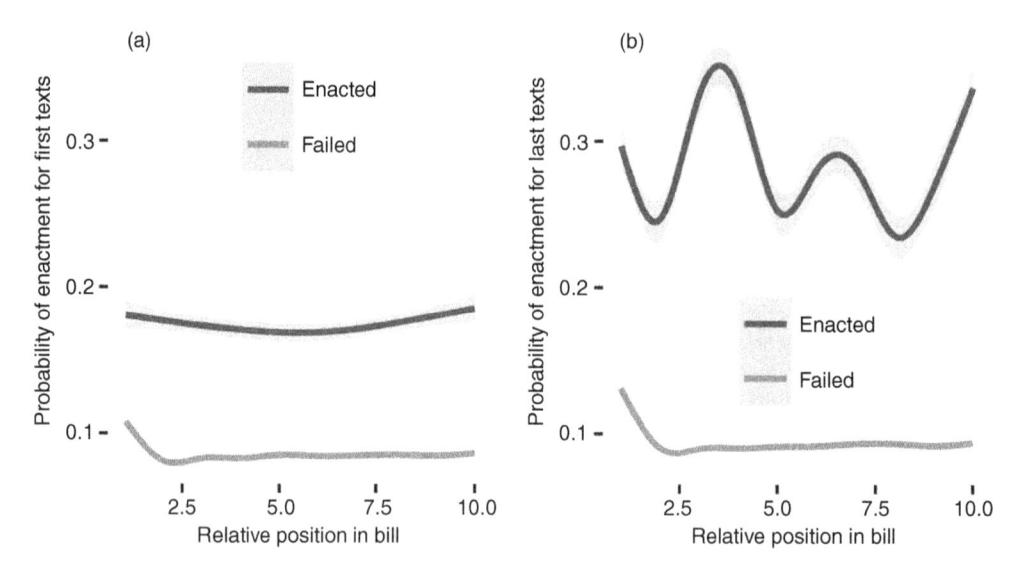

FIGURE 3.10.1 Sentence probabilities across bills for first data (a) and last data (b). For each bill, we converted the variable length vectors of predicted sentence probabilities to n-length vectors by sampling n evenly spaced points from each bill. We set $n = 10$ because almost every bill is at least ten sentences long. Then we loess-smoothed the resulting points across all bills to summarize the difference between "Enacted" and "Failed" and first and last texts.

one: A function is designed to attempt to recall the most likely answer to a question from a predefined set of answers. These answers are based on the pairs of answers and questions the model has been trained to recall.[8]

The second approach uses complex models that can actually generate words in new and creative ways, instead of relying on predefined answer sets. Based on past example answers and questions, the model learns to encode a question into mathematical space and then decode that representation into a sequence of words that addresses the question.

These techniques for answering questions can be applied to a whole range of functions, such as designing chatbots that can answer simple legal questions by training models on past examples of legal questions and answers. In the case of *Gov2Vec*, there is vast potential to improve our understanding of the legislative drafting process, supplying both law makers and the citizens they serve with new tools that can help achieve the daunting task of producing comprehensive legislation with broad political support.

---

[8] Minwei Feng, Bing Xiang, Michael R. Glass, Lidan Wang, and Bowen Zhou, "Applying Deep Learning to Answer Selection: A Study and an Open Task," in *2015 IEEE Workshop on Automatic Speech Recognition and Understanding (ASRU)*, Scottsdale, AZ, USA, December 13–17, 2015, 813–820, available at: https://arxiv.org/pdf/1508.01585.pdf.

3.11

Representation and Automation of Legal Information[1]

Katie Atkinson

This case study demonstrates in more detail how one particular technique – computational argumentation – can be effectively used to build automated reasoning tools that provide decision support capabilities for legal practitioners. This case study will also demonstrate how legal cases can be represented and interpreted through computational models of arguments, and how this enables software programs to generate and reason about the relevant arguments for deciding a case, akin to human judicial reasoning.

I CASE STUDY OVERVIEW

This section provides an in-depth case study to demonstrate how computational models of argument can be used to model reasoning in legal cases.[2]

A Automating Reasoning about Legal Cases

There have been a variety of projects over the past three decades aimed at developing systems for reasoning with legal cases. Over the same time period, there have been developments in the computational modeling of arguments. The work described in this case study demonstrates how established ideas from the field of legal case-based reasoning have been married with developments from the literature on computational models of argument to produce a methodology called Angelic.[3] Angelic is used for reasoning with legal cases, and has yielded successful results in replicating the decisions in legal cases within three application domains: US trade secret law; possession of wild animals; and the US automobile exception to the Fourth Amendment.

B Factor Based Reasoning

The starting point for this body of work is the CATO system, described in more detail at the end of Chapter 2.2. CATO's core goal is to describe cases in terms of factors (legally significant abstractions of patterns of facts found in cases), and to build these base-level factors into

---

[1] Refer to Atkinson – Representation of Legal Information, *supra*, for approaches to representation of legal information, and for an overview of CATO and ADF.
[2] The case study herein is a summary of the larger body of research reported in Latifa Al-Abdulkarim, Katie Atkinson, and Trevor J. M. Bench-Capon, "A Methodology for Designing Systems to Reason with Legal Cases Using Abstract Dialectical Frameworks," *Artificial Intelligence and Law* 24 (1) (2016): 1–49.
[3] ANGELIC is an acronym that stands for: ADF for kNowledGe Encapsulation of Legal Information from Cases.

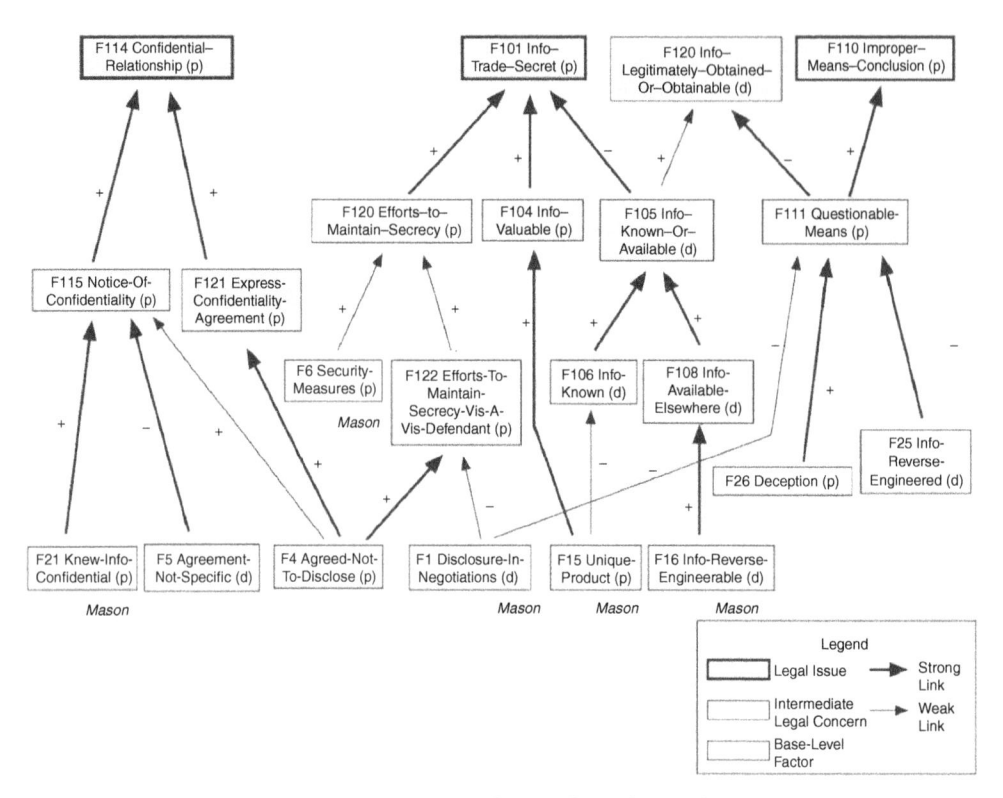

FIGURE 3.11.1 CATO abstract factor hierarchy.[4]

a hierarchy of increasing abstraction, moving upward through intermediate concerns (abstract factors) to issues representing the main matters to be resolved in the cases. The specific domain used within CATO is US trade secret law. An example of such a factor hierarchy, showing details of the support and attack relations between the factors, is shown in Figure 3.11.1. The 26 base-level factors used in CATO are listed in Table 3.11.1 (note that there is no factor "F9"; this will be addressed later).

Within CATO's factor hierarchy, each factor favors either the plaintiff or the defendant, and precedent cases are matched with a current case to produce arguments in three layers. First, a precedent with factors in common with the case under consideration is cited, suggesting a finding for one side. Then, the second side cites precedents with factors in common with the current case, but with a decision for their side as a counterexample, all while also distinguishing the cited precedent by pointing to factors not shared by the precedent and current case. Finally, the original side rebuts the second side by downplaying the distinctions they mentioned. The original side cites cases to prove that these weaknesses are not fatal, and distinguishes counterexamples. The representation yielded by CATO is intended to assist law school students in forming case-based arguments in order to reason better about cases.

As can be seen from Figure 3.11.1 and Table 3.11.1, within CATO there is no single root for the factor hierarchy. Instead, there is a collection of hierarchies, each relating to a specific issue. These hierarchies are tied together within the issue-based prediction (IBP) system that

---

[4] Figure 3.11.1 has been reproduced directly from Vincent Aleven, "Teaching Case-based Argumentation through a Model and Examples," (PhD thesis, University of Pittsburgh, 1997), available at: https://pdfs.semanticscholar.org/8995/bf5e9d0a686e635d0099976c18cb47f05172.pdf.

TABLE 3.11.1 *Base-level factors in CATO.*

ID	Factor
F1	DisclosureInNegotiations (d)
F2	BribeEmployee (p)
F3	EmployeeSoleDeveloper (d)
F4	AgreedNotToDisclose (p)
F5	AgreementNotSpecific (d)
F6	SecurityMeasures (p)
F7	BroughtTools (p)
F8	CompetitiveAdvantage (p)
F10	SecretsDisclosedOutsiders (d)
F11	VerticalKnowledge (d)
F12	OutsiderDisclosuresRestricted (p)
F13	NoncompetitionAgreement (p)
F14	RestrictedMaterialsUsed (p)
F15	UniqueProduct (p)
F16	InfoReverseEngineerable (d)
F17	InfoIndependentlyGenerated (d)
F18	IdenticalProducts (p)
F19	NoSecurityMeasures (d)
F20	InfoKnownToCompetitors (d)
F21	KnewInfoConfidential (p)
F22	InvasiveTechniques (p)
F23	WaiverOfConfidentiality (d)
F24	InfoObtainableElsewhere (d)
F25	InfoReverseEngineered (d)
F26	Deception (p)
F27	DisclosureInPublicForum (d)

was produced subsequent to CATO but with a different aim: not simply enabling students to discover and present arguments, but going beyond this to predict the outcomes of cases.

C Issue-Based Prediction

In IBP, the issues of CATO's hierarchy are tied together using a logical model derived from the Uniform Trade Secrets Act, which has been adopted by nearly all US states and territories, as well as the Restatement of Torts. This model is shown in Figure 3.11.2.

To determine the effectiveness of the IBP program in predicting the outcomes of cases, an evaluation was conducted using 186 cases, comprising 148 cases analyzed by CATO and 38 analyzed specifically by IBP. According to Bruninghaus and Ashley, IBP correctly predicted the outcome of 170 cases, made 15 errors, and abstained only once.[5] The evaluation also considered IBP's performance by comparing it to a number of standard, easily accessible machine learning algorithms; however, none of these other algorithms matched IBP's accuracy. The closest was the naive Bayes algorithm, with an accuracy of 86% compared with IBP's accuracy of 91%.

---

[5] *Ibid.*

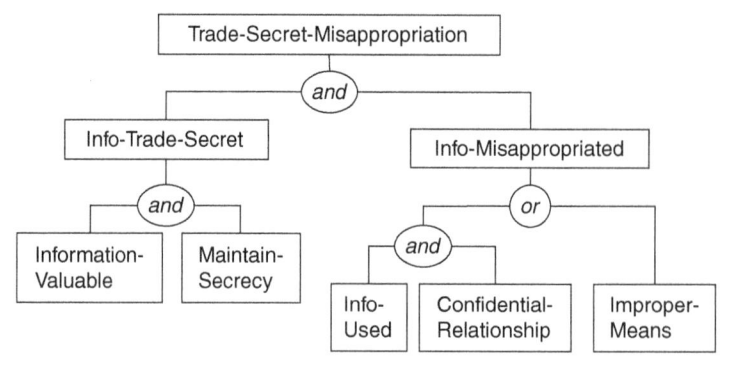

FIGURE 3.11.2 IBP logical model.[6]

D Abstract Dialectical Frameworks

The work on CATO and IBP has been valuable in driving research on systems for supporting legal reasoning, but it has subsequently been taken further by combining factor-based approaches with new representation methods from the field of computational models of argument, particularly abstract dialectical frameworks (ADFs).[7]

A large body of work from the field of computational models of argument has focused on abstract argumentation frameworks (AFs), which were originally introduced as a method for evaluating sets of arguments with respect to how well they defend themselves against attack and defeat by other arguments.[8] Arguments in these frameworks are intended to be abstract: We are not concerned with the internal structure or content of the argument, merely that attack relations between the arguments exist. As such, an AF can be represented as a graph in which the nodes represent arguments and the edges represent attack relations between the arguments. An example of such a graph is given in Figure 3.11.3.

We read Figure 3.11.3 in the following way. Argument E has no attackers. Arguments C and D attack each other and each attacks argument B. Argument B attacks argument A. Given the arguments and the attack relations between them, the acceptability status of an argument can be evaluated by considering whether or not it can be defended from attack by other arguments. Argument E has no attackers and so is acceptable. If we choose to accept argument C, this defeats arguments B and D. On the contrary, if we accept argument D, this defeats C and B. Regardless of whether we accept argument C or argument D, argument B is defeated. Once B is defeated, the attack on argument A is removed, making A acceptable. So, arguments A, C, and E can together be seen as an acceptable set of arguments. Another acceptable set of arguments is A, D, and E.[9]

---

[6] Image from Stephanie Bruninghaus and Kevin Ashley, "Predicting Outcomes of Case-based Legal Arguments," in *9th International Conference on Artificial Intelligence and Law (ICAIL), Scotland, UK, June 24–28* (New York, NY: ACM, 2003), 233–242.

[7] See Gerhard Brewka and Stefan Woltran, "Abstract Dialectical Frameworks," in *Twelfth International Conference on the Principles of Knowledge Representation and Reasoning, Toronto, ON, Canada, May 9–13* (Menlo Park, CA: AAAI Press, 2010).

[8] Phan Minh Dung, "On the Acceptability of Arguments and its Fundamental Role in Nonmonotonic Reasoning, Logic Programming, and n-Person Games," *Artificial Intelligence* 77 (1995): 321–357.

[9] Dung provides a more in-depth, formal description of the reasoning provided in this example, *ibid*.

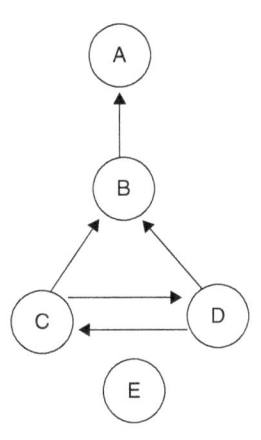

FIGURE 3.11.3 Example abstract argumentation framework.

Since the introduction of AFs, researchers have worked to develop them as a representation format. Abstract dialectical frameworks are one such development.[10] These provide a generalization of abstract AFs like the one in Figure 3.11.3. Like AFs, ADFs consist of a set of nodes and directed links between them, but whereas the links in an AF have a uniform interpretation (i.e., that one argument defeats another), the links in an ADF can have a variety of interpretations. Moreover, in ADFs the nodes are general statements rather than specifically abstract arguments. Abstract dialectical frameworks also enable representation of a second relation – a support relation – in addition to the attack relation of AFs. Whereas AFs only express attack relations, the support relations in ADFs express statements that support statements they link to. A statement's acceptance is determined through the specification of conditions for the acceptance or rejection of a statement in terms of the acceptance or rejection of its children. The next section illuminates how these ADFs are used to represent and reason about legal cases.

E Abstract Dialectical Frameworks for Legal Reasoning

If we bring together the factor hierarchies of CATO and IBP (Figures 3.11.1 and 3.11.2, and Table 3.11.1), and the representation format of AFs (Figure 3.11.3), we can instantiate an ADF to encapsulate the legal domain knowledge as represented by the factor hierarchies, as follows:

- **Statement:** The statements of the ADF form the set of all the issues, intermediate concerns, and base-level factors in the factor hierarchy.
- **Links:** The set of links where $L+$ are the supporting links labeled "+" and $L-$ are the attacking links, labeled "–".
- **Acceptance conditions:** For each abstract factor (non-leaf node), acceptance conditions are defined by how their supporting and attacking children reflect the decisions in precedent cases. The acceptance conditions expressed in this way form a set of tests. The order of the tests expresses preferences. If no test is satisfied, the node (abstract factor) is assigned to a default value.

---

[10] Gerhard Brewka, Stefan Ellmauthaler, Hannes Strass, Johannes Peter Wallner, and Stefan Woltran, "Abstract Dialectical Frameworks Revisited," in *Proceedings of the Twenty-Third International Joint Conference on Artificial Intelligence, Beijing, China, August 3–9, 2013* (Cambridge, MA: AAAI Press, 2013), 803–809; *see also* Brewka and Woltran, "Abstract Dialectical Frameworks, *supra* note 7.

Once the ADF is instantiated, it encapsulates the relevant domain of case law. Once instantiated, an ADF allows for reasoning of individual cases, taking into account the specific factors relevant to each case. To perform this reasoning, a software program written in the Prolog language codes the acceptance conditions associated with each node in the instantiated ADF.[11]

Using the complete factor hierarchy from Figures 3.11.2 and 3.11.3, we can produce an ADF that has as its leaf nodes the base-level factors of CATO (see Table 3.11.2 for a tabular form of these factors). The roots of CATO's hierarchies correspond to the leaves of the IBP logical model; we can therefore combine them into a single ADF by using this structure. The relevant additions to the ADF needed to integrate the IBP model are shown in Table 3.11.3.[12]

In Tables 3.11.2 and 3.11.3 we can see 18 nodes that provide us with acceptance conditions. These are written as a set of tests for acceptance and rejection, to be applied in the order given, and thus expressing a priority between them. The last test will always be a default. Thus, the reasoning can be characterized as follows:

```
Accept Parent if Child.
Reject Parent.
```

TABLE 3.11.2 *CATO as ADF.*

ID	S	L+	L−
F_{102}	EffortstoMaintainSecrecy	F_6, F_{122}, 123	F_{19}, F_{23}, F_{27}
F_{104}	InfoValuable	F_8, F_{15}	F_{105}
F_{105}	InfoKnownOrAvailable	F_{106}, F_{108}	
F_{106}	InfoKnown	F_{20}, F_{27}	F_{15}, F_{123}
F_{108}	InfoAvailableElsewhere	F_{16}, F_{24}	
F_{110}	ImproperMeans	F_{111}	F_{120}
F_{111}	QuestionableMeans	F_2, F_{14}, F_{22}, F_{26}	F_1, F_{17}, F_{25}
F_{112}	InfoUsed	F_7, F_8, F_{18}	F_{17}
F_{114}	ConfidentialRelationship	F_{115}, F_{121}	
F_{115}	NoticeOfConfidentiality	F_4, F_{13}, F_{14}, F_{21}	F_5, F_{23}
F_{120}	LegitimatelyObtainable	F_{105}	F_{111}
F_{121}	ConfidentialityAgreement	F_4	F_{23}
F_{122}	MaintainSecrecyDefendant	F_4	F_1
F_{123}	MaintainSecrecyOutsiders	F_{12}	F_{10}
F_{124}	DefendantOwnershipRights	F_3	

TABLE 3.11.3 *IBP logical model as an ADF.*

ID	S	L+	L−
F_{200}	TradeSecretMisappropriation	F_{201}, F_{203}	F_{124}
F_{201}	InfoMisappropriated	F_{110}, F_{112}, F_{114}	
F_{203}	InfoTradeSecret	F_{102}, F_{104}	

---

[11] For full details of this coding, *see* Al-Abdulkarim et al., "A Methodology for Designing Systems to Reason with Legal Cases Using Abstract Dialectical Frameworks," *supra* note 2.

[12] Note that Factor F_{124} is not discussed in Bruninghaus and Ashley, "Predicting Outcomes of Case-based Legal Arguments," *supra* note 6.

Six nodes (F105, F108, F114, and F124 in Table 3.11.2; F201, F203 in Table 3.11.3) have only supporting links (i.e., "+" signs). These "+" links can be straightforwardly represented using AND and OR relations (we also make use of NOT where needed).

Here is an example of the reasoning applied for InfoMisappropriated (F201):

```
Accept InfoMisappropriated if F114 AND F112.
Accept InfoMisappropriated if F110.
Reject InfoMisappropriated.
```

Moving on, we have five nodes (F110, F120, F121, F122 and F123) that have one supporting and one attacking link. These form an exception structure where the reasoning is as follows: Accept the parent if, and *only* if, there is a supporting child, *unless* there is an attacking child. The reasoning here is characterized as follows:

```
Accept Parent if Supporter AND (NOT Attacker).
Reject Parent.
```

Seven nodes now remain, and these require a more complex encoding than the previous ones. Let us look at F200 as an example, since this encodes the high-level reasoning as to whether a trade secret was misappropriated. The reasoning about this node is as follows:

```
Accept Trade Secret Misappropriation if
     Info Trade Secret AND
     Info Misappropriated AND
     (NOT Defendant Ownership Rights).
Reject Trade Secret Misappropriation.[13]
```

F Implementation

Once the acceptance conditions for each node are defined, these can be transformed into a software program to reason about cases relevant to the domain. The program is executed by supplying it with a query whose input is the first factor to be decided in the case, as well as its base-level factors. The program works through the factor hierarchy, recording the factors present and the effects of those factors when the acceptance conditions for each node are considered. To provide an insight into how the program works, consider the sample given here, focusing on one specific case – the Boeing case.[14] The program is fed a list of base-level factors relevant to the case (with the factor IDs mapping to factors as previously given in Table 3.11.1):

```
case(boeing,[f4,f6,f12,f14,f21,f1,f10]).
```

Feeding this starting list of factors to the program kicks off the reasoning over the full factor hierarchy and gives the following output reflecting the reasoning:

```
accepted that defendant is not owner of secret
efforts made vis a vis outsiders
efforts made vis a vis defendant
there was a confidentiality agreement
defendant was on notice of confidentiality
there was a confidential relationship
```

---

[13] For analysis and reasoning about the remaining nodes, see Al-Abdulkarim et al., "A Methodology for Designing Systems to Reason with Legal Cases Using Abstract Dialectical Frameworks," *supra* note 2.
[14] *The Boeing Company v. Sierracin Corporation*, 108 Wash.2d 38, 738 P.2d 665 (1987).

```
accepted that the information was used
questionable means were used
accepted that the information was not available
    elsewhere
accepted that information is not known
accepted that the information was neither known nor
    available
accepted that the information was valuable
not accepted that the information was legitimately
    obtained
improper means were used
efforts were taken to maintain secrecy
information was a trade secret
a trade secret was misappropriated
find for plaintiff
boeing[f200, f201, f203, f102, f110, f104, f111, f112,
    f114, f115, f121, f122, f123, f4, f6, f12,
    f14, f21, f1, f10]
decision is correct in accordance with the actual
    decision
```

Inspecting the above output, one sees that the factors and the acceptance thereof are reported. The program finishes with the decision in the case ("find for plaintiff"), then lists all the factors of the case and finally reports whether the decision the program has reached matches that from the actual case.

The Boeing case is just one of a number of cases that have been used to evaluate how effectively the ADF software can replicate the real decisions made in the US trade secrets domain. A fuller evaluation exercise using 32 cases from the domain has been conducted and reported as well.[15] In that exercise, the final version of the program was able to match the decisions in the real cases 96.8% of the time.

One other evaluation pertaining to another important domain that is well studied in the artificial intelligence (AI) and law literature – the US Fourth Amendment's "automobile exception" – is examined next as part of a wider discussion about the development environment for ADFs and their analytical software.

The US Fourth Amendment's "automobile exception" rule covers a serious, large-scale problem. The Fourth Amendment protects the "right of the people to be secure in their persons, houses, papers, and effects, against unreasonable searches and seizures." A search is considered reasonable if there is a warrant. However, in some urgent situations where there is a high probability of losing evidence, obtaining a warrant in time may be impossible. The automobile exception refers to such an urgent situation, where an automobile can be easily moved from its known location, and relevant evidence potentially hidden, removed, destroyed, or otherwise rendered undiscoverable by any search warrant. This domain is complex, and considers the interaction of two competing considerations: enforcing the law and maintaining a citizen's right to privacy.

An ADF was produced to model the factors in this domain. The associated software program was evaluated using ten cases from this domain, and the software program decided nine of the ten cases correctly. The single incorrectly decided case occurred due to a change

---

[15] Al-Abdulkarim et al., "A Methodology for Designing Systems to Reason with Legal Cases Using Abstract Dialectical Frameworks," *supra* note 2.

in understanding of the law that can be accounted for by using a portion of precedent cases. This apparent error highlights the fact that temporal context can be handled and accounted for in the computational model.[16]

G Development Environment

Given the high success rate in modeling the reasoning in the example domains, the next hurdle is turning this tool into something legal practitioners can use. This usage problem is greatly alleviated by Angelic's solid methodology, which allows a variety of problems to be modeled in a systematic and reproducible manner.[17]

The development environment consists of a database that stores the domain theory produced by the Angelic methodology, as well as an extensible set of tools that display and use the stored knowledge to support development, verification, and refinement. The database tables hold all the information produced by the Angelic analysis. This covers the domain theory expressed as an ADF, the domain itself, and the individual cases within the domain. In addition to the database tables, there are also facilities to support development in the Angelic environment. These tools are intended to be extensible, and developers can write programs to use information in the database in any way they find useful. The tools support visualization of a domain; entry of facts relating to a particular case; retrieval of additional information about cases (e.g., descriptions or links to external sources); and generation of the underlying knowledge base that captures the domain.

Figure 3.11.4 shows a snapshot of the interface visualization when applied to the domain of warrantless search under the Fourth Amendment's automobile exception.[18] The issues concern finding a balance between exigency – the practical issue of whether a warrant can be obtained or whether the evidence would simply be driven away – and privacy. Expectations of privacy are considered lowered for automobiles relative to dwellings. A case that has been widely discussed in AI and law is *California v. Carney*.[19] That case related to the search of a mobile home, which was capable of use either as a vehicle or a dwelling. The majority found for California, because the mobile home was in use as a vehicle at the time of the search, in a public short-stay car park. The minority opinion argued, however, that because it was daytime in downtown San Diego, a warrant could have been obtained without risk of losing evidence. The visualization of this domain given in Figure 3.11.4 shows the factors relevant for this and other cases within the domain. Tools related to further tasks within the development environment are accessed by buttons on the left-hand pane, and the larger pane is a display and working area.

---

[16] Ibid.
[17] For a fuller description of a development environment for the Angelic methodology, see Sam Atkinson, Latifa Al-Abdulkarim, Katie Atkinson, and Trevor Bench-Capon, "Angelic Environment: Demonstration," in *Proceedings of the Sixteenth International Conference on Artificial Intelligence and Law, ICAIL 2017, London, UK, June 12–16, 2017* (New York, NY: ACM Press, 2017), 267–268.
[18] A series of Supreme Court cases relates the exceptions for automobiles; see Trevor J. M. Bench-Capon, "Relating Values in a Series of Supreme Court Decisions," in *Legal Knowledge and Information Systems JURIX 2011: The Twenty-Fourth Annual Conference, University of Vienna, Austria, December 14–16, 2011*, ed. Katie Atkinson (Amsterdam: IOS Press, 2011), 13–22, available at: https://cgi.csc.liv.ac.uk/~tbc/publications/tbcJurix11.pdf.
[19] See, e.g., Alexander Boer, Radboud Winkels, and Fabio Vitali, "Metalex XML and the Legal Knowledge Interchange Format," in *Computable Models of the Law, Languages, Dialogues, Games, Ontologies*, eds. Pompeu Casanovas, Giovanni Sartor, Nuria Casellas, and Rossella Rubino (New York, NY: Springer, 2008), 21–41.

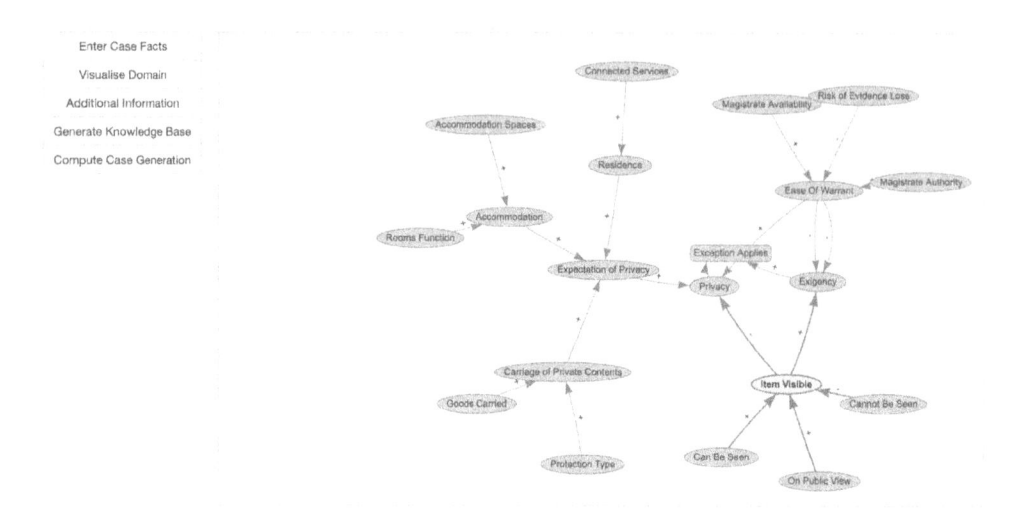

FIGURE 3.11.4 Visualization of automobile exception domain addressing the question "Can an automobile be searched without a warrant?"

Figure 3.11.4 illustrates one aspect of one domain modeled using the Angelic methodology. At the time of this writing, the tool has moved beyond academic testing and is being investigated for deployment in the field using cases from a UK law firm.

II SUMMARY

These case studies provide an in-depth look at how research in the AI and law community on representing and reasoning about legal cases has been developed, implemented, and deployed. The tools outlined in this chapter represent an important step in transitioning a computational model of argument from academic research to a usable tool that can be deployed in practice and tailored to a domain as needed. The Angelic environment described here is an example of a tool that can be used to provide automated support for a variety of tasks: decision support tools for assessing case outcomes, advising on strong and weak arguments in a case, comparing current cases with previous cases, assisting in decisions on whether to take on a case, and for training law students. The case study provided here is just one of a number of lines of research from the field of AI and law that is being investigated with the aim of visually representing legal knowledge.

D.

Dispute Resolution and Access to Justice

3.12

Online Dispute Resolution

Dave Orr and Colin Rule

One concept that has seized the popular imagination is the idea of the digital judge. There is something intuitively appealing about the concept that one day our unruly, chaotic human disputes will be resolved by the cool, all-knowing rationality of a fair and impartial electronic decision maker. While the concept may be enticing, this leap from human-powered justice to electronic justice is a pretty big one. Much like the concept of self-driving cars or watches we can talk into, many people seem to have concluded that this future is inevitable, even when we don't yet have the technology that could make it come to pass. Right now we're just biding time, waiting for the future to arrive.

There are several reasons why we feel the arrival of the digital judge is inevitable. First, we humans generate billions of disputes each year, soon to be tens of billions. This growth shows no signs of stopping. We cannot help ourselves; we love to fight with each other. Despite this love of fighting, the idea that current, inefficient, human-based resolution processes could resolve all these disputes strains credulity. Faith in our very ability to be fair and impartial arbiters weakens under this strain, and it is undermined even further by what we continue to learn about how our brains work. Alongside these developments, computers continue to become more powerful and more deeply integrated into our everyday lives. It stands to reason, then, that if current trends continue, computers will one day be better at fairly resolving our disputes than we are. Considering this, one thing becomes clear: If computers are going to resolve our disputes, they are going to go about it in a very different way than we have up until now.

I TECHNOLOGY, DISPUTE RESOLUTION, AND THE FOURTH PARTY

Online dispute resolution (ODR) is the use of information and communication technology to help people prevent and resolve disputes. Like its offline sibling, *alternative dispute resolution* (ADR), ODR is characterized by its extrajudicial nature. In a sense, dispute resolution is defined by what it is not: It is not a legal process. Any resolution outside of the courts is dispute resolution. If you and your counterparty decide to resolve your dispute by consulting tarot cards, that is ADR. If you decide to resolve your dispute with a game of checkers, that is also ADR. However, if you decide to resolve your dispute with a game of *online* checkers, that is ODR. Either way, in the dispute resolution world, we paint with a pretty big palette.

As ODR has developed over the past 20 years, a few core concepts have emerged. One of the most foundational concepts is that of the "fourth party." Originally introduced by Ethan Katsh and Janet Rifkin in their book *Online Dispute Resolution*, the fourth party describes technology as another party sitting at the table, alongside party one and party two (the disputants) and the third party (the neutral human, such as a mediator or arbitrator).[1] You may be forgiven for picturing the fourth party as a friendly robot sitting next to you at the negotiating table and smiling patiently. Bear in mind, though, that this fourth party could just as easily be a black cylinder sitting on the table – *a la* Amazon Echo – or just software floating somewhere in the cloud. The form of the fourth party is irrelevant to the function the fourth party provides.

The fourth party can play many different roles in a dispute. In most current ODR processes, the fourth party is largely administrative, handling tasks like case filing, reporting on statistics, sharing data, and facilitating communications. We ask our friendly fourth party robot to take notes, or to dial in someone who could not join us at the table in person. But it is obvious to those of us in the ODR field that the fourth party is capable of much more. While we humans pretty much work the way we always have, with our cognitive biases and attribution errors, computers are getting more powerful all the time. It is inevitable that at some point we will ask our fourth party robot to help us resolve our issues, or maybe even to just handle it for us outright. The fourth party is just getting started.

II GETTING USED TO THE MACHINES

There was a time when technology was perceived as very dehumanizing. Dispute resolvers in particular resisted the idea that algorithms had any useful role to play in helping disputants find solutions to their disagreements. But technology has become much more accessible and integrated into our lives, and we now use technology in ways we never would have considered ten years ago. People take to the internet to find their spouses, to find information on where to go to church, to choose the best school to send their kids, and even to seek out a cardiac surgeon. The younger generation is even more comfortable: They ask each other to prom via text, break up over Twitter, and Snapchat their friends embarrassing pictures from last night's party.

Individuals have come to trust information presented to them by an algorithm more than they trust information presented by a human. While this might seem initially jarring, upon reflection it makes some sense. If you are thinking about getting a divorce, you may want to consult a lawyer to learn about your rights and the required steps. Perhaps in the consultation with that lawyer, you feel they are judging you in some way – maybe for your age, or for your ethnicity, or even for your perceived ability to pay. Maybe you suspect that the lawyer is wondering whether the divorce is your fault, or is tailoring the information he or she presents to you in order for you to pick a resolution process that the lawyer feels is more appropriate in your particular situation. That feeling can be very uncomfortable.

Now think about an algorithmic consultation. You go to Google and type "divorce." The search returns hundreds of millions of results, and you scan through the first 25 to see if any appear to be on target. You select, somewhat at random, a guide published by a legal service bureau a few counties away from you. This online guide was clearly not created specifically for you – it was put online several years ago, long before you ever thought you would need to consult it. None of your personally identifiable information is required to navigate the guide. You can answer high-level questions about your situation (e.g., whether you have kids, whether you are both employed) without providing your name. After six or seven minutes

---

[1] Ethan Katsh and Janet Rifkin, *Online Dispute Resolution* (San Francisco, CA: Jossey-Bass, 2001).

of navigation and simple questions, the guide shares its conclusions about the likely steps that would be involved in your divorce. If the result seems questionable, you can merely reload the homepage and start again, perhaps providing different answers to see how your changes alter the final results. In any event, this algorithmic process does not judge you on the basis of your race, sex, age, income, or other characteristics – largely because it knows nothing other than what you tell it. It stands to reason that people might be more comfortable using assessment tools such as this one when they are trying to get their questions answered. In addition, that algorithm is probably free, while a lawyer will probably charge an hourly rate for the same service.

III THE RISE OF ARTIFICIAL INTELLIGENCE

Technology is likely to alter many areas of professional services, from financial planning to medical care. But in the justice sector, this development may prove particularly significant. Government has an interest in the consistent resolution of disputes, and to that end, government funds the courts. But it is unlikely that the government will be the sole provider of algorithms used in these ways. Just as the internet has weakened the role of the public sector in many areas of the economy (e.g., Bitcoin has made financial transactions stateless and invisible to regulators), it may also weaken the role of the public sector in providing justice.

A shorthand for the expansion of technology into these realms formerly dominated by humans is the term *artificial intelligence*, or AI. People often envision AI working the way humans work, perhaps taking the form of a humanoid robot in the front of a courtroom, wearing a powdered wig on his metal head and wielding a gavel in his little robot hand. That image may be drawn more from old episodes of *The Jetsons* than from technological necessity, but sometimes there is value in matching people's expectations. If that form is more satisfying to people, it certainly is doable. In reality, though, the action in AI takes place in software, no powdered wigs necessary.

Artificial intelligence uses software algorithms to tackle complex tasks that have been traditionally handled by non-artificial intelligences (i.e., us, the humans). Humans have their own ways of understanding problems and devising solutions. Artificial intelligence also has to understand problems and devise solutions, so that it can deliver outcomes equivalent to, or better than, human-devised outcomes. But algorithmic intelligence doesn't go about devising those outcomes in the same way as human intelligence would.

We've all heard about IBM's Watson winning *Jeopardy!* over the top human players in the world. Many of us might presume that Watson works like an electronic human brain, mimicking the same types of connections that happen in the human players' brains during the game. But that isn't the way Watson is programmed to operate. As Alex Trebek is reading off each word of the question, Watson is guessing what the question is getting at, and instantly generating thousands of possible responses to the possible question. Watson is scoring all of those possible responses in real time, estimating the likelihood that each one is the right answer. As soon as Watson finds an answer with the highest likelihood of both (1) the question being the right question, and (2) the answer being the correct answer to that question, Watson buzzes in. The other human players are trying to make connections in their brain that generate the one best answer, but Watson is generating thousands upon thousands of answers and scoring them all to see which one is best. This is similar to the way computers win chess matches: They evaluate all possible moves one move out, two moves out, and three moves out; score them all; and then decide which move is best in each situation. This is fundamentally different from the way a human plays chess or plays *Jeopardy!*, but the result is equivalent to or even better than a human's performance.

When an AI is first created, it is a blank slate hungry to learn. But as we can see from the above examples, an AI learns in a very particular way. It learns by looking at data, and this data must be structured into a format that the AI can make sense of. The AI can then look at this data in order to formulate some observations, but to train an AI to make these observations, you must always first provide the AI a corpus of data.

For example, imagine an AI is asked to decide the appropriate penalty payment owed by a business for inappropriately sharing a consumer's private information. Maybe there is a large database of prior cases that contains more than 10,000 decisions made by customer service representatives about penalty payments. The details of each of these violations (such as severity, scope, and type of information shared) are stored in the database. The algorithm then crawls through all of the cases and creates a set of rules that correlate the decision rendered in each case to the details of each case. With this setup, when a new case is presented to the AI, it will consult the rules it already created when it learned from the corpus, and it will then make a determination as to the appropriate payment amount.

This algorithm is built from determinations originally made by the customer service representatives. Let's say the reps were very skilled at making their determinations, but were still wrong about 10% of the time. Because the algorithm trains itself based on these decisions, the AI cannot make the correct decision more than 90% of the time. The algorithm cannot use the data in the corpus to train itself to be *better* than the data set it was presented. But the bigger the corpus, the more specific the AI will be in crafting rules, and that will enable the AI to get ever closer to that 90% accuracy level.

Sometimes a corpus of data might not exist around a particular decision type. For example, imagine there is a need to decide if a certain online review is specific enough for inclusion on a hotel rating website. No database exists that contains prior evaluations of reviews to determine if they meet the standards in question. But perhaps the hotel rating website starts a crowdsourced process to evaluate reviews. Members of the website are repeatedly asked if a particular review is specific enough for inclusion. Every time they log in they get another review to evaluate. Maybe customer service reps also decide some cases as well, in addition to the users. Slowly but surely, website members and customer service reps would generate a corpus of data. As each decision is rendered, the AI could be watching and learning from each new case. Again, maybe the users only get it right about 90% of the time, but by observing enough of these evaluations, and by capturing all of the outcomes from the crowdsourced process in a structured database, the AI algorithm could train itself what to look for, and eventually be able to make decisions about future online reviews at a similar level of accuracy. At this point, the human-powered crowdsourced decisions could taper off, and the AI algorithm could increasingly take over.

When AIs come up with rules, it may seem like magic. You might even want to open the hood and see just what these miraculous rules are, so that you can leverage them in your own decision making. Don't bother. Most humans cannot make heads or tails of the rules AIs glean from a large corpus of data. For example, an AI may decide that a review that has the word "actually" within eight words of the word "budget" is likely to be a trustworthy review. Now why is that? Our simple little human brains might not be able to come up with a good explanation as to why that may be true. But the AI has found a pattern, and that pattern may have truth undergirding it that a human is not able to comprehend. In fact, if you look at most rules generated by AIs, they appear to us humans as gobbledygook. But that is only because humans think like humans, and AIs think like computers. There may be insight in those rules that we are simply unable to understand. The proof is in the pudding, and if the output is of high quality, then the logic generated by AIs is quality, even if to humans it doesn't seem all that logical.

IV BUILDING THE CORPUS

The challenge is not necessarily to think about how to train an AI to decide a dispute. As we've already described, we know how to program an AI so that it can take on that task. The real challenge is: How do you categorize the world's resolution information into a format an AI can make sense of, and not only make sense of, but also learn from?

There is no shortage of raw data in the world. There are lots of court decisions that we could give an AI to read, for example. There are also many companies out there trying to make sense of court cases via AI. The problem lies in finding ways for AI to process this data. Currently it is very difficult to do. There is a lot of structure to the law, but it is not the kind of structure that can easily help an algorithm learn and identify patterns and rules. We are still a long way away from giving an AI LexisNexis access and then asking it to serve on the Supreme Court.

So what do we do? If we want to train AIs to be better decision makers, we need to build data sets. Since so many cases are now being decided on ODR platforms, one task AIs could take on in the near term would be to help build these data sets through case classification. Humans would negotiate, mediate, and arbitrate new cases, and AIs would review the outcomes and structure the data they generate in real time. This would give us a good head start on building a large corpus we could use to train future AI algorithms. AIs are very good at labeling data and storing it in a structured way that will make sense to future algorithmic analysis. If an AI labels and classifies millions of traffic court decisions in real time, for example, then we can open that database to other algorithms that could then use that data to educate themselves about traffic cases. This could potentially teach all those algorithms how to accurately decide traffic court cases moving forward. It's a long way from the Supreme Court, but it's a start.

This is an important point, and an important limitation to consider. An AI must focus on similar baskets of cases. It is very difficult for an algorithm to get a database of many different kinds of cases (e.g., workplace, traffic, divorce) and then somehow glean rules that could make sense out of any possible new case. Specialization into specific case types (e.g., traffic) is very important for accuracy in rules. General decision-making systems (humans) still need to be able to determine the classification of each new case, and then apply the rules relevant to that specific case type. Artificial intelligence is not there yet, but perhaps one day a team of AIs will work to resolve cases, with the first AI routing each incoming case to the appropriate queue, and a second AI determining the appropriate outcome for cases of a particular type.

V CHANGING HOW WE THINK ABOUT JUSTICE

The techniques we are describing are feasible today. But if that's the case, where are all of the algorithmic judges? The truth is that they are out there, silently churning away, but currently they are primarily focused on answering relatively simple data-based questions.

The reason for this is that AI algorithms are still not very good at making sense of unstructured data. For example, if we were to show the transcript of a negotiation session to an AI and ask that AI to suggest a fair resolution, that would require some pretty advanced capacity on the part of the AI. In the near term, the speech transcription of the session is being solved, so the AI can probably learn the words said in the session. But words are only part of what is communicated in a negotiation. Identifying the truly important points of disagreement in a dispute, and comprehending the subtexts and assumptions behind each of those points, is much harder. Teaching an AI to contextualize unstructured communication may be possible in 10–20 years, but at the current moment AI may get just as confused by legalese as a layperson.

What breakthroughs are required to help AIs get over that hump? How could an AI gather more understanding to fill in the blanks in a negotiation? Maybe AIs can be taught to ask the disputants questions, the same way a judge or a mediator might, in order to get at more subtle points of meaning. Perhaps the AI could educate itself by reading the internet, or looking through case databases to try to learn from similar matters. The AI could then bring conclusions drawn from other cases into each new conversation, which could help it parse points of confusion without constantly asking the parties to explain what they mean by each comment they contribute.

One way we could make it easier for algorithms to resolve our disputes is to structure our negotiations into questions that are more easily answerable by computers. For example, instead of asking an algorithm to simply issue a decision from scratch in a disagreement, perhaps the two parties in a disagreement could be asked to put forward their last, best offer, and the algorithm would be asked which of the final offers is more appropriate. In this design, the algorithm would conduct research in databases around the world, return a result, and then see which of the proposals is the closest to its template resolution. The parties would also have an incentive to be as reasonable as possible in putting their offers on the table, because they would want the AI to pick their suggested resolution over the other party's proposed solution. This kind of technology-assisted final offer arbitration could be a shortcut to AI-powered resolutions, because this design plays to algorithmic strengths and avoids difficult, more nuanced questions that might trip it up. It also avoids the possibility that the AI really gets it wrong and delivers a resolution that is wholly unjustified, frustrating both of the parties.

There are intermediate steps on the road to the digital judge. AIs do not have to serve as the final decision maker right out of the box. They could start out by evaluating cases and coming up with suggested resolutions that human decision makers might consult on an advisory basis. Parties could also run their cases by an algorithm in advance of a human-powered arbitration to see what resolution the algorithm might consider fair. Even the best arbitrator can only keep a couple hundred case outcomes in their mind, but an algorithm can consult millions or tens of millions of cases and factor all of that information into its suggested resolution. Consulting AIs in this way could not only help to improve the quality of AIs, but also increase confidence in the ability of AIs to render trustworthy decisions. Once the AI has proven itself effective – perhaps after consulting on millions of cases – then it could be put into the final decision-making role.

VI DECIDING WHAT AIS CAN CONSIDER

AIs act very differently from people, but these differences may actually be beneficial. They can be programmed in a way that makes them more "fair," by ignoring information that system designers and programmers deem to be outside the scope of the question at hand. For example, you can never be sure whether your jury was swayed by some unforeseen factor, like your accent or your hemline. The jury may not be sure themselves as to why they feel compelled to decide your case one way or the other, but a computer algorithm can not only be explicitly instructed to ignore certain factors (e.g., accent, hemline), but it can also be prevented from even knowing those bits of data in the first place. There is no way for a jury to ignore such factors, not even after explicit instructions from the judge not to pay attention. There is a surefire way, though, to prevent the AI from knowing them.

This leads to some interesting design choices – and complex ethical and moral ramifications – for building dispute resolution AI. For example, computers have gotten very good at reading human facial expressions. Is it reasonable for a computer to closely watch a disputant explain their actions, and then to determine based on the observed facial expressions whether the explanation is a lie? What if the computer could conduct an MRI on the disputant as they offer their explanation, and from that MRI provide certifiable evidence that the statement is a lie? Should that information be factored into the computer's decision-making process, or should the AI be forbidden from considering it? It is up to the AI's programmer to determine if that information is relevant, as well as whether the algorithm will even be capable of gathering this kind of data during the dispute. There may be a certain ick factor in giving computers so much visibility into things that we as humans cannot perceive ourselves. But we may conclude that the accuracy and accountability that comes from these new capabilities may outweigh the ick factor, and our instinctual resistance may ease over time.

On the other side of the coin, AI systems might make egregious mistakes that humans would never make. This may, however, be due to their systems designers failing to integrate all of the information required to avoid such mistakes. For example, Google's self-driving car follows the explicit laws on the books that regulate driving, but it does not follow the *implicit* rules that so often conflict with the laws on the books.[2] A human understands both these sets of rules, and appropriately contextualizes them in real time. A machine might not know both sets of rules unless there is some way to integrate them into the algorithm. To picture the problems of this lack of context, imagine a human driver seething behind a row of Google cars all driving at the exact speed limit.

Sometimes AIs may make decisions that seem odd or ill-advised to a human observer, and it can be very hard to understand the reasoning behind an AI's decisions. By carefully deciding the information AIs are given, and by working out the kinds of decisions AIs are allowed to make with that information, all of these kinks can eventually be worked out, and AIs can gradually become more integrated into the decision-making process.

---

[2] Matt Richtel and Conor Dougherty, "Google's Driverless Cars Run into Problem: Cars with Drivers," *New York Times*, September 1, 2015, available at: www.nytimes.com/2015/09/02/technology/personaltech/google-says-its-not-the-driverless-cars-fault-its-other-drivers.html?_r=1.

3.13

Access to Justice and Technology

Reaching a Greater Future for Legal Aid

Ronald W. Staudt and Alexander F. A. Rabanal

I INTRODUCTION: THE CIVIL ACCESS TO JUSTICE PROBLEM IN THE USA

The justice system in the USA is modeled on that of the UK: The rule base is made up of common law derived from cases and statutes. The US system differs, though, because it is controlled by a written Constitution that sets out the operation of the courts and controls some of the core relationships between people and government. In all serious criminal cases where the government is the plaintiff, the accused are generally entitled by the Constitution to free representation by appointed lawyers. However, there is no corresponding constitutional right to representation by lawyers in *civil* cases.

Civil cases in the USA involve all types of very serious disputes, such as divorce, child custody, eviction from rental housing, reduction or elimination of government income and food assistance, mortgage foreclosure, and bankruptcy. In these civil cases, the Constitution does not guarantee low-income people access to free or subsidized legal assistance. Therefore, millions of low-income people in millions of civil cases are forced to represent themselves or simply default.

Lawyers and judges know that self-represented people are very likely to suffer in an adversarial court system when their disputes are litigated without professional representation. To help blunt this gross injustice, a patchwork of federal, state, and private sources have helped to fund a small number of lawyers who devote their entire professional efforts to representing low-income people in civil cases. Since 1974, the federal government has appropriated about $350 million each year to the Legal Services Corporation (LSC) for civil legal aid. In many states, courts have even consolidated and applied interest on lawyers' trust funds in order to support legal aid to the poor. In other areas, some state and local governments devote a small part of their tax revenues to help people in need of legal assistance. Lawyers provide some help for these unrepresented litigants through donations to their bar associations and through pro bono work. Charities and foundations also fund some legal aid efforts. Nevertheless, these sources of aid are inadequate to meet the huge demand for civil legal aid to the poor.

Over the past 40 years, there have been dozens of studies of the civil legal needs of the poor.[1] These studies have consistently found that at least 80% of the civil legal needs of the poor are not met, leading to a massive justice gap. Millions of poor people each year are evicted, lose

---

[1] *See, e.g.*, Legal Services Corporation (LSC), "Documenting the Justice Gap in America: The Current Unmet Civil Legal Needs of Low-Income Americans," 2009, available at: www.americanbar.org/content/dam/aba/migrated/marketresearch/PublicDocuments/JusticeGaInAmerica2009.authcheckdam.pdf.

custody of their children, or pay unnecessary fines and judgments all while facing a confusing, complex, and unfriendly legal system that they do not understand and cannot navigate. This justice gap extends into the middle class, as the cost of legal representation and the complexity of our justice system leaves 60–70% of middle-income people without the legal help they need.[2] Priced out of private legal representation and earning too much to qualify for legal aid, middle-income people also face critical legal problems affecting health, housing, safety, and financial well-being without the benefits of attorney representation.[3]

The scale of the civil justice gap in the USA is daunting, and with it comes the likelihood that the government will not provide the funds necessary to hire enough lawyers to meet this need. The LSC attempts to correct this. It is a non-profit corporation founded by Congress in 1974 to provide equal access to justice, and is the largest funder of civil legal aid in the country. But the Corporation's ability to support legal aid lawyers has been declining each year for decades, and each year is a struggle to ensure the Corporation survives budget cutting or more direct political attacks. Other sources of legal aid now exceed the total provided by the Corporation, yet the totality of funds and volunteer efforts from the LSC and these other sources, combined, meets at best 20% of the need. Without a paradigm-breaking set of innovations, there is no prospect that the justice crisis will ever be resolved.

II TECHNOLOGY AS A SOLUTION FOR THE ACCESS TO CIVIL JUSTICE PROBLEM

In 2000, Congress appropriated special funds to the LSC for the Technology Initiative Grants (TIG) program. This program's goal is to use technology more effectively to meet the legal needs of low-income Americans. Between 2000 and 2017, Congress authorized a total of $57 million for LSC to issue grants for more than 670 technology projects aimed at the justice crisis.[4] Over this 17-year period, TIG funds represented about 1% of the grants made by LSC. Most of the rest of LSC grants ($300–400 million each year) were basic field grants that paid the salaries of lawyers for low-income people.

The projects funded by TIG have explored all types of technology, including mobile offices, videoconferencing, data analysis, cloud computing, pilot projects to evaluate satellite communications, and many other ideas. Three clusters of projects have proved to be consistently effective: (1) grants to build and maintain statewide legal aid websites; (2) grants to build and support a national document assembly server; and (3) grants to build and support a new client-facing interview builder called A2J Author. These three project clusters are interdependent and mutually reinforcing, and the combination has proved to be quite successful. Millions of people have been able to achieve their justice aims because of these three technology initiatives.

---

[2] Ibid.
[3] American Bar Association, "Report on the Future of Legal Services in the United States,", 2016, available at: http://abafuturesreport.com/2016-fls-report-findings.pdf; Rebecca L. Sandefur, "What We Know and Need to Know about the Legal Needs of the Public," *South Carolina Law Review* 67 (2016): 443, 445; *see also* Barbara A. Curran, *The Legal Needs of the Public: The Final Report of a National Survey* (Chicago, IL: The Foundation, 1977); Deborah L. Rhode, "What We Know and Need to Know About the Delivery of Legal Services by Nonlawyers," *South Carolina Law Review* 67 (2016): 429; Deborah L. Rhode, *Access to Justice* (Oxford: Oxford University Press, 2004).
[4] Legal Services Corporation, "Technology Initiative Grant Program," available at: www.lsc.gov/grants-grantee-resources/our-grant-programs/tig.

A Statewide Websites

When the TIG program was launched in 2000, legal aid lawyers were infrequent and inefficient users of technology. Many legal aid organizations had websites, but the sites were little more than confusing online brochures, only sometimes enriched with information on legal problems frequently facing low-income people. States with small populations of low-income people and only a few legal aid lawyers had little or no internet presence. Populous states, meanwhile, frequently had dozens of legal aid organizations in addition to the two or three supported by the LSC, but each of these organizations had a separate website with confusing branding and incomplete information about the legal issues faced by low-income people. The situation was a mess.

The LSC's first challenge was to untangle the inadequate array of legal aid websites. Using modest TIG grants – usually no more than $30,000 each – the LSC prodded states to coordinate all their legal aid organizations in order to build and launch a single statewide website aimed at low-income people needing civil legal assistance. To obtain the money, legal aid organizations had to agree to coordinate information for the public on a single website, use one of two approved website templates, and participate in a national branding initiative. Over several years, all states involved built a conforming statewide legal aid website for low-income consumers, with all the sites loosely coordinated under the brand "LawHelp.org." One of the LSC-approved template builders was Pro Bono Net, a New York charity that has maintained the national LawHelp.org site, from which all statewide sites could be reached. The LSC's master stroke came when it amended its Grant Assurances, the rules that all the basic service grantees must agree to follow. Now these Assurances require that grantees:

> "work with other LSC and non-LSC-funded legal services providers in the State to ensure that there is a statewide website that publishes a full range of relevant and up-to-date community legal education/pro se related materials and referral information, at least covering the common topics facing the client communities on the subject matters that are the Applicant's priorities."[5]

The LSC's sequencing of carrots and sticks is a great example of the influence and impact that modest stimulus grants can have when followed by effective regulatory reform. Today, every state has a statewide website with authentic, relevant information on the legal rights of poor people facing difficult civil legal challenges. These sites have referral resources to help locate legal aid lawyers and pro bono volunteers. The more advanced sites serve as platforms for delivering legal services by hosting extensive self-help resources, such as document assembly templates that help people draft their own forms, as well as A2J Guided Interviews that inform and support self-help processes.

B Document Assembly: Standardized and Coordinated

From the beginning of the TIG era, the LSC has focused on bringing the power of document assembly to its legal aid agencies. The TIG staff, especially Program Counsel Glenn Rawdon, believed that legal aid agencies are the perfect place for document assembly because of their repetitive nature. Hundreds of thousands of documents are prepared each year for divorces,

---

[5] Legal Services Corporation, "Grant Assurances," available at: www.lsc.gov/grants-grantee-resources/grantee-guidance/grant-assurances.

evictions, mortgage foreclosures, debt collections, and child custody disputes. Document assembly offers enormous efficiencies because of this high volume of structurally similar cases.

In 1999, the LSC convened a group of experts to evaluate the document assembly software that lawyers were using in private practice. The ensuing report required all legal aid agencies wishing to apply for TIG grants to automate documents using one software tool – HotDocs, then the leading document assembly software in private law firms. HotDocs software aided lawyers and their assistants in building document assembly templates, allowing users to then create individual documents from those templates. In addition, HotDocs also sold server software so that document templates could be run from a website interfaced for consumers who needed such documents.

Through a generous donation from LexisNexis (then the owner of HotDocs), the LSC obtained HotDocs authoring software for every state, and server software for a national central HotDocs template server. TIG grants to an Ohio legal aid organization supported the creation of a single national server to house all the HotDocs templates built by legal aid societies. In addition to avoiding duplication of infrastructure and providing some benefits of scale, the single national server enabled all LSC agencies across the country to share templates. This national server is now managed by the LawHelp Interactive (LHI) division of Pro Bono Net.[6]

C A2J Author: The Missing Piece of the Access to Justice Puzzle

TIG grants and HotDocs software created a theoretically usable system, but now the market needed a tool that could bridge the gap between the standard technologies and the special needs of low-income consumers. Many consumers of legal aid services found the interface of HotDocs templates too complicated to easily use; HotDocs templates were well suited for advocates who prepared repetitive pleadings and other documents, but not as well suited for users of do-it-yourself websites. To address this concern and others, the State Justice Institute, the Illinois Institute of Technology, the Open Society Institute, and other charities funded a two-year study of the legal needs of self-represented people. IIT Chicago-Kent College of Law (Chicago-Kent), the IIT Institute of Design, and the National Center for State Courts worked together to create a prototype user interface that combined consumer education and very simple design for graphical information gathering. The prototype tested well with low-income self-represented litigants. With additional funding from LSC's TIG program, Chicago-Kent and the Center for Computer-Assisted Legal Instruction (CALI) built an authoring tool in Adobe Flash called A2J Author. A2J Author was designed to be a tool for building graphical interfaces that low-income people can use to prepare documents, apply for legal aid, and learn their rights.

A2J Author was the necessary missing piece to build B-to-C solutions for delivering web-based legal services directly to low-income people. With A2J Author, legal aid lawyers and their assistants could now build consumer-facing applications that educated low-income people about their rights and guided them through the creation of documents needed to seek legal solutions to their problems. A2J Guided Interviews even help prospective clients apply online for the assistance of legal aid lawyers. Statewide legal aid websites are perfectly positioned to use the web to reach legal aid consumers at any time and at any place. With a national server providing efficient and non-duplicative infrastructure for document

---

[6] For more on document assembly, *see* Lauritsen – Document Automation, *supra*.

assembly, A2J Guided Interviews can deliver information that helps low-income people handle their own problems.

This trio of projects has made it possible to begin to create layers of help for low-income people in need of legal assistance. At the first layer, the texts, videos, and other educational material on statewide websites gives people information necessary to understanding and solving their own legal problems. When the assistance available from the educational material on the websites runs out or proves to be inadequate for more complex issues, the website can link to an A2J Guided Interview to provide more targeted and detailed assistance tuned to a user's specific needs. If the linked A2J Guided Interviews are not enough to solve the user's legal problems, the websites can aid these consumers yet further by helping them apply for legal assistance from staff lawyers who are experts in their legal problems.

III A2J AUTHOR CASE STUDY

A2J Author is a software-as-a-service (SaaS) program co-developed by CALI and Chicago-Kent that allows self-represented litigants to complete legal forms in a simple way. Instead of manually filling out a complex court form typically written in legal jargon, an A2J Guided Interview user is asked straightforward step-by-step questions that gather information needed to complete the forms. The program allows content developers – attorneys, technologists, or law students – to create A2J Guided Interviews that consist of question screens supplemented by visual aids. Users progress through the A2J Guided Interview based on their response to each question screen. To facilitate meaningful progression, content developers write questions and informational text in plain language to minimize ambiguity about phrasing and corresponding user inputs.

A2J[9] Author, like an expert system, enables domain experts (attorneys) to capture and deliver their expertise and legal solutions to a wider group of people beyond just their clients.[7] Just like in expert system development, A2J Author developers act as knowledge engineers, taking information from a domain expert and mapping that expertise onto the A2J Guided Interview. The attorney's knowledge of substantive and procedural law and the attorney's own experiences and heuristics are captured in the A2J Guided Interview in the logic flow of the questions and the scripts that branch users to the correct set of questions needed to solve their problems. As is typical in expert systems, the knowledge engineer and the domain expert are often two different professionals, but in A2J Guided Interview development, the two can sometimes be one and the same.

The A2J Guided Interview functions as a decision tree based on the captured expertise within the knowledge base. Decision making about interview progression, for example, can be done using buttons for simple branching, or by using conditional logic for more complex branching. In an A2J Guided Interview for temporary custody of a minor, for example, the interview might ask whether the person for whom the petition is being filed is under the age of 18. The developer can dictate branching simply by creating two buttons, "Yes" and "No," and designating destination pages for each. If the answer is "Yes," the user continues with the interview, and if the answer is "No," the user navigates to a screen that informs them that they do not qualify to continue. Where navigation goes beyond simple binary evaluation, the developer can use conditional logic. In the same A2J Guided Interview, the end-user may be

---

[7] See Conrad Johnson and Brian Donnelly, "If We Only Knew What We Know," *Chicago-Kent Law Review* 88 (3) (2013): 729, 742.

FIGURE 3.13.1 Conditional logic to determine judicial district in IL.[8]

asked why the court granting temporary custody to the end-user would be in the child's best interests. If the end-user is then presented with several preset answer options, conditional logic expressed as IF/THEN statements can determine the next screen the user sees as a follow-up to the initial question. Furthermore, conditional logic can be used to make decisions about the values of certain variables. For example, an A2J Guided Interview might ask for the county in which the end-user lives, in order to determine the appropriate judicial district for filing the form. In Figure 3.13.1, the variable for judicial district is determined by the value of the variable for the user's county.

Additionally, an A2J Guided Interview almost always asks for the end-user's full name, stored as a variable expressed as the combination of their first, middle, and last names. Because middle names are optional, a developer may script logic that evaluates whether the end-user has entered a middle name, and if so, to construct the full name as a combination of the first, middle, and last names. Otherwise, only first and last names are used (Figure 3.13.2).

To allow the developer to visualize connections between and among each of the screens and the individual components of each screen (e.g., text boxes), A2J Author has the *map* tool. This tool creates a visual aid of any decision tree the developer creates (Figure 3.13.3).

The expertise of legal aid attorneys captured in an A2J Guided Interview must be communicated effectively to a customer base unfamiliar with law and legal process. When breaking down a complex legal process for a self-represented litigant, it is imperative that developers draft Guided Interview text in plain language. A2J Author has features that help the developer articulate attorney expertise clearly and concisely. The *report* tool assesses all text in the Guided Interview and provides a readability score from multiple indices, most notably the

---

[8] Figures 3.13.1 and 3.13.2 derived from A2J Author Guided Interviews; *see generally*, www.a2jauthor.org.

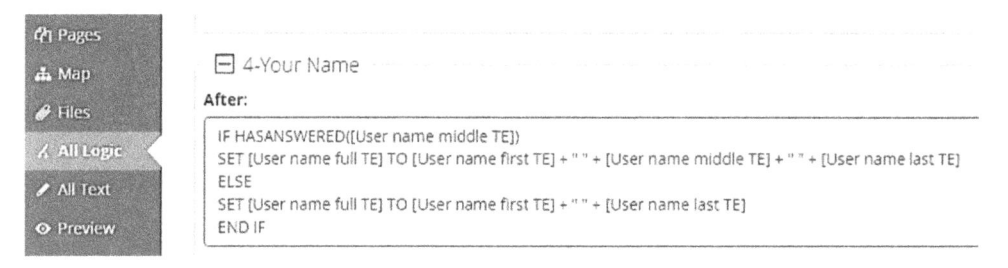

FIGURE 3.13.2 Conditional logic to determine the end-user's full name.

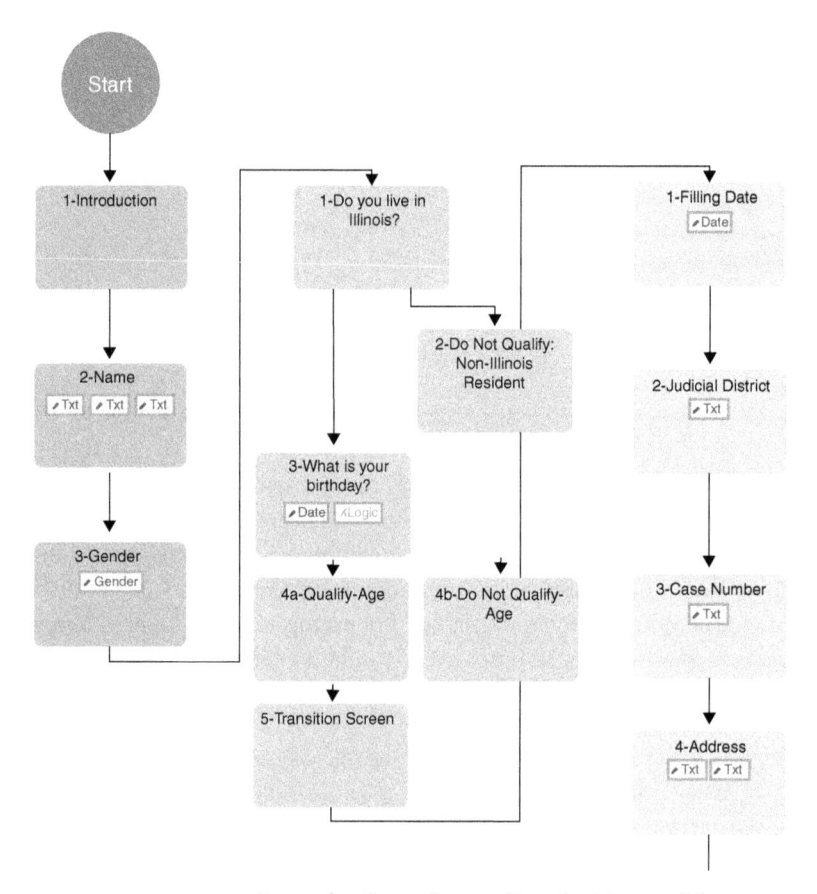

FIGURE 3.13.3 Example of map feature (i.e., decision tree).[9]

Flesch–Kincaid Grade Level and Reading Ease scores (Figure 3.13.4). The report also includes scores from the Gunning Fog, Smog, and Coleman–Liau Indices, as well as a total word count and average words per sentence.

Sometimes, however, legal aid users are unable to speak and read English well. Large populations of low-income people in the USA speak only Spanish, or one of a dozen other languages. A2J Author supports multiple languages for program-specific text, such as the progress bar (Figure 3.13.5). This allows a user to choose a display in one of over a dozen preselected languages. A2J Author does not, however, have an in-built translation feature, so to develop a Guided Interview for people who speak languages other than English, the Guided

---

[9] Figure 3.13.3 derived from A2J Author's map tool; *see generally*, www.a2jauthor.org.

Text Statistics

The F-K Grade for all questions and help in this interview is 7.2 (< 7 is Good)
Flesch Kincaid Grade Level: 7.2 and Reading Ease: 66.1; Gunning Fog Score: 10.1; Smog Index: 7.8; Coleman–Liau index: 11; Word Count: 2240; Average Words Per Sentence: 12.947976878612717

FIGURE 3.13.4 Report feature – readability score.[10]

Mi Progreso: Hola, bienvenido a A2J Author!

FIGURE 3.13.5 A2J Guided Interview progress bar in Spanish.[11]

FIGURE 3.13.6 Example of a question screen in A2J Author.[12]

Interview text must first be translated. The report tool can generate a transcript of the Guided Interview text, which can then be given to a translator.

Though A2J Author offers a robust authoring feature set, it is best known for its unique end-user interface. While other form automation programs also use rules and programming scripts to help users complete forms, A2J Author is the only program that visually situates the user within a recognizable visual setting: going to a courthouse (Figure 3.13.6). Framed as a metaphorical walk down a path toward a courthouse, A2J Guided Interviews display graphics that make the task of completing a legal form less daunting. The virtual guide avatar, user avatar, path, and courthouse reduce the intimidation users might otherwise feel if they had to answer the questions as written on a form.[13] Reaching the courthouse symbolizes successful completion of the form, which users may then print for later filing. Like an expert system, the program is designed to simulate a personal interview that a user might encounter in a legal consultation with a domain expert attorney. While a personal legal consultation may be out of reach for the user, the A2J Guided Interview models a personal interaction within a computer or mobile device screen. It represents a twenty-first century paradigm for legal services that places less emphasis on in-person consultations and more emphasis on delivering critical legal information through an accessible medium.[14]

[10] Figure 3.13.4 derived from A2J Author's reports tool; see generally, www.a2jauthor.org.
[11] Image derived from A2J Author, *supra* note 8.
[12] Image derived from A2J Author, *supra* note 8.
[13] Rochelle Klempner, "The Case for Court-Based Document Assembly Programs: A Review of New York State Court's 'DIY' Forms," *Fordham Urban Law Journal* 41 (4) (2015): 1190–1200.
[14] Jeanne Charn, "Celebrating the 'Null' Finding: Evidence-Based Strategies for Improving Access to Legal Services," *Yale Law Journal* 122 (2013): 2206, 2213.

In addition to being a front end for document assembly, A2J Guided Interviews can also be used as standalone guides or front ends for legal aid intake or court e-filing.[15] Answers to questions in an A2J Guided Interview are stored in extensible markup language (XML). Through this XML transformation, the data in an A2J Author answer file can be converted for use in an alternate XML format used by case management and electronic filing systems. This process can streamline legal aid intake by prequalifying applicants and, more importantly, screening out those who do not qualify. Reducing transactional friction is integral to lowering barriers to justice, and as more jurisdictions adopt mandatory e-filing in civil cases, there will be more opportunities to use A2J Author as a potential front end for e-filing.[16]

Historically, A2J Guided Interview developers needed to learn two software programs to create a unified self-help resource. A2J Author features a distinct and effective front end, but up until recently it did not have its own document assembly tool. Instead, a developer had to create a document assembly template in a separate program, HotDocs, and map the corresponding variables on the template to questions in the A2J Guided Interviews. The need for dual development in two separate software authoring environments made automating a suite of forms complex and time-consuming. A2J Author 6.0, the latest version, seeks to streamline this process by integrating its own Document Assembly Tool with a revamped front end. The same conditional logic applied within the Guided Interview itself can now also be applied to the corresponding template created in the Document Assembly Tool. There, a particular document can be inserted into the template based on the end-user's response to certain questions within the A2J Guided Interview. The first generation of the 6.0 Document Assembly Tool can create templates with non-complex formatting, and this capability opens the door for developers to create end-to-end solutions for simple documents like demand letters and uncomplicated pleadings.

Since 2005, A2J Author has successfully helped self-represented litigants complete important court forms. A2J Author has been used over four million times and has helped assemble over 2.5 million documents. To date, 42 states have posted A2J Guided Interviews on LHI for use by self-represented litigants. A2J Guided Interviews are also used by consumers in Canada, Australia, Puerto Rico, Guam, and the US Virgin Islands.[17]

One of A2J Author's most important attributes is that self-represented litigants can use it at various access points. Statewide legal aid portals – such as Illinois Legal Aid Online (ILAO) – have posted several A2J Guided Interviews for use on the web.[18] Additionally, mobile-responsive A2J Guided Interviews have been available on the LawHelp platform since April 2017. This is an important development, not only because of the nearly ubiquitous use of mobile devices, but also because a small but growing number of Americans are smartphone-dependent, only accessing broadband through their mobile device. Among those who are smartphone-dependent, a significant number are low-income individuals for

---

[15] See Ronald W. Staudt, "All the Wild Possibilities: Technology that Attacks Barriers to Access to Justice," *Loyola Law Review* 42 (2009): 1135–1139. For an example of an A2J Guided Interview used for legal aid intake, *see* the Iowa Legal Aid Online Application at: www.iowalegalaid.org/resource/introduction-to-online-intake?lang=EN. For an example of an A2J Guided Interview used as the front end for e-filing with a court, *see* the United States District Court for the Eastern District of Missouri E-Pro Se programs atwww.moed.uscourts.gov/e-pro-se.

[16] See, e.g., Supreme Court of Illinois, *In re: Mandatory Electronic Filing in Civil Cases*, M.R. 18368, available at: http://illinoiscourts.gov/SupremeCourt/Announce/2016/012216.pdf.

[17] A2J Author, "Where is A2J Author used?" available at: www.a2jauthor.org/where_is_A2JAuthor_used.

[18] See, e.g., ILAO, "Name Change for Adult," available at: www.illinoislegalaid.org/legal-information/name-change-adult.

whom A2J Guided Interviews may be particularly helpful.[19] For those without access to a personal computer or mobile device, A2J Author is also available for use at courthouse self-help kiosks. Visitors to the Self-Help Web Center (SHWC) at the Daley Center courthouse in Chicago, for example, can use one of the computers there to access A2J Guided Interviews, and can seek computer assistance from Chicago-Kent law students who staff the help desk.[20] In New York, the State's Access to Justice Program has enjoyed tremendous success through its use of A2J Author to create its "DIY Forms," accounting for 28% of form assemblies on the LHI server in 2016, or 138,730 total assemblies.[21]

Notwithstanding A2J Author's effectiveness at narrowing the justice gap, its ability to create a larger corpus of A2J Guided Interviews has been limited both by its small cadre of developers and by the small number of people who know how to use both A2J Author and HotDocs together effectively. Professor Ronald Staudt of Chicago-Kent College of Law, one of the authors of this chapter, sees law students as a new group of developers that could help enlarge the number of Guided Interviews for use by legal aid organizations and courts. In 2010, Professor Staudt offered the Justice & Technology Practicum for the first time at Chicago-Kent. A hybrid course, the Practicum has elements of a clinic, seminar, and legal writing course, and for their semester project students must develop an A2J Guided Interview for a legal aid organization or court. Students research the substantive legal issue, design a storyboard to map out questions, build the interview, and then test iteratively. Since the introduction of this course at Chicago-Kent, a dozen other law schools have experimented with curricula that incorporate instruction and use of A2J Author.[22]

Apart from creating more A2J Guided Interviews for public use, Professor Staudt's course, and the paradigm of incorporating A2J Author into other law school courses, has presented real educational benefits.[23] Students are assigned foundational reading for an overview of how technology has changed the way legal professionals provide services. Students learn technical skills through software immersion, which is particularly important since effectively leveraging technology has proven crucial to providing value in the legal services market. And while students currently learn how to use A2J Author as the signature software offering, in years past they also learned how to create document assembly templates in HotDocs, enabling them to develop methods for integrating different technology tools in service of a semester-long project. In a course with many components, including various project deliverables and software tools, students have also gained skills in project management at a time when legal project management and process improvement are gaining added importance in legal organizations.[24]

Students in the course also learn empathy and client-centered professionalism. Throughout the semester, they are required to complete fieldwork hours, which can be achieved through court observations or volunteering at the SHWC. The Justice &

---

[19] Aaron Smith, "Record Shares of Americans Now Own Smartphones, Have Home Broadband," Pew Research Center, January 12, 2017, available at: www.pewresearch.org/fact-tank/2017/01/12/evolution-of-technology.

[20] See Chicago-Kent College of Law's Self-Help Web Center at: www.kentlaw.iit.edu/institutes-centers/center-for-access-to-justice-and-technology/self-help-web-center.

[21] New York State Courts Access to Justice Program, "Working Toward 100% Meaningful Access to Justice: Report to the Chief Judge and the Chief Administrative Judge of the State of New York," 2016, available at: www.nycourts.gov/ip/nya2j/pdfs/NYA2J_2016report.pdf.

[22] Ronald W. Staudt and Andrew P. Medeiros, "Access to Justice and Technology Clinics," *Chicago-Kent Law Review* 88 (2013): 695, 715–717.

[23] Ibid.

[24] See, e.g., Roy Strom, "Legal Project Managers: The New Rainmakers?" Law.com, September 22, 2016, available at: www.law.com/sites/almstaff/2016/09/22/legal-project-managers-the-new-rainmakers.

Technology Practicum has served as a model for courses at over a dozen other law schools supported through the A2J Author Course Project, which provides monetary support for teaching A2J Author courses. These courses have helped to make a modest contribution to the number of A2J Guided Interviews available for use nationwide.

IV ONGOING CHALLENGES FOR ACCESS TO JUSTICE TECHNOLOGICAL PLATFORMS

As the foregoing case study illustrates, the technologies identified in this chapter are effective at narrowing the civil justice gap. Using these technologies, millions of people over the past several years have prepared their own court documents or other legal papers, and this success has been due to the combination of coordinated statewide websites, national software hosting services for document assembly templates, and an array of tools for building educational graphical interfaces and gathering information directly from low-income people. And from the case study we also know that these solutions scale to more than half a million uses per year.

Figure 3.13.7 shows the steady growth in A2J Guided Interview use on the LHI national server once the integrated set of technology solutions was rolled out in 2008. In 2009, 2010, and 2011, use nearly doubled each year. At that rate, some of us involved in these projects from the start had dreams of a "hockey stick" growth pattern that would yield four or five million uses a year by 2015.

The aggressive expansion of A2J Guided Interview use on LHI tapered off in 2012, and the rate of growth reversed entirely in 2015. National use of LHI grew again in 2016, but at a level that failed to match the height of usage that occurred in 2014. Early reports in 2017 point to a flat year, with use about the same as 2016, matching a level already reached in 2013. Achieving only 500,000 to 600,000 uses each year after 2011 is disappointing. While we know A2J Guided Interviews helped more than two million people in those four years, the pool of potential users was much higher, and we had hoped to reach 20 million.

What caused this plateau? There are several plausible explanations. Adoption of these three technologies has possibly hit the "chasm," the gap between early adopters and the early majority that often occurs when selling new technology.[25] This phenomenon would perhaps explain the plateau, but cannot explain the decline in 2015 or the slow recovery apparently starting in 2016 and extending into 2017.

A more focused study yields better answers. There were some specific problems in several states that caused large drops in growth, as well as large drops in aggregate use. Thousands of consumers in Texas, for example, were knocked off the system by a state decision to refocus document assembly efforts for court forms on the tool provided by its own court automation company. Texas simply turned off its successful A2J Guided Interviews, and Texas' use of its A2J Guided Interviews on LHI fell dramatically. The loss of the Texas consumer population closely maps to the 2015 decline, and due to Texas' size, may perhaps by itself adequately explain the first ever drop in total uses in that year. It would not, however, explain the slowing growth in 2012, 2013, and 2014. After usage growth of 40–50% in 2009, 2010, and 2011, the growth curve began to level off in 2012, long before Texas withdrew.

In 2012, LHI began to change its infrastructure, and this may have caused too many interruptions in the service to support growth among conservative new authoring prospects.

---

[25] Geoffrey Moore, *Crossing the Chasm: Marketing and Selling High-Tech Products to Mainstream Customers* (New York, NY: HarperBusiness, 2006).

The national template server, LHI, began a complete redesign of its infrastructure in 2013, an absolute necessity in order to scale to millions of uses per year. In its early years, the server depended on a patchwork of systems that needed to be streamlined and replaced with modern modular code delivered on a cloud infrastructure. Implementation of this redesign was complicated and time-consuming. Occasional interruptions of service were not uncommon during this retooling period. These infrastructure issues, and the subsequent outages during the redesign, might be related to the pattern of slowing growth starting in 2012. Still, these interruptions were quite modest in length of "down time." Statistics might even show *more* use caused by outages if the same customer were bumped off and thus had to start over, making two attempts to do what one uninterrupted sign-on would have accomplished.

At the end of the LHI redesign in 2016, a more robust and standardized server infrastructure was completed and delivered to the states and courts that were the primary consumers of LHI. While LHI had worked on its redesign, CALI led a multi-year effort to completely retool and reprogram a new version of A2J Author and the accompanying consumer interface. From 2014 to 2016, the programming team for A2J Author at CALI built two complete replacements for the Adobe Flash authoring system. In late 2016 and early 2017, CALI rolled out A2J Author 6.0, a cloud-based authoring system. This system features a mobile-responsive design that adapts to the devices of end-users, and it also had an early version of an integrated document assembly tool. On April 6, 2017, LHI's redesign and CALI's new system were presented to consumers, and LHI announced that beginning April 10, 2017, states would be able to upload A2J Author 6.0 Guided Interviews into the LHI production environment to make those interviews available for public use.

During the entire development period of A2J Author 6.0, the LHI server supported legacy Flash-based A2J Guided Interviews (version 4.0). LawHelp Interactive hosted approximately 1000 A2J Guided Interviews in version 4.0, and these were used between 500,000 and 600,000 times each year. The Flash-based A2J Guided Interviews were robust enough to support half a million uses; more importantly, no obvious constraint exists in the software that would stop user growth from running up to as many as 20 million. This may provide yet another partial explanation of the usage plateau. It is possible that the existing 1000 A2J Guided Interviews had reached a saturation point; there were only 500,000 to 600,000 annual users who needed the particular justice solutions embodied in those A2J Guided Interviews. To find new demand and increase the number of users of A2J, it may be necessary for new states to prepare forms and documents and other automated solutions for new consumers not already served by the 1000 currently existing interviews. The

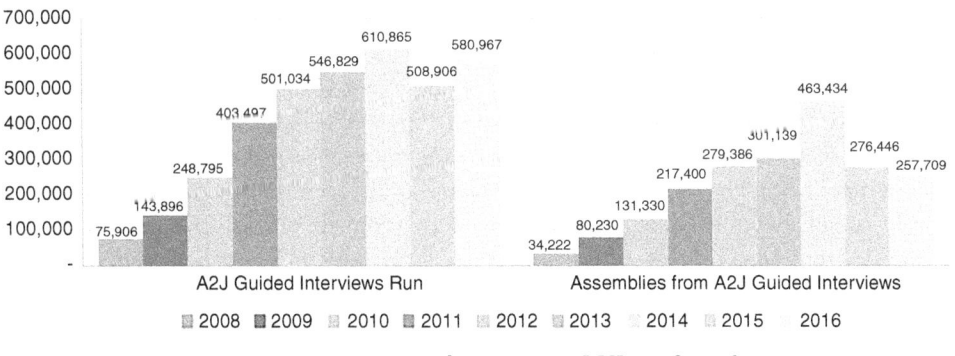

FIGURE 3.13.7 A2J Author usage on LHI, 2008–2016.

number of active A2J Author developers has always been limited. As described in the above case study, CALI and Chicago-Kent built courses and tried to stimulate authorship by using cash incentives for law schools to incorporate A2J Author into clinical and other courses. While more than a dozen law schools offered new courses with A2J Author integrated into the curriculum, the number of new A2J Guided Interviews developed by these faculty members and their students has been quite modest.

Yet another possible explanation for A2J's unforeseen slow growth could be that established authors simply held off on building new content. As explained above, from 2014 to 2017, CALI worked to create a new authoring system that was cloud-based, mobile-ready, and more reliable than the previous iteration. States and authors may have decided to wait for this new version to be released before investing in new systems for their consumers, thus blunting demand and enthusiasm among existing and potential developers of A2J Guided Interviews.

The atrophy in user population growth may have been because these technologies did not adapt rapidly enough to support mobile phones and tablets. As we pointed out earlier, half of potential low-income consumers of A2J Guided Interviews connect to the internet with a mobile device. But the first fully functional mobile-responsive viewer was only available with A2J Author 6.0, released in early 2017. While conversion of the existing library of 1000 state forms and documents to the new version of A2J Author is not difficult in most cases, it is still a barrier to easy access for the large population of mobile users. From the project's inception until early 2017, the consumer-facing A2J Author viewer was not mobile-responsive. New growth may not require new interviews, new marketing, or better outreach. The full conversion of all live A2J Guided Interviews to a mobile-ready application may be all that is required to restart the previously rapid growth of A2J Author usage.

V THE FUTURE OF LEGAL AID USING LEGAL INFORMATICS

The most important lesson taught by these examples, and by our speculation on the performance of these tools, is that the reasons for the observed use patterns, and the subsequent plateau of adoptions of A2J Guided Interviews by the low-income public, still elude us. This information gap makes it clear that data gathering has been weak and haphazard, a detriment to a better analysis of our data. We know the gross number of times that end-users from LHI called up A2J Guided Interviews, and we know whether or not a document was generated by LHI after the end-user completed the interview. That is about as far as our data goes. Both HotDocs and A2J Author 4.0 were fire-and-forget applications. Once a customer called up the A2J Guided Interview from LHI, there was no interaction with that customer unless the customer asked to save answers or launch a document.

We need more specificity. For example, assume that a critically important divorce A2J Guided Interview had a confusing or offensive set of questions in the middle of the interview that caused many users to abandon the interview out of irritation or frustration. Current data on customer behavior cannot identify that problem. The data currently available cannot even provide insight about the impact of unreliable internet connections, server instability, or lack of a device-responsive display of the interviews. Interviews are launched from statewide websites that keep some data, probably analyzed by Google Analytics. LawHelp Interactive keeps some data on the number of existing templates, on the A2J Guided Interviews stored by each state, and how often each interview is called each month and how often a document is assembled from each use. However, a lot more information is needed for us to be able to fine-tune this multilayered justice solution.

James Greiner, head of the Access to Justice Lab at Harvard Law School, has authored most of the experimental work examining the operations and effectiveness of the current legal aid delivery systems. He is emphatic in urging legal aid leaders to gather better information about the tools and the techniques currently used to deliver legal aid to the poor:

> "We need to know more about outreach and intake. The implementation, coherence, and results of the systems LSPs [Legal Services Programs] rely on to address the extreme scarcity that characterizes all aspects of the civil legal assistance system depend on something about which we know almost nothing. Under such circumstances, we have as much hope of having a modestly effective civil legal assistance system as a stopped clock has hope of telling the correct time. For a community that purports to care about the population it services, such a situation is intolerable."[26]

It is similarly intolerable to be so completely ignorant of the operation, processes, and customer behavior inherent in the successful technologies we have arrayed to serve the poor. One benefit of the cloud-based solution at the heart of A2J Author 6.0 is the ability to track and store every keystroke in every customer interaction with a Guided Interview. The next step is for us to gather this data and other corresponding data that can help explain the impact of our investments in technology to serve the needs of the poor. We know millions have been served. Now it's time for us to find out how to ramp up demand, scale the delivery of services, cross the innovation chasm, and make the product attractive to any and all potential users. The hurdles ahead are far from insurmountable. Donors and taxpayers, but most importantly the low-income people in need of access to justice, want a system that works, and works well. We owe it to those in need of help to get this right.

---

[26] D. James Greiner, "What We Know and Need to Know About Outreach and Intake by Legal Services Providers," *South Carolina Law Review* 67 (2016): 287, 294.

3.14

Designing Legal Experiences

Online Communication and Resolution in Courts

Maximilian A. Bulinski and J. J. Prescott[1]

I INTRODUCTION

Technological advancements are improving how courts operate by changing the way they handle proceedings and interact with litigants. Court Innovations is a socially minded software startup that enables citizens, law enforcement, and courts to resolve legal matters through Matterhorn, an online communication and dispute resolution platform. Matterhorn was conceived at the University of Michigan Law School and successfully piloted in two Michigan district courts beginning in 2014. The platform now operates in over 40 courts and in at least eight states, and it has facilitated the resolution of more than 40,000 cases to date.[2] These numbers will continue to grow as new categories of disputes and other legal matters become eligible for online management and resolution and as more court systems recognize the economic and social benefits of adopting online platform technology.[3] This case study chronicles the development, implementation, and refinement of Matterhorn.

Implementing software in the legal world can be cumbersome, especially when adoption requires the coordination and agreement of multiple public entities with overlapping – but not identical – goals. We hope that by sharing the story of Matterhorn's creation and growth over the last few years, we can light the way for the next generation of court-focused technology and e-governance tools, especially those that relate to the criminal justice system. We also hope to offer valuable lessons for transitioning ideas for progress into realized change.

First, we outline the social problem that Matterhorn was initially designed to address – minor warrants – and how that focus led to Matterhorn's now-broader aim of improving court access generally. Second, we describe Matterhorn and how it works in practical terms. Third, we present an analysis of the platform's underlying design philosophy and objectives. Fourth, we address two challenges that Court Innovations encountered and overcame in implementing Matterhorn in a variety of courts with diverse stakeholders. We conclude that Matterhorn has demonstrated the value of using online platform technology to resolve disputes in courts and has succeeded in producing measurable improvements in court accessibility and efficiency.

---

[1] Prescott is a co-founder and equity holder of Court Innovations Inc., a University of Michigan startup that develops and implements online case resolution systems.
[2] For current information on where Matterhorn operates, visit www.getmatterhorn.com.
[3] See Maximilian A. Bulinski and J. J. Prescott, "Online Case Resolution Systems: Enhancing Access, Fairness, Accuracy, and Efficiency," *Michigan Journal of Race & Law* 21 (2016): 205, 249.

II THE INSPIRATION

In Michigan, over one million arrest warrants were active as of 2014.[4] Although some of these warrants sought the arrest of individuals accused of committing felonies, the majority were what we refer to as "minor warrants" and were issued for something much less serious and even mundane:[5] either failing to appear in court to deal with a minor legal issue or failing to pay a court-ordered fine.[6] On this score, Michigan is no outlier among the states; in fact, there are other state court systems that issue even more minor bench warrants on a per capita basis.[7]

Again, these "minor warrants" are not search warrants or arrest warrants for serious crimes. A failure to appear in court or to pay a court-ordered fine, while certainly not laudable, does not carry the same social condemnation as does a traditional or even minor criminal act. Nevertheless, warrants for these minor failures still have significant economic and social consequences for people. The threat of arrest and the confusion about how to resolve the situation leads people with outstanding warrants to avoid police, courtrooms, and other government officials.[8] People with warrants are less likely to report crimes and serve as jurors or witnesses in legal proceedings, and are more likely to withdraw from public life by refraining from voting or engaging in civic activities.[9]

People typically resolve minor warrants by physically entering a courthouse and effectively self-surrendering. This is a trickier process than many people might expect. Even after overcoming the associated fear and confusion and any other barriers to appearing in court, the wait to see a judge is often lengthy and of uncertain duration. If someone is unable to pay or has no credible reason for missing a court date, showing up to court with a failure-to-appear or failure-to-pay warrant outstanding can result in arrest.[10] Even in courts where incarceration is rare, arrest and detention are still real possibilities, and people often believe that they will be arrested if they self-surrender without sufficient resources to pay what they owe or a good explanation for their failure to appear.[11] The prospect of being arrested at the courthouse conjures up images of missing work, losing employment or benefits, and being unable to take care of family. It is therefore unsurprising that many people decide against physically appearing in court to attempt to resolve an outstanding minor arrest warrant.

---

[4] Brad Heath, "For a Million Fugitives, Freedom Starts at County Line," *USA Today*, 2014, available at: www.usatoday.com/story/news/nation/2014/08/06/fugitives-las-vegas-wont-pick-up/13607595.

[5] *Id.*

[6] *See* Daniel J. Flannery and Jeff M. Kretschmar, "Fugitive Safe Surrender: Program Description, Initial Findings, and Policy Implications," *Criminology & Public Policy* 11 (2012): 437, 449.

[7] At the extreme end of the spectrum, the municipal court of Ferguson, Missouri, issued over 9000 warrants in 2013 in cases stemming in large part from minor violations such as parking infractions, traffic tickets, or housing code violations. The population of Ferguson is roughly 21,000. Civil Rights Div., US Dep't of Justice, "Investigation of the Ferguson Police Department" March 4, 2015: 12. Outstanding minor warrants are an issue in many states. "To take just a few examples: The State of California has 2.5 million outstanding arrest warrants (a number corresponding to about 9% of its adult population); Pennsylvania (with a population of about 12.8 million) contributes 1.4 million more; and New York City (population 8.4 million) adds another 1.2 million." *Utah v. Strieff*, 136 S Ct. 2056, 2073 (2016) (Kagan, J., dissenting). Michigan's population is currently just under ten million. Kristi Tanner, "Michigan's Population Increased for the Fifth Straight Year in 2016," *Detroit Free Press*, December 20, 2016, available at: www.freep.com/story/news/local/michigan/2016/12/20/michigan-population-increase-census/95631726.

[8] *See* Meagan Cahill, "Focusing on the Individual in Warrant Clearing Efforts," *Criminology & Public Policy* 11 (2012): 473, 476.

[9] Barry H. Weinberg and Lyn Utrecht, "Problems in America's Polling Places: How They Can Be Stopped," *Temple Political & Civil Rights Law Review* 11 (2002): 401, 431.

[10] Flannery and Kretschmar, "Fugitive Safe Surrender," *supra* note 6, at 446.

[11] *Id.* at 449.

These long-standing warrants are clearly problematic for the people facing them, but courts would also like to resolve these lingering cases. The number of cases resolved by a court, and the speed and efficiency with which judges and court staff resolve them, can affect the perceived success of the court.[12] Moreover, outstanding court debt usually has implications for a court's budget, as courts are often partially funded by the fines and fees they collect.[13] Thus, courts are usually happy to forego arrest and work with people who have minor warrants to identify a mutually beneficial way to resolve the dispute.

Yet even though resolving these warrants has benefits for both litigants and courts, and even though resolving them should be painless, relatively few of them are actually resolved in a timely way, if at all. If people with warrants are fearful and therefore unwilling to self-surrender, law enforcement must expend resources to locate, apprehend, and bring these individuals to court. This is a problem, though, because the execution of these warrants is a low priority for resource-pressed police departments focused on more serious crime in their communities, and courts are likewise unable to afford more active ways of resolving these cases. Thus, many warrants that could easily be resolved if individuals and judges could communicate with each other in a low-risk, low-cost way instead remain outstanding for months or years.

In response, some courts have developed amnesty programs to help reduce the number of outstanding minor warrants.[14] But amnesty programs can be costly and time intensive, and there is a limit to how often they can be used without sapping the legitimacy of court orders. Forgiveness, although helpful to the people whose warrants are waived or treated favorably, is only a temporary and somewhat arbitrary patch that fails to address the real problem: the significant hurdles that keep people from using courts to resolve their cases.

Minor warrants are undoubtedly a significant issue nationwide, but in an important sense, warrants are just the tip of the iceberg. Working with courts and other stakeholders soon made it clear that Matterhorn had the potential to do far more than address the deluge of minor warrants in the USA. It was poised to enhance access to justice generally. To see this, consider that by the time an unpaid fine becomes a warrant, a person has already struggled, sometimes for months, to address the legal issue that underlies the warrant. These are usually legally straightforward disputes – such as traffic or parking tickets, or disagreements over property or income tax assessments – but they present outsized difficulties for community members and constitute an important court-access issue themselves.[15] Some individuals may not be able to use their courthouse's resources effectively because they have a rigid employment schedule or cannot make alternative family-care arrangements. Limited access to affordable transportation or a disability can present additional obstacles to accessing a courthouse, both physically and financially. And even if a person manages to make it to court, they may struggle to

---

[12] At a minimum, a large number of outstanding warrants or other matters that take a long time to resolve make a court *appear* less administratively efficient and therefore less successful.

[13] Arthur W. Pepin, "The End of Debtors' Prisons: Effective Court Policies for Successful Compliance with Legal Financial Obligations," presented at the *Conference on State Court Administrators*, July 25–29, 2015, Omaha, NE.

[14] Amnesty programs are often run in community centers, churches, or other "safe" places. *See, e.g.*, James Orland, "Warrant Amnesty Programs," OLR Research Report, 2016, available at: www.cga.ct.gov/2016/rpt/2016-R-0315.htm.

[15] *See* Bulinski and Prescott, "Online Case Resolution Systems," *supra* note 3, at 217–235; Monica Llorente, "Criminalizing Poverty Through Fines, Fees, and Costs," American Bar Association, October 3, 2016, available at: www.americanbar.org/groups/litigation/committees/childrens-rights/articles/2016/criminalizing-poverty-fines-fees-costs.html.

resolve the issue in a single visit. Often, people discover the lines are too long, they come on the wrong day or at the wrong time, or they do not have the proper paperwork.[16]

Because of these hurdles, many people have no practicable way to contest or negotiate what amounts to a government accusation made against them in the form of a tax assessment, a civil infraction summons, a family court show-cause hearing, or a minor misdemeanor charge.[17] The same is true of a claim made against someone by a private party in a small claims setting. And even if someone is able to resolve their case in front of a judge, the social problem remains that using courts to address relatively minor issues requires considerable industry and an enormous outlay of resources before a judge and a court user can interact one-on-one.

Clearly, logistical and social impediments often make it challenging for citizens to resolve warrants, civil infractions, and minor misdemeanors before a judge in a physical courthouse. Unresolved legal issues can become a social problem, especially when jurisdictions allow unpaid civil fines to transition into arrest warrants. These disputes are relatively easy to rectify if a litigant and a judge can communicate in person, even if just for a few moments, but arriving at this final stage often requires great effort and sacrifice for the litigant – relative to the stakes of the legal issue – as well as significant time and coordination effort on the part of judges and court staff. As a result, this meeting too often does not happen. If and when it does happen, it has almost always been a long and costly slog for both sides.

Matterhorn's premise is that online technology can facilitate the dispute resolution process by reducing communication and coordination costs between courts and citizens. To that end, Matterhorn offers an online environment in which people with pending legal issues can converse with judges (or prosecutors, police, other parties, etc.) in an efficient and structured way, and contest, negotiate, and resolve claims that affect them without fear of arrest or the inconvenience and costs of accessing a brick-and-mortar courthouse.

III HOW MATTERHORN WORKS: THE BASICS

At its core, Matterhorn is an online platform that allows citizens to communicate with judges, prosecutors, law enforcement, and other decision makers, as well as other private parties. The primary goal of this communication is to resolve an existing legal matter accurately and efficiently, so the structure of the platform directs communication toward that end. During this communication, there may also be other intermediate aims – such as educating litigants, collecting case information, and giving citizens an opportunity to record their views on a case – all of which may be valuable even if the case is not resolved through the system.

Matterhorn is easy to use and understand, but the specific variant of Matterhorn a litigant will experience depends on the facts of the case, the type of case, the court, and possibly the judge. For example, resolving an active minor warrant may only require communication with a judge (who may ask different questions than another judge), whereas resolving a civil infraction or minor misdemeanor will regularly include law enforcement or prosecutorial

---

[16] The costs of unresolved legal issues tend to grow exponentially over time, as citations lead to bench warrants and exploding financial penalties when litigants fail to appear in court or negotiate an agreement with the court on how to resolve their outstanding debt. People who accrue multiple outstanding warrants will face even higher access barriers (e.g., greater fear of arrest), making them even less likely to appear in court as the situation escalates, which in turn increases courts' administrative burdens.

[17] For many, the ultimate difficulty is affording the court-ordered fine. Failure to pay fines (if one has not demonstrated their inability to pay) usually leads to the issuance of a warrant and its associated costs and other consequences. See Civil Rights Div., supra note 7, at 3, 42.

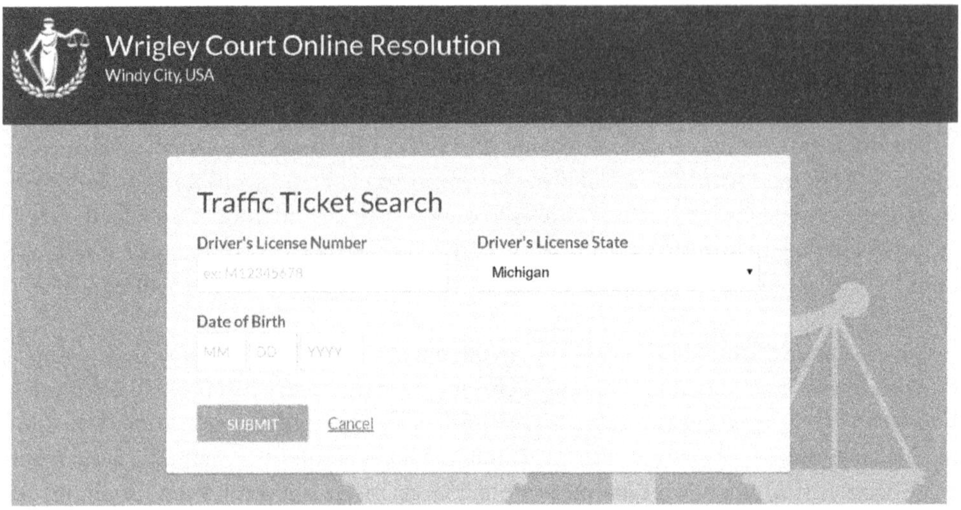

FIGURE 3.14.1 Matterhorn litigant access.[18]

participation in addition to judicial involvement. Despite this heterogeneity, it is possible to provide a basic overview of how litigants access Matterhorn, what Matterhorn does, and how decision makers interact with litigants through the platform.

To begin the resolution process, a litigant must access Matterhorn from the court's website. Once there, a litigant must search for their case using identifying information such as their driver's license number (Figure 3.14.1). Matterhorn uses the entered information to search active databases for cases that pertain to the individual in question. If the search locates any open cases, the platform applies criteria formulated by the relevant court or judge to these matters to determine which of them, if any, are eligible for online resolution. Eligibility criteria typically relate to the nature of the offense and the litigant's previous interactions with the justice system.

If a case is eligible for online resolution, Matterhorn presents the litigant with their procedural options (Figure 3.14.2). These options typically include doing nothing, retaining the option of going to court in person to resolve the matter, and seeking an online review of the case in the hopes that communicating with a decision maker will result in a favorable outcome. When litigants choose to use Matterhorn to attempt to resolve their legal issues, the system establishes a communication channel with individuals by asking them to provide their contact information (e.g., email address or mobile phone number), so the court can electronically deliver information, instructions, requests, and/or any decisions to them at a later point in time.

Matterhorn next presents the litigant with a series of questions and requests and collects the litigant's responses. Matterhorn is configurable, which means a court's requests can target any information deemed relevant to how a decision maker processes or decides a case. The court and its judges design these queries with the needs and obligations of the court in mind, and question content is specific to the facts and law of the case. These inquiries can be "smart," appearing only when they are relevant based on answers to previous questions. One uniformly included request directs litigants to provide a statement explaining their reasons for accessing the court using Matterhorn – i.e., the remedy they seek, such as an offense reduction or the

---

[18] Figures 3.14.1–3.14.3 derived from Matterhorn, used with permission.

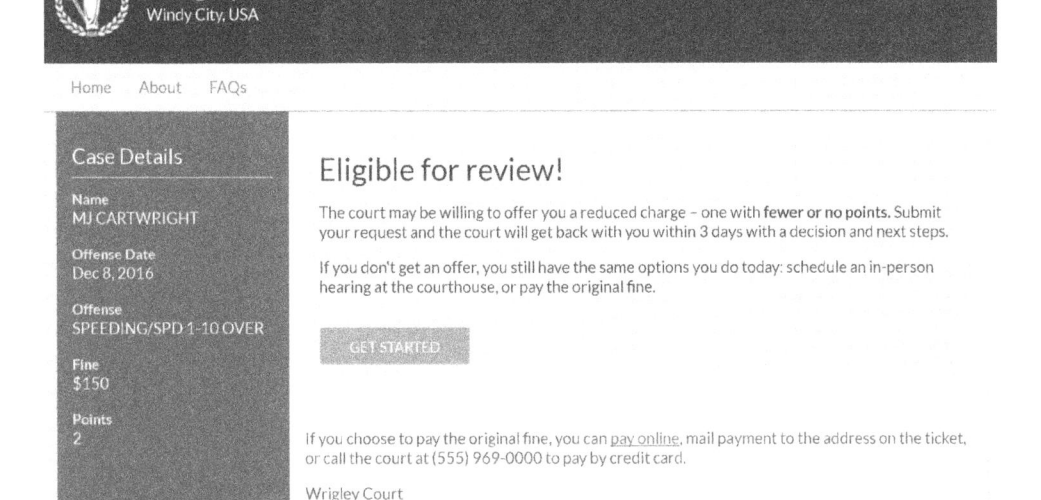

FIGURE 3.14.2 Eligibility for review.

withdrawal of an outstanding warrant – and why they believe their application should be granted.

The stage concludes with the system informing litigants that any offer of resolution (e.g., a reduced fine amount) is conditional on compliance (e.g., paying the new fine amount promptly). Once the case has been submitted through Matterhorn, it is presented digitally and directly to a court clerk, prosecutor, law enforcement officer, magistrate, or judge – whomever is appropriate for the court, the type of case, and the facts of the case. These decision makers then determine how to resolve the request based on the data presented to them by Matterhorn, including information submitted by the litigant, records already in the case file, or data compiled from other germane databases (Figure 3.14.3). Often relevant in a traffic case, for example, are the specifics of the charged infraction, the surrounding circumstances, the content of the request, the litigant's past infractions, and the litigant's interactions with the court via the system.

Finally, Matterhorn notifies the litigant of the decision. If the decision maker wishes to resolve the case by making an offer (e.g., a reduced sanction), Matterhorn provides the litigant with the option to accept or reject the decision maker's proposal. If the litigant accepts, the system directs the litigant to comply as soon as possible (e.g., pay any prescribed fines or fees via a link to the court's online payment portal). If the litigant declines the decision maker's offer – or accepts it but does not comply with its requirements within the time frame specified by the court or judge – the system automatically rescinds the offer, informs the litigant of the rescission, and restores the original charge. This latter outcome returns the litigant to the status quo ante, as if the online proceeding had never occurred.

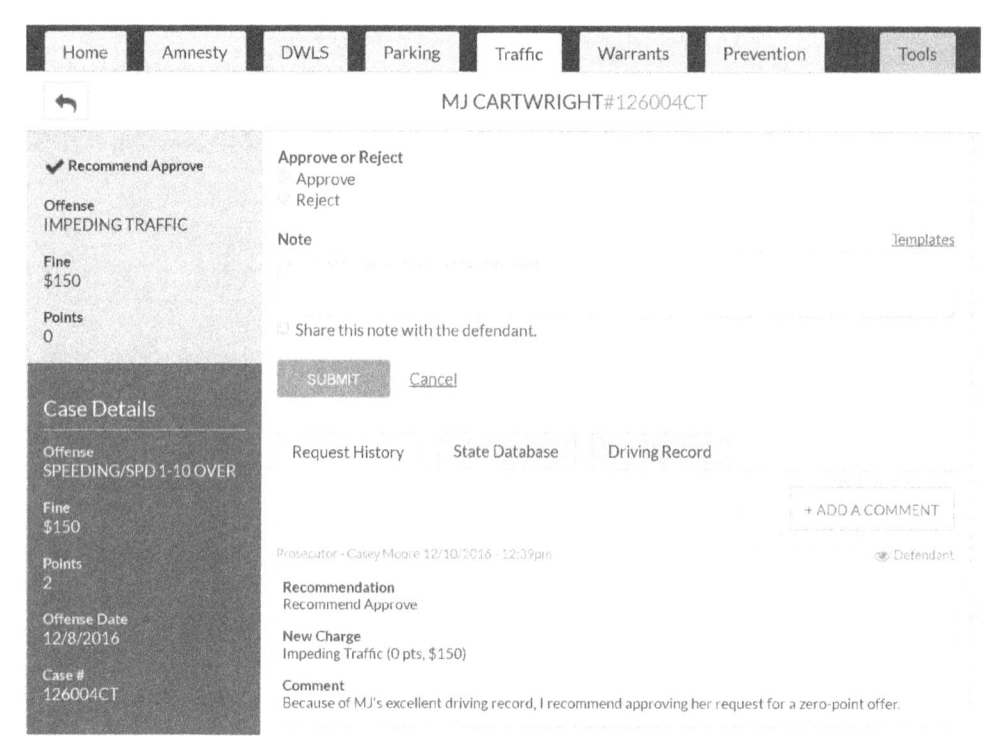

FIGURE 3.14.3 Judge's reviews of a litigant's request.

IV DESIGN PHILOSOPHY AND GOALS

Matterhorn was fashioned to make courts – and therefore justice – easier to access and to improve the efficiency and accuracy of legal outcomes. Accomplishing these goals requires that both litigants and decision makers perform their essential roles in resolving disputes easily, quickly, and well. Improved performance, in turn, requires replacing or eliminating extraneous features of the system that are now outmoded for some types of disputes.

In today's courts, people find it difficult to address and resolve even minor legal issues. Many of these difficulties involve barriers to accessing the courthouse, fear or confusion related to appearing in court in person, and the inability to take time off from work or other responsibilities to visit a courthouse during its business hours. Technology can help people overcome these difficulties most of the time.[19] In the end, the critical one-on-one stage with a judge or other decision maker – during which a litigant conveys substantive concerns and contentions, seeks understanding, answers material questions, presents relevant evidence, and chooses how to proceed – is the only stage *necessary* to fairly and accurately resolve a legal dispute. For this reason, it seems logical that litigants should have a communication platform of some kind that decision makers find useful and credible.

---

[19] Many of the challenges of access to justice that relate to getting to the courthouse can be avoided entirely if a one-on-one, in-person interaction with a judge is no longer considered essential. Likewise, fear of arrest if one presents oneself to the court disappears for all but those who might view an online platform as a means by which the government can discover their location and arrest them. Other barriers (e.g., confusion about the legal issues involved in one's case or the difficulty in conveying one's views to a judge) change and likely improve, but do not disappear.

Matterhorn seeks to enhance litigants' ability to provide information and evidence that is material to an issue, express their opinions and make their arguments, understand their options, and ultimately resolve or manage the dispute. In place of an inefficient courthouse, Matterhorn offers a simple, easy-to-use online interface with straightforward instructions and targeted information requests specific to a case or claim. The platform's goal is effective communication with decision makers, and these features all work toward that end. Matterhorn is available at any time from any mobile device and allows a litigant to communicate with a decision maker asynchronously. A litigant can respond to a communication from a court via Matterhorn at night after his children have gone to bed, and the judge can respond in the morning during normal business hours. Matterhorn also incorporates reminders of upcoming deadlines and offers guidance on procedures and resources. These features help to mitigate, or even eliminate, the traditional burdens of going to court.

Many district judges, for their part, face a never-ending stream of minor cases to resolve, sometimes dozens or hundreds in a day. Even minor delays or inefficiencies in scheduling, accessing case information, waiting for someone to speak, and dealing with confusion and fear can waste hours per day. Waiting, repeating directions, searching for information, recording a decision in longhand, even banging a gavel – not one of these acts is essential to "judging."[20] These administrative tasks may plague a judge's day, though, and the ability to complete such tasks is not why society values judges – or why, for that matter, a voter chooses one judge over another. What is critical is that judges learn the facts and the law relevant to resolving the case at bar, weigh the arguments and evidence, and then make a decision that will hopefully end the dispute. Society relies on judges to make judgments, not to recite rules by rote or file administrative paperwork.

If technology can alter or replace the outmoded exoskeleton originally constructed to support the essential decision-making process, judges will have greater capacity to handle tougher cases, enabling them to better fulfill their core functions as judges. In the remainder of this section, we describe how the Matterhorn platform has been structured to enhance the efficiency and accuracy of judicial decision making.[21]

If rendering legal determinations is the heart of what judges do, the first step in building a successful platform is to ask how judges approach decisions in minor cases. Judges face a high volume of minor cases, so they often make their legal determinations quickly based on little information. Given their time constraints, this approach is understandable: Judges struggle to keep up with their caseloads if they spend more than a few moments on each case.[22] To succeed, judges commonly employ rules of thumb, but the specifics of these rules

[20] Admittedly, judges serve other public functions, and making or at least announcing noteworthy decisions in person in open court – regardless of the content of the substantive decision itself – may also be important. Even so, in the context of an uncountable number of minor issues that are individually of no interest to the public, rendering an accurate and fair decision is ultimately the touchstone of the judge's role.

[21] Matterhorn was built to provide many of the same benefits to judges and other decision makers as it does to litigants. Judges can access the platform from anywhere, and the technology is quick and easy to use on their end as well. Matterhorn is highly configurable to a judge's individual preferences, eliminating many efficiency losses that result from structures that are designed to accommodate the desires of the average or median judge. Perhaps most important, judges can handle cases more quickly because in-person process inherently involves delay and diverse approaches to how evidence is presented. Judges must necessarily entertain irrelevant arguments and evidence, sifting through them for the relevant tidbits.

[22] The size of most traffic judges' dockets makes it infeasible to spend more than a few moments on a case without falling substantially behind. *See, e.g.,* Bobby Allyn, "Speeders Have Made Milwaukie's Municipal Court the Busiest in Clackamas County," *The Oregonian*, November 18, 2010, available at: www.oregonlive.com/milwaukie/index.ssf/2010/11/speeders_have_made_milwaukies_municipal_court_the_busiest_in_clackamas_county_1.html.

can vary significantly across courts and judges.[23] At the same time, judges may also desire information beyond what a case file contains, despite the fact that the standard approaches to obtaining such information – such as asking the litigant to provide a document or answer a question – may prove either too costly or too time intensive to justify whatever value it might afford to the judge's decision-making process. Moreover, dissecting new documents or other sources of potentially useful information can be cognitively challenging, and judges may pass up the opportunity to access and use additional information when the costs of doing so exceed the benefits.

Matterhorn cuts through this laborious process, enhancing judicial decision making and enabling judges to thrive within the constraints of their institutional role. Matterhorn endeavors to free judges to spend more of their time actually judging by providing them many of the same benefits that it offers to litigants as well as giving them the power to configure their decision-making environment to suit their own judicial philosophy, preferences, experience level, and skill set. Matterhorn's goal is not to make courts more efficient at the expense of judicial discretion and flexibility or by somehow automating the decision-making process. Rather, its goal is to make judging more efficient and accurate while leaving a judge's discretion intact. Matterhorn is thus easy to use and customizable by design, and was created with the view that technology should empower, not constrain, decision makers. Specifically, by supporting effective gathering, filtering, and delivery of information, Matterhorn frees judges to spend much more of their time deliberating and eventually arriving at better judgments.[24]

A *Gathering Information*

With respect to more effectively gathering information, Matterhorn takes as given that judges often receive very little information when making decisions, especially in minor cases. Matterhorn's development team regularly speaks with judges, prosecutors, and other decision makers about how best to provide them with more useful information and in a more useful format, while avoiding useless detail and visual clutter that will serve only to distract the decision maker and delay or distort the decision.

What information would judges like to know when deciding, for example, whether to reduce a charge? Currently, judges have limited access to court-related data from outside of their districts, including relevant information about the parties. The amount of shared data depends in large part on the organization of the courts. A unified court system is one in which a state has effectively consolidated many local courts into one all-encompassing court system that is centrally governed, usually with shared software and data systems. In states that have unified court systems, data availability may be less of an issue, but central management of data does not necessarily mean that courts will have access to the full spectrum of that data. The information may only be available to the central administrative agency and not incorporated into the daily operations of courts. In non-unified systems, the problem is even worse.

---

[23] In the context of mediating a traffic ticket, for example, some judges may be willing to agree to the reduction of a ticketed charge to a less severe infraction if the litigant has accrued no more than three tickets in the past few years. For other judges, though, the number may be only one ticket over the same period. See Richard A. Ginkowski, "Traffic Court 101: Practical Pointers from the Bench," *Criminal Justice* 29 (2014–2015): 11, 13.

[24] The benefits of enhanced decision making redound not only to citizens facing outstanding warrants, traffic fines, and the like, but also to those with matters that are more complicated and require in-person, traditional procedures and hearings. With Matterhorn, judges can spend less time on minor cases and therefore more time on cases and issues that require their sustained attention and expertise.

Different courts may utilize different software and data standards, resulting in different methods of data collection and record-keeping. Thus, even if two neighboring district courts want to share their data, they are likely to run into technical compatibility challenges right at the outset.

Michigan, where Matterhorn was first implemented, lacks a unified court system. However, as is the case with some other states, Michigan does have a statewide data repository, the Judicial Data Warehouse (JDW), that aggregates specific data from district courts across the state and translates them into a common format to make it possible to assemble cross-court comparisons.[25] Although the JDW has proven to be useful for state-level court administrators who are interested in analyzing statewide trends and evaluating the relative performance of individual courts on certain metrics, district courts appear rarely to use JDW data, and generally there is no practical way for judges to access data from other courts for use in their decision making. Courts in Michigan and in many other states effectively operate in information silos.

Thus, Matterhorn was designed against a background in which judges in traffic cases often make decisions based solely on a paper print-out of a litigant's driving record and what is written on the ticket by a police officer, and in which judges make decisions about canceling minor warrants without being able to check whether the individual in question has outstanding warrants in other district courts. Early versions of Matterhorn sought to improve the information resources of judges by incorporating useful JDW information into the judicial dashboard. Later versions of Matterhorn integrated Michigan's driver and driving history information into the platform, making critical information easy to digest and immediately accessible to judges.

Judges also have no ability to access data from any of the dozens of other government databases that exist in Michigan and in other states, many of which contain information that is pertinent to common judicial inquiries. For example, judges often evaluate an individual's ability to pay court-assessed fines and fees, and may consider whether to allow the person to comply with an obligation via a payment plan.[26] Other state agencies collect data on individual income, employment, receipt of public benefits, and more, all of which are relevant to ability-to-pay determinations and structuring payment plans. But if judges want such information, courts must collect it by hand on a case-by-case basis from each litigant. The process is daunting for all parties. It precludes many litigants from making otherwise reasonable requests and, even when they do, it often circumscribes the information judges have available to them in making these common, yet important, decisions.[27]

Matterhorn offers a richer data environment in which judges need only exert minimal effort to integrate more useful information into their decision-making process.[28] From a technical standpoint, incorporating data into the platform from another source in

---

[25] Michigan Courts, "Technology: Supporting Timeliness, Efficiency, Access," available at: http://courts.mi.gov/education/stats/dashboards/pages/dashboard-jdw-why.aspx.

[26] See Meghan M. O'Neil and J. J. Prescott, "Targeting Poverty in the Courts: Improving the Measurement of Ability-to-Pay Fines," Law & Contemporary Problems 82 (1) (2019): 199–216.

[27] Ibid. Court Innovations has recently piloted an online Ability-to-Pay Assessment Tool which, despite not linking directly to other government databases, does streamline and standardize the data collection and analysis processes while at the same time making it easier for litigants to request relief from court-ordered debt.

[28] Matterhorn is also capable of automating and delivering *analysis* of data that decision makers consider relevant to the resolution of a case. To illustrate, if courts have access to data from other districts and other relevant agencies, Matterhorn can present useful comparative or predictive information that may improve judicial decision making. Rather than just evaluating an individual's driving record through the prism of their own experience, judges might prefer to compare the record of the driver to *all* other drivers in the district, county, or state, or use all driving records and traffic safety data to predict how likely the litigant in question is to be involved in a driving accident in the next year, for example.

a scalable way is not very difficult. But there are other hurdles. Obtaining permission from relevant agencies or other data "owners" can be challenging for a host of reasons. Stakeholders have raised privacy concerns, and agencies may be wary of giving data to developers who operate as private companies. The permission and access problem is compounded if information needs to flow both ways. For example, if Matterhorn pulls data from a source regarding a litigant's history (e.g., past infractions) to inform a judge's decision, this source may need to be updated *ex post* to account for the judge's eventual finding. The combination of technical, procedural, and political concerns about how, when, and where data can flow across agency and court boundaries complicates implementing court-related software like Matterhorn.

B Filtering Information

When it comes to filtering the information presented to a judge, Matterhorn seeks to improve the decision-making environment in at least two ways. First, Matterhorn can reduce cognitive overload and information fatigue by curtailing the delivery of irrelevant information, which might delay and perhaps skew the outcome of a case. Second, Matterhorn is configurable, meaning that judges and other decision makers can modify how Matterhorn works to fit their preferences, such as specifying the precise information litigants are required to provide to the court, altering how cases are flagged, and streamlining how information is presented so that each judge has only what is needed and only when it is needed. We turn now to how Matterhorn approaches these filtering tasks.

Although limited access to pertinent information may be an obstacle to high-quality and efficient decision making, minimizing the availability of irrelevant information to decision makers is also important to well-functioning courts. Simply put, reading documents or examining data that have been made part of a case file for the sake of completeness, but that are irrelevant to resolving the issue at hand, takes time and can distract and exhaust a decision maker.[29] Cognitive resources are limited, and decision making can become less accurate as judges fatigue.[30] By structuring the decision-making environment to minimize the waste of judicial attention, Matterhorn both speeds up and improves the accuracy of case resolution.

Obscuring irrelevant information in the decision-making process can also reduce bias – and the perception of bias – in the judicial system. One well-documented source of distrust of the legal system is the perception that judges themselves are biased (whether explicitly or implicitly) in their decisions because of their awareness of a litigant's race, gender, appearance, or social class.[31] Matterhorn's ability to structure what judges "see" means that information that is socially charged or likely to produce bias can be removed from view. How this is done can be determined at the judge, court, or case level. Assigning a judge a case file replete with all relevant information, but stripped of any irrelevant or potentially prejudicial information, may work to restore public faith in the fairness of courts. If people trust judges, court personnel, and the judicial process itself, they are more likely to participate in the justice

---

[29] John Tierney, "Do You Suffer from Decision Fatigue?" *New York Times*, August 17, 2011, available at: www.nytimes.com/2011/08/21/magazine/do-you-suffer-from-decision-fatigue.html.

[30] Shai Danziger, Jonathan Levav, and Liora Avnaim-Pesso, "Extraneous Factors in Judicial Decisions," *Proceedings of the National Academy of Sciences* 108 (17) (2011): 6889, 6890.

[31] *See* Richard R. W. Brooks and Haekyung Jeon-Slaughter, "Race, Income, and Perceptions of the U.S. Justice System," *Behavioral Sciences & the Law* 19 (2001): 249, 251–252.

system and comply with its commands.[32] Procedures that build trust of this sort effectively remove a barrier to access; they keep people coming to court to resolve their issues.

Matterhorn's configurability also helps courts manage case volume by allowing judges to automate certain judge-specific preferences. For example, judges can choose *ex ante* which cases will be presented to them through Matterhorn and which require a face-to-face setting. Furthermore, if a court or a judge has criteria for determining whether a litigant must appear in court or instead can address the dispute using Matterhorn, these eligibility rules can be implemented directly within Matterhorn. Judges can also configure Matterhorn to emphasize certain case characteristics considered important to a case's resolution so they are not overlooked, and judges can even directly implement individualized decision rules that turn on those characteristics (e.g., automatically providing a litigant found in violation of a law with the judge's individual explanation of how a particular law works). Thus, judges can use Matterhorn to buttress their individual approaches to judging, allowing them to avoid reinventing the wheel for each case, and therefore resolve cases more quickly and accurately.

To see how judges can use Matterhorn's configurability to better manage dockets, consider the following scenario: Three judges in a district have different standards for when they will even *consider* reducing a charge to a lower offense. Judge A will consider anyone who has three or fewer tickets in the past six months. Judge B contemplates offense reduction only for individuals who have not had a ticket in the past month. Judge C takes a long-term view and considers reducing charges for anyone who has had fewer than five tickets in the past two years. Satisfying a judge's criterion may not be a sufficient condition for the judge to offer a reduction, but it is a necessary condition before the judge will consider other factors. Among those cases the judges will consider, there are some that are closer calls and others for which the outcome, based on a judge's sanctioning philosophy, is obvious.

How much time should each judge spend evaluating the driving record of Jane Smith, who had three tickets last month? Does the answer depend on whether last month was a typical or atypical month for Jane? A computer algorithm can quickly inform these judges where Jane falls, given their rules, and whether they should take time to consider adjusting her ticket. Judge B will presumably deny the request and can configure Matterhorn to alert him to the issues he considers dispositive. That way, he will not waste time reviewing other aspects of the case. Judges A and C will presumably look at the case more closely, perhaps configuring Matterhorn to highlight other case characteristics – and, importantly, not necessarily the same characteristics – that the judges view as relevant in a case like Jane's.

In all cases, Matterhorn enables judges to do what it took them longer to do, and with less consistency, without Matterhorn. Still, the varying approaches the three judges take toward cases raises an important philosophical issue: Is it *fair*? Should similarly situated individuals expect equal outcomes regardless of the judge they are assigned and the court in which they appear? Our legal system trusts that judges are knowledgeable and deserving of discretion in managing their dockets and making judgments, and it explicitly contemplates that judges may hold different perspectives on the efficacy of different approaches to punishment and civil sanctions. Even so, social or political tolerance of variation of this sort presumably has limits, and Matterhorn can help us better understand and perhaps police its scope.

Regardless of whether judges should make more uniform judgments, Matterhorn presents opportunities to improve how decision makers function. If judges ought to be free to structure their decision-making environment, Matterhorn can make their lives easier and their

---

[32] Sara C. Benesh, "Understanding Public Confidence in American Courts," *Journal of Politics* 68 (2008): 697, 704.

decisions more consistent by eliminating the repetitive administrative tasks of gathering the information the judge considers relevant and removing or obscuring data that the judge considers likely to distract, delay, or prejudice. But if consistency *across* judges is important, sharing how each judge uses Matterhorn with other judges (or with the public) may nudge their decision-making philosophies toward some shared norm.[33]

Judges may be unfamiliar with how their approach to resolving cases compares to how other judges operate in their roles beyond what is dictated by statute. In the process of formalizing these judge-made eligibility and decision rules and standards for implementation within Matterhorn, judges in courts using Matterhorn have been made privy to other judges' assumptions, and to the information other judges feel they need in order to make accurate decisions. Formalizing these ideas into a software platform can encourage conversations between judges and across courts about their relative merits. By enabling judges to become more aware of how their fellow judges exercise their discretion, Matterhorn encourages communication and learning among judges as to the logic underlying their varied methods, perhaps prompting some to adapt and hopefully improve their approaches.

C Delivering Information

With respect to delivering information, once the appropriate informational content for a particular case and judge is determined, Matterhorn can augment decision making by delivering this content instantaneously in ways designed to improve understanding and reduce inefficiency. These delivery improvements include not just flexibility in how judges receive case information – on their cell phones, tablets, etc. – but also the conscious exploration and use of strategies designed to improve a judge's experience, increase comprehension, reduce fatigue, and so on. Matterhorn's future trajectory will likely include ongoing incremental refinements designed to reduce the time and energy judges spend on activities that are *not* judging, so the public can maximally benefit from their expertise.

V IMPLEMENTATION CHALLENGES

Once Matterhorn's design philosophy and goals were ironed out, the many technical and training-related aspects of implementing Matterhorn in courts proved to be relatively simple. These undertakings included constructing the platform, teaching court users to use and understand the platform, configuring the platform to fit varying court preferences, and integrating the platform with other software and data sources already in use. Potential concerns in these categories were easy to predict and navigate. Matterhorn's key implementation challenges thus became: (1) convincing courts and other stakeholders of the value of Matterhorn and ultimately swaying them to adopt it; and (2) ensuring the availability of Matterhorn to citizens as a way of accessing justice and inducing them to use it.

A Persuading Courts to Adopt Matterhorn

Designing, marketing, and implementing technological change in public sector institutions differs in important ways from creating and implementing technology for the private sector.

---

[33] Of course, if it were desirable, court administrators or state supreme courts could use Matterhorn to impose greater consistency across judges by homogenizing the information environment and eligibility criteria and by making these choices public.

In particular, persuading *courts* to pilot and commit to new solutions, especially technological ones, requires lining up a lot of ducks, and in some cases identifying, convincing, and leveraging a champion from within the courts to bolster the effort.

Generally, government organizations move at their own pace.[34] Courts have historically been slow to enact litigant-oriented institutional change.[35] Although judges, especially chief judges, have significant control over their courthouse's administration,[36] they are already familiar and comfortable with how their courts work. They have developed their own approaches to their dockets, and though their methods may not be perfect, they generally get the job done. Moreover, we do not typically imagine judges as savvy business types who focus on balance sheets, customer service, and efficiency. Judges think of themselves as jurists; they interpret laws, decide cases, and do justice. Judges also understand at some deep level that courts are essential government services and therefore will never go out of business. Accordingly, reform and technology adoption tend to proceed slowly in courts.

That said, courts do have a bottom line. They face the market pressure of competing government priorities and are often assessed using quantitative metrics. Judges are public officials, and government waste is rarely popular with voters. Furthermore, judges independently value providing high-caliber procedures and accurate outcomes, and so will often consider even costly reforms that are capable of improving the quality of their court's work. Therefore, even if judges are typically averse to change, it may be surprising when courts are slow to adopt even technology that seems to check every box by reducing costs, saving the time and effort of court personnel, and providing swifter and more accurate justice. Courts were particularly hesitant initially to adopt Matterhorn for two reasons: (1) political risk and legal uncertainty; and (2) consensus-oriented management and the involvement of other stakeholders.

Judges appear to view new technology as politically risky. This is particularly true for technology that at first seems complicated or that could potentially alter case outcomes in unexpected ways.[37] Judges, whether elected or not, are public officials, and may be particularly sensitive to the possibility of *public* failure.[38] Unlike most court technology, Matterhorn is technology that litigants – members of the public – use. If it works poorly, constituents may punish a judge at the polls. Chief judges might also worry about the career and social consequences of failing in front of their judicial peers. Judges likely fixate on the worst-case scenario; even when there is a strong possibility of the technology making their processes significantly better, judges may conclude adoption is not worth the risk.

A corollary to the idea that judges fear public failure is the idea that judges fear making an embarrassing *legal* mistake. From Matterhorn's beginning, judges have worried that the platform's approach may not be lawful or, even if lawful, might be at odds with the spirit of certain laws. These judges have feared that implementation might generate a response from the legislature that would undo their efforts. For example, a couple of judges have expressed concerns in casual conversations that hearings may technically be defined as "in-person" events, though court rules often do not specify and are open to interpretation. Matterhorn is

---

[34] James Joyner, "Why Government IT Sucks," Outside the Beltway, October 13, 2013, available at: www.outsidethebeltway.com/why-government-it-sucks.

[35] Consider the adage, "if it's not broken, don't fix it."

[36] *See generally* Catherine D. Perry, "From the Bench: Lessons Learned as a Chief Judge," *American Bar Association Litigation Journal* 38 (1) (2011).

[37] *See* "The 'C.S.I. Effect'," *The Economist*, April 22, 2010, available at: www.economist.com/node/15949089.

[38] *See* Adam Liptak, "Judges Who Are Elected Like Politicians Tend to Act Like Them," *New York Times*, October 3, 2016, available at: www.nytimes.com/2016/10/04/us/politics/judges-election-john-roberts.html?_r=0.

innovative, and seems in some ways to be an obvious way to improve how courts operate. For some judges, it seems too good to be true, and the sheer fact that Matterhorn is not *already* in place is interpreted as evidence that Matterhorn must violate some rule, and they worry they risk revealing ignorance about the nature of that constraint if they adopt it without explicit permission from someone with authority.

Consequently, Court Innovations has from the very beginning worked hard to persuade courts that Matterhorn is in fact compliant with the law, including local court rules and relevant state statutes. Matterhorn's earliest adopters hesitated to consider Matterhorn for fear of running afoul of a rule or statute because, in that case, subsequently *reforming* court rules or state statutes to be consistent with Matterhorn's use would presumably require a significant investment of time and resources. Over time, Court Innovations has been able to address these concerns either through software design or collaborative legal research, and no conflicts or difficulties with court rules or state statutes have emerged to date. Nor has Court Innovations had to seek legislative reform or other sorts of rule changes.

Another obstacle to implementation concerns how courts make decisions to innovate, especially when those decisions require the acceptance, if not the enthusiastic endorsement, of other stakeholders, such as prosecutors. Even excluding outside partners, if a chief judge is confident that a software solution will be beneficial, but other judges are skeptical or court personnel are wary, adoption is at least likely to be significantly delayed. Although a few courts have a single chief judge who can simply choose to change a process or adopt new technology, many courts essentially operate by consensus. The democratic nature of consensus-driven courts makes them slower to adopt new technologies; getting everyone on board consumes a lot of effort and time, which some chief judges may decide is simply not worth it.

Matterhorn is not merely technology for use in the internal management of courts; it is also intended to facilitate litigant communication with parties other than judges and court personnel. The adoption and implementation process therefore requires the buy-in of prosecutors, city attorneys, law enforcement, and other entities. Every court operates in a unique way, and each court may interact with many prosecutors' offices and law enforcement agencies. To make matters more complicated, the set of relevant stakeholders may differ from one type of case to another. For each case type (other than warrants), coordinated acceptance by at least several of these outside agencies appears necessary both for Matterhorn to be useful in a sufficiently large number of cases and to lend legitimacy to the court's decision to use the software. Figuring out whom to approach, and when, is its own strategic puzzle that takes time to solve.

A final hurdle to adoption by courts is rooted in judges' discomfort in using unfamiliar technology and in a common initial assumption that Matterhorn "resolves cases" for courts on its own, eliminating decision makers from the process, or at least downgrading their role. In reality, Matterhorn does nothing of the sort. Matterhorn's *sine qua non* is to enhance and improve decision making, not to replace it with some computer-based algorithm. Overcoming this misinterpretation of Matterhorn's goals and operation has required thinking about how best to frame the way Matterhorn works, and to emphasize that the platform is configurable to the point of allowing a judge to decline to use Matterhorn altogether. In other words, stressing that judges are always in control, and that the platform is simply a tool that improves decision making and ultimately makes judges better, has proven to be critical.

B Persuading Citizens to Use Matterhorn

Even a well-designed online platform for resolving legal issues will fail if citizens do not use it. There are a few dimensions to this problem. First, Matterhorn was designed in part to benefit a group of citizens with whom courts have no current connection (e.g., individuals with outstanding minor warrants). How do you make these potential users aware of Matterhorn's availability? Second, even when a means of communication exists, citizens are busy and typically already have a preconception of what it means to go to court – that is, physically walking into a courthouse. A mention of a new online option in a letter or in the small print on a ticket may not be sufficiently conspicuous. Third, Matterhorn operates as an *additional* means of accessing courts. Litigants retain all the traditional options and can still choose to come to court in person or simply ignore their issue if the platform does not seem fair or easy to use.

One of the chief aims of Matterhorn has been emptying the ocean of outstanding minor failure-to-pay and failure-to-appear bench warrants in this country. These warrants result from a person's earlier inability to resolve a legal issue in a timely fashion. Law enforcement or courts can often confirm or collect a litigant's physical mailing address when the issue originally materializes (e.g., when someone receives a ticket alleging an infraction), but it is common for socioeconomically disadvantaged people to move frequently,[39] and so by the time a bench warrant is issued (often because the person is unable to pay a legal fine), courts regularly cannot reach the litigant in question – even with the good news of a new way to access the court and resolve their delinquent obligation online. An ongoing challenge for Matterhorn, therefore, has been making the public aware of its availability. This is critical because even a flawless interface will fail if citizens are unaware of it.

Increasing awareness of Matterhorn has been complicated. Although traditional advertising can theoretically reach a large audience, it is often expensive and can fail to convey the critical message.[40] Public service announcements are a clear precedent, but there is also something that feels a bit untoward about courts, which are funded by taxpayers, taking out advertisements.[41] People with warrants might smell a trap, and others might be suspicious because courts are dependent on fines and fees. Overall, though, the primary limitation is resources. In a world with unlimited resources, targeted advertising and educational campaigns would do wonders.[42] But in the real world, the stumbling block continues to be how to most efficiently get the word out to the right people in a format they can understand and trust.

This hurdle is exacerbated by the fact that Matterhorn has not yet been adopted across an entire state. Instead, it has been implemented court by court, following an S-curve adoption pattern.[43] Furthermore, courts that have adopted the software are often geographically dispersed, and many court districts are small (generally, tied to county lines or even smaller). This produces two problems. First, broad advertising will reach citizens who do not yet have

---

[39] Rebecca Cohen and Keith Wardrip, "Should I Stay or Should I Go?," Center for Housing Policy, 2011: 3, available at: http://mcstudy.norc.org/publications/files/CohenandWardrip_2009.pdf.

[40] *See* Elaine K. F. Leong, Xueli Huang, and Paul-John Stanners, "Comparing the Effectiveness of the Web Site with Traditional Media," *Journal of Advertising Research* 38 (1998): 44, 53.

[41] *See* James L. Gibson, Jeffrey A. Gottfried, Michael X. Delli Carpini, and Kathleen Hall Jamieson, "The Effects of Judicial Campaign Activity on the Legitimacy of Courts: A Survey-based Experiment," *Political Science Quarterly* 64 (2010): 1, 10.

[42] *See, e.g.*, "The Real Cost Campaign," FDA, January 19, 2017, available at: www.fda.gov/TobaccoProducts/PublicHealthEducation/PublicEducationCampaigns/TheRealCostCampaign.

[43] *See generally* John M. Golden, "Innovation Dynamics, Patents, and Dynamic-Elasticity Tests for the Promotion of Progress," *Harvard Journal of Law & Technology* 24 (47) (2010): 83–84.

access to Matterhorn. Second, issues might not always occur in a citizen's residential district, and most citizens interact seldom enough with the courts that it is easy for them to get confused about courthouses and districts, and which options are available where. Wide advertising efforts such as public radio service announcements, television advertisements, or social media announcements may confuse or frustrate the public if they reach counties that have yet to adopt the software, or reach individuals who have access to Matterhorn at some courts but not others. These techniques may well increase awareness of Matterhorn generally, and even drive court interest in adoption, but on the whole, broad messaging is a mixed bag.

An alternative to widespread advertising of Matterhorn is to notify litigants directly. Posting notices in courthouses is one logical way to go about this, but it may undercut some of the efficiency gains of the platform. If a litigant must come to court to find out that they may not have had to come to court, some will be understandably irritated – but not as irritated as they might be if they then leave the court and attempt to log in at home, only to find that their case is not eligible to be resolved online. Thus, notice must be carefully crafted or occur in a way that encourages litigants to experiment with Matterhorn in a low-stakes way.

But appearing in court to resolve an outstanding issue is not the first interaction that an individual has with the legal system. In traffic cases, for example, a person is issued a citation. At least for new cases, a paper citation is an opportunity to inform citizens about the availability of Matterhorn, and to this end, Court Innovations has partnered with law enforcement agencies to print information about Matterhorn on traffic and parking tickets. This is a more direct way to inform only the most relevant people, and to reach them before they have invested time, money, and effort heading to a court or before they have given up because the costs of accessing justice are too high. Using tickets or summons is also more cost-effective than many other options like reaching out through community groups or sending mailers.

On the other hand, this approach is far from perfect. Many citizens do not read the small print,[44] and many legal issues do not involve a form of communication at the outset of the dispute. Court Innovations continues to make efforts to make printed information more salient and to devise strategies to reinforce this notice, such as encouraging police officers to inform citizens verbally of the availability of Matterhorn.

Besides, awareness of Matterhorn-like technologies alone is hardly sufficient to ensure that most or even many people will use them to access courts. For a system to succeed, it must be accessible to the public, trusted, and easy to use. Usability and user acceptance testing are therefore critical components of successful platform implementation.[45] Questions evaluated during testing include: Do people understand what they are doing? Is the software credible? Do they understand where they are in the process and the status of their case at any point in time? If they are not native English speakers, does the software seamlessly translate into their preferred language? Would they recommend it to a friend or family member? And perhaps most importantly: Do they feel that they were heard?[46]

There are many legal considerations as well. Implementation responsibilities include staying in compliance with and abreast of changes to relevant regulations, for example.

---

[44] See, e.g., Andy Greenberg, "Who Reads the Fine Print Online? Less than One Person in 1000," *Forbes*, April 8, 2010, available at: www.forbes.com/sites/firewall/2010/04/08/who-reads-the-fine-print-online-less-than-one-person-in-1000/#2d92c4307017.

[45] Abhijit A. Sawant, Pranit H. Bari, and P. M. Chawan, "Software Testing Techniques and Strategies," *International Journal of Engineering Research and Applications* 2 (2012): 980, 985.

[46] Bulinski and Prescott, "Online Case Resolution Systems," *supra* note 3, at 231.

The US Department of Justice is increasingly interested in how web interfaces, either government-based or privately hosted, meet emerging accessibility requirements, particularly with regard to the Americans with Disabilities Act.[47] A well-designed user interface requires an unwavering commitment by software designers to abandon their own notions of the "right" design or approach and to engage in frequent, aggressive user testing that employs a variety of methods to discover the most effective approach for different audiences.

One of the primary motivations behind Matterhorn's design was enabling people to go to court when they otherwise would be unable to do so. But, lamentably, not everyone has access to the internet, and if citizens are unable to access the platform via the internet, an online solution is limited in its ability to increase access to the justice system and courts specifically. This poses both practical and philosophical problems.

The first step in addressing this challenge is measuring internet access in the relevant populations to determine the extent of the lack of internet access. The digital divide has been well documented, of course,[48] but fortunately it has narrowed significantly in recent years.[49] Moreover, internet use among minority groups is rapidly approaching parity with the rest of the nation.[50] Smartphone ownership trends also indicate that the digital divide is becoming less of a problem over time.[51] In a recent survey, the number of mobile phone users who own internet-enabled smartphones increased by almost 10% in a single year,[52] with more than 50% of adults in the USA having access to the internet through their phone in 2013, and significant growth occurring at the lower end of the income distribution.[53] Designing internet solutions is valuable, but as this data shows, accessibility can be enhanced by ensuring that the technology can be used on mobile devices. This will only become more true over time. Accordingly, Matterhorn has been fully functional on mobile devices from day one.

The digital divide appears to be closing, particularly with the rise of smartphones, but there will always be people who lack the means to access new technologies. Developers should be mindful of disparities in internet availability and consider the implications for tools that are designed to improve access to justice for those who are often disadvantaged or disenfranchised. A system that benefits some portion of the population and puts no one in a worse position is a good thing from some perspectives. But if not everyone is able to experience the gains from a system, technology designed to enhance access may aggravate disparities and seem unfair,[54] which is a principal concern when dealing with courts and the opportunity to be heard.[55] For this reason, Court Innovations continues to work to ensure that Matterhorn is

---

[47] Jonathan Lazar and Harry Hochheiser, "Legal Aspects of Interface Accessibility in the U.S.," *Communications of the Association for Computing Machinery* 56 (12) (2013): 77.
[48] *See, e.g.*, Council of Economic Advisers, *Mapping the Digital Divide* (Washington, DC: Council of Economic Advisers, 2015); *see also* US Census Bureau, "Measuring America: A Digital Nation," March 23, 2016, available at: www.census.gov/library/visualizations/2016/comm/digital_nation.html.
[49] *See* Pew Research Center, "Internet/Broadband Fact Sheet," January 12, 2017, available at: www.pewinternet.org/fact-sheet/internet-broadband.
[50] *Ibid.*
[51] Bulinski and Prescott, "Online Case Resolution Systems," *supra* note 3, at 236–237.
[52] *Ibid.*
[53] *See* Aaron Smith, "Record Shares of Americans Now Have Smartphones, Own Broadband," Pew Research Center, January 12, 2017, available at: www.pewresearch.org/fact-tank/2017/01/12/evolution-of-technology.
[54] *See generally* Kentaro Toyama, *Geek Heresy: Rescuing Social Change from the Cult of Technology* (New York, NY: Public Affairs, 2015), 49.
[55] At the same time, Matterhorn may approximate a second-best solution, given the difficulties many face when trying to access justice at courthouses. Currently, many citizens have effectively no access to our justice system as a result of its outmoded design and reliance on physical courthouses. Systems that differentially improve the lot of those disadvantaged by the existing arrangement may reduce disparities on the whole.

broadly available to all segments of the population – especially those who suffer the most from limited access – through one's computer, a public computer, one's smartphone, or even a friend's smartphone.

Implementing Matterhorn has been an adventure for Court Innovations. Progress has required time, patience, and imagination. Overall, the technological issues have been predictable, generic, and relatively easy to resolve. Convincing judges, prosecutors, law enforcement, and the public to embrace and use Matterhorn, however, has proved far more challenging (though perhaps not more than was expected). Nonetheless, Court Innovations has made great progress. Along the way, it has discovered unexpected dimensions to more predictable implementation impediments, and has also managed to work out creative solutions to manage these issues, offering lessons that will be useful to those who seek to innovate and improve our justice system.

VI CONCLUSION

Matterhorn enables citizens to communicate with judges, prosecutors, law enforcement, and other decision makers, including private parties, to resolve legal issues. Court Innovations conceived of Matterhorn to target the large volume of outstanding minor warrants in this country, but quickly realized that such a platform could also generally improve court access and efficiency and enhance the decision-making environment of judges. In many ways, Matterhorn is sensible and predictable, and undoubtedly all courts will eventually use platforms like Matterhorn. Indeed, by many metrics, Matterhorn has already transformed the courts in which it currently operates: default rates are lower, cases close faster, and litigants report better access.[56] Nevertheless, court technology is a difficult area in which to successfully innovate. Persuading judges to use Matterhorn and alerting the public to its value have been significant obstacles. Court Innovations' success, however, demonstrates that progress is possible, and its story offers useful lessons for future innovators.

---

[56] Court Innovations, "Online Resolution Outcomes: Putting Court Access Technology to Work," 2016: 3, available at: http://getmatterhorn.com/static/Matterhorn_Outcomes_White_Paper_2016.pdf; J. J. Prescott, "Improving Access to Justice in State Courts with Platform Technology," *Vanderbilt Law Review* 70 (2017): 1993–1994.

PART IV

Legal Informatics in the Industrial Context

A.

Challenges Facing Innovation in Law

4.1

Adaptive Innovation

The Innovator's Dilemma in Big Law

Ron Dolin and Thomas Buley[1]

Big Law has been described as being in the throes of a painful transformation brought about by factors such as globalization, the increased use of technology, and a transition from a supply-driven market to a demand-driven one. A common framework for such upheaval is Clayton Christensen's *The Innovator's Dilemma*, which generally portends an inevitable collapse of market incumbents when they cater to the performance requirements of their high-value customers' demands.[2] Big Law is not immune to the principles of *The Innovator's Dilemma*. However, neither the disruptive nor sustaining innovation described in Christensen's work seem to adequately characterize the changes occurring. In this chapter, we describe a hybrid model, *adaptive innovation*, that takes into account the opposing forces in play. As with most other sectors, lawyers have argued that Big Law is different.[3] This chapter reviews some of the most cited factors predicting and denying the demise of Big Law. We argue that market-imposed values such as quality, efficiency, and ROI will likely dominate over reputation and comprehensiveness, forcing a fundamental change in many common features of Big Law. However, law firms will likely remain an inevitable mechanism for the delivery of services, albeit under a different model.

I INTRODUCTION

In the summer of 2013, Norm Scheiber heralded "The End of Big Law" in a controversial cover story in *The New Republic*.[4] Spotlighting Mayer Brown as a representative of Big Law more broadly, Scheiber described an unsustainable law firm model racked with in-fighting, threats of partner flight, and unsatisfied associates. Scheiber is not alone in highlighting the headwinds facing the industry, and the zeitgeist suggests that Big Law is on the brink of

---

[1] This work was originally done through Stanford Law's Center on the Legal Profession. Disclaimer: Dolin is an angel investor in legal technology and invests in some of the companies discussed in this chapter. The authors would like to acknowledge the assistance of Stephanie Kimbro for her contribution to this chapter.
[2] Clayton M. Christensen, *The Innovator's Dilemma: The Revolutionary Book that Will Change the Way You Do Business* (New York, NY: HarperBusiness, 2011).
[3] We define "Big Law" as those law firms that are among the top 200 by revenue or number of lawyers. Another workable definition is firms of 500+ lawyers whose clients include Fortune 100 companies for common corporate and litigation services. Note that while, to date, most/all Big Law firms work with Fortune 100 companies, it is not clear that firms employing hundreds or thousands of lawyers will not increasingly work within lower-cost consumer law frameworks similar to H&R Block, or other consumer-oriented law, like Jacoby & Meyers (www.jacobymeyers.com).
[4] Noam Scheiber, "The Last Days of Big Law," *The New Republic*, July 21, 2013, available at: www.newrepublic.com/article/113941/big-law-firms-trouble-when-money-dries.

collapse.[5] *The American Lawyer's* annual rankings of firms' profitability paints a different picture of the industry: Firms are watching their profits-by-partner return to, or exceed, pre-crisis levels, and even the much maligned Mayer Brown saw record profits for 2013, the year of its profile in *The New Republic*.[6]

Among the commentary on the future of Big Law and legal services have been calls for the industry's "disruption," in the parlance made famous by Clayton Christensen of Harvard Business School. Legal technology companies like LegalZoom threaten to undermine the traditional delivery of legal services, while legal process outsourcing (LPO) companies such as Axiom[7] have worked to take rote work like document review or e-discovery away from law firms.[8] Even Christensen has noted the disruption of Big Law embodied in the development of in-house legal departments to handle matters that normally would have been assigned to outside counsel.[9]

Christensen, in his seminal work *The Innovator's Dilemma*, identifies "sustaining" and "disruptive" as two distinct classes of innovation. *Sustaining innovation* allows incumbents to better serve their high-value customers, making it difficult or impossible for new entrants to get a footing in an established market. *Disruptive innovation* – where a business uses a new methodology and/or technology to focus on creating a new market or on providing low-cost alternatives to lower-value customers – often overtakes established players who do not react fast enough to compete. As noted by Christensen, established companies in every industry have argued that their industry is unique and thus they are not amenable to disruptive competition.[10] We ask the question as to whether Big Law is distinguishable in some fundamental structural way that renders it immune from typical notions of disruptive innovation. We argue that Big Law seems to be characterized best as a hybrid on an innovation spectrum – what we call "adaptive" innovation – that would leave some form of Big Law in place, while potentially vastly restructuring much of its current common elements.

We will first review Christensen's disruptive innovation framework and identify Big Law's structural defenses to disruption. We then contextualize adaptive innovation and offer examples of its nascent existence in Big Law. Finally, we address what Big Law could be doing additionally, and what it stands to gain from embracing adaptive innovation.

II DISRUPTIVE INNOVATION AND *THE INNOVATOR'S DILEMMA*

In *The Innovator's Dilemma*, Christensen identifies two innovative forces in the market: sustaining and disruptive innovation. Sustaining innovations improve existing products or services according to accepted notions of performance, and, regardless of the identity of the first mover, benefit the established incumbents in a particular industry. Disruptive

---

[5] See, e.g., Scheiber, *ibid.*; see also Larry E. Ribstein, "The Death of Big Law," *Wisconsin Law Review* 749 (2010); see also Steven J. Harper, *The Lawyer Bubble: A Profession in Crisis* (New York, NY: Basic Books, 2013); see also Richard Susskind, *The End of Lawyers? Rethinking the Nature of Legal Services* (Oxford: Oxford University Press, 2010).

[6] Ross Todd, "Mayer Brown: Record Profits Follow Some Bad Press," *The American Lawyer*, April 28, 2014, available at: www.law.com/americanlawyer/almID/1202651706664/?slreturn=20180723133225.

[7] www.axiomlaw.com.

[8] See also Daniel Fisher, "Legal-Services Firm's $73 Million Deal Strips the Mystery from Derivatives Trading," *Forbes*, February 12, 2015, available at: www.forbes.com/sites/danielfisher/2015/02/12/legal-services-firms-73-million-deal-strips-the-mystery-from-derivatives-trading.

[9] Clayton Christensen, Dina Wang, and Derek van Bever, "Consulting on the Cusp of Disruption," *Harvard Business Review* 91 (10) (2013): 106–150.

[10] Christensen, *The Innovator's Dilemma*, supra note 2.

innovations, on the other hand, are usually less effective in terms of existing performance metrics, but offer different attributes that attract a different segment of the market by redefining quality metrics.[11] The disruption occurs when these cheaper, less powerful products evolve to the point of capturing mainstream customers, displacing incumbents, often redefining concepts of performance. For an illustration of the difference between the two types of innovation, consider camera technology.[12]

Film-based cameras differentiated themselves ultimately in the quality of the pictures the camera could take based on the lens quality, available shutter speeds, and intrinsic film quality, for example. Digital cameras came onto the market taking pictures whose quality was considerably worse than that of film, but redefined the relevant performance metrics to include the ability to view pictures instantly on a screen and later triage which pictures to print after reviewing them on the camera or a computer. This new performance metric helped capture a new segment of the market – those who wanted "good enough" pictures with the ability to review instantly and triage later. Eventually, digital camera and printing technology improved to the point at which digital pictures were of the same quality as film pictures, if not even better based on digital editing abilities. At some point, for most consumers, the hassles of dealing with film were too great compared to the convenience of digital photographs. Similarly, cell phone cameras disrupted digital cameras, redefining performance to include the ability to capture a moment without the foresight of bringing a standalone camera, and the ability to share the moment immediately with others. Cell phone cameras have improved to the point that the picture quality is similar to a traditional (low-end) digital camera, but the cell phone enjoys an advantage in the new quality metric of portability and ability to share quickly. The convenience of an all-in-one pocket device became increasingly more important than the high-end features offered by standalone digital SLR cameras, to all but serious photographers. Time and again, the feature set at the high end overshoots the needs of the market, leaving it ripe for disruption.

There are two major categories of disruptive innovations: low-end disruptions and non-consumption disruptions. Low-end disruptions provide a simpler and cheaper version of a product to less demanding, typically lower-value customers. Mainstream products outperform the needs of these customers, so new entrants can create new solutions that address these simpler needs. Over time, these solutions improve in performance and begin to penetrate the higher-value end of the market. An example of this that Christensen predicted in 1999 is Google Sheets. Microsoft Excel, Christensen hypothesized, contained far greater functionality than most customers needed.[13] The market was ripe for a streamlined spreadsheet application. Google Sheets does not have the same functionality as Microsoft Excel that demanding corporate clients may require, but it offers simplicity of use, easier sharing, and cloud access – and it is free. These qualities redefine the "performance" of spreadsheet software and appeal to different customers. Eventually, the product gained traction even with the higher-value corporate clients.

Non-consumption, alternately, creates a product or service for consumers who previously did not have access to a mainstream version of it. The personal computer (PC) is an example: it was far less functional than the mainframe computers existing in large corporations and universities at the time, but it opened up an entire new market – that of individual

---

[11] For more detail on quality metrics in law, see Dolin – Measuring Legal Quality, *supra*.
[12] James Euchner, "Managing Disruption: An Interview with Clayton Christensen," *Research-Technology Management* 54 (1) (2011): 11–17, available at: www.tandfonline.com/doi/abs/10.1080/08956308.2011.11657668.
[13] Christensen, *The Innovator's Dilemma*, *supra* note 2, at 230.

consumers – to computing. PCs facilitated common tasks such as word processing, document storage, and printing, as well as simple gaming and office functions – activities not previously available in such a manner.

Another insight that informs much of Christensen's analysis of disruptive innovation is that of values, processes, and resources (VPR). The VPR of a given company defines its capabilities, and Christensen argues that the VPR of successful incumbents necessarily makes it harder to adopt or create disruptive innovations. For example, if a camera company defines itself based on the quality of its film prints, fosters distribution networks and processes to emphasize quality of photos, and allocates capital to projects that improve film prints, it would be futile to try to develop digital camera technology in that organization.[14] Efficient organizational decision making requires embedding decisions into processes and employee values; the different decisions required in the face of disruption are thus slowed down or simply precluded. A marketing and distribution network that depends on high profit margins, for example, cannot easily be rebuilt in the face of a low-cost provider. This was critical to Christensen's insight that great companies fail precisely because they are great; the VPR that made them great often does not allow them to disrupt.

III *THE INNOVATOR'S DILEMMA* FRAMEWORK AND BIG LAW'S PROTECTIONS

Big Law, and legal services more broadly, are unique and enjoy structural peculiarities that reinforce their incumbency and mitigate the effects of full-blown disruption. First of all, law firms are not selling products, but rather are offering regulated professional services. The Model Rules of Professional Conduct, and its counterpart in state legislation, regulate who can offer legal advice and who can own law firms.[15] Big Law also enjoys the advantages of information asymmetry that define professional services: Clients come to law firms precisely because they cannot do the job on their own. Finally, the concept of outside counsel serves a vital role in offering both specialized services to a broad set of clients and a degree of liability insurance for clients. The law firm, as a provider of outside counsel services, is a logical delivery method based on reputational bonding as a signal of quality that reduces adverse selection in the market for legal services.

The ABA's ethical rules and their statutory counterparts provide regulatory protection for Big Law. In particular, the rules against the unauthorized practice of law (UPL) and the non-lawyer ownership of law firms help entrench existing law firm structures and the structure of the Big Law market more broadly.[16] UPL statutes prevent non-lawyers from offering legal services with the stated goal of protecting the public, but judicial decisions and enforcement proceedings at the state level suggest that protecting the profession is the more salient goal.[17] The ethical rules also restrict law firm ownership to lawyers, preventing analogous professional advisors such as consultants and investment bankers from competing with Big Law despite their similar connections to corporate boardrooms. These rules are strict barriers to

---

[14] Euchner, *supra* note 12.
[15] *See, e.g.*, American Bar Association (ABA), Center for Professional Responsibility, Model Rules of Professional Conduct Rule 5.5; see *also* California Business and Professions Code § 6125 ("No person shall practice law in California unless the person is an active member of the State Bar.").
[16] Daniel Fisher, "Non-Lawyers Find It Hard to Avoid Breaking Bar's Vague Rules," *Forbes*, July 25, 2011, available at: www.forbes.com/sites/danielfisher/2011/07/25/non-lawyers-find-it-hard-avoid-breaking-bars-vague-rules.
[17] *See generally*, Deborah L. Rhode and Lucy Buford Ricca, "Protecting the Profession or the Public? Rethinking Unauthorized-Practice Enforcement," *Fordham Law Review* 82 (6) (2014).

entry in the legal market, reducing the number and efficacy of new entrants with alternative value propositions for clients.[18] The practice of law, in a sense, is the delivery of intellectual property maintained at an individual or firm level, and UPL statutes ensure that even if one could extract that IP, only a lawyer can legally monetize its delivery. The equivalent governing bodies of Australia and the UK relaxed their ethical rules regarding law firm ownership, allowing for the expansion of alternative business structures (ABS) in these markets.[19] ABS provisions maintain standards for legal service delivery, and there have been few complaints about the services ABS companies provide.[20] The performance of these companies in the coming years, both financially and in the quality of service provided, will be instructive for their potential in the USA. But the ABA's Commission on Ethics 20/20, a special commission created to examine changes in the legal profession as a result of technology, determined in its final report in 2012 that it will not move forward with policy changes related to non-lawyer ownership of law firms.[21] Other Model Rules that help entrench the existing structure of Big Law include advertising and referrals (Model Rule 7.2), fee splitting (Model Rule 5.4), and imputed conflicts (Model Rule 1.10).[22] Proposals to revise these rules came up during the proceedings for the Commission on Ethics 20/20 but were rejected by a number of sections and divisions within the ABA through comments submitted to the Commission. In several of these comments, the protests to update the rules based on the impact of technology on law practice were blatantly protectionist of traditional law firm operations, and they effectively halted the potential for the Ethics Commission to make any substantial Model Rule revisions.[23]

---

[18] See, e.g., Susan Beck, "Emerging Technology Shapes Future of Law," *The American Lawyer*, August 4, 2014, available at: www.law.com/americanlawyer/almID/1202664266769.

[19] See generally, Laura Snyder, "Does the UK Know Something We Don't About Alternative Business Structures?" *ABA Journal*, January 2015, available at: www.abajournal.com/magazine/article/does_the_uk_know_something_we_dont_about_alternative_business_structures. Two notable UK firms to win approval for an ABS license are Irwin Mitchell and Kennedys, both among the top 30 UK-based firms by revenue. In their press releases announcing the ABS approval, both cited access to capital necessary to grow their businesses, and the ability to have non-lawyer management; see "Irwin Mitchell Approved as an Alternative Business Structure," press release, August 20, 2012, available at: www.irwinmitchell.com/newsandmedia/2012/august/irwin-mitchell-approved-as-an-alternative-business-structure.

[20] At a conference held at Harvard Law School in March 2014, Chris Kenny, the chair of the Legal Services Board, spoke remotely about how successfully ABS is working in the UK. This paper's authors were present to hear Kenny attest to the success of ABS in the UK. The website for this event may be accessed at: https://clp.law.harvard.edu/event-post/disruptive-innovation-in-the-market-for-legal-services. Kenny stated: "The case for some kind of supply-side reform to ensure that social and economic need is met is actually pretty overwhelming. In addition, there's no evidence that ethical standards have been lowered or that customer service has suffered. Deregulation needs to happen because unmet need for legal services is still great." As reported by Lewis Rice, "Conference Examines 'Disruptions' in Law and Marketplace," *Harvard Law Today*, March 19, 2014, available at: http://today.law.harvard.edu/conference-examines-disruptions-law-marketplace-video/.

[21] See Letter from ABA Commission on Ethics 20/20, April 16, 2012, available at: www.americanbar.org/content/dam/aba/administrative/ethics_2020/20120416_news_release_re_nonlawyer_ownership_law_firms.authcheckdam.pdf.

[22] See American Bar Association (ABA), Center for Professional Responsibility, Model Rules of Professional Conduct Rule 7.2, available at: http://www.americanbar.org/groups/professional_responsibility/publications/model_rules_of_professional_conduct/rule_7_2_advertising.html; Model Rule 5.4, available at: http://www.americanbar.org/groups/professional_responsibility/publications/model_rules_of_professional_conduct/rule_5_4_professional_independence_of_a_lawyer.html; and Model Rule 1.10, available at: http://www.americanbar.org/groups/professional_responsibility/publications/model_rules_of_professional_conduct/rule_1_10_imputation_of_conflicts_of_interest_general_rule.html.

[23] See, e.g., a letter to the Commission on Ethics 20/20 entitled "Comments of Nine General Counsel on the ABA Commission on Ethics 20/20's Discussion Paper on Alternative Law Practice Structures," February 29, 2012, at www.americanbar.org/content/dam/aba/administrative/ethics_2020/ethics_20_20_comments/ninegeneralcounselcomments_alpschoiceoflawinitialdraftproposal.authcheckdam.pdf. As another example, the ABA Standing Committee on the Delivery of Legal Services proposed that the Commission consider the deletion of Model Rule

Beyond the regulatory protections it enjoys, Big Law enjoys protections from the information asymmetry that underpins the very nature of its work. Clients are at a necessary information disadvantage when seeking legal advice from a specialist – they have retained outside counsel precisely because they do not have the necessary ability to solve a problem on their own. Lawyers can rely on the opacity of their work product and the agility with which they can respond to client needs to amplify the sense of necessity regarding their work.[24] The information asymmetry is an important advantage to clients in one respect, though. By retaining outside counsel, acknowledging a lack of expertise, a company takes on a measure of liability insurance. For example, if a company wants to employ a legally risky transaction structure, the third-party expert approval of outside counsel can help protect the company from shareholder suits if the structure becomes problematic, in a way not available if the company used only in-house lawyers. It is important to note, however, that the information asymmetry protecting law firms has narrowed with the growth of in-house legal departments, and the opacity of a law firm's work product will continue to diminish as more lawyers transition from law firms to in-house counsel roles.

As an organizational form, the structure of the law firm serves an important function in the marketplace for legal services, conferring additional protections to Big Law's incumbency. Information asymmetry naturally exists in any marketplace for expert services because a lay consumer will not be able to properly evaluate the expert's quality. The structure of a law firm, which organizes groups of specialists under one umbrella organization, reduces the information asymmetry and associated agency costs through reputational bonding.[25] Rather than an individual lawyer convincing a client that she can provide suitable legal services, the lawyer can point to the firm name on her business card as a signal of quality. A law firm with a reputation for quality has a vested interest in continuing to hire competent lawyers who can continue to deliver quality services. The client need not do the same level of due diligence in hiring outside counsel because he knows the reputation of the law firm that has hired this particular lawyer. Agency costs are reduced, benefiting both parties.[26] Further, law firms relying on reputational bonding are best organized as partnerships of lawyers, because nonexperts would be unable to monitor the lawyers effectively to maintain the reputational bonding. This need for oversight to ensure quality also motivates in part the ethical rules regarding non-lawyer firm ownership.[27]

Finally, law firms are efficient within a societal legal system from an informatics perspective. If we look at law firms through a data flow model, the processing that goes on there between the various inputs and outputs can be viewed as a series of operations. Some of these

---

7.2(b) in light of the impact of technology and the internet on lawyer advertising. *See* the Standing Committee's letter at: www.americanbar.org/content/dam/aba/administrative/ethics_2020/ethics_20_20_comments/abastandingcommitteeondeliveryoflegalservices_revisedproposaltechnologyandclientdevelopment.authcheckdam.pdf. This proposal was rejected by several sections and individual lawyers in comments submitted to the Commission related to 7.2 at: www.americanbar.org/content/dam/aba/administrative/ethics_2020/technology_working_group_comments_chart.authcheckdam.pdf.

[24] *See* Christensen et al., "Consulting on the Cusp of Disruption," *supra* note 9.
[25] Law has not (yet) moved to empirical quality metrics, standards, or certification, so a proxy for quality is generally reputation and pedigree. *See* Kenneth Grady, "Debunking the Legal Service Quality Myth," SeytLines Seyfarth Lean Consulting LLC Blog, April 2, 2015, available at: www.seytlines.com/2015/04/debunking-the-legal-service-quality-myth; *see also* Ron Dolin, "Getting to New Law: Standardized Quality Metrics," Radical Concepts Blog, March 25, 2015, available at: http://radicalconcepts.com/239/getting-to-new-law-standardized-quality-metrics. For more on quality metrics, *see* Dolin – Measuring Legal Quality, *supra*.
[26] For greater detail on the reputational bonding justification for the structure of the law firm, *see* Ribstein, "The Death of Big Law," *supra* note 5, at 750, 753–755.
[27] *Id.* at 754–755.

operations are more efficiently performed as the equivalent of callable routines. Imagine a given lawyer or practice group with unique expertise. The number of matters drawing on that expertise within a given client corporation may be quite limited. However, where that lawyer or practice group is able to apply that skill set across many clients, the overhead costs of maintaining the expertise drop. That is, it is more sustainable for some specializations to exist within a neutral law firm model available to multiple clients than for each of those clients to maintain that level of expertise directly. Since the expertise lives in the heads of the lawyers, some form of law firm model is simply efficient. However, where the level of inefficiencies of the law firm itself (e.g., the billable hour) increase the overhead of the availability of such expertise, it becomes more cost-effective for clients (large clients in particular) to move those lawyers in-house. This would remain true until the law firm model becomes sufficiently efficient (something on par with what in-house does) such that it becomes, yet again, more cost-effective to work within the law firm structure. Thus, the client goal is not inherently toward dismantling law firms as groupings of experts working together. Instead, the push is toward increased efficiency with different cost and quality controls, within the law firm. Not only is there economy of scale at a law firm in terms of the utilization of human capital, but also in working with various legal service providers. For example, for all but the largest corporate clients, the frequency of litigation may be variable. One can imagine that such clients may not be able to attract the same pricing from LPOs and e-discovery vendors, for example, as a law firm that is pooling the work of many clients.

There are several factors working to keep Big Law in place. Some, such as the ethics rules, are more oriented toward maintaining the current model. Others, such as the inherent efficiency of independent practice groups, are more focused on Big Law's substantive contribution. Protecting the status quo derives from a model focused on the billable hour, with associated "productivity" measured as the number of hours billed per lawyer. One justification for this type of business model is the comprehensiveness of the work product. In contrast, the benefits of reducing societal redundancy derive from the goal of having high-quality, efficient delivery of Big Law expertise. The disruptions occurring are not necessarily focused on the core values that Big Law ideally presents.

IV ADAPTIVE INNOVATION AND BIG LAW

The question arises, therefore, as to whether the current framework that protects the existing Big Law model is likely to maintain the status quo indefinitely. Several trends point to increasing challenges to Big Law regardless of the existing protections. As previously discussed, the percentage of corporate clients' legal spend going to Big Law is decreasing, and Big Law revenue for all but the very top firms has been basically flat for years.[28] In addition to unbundling of legal services by corporate in-house departments and taking key areas of work away from Big Law firms, there are also new models of legal interaction that simply do not require a Big Law solution.[29] For example, new forms of dispute resolution simplify the process.[30] While much, though certainly

---

[28] See, e.g., William D. Henderson, "From Big Law to Lean Law," *International Review of Law and Economics* 3 (2013), available at: http://papers.ssrn.com/sol3/papers.cfm?abstract_id=2356330##.

[29] Note that in-house legal departments are free to use alternatives that might otherwise fail under the existing regulatory framework, since the work is overseen by licensed in-house attorneys.

[30] See, e.g., Tyler Technologies (formerly Modria; http://modria.com), providing technology-assisted (algorithmic) settlement mechanisms in conjunction with, for example, Lex Machina or Ravel, to arrive at reasonable settlement range propositions. Lex Machina, https://lexmachina.com; Ravel, www.ravellaw.com. See also Orr and Rule – Online Dispute Resolution, *supra*.

not all, of this work focuses on consumer, low-end, or commodity work, it will continue to move up market. Within an *Innovator's Dilemma* framework, not only are there new alternatives to the current procedures for transactional and litigation issues, there are increasingly new procedures and mechanisms for which the traditional law firm is currently ill prepared, and for which viable alternatives exist. As a result, the existing regulatory framework is likely inadequate to hold back the tides of innovation being demanded by clients.[31]

Structural defenses against disruption suggest that Big Law cannot suffer large-scale disruption in the way the film camera industry did, or the integrated steel manufacturers did in Christensen's *The Innovator's Dilemma*.[32] The required license to practice and to own – the UPL and law firm ownership statutes – are steep barriers to entry that help insulate law from disruption. This license reflects the expertise inherent in the profession, and as long as there is an information asymmetry between consumers and providers of legal services, there continues to be a need to retain licensed lawyers.[33] And while the growth of in-house legal departments is a step toward disrupting Big Law, few companies, if any, have the need or resources to maintain a fully functional law firm in their organizations. A large corporation could hire a team to handle all M&A work without the help of outside counsel, but it is hard to justify that allocation of capital if deal activity slows. An in-house litigation team would fail under similar scrutiny if the team does not have the case flow required to remain sharp, or has a sudden influx of cases it does not have the bandwidth to handle. Big Law will continue to offer specialized services, providing the liability insurance and staff augmentation capacities that its clients' in-house departments need. And the law firm as a reputational bonding vehicle will continue to mitigate search and monitoring costs in retaining outside counsel.

Total disruption is not likely to be on the horizon for Big Law, but the industry would benefit from the lessons of *The Innovator's Dilemma*, even embracing a middle ground of "adaptive innovation." Adaptive innovation would require a hybrid approach to innovation, acknowledging the peculiarities of the industry that prevent total disruption, while embracing tenets of disruptive innovation to help cement the incumbents' position in the market, augmenting and amplifying the services they provide.[34] In this section, we highlight four

---

[31] Note that usually it is not the largest customers that instigate disruption. To the degree that there is pushback by Fortune 500 legal departments that Big Law work under a different, more efficient and value-driven model, the landscape for Big Law is atypical of the classic circumstances described by *The Innovator's Dilemma*. As an example of such value-driven external counsel management, see the Association of Corporate Counsel's "Guide to Managing Outside Counsel," 2011, available at: www.accvaluechallenge-digital.com/accvaluechallenge/acc-guide-to-managing-outside-counsel.

[32] For Christensen's description of disruptive innovation in the steel industry, *see* Christensen, *The Innovator's Dilemma*, *supra* note 2, at 101–108; for disruptive innovation in digital cameras, *see* Euchner, *supra* note 12.

[33] Waxing futuristic, the licensing of attorneys can be augmented with the certification of support software; *see* Ron Dolin, "Guest Post: Using a Document Automation System – Authorized Practice Of Law?" MyCase Blog, August 28, 2013, available at: www.mycase.com/blog/2013/08/guest-post-using-a-document-automation-system-authorized-practice-of-law.

[34] Sustaining innovation generally refers to those changes that strengthen a company's existing VPR. For Big Law under the billable hour model, efficiency hurts the firm and can cause it to fail. The underlying values of existing firms cannot easily accommodate innovations such as document automation, TAR, etc. Some, but not all, of the values of Big Law would need to change in order to compete with new entrants. However, core values, such as quality and expertise, are not antithetical to efficiency-based models. Thus, these innovations neither sustain common practice, nor disrupt core values; they are adaptive in nature for those firms that incorporate them.

The definition of disruption in the case of Big Law is challenging. In an extreme hypothetical, suppose that all AmLaw 200 firms failed, but that all the lawyers in those firms moved to the new firms that then made up the AmLaw 200, but under a predominately AFA structure. Rather than looking at firm names, we could look at the percentage of individual attorneys who still work in the new AmLaw 200 firms, consistent with the notion of a law firm as a partnership. If there were a 50%-plus overlap, would that be considered disruptive?

areas in which embracing adaptive innovation would benefit Big Law. First, Big Law could embrace the exodus of lawyers to in-house legal departments and the changes clients are attempting to drive, partnering more proactively with clients. Second, rather than abandon commoditized work in a retreat to bespoke, high-value work, Big Law could look for ways to alter its delivery mechanism to make rote work profitable, and high-end work more efficient. Third, Big Law could consider changes to its incentive structure to encourage reinvestment in the firm and continuing training for lawyers. Finally, Big Law could embrace the development of standardized quality metrics to directly measure the quality of work product rather than indirectly (and inaccurately) associating quality with reputation or pedigree.[35]

Christensen has pointed to the growth of in-house legal departments as an example of disruptive forces at work in Big Law. While an in-house department could certainly obviate the need for outside counsel for certain tasks, the structural defenses mentioned prevent in-house departments from entirely ousting Big Law. Embracing the disruptive elements of in-house legal departments in a way to create new bonds between law firms and their clients would be an effective adaptive innovation that could help sustain Big Law firms. Firms, for example, could offer legal consulting services to help their clients grow their in-house departments.[36] This would open up a new revenue stream for Big Law firms, profiting off of the seemingly disruptive move of clients in-sourcing legal work. While associates and partners are valuable assets to a firm, representing tens or hundreds of thousands of dollars of investment in infrastructure and training, facilitating moves between the firm and a client could be a valuable adaptive innovation in the long run. Rather than force associates to engage in a clandestine search for in-house positions, law firms' human resources staff could partner with their counterparts at clients to help fill staffing needs on either short-term secondment basis or through full-time moves.[37]

Part of the irony of disruptive innovation for Christensen is that it results in the failure of well-managed companies that successfully cater to their highest-value clients.[38] The lesson in part is not to abandon low-margin work and retreat to high-value customers when a new competitor enters the marketplace. Commentary pieces on the prospects for Big Law often either predict or counsel a retreat toward bespoke, high-value practice areas like white-collar crime, banking regulation, and private equity. Christensen's framework spotlights the pitfalls of this path though. Rather than abandoning low-margin work, law firms could be tweaking delivery models to make low-margin work more profitable. Some types of expertise from an individual lawyer can be extracted and encoded in a software platform, allowing for an element of leverage that provides such knowledge at a reduced cost compared to having to engage the lawyer directly. In this way, work product that clients are not willing to pay Big Law prices for become available at a lower cost to a greater number of clients. The expertise is still required, but the impact is amplified, and the market is expanded. Working with clients

---

[35] See Grady, "Debunking the Legal Service Quality Myth," *supra* note 25; and Dolin, "Getting to New Law: Standardized Quality Metrics," *supra* note 25. See also, Dolin – Measuring Legal Quality, *supra*.
[36] The authors do not assume that this and other suggestions may not be occurring already in some firms, but they are not aware of widespread adoption among most firms.
[37] Note the development of law firm APIs to allow complex or micro questions from a client that do not require the direct intervention of a firm attorney.
[38] In fact, in the subtitle of *The Innovator's Dilemma*, Christensen notes that disruptive innovation causes "great" firms to fail.

on alternative fee arrangements (AFAs) and unbundling of legal services is essential to embracing the potential profitability of lower-value work.[39]

Even for custom work, there are interplays between the commodity aspects (components, process flow, quality control) and the finished product that allow for more efficient delivery. Borrowing from hi-tech, Intel has moved from solely commodity work and is increasingly accommodating custom chip making, but with a commodity-based production mechanism:

> "The demand [for custom chips] may be clear, but the economics of this business seem odd: Intel has long profited by turning out tens of millions of the same thing. Why go over to custom work?
>
> The reason is, again, computers. Intel's chip fabrication plants are now so automated that leaving out an unwanted core, or changing other properties, is a matter of a few new commands to the machine. Customers are willing to pay a little more for the special run of chips, or pay an engineering fee for the special service. [...]
>
> While most of Intel's chips still go into PCs, about one-quarter of Intel's revenue, and a much bigger share of its profits, come from semiconductors for data centers. In the first nine months of 2014, the average selling price of PC chips fell 4 percent. But the average price on data center chips was up 10 percent, compared with the same period in 2013."[40]

The lesson for future high-end legal service delivery, with a decreasing emphasis on the billable hour, is to make efficient not only the AFA-related components, but also the interaction between the two. The typical argument that legal work is too fact-intensive, or that lawyers' workproduct is too specialized to be susceptible to the pressures of technology, assumes that all aspects of the workflow must be done manually and redundantly. A more sophisticated, hybrid model balances efficiency with flexibility while maintaining quality.

Third, to facilitate any move toward innovation, Big Law needs to reevaluate its incentive and pay-out structures at both the individual and firm levels. The ability to deliver technological solutions to clients and revamp the breadth of services offered requires law firms to reinvest capital into larger R&D budgets. A partnership model merges the roles of manager and shareholder, as viewed from the perspective of a corporate structure. It also encourages the annual pay-out out of what would be considered dividends, at the cost of what might otherwise go to R&D within a corporate setting.[41] At the individual level, law firms should incentivize associates and partners to retrain for a marketplace in which the percentage of low-value work the firm delivers clients increases with respect to the high-value, bespoke, hourly work. Training lawyers to work with technology and to embrace solutions that can leverage an individual lawyer's expertise requires the firm to put in place an appropriate

---

[39] See American Bar Association Standing Committee on the Delivery of Legal Services, "Perspectives on Finding Personal Legal Services: The Results of a Public Opinion Poll," February 2011, 19–20. These results show that while the majority of the respondents to the poll were not aware of unbundling as an alternative form of legal service delivery, once made aware of the availability they found it an important factor in deciding to select a lawyer. www.americanbar.org/content/dam/aba/administrative/delivery_legal_services/20110228_aba_harris_survey_report.authcheckdam.pdf; See also Paul Bonner and Deborah McMurray, "Alternative Fee Arrangements that Work for Clients and Lawyers," Law Practice Magazine 40 (3) (2014), available at: www.americanbar.org/publications/law_practice_magazine/2014/may-june/alternative-fee-arrangements-that-work-for-clients-and-lawyers.html.

[40] "Intel Betting on (Customized) Commodity Chips for Cloud Computing," New York Times, December 19, 2014.

[41] Ron Dolin, "Big Law as Legal Fiction and the Lack of Innovation," Radical Concepts Blog, January 18, 2015, available at: http://radicalconcepts.com/156/big-law-legal-fiction. Note that the partnership structure was integral in providing reputational bonding as a way of guaranteeing a high-quality talent pool. The same structure, however, presents incentive challenges to innovation. This is an example of how the VPR of a well-run firm under an existing market structure presents problems in transitioning to a new market structure.

incentive structure.[42] Or more directly, requiring technological training as a precursor to promotion, or as part of an annual billable hours goal, would introduce both a carrot and stick.

Finally, another adaptive innovation for Big Law would be the establishment of standardized quality metrics.[43] As described by Christensen, market maturity is measured in part by a move from all-encompassing integrated solutions to componentized, modular ones.[44] The ability to plug in components facilitates finer-grain competition via interface standards. In law, such componentization is referred to as unbundled services.[45] Benchmarks are important to unbundling because they allow an apples-to-apples comparison of various component suppliers. When different quality metrics are used by different suppliers, there is simply no straightforward way to compare components. With standardized quality metrics in place, components can be used based on a value curve allowing someone to piece together an appropriate level of quality within a given cost framework.[46] The competition at the component level allows us to buy commodity products of varying capabilities and price points while the quality benchmarks help guarantee that the overall system will function correctly. Taking an example from Christensen, rebar is a commodity steel product and all material aspects of it fall within quality standards.[47] The competition at the component level allows us to buy commodity products of varying capabilities and price points while the quality benchmarks help guarantee that the overall system will function correctly. This allows for competition based on cost, time, and, say, customer service.

While general benefits from standards are well established,[48] the question is whether any benefits would fall to Big Law as a whole, or even to any individual incumbent. Battles over standards in general date back to at least the US Civil War, and the company setting the standard tends to have multiple advantages: control over an installed user base, IP rights, greater ability to innovate, first-mover advantage, brand recognition, greater access to complements and add-ons, etc.[49] The economic impact on incumbents of quality standards and

---

[42] From the authors' personal experience, it can be challenging to get lawyers at all levels of a firm to participate in training, workshops, etc., and the reasons are not clear. At first blush, one may assume that it has to do with a lack of billable hours at such events, or a busy schedule. It may be an issue of attitude; pilot projects come and go, and lawyers really do not like to change what has been working for them. No matter the reason, however, where innovation is required, the incentive structure needs to reward staff participation.

[43] See Grady, "Debunking the Legal Service Quality Myth," *supra* note 25; and Dolin, "Getting to New Law," *supra* note 25. See also, Dolin – Measuring Legal Quality, *supra*.

[44] See Clayton Christensen and Michael E. Raynor, *The Innovator's Solution: Creating and Sustaining Successful Growth* (Cambridge, MA: Harvard Business Review Press, 2003), 125–142 (describing the rise of modularity in product architectures as a market matures and the subsequent rise in specialized, interdependent architectures as new products redefine quality metrics).

[45] Revised in 2002, the ABA Model Rule 1.2(c) entitled "Scope of Representation" formally allows for the unbundling of legal services by stating "(c) [a] lawyer may limit the scope of the representation if the limitation is reasonable under the circumstances and the client gives informed consent." Available at: www.americanbar.org/groups/professional_responsibility/publications/model_rules_of_professional_conduct/rule_1_2_scope_of_representation_allocation_of_authority_between_client_lawyer.html. Unbundling has been adopted or modified by 42 states since its addition to the Model Rules. Unbundling is also termed limited scope services, à la carte legal services, discrete task representation, or disaggregated legal services. See generally, Stephanie Kimbro, *Limited Scope Legal Services: Unbundling and the Self Help Client* (Cleveland, OH: ABA Book Publishing, 2012).

[46] This is why, for example, we see benchmarks for computer components, such as CPU floating-point operations per second (FLOPS), or mean time to failure (MTTF) for memory or hard drives.

[47] See generally, "Rebar Grades," *Wikipedia*, available at: http://en.wikipedia.org/wiki/Rebar#Grades (accessed June 9, 2020).

[48] International Organization for Standardization, "The Main Benefits of ISO Standards," available at: www.iso.org/iso/home/standards/benefitsofstandards.htm.

[49] Carl Shapiro and Hal R. Varian, "The Art of Standards Wars," *California Management Review* 41 (2) (1999).

third-party quality certification is complex and outside the scope of this chapter.[50] However, in an environment in which quality metrics are inevitable, it is in the incumbents' interests to help establish the standards. Furthermore, where standards are established, the importance of reputation moves from the producer to the standard certifier. That is, even if the direct benefits of quality benchmarks may seem elusive, it is likely that not being able to excel within emerging standards would be harmful.

V EVIDENCE OF ADAPTIVE INNOVATION

Much has been written[51] about the changing landscape of Big Law and the pressures coming from disruptive legal service providers, including smaller mid-size firms,[52] LPOs,[53] and upwardly mobile new entrants,[54] as well as the trend of more legal work moving in-house.[55] From an *Innovator's Dilemma* perspective, these alternates represent lower-margin competitors, as well as new entrants initially focused on prior non-consumption, who can be expected to move up-market and increasingly compete for Big Law's more lucrative clients. And certainly, in a classic response to disruptive innovation, there has been talk among Big Law firms about dropping lower margin work and moving up-market.[56] *The Innovator's Dilemma* highlights that there simply is not room up-market to accommodate all the Big Law firms, and that under such an approach, most of those firms would not be expected to survive.[57] But under an adaptive innovation framework, we would expect to see Big Law starting to incorporate disruptive methodologies and migrate their VPR to adapt to changing market demands such as efficiency and evidence-based analysis. Is there evidence of this among Big Law firms?

There are some well-publicized examples of law firm innovation awards and rankings, such as ILTA and the *Financial Times*. Professor William Henderson of Indiana University Law School describes the 2014 ILTA Big Law innovation winners:[58] Bryan Cave (realistic financial performance data, integrated technology training), Seyfarth Shaw (client-focused interdisciplinary R&D), and Littler Mendelson (workflow optimization and client-available KM). "It is time to put down the broad brush used to paint BigLaw as inefficient and out of touch," he says. "As it turns out, BigLaw has on balance a surprisingly good hand to play. Many will thrive, but at the expense of taking market share from the rest." However, there are also commentaries (e.g., by Ron Friedmann) explaining that so-called innovation at many/most law firms might be best described as the uptake of technology or methodologies that have been common in other industries for years. As Henderson says, "what is missing at some firms,

[50] *See, e.g.*, Huishuang He, "The Strategic Entry Behavior Choices of Firms under Minimum Quality Standard," *Theoretical Economics Letters* 4 (9) (2014); and Ram Kumar Phuyal and Sang-Ho Lee, "Strategic Entry Deterrence with New Technology under Quality Regulation in a Vertically Differentiated Industry," in the *Third International Conference on Addressing Climate Change for Sustainable Development*, 2011.
[51] *See, e.g.*, William D. Henderson, "From Big Law to Lean Law," *supra* note 28.
[52] Jennifer Smith, "Smaller Law Firms Grab Big Slice of Corporate Legal Work," *Wall Street Journal*, October 22, 2013, available at: www.wsj.com/articles/SB10001424052702303672404579149991394180218.
[53] *See, e.g.*, Rama Lakshmi, "U.S. Legal Work Booms in India," *The Washington Post*, May 11, 2008, available at: www.washingtonpost.com/wp-dyn/content/article/2008/05/10/AR2008051002355.html.
[54] *See, e.g.*, Dolin, "Big Law as Legal Fiction and the Lack of Innovation," *supra* note 41.
[55] *See* Joe Patrice, "Another Day, Another Dose of Bad News for Biglaw," Above the Law Blog, November 11, 2014, available at: http://abovethelaw.com/2014/11/another-day-another-dose-of-bad-news-for-biglaw.
[56] Dolin, "Big Law as Legal Fiction and the Lack of Innovation," *supra* note 41.
[57] *See* Christensen, *The Innovator's Dilemma*, *supra* note 2.
[58] William D. Henderson, "Ahead of the Curve: Three Big Innovators in BigLaw," August 26, 2014, available at: www.littler.com/files/press/pdf/Ahead-Of-Curve-Three-Big-Innovators-In-Big-Law-August-2014.pdf.

but clearly not all, is the will, courage, and leadership to seize the opportunity." In fact, he estimates that only 10–15% of large law firms have embarked on strategic initiatives that take into account the "New Normal." While this pattern of trend-setters and laggards is normal in the adoption of technology and innovation (e.g., *Crossing the Chasm*), the reasons likely vary sector by sector.

Firms are experimenting with AFA, leveraging technology, and partnering more with in-house departments.[59] Likewise, suppliers to law firms are making strides in the technology space that will allow Big Law to make the changes it needs to make. One example of AFA to embrace low-margin work is the innovation in Silicon Valley over the last few decades to address the legal needs of startups. While a Fortune 500 company may be able to afford four-figure-per-hour rates for legal advice, a startup that is little more than two founders and a good idea likely cannot. Law firms in the Valley began offering a suite of startup services like incorporation documents, shareholder agreements, and IP advising on a flat, deferred fee basis, or in some cases, in exchange for equity in the company.[60] These innovations allow law firms to make the low-margin work of incorporating a company profitable by using it as a hook for a longer relationship that ideally involves negotiating a sale to a strategic buyer, or advising on an IPO and future securities regulation compliance. Firms like Orrick, Herrington & Sutcliffe LLP and Fenwick & West LLP have taken this a step further, using technology to better leverage the associate and partner resources required to deliver these startup services.[61]

In the world of suppliers to Big Law and in-house departments, legal technology startups are making large strides that, if Big Law chooses to embrace the changes, can help Big Law further defend its position in the delivery of legal services. For example, Allegory Law, founded by a former litigation associate at Gibson and Dunn LLP, simplifies the case management process for a litigation team, making the team more efficient and productive, and increasing the value of the services it is delivering a client. Lex Machina has positioned itself as the dominant patent litigation database, using big data to help predict outcomes and identify salient issues in patent infringement claims. Ravel Law has received a lot of press coverage about its legal research tool. Part of the significance of these suppliers' offerings is that in embracing an efficiency-based value system, they will likely force the way big suppliers like Thomson Reuters will deliver and charge for services.[62]

We see the concurrent patterns of pressure by external forces and an increasing response by Big Law, including a shift toward increasing AFA and efficiency, and a change in financial metrics redefining productivity to be based on work product. The trends seem to indicate that disruptive innovation is abundant, and that law firms are fundamentally changing in response by adapting to the market changes, rather than by simply collapsing and yielding to new entrants. This is what we would expect to see under an adaptive innovation framework.

---

[59] *See, e.g.*, Kirkland and Ellis' discussion of its alternative free arrangements, available at: www.kirkland.com/sitecontent.cfm?contentID=341; and Wilson Sonsini Goodrich and Rosati's automated term sheet generator, available at: www.wsgr.com/WSGR/Display.aspx?SectionName=practice/termsheet.htm.

[60] *See* Timothy Hay, "Lawyers Get Smarter about Betting on Tech Clients," *Wall Street Journal*, June 27, 2012, available at: www.wsj.com/articles/SB10001424052702304782404577487360810848668.

[61] *See, e.g.*, Orrick's startup services, www.orrick.com/Total-Access/Tool-Kit.

[62] For example, as Fastcase or legal research startups move toward comprehensive coverage of case law, at a greatly reduced cost structure, with useful additional features, the older methods are no longer viable. The same holds for the disruptive impact of cloud-based e-discovery. A change in values among Big Law firms that incorporate efficiency forces those changes down the supply chain.

VI CONCLUSION

Law often portrays itself as substantially distinguishable from other industries. While in many regards that may well be true, it is also true that in many material ways, law is quite similar. It seems quite unlikely that law would be able to avoid the deep re-implementation resulting from technology, globalization, etc., as seen elsewhere. Big Law may have a unique response to such drivers, but it is not immune to them. Adaptive innovation is a framework that integrates those aspects of law that are necessary with those implementation details that are likely to change.

4.2

Legal Data Access

Christine Bannan

I INTRODUCTION: AN IDEAL, FREE, AND OPEN LAW SYSTEM

The law is not free in either sense of the word: It is costly to access, and there are restrictions on its use. An ideal system would allow any member of the public free online access to all official primary law – cases, statutes, and regulations. In the twenty-first century, a digital-first court publishing system, and primary law in general, should be online, free, open, comprehensive, official, citable, and machine-readable. A modern online law system should also have eight additional, more specific characteristics: digital signing, versioning, good structure, medium-neutrality, archives, a search function, bulk conveyance, and an application program interface (API).[1] Unfortunately, such an ideal system remains a distant aspiration in most jurisdictions.

There are several barriers to accessing primary legal information: index and cataloguing, citation, use of citators, formatting, presence of archives, version control, bulk conveyance, copyright and corporate control, expenses, and search.[2] This chapter discusses issues of access to law more generally, including federal law and statutes and regulations (as of 2017). Some barriers may be more pronounced than others for different types of law, but all these problems pervade the entire legal publishing system. Section II discusses the reasons for the relatively high costs of accessing law, including court documents, statutes, regulations, and other related materials. Section III focuses on the existing barriers to changing the delivery mechanisms. Finally, Section IV explores the potential role of government in achieving an open law framework, as well as the possibilities that might result from such changes.

II MAKING THE LAW FREE

Americans must obey the laws of the USA, but it is common for the text of laws to only be accessible to those who can afford to pay for that access. For example, many corporations control access to the law through restrictive licensing agreements and assertions of copyright. Oftentimes, this means that members of the public pay for the law twice. First, they pay taxes, and through taxpayer money the government performs its duties, such as legislation. After paying taxes so the government can create the laws, the public then pays a second time if and

---

[1] Adam Ziegler, Harvard Library Innovation Lab, phone interview, December 5, 2016.
[2] *See generally*, Sarah Glassmeyer, "State Legal Information Census: An Analysis of Primary State Legal Information," at 5, available at: www.sarahglassmeyer.com/StateLegalInformation/wp-content/uploads/2014/04/GlassmeyerStateLegalInformationCensusReport.pdf.

when they need to read those laws. It is expensive to provide free public access to the law, but it does not need to be as expensive as it is now.

A The WestLaw/LexisNexis Duopoly

Many states have exclusive licenses with either WestLaw or LexisNexis to publish their cases, statutes, and regulations.[3] Some states save money by giving a commercial publisher sole rights to publish their laws, but by doing this they relinquish their responsibility to make the law available to their citizens to read. Large states like New York and California have contracts with commercial publishers that allow them to have their law reports published for free, and also receive computer equipment and other goods and services for free. The catch is that, in exchange, WestLaw and LexisNexis impose licensing requirements restricting use to personal, non-commercial purposes.[4] Small states that are not offered such favorable contract terms by commercial publishers are more likely to retain the responsibility of publishing their law reporters, but currently only 13 states do so. The rest all have contracts with private publishers to perform at least some, if not all, editorial functions.

In 2009, Arkansas became the first jurisdiction in the USA to switch from law report publication to official legal data distribution. The deciding factor for Arkansas was the cost savings resulting from the transition to digital publication. Several circumstances contributed to this transition. Unlike most states, Arkansas always retained complete control of its system of case law dissemination. This made the decision easier, because there was no contract with WestLaw or LexisNexis to negotiate or break. This is partly due to WestLaw and LexisNexis not offering smaller states agreements to publish their law reports free of charge. Larger states, such as New York and California, have been slower to develop official online legal resources, and this may be because it would mean giving up the perks of their contracts with commercial publishers.

When governments grant WestLaw or LexisNexis exclusive rights to publish their laws, they are perpetuating a business model that requires everyone to pay to access essential legal information that citizens are required to know in order to avoid breaking the law. There are alternatives, however. Governments can turn to startups that use different business models, or they can renegotiate the terms of their contracts to be non-exclusive so that other publishers can also have access to the primary law data.

B Copyright

Open access to the law cannot occur until governments and corporations stop asserting copyright interest in the law. Government edicts are not even copyrightable.[5] Nevertheless, many state websites claim copyright protection in their statutes and other forms of law.[6] The

---

[3] Peter W. Martin, "Abandoning Law Reports for Official Digital Case Law," *The Journal of Appellate Practice and Process*, 12 (1) (2011): 34, available at: http://scholarship.law.cornell.edu/cgi/viewcontent.cgi?article=2472&context=facpub.

[4] Ibid.

[5] See, e.g., Katie Fortney, "Ending Copyright Claims in State Primary Legal Materials: Toward an Open Source Legal System," *Law Library Journal* 102 (1) (2010), available at: http://escholarship.org/uc/item/3kpog81h. Several courts that have addressed this issue have concluded that edicts of government are not copyrightable.

[6] See Glassmeyer, "State Legal Information Census," *supra* note 2, at 24. One example: "The Arkansas Code of 1987 is copyrighted by the State of Arkansas. By using this website, the user acknowledges the State's copyright interests in the Arkansas Code of 1987. Neither the Arkansas Code of 1987 nor any portions thereof shall be reproduced without the written permission of the Arkansas Code Revision Commission ... "

Copyright Act specifically excludes works of the federal government from copyright protection, but does not mention the copyright status of state and local government works.[7] This leaves the copyright status of government works in various states rather murky, and the Harvard Library Copyright Office has created a guide to deciphering these varying protections.[8] A bipartisan group of Congress members has also expressed concern over copyright as a barrier blocking citizens from accessing the law.[9]

Both governments and private corporations have made copyright claims in annotations and other editorial content published alongside the primary law. WestLaw embeds cases with its own editorial content, such as case synopses and keynotes, so that the public domain law cannot be extricated from its copyrightable material without great expense and effort.[10] At the bottom of any WestLaw document, there is a copyright notice with a disclaimer: "© 2017 Thomson Reuters. No claim to original U.S. Government Works." This disclaimer, however, has little meaning due to the difficulty of separating the public domain from WestLaw's accompanying copyrighted editorial content.

Some states have taken similar approaches.[11] Georgia, for example, claims copyright in the Official Code of Georgia Annotated. When Carl Malamud posted the Official Code of Georgia Annotated on public.resource.org, he received a cease-and-desist letter from Georgia. When he refused to take the code down, he was then sued by the state for copyright infringement.[12] Georgia claims that it owns the copyright in its annotations, but Malamud argues that since the annotated code is the only official version of the code, the annotations are equivalent to law and cannot receive copyright protection.[13] Unlike Georgia, most states have not been willing to undertake litigation to enforce their copyright claims.[14] Even if similar copyright claims – by public or private entities – are not enforced, though, this makes users unsure of what they are legally permitted to do with legal information, which can hinder innovation and public access.

Commercial publishers also assert copyright in private standards that are incorporated into law by local, state, and federal legislators and regulators. The problem of access to private standards is more widespread than one might think. Building inspectors, fire marshals, and county supervisors must have access to various private standards to perform their jobs, and they are responsible for buying access to those standards.[15] For example, the American

[7] 17 U.S.C. § 105 (1976).
[8] "State Copyright Resource Center," Copyright at Harvard Library, http://copyright.lib.harvard.edu/states/.
[9] "US Reps: Congress Must Address Copyright-Restricted Laws, Legal Codes & Standards," OpenGov, last accessed July 18th, 2017, http://opengovfoundation.org/us-reps-congress-must-address-copyright-restricted-laws-legal-codes-standards-release/.
[10] Glassmeyer, "State Legal Information Census," supra note 2, at 25.
[11] See, e.g., State of California Office of Administrative Law, "Paperwork Reduction Act Response to Public.Resource.Org," June 4, 2009, available at: https://public.resource.org/scribd/17358146.pdf (California asserts copyright over the California Code of Regulations); Cory Doctorow, "Oregon: Our Laws Are Copyrighted and You Can't Publish Them," BoingBoing, April 15, 2008, available at: https://boingboing.net/2008/04/15/oregon-our-laws-are.html.
[12] Joe Mullin, "If You Publish Georgia's State Laws, You'll Get Sued for Copyright and Lose," Ars Technica, March 30, 2017, available at: https://arstechnica.com/tech-policy/2017/03/public-records-activist-violated-copyright-by-publishing-georgia-legal-code-online.
[13] Ibid.
[14] Carl Malamud filed a notice of appeal with the US Court of Appeals for the Eleventh Circuit on April 21, 2017, available at: https://law.resource.org/pub/us/code/ga/pro_v_georgia/appeal_11th_circuit/gov.uscourts.ca11.17-11589.01109501297.pdf.
[15] See, e.g., Public.resource.org, "Show Me the Manual," available at: https://law.resource.org. The head building inspector for Sonoma County, California stated that it cost his department $30,000 to purchase the codes they needed for the last code cycle.

National Standards Institute (ANSI) develops standards for various industries that are later incorporated into the United States Code, making those standards legally binding on all citizens and residents of the USA. But since those standards are not printed in the code itself and are instead incorporated into the law by reference, anyone who needs to know what the law requires needs to buy access to ANSI standards. A section of those standards contains safety requirements for portable metal ladders, and was incorporated into the Code of Federal Regulations. Noncompliance with these standards can lead to criminal penalties.[16] ANSI sells their standards in a PDF for $1500.[17]

The exclusive rights that copyrights grant authors are meant to incentivize authors to produce more works, and standards bodies claim that they would not be able to continue developing standards if they could not receive copyright protection for them. An ANSI board member compared the push for free access to legal standards to "clamoring for free beer and free sex."[18] This is a fallacious argument and completely misses the point. Access to law should not be compared to random free stuff. The law binds us all, and ignorance of it can lead to serious civil or criminal penalties. Once a private standard is incorporated into a law by reference, it becomes part of the law and it ceases to matter that it was originally developed by a private standards body rather than a legislature. While it undoubtedly costs standards bodies like ANSI time and money to develop good industry standards, copyright is not the only way for them to be compensated for their efforts, and the current business model of locking legally binding standards behind a paywall is not inevitable.[19]

Until this legal issue is settled, there are ways for state and local governments to clearly indicate on their websites that their laws are in the public domain. The DC Code is one such example. The DC Code states that it is "available for use under CC0" and provides a link to the wiki explaining what that means.[20] Creative Commons provides HTML code that can be copied and pasted into a website and displays a simple logo that is hyperlinked to the explanatory wiki. This is a simple way for state and local governments to convey clearly that the law belongs to the people.

C Expense

Corporate control and copyright are major reasons for the high cost of accessing the law. The biggest challenge for the Case Law Access Project, for example, has been the cost of employing the team and the scanning equipment; even Harvard could not afford this huge undertaking on its own and partnered with Ravel Law to help with expenses.[21] These costs are necessary and inherent in converting books to usable digital publications, and while a digital-first publishing system is now possible and can make these costs avoidable in the future, they

---

[16] 29 CFR 1917.119, 1918.24.

[17] American National Standards Institute (ANSI), "ANSI ASC A14 Ladder Standards Package," available at: http://webstore.ansi.org/RecordDetail.aspx?sku=ANSI+ASC+A14+Ladder+Standards+Package.

[18] Mike Masnick, "Standards Body Whines that People Who Want Free Access to the Law Probably Also Want 'Free Sex'," Techdirt, July 7, 2016, available at: www.techdirt.com/articles/20160702/07240834879/standards-body-whines-that-people-who-want-free-access-to-law-probably-also-want-free-sex.shtml.

[19] Corynne McSherry, "The Law Belongs in the Public Domain," Electronic Frontier Foundation, January 14, 2014, available at: www.eff.org/deeplinks/2014/01/law-belongs-public-domain. Much of the work that goes into developing private standards is done by volunteers and government officials, and courts have acknowledged as much.

[20] Creative Commons, "CC0 FAQ," available at: https://wiki.creativecommons.org/wiki/CC0_FAQ.

[21] Ziegler, *supra* note 1.

still represent a significant barrier for digitizing laws that were printed first or are controlled by a commercial publisher.

PACER (Public Access to Court Electronic Records) charges ten cents per page for documents, for search results, and for docket listings. It is cost-prohibitive to use PACER for data mining or other mass analytic purposes: It would cost half a billion dollars for researchers who need access to the full corpus of PACER.[22] Yet in a survey conducted by a Stanford Law librarian, only 3 out of the 66 (4.5%) academic law library respondents stated that they did not limit or ration patron access to PACER.[23]

Due to technological advancements, providing electronic public access to law does not need to be as expensive as it currently is. PACER is run on a highly inefficient decentralized infrastructure: every court runs its own instance of PACER software, requiring its own hardware, network connection, and support staff.[24] While the law only allows the government to charge fees that reimburse costs,[25] there is evidence that the current fees are greater than the cost of providing the services.[26] The US General Services Administration (GSA) has a streamlined government procurement system for cloud hosting that could make PACER much more efficient and cost-effective.[27] Princeton's Center for Information Technology Policy and the Free Law Project have also developed a workaround: a browser plug-in that allows anyone to automatically upload PACER documents to a free database maintained by the Internet Archive.[28]

When DC undertook a project to put its legal code online as open data,[29] the Council of DC first had to remove the WestLaw logo from the header of their documents because they had previously contracted with WestLaw to publish its code.[30] The logo was in the header of the approximately 50 documents that make up the DC Code, but since the header was specified independently for each section of the code, there were thousands of logos to remove.[31] This extra work makes digitizing legal texts more expensive than it would be otherwise.

---

[22] Stephen Schultze, "Making Excuses for Fees on Electronic Public Records," Freedom to Tinker, February 7, 2013, available at: https://freedom-to-tinker.com/2013/02/07/making-excuses-for-fees-on-electronic-public-records.

[23] Erika Wayne, "PACER Spending Survey," Legal Research Plus, August 28, 2009, available at: https://legalresearchplus.com/2009/08/28/pacer-spending-survey.

[24] Between district, bankruptcy, and circuit courts, these resources are duplicated approximately 200 times. See Stephen Schultze, "What Does It Cost to Provide Electronic Public Access to Court Records?" openpacer.org, available at: www.openpacer.org/hogan/Schultze_PACER_Costs.pdf.

[25] Note to 28 U.S.C. § 1913: "The Judicial Conference may, only to the extent necessary, prescribe reasonable fees ... for collection by the courts under those sections for access to information available through automatic data processing equipment."

[26] Schultze, *supra* note 22.

[27] The GSA-developed cloud-based infrastructure has agreements with agencies that allow them to buy cloud storage, virtual machines, web hosting, and data center services. See GSA, "Infrastructure as a Service (IaaS)," available at: www.gsa.gov/portal/content/112063.

[28] The Free Law Project, https://free.law.

[29] *See* Council of the District of Columbia, "District of Columbia Official Code," September 2013, available at: http://dccouncil.us/UnofficialDCCode.

[30] Joshua Tauberer, "DC Opens Its 'code,' Embracing Principles of Open Laws," personal blog, April 4, 2013, available at: https://razor.occams.info/blog/2013/04/04/dc-opens-its-code-embracing-principles-of-open-laws.

[31] 17 U.S.C. 105; *ibid*.

III MAKING THE LAW OPEN

Free online access to law is necessary, but more must be done to make that access have a meaningful impact. Addressing the following issues will make the law easier to access and use, and will also expand the possible uses of legal information.

A Format

The format used to deliver the text of a law to a user determines how that text may be used. PDFs are the most common format governments use to digitally publish their laws, but PDFs are often nothing more than images of printed documents that are read-only. Text in this format is not machine-readable, so it cannot be copied or searched; this makes it difficult to republish the law in any useful way. Additionally, it precludes other uses, such as copying and pasting a quote from a case into a court filing, or use of screen reader software that can read text aloud to visually impaired people. The text in PDFs can be converted into a better format. However, techniques such as optical character recognition (OCR), which automatically convert images of text into machine-encoded text, are time-consuming, potentially expensive, and imperfect.[32] Text must first be extracted from a PDF, which can result in problems such as extensive whitespace formatting, underlines appearing as underscores, footnotes being included in the main text, and single words being split onto two lines.[33]

It is much better for original legal texts to be in a machine-readable format than to require conversion, and there is a spectrum of acceptable machine-readable formats that can be used. Digitally created (i.e., not scanned images of printed text) PDFs are the bare minimum to satisfy Harvard's guidelines for the digital publication of court decisions.[34] Federal agencies have also begun work on improving access. The Consumer Financial Protection Bureau and 18F have created eRegulations to improve online access to federal regulations. Their guidelines state that Microsoft Word (.doc or .docx) is an acceptable format, but that XML or markdown HTML are ideal formats.[35] The structured formats of XML and HTML make it easier and more affordable for third parties to gather and parse this data.

B Bulk Conveyance

Format concerns *what* the legal information is contained in. Conveyance, meanwhile, concerns *how* that legal information is contained. A government body may choose to make its legal information available in print, web, or bulk access. As with format, conveyance may determine the potential uses of the information. For example, nowadays it is common to have both a print and a web version of the same set of laws. As discussed above, the print version may be the only "official" version of a law, but the web version is how most lawyers and members of the public actually access the law. Generally, the conveyance of laws via the web is not the issue; rather, problems arise because of the format of the information and the unofficial status of that information on the internet.

---

[32] *See, e.g.*, Michael Jay Lissner, "Converting PDF Files to HTML," February 6, 2010, available at: http://michaeljaylissner.com/posts/2010/02/06/converting-pdf-files-to-html.

[33] *See* Rowyn McDonald and Karen Rustad, "The Berkeley National Reporter: Building a Free, Open Source Legal Citator," University of California, Berkeley, 2012: 19, available at: www.ischool.berkeley.edu/sites/default/files/student_projects/mcdonald_rustad_report.pdf.

[34] Ziegler, phone interview, *supra* note 1.

[35] eRegulations, "Writing rules and regulations," available at: https://eregs.github.io/guidelines.

Bulk conveyance would streamline the conveyance process and make sure all formats are consistent. Third parties need to be able to download and repurpose legal information, and the consistency of bulk conveyance would greatly aid this process. Bulk conveyance of laws is rare, though. Most states do not allow bulk access to their legal information publications, and some even have prohibitions against bulk access tools in their terms of use.[36] New Mexico's Case Lookup, for example, prohibits downloading multiple cases at the same time.[37] The CourtListener service is trying to correct this deficiency by creating bulk files for jurisdiction–object pairs (e.g., Ninth Circuit opinions).[38] But the fact remains that more affirmative measures must be taken to create and maintain bulk access to statutes and regulations in order to reduce costs for third parties seeking to republish.[39] If governments do not convey laws to the public in bulk form, they are limiting the amount of usable data, making it little more effective than an obsolete print book.

C Official Versions and Authentication

There are currently no uniform standards determining how a version of a law becomes official or how it can be authenticated.[40] The official versions of many laws are often only available in print.[41] There are multiple methods to make online publications of laws official despite this lack of standard requirements.[42] Some states clearly say on their websites that the online version is official law: Maryland, New Mexico, Tennessee, and Virginia have all passed statutes specifying that online publications of laws are official.[43] The judiciary also possesses the authority to designate digital publications of laws as official. Arkansas once had statutory requirements for the print publication of its official reporter, so legislative amendments were required to switch to electronic publication.[44] However, the Arkansas Supreme Court later ruled that print publication of the Arkansas Reports would end with volume 375 and that the "official report" of all decisions issued after that cutoff would be the "electronic file created, authenticated, secured, and maintained by the Reporter of Decisions on the Arkansas Judiciary website."[45] Some states have statutes or policies indicating that online publications are official, but the implementation and labeling of these digital documents makes their official status ambiguous.[46] For this reason, some states place disclaimers on their websites warning users that the cases, statutes, or regulations on their website are not the official versions.[47]

---

[36] See Glassmeyer, "State Legal Information Census," *supra* note 2, at 18. Her research found that only 2% of case law websites, 6% of regulation websites, and 8% of statutory websites allowed for bulk access, and that some of these bulk access options required payment.

[37] New Mexico Courts, "Case Lookup," available at: https://caselookup.nmcourts.gov/caselookup/app.

[38] Michael Jay Lissner, "Updating Bulk Data in CourtListener … Again," personal website, November 6, 2014, available at: http://michaeljaylissner.com/posts/2014/11/06/updating-bulk-data-in-courtlistener-more; see also Court Listener, "Bulk Data," available at: www.courtlistener.com/api/bulk-info.

[39] Martin, "Abandoning Law Reports for Official Digital Case Law,"*supra* note 3, at 84–85.

[40] See American Association of Law Libraries, "Guide to Evaluating Legal Information Online," July 2016, available at: www.aallnet.org/mm/Advocacy/access/evaluatelegalinfoguide.html.

[41] See Glassmeyer, "State Legal Information Census," *supra* note 2, at 28.

[42] Richard J. Matthews and Mary Alice Baish, "State-by-State Report on Authentication of Online Legal Resources," American Association of Law Libraries, March 2007, at 22–24, available at: www.aallnet.org/Documents/Government-Relations/authen_rprt/authenfinalreport.pdf.

[43] Id. at 45–47.

[44] Martin, "Abandoning Law Reports for Official Digital Case Law," *supra* note 3, at 43.

[45] Id. at 42.

[46] Id. at 51.

[47] Glassmeyer, "State Legal Information Census," *supra* note 2, at 28.

Only the governments writing the laws – courts, legislatures, and administrative agencies – have the power to determine what makes a publication official. If government bodies at the federal, state, and municipal levels provided raw data that constituted the official statements of law, this would enable greater public access to law. Digital versions of official laws would help achieve the medium-neutral objective, and would also eliminate the need to digitize books of laws in the future because there would already be an official online version.[48]

In order to accomplish the medium-neutral objective, legal publishers need a way to establish that the legal information they provide is authentic. Multiple authentication methods have been suggested and tried, such as watermarks, certificates, and digital signatures. For example, Arkansas places the state seal on all official (i.e., non-slip) opinions with text beneath stating "official court opinion."[49] This is essentially a watermark, and it is sufficient authentication for documents hosted on the state's website. Digital signatures like these could also be used to assure legal practitioners that online publishers' chain of custody leads back to the original official government source. The signer, which here would be the government entity releasing the law, creates the digital signature, and this signature can then be verified by another party to confirm that the information accompanying the signature could only have been sent by the signer and has not been changed since it was sent. The source of the information could be in the document metadata, by using the TEI <sourceDesc> and <revisionDesc> tags, or something similar.[50] This opens up options for lawyers who want to use reliable third-party sites that are innovating new tools to use with government data.[51]

It may not even be necessary for the legal community to develop complex authentication methods for primary legal materials. Law librarians have expressed concern that digital files are much more susceptible to corruption and maintenance lapses compared to print editions of laws, claiming that, "[t]he disappearance of print official legal resources without an authentic online substitute critically erodes the bedrock of trustworthy statements of the law."[52] This is not necessarily true, though. Westlaw and LexisNexis often only provide unofficial versions of laws, and the authenticity of their content has not been questioned. Meanwhile, the Cornell Legal Information Institute – among other relatively new legal publishers, such as Justia – collect their documents from the same unofficial court sources as Westlaw and LexisNexis.[53] Therefore, it seems that distrust of those publishers comes from custom rather than any substantive reasons. But this is not an insurmountable obstacle, considering the Cornell Legal Information Institute has become the most linked-to legal website in the world.[54] Thus, a reputation for trustworthiness combined with a standard method for obtaining unofficial legal materials could be an adequate substitution for authentication tools.

---

[48] This is what Harvard is currently working on for case law. *See* Ziegler, *supra* note 1.

[49] *See, e.g., Jerry Lard v. State of Arkansas*, 2014 Ark. 1, available at: http://opinions.aoc.arkansas.gov/WebLink8/o/doc/319825/Electronic.aspx.

[50] John Joergensen, "Authentication of Digital Repositories," VoxPopuLII, May 14, 2009, available at: https://blog.law.cornell.edu/voxpop/2009/05/14/authentication-of-digital-repositories.

[51] *See* David Robinson, Harlan Yu, William P. Zeller, and Edward W. Felten, "Government Data and the Invisible Hand," *Yale Journal of Law and Technology* 11 (2009): 174–175; *see also* Joergensen, "Authentication of Digital Repositories," *supra* note 49, who argues that this type of digital signature is overkill because it is only necessary when users are concerned about the transmission of information.

[52] Matthews and Baish, *supra* note 42, at 10, 56.

[53] Joergensen, *supra* note 50.

[54] Cornell Legal Information Institute, "About LII: Who We Are," www.law.cornell.edu/lii/about/who_we_are#reliability.

D Version Control

Version control is necessary for establishing the official status of digital legal publications. The switch to digital raises the issue of how to treat unpublished opinions and slip opinions. A *slip opinion* is a temporary version of an opinion, typically published online when a decision is first issued so that people can access a decision without having to wait for final edits, which are often time-consuming and must be made before the final decision can be published. Access problems arise from this because courts commonly publish slip opinions online without indicating later changes.[55] Arkansas provides a helpful model for solving this problem. When decisions are first released, Arkansas uploads slip opinions to its website with a watermark reading "SLIP OPINION" on every page of the document.[56] Once the final versions of the laws are ready, they are uploaded and the slip opinions are removed. Importantly, only the *final* versions have the deciding court's seal and digital signature. This approach retains the convenience and timeliness of having immediate access to slip opinions, while also making sure that the public has access to the fully edited version once it is ready, eliminating confusion by removing the slip opinions.

When Arkansas transitioned from publishing official cases in print reporters to publishing them online, it decided to eliminate the "unpublished" decision category at the urging of the bar association and state legislature.[57] Traditionally, the high cost of printing law reports prevented states from publishing all opinions, and since there was no official version of these unpublished opinions, they could not be cited as precedent. Since digital publishing is significantly less expensive than print publishing, the main justification for leaving decisions unpublished disappeared once Arkansas began publishing all decisions online.

This problem is slightly different for regulations and statutes, which do not have slip or unpublished versions but do have subsequent amendments. Timestamps and currency dates are not always stated on a website of legal codes, which has led some lawyers to call state legislative offices to find out when they last updated the code.[58] Future statutes or policies that list the requirements for digital official laws could stipulate that government websites include the date of the last update, which would help prove to users that the information is reliable. The usage of a version control system such as Github could be especially helpful for statutes and regulations. Version control systems record changes to a file without replacing the earlier versions. This makes sense, because we do not want to delete evidence that an earlier version of a statute existed; we simply want access to older versions of statutes in order to have a more complete understanding of a case. In this way, version control could be especially helpful for interpreting legislative history. Once a bill is drafted, it goes through many stages of study, debate, and revisions. The ability to clearly see the different stages of legislative drafting would help courts interpret the legislature's intent. For example, if the first draft of a statute included a list of items that it applied to, and the final version removed one of those items, a court could infer that the exclusion of that item was intentional, and thus come to a more precise interpretation of it.

---

[55] Glassmeyer, "State Legal Information Census," *supra* note 2, at 29.
[56] Martin, Abandoning Law Reports for Official Digital Case Law," *supra* note 3, at 39.
[57] *Id.* at 40. This category still applies for cases decided prior to 2009.
[58] Courtney Minick, "Universal Citation for State Codes," VoxPopuLII, September 2, 2011, available at: https://blog.law.cornell.edu/voxpop/2011/09/01/universal-citation-for-state-codes.

E Citation

Proprietary citation systems are another reason it has been so difficult for new companies to break into the legal publishing market. The idea of universal citation – also referred to as vendor-neutral, medium-neutral, or public domain citation – is not new, but the US legal community has been slow to implement it. The American Association of Law Libraries developed and published the *Universal Citation Guide* in 1999 and released an updated version in 2004, but only 16 states assign universal citations to their highest court opinions.[59]

Eleven states require use of *The Bluebook: A Uniform System of Citation*, but *Bluebook* is a proprietary system owned by the Columbia Law Review Association, Inc., the Harvard Law Review Association, the University of Pennsylvania Law Review, and the Yale Law Journal Company, Inc.[60] *The Bluebook* always requires citations to the West National Reporter System, so a lawyer submitting a brief to a court requiring *Bluebook*-style citations must pay for both the reference guide and a subscription to a commercial publisher, just to access and cite public domain work. Judge Richard Posner considers this uniform system of citation anticompetitive, and argues that *The Bluebook* should not have a monopoly on legal citation.[61] One suggested solution to this problem is a parallel citation table that shows the universal citation alongside a commercial reporter citation.[62]

Allowing lawyers to cite other publishers would make the market for legal publishing much more competitive. If lawyers already have to cite to the WestLaw version of a case, they would probably not pay for another subscription service – even one with better features – because it would still be necessary for them to pay for a WestLaw subscription. A universal citation system would allow lawyers to access the law through various publishers, because citing to any particular publication of an opinion would not be required.

Current methods of citation have not adapted adequately to the online ecosystem of legal information. *The Bluebook* and other citation systems were developed when books were the primary resources for legal research. This makes them ill-suited guides for internet sourcing. Currently, court decisions do not have a unique and universal identifier that can be easily expressed as searchable metadata, which is necessary for a workable online system. If there were a non-proprietary universal form, companies could build citation tools so that attorneys and paralegals would not need to spend valuable time formatting citations. Other fields that use non-proprietary citation systems already have such tools. For example, there are online citation machines that allow users to search for a source as they would on Google, and once they select the source a citation is automatically generated in accordance with the selected standard, such as MLA or Chicago style.[63]

Link rot and reference rot are also serious problems in legal citations. *Link rot* refers to instances when a cited URL no longer contains any material, and following the link returns an HTTP status code such as "404 Not Found." *Reference rot* refers to instances when a cited URL serves up material, but the material cited has changed or is no longer present. This is a pervasive problem: 50% of the URLs cited in US Supreme Court opinions suffer reference

---

[59] Ibid.
[60] "The Bluebook: A Uniform System of Citation," available at: www.legalbluebook.com/default.aspx. The copyright claims are dubious, because the Copyright Act specifically provides that systems are not to receive copyright protection and the word "system" is used in this book's title.
[61] Richard A. Posner, "The *Bluebook* Blues," *Yale Law Journal* 120 (2011): 850–862, available at: www.yalelawjournal.org/review/the-bluebook-blues.
[62] Courtney Minick, "Public Domain Legal Citations," Justia Law Blog, December 17, 2010, available at: https://lawblog.justia.com/2010/12/17/public-domain-legal-citations.
[63] See, e.g., EasyBib, www.easybib.com.

rot.[64] These problems undermine the value of the sources cited in judicial opinions. In the pre-internet era, all sources cited were in printed books. Those books may have been obscure and difficult to track down, but the nature of books ensured that they would remain unchanged. Now, we have the opposite problem: Hyperlinks make it easy to track down sources, but there is no guarantee that the information at that location will be the same as when the source was cited.

Permanent links offer a solution to link rot and reference rot. When citing online sources in briefs, some lawyers have resorted to printing out webpages and inserting the printouts as addendums in PDFs, because they do not want the court to struggle to find the source they cited.[65] Harvard Law School Library developed a tool to address link rot and reference rot called Perma.cc, which it maintains in conjunction with other law libraries. Perma.cc is user-friendly: A user just needs to enter the URL of the page she wishes to preserve and cite, the software visits that URL, preserves the page by depositing it into the collection, and then the software gives the user a unique URL.[66] This tool is preferable to other proposed solutions, such as adopting digital object identifiers or using the Internet Archive, because Perma links are simple and the project is reliably funded.[67] Courts and other government organizations qualify for unlimited free accounts to Perma.cc and are therefore able to take advantage of this valuable resource for their citations.[68] As important as it is for the citations in opinions to be permanently preserved, it is even more important for the primary law itself to be stored at a permanent link.

F Citators

Citators are essential tools for case law research because they indicate whether a case is still good law. For a given case, a citator identifies what other cases cite that case, and also shows the depth of treatment the given case receives from those other cases. A citator also indicates the relationship between the given case and the cases citing it: whether the treatment is positive, upholding the doctrine; or negative, overruling the doctrine. This function of determining the relationship between cases is known in lawyer jargon as *Shepardizing*. Shepardizing is named for Frank Shepard, who originally developed a citation system in a series of books called *Shepard's Citations*.[69] LexisNexis acquired Shepard's in the late 1990s and it is now a feature of its digital subscription service. WestLaw has also developed its own proprietary citator, called KeyCite. These citators, however, are only available to subscribers to LexisNexis and WestLaw.[70]

There have been a couple attempts at building a free and open-source legal citator, with mixed success. A team of Berkeley researchers built a free and open-source citator for

---

[64] Jonathan Zittrain, Kendra Albert, and Lawrence Lessig, "Perma: Scoping and Addressing the Problem of Link and Reference Rot in Legal Citations," *Harvard Law Review Forum* 127, March 17, 2014: 176, available at: http://harvardlawreview.org/2014/03/perma-scoping-and-addressing-the-problem-of-link-and-reference-rot-in-legal-citations.

[65] Marilyn Odendahl, "Attorneys Finding More Link Rot Online," The Indiana Lawyer, January 29, 2014, available at: www.theindianalawyer.com/attorneys-finding-more-link-rot-online/PARAMS/article/33336.

[66] Perma.cc, "Overview," available at: https://perma.cc/docs#how-does-perma-work.

[67] Zittrain et al., "Perma," *supra* note 64.

[68] Perma.cc, "Perma.cc Basics," available at: https://perma.cc/docs#create-account.

[69] *See generally*, "Shepard's Citations," *Wikipedia*, available at: https://en.wikipedia.org/wiki/Shepard's_Citations (accessed June 9, 2020).

[70] Thomson Reuters WestLaw, "KeyCite," available at: https://legalsolutions.thomsonreuters.com/law-products/westlaw-legal-research/keycite.

CourtListener, using Linux, Apache, MySQL, Python, and Django for the main site, Solr for the search engine, and Celery and RabbitMQ for distributed task management.[71] Their research discovered that lawyers found depth of treatment the most important feature of a citator, because many lawyers are skeptical of Shepard's and KeyCite's categories and so will often read cases for themselves.[72] The researchers identified a few features that could be added to improve their citator in the future: modifying the algorithm to identify short forms of citations so that it could recognize subsequent citations in a case for a depth-of-treatment signal; using natural language processing to analyze the text surrounding a citation in order to determine whether the case agrees or disagrees with the citation; and using Bayesian algorithms that could train the computer to identify citations, rather than their current approach of hard-coding for citation recognition.[73]

There are further improvements to free and open-source citators that could make them more appealing than Shepard's or KeyCite. For example, it is not just the number of times a case is cited, but the amount of words devoted to discussing it, that determines how deeply a case has been treated in an opinion. For this reason, a word count algorithm could be included to make the depth of treatment signals more accurate. Currently, both Shepard's and KeyCite show a single signal next to each case name, even though a citing case may only supply a positive or negative treatment of a very small part of the case. More robust citator algorithms could fill these information gaps.

A high-quality citator is necessary for any legal research startup striving to compete with WestLaw and LexisNexis. Lois Law and Fastcase compete with the duopoly on other metrics, but their lack of legal citators is a big reason why firms may not switch.[74] Lawyers will be attracted to new citators if they are able to do one thing well, instead of trying to do everything that WestLaw and LexisNexis do poorly.[75] The citator issue can only be solved if greater emphasis is placed on context. Citators express relationships between different cases, putting a single case into the broader context of its subsequent treatment. It would be useful, then, for citators to have the option of including statutes and regulations in addition to case law. A lawyer researching a state law issue may need to visit three or more different websites to access cases, statutes, regulations, and any updates to them.[76] It would be far better if a lawyer only had to visit one location in order to find all the most relevant citations.

G Index, Cataloguing, and Search

A legal website's organization and search features have a significant impact on the public's ability to access the law, and government websites have largely failed in these efforts. Not all primary law websites have search capabilities, and many that do search all of the information on the site without an option to limit a search to the primary law.[77] For example, some materials on the Federal Communications Commission's website are not full-text searchable, even for texts that are in a searchable file format.[78]

---

[71] See McDonald and Rustad, "The Berkeley National Reporter," *supra* note 33 at 19.
[72] *Id.* at 10.
[73] *Id.* at 23.
[74] For more on Fastcase and the competitive tools it brings to the market, see Walters and Asjes – Fastcase, and the Visual Understanding of Judicial Precedents, *supra*.
[75] McDonald and Rustad, "The Berkeley National Reporter," *supra* note 33, at 11.
[76] Glassmeyer, "State Legal Information Census," *supra* note 2, at 14–15.
[77] *Id.* at 31.
[78] See Robinson et al., "Government Data and the Invisible Hand," *supra* note 51, at 162.

Cataloguing and search problems are partially caused by citation issues. The current citations for court decisions cannot be used as unique identifiers to construct a usable primary key for a metadata system for a digital repository.[79] A reformed citation system would make it easier to develop the metadata necessary to properly organize huge collections of cases and make them searchable.

H Archives

Ideally, the total corpus of American law would be fully free and open online, satisfying our previously stated guideline of comprehensiveness. Archives are necessary because very dated cases, statutes, and regulations may still be good law. Accessing these archives will be exceedingly difficult to accomplish without conveyance via bulk access, which could enable the use of tools like web scrapers. Harvard and Ravel's collaboration is creating archives of all case law,[80] but there are currently no similar projects for statutes or regulations.

IV THE GOVERNMENT'S NEW ROLE IN LEGAL TECH AND PUBLISHING

There are many different roles governments can play in the online publication of law while still enabling free and open access for their citizens. Some governments have had great success self-publishing. Illinois and Arkansas are successful examples of a digital-first case law publishing regimes delivered by states.[81] The US Government Publishing Office has created an interface for the Electronic Code of Federal Regulations (e-CFR) that is current and relatively user-friendly, but it is not official.[82] These are some notable successes of governments spearheading open access to law, but for every success story like these, there are several examples of government bodies with primary law websites that are outdated and difficult to use.[83]

Federal webmasters face more challenges than private webmasters, because there are 24 different regulatory regimes with which all public federal websites are required to comply.[84] Furthermore, First Amendment considerations make some website features – such as wikis, discussion boards, and group annotations – nearly impossible for the government to manage.[85] Sarah Glassmeyer does not see government websites as the best model: "In an ideal world, states would publish their information digitally in such a way that is acceptable by secondary organizations, like nonprofits. I really don't trust the states to create resource portals that would be useful."[86]

---

[79] Cornell University Law School Legal Information Institute, "Citations, AALL Citations and Primary Keys," VoxPopuLII, available at: www.law.cornell.edu/wiki/lexcraft/citations_aall_citations_and_primary_keys.
[80] Harvard Law School, "Harvard Law School Launches 'Caselaw Access' Project," October 29, 2015, available at: https://today.law.harvard.edu/harvard-law-school-launches-caselaw-access-project-ravel-law.
[81] Ziegler, *supra* note 1. Ziegler notes, however, that their use of digitally created PDFs was not ideal and XML or HTML would be preferable.
[82] US Government Publishing Office, "Electronic Code of Federal Regulations," available at: www.ecfr.gov/cgi-bin/ECFR?page=browse.
[83] Robinson et al., "Government Data and the Invisible Hand," *supra* note 51, at 161.
[84] *Id.* at 162–163.
[85] *Id.* at 165.
[86] Stephanie Francis Ward, "Sarah Glassmeyer: Opening a Window on Closed Data," ABA Legal Rebels Profiles, September 22, 2016, available at: www.abajournal.com/legalrebels/article/sarah_glassmeyer_profile/?utm_source=dlvr.it&utm_medium=twitter&utm_campaign=site_rss_feeds.

Luckily, it is not necessary for the government to take full responsibility for controlling all aspects of the editorial process. The public office of law reporter is a declining breed,[87] and it is a common misunderstanding that the government's responsibility is to create a website containing the laws.[88] Governments can choose how open their data is, and whether they will prioritize changing the technical infrastructures to make open data a reality. Instead of recognizing this, governments still invest a lot of resources in development of their websites. A government's responsibility is to make the law free and open, though, not to build online legal research tools. Governments can redefine their role in online legal publishing as the providers of reusable data by relying on the engineering principle of separating data from interaction. One way to make this work would be for the government to store data in a MySQL database, and then leave it to third parties to build websites with interactive access to the public, using a web server such as Apache.[89] The US Government Publishing Office has done an excellent job with the CFR: Anyone can download the bulk data of the code in XML.[90] Private publishers have more resources and fewer legal restrictions than the government, making them better suited to transform raw data into useful research services. Ideally, all governments would follow one standard or protocol, but the Harvard Library Innovation Lab has not tried to impose specific requirements and has instead focused on general principles; ultimately, courts, legislatures, and government agencies will have to implement the standards.[91]

V CONCLUSION: LOOKING AHEAD

Wikipedia and Google have democratized most of the world's knowledge, but there are still many hurdles to overcome before the law is fully democratized. Restrictions created by private companies and governments have outlived the usefulness they once provided. Legal technology has the potential to transform the study and practice of law in countless ways, some of which are difficult to imagine now because the law is not free and open yet. With open access to legal data, anyone and everyone will be able to create applications that both promote access to justice and support innovative tools. Removing barriers to legal access will enable empirical legal studies, data visualization, predictive analysis, custom applications, search engines for specific practice areas, and much more.

---

[87] *See* Martin, "Abandoning Law Reports for Official Digital Case Law," *supra* note 3, at 28–34.
[88] Molly Schwartz, "Public Access vs. Open Access," Congressional Data Coalition, April 17, 2014, available at: http://congressionaldata.org/public-access-vs-open-access.
[89] Robinson et al., "Government Data and the Invisible Hand," *supra* note 51, at 161.
[90] US Government Publishing Office, "Code of Federal Regulations (Annual Edition) – Bulk Data," available at: www.gpo.gov/fdsys/bulkdata/CFR.
[91] Ziegler, *supra* note 1.

B.

Large Firm and Corporate Legal Informatics Case Studies

4.3

A History of Knowledge Management at Littler Mendelson

Scott Rechtschaffen

I INTRODUCTION

The development of knowledge management and the early adoption of innovative technology into Littler Mendelson's practice did not occur by chance, or as a reactionary response to "everyone else doing it." Littler launched a robust and comprehensive knowledge management program and adopted new technology in order to support its long-term strategic plans, help achieve its vision of becoming a global law firm, and uphold its commitment to meeting clients' needs. By making both knowledge management and technology adoption an integral part of the firm's strategic plan, rather than an *ad hoc* response to episodic changes in the market, Littler has fully integrated both into the way the firm does business and serves its clients.

Several factors have influenced Littler's decision and approach to adopting knowledge management and technology: Littler's pre-digital era history of innovating and supporting entrepreneurial projects; Littler's strategic growth plans, both domestically and globally; and the changing nature of its practice as more clients have come to perceive employment law as a commodity.

From its inception, Littler's business model was an innovative concept for a law firm. Littler was one of the first "boutique" law firms, singularly focused on one area of law: management-side labor and employment law. Littler also had an entrepreneurial approach to how a law firm should market and deliver its services, breaking ground that other firms had not considered. Littler was a pioneer in content marketing; it was among the first firms to put on client conferences, distribute client alerts, self-publish comprehensive books in its subject area, and develop unique legal products like videos and early-stage software products. Littler was also one of the first law firms to create a standalone business to offer its clients ancillary services. All of this was done to establish the Littler brand as the authoritative expert in its field.

Littler created a standalone business to offer clients ancillary services, and developed several technology products, but it also had a vision of how a "boutique" firm could become a global firm, and had the foresight to see how the legal market would soon change and begin requiring firms to adjust to the commoditization of legal services. Littler considered how knowledge management and technology could address these concerns, and realized that becoming a global firm with far-flung offices required technology and knowledge management practices that connected attorneys and offices, avoided duplication of effort, and provided clients with consistent and uniform services across offices. Building a global network of offices and attorneys required, among many other things, a substantial investment in both technology and knowledge management resources.

Littler recognized the growing influence of commoditization at the same time as many of its larger corporate clients. Developing HR policies or employment-related documents, providing advice and information regarding local laws, handling administrative charges, litigating single plaintiff lawsuits, and even handling wage-hour class actions were increasingly becoming seen by clients as routine work that should be performed on a predictable flat-fee basis. Littler responded to these concerns by developing innovative approaches to the delivery of its services: it developed client-facing subscription information services; developed or deployed internal knowledge management systems that would make its attorneys more efficient in delivering their services; developed an entirely re-engineered process for managing and handling litigation and litigation-related services; and partnered with a software provider to create a standalone company to develop legal technology solutions.

Convincing Littler's attorneys to adjust the firm's business processes to reflect the changes in the legal marketplace has not come without challenges, though. While Littler may have had some inherent or acquired advantages, it also encountered many issues that virtually every large law firm confronts when trying to change the working behavior of professionals who still believe in the approach and results of their entrenched business model. This was not the only problem, though. Another major challenge for Littler, and one other large firm's experience as well, involved compensation and capital structures that did not reward efficiency, support substantial investment in research and development, or allow for expensive enterprise-scaled technology systems. Finally, and not surprisingly, it is always difficult to get professionals to change the way they do things when that change, instead of helping them do their jobs better, might actually *eliminate* their jobs or make them unnecessary.

This case study reviews the strategic imperatives that forced Littler to become an early adopter of knowledge management and legal technology, and how those imperatives shaped that adoption. It also reviews the innovative approaches to knowledge management and legal technology Littler pursued, and some of the internal challenges Littler confronted in the process.

II BRIEF HISTORY AND DESCRIPTION OF LITTLER MENDELSON

Littler Mendelson began in 1942 in San Francisco. At that time, it was a small, two-attorney law practice focused exclusively on management-side labor law. The firm grew slowly over the decades; by the end of the 1970s, Littler had fewer than 40 attorneys in five offices, all in California. In the 1980s, labor law (i.e., union–management relations) was overtaken by the burgeoning field of employment law, with the emergence of wrongful termination and employment discrimination litigation, ERISA and employee benefits law, and human resources advice and counseling. The firm expanded rapidly under these conditions, but remained exclusively focused on the employer–employee relationship even as the legal issues arising from that relationship began to increase exponentially.

The pace quickened in the 1990s, and the firm expanded outside of California to several major US cities. By the end of the millennium, Littler had over 350 attorneys in 24 offices, including New York, Washington, Dallas, Chicago, and Atlanta. By 2010, the firm had opened another 20 offices, and doubled the number of its attorneys.

Responding to clients' increasingly globalized needs, Littler opened its first international office in Caracas, Venezuela in 2010. Littler subsequently opened two offices in Mexico and continued to expand throughout Central and South America. More recently, Littler opened offices in Canada, Germany, France, and the UK. Today, the firm has over 1200 attorneys working in 75 offices (including 22 offices outside of the USA), making it the largest law firm in the world exclusively devoted to representing management in employment, employee benefits, and labor law matters.

In recent years, Littler has developed a very prominent reputation as one of the most innovative law firms in the USA. It has been recognized or has received awards for innovation by the *Financial Times*, American Lawyer Media, Law Technology News, the International Legal Technology Association, the College of Law Practice Management, BTI Consulting, the *ABA Journal*, and Bloomberg BNA. Legal industry leaders and consultants speaking at conferences and meetings frequently cite Littler as an example of an innovative law firm.

Littler's innovative products and services include: Littler GPS®, a client-facing subscription database of multi-jurisdictional US employment law; toolkits such as HR PolicySmart, X-Celerator, and the Franchise Compliance Toolkit, all of which address specific legal or industry-specific issues; Littler CaseSmart®, an award-winning and cost-effective platform for managing litigation; and ComplianceHR, a joint venture with a legal technology software company that develops expert system software to assist organizations in assessing their legal risks in employment decision making.

Littler has overcome obstacles that many law firms confront when trying to reshape their business models. The firm's interest in innovating – and its ability to do so effectively – is a product of Littler's history of growing from a small boutique practice to becoming a global "Big Law" firm.

III BRAND-BUILDING THROUGH CONTENT AND ENTREPRENEURIALISM

When it began its expansion outside of California, Littler frequently encountered what its attorneys colloquially referred to as the "Littler who?" problem. By 1990, Littler had over 100 attorneys in a dozen California offices, and had established itself as a major regional firm with a developing reputation in the employment and labor field. Littler was not a general practice firm, however, and this made it a lesser-known name in the legal marketplace outside of California. When it opened new offices in cities outside of California, particularly on the East Coast, Littler was an unknown entity to corporate decision makers. Attorneys opening up Littler's new offices often had to compete against more established firms, including many regional and local employment and labor boutiques. Over time, and with the addition of new attorneys and the overall growth of the firm, this problem eventually resolved itself. This was due in part to Littler's understanding that marketing – particularly content marketing and developing a reputation for innovation – could help them become more established and well-known.

Littler became more entrepreneurial as it expanded. They experimented with content marketing, video training products, and partnerships with early-stage software vendors. In 1983, Littler launched The Employer® conference, an annual gathering of human resources professionals and in-house employment counsel that eventually would attract over 1000 attendees at each year's event. In 1984, the firm began publishing The National

Employer®, an annual compendium of labor and employment law information that would eventually cover 26 topics over more than 3000 pages.[1]

These projects met with initial resistance from many of the firm's attorneys. At the time, few law firms held client conferences at which their most experienced attorneys openly discussed legal developments and practical strategies clients could implement to avoid legal risk. Few law firms published how-to books setting forth their insightful analysis of the state of the law and the most critical cases and legislation, let alone offering practical self-help tools such as checklists, model forms, and templates. Several of Littler's leaders strongly objected, arguing that they billed clients thousands of dollars for memoranda analyzing the state of the law and recent developments. They routinely charged clients for practical tools such as checklists, forms, and templates. These ventures produced a clear conflict, but they were part of Littler's belief in the value of content marketing. Content marketing is a concept espoused most prominently by Garry Mathiason, one of Littler's visionaries on the future of legal services. Mathiason understood that clients would come to expect "content" from their attorneys; a prescient insight when one considers the rise of the internet, where content would become something available for free. Mathiason recognized that content and legal information would be more valuable in building Littler's reputation for authoritative expertise on employment and labor law. When Littler's National Employer book series was first published in 1984, Littler had no offices outside of California. Yet this publication helped establish Littler's reputation as a "national" firm. Similarly, Littler would publish its Guide to International Employment Law starting in 2008, before it had a single office outside of the USA. This publication helped establish Littler's reputation for knowledge of global employment law. In Mathiason's view, the value of establishing Littler's brand of authoritative expertise through content marketing was worth far more than the revenue that could be derived from billing clients for individual memoranda.

Along with its conferences and publications, Littler also began to consider creating employment law "products." As Littler's reputation for having a deep bench of subject matter experts and a willingness to explore creative ideas grew, opportunities arose to partner with third-party companies. Many of these companies operated in the human resources space, and were eager to partner with Littler. In the early 1990s, Littler partnered with various companies to create, among other things, a telephone "fax-back service" in which employers could use their telephone touch-tone keypads to ask questions through a decision tree, which resulted in a facsimile of a legal memorandum on their topic of interest. Littler also partnered with other companies to develop software that could generate employee handbooks and employment agreements, and they also developed one of the first online background check services.

One of these partnerships foreshadowed how Littler would structure its relationships and investments in the future. A video production company approached Littler about collaborating on a series of managerial training videos on human resources and employment law. The production company asked Littler to share the production costs in exchange for an ownership interest in the intellectual property rights. As most law firms would have at the time, Littler responded that it could not justify investing outside of its core business. Instead, Littler counteroffered. The production company would put up the required capital to cover production and retain full ownership of the intellectual property. In exchange, Littler would receive a small royalty on sales of the video. One of the videos, *Avoiding Litigation Landmines*, became a bestseller, generating huge profits for the production company. Littler enjoyed

---

[1] *See* "The Littler National Employer Library," available at: www.littler.com/bookstore.

royalties from that video for many years, but despite this, some of Littler's attorneys believed that the firm had left a lot of money on the table by not initially investing in the production costs. This would prove incredibly instructive for how Littler would structure its next venture.

In 1996, with financial backing from the firm, individual firm attorneys, and outside venture capital, Littler became one of the first law firms to launch a standalone ancillary business: Employment Law Training (ELT). Established as an independent company with its own management team, sales and marketing professionals, trainers, and technologists, ELT offered clients in-person and online training in areas such as workplace harassment prevention, workplace violence avoidance, and effective HR management skills. ELT helped establish Littler's reputation for innovation, while also generating revenue for the firm through the sale of in-person training delivered by Littler attorneys. ELT also introduced Littler attorneys to many companies with whom they might not have otherwise connected. Most importantly, ELT was eventually acquired by a private equity firm and the sale resulted in a substantial return on investment for the firm and its attorneys. This return on investment in an ancillary business would help reduce some internal resistance years later to establishing another ancillary business: ComplianceHR.

The firm's early embrace of content marketing and entrepreneurialism proved critical to the firm's decision many years later to elevate its innovation as the main feature of its brand and its competitive advantage. Innovative client-facing products, such as subscription services and online client services, were simply a natural extension of the firm's early forays into client conferences, publications, innovative products, and ancillary businesses. These efforts also produced another benefit, one that would greatly enhance the firm's knowledge management initiatives: a culture in which attorneys understood that they were expected to contribute time and effort to firm-wide projects. Attorneys at Littler understood and accepted that part of their job, beyond billing hours to clients, was to contribute content – their personal knowledge – to the firm's marketing and branding efforts and the firm's collective knowledge base. They were expected to write chapters for the *National Employer* books, spend time preparing and delivering presentations at the firm's client conferences, and collaborate with their colleagues by sharing their work product and subject matter expertise. The importance of the culture of knowledge sharing that developed cannot be overstated. Littler's culture would eventually accelerate the firm's knowledge management initiatives as many attorneys began to see the value proposition of sharing and collaborating in exchange for the ability to draw upon the equivalent contributions of their colleagues.

IV STRATEGIC GROWTH AND THE NEED FOR INNOVATION AND KNOWLEDGE MANAGEMENT

By 2002, Littler had grown to hundreds of attorneys in about a dozen offices, still mostly in California but with a few offices outside of California, in New York, Chicago, and Dallas. Its aspirations were far larger, though. That year, the firm held a strategic planning summit, bringing together key firm leaders to discuss the firm's future. The summit also included consultants and individuals from outside businesses with whom Littler had partnered in the past.

At this meeting, firm leaders envisioned Littler as not only a national firm, but as a global one, with over 1000 attorneys across dozens of offices in cities across the globe. One of the critical topics of discussion was how the firm would maintain quality and consistency across this global platform. The goal was to build an integrated and unified law firm that could operate cohesively regardless of the number of offices and their distant locations. The goal was also to avoid having individual franchise-type offices that operated on their own without observing the quality service levels, firm standards, and branding that had made Littler so successful to date.

This consistency is a difficult task for any rapidly growing organization in any industry, but is particularly challenging for law firms because of the way most law firms work. As leaders of most law firms will attest, attorneys, particularly those who have reached partner or shareholder status, expect tremendous autonomy in how they serve their clients and run their individual practice or practice groups. This is one reason many firms have traditionally been reluctant to mandate the use of standardized documents, specific case-handling methodologies, or "best practices." This can be ameliorated to some extent if attorneys work closely together, ideally in the same office, learning from and mentoring each other. Common practices easily develop between attorneys working together in close proximity who might only have to walk down the hall to ask a colleague for information and support. But what about when attorneys are scattered across 70 offices? That natural dynamic can easily dissipate.

The concern for anyone focused on their firm's future growth strategy is how to ensure that the services clients receive in New York are of the same quality as what they would expect from attorneys in San Francisco, Atlanta, or Mexico City. To serve national and global clients that the firm aimed to attract, Littler had to ensure that, for example, answers to complaints drafted in different offices of the firm did not look like they had been drafted by attorneys at different law firms. Clients needed to know that the knowledge of Littler's business and matters could be communicated across all offices and all attorneys with whom the client worked. For its part, Littler wanted to avoid "knowledge silos," where substantive knowledge and experience remain trapped within the minds of attorneys, in their file drawers or on their local hard drives. The firm wanted to ensure that attorneys across the firm had ready access to the collective knowledge and experience of subject matter experts, and of those with the most knowledge of the firm's clients and their businesses, regardless of where those keepers of knowledge resided.

At about this point in the strategic summit, Garry Mathiason, one of Littler's most senior attorneys and key visionaries, proposed that Littler investigate the burgeoning field of "knowledge management," find out what it entailed, and perhaps invest in it. Knowledge management would not be enough on its own, though. Building a firm with over 1000 attorneys and a global geographical footprint would also require a significant investment in information technology infrastructure. To build this knowledge management program, Littler asked Scott Rechtschaffen to develop a strategic plan and incorporate the many products and services (publications, products, training programs) already on offer to its clients.

The first step in developing a strategy to enhance knowledge sharing and collaboration among far-flung attorneys was to build the basic foundation of any good knowledge management program: precedent libraries hosted on a curated intranet, with enterprise search and targeted databases that respond to the inquiries most often posed by attorneys and practice groups. Examples of this kind of technology infrastructure include: multi-jurisdiction substantive surveys; Yelp-like databases containing reviews of often-used resources such as arbitrators, mediators, and expert witnesses; and team sites and extranets that enable collaboration among case or client teams and their clients. Littler was among the first US firms to license a cutting-edge document automation tool, DealBuilder (now called ContractExpress), that enabled its users to efficiently generate commonly used and repetitive documents.

In developing its strategy, Littler did two things that would greatly enhance acceptance of knowledge management by the firm's attorneys and differentiate its knowledge management program from that of other law firms. First, the firm developed knowledge management products that were client-facing and designed to either generate revenue or enable attorneys to direct more business to their core legal service offerings. For example, Littler developed a product called Littler GPS, a service that informed employers of recent changes in employment law legislation and provided a database of multi-state surveys. This product was critical for national employers, given that so much of employment law is based on state or local legislation. Littler GPS was sold to clients on a subscription basis for an annual fee, and it became an independent revenue stream and a marketing differentiator. Critically, by offering Littler GPS to clients and deriving revenue from its subscription base, Littler was able to invest firm resources in a technology product that also substantially benefited the firm's attorneys; they now had access to a unique tool and could use it in serving their clients, even if their clients were not full subscribers. This was an opportunity for the firm's attorneys to appreciate the value of a technology solution that could generate independent revenue (through subscription sales) or enhance their ability to serve their clients on an hourly basis (by giving them ready access to the needed information about clients' substantive questions).

The second thing that greatly enhanced attorney acceptance of knowledge management was the firm's recognition that an effective knowledge management strategy could not just be about technology. Many attorneys would not readily accept and adapt to new technology without some kind of support. Marko Mrkonich, Littler's managing director from 2004 to 2012, believed that an effective knowledge management program had to include human resources – trusted professionals with substantive experience who could become trusted knowledge resources for their less tech-savvy colleagues and guide them through the maze of technology resources being developed. To achieve this, the firm created the position of knowledge management counsel and began hiring Littler associates who wished to find an alternative career path that provided flexibility, but still offered challenging work. Modeled after the professional support lawyer position common in the UK, Littler created a unique role for experienced employment law attorneys to support practice groups or case teams and provide substantive support for client-facing or internal technology projects.

A critical benefit of employing knowledge management counsel – most of whom were resident in practice offices across the firm – was that they became the real-life interface between the principles and practices of knowledge management and the firm's practicing attorneys. Rather than perceiving knowledge management as merely some technology tool (and, perhaps, a threatening tool), Littler attorneys came to think of "knowledge management" as a real-life attorney, sitting in an office or attached to their practice group, who could assist them in accessing critical resources or finding documents or answers their clients needed. Over the years, as the number of knowledge management counsel expanded to over 15 full-time counsel and the mission of the Knowledge Management Department broadened, the department created additional support positions. To aid its publishing efforts and its need to keep client- and attorney-facing products up to date, the Knowledge Management Department hired research attorneys, legal writers, and editors. The firm also needed to support the various content publishing platforms the department was responsible for: SharePoint for internal use and client extranets; Drupal for the firm's public-facing website and products such as Littler GPS; and external platforms hosted by third-party publishers. To manage this, the department hired content and technical support administrators, with the latter also responsible for supporting many of the software solutions the knowledge management counsel routinely used, such as ContractExpress for document automation, KMStandards for document analysis, and Neota Logic for developing expert systems. Eventually, the firm's Library and Research Services Department was fully integrated into the Knowledge Management Department, exponentially expanding the department's research, monitoring, and publishing capabilities.

Marko Mrkonich's belief that knowledge management had to incorporate both technology and full-time attorneys and staff may have stemmed from his oft-repeated management philosophy: "If you want something done, make it somebody's job." While many law firms form committees to study and discuss issues, committees are typically only effective in making decisions and developing strategies; they often struggle to effectively implement those decisions and strategies. By contrast, Littler's approach to firm management – espoused by Mrkonich and continued by his successors – stressed implementation, expressed by the firm's decision to charge Scott Rechtschaffen with implementing Littler's knowledge management strategy. Littler had initially formed a committee to develop a knowledge management strategy, but it was Rechtschaffen's job to execute the strategy the committee developed. This is not the only example of Littler using the "make it somebody's job" approach to innovation – a similar approach was taken by the firm to deal with class and collective action changes made in 2005 by the Fair Labor Standards Act, which resulted in significantly increased exposure to liability.

Mrkonich next tackled e-discovery. In recent years, e-discovery has transformed employment litigation due to the sheer volume of electronic evidence involved in virtually every case (e.g., emails, instant messaging, HRIS systems, payroll records, text messages, social media, etc.). Mrkonich recognized the need for dedicated expertise, so he hired Paul Weiner, who had previously been a litigation partner at Buchanan Ingersoll, to lead Littler's e-discovery efforts. Weiner was already considered one of the foremost practitioners in the field; his work was cited in the landmark opinion in *Zubalake v. UBS Warburg LLC*, a seminal case recognizing the critical role of electronic evidence in litigation that jump-started the entire field of e-discovery. Mrkonich tasked Weiner with building a team of e-discovery attorneys who could help firm attorneys with e-discovery-related issues. Weiner developed a team of litigation support project managers, developers, data analysts, and database administrators, and built a National Data Center to handle electronic evidence processing and hosting activities using best-of-breed technologies and quality assurance workflows. His primary focus was on developing a team of attorneys that could assist clients with handling of electronic evidence. Simply stated, Mrkonich and Weiner recognized that law firms needed dedicated teams of attorneys with deep expertise in e-discovery to address cutting-edge legal issues surrounding the rapidly developing area of e-discovery.

Littler's e-discovery lawyers focus *only* on this critical subspecialty of the law, allowing them to remain current on the latest e-discovery developments and to proactively provide leading-edge solutions to clients. Littler's e-discovery lawyers are particularly adept at marrying technology skills, litigation experience, and deep subject matter knowledge to provide targeted advice, strategy, and hands-on assistance to advise clients on managing litigation holds, preparing for and attending "meet and confer" conferences, handling court appearances addressing e-discovery matters, taking and defending depositions of IT professionals, and developing strategies for effective harvesting, protection, culling, searching, review, and production of electronic data. Today, most AMLAW 200 firms have come to recognize the importance of hiring lawyers who focus only on e-discovery, and the importance of bulking up their internal litigation support capabilities so they can compete in the marketplace of digital skills. But once again, through the vision and ability of its leadership, Littler was able to "look around the corner" to anticipate future trends and pain points for clients. Littler was one of the first firms in the USA to hire an attorney like Weiner at the shareholder level to focus exclusively on e-discovery, and they have continued to dedicate resources to maintaining a dominant position in this field as it has matured over the course of the last decade.

Littler continues to develop innovative practice areas and bring in expert practitioners in these fields. As recently as 2016, Littler saw the growing significance of "big data" both in how its clients were using predictive data analytics in their HR business decisions, and in how law firms could use data analytics to guide their litigation strategies. To address this burgeoning field, Littler's managing directors hired Dr. Zev Eigen, a nationally recognized expert in data analytics, to lead the firm's big data initiative. Not only had Dr. Eigen been a practicing employment attorney, initially at Littler and then as an in-house employment counsel, but he had also received his PhD from MIT and had taught at Northwestern, Yale, and NYU law schools. Dr. Eigen's combined experience as a practicing employment lawyer and his expertise in complex data analytics and social scientific research made him uniquely qualified to develop Littler's practice in predictive analytics. He has implemented artificial intelligence, machine learning algorithms, statistical analysis, and econometric modeling for issues arising out of class actions, and has also used statistical analysis for data related to labor, employment, and HR.

V THE COMMODITIZATION OF EMPLOYMENT LAW IMPACTS THE NEED TO INNOVATE

Another significant aspect of Littler's history that shaped its future approach to innovation was the decision, made early on by firm leaders, to maintain focus on a narrow and specific subject area: management-side labor and employment law. Focusing exclusively on labor and employment law helped the firm develop its reputation for authoritative expertise and market positioning. Littler does one thing, and it does it really well. However, this specialization has brought several disadvantages from a business perspective.

Labor and employment is not perceived by clients as a high-value practice area – particularly when compared to areas such as corporate, mergers and acquisitions, tax, or real estate. For some in-house counsel, employment litigation is just barely one step above slip-and-fall claims, and labor law just makes them nervous. Additionally, for in-house counsel most employment-related issues are time-intensive but rarely pose the risk of significant liability – except for wage-hour class actions or matters involving high-level executives. As a result, employment and labor law firms felt the economic pressures of commoditization long before other practice areas, and long before the effects of the Great Recession of 2008–2009.

Other firms began to address the demand for alternative fee arrangements after the Great Recession (the so-called "death of the billable hour"), but these concerns were not new for employment and labor law firms. Clients had been asking for flat-fee labor arbitration engagements going back 20 years. There was a time when employment firms practically owned the human resources practice area: Clients would not issue human resources policies or forms (e.g., job applications, employee handbooks, employment agreements) without running them by their employment law counsel, sometimes even asking their outside employment counsel to draft these documents themselves. For many employers, employment decisions were not implemented without approval by outside employment counsel, and employers routinely asked their outside employment counsel whether they could engage an individual as an independent contractor, designate an employee as overtime-exempt, or terminate an employee without cause.

In recent years, this dynamic has changed dramatically. Employers have abundant options for obtaining human resources policies, forms, and agreements. There are numerous online resources and consultants to provide basic template documents. Industry associations, such as the Society for Human Management Resources and the Association of Corporate Counsel, can readily provide these types of document resources. Similarly, the thought of calling outside counsel – at $400+ per hour – to ask whether a given individual out of perhaps 100 similarly situated individuals is employable as an independent contractor is a non-starter from a cost perspective. And asking outside counsel to review whether individuals can be employed as overtime-exempt seems equally nonsensical, given the number of employees or job positions that often must be classified.

In the litigation arena, companies have also begun reevaluating their relationships with, and the work they send to, outside counsel. Companies have begun to disintermediate the litigation process by relying more heavily on legal process outsourcers (LPOs) that focus on basic legal tasks – document review, legal research, legal document drafting – and deploying improved business processes to perform these tasks at lower prices than those offered by traditional law firms. The basic value proposition of LPOs to in-house counsel is that they can provide the basic legal "blocking and tackling" – the commodity work – at lower rates, enabling in-house counsel to reserve the more strategic litigation tasks for higher-priced outside counsel. Similarly, corporate legal departments have begun keeping more basic legal tasks in-house. Responding to administrative agency charges, drafting legal documents, or providing advice and counsel can realistically stay in-house, even if that means increasing the number of lawyers and paralegals on staff.

The Great Recession greatly accelerated the trend of legal departments looking for ways to reduce costs through disintermediation and bring more work in-house as they came under enormous pressure to reduce their budgets and gain control of their legal spend on outside counsel. For Littler, because it had been responding to these types of pressures for decades, this actually proved to be as much of an opportunity as a challenge.

A Littler CaseSmart®

In 2009, one of Littler's largest clients asked all of its outside counsel to help identify ways to reduce legal spend and provide more value for less. At this time, Scott Forman, Littler's shareholder responsible for this client relationship, had started to see this theme emerge in the legal market as a result of the recession. He had already been contemplating a solution to this client's request, and the timing was thus perfect. Forman responded with an innovative idea that would redesign the way Littler provided legal services to this client by not only reducing spend, but also providing the client with greater efficiency in the management of agency charges through a unique combination of people, process, and technology. When the client accepted Forman's proposal, Littler CaseSmart® (LCS) was born.

Working with Littler's chief operating officer, chief knowledge officer, and over 60 individuals from Littler's various corporate departments, Forman began developing LCS by redesigning the way Littler handled administrative agency charges. The multidisciplinary team created a series of process maps depicting the current state of matter management, and then analyzed in great detail how the work could be performed more efficiently. They asked themselves which legal tasks were necessary to perform, what type of expertise was required to perform each task, how the firm could better leverage technology, and what Littler could provide to help employers be more effective and reduce future risk. The multidisciplinary business analysis team identified work process inefficiencies and developed technology solutions to improve workflows. The end result was Littler CaseSmart – Charges™, a new approach to managing administrative agency charges premised on an efficient workflow, a unique staffing model, and cutting-edge proprietary technology. It was a complete reimagining of how the firm handled administrative agency charges, combining legal process improvement principles, a proprietary technology platform, and an alternative staffing model.

The attorneys working on the model would have access to client-specific team sites that enabled them to quickly access information, as well as document automation so they could easily generate frequently used documents. Supervising attorneys could also access dashboards to monitor the status of matters. And, in what became one of its most popular features, the Littler CaseSmart model offered dashboards to clients as well, enabling them to review the status of matters, including both individual charges and their entire portfolio of pending or completed matters. For most clients, this was data they had never been able to collect or readily access. One client reported that their legal department's quarterly report to the company's executive committee of pending administrative charges had previously taken them *two weeks* to prepare on Excel spreadsheets. With the Littler CaseSmart dashboards, they were able to run reports – and even filter the reports by division, region, or down to the business unit level – within *minutes*.

As part of this redesigned process, Littler created an alternative career path, the flextime attorney (FTA), to perform the majority of work related to a charge. The role was designed for experienced attorneys looking for interesting and challenging work with a more flexible schedule and greater work–life balance.[2] The "flexibility" of the position came from the ability of FTAs to work from home and set their own schedules outside the confines of the traditional attorney workday. The FTA role also provided greater flexibility because there were limited non-billable requirements compared to those required of attorneys on a shareholder track. This allowed FTAs to focus on specific areas within a charge process in order to hone their skills and work more efficiently. Working this way, FTAs could become extremely proficient in handling charges, and develop a deep understanding of agency practices and effective defense strategies. They would also become intimately familiar with their assigned clients, understanding their litigation philosophy and risk tolerance, learning who to contact at the client company for specific information, and learning the company's unique terminology, culture, and business processes. From a legal process improvement perspective, this was critical; FTAs were able to reduce time wasted on asking redundant questions, contacting the wrong client representative, or learning the client's business processes (e.g., their HR policies, training programs, or disciplinary practices).

In developing the FTA role, the firm deliberately decided not to use contract attorneys; FTAs are full-time Littler employees working on technology provided by the firm, entitled to firm benefits, and eligible for advancement on a defined career path. This has been important in enabling the firm to maintain and ensure the quality of their legal work product. Littler realized it had an untapped market of experienced attorneys seeking some type of alternative career, and for many, events in their lives – such as raising children, caring for elderly parents,

---

[2] FTAs average 13 years of employment and labor experience. Some FTAs are former shareholders and associates, while others are former clients.

physical disabilities, or dissatisfaction with the rigors of a traditional law firm career path – meant that they might otherwise be leaving the firm or leaving the practice of law altogether. The FTA model has become an attractive position for many talented attorneys and has enabled Littler to capture an important sector of the workforce.

A key factor in the success of the FTA staffing model is the implementation of the client-dedicated teams mentioned above. In addition, to ensure effective collaboration, LCS teams leverage technology-based tools to communicate and access the details of their matters on a 24/7 basis. Working alongside Littler's in-house application and development team, Scott Forman led the creation of the proprietary, secure, web-based dashboard. This dashboard is accessible to the client 24/7, and is configured to each client's business model and acts as a case management system, enabling the client to track and monitor the status of matters in real time. Critically, it also tracks data points associated with every matter, providing clients with "privileged analytics" – data-driven insights across their portfolio of matters. Having access to key performance indicators enables employers to better identify patterns of potential risk and adjust their business or operational response accordingly under the protection of attorney–client privilege. FTAs are also supported by an internal site where the firm's collective knowledge about a client resides. From a legal process improvement perspective, this has been critical in ensuring consistent work product across a client's portfolio of matters, and reducing time spent on asking clients redundant questions.

The Littler CaseSmart – Charges model thus offered a mutual value proposition for the client and the firm. The client would have greater predictability and reduced costs because of the flat fee pricing, and Littler would increase its revenue from the client because of the substantial increase in the volume of work. Critically for clients concerned with maintaining and ensuring quality of work product and results achieved in settlement and litigation, Littler's approach to reducing its legal spend did not involve outsourcing the work overseas, pushing the work down to lower inexperienced attorneys, or reducing the amount of supervision provided. The cost savings were produced by the legal re-engineering, technology, and alternative staffing approach.

Prior to the proposal that led to LCS – Charges, Forman was handling about one-quarter of the client's agency charges. When LCS – Charges launched in August 2010, the client decided to move all of their charges to the platform. Working with the client to determine a pricing model that would meet their needs, Forman proposed a flat fee per charge that would provide them with greater predictability and ultimately reduce spend by up to 30%. The result was a successful business partnership: The client realized the goals they had set out to achieve, and Littler strengthened its relationship with its client while also increasing revenue.

Over the last seven years, many clients have embraced LCS, and Littler has managed well over 18,000 agency charges on the platform. In 2014, Littler applied the same successful methodology to single-plaintiff litigation and launched Littler CaseSmart – Litigation™. This model required Forman and his team to expand the role of the FTA. Under the charges model, FTAs could manage virtually all aspects of a matter due to its confined scope. However, because single-plaintiff litigation includes multiple stages and more specialized tasks, Littler created four FTA roles, each one addressing different areas of litigation that can be routine, yet time-intensive and potentially expensive for clients: research, early case evaluation, written discovery, and brief writing. In the three years since launching this service line, a significant number of clients have adopted the model and the firm has managed over 700 matters on the platform.

Based on the continued success of the LCS platform, and the increasing competitiveness of the legal landscape, in early 2017 the firm launched Littler CaseSmart – Class Action™ to manage wage-hour class actions. This solution has not only created greater efficiencies when managing wage and hour class or collection actions, but it has also ensured that the highest quality strategies are being deployed on complex matters. This new platform also created new in-house roles in the form of data analysts, and in a new committee, the Strategic Review Committee (SRC).[3]

By the middle of 2017, Littler had handled nearly 20,000 employment matters with more than 100 different clients across all LCS service lines, helping clients to reduce spend and providing them with greater insights into their businesses. The LCS platform continues to evolve and has enabled the firm to aggregate data from the thousands of matters managed on the platform. In Littler's view, the ability to use innovative tools and data analytics to inform clients of the relative value of their matters and their potential liability, benchmarked against similar matters, is critical knowledge that improves clients' ability to make important and strategic business decisions. The LCS approach does much more than reduce legal spend; it moves litigation decision making from mere guesswork to rigorous analysis informed by actual statistical evidence and data analytics.

B ComplianceHR

Littler CaseSmart has provided an innovative approach to litigating employment cases with administrative agency charges, single-plaintiff litigation, and wage-hour class actions. But Littler has seen yet more opportunities to reclaim other types of transactional work that have been lost to alternative legal and HR service providers.

Increasingly, employers have not been calling their outside employment counsel to obtain answers to routine employment law questions. Additionally, companies have not been calling their employment lawyers to obtain basic employment documents such as employment applications, offer letters, non-compete agreements, and NDAs. For many employers, this failure to consult with employment counsel to draft these agreements has proved problematic, since these documents are governed by a myriad of state laws, and multi-state compliance is quite complex.

Back in 2011, Scott Rechtschaffen, Littler's chief knowledge officer, became convinced that there was a developing market and a need for Littler to create an online, client-facing application to answer repetitive legal questions, generate routine legal documents, and automate other basic employment law tasks. Even before then, Rechtschaffen had advocated internally that the firm recognize the coming disruption of the legal marketplace and begin to develop more digital tools to enable clients to more effectively transact business with their law firms. Purchasers of legal services, typically in-house counsel, were no different than anyone else in that they now lived online: they got their news, checked their bank accounts, connected with friends, and made restaurant, airplane, and hotel reservations online. Rechtschaffen pointed out that the generation of digital natives was now in the workplace and making decisions. How much longer would they be satisfied working with law firms that did not readily facilitate transacting business online?

---

[3] The SRC is a team of Littler's national thought leaders who practice extensively in wage and hour class and collective action litigation and provide input and strategic direction on each matter defended on the platform. The SRC reviews key pleadings and filings in a matter to assist with the development of defenses and arguments that fully capture the latest developments in class action litigation.

Littler knew it had to start developing online services beyond just databases of legal information, or access to matter status information. They also needed to implement new ways for their clients to obtain services. The Great Recession's impact on the legal industry made it increasingly unlikely that in-house legal and HR departments would be willing to continue paying hourly rates to outside counsel for basic services. To the contrary, it was far more likely that they would keep this work in-house or look to alternative resources already present on the internet. Google, for example, may be the most used application for obtaining basic documents like employment applications or employment agreements. Legal technology companies (e.g., LegalZoom, RocketLawyer) have emerged as well, focused where most classic disruptive innovation begins: the consumer market. If consumers could draft their wills and incorporate their small businesses online, how long would it be before similar services emerged to serve the corporate marketplace?

Rechtschaffen had previously used a software product called Jnana. Jnana enabled the creation of complex decision trees with weighting factors. He searched for months to find that company, only to learn that it had gone out of business. He did learn, however, that the Jnana software had been purchased by a startup called Neota Logic and, coincidentally, one of Neota Logic's founders was Michael Mills, an old friend of his who had served for many years as the chief knowledge officer at Davis Polk. Rechtschaffen began talking with Mills and, working with a re-engineered version of the expert system software, built an early prototype of an independent contractor analysis application. Through that process, Rechtschaffen began to further formulate and refine the idea of a suite of applications that would deliver online answers to repetitive employment law questions.

In August 2012, he proposed to Mills and John Lord (another Neota Logic founder) the idea of Littler and Neota Logic forming a joint venture to bring these applications to market. Initially, Mills and Lord were not interested in developing applications; given Lord's background as a software entrepreneur, he was focused more on software licensing than on developing and selling specific applications or products.

After this minor setback in the joint venture discussions, Littler looked for opportunities to develop applications on its own as proofs of concept. Rechtschaffen worked with Steve Friedman and Ilyse Schuman, two of Littler's practice group chairs, and with Meghann Barloewen, one of Littler's knowledge management attorneys, to develop the Health Care Reform Advisor (HCRA). The HCRA was an online application that enabled employers to determine whether they would be better off under the Affordable Care Act providing their employees with employer-paid health insurance coverage, or instead paying the ACA's penalties. The HCRA also estimated the amount of penalties the employer would have to pay if it elected to forego providing health insurance coverage. The success of this proof of concept demonstrated that the firm could take complex legal questions, embed the subject matter expertise of its attorneys into Neota Logic's software, and create a viable risk analysis application. From this initial work, Lord began to realize that creating specific products could benefit Neota Logic by demonstrating to the market that its software could be adapted to complex scenarios. Following opportunities to assess market reaction to such products – most notably at Littler's annual Executive Employer Conference – Lord became convinced that a joint venture would benefit both Littler and Neota Logic.

In 2015, Littler and Neota launched their joint venture: ComplianceHR. This standalone company was designed to develop a suite of applications that would combine Littler's subject matter experience and Neota's software development expertise. Over the next two years, ComplianceHR would develop and bring to market applications that could provide a risk analysis of classifying workers as independent contractors or as overtime-exempt, provide answers to frequent wage-hour questions (e.g., "What is the minimum wage in Georgia?"), and generate often-used documents such as employment applications, NDAs, and offer letters. By 2017, ComplianceHR had developed and launched a suite of 20 employment law compliance applications, and had also developed an extensive and impressive client base of over 1500 companies and 7000 individual users.

ComplianceHR, along with Littler CaseSmart, Littler GPS, and other innovations, offered Littler attorneys the ability to demonstrate to their clients and prospective clients a key differentiator for Littler: its willingness to innovate and develop new approaches to delivering legal services. Law firm client pitches occur in a competitive environment, and Littler has robust and tangible ways of distinguishing itself from other firms in that environment. It has repeatedly affirmed that innovation and technology are powerful differentiators between it and other firms, something that goes beyond a potentially dubious statement of having "great lawyers." These client services are not mere marketing devices; they represent Littler's efforts to re-engineer the delivery of legal services. For their part, clients and prospective clients have recognized the difference: they know when a law firm is simply mouthing about marketing innovation, and when a law firm has truly committed to the evolution of legal service delivery.

VI CONCLUSION: OVERCOMING TWO CONTINUING CHALLENGES

A "If It Isn't Broken, Don't Fix It"

In Big Law, efforts to innovate or change the delivery of legal services invariably encounter a major obstacle: the belief among many attorneys that their business model has been successful all along, and thus does not need to change. How exactly do you approach a senior partner who has been earning hundreds of thousands of dollars each year – if not millions – and say, "Your business model is broken"?

Following the Great Recession of 2008–2009, many law firm leaders who paid close attention to the buyers of their services understood the changes taking place in the legal marketplace. Clients sought to drastically reduce their legal spend by bringing more work inhouse and disintermediating the legal services they purchased by looking to alternative providers such as LPOs. Online services such as West's Peer Monitor – a tool that enables firms to compare their financial performance against the industry at large and against peer firms – enabled firm leaders to see, among other things, the leveling off of demand for legal services. The challenge became how firm leaders could convince attorneys, particularly highly successful and prosperous attorneys, that the legal marketplace was changing and that these long-term trends would perhaps inevitably impact firm revenue and profitability.

Many firms tried to drive home the message by bringing in industry consultants to speak at annual partners' meetings and preach the gospel of doom and gloom. These consultants would put up graphs showing the reduction in billing realization, the flattening of hourly rates, and the downward trend in client demand. They would quote Richard Susskind, Jordan Furlong, and other industry prognosticators, and they would show the research of academics such as William Henderson and David Wilkins, predicting the inevitable change in buyer demand and the coming wave of new service providers such as LPOs, legal tech startups, and artificial intelligence disruptors. They would show the increase in head count of in-house legal departments, and the increasing market share of major accounting firms providing "legal-type" services. Despite this, most law firm partners attending those meetings would yawn and say, "What does this have to do with me and my practice?"

Littler also tried this approach to convince its attorneys of the coming changes. During and following the Great Recession, at its annual shareholder meetings Littler's leaders discussed the changing demand for legal services, the realization challenges, and the downward pressure on rates; they presented numbers showing the impact on the overall legal industry, particularly the flattening of demand in the labor and employment sector; and they brought in industry consultants to provide the third-party perspective so often necessary to convince those within an organization of the veracity of what their internal leaders are telling them. While many Big Law attorneys, including those at Littler, remained resistant in the face of the fundamental changes in the legal industry accelerated by the Great Recession, and also rejected the call to adjust their business models and methods of delivering legal services, a small number of attorneys began to recognize that change was necessary. At Littler, two factors proved critically important to this gradual recognition.

First, Littler had seen this movie before. As discussed previously, the field of labor and employment law had been viewed as a commodity practice for decades, and had long been subject to the economic pressures accelerated by the Great Recession. Littler's attorneys had seen their work become routinized, standardized, and commoditized. Alternative providers could provide the types of services that had long been the primary, if not exclusive, bailiwick of Littler's employment lawyers (e.g., drafting employment policies, employee handbooks, and employment agreements; answering questions about employment law; advising on the impact of employment law on employment decision making).

Second, Littler's leaders – specifically its managing directors Tom Bender and Jeremy Roth, and chief operating officer Robert Domingues – did not focus solely on discussing pending financial challenges and forecasts of the coming economic downturn; instead, they began to demonstrate how the firm could successfully adapt to meet the changing market. In essence, they focused not on the crisis, but on how to turn the crisis into an opportunity. They embraced and advocated for the firm's innovations, described previously, such as Littler CaseSmart and ComplianceHR. While not mandating that attorneys adopt these approaches, they rarely missed an opportunity at a shareholder meeting, an office-level meeting, or a web-cast town hall meeting to urge attorneys to consider these solutions and propose them to their clients. Tom Bender constantly reminded his colleagues that clients frequently questioned why they had to ask their attorneys for new approaches, rather than their attorneys proactively proposing new and innovative solutions.

None of Littler's innovative solutions were adopted overnight, though. Launched in 2010, Littler CaseSmart had only a handful of clients through 2014. However, the firm's leaders persisted in highlighting, at every opportunity, how Littler CaseSmart was successfully responding to clients' demands for greater efficiency, reduced cost, and maintenance of quality, and how it was expanding revenue and facilitating new business development. Over time, more and more shareholders saw how including Littler CaseSmart in client pitches and responses to requests for proposal (RFPs) increased their success rate and demonstrated the firm's (and, thereby, the attorney's) commitment to innovation and enhancement of client relationships.

B Financial Obstacles to Innovation

Perhaps the single greatest impediment to innovating the way Big Law delivers legal services and improves the value received by clients lies in a well-entrenched financial compensation system. Old systems, as many legal industry commentators have noted, reward inefficiency, disincentivize collaboration, and do not necessarily work in clients' best interests. A financial system based on hourly billing rewards inefficient practices, can lead to overstaffing, and can cause underutilization of available technology, not to mention reduced interest in the development of new technological applications. The death of the billable hour has long been predicted, and the justification for its demise has been explained in great detail by numerous legal industry observers and academics. Yet it remains. There are many reasons for this: institutional inertia; the historic success of the billable hour model; the lack of client demand for change, until recently; dissatisfaction with alternative fee structures; and the inability of law firms to develop valuable performance metrics other than hours billed and revenue dollars generated.

These issues have not been fully resolved at Littler. Many attorneys continue to perceive innovative practices and technology as reducing their opportunity to bill hours. Many attorneys continue to focus on "selling" their own billable hours, rather than selling technology-based products. Littler has had some success, however, in demonstrating the potential return from its investment in technology. This success has been due to several factors. Some of these factors have already been discussed: Littler's long history of using innovation and content marketing to grow its market share and geographic reach, and the impact of commoditization on the labor and employment practice which has made attorneys more willing to incorporate products and alternative legal service delivery into their marketing efforts. When submitting responses to RFPs, most attorneys insist on including Littler GPS, complimentary passes to Littler's conferences, access to Littler's publications, and other "freebies" to provide a value-add for the client, and generally distinguishing Littler's overall service offering from its competitors. More recently, attorneys have begun to include Littler CaseSmart and ComplianceHR, for the same reasons. Significantly, the responses from clients to these offerings have been overwhelmingly positive and, in some cases, have been identified as the major reason Littler was awarded the work that was the subject of the RFP. In one recent example, during a convergence process where the client was significantly reducing the number of outside counsel with whom it worked, the general counsel questioned why every law firm was not offering these alternative service delivery options.

Littler has also achieved success in promoting innovation because, many years ago, Littler's culture of sharing and collaboration was extended to its business development efforts. Attorneys were actively encouraged, and the client origination system was re-engineered, to collaborate in developing new clients and new work from existing clients. Attorneys were encouraged to share new client origination credits, gradually phasing out the historical "tattoo" system of marking clients as belonging to one attorney forever. Attorneys came to realize that collaborating with one another in business development efforts could help develop more new business, even if their individual share of the new work was lessened. The company mantra became, "50% of some work is better than 100% of no work."

In addition, attorneys have become accustomed to including Littler's wide range of "specialists" in their business development efforts. Some of the individuals discussed previously, such as Allan King, head of the Class Action Practice Group, and Paul Weiner, Littler's national e-discovery counsel, have been routinely included on pitch teams without any expectation on their part that they would receive a share of the origination credit. Because of this, it became natural for attorneys to include knowledge management, technology, and products as enhancements to their marketing pitch. Interestingly, some of the strongest proponents and "salespersons" of Littler's approach to innovative products and services are the firm's largest rainmakers.

A related obstacle is that firms often confront difficulty when searching for the capital necessary to invest in innovation and technology. While every law firm recognizes the need to invest in the technological infrastructure necessary to operate the firm (HR, payroll, finance, billing, document management systems), technology that lies outside of run-the-firm systems can be a challenge. Law firms distribute their earnings at the end of the year to their partners or shareholders; they do not retain excess capital. Because of current state bar rules and ethical restrictions, law firms cannot permit non-attorney ownership and therefore cannot raise outside capital. Thus, every dollar spent on technology is one less dollar available to distribute to the partners or shareholders at the end of the year.

Littler addresses this financial obstacle using its unique history of innovation successes. Their history of successful innovation, and the centrality of innovation to the firm's overall strategy and branding, presents a compelling case for investment in innovation and technology. Littler's past return on investment in these sorts of ventures strengthens the case internally for greater technology use. Littler's past investment in an ancillary company, ELT, produced significant returns for the firm's shareholders when the firm sold its equity stake.

Although Littler's history of technology implementation would seem to justify the investment in research and development or technological innovation that a well-capitalized public or private company might make, this is not always sufficient in and of itself. Littler's approach involves being fairly conservative and transparent with its investments. The firm tracks precisely how much it is spending on "future investment" activities, versus what the firm spends on "run-the-firm" technology resources. The firm's management committee budgets and approves these investments, and major decisions and expenditures – such as the decision to invest in the ComplianceHR joint venture – are submitted to Littler's board of directors. The firm constantly balances the need to invest in innovation and technology with the expectations of the firm's shareholders for a reasonable return for their efforts. Generally, the firm's management committee has successfully balanced these concerns, delivering both innovative legal services and strong financial performance. Most importantly, the firm's management committee has been open and transparent with shareholders about the firm's innovation strategy and its financials.

The most compelling explanation for how Littler justifies and defends its decision to invest in innovation and technology is that the firm's leadership strongly believes that the future of the law firm and of the legal industry depends on these kinds of innovation. If law firms do not make these investments – either in developing technology in-house or licensing already available technology – they will be left behind. There are too many legal technology companies in the market, and a significant amount of venture capital focused on the legal industry. Littler's leadership not only believes, but has seen firsthand, that the long-term future of the firm requires developing new and innovative approaches to delivering legal services.

4.4

Legal Operations at Google

Mary O'Carroll[1] and Stephanie Kimbro

I INTRODUCTION

Google's Legal Department addresses cutting-edge issues that run from driverless cars to green-energy power cables for the Eastern Seaboard and legal hot spots from China to Turkey. Our legal department today consists of more than 900 legal team members, a significant growth from the one lawyer that made up the legal department in 2001. The unique culture of Google itself has inspired the legal department to innovate in ways that are more progressive than most companies of a similar size. The Google Legal Team supports the vision of the company's engineers who are trying to create new technologies that will have an international impact on the lives of people. Accordingly, our legal team focuses its support on the interests of the users of the company's technology and defends Google so that it can continue to focus on the company vision.

Google's Legal Operations (Legal Ops) function was established in 2008. Its purpose is to optimize the balance of speed, cost, and quality of legal work at Google. Its mission is to make Google Legal the most efficient, effective, and innovative legal department in the world. While still fairly new and unknown at the time, the role of Legal Ops has grown tremendously in prevalence, scope, and seniority over recent years. Legal operations functions are taking root in corporate law departments that are increasingly charged with running efficiently and effectively, freeing up general counsel to focus on the bigger strategic picture. If the general counsel (GC) is the CEO of Legal Ops, think of this as the COO for the department. They focus on the intersection of people, process, and technology. These roles are the right hand of the GC and are deeply involved in setting the strategy and executing on it. The Legal Ops director manages all the operations of the department so that the lawyers, including the GC, can focus on the legal counseling. It has been a challenging role to hire for because of the breadth of skills attached to the role and lack of training that exists for it. Not only does one need to understand the legal industry, but one also needs to have a solid understanding of how to run a business, including financial management, project management, an interest in or passion for technology, and of course process improvement. Because of the senior level of the people this role interacts with, the soft skills are necessarily as important. These include leadership skills, persuasiveness, change management, communication skills, problem solving, negotiating, planning, and creative thinking.

---

[1] Google Inc. is headquartered in Mountain View, California. Mary O'Carroll is Head of Legal Operations and co-author of this chapter.

With an increased appreciation for what a Legal Ops professional can bring to the table, GCs are realizing the value of adding this function in the legal department. Most large legal departments now have this role and it is increasing in clout and seniority. Interestingly, more and more small-sized legal departments are adding this role, and earlier as well – some even consider it the first legal department hire after the GC. Amid this legal ops movement, the Corporate Legal Operations Consortium (CLOC) emerged as an organization to act as a driver for change and a way to bring the community together. CLOC is an organization with corporate Legal Ops leaders as members who aim to optimize legal services delivery models and share knowledge. As it has grown, the group's work has helped define what skills and focuses are needed for law departments to make Legal Ops work and allowed a community to form around operations. The group formed in early 2016 and its own growth is reflective of industry trends. Within 16 months of CLOC's establishment, membership grew from 40 to over 650 globally and it attracted 1000 attendees to its annual event.

The drivers of this growth can be attributed to the economic downturns of the early 2000s, which have caused more pressure from the CEO and CFO of corporations to manage company resources responsibly. As a result, GCs are feeling financial pressures and being forced to run the legal function more like a business than in the past. Years ago, almost all of legal department spending was with outside counsel and traditional law firms. Today, bringing much more of it in-house is normal practice because it is more cost effective.[2] From this shift in practice came the growth of the in-house sector and, with it, the need for the field of Legal Ops. With business-minded professionals now guiding the direction of corporate legal departments and putting increasing pressure on traditional law firms, the landscape started to change as opportunities brought the entrance of new market players.

Technology, globalization, and growing economic pressure have changed the ways many industries operate, and the legal industry is no different. Technology is enabling law firms and legal departments to finally gain insights into productivity and value. This transparency is leading GCs to question the way legal services are being delivered, which is resulting in big changes in the legal landscape. The question of *value*[3] is at the forefront of the mind and legal services are being disaggregated or unbundled. In the past, there were only two ways to get legal work done – either it stayed in-house or got sent to outside counsel. Now there are a tremendous number of models and mixes, including onshore and offshore options.

One big driver of innovation in the industry is the GC's changing role from risk manager to trusted advisor. Before the 1990s, GCs were hired to be the risk managers or top lawyers for their companies. They fought fires and hired outside counsel. During the 1990s, their roles started to expand in breadth and depth and C-Level suite started to look at the GC as a business partner. They started to have a seat at the executive table.

The GC of today's role includes personnel management and career development; budgeting; financial management; vendor management; systems and tools; efficiency and metrics, and more. One challenge is that lawyers generally receive no exposure to business management principles in law school or at law firms. Moreover, many of these management issues are things that GCs and other lawyers may not find appealing, yet know are critically

---

[2] It is curious that in-house would be more efficient than an outside law firm. If law firms were run well, they should be able to be more cost-effective than a lot of the work going on in-house currently. The section in this book on adaptive innovation (Dolin) discusses why law firms are inefficient and whether that is likely to change. Some work that has moved in-house may well move back to law firms if/when they incorporate efficiency among their core values.

[3] Value, often defined as benefit / cost, is discussed in the chapter on quality metrics: Dolin – Measuring Legal Quality, *supra*.

important. They are also facing increasing pressure from CFOs to manage the department more like a business and manage finances and resources more effectively. The GC needs to focus on being integrated with the business, something new if he or she has come from a law firm. This responsibility for increased management creates the need for the role of the legal operations director, which allows the GC to focus on the business and substantive issues.

II INNOVATION AT GOOGLE LEGAL OPS

Taking both the background and mindset of the existing legal industry and looking at areas ripe for innovation and disruption, Google Legal Ops has progressed four main areas of focus that resonated with the overall company mindset: culture, people, resources, and technology.

A Focus on Culture

Cultivating a culture that encourages innovation requires the creation of physical spaces that invite collaboration and communication among members. In 2010, Google completed an office remodel for the Legal Department. In an effort to increase teamwork and collaboration, we redesigned our building to reflect a more open approach. Legal team members have abandoned walls and traditional offices and moved to uniform open work spaces. Everyone works in open-plan layouts, reflecting that approach. We don't have an "open door" policy; we have a "no door" policy. With a variety of alternative work areas including nooks, huddle rooms, cafes, lounges, phone booths, and a library, we try to encourage people to work in more collaborative ways.

To maintain an open mindset, members of Google Legal do not have the hierarchical structure of the typical in-house department. Instead, members are expected to treat each other as equals without the encumbered decision making of unnecessary hierarchy – hence the "no door" policy. Opinions matter regardless of level or position, and Google values transparency and learning across the company. For example, we launched a series of company-wide "Legal Hot Topics" sessions. These were all-employee meetings that provided opportunities for employees to discuss some of our most interesting and controversial legal issues with senior members of the Legal Department. Within Legal, we have quarterly "Legal All-Hands Meetings" and additional Hot Topics sessions for the Legal Department.

B Focus on People

Google Legal is made up of team members who all went through the same on-boarding process and who continue to go through programs designed to promote educational and professional growth. New hires go through a formal on-boarding process first at the company level, then at the department level, and finally at the team level. Google has countless company-wide programs that promote personal growth. This is an important component of the company culture in general, and thus influences the culture in the Legal Department. At the Legal Department level, we have created a program that includes an overview of our organizational structure, team descriptions, insight into our culture, a video message from our leadership team, and essential tools and resources for navigating Google. We also assign new members, or "Nooglers," a buddy, who is a peer from their team, for the first month to help them navigate the department.

Continuing legal education for members of our Legal Department includes four components: (1) education about the core company and the department; (2) professional skills building; (3) education on areas of the law that are central to our business; and (4) team-specific legal issues.

We have developed a Google Essentials program that includes everything a new member needs to know about Google, the Legal Department, and how the two fit together. Professional skills including critical soft skill training focuses on building and improving skills such as communication, presentation, negotiation, and project management. Members have access to continuing legal education through our "101" sessions. These programs are designed with the entire department in mind and introduce the basics in areas of law that are central to our business. This series of in-person sessions is led by senior leaders/counsel and provide an exploration of some of the most interesting and challenging legal, policy, and ethical issues facing internet businesses today. These include novel issues of international law, privacy, copyright, competition, law enforcement, patents, and more. In addition to this continued legal education, there are team-specific programs for members of Legal that dive deeper into particular legal issues a member may be tasked with working on. These include programs such as the Rotation Program, which encompasses both role and geography changes.

One of the goals of continuing legal education for Legal is to increase members' exposure to new and different areas of law and their legal practice. We do this by facilitating 3–6-month assignments to other groups. Rotations are opportunities for people to learn new skills, make lots of connections, and share know-how with a team down the hall or in another part of the world. We believe that the knowledge and fresh perspective a member brings during a rotation will be a huge asset to a host team, and the insights and relationships developed while away will make people better at their jobs when they return home.

C Focus on Resources

As discussed above, in the early 2000s a shift occurred in which there was increased pressure from the CEOs and CFOs of corporations to manage company resources responsibly. General counsel is expected to run the legal function of a company like a business. Accordingly, attention to resources and efficiency have become critical to the mix of running an innovative legal department. For example, in-house teams must ask themselves how to match the right work with the right people using a mix of internal and external resources.

Using resources as effectively and efficiently as possible requires forethought, careful planning, and the right tools. Establishing the right approach for managing resources can improve the department's performance and generate significant cost savings. The analysis required to balance resources starts at the lowest levels by determining the value of a resource or task. This includes assessing the risk of the task at hand, clearly defining the scope of the work, and determining what level of quality is either required or acceptable. One should question whether it is possible to simply stop doing that task or using that resource. At the most commoditized levels, there are technologies and automation that we can leverage to maximize efficiency, such as workflow tools, client self-service, e-signatures, NDAs, etc. Using these systems and technologies may free time from administrative tasks, paralegal work, or even attorney hours. Further along on this analysis it becomes more complex and includes the possibility of good offshore solutions in India, Manila, etc. for document review, production, patent filings, etc. At these mid-levels, one should consider whether the work needs to be performed by attorneys or not. Following that may be an analysis of on-shore options for low-cost contract managers or attorneys in lower-cost areas like Fargo or Tempe. It may be possible to retain sophisticated work from lawyers in smaller cities for much lower cost than traditional firms. Finally, for complex, sensitive, high-profile, or "bet the company" type work, the reliance on Big Law will continue.

In-house legal departments are forcing law firms to work differently and driving the changes in how corporate legal services are delivered. Legal operations teams can no longer rely on firms to bill by the hour for commodity-type work or routine tasks. The benefits of "right sourcing" can often mean lower cost, more pricing certainty, faster turnaround times, and improved quality as specialization and focus on particular tasks can lead to optimization.

D Focus on Data and Technology

Google Legal uses technology not unfamiliar to larger law firms that have invested in quality legal technology solutions, many of which have been used in practice for over a decade, including e-signatures, e-billing systems and matter management solutions, entity management, contract management, IP management, document management, and e-discovery methods. These are foundational systems that legal departments should invest time and money in implementing. Each of them can be multi-year projects to launch, but the return on investment if done correctly can be quite significant.

Google Legal Ops is innovative in the way that it leverages technology to solve operational issues. Specifically, we describe four initiatives that Google's Legal Ops team focused on: (1) real-time dashboards designed to empower decision making through metrics; (2) expert systems to improve service to the rest of the business and eliminate low-value work; (3) a knowledge management system to leverage our useful resources; and (4) machine learning to accelerate and scale repeat processes. It is in these areas of leveraging technology that we have developed custom, in-house solutions that address operational issues.

1 Real-Time Dashboards

First, we needed real-time visibility into outside counsel (OC) spend in order to make informed decisions. We realized that we were not able to easily answer questions such as:

- Are we getting good value for our money?
- Who are our top spend firms and how many matters are they on?
- How are we doing against budget by matter?
- What do we spend on an average phase/case/motion/etc.?
- How does one firm compare to another on budgeting/staffing/rates?
- How many timekeepers are on that matter?

We knew we had the data in our invoices, but we could not analyze it well nor confidently draw conclusions. To address this, we built the Outside Counsel Dashboard (OCDB), a simple and easy-to-use online tool that gives attorneys a near real-time view of their OC spending activity across their matters. OCDB displays both summary and detailed views at the aggregate level, by firm, and by matter. Users can see clear visual representations of trends over time, budget analyses over time and by phase or task code, timekeeper staffing ratios, details and rates, and vendor details. The impact of this real-time dashboard has been to empower informed decision making when evaluating bills, managing how individual matters are staffed, and selecting OC. Analytics has helped us move towards more alternative fee structures because we are in a better position to know how much tasks might cost and how they should be staffed. Additionally, the OCDB allows attorneys to get the information they need when they need it, thus eliminating the delay and reliance on analysts to produce ad hoc reports.

Many third-party data analytics systems have become available since, but at the time, the options were quite limited, which led to the development of our own dashboards. This took many years. We were collecting data, but it was neither structured nor clean. Due to the lack of industry standards and even department-wide standards, we spent much time and effort defining data fields and redesigning processes and systems to capture those fields in an accurate and timely manner. This included defining matters, timekeeper types, product areas, phases of work (which mapped to task codes), and more.

2 Expert Systems

Second, Legal Ops was challenged in meeting the needs of a growing client base with limited headcount. This is a common problem for departments like Google's who experience hypergrowth because the roles and responsibilities of team members of a small and nimble legal department do not always scale well. The result is a department where existing processes need to be examined and often re-engineered. In this case, a particular practice area lead approached the Legal Ops team because she wanted to focus attorneys on higher-value work to keep them happy and engaged and to ensure that their team could scale effectively. To understand the challenge, we conducted interviews, analyzed team emails, and applied data analytics to uncover the fact that too many emails were directed to the team unnecessarily. We went about understanding team work drivers and workflows to identify pain points and find high-value areas for greater efficiencies to develop solutions for improvement.

What we found for this team is that they are often the first point of contact on an issue. Much of this is due to legacy relationships as internal clients from within the company come to them because they know the team will help, even if it is an issue that should have been escalated somewhere else first. From our study on email traffic, we found that only 34% of the alias traffic were legal issues. Often, requests were just for another set of eyes, for help with what should be done next, or for something that was eventually forwarded and handled by a non-legal team. We also followed the email threads and found that when it was appropriately sent to this team, there was still a lot of back and forth and information gathering before getting to the right answer.

We concluded that we needed to provide better, faster, and more efficient advice. In order for us to turn our focus to what we felt were the most important issues, we knew we would have to develop some resources to direct our clients to in order to give them more ownership in decision making. We decided to create expert systems/decision trees to solve our problem and give our clients some self-service resources.

Once that was decided, we moved into developing the content. We focused on the most-asked topics that we advise on, then we worked with our lawyers around the world to get their input. We wanted unified agreement, given that some lawyers handle issues slightly differently than others. We had to get everyone on the same page. The key thing here was to remove the gray area. We wanted to have a resource that we could point clients to. It was not going to help them if we said, sometimes this, sometimes you may want to contact Legal. We had to make a lot of choices about drawing bright lines: You either contact us or you do not. On top of all this content development, we developed ancillary resources to go with it. These resources give answers and remove the need to contact a lawyer every time.

Our benchmark of success for this project was that we drove down the percentage of inquiries to the legal team that do not require legal advice. This was an indicator that our team is handling more substantive work, and we were also able to measure a much faster response time to legal inquiries sent to this team. We developed a robust self-service site to deliver answers or better direct the user. Looking at the first 12-month impact of implementing the self-service tools expert system, we saw 26,000 page views, 1475 unique visitors from 29 countries, a 33% decrease in inquiries not requiring legal advice, and five times faster response time to legal inquiries. We are now looking to leverage this project and technology to other teams within Legal.

3 Knowledge Management

Another focus of utilizing technology and data in-house was to evaluate our use of knowledge management systems. We are facing some unique challenges that result from hyper-growth. When you get bigger, communication is harder, collaboration is harder, and decision making slows. We have really smart people doing amazing work, but how do you make it easier for people to share and find relevant information? To address this, we put a lot of focus on knowledge management and how technology can enable better communication and collaboration. The long-term vision is to make the collective knowledge of the department and our external resources (including OC) available to our team members at the tips of their fingers – to us, that means universal search, where a user enters in some keywords and their pertinent results appear. Just like Google Search indexes the internet, Legal Search has to index the information we have available in all our internal Legal systems. This is easier said than done, so that is the end goal, which will take several years. First, we have to collect or curate the information/knowledge, then unify the systems, and then build interfaces.

The Legal Department's business requires and generates in-depth research and analysis on a variety of topics. Many Legal Department employees are also quintessential "knowledge workers," trading in research, understanding, and communication of the law and risks. Much of this information bought or gained by team members is never shared. One project Google's Legal Ops team was tasked with was to improve retention of expensive knowledge capital in a system that could benefit all. As much as possible, we wanted to tap into the existing workflows of team members to provide the department with a quick, powerful tool that is as easy to contribute to as it is to search. We, like most departments, have been frustrated by the state of legal knowledge sharing. We lacked a centralized database to store and manage broadly useful legal advice documents. This resulted in redundant work and loss of thought capital. Several years ago, a group of legal assistants tried to address this by creating a homegrown document-sharing repository as a side project to make it easy to store and share documents that would be of benefit to other teams in the department. While it was a great idea, the platform that it was built on was not ideal and not scalable. We took this idea and partnered with our IT/engineering team. We endeavored to make it easier, to make it more in the normal flow of work, and not something over the top that lawyers need to do. In the end, we built a department-wide research repository containing all of our useful, reusable intellectual capital content, including outside counsel memos, product or internal advice memos, and best practices. Goals for our knowledge management system included: (1) recycle expensive thought capital (external and internal); (2) reduce redundant OC requests;

(3) build knowledge base on core topics; and (4) help others find answers to questions regarding core topics as quickly as possible. Through these upgrades we achieved our goal of having a metadata-rich repository of documents.

What we learned from this project was that knowledge management continues to be one of the biggest challenges facing legal departments today. Even with dedicated resources and a robust technology system to support it, it is difficult to get around the "KM freeloader" problem – everyone wants to access the database, but without a carrot or stick, it is impossible to get people to take the time to create content and to contribute or update it.[4] It is the authors' belief that it will require the use of machine learning to ultimately solve the Legal Department knowledge management issue.

4 Machine Learning

Machine learning is another area of focus for innovation of our use of technology and data. This started because we wanted visibility into our massive patent portfolio and those owned by other companies. Additionally, answering basic questions required us to manually label thousands of patents. To address these issues, we leveraged an internally built machine learning system. This system can be trained to classify thousands of patents at a fraction of the cost/time and still deliver accurate results. The tool allows our Patents team to proactively classify Google patents and patents owned by other companies, which, in turn, allows our Patents team to make informed business decisions. The impact of this system has been the rapid classification of documents with high accuracy and significantly reduced labor costs. This methodology is now being leveraged by other internal teams, including e-discovery and contract analytics.[5]

Google has a home-grown contracts management system that has limited search capabilities. We relied on manually entered and inconsistently maintained metadata and manually tracked obligations through spreadsheets. Following our success with the Patents team, we embarked on improving three different areas for contract analytics: (1) search and discovery; (2) targeted diligence; and (3) robust reporting.

With search and discovery, one of the biggest pain points of our end-users was simply not being able to search for what is inside our contracts. We were often wasting significant amounts of time pulling reports and reviewing documents with no relevance to the original question being asked. We also wanted to enhance our product diligence processes, where the ultimate goal is to be able to perform thorough research on our current obligations and identify any high-risk contracts that may be impacted by future product or feature launches (for example, does X type of language appear in any partner agreements?). Lastly, with robust reporting, our goal was to be able to provide real-time insight on a large number of terms with the ability to filter and report extracted clause-level data and discrete values with confidence (for example, obligation tracking). To date, we have loaded our executed contracts into the system and are still in the early days of building and testing. We have been happy with the results to date, but recognize that a lot of investment in human time (and legal process outsourcers) are required to make projects like this work. It is a lot of upfront investment and we are hopeful that it will pay off.

---

[4] For more on incentivizing such behavior, see Kimbro – Gamification of Work and Feedback Systems, *supra*.
[5] See, e.g., Zander from ICAIL 2015 in San Diego.

III MINDSET AND CONCLUSION

The legal industry is uniquely resistant to change and disruption for many reasons. Law firm profitability and the traditional law firm business model are not motivated by efficiency. Regulations, including partnership structures and consensus markets, create barriers for law firms to innovate and in many cases de-incentivize innovation in the firm. Accordingly, law firms have been known to turn away from systems and tools that make things better, faster, and cheaper. There is also legitimate skepticism from many law firms about the ability of machines to help with or replace the skill and specialization of lawyers in practice. They might argue that if you find ten people doing the same transaction, you will find ten ways to do that transaction. To some, it is challenging to understand how the practice of law could be made more efficient through some level of standardization and commoditization and the use of technology and still retain the quality that they believe can only come from a skilled and specially trained lawyer.

We are currently in a time of disruption and opportunity for the corporate legal services industry, and it is exciting to watch the transformation slowly unfold. Those that deny that something is happening will be left behind, while those that recognize it can lead the way to the future.

While most would agree that these things are happening and that something needs to be done, there is certainly no agreement on what needs to be done or how. For those in legal operations or law firms interested in innovating, there are three things to keep in mind when faced with an environment that may be hostile to change. We have a saying: Just because it's obvious, doesn't mean it's easy. First, innovation can mean a lot of things. A lot of legal operations are complex, for sure. But a lot of what we do is putting common sense into motion. It is finding a way to do the things that might seem obvious but require massive change. Innovation does not have to mean advanced technology or AI or robot lawyers taking over human lawyer positions and roles in practice. In fact, it does not even have to be technology at all. Sometimes it just means changing the lens on how something is done and bringing other people to see the world the way you do. And you have to work patiently to convince them. Second, think big, but with any experiments or changes, start small. Change is hard and it takes time. This particular industry faces a lot of unique barriers to change. We are not going to come up with new models overnight, so start small. Try different things. As we say at Google, "launch and iterate." Finally, we believe that law firms and legal departments should be working together more closely to find ways to innovate together. We can do it better, faster, and cheaper with collaboration, and there are ways that all parties involved can all achieve our goals. Better outcomes with less effort are good for everyone. Share, collaborate, and be transparent.

The goal of innovation at Google Legal Ops is to optimize the balance of speed, cost, and quality of legal work at Google by leveraging people, process, and technology in the ways discussed above. Going forward, Google intends to continue to challenge the status quo by defining the future of the field and pushing technology to work in new areas of legal practice.

For EU product safety concerns, contact us at Calle de José Abascal, 56–1°,
28003 Madrid, Spain or eugpsr@cambridge.org.